October 30, 2015
My friend G
was a brilliant
didn't even know how
brilliant until after he died
very unexpectedly on
Oct 19, 2015 at the age of 53.
I purchased this book in
his memory & his honor.
RIP Glenn

Susie Compton

THE IRONY OF THE
SOLID SOUTH

THE IRONY OF THE
SOLID SOUTH

Democrats, Republicans,
and Race, 1865–1944

Glenn Feldman

THE UNIVERSITY OF ALABAMA PRESS
Tuscaloosa

Copyright © 2013
The University of Alabama Press
Tuscaloosa, Alabama 35487-0380
All rights reserved
Manufactured in the United States of America

Typeface: Goudy and Goudy Sans

Cover photograph: College students from around the South celebrate at the Dixiecrat Convention, held at Birmingham's Boutwell Municipal Auditorium, July 16, 1948. Courtesy of the *Birmingham News*.
Cover design: Erin Kirk New

∞

The paper on which this book is printed meets the minimum requirements of American National Standard for Information Sciences—Permanence of Paper for Printed Library Materials, ANSI Z39.48-1984.

Library of Congress Cataloging-in-Publication Data

Feldman, Glenn.
  The irony of the solid south : Democrats, Republicans, and race, 1865-1944 / Glenn Feldman.
    pages cm
  Includes bibliographical references and index.
  ISBN 978-0-8173-1793-5 (trade cloth : alk. paper) — ISBN 978-0-8173-8670-2 (ebook) 1. Southern States—Politics and government—1865-1950. 2. Democratic Party (U.S.)—History—20th century. 3. Republican Party (U.S. : 1854-)—History—20th century. 4. Southern States—Race relations—History—20th century. I. Title.
  F215.F43 2013
  975'.04—dc23
                    2012036142

For Hallie, my heart, and Rebecca, my soul . . .

Contents

Acknowledgments ix
Preface xi
1. The "Reconstruction Syndrome" and the Calcification of Conservative Culture 1
2. Elements of Democratic Solidarity *and* Discontent: Industry, Economics, Calvinist Religion, and Jim Crow 21
3. For Blacks Only: The Perversion of Alabama Progressivism 41
4. Race over Rum, Romans, and Republicans 67
5. Placing Culture on Hold: The New Deal Coalition, Its First Cracks, and the "Great Melding" Takes Shape 87
6. Splitting the New Deal Coalition Open 123
7. The "Liberal South" and the Central Tragedy of Southern Politics 163
8. Cheap Labor, the FEPC, and Frank Dixon as Knight-Errant of the South 184
9. Racial Challenge, White Reaction, and Chauncey Sparks as the New Champion 208
10. Race, Religion, and the "Status Quo Society" 247
11. Liberals, Friends of the Negro, and Charging Hell with a Toothpick 266
Epilogue: Since 1944 291
Notes 313
Selected Bibliography of Primary Sources 413
Index 429

Acknowledgments

There are a great many people who have my sincere gratitude for helping make this book possible. First, I would like to thank Curtis Clark, director, and Dan Waterman, editor-in-chief, of The University of Alabama Press for the faith, encouragement, guidance, and support they have demonstrated from the beginning. I am deeply grateful to them both. Everyone at The University of Alabama Press was wonderful to work with again. Jenn Backer provided excellent copyediting.

I am especially indebted to my family, whose support is vitally important to me. My wife of a quarter century, Jeannie, and my daughters, Hallie and Rebecca, are the world. Hallie is my sunshine; Rebecca is my music. My brother, Richard, has been my constant companion and friend in all. My parents, Brian Feldman and Julia Garate Burgos Feldman, are the best parents one could hope for. My sister and brother, Vicky F. Menke and Danny Feldman, have always been very supportive of me and my work, as are my cousins Ronnie Feldman and Eulogio and Luz Pena. I am immensely grateful for all of them.

I am blessed to have so many good friends, people whose enduring friendship is more important to me than they probably realize: Johnny Sherman, Jak and Judy Karn, Becky and Owen Stayner, Jimmy and Tracy Wooten, Glenda Curry, Debbie Donaldson, Mary and Vince Morgan, Kurtie Hutto, Stephanie Diethelm, Kaki O'Flinn, Lori Jack, Natalie Motise Davis, Matt Farrar, Preston Lovinggood, Irina Oshinsky, Mo Hajialilu, Marc L. J. Dierikx, Bill Trimble, Larry Gerber, Lois McFadyen Christensen, Flowers Braswell, Guy Beckwith, Allen W. Jones, Jack Owens, Jody Coombs, Carol Ann Vaughn Cross, Kristine Wirts, Julie Ryan, Burt Nabors, Mark Westfall, Yvonne Carlson, Tim Hays, the late Jeff Prugh, Jim Baggett, Larry Dennis, Melvyn "Smooth" Parker, Jo Fowler, Colin Davis, Brian Steele, Bryan Vroon, Frank LaRussa, Fred Renneker III, Michael Gallo, Sam Harper, George Theodore, and Richard Grooms.

A generous faculty development grant from the University of Alabama at Birmingham (UAB) helped immensely with out-of-state research. I especially want to thank the dean of the College of Arts & Sciences at UAB, Tom DiLorenzo, and Associate Dean Rebecca Bach for being so supportive of my research. I must thank the army of archivists, librarians, and others who provided research assistance to me, especially Norwood Kerr, Debbie Pendleton, and Ed Bridges at the Alabama Department of Archives and History, Jim Baggett at the Birmingham Public Library Archives, Liz Wells at Samford University, Peggy Greenwood at the Missouri Historical Society in St. Louis, Ned Dirlik at the Columbia University Oral History Collection and the New York Public Library, both in New York, Paul Crater at the National Archives, Southern Regional Branch, East Point, Georgia, Dwight M. Miller at the Herbert Hoover Presidential Library, Iowa City, Iowa, and Brad Bauer and Dennis E. Bilger at the Harry S. Truman Presidential Library in Independence, Missouri.

Glenn Feldman

Preface

The very things that made the South solid for the Democratic Party after 1865—white supremacy, religious and cultural conservatism, a boundless devotion to market values—also "made" the South begin to become, by 1936, disillusioned with the Democratic Party of Franklin Roosevelt and the New Deal. This was a disenchantment that would only simmer and grow in strength until it erupted in party revolt, third-party rebellion, and, ultimately, realignment in much of the South to Republicanism (especially in statewide and up-ticket elections). The implications have been national, and they have been profound. This constitutes the first irony of the Solid South.

Actually there was nothing inherent or intrinsic about the South's affinity for the Democratic Party after 1865. The worshipful allegiance white southerners gave to that party emanated most fundamentally from the deep-seated, pervasive, almost indelible cultural conservatism of the region—the same cultural conservatism that would, one day, ironically, dictate a *rejection* of the national Democratic Party and crack the Solid South wide open.

White southerners didn't become Republicans so much as they stopped being Democrats. This was a function of the primacy of ideology over party, of the enduring nature of politics and culture over temporal partisan allegiances, of . . . continuity. This, more than anything else, is the story of the New South.

Even in the face of seeming modern political realignment to Republicanism, the South did not change in an elemental sense. The two major parties essentially changed in the middle of the twentieth century, especially on matters of race and culture. The white South merely chose to stay loyal to the most viable conservative party alternative available—be it a Dixiecrat rump group within the Democratic Party, a more formal third-party revolt of

States' Righters, the independentism of George Wallace, or, eventually, the GOP itself. This is the second and overarching irony of the Solid South.

The third major irony of this story, which runs counter to traditional understandings, is that the New Deal held within it the seeds of its own destruction. That is, at the precise moment when most scholars (correctly) identify the height and apex of Democratic strength in the South (the 1930s), a silent and largely invisible cancer was also growing within the party, one that would eventually eat away its foundations and doom its prospects for long-term survival in the South.

The New Deal Coalition's strength in bringing together Democrats of varying culture and color in the tempest that was the Great Depression virtually preordained that the coalition could not be held together once the storm had passed. When the unprecedented economic crisis of the Depression lifted, white southerners were free to return to "normalcy," to go back to putting race regularity and white supremacy above all other competing factors—something they had held in abeyance during a crisis that threatened material ruin and actual survival.

The New Deal (and its vaunted coalition) was not so much American politics at normality but an aberration in which economic conditions were so terrifying, so oppressive, and so unprecedented, at least in the United States, that people (including white southerners) were willing to temporarily subsume traditional racial and cultural concerns to immediate class imperatives. They were willing to suppress a rampant and deep-rooted individualistic impulse—and, more important, the mythology that surrounded it—to supplicate for public aid, lobby for state activism, and tolerate collective action. Thus the coalition to deal with crisis that was so hastily put together was (1) so heterogeneous and so variegated that it could not last and (2) understood by many of its participants to be exactly that: a temporary stop-gap measure allowing massive, liberal, government activism, not a permanent solution to politics or economics—especially in the still fundamentally conservative South.

Beginning in earnest in the 1930s a phenomenon that may be termed the "Great Melding" took place in the South and eventually would radically realign politics in America. By 1980 the first Great Melding, and a subsequent one, would result in a national Republican ascendance based on a bedrock of southern support. Three decades after that the ascendance (with its meldings) would lead to a previously unthinkable assault on the modern welfare state, an unfortunate term of disparagement for a more just vision of society. The assaults would result in record levels of poverty, staggering disparities and wealth inequality, and a ferocious attempt to eviscerate America's safety net along with any real devotion to the common good, the public interest, or the general weal.[1]

In actuality, there were two great meldings—both variations on a theme and both perfected in the American South—long before they were ever recognized, or attempted, by different names on a national stage: names such as "fusionism" or "movement conservatism."[2] The meldings were southern in origin long before they succeeded in radically pushing American politics at least a full category or more to the right. Decades before people ever heard of Tea Parties, Sarah Palin, Rick Perry, Michelle Bachmann, or even Ronald Reagan, Dixie had already tested and approved the blueprint, the roadmap, the model for it all.

The first Great Melding began in response to the racial liberalism of Franklin Roosevelt and his New Deal. Before it was over, it would encompass "massive resistance" to desegregation and civil rights—all of which would provide a rocket booster for the development of the modern Republican Party in the South and, later, the nation.

This first melding was, at its heart, the ingenious fusing by elites of economic conservatism (even fundamentalism) with the sacred cow of white supremacy. A shared aversion to the federal government would provide the essential glue for the union. This anti-federalism would commonly take euphemisms such as "states' rights," "home rule," "local rule," "constitutionalism," and "Americanism," among others. But it had its roots in the nineteenth-century South.

The melding (and its brother) solved the nagging, primordial problem that all oligarchies face: how to rule "the people" and effect a program that retains its richest rewards for the very few while also existing in a democratic republic that has, as its most fundamental prerequisite, the approval of the people at the polls.

Up until the two versions of the Great Melding took hold, popular spasms against elite rule tended to temporarily but seriously disrupt the planting and industrial elite that controlled wealth and power in the post–Civil War South. We should be clear that there was a contest. The conflation of rightist economics and racial arguments did not occur without a struggle—sometimes a ferocious one—beginning with Unionist whites who initially, at least, supported the "black" Republican Party of Reconstruction. Other sporadic irritants to the southern aristocracy and their northern financial backers found form under various names—foremost among them the Knights of Labor, the Greenbackers, the United Mine Workers, and the Populist (or People's) Party of the 1890s—and were usually based on some difficult extraction of biracial cooperation between working-class whites and blacks.

But the melding allowed elites, especially in places like Alabama, to repackage the bitter pill of fiscal retrenchment and a public austerity that benefited private wealth with the appealing sugarcoat of racial regularity and even a sectional type of patriotism. The fusing of economic conservatism with racial conservatism (actually, the almost-complete appropriation of white supremacy by the planters and industrialists away from the region's populists and economic progressives) allowed the bosses to win over en masse the votes of plain-white people who had, until then, too frequently (if ineffectively) challenged their rule.

The move was brilliant. It allowed the besieged forces of wealth, privilege, extreme laissez-faire, and even a kind of state-sponsored corporatism to recast their affinity for economically rightist fundamentalism as something indissolubly bound to the holiest of cultural holies: white supremacy. And in doing so, it eventually doomed economic liberalism in the South. It would, finally, become untenable to continue to profess economic liberalism and still insist that one was okay on race. Further, it supplied the eventual prototype the modern GOP would use to emerge triumphant in the South after the possibility of a second Dixiecrat Revolt was ruled out by conservative maneuvering to control state party machinery.

The second version of the Great Melding actually took form and substance in the South contemporaneously with the first. It should be considered a "second" Great Melding, though, because it would not appear to a great extent on the national level until the late 1970s ascension of Ronald Reagan, the Religious Right, and figures from Jerry Falwell, Pat Robertson, and George W. Bush to the Tea Party favorites of recent vintage. Nor was this melding wholly unrelated to the first. There was obvious and distinct overlap in Dixie. There would be less obvious but still distinct common ground nationally.

The second version melded economic fundamentalism with the religious kind (instead of and in addition to the now more subtle racial kind) and used a deep and powerful aversion to democracy and democratic institutions as its essential glue (instead of just the out-and-out anti-federal adhesive used by the first variation). To be sure, it included hearty doses of the anti-federal animus, now most commonly appearing under the euphemisms of "freedom" and "liberty." But like the first, it too could trace its roots to the nineteenth-century South—specifically the Calvinist Protestantism that gave Baptist and Methodist Dixie so much of its conservative hue. In its more extreme manifestations, it contained more than a whiff of the thoughts and beliefs of Rousas John Rushdoony, Dominionism, and the Christian Reconstructionists.[3] But this religious view, once considered to occupy the furthest fringes of theological thought, would gain ground during the twentieth century, increasingly so in the century's closing decades and the opening ones of the twenty-first.

Both versions of the melding gave sinew and flesh to what was generally and perhaps more popularly understood as Social Darwinism. And while the second melding took root and matured in the South, it would have to wait until 1980 to receive national entrée and acceptance—and then in the thoughts, words, and deeds of Ronald Reagan, F. A. Hayek, Milton Friedman, Margaret Thatcher, and M. E. Bradford—along with those of the far Calvinist right.[4] At the moment it is enjoying a renaissance in the newfound celebrity of novelist Ayn Rand and her legion of libertarian followers as well as the Tea Party. The irony of Rand—an atheist who accepted Social Security checks and Medicare benefits—serving as the posthumous front for a melding of economic and religious fundamentalism is one for the ages. In fact, as this story unfolds it will become clear that "the irony" of the Solid South is not just one, two, three, or even four ironies but perhaps even more, some as important as the others.[5]

In sum, the two most important political movements of the last half century (both of which have led to a national conservative and Republican ascendance that has mutated into something glaringly extreme) may actually locate their roots decades earlier in the soil of the American South. They are a first melding of economic and racial rightism on the shared basis of antipathy to the federal government and a second melding of economic and religious fundamentalism based on (in addition to the anti-federal animus) a profound disdain for democratic institutions and popular participation in government.

It is important that we pause to note that none of this happened by accident. The present-day Republican assaults on Social Security, Medicare, birth control and contraception, public schools and employees, the post office, and even federal storm aid for hurricane, tornado, and disaster victims (unthinkable just a few years ago) are the national fruit of one of our two major parties adopting a decades-old, extreme rightist regional mutation of the democratic experiment.[6]

That is, southern elites, so long frustrated by the repeated flirtations of plain people with biracial liberalism in the form of the 1880s Greenback-Labor Party, the 1890s Populists, and various labor unions such as the United Mine Workers, skillfully appropriated the race issue away from white, southern, economic liberals in places like Alabama and learned to use it to their advantage to meld the cause of undiluted laissez-faire to white supremacy in Dixie. This marriage—aided by exorbitant funding, determined activism, and peerless organization in the areas of propaganda, mass reeducation, and the inculcation of pro-business, conservative market values—eventually led to "liberalism" itself becoming a dirty word in the South (and, with time, in many other places around the country). Southern economic liberals thus found it increasingly difficult to differentiate themselves from the national Democratic Party—to insist that they were still conservative on race (and, thus, "true southerners") while being liberal on economic issues.

This led to the severe weakening of the prospects for continued Democratic vitality in Dixie as white southerners increasingly conflated the racially and culturally liberal national Democratic Party with state and local Democrats. In part this provides a crucial missing link in the story of how the South—once the bastion of solid Democracy—went Republican. In short, southern liberalism was never what it was cracked up to be—either by its adherents, admirers, the hopeful, or later scholars. It was "soft" on the inside. In other words, its apparently solid outer crust was economic (and white) in nature. But its center, its essential being, was depressingly vulnerable in its stubborn adherence to racial conventions such as segregation, white supremacy, and other forms of cultural conservatism—a fatal and regionally distinctive flaw that led, repeatedly, to the primacy of race and other emotional issues over class concerns for the whites who made up the majority of the South. It was a core that eventually won out after racial crisis (and a return to prosperity) eclipsed the material cataclysm of the Great Depression.

Unfortunately this was true for all rank and manner of southern whites: Democratic loyalists and New Dealers as well as Dixiecrats, southern rebels, and outright bigots. And it was especially (if surprisingly) true of even the most celebrated southern liberals of the time: men such as Lister Hill, John Sparkman, George Huddleston, and John McDuffie.

Another (and related) part of the missing link in the story of how the South became Republican involves a simple but important lapse in popular and collective memory. In Deep South settings such as Alabama, the Democratic Party was never simply *the Democratic Party*—not until the New Deal anyway. It was founded and named—formally and far more accurately—the Democratic *and* Conservative Party.[7] Thus, when sectional realignment to the modern GOP finally came (after the national Democratic Party embraced economic *and* racial liberalism), the South's adoption of Republicanism (and its contrasting conservatism) should not have been as shocking as it has proven to be. After all, the GOP made certain it was the party of conservatism by expelling its northern and liberal wing after the Miami convention of 1964. Once George Wallace passed from the scene, where was the Democratic *and Conservative* South to go?

Even more, perhaps, the two variations of the Great Melding led to a fundamental reordering of villains in American society, one that has had profound and national implications. Specifically, and most important, the traditional American suspicion and enmity to bigness was consciously shifted away from Big Business (and its "fat cat" stereotypes) to Big Government. While white southerners benefited more than any other group from New Deal policies, by 1936 they had become increasingly alienated by the attendant racial and cultural liberalism of FDR and his closest advisors, principal among them Eleanor Roosevelt, Harold Ickes, Henry Wallace, and Aubrey Williams. By the end of World War II, and the succession of Harry Truman and his Fair Deal, this disillusionment portended great partisan disturbances both in the South and in the nation at large: yet another irony for us to consider.

While I recognize, of course, that the present study is not the last word on the subject, it is my hope that this book will encourage scholars and a general educated readership to engage in a serious reexamination of some of their most basic understandings of how and why the South became solidly Democratic; how the seeds for the destruction of that solidarity were present as early as 1865; how the South's apparent political realignments belie a continuous devotion to conservative culture and ideology born in the cauldron of war and Reconstruction; how the New Deal both thrived and was being eaten alive from within in the South; how economic and business conservatives purposefully and successfully snatched away the standard of white supremacy from their economically liberal adversaries, thus largely dooming economic liberalism to eventual irrelevance (and, worse, cultural opprobrium) in the South; how emotional political issues have been used repeatedly by southern elites to distract plain whites from their material interests and undermine attempts at biracial political and economic action; how an actual "Southern Religion"—based on a fusing of Calvinist conservatism with Austrian economics, patriotism defined as knee-jerk militarism, and an indifference to social and collective solutions to society's problems—has worked to make it difficult for liberalism to survive in the South among the rank and file of religious believers and working people;[8] and how the South's underlying conservatism, formed long ago, has intimately bound enduring regional conventions not only on race but also on gender, economics, patriotism, militarism, and a whole host of important subjects, eventually facilitating the rise of the modern Republican Party in the South and in America.

This study spans the period 1865 to 1944, principally in Alabama, because it allows us to study closely the advent of a Solid Democratic South in the Reconstruction period against the "party of Lincoln." The winding down of World War II is a logical end point for the study as the changes associated with the onset of peace in 1945 are overwhelming.

By focusing on Alabama we are susceptible to the criticism that our lens is too narrow, too focused on an extreme and racially reactionary southern state. No doubt there is some truth to this view. But there is a great deal more about the state that justifies our examination of it—indeed, even compels us to do so—namely because, at one time, Alabama was considered the most liberal garden spot in the South. Due to its high level of industrialization it has consistently ranked as one of the most unionized southern states. Its congressional representatives were considered at one time to be the most liberal in the South, and its potential as a vanguard for the rise of Dixie liberalism served as a source of hope to many progressives. Thus Alabama's succumbing to the siren call of racism and religious reaction is the most tragic of stories because it was not inevitable and did not occur without a struggle. And it took place in a setting that once suggested economic (if not social) possibilities of far more progress and light.

While the book does focus on Alabama and race, it is no one-dimensional study. Instead it is filled with abundant comparisons and material regarding the other southern states as well as insights into the uses of emotional issues other than race that have been employed time and again to distract plain whites from their economic, material, and real interests.

In Alabama we are able to trace the GOP's rise from leprous origins to great influence. The trauma of Republican Reconstruction left the state and the region with an implacable, and seemingly unquenchable, hatred for everything black, federal, liberal, and Republican. For eighty years the Solid South was almost completely Democratic in its politics. Any whiff of Republicanism was anathema in the South, indelibly associated with the traumatic, caricatured, and largely canted memory of corrupt and incompetent black rule backed by the bristling bayonets of a federal army of northern aggression. From 1874 on, Republicans received only a smattering of votes in Alabama and the other southern states. That is, until, the election of 1928—and later the rise of Franklin Roosevelt and the New Deal.

Perhaps the biggest lesson here is that the American South is not Republican or Democratic by choice but largely by default. In the South, to a greater extent than in any other section of the country, culture determines politics—not the other way around. The enduring goal of the region, broadly defined, has been to find a partisan vehicle that reflects cultural continuities and verities, and to give its support unwaveringly until that party ceases to do so. This is the story of how the Democratic Party—a conservative party in the South—did that for nearly eight decades.

The terms, concepts, ideas, and themes that are the fruit of the two forms of Great Melding in the American South will appear again and again in what follows. Different chapters will mention and discuss, to various degrees, terms, buzzwords, and colloquialisms that have reached the level of the sacred in the U.S. South—and, increasingly, in modern American society: personal responsibility, freedom, states' rights, local rule, Americanism, constitutionalism, individualism, religion, white supremacy, liberty, fealty to a "southern way of life," the almost metaphysical belief in the power of free markets, the omniscience and heroic stature of bosses and payroll makers, the inherent inferiority, suspect patriotism, and trouble-making nature of labor unions, reverence for a social stratification with every cog, gender, and minority in its place, and more. And they will stem directly from the racial, religious, and economic rightism of the South that was once considered to be quite extreme and at great odds with the dominant ethos of the rest of the country.

Torched by the trauma of war, defeat, "foreign" occupation, and Reconstruction, white southerners (and, to a lesser extent, some blacks) took in these ideas with their mother's milk and thought them just as natural, immutable, and heavenly ordained as anything could be. It would take time, sweat, money, organization, military defeat, social convulsion, and a zealotry bordering on the fanatical to export these extremisms to the rest of the country. But, eventually, it would happen. It is important, though, in a time of national acceptance of many of these ideas as mainstream, conservative, and even normal not to miss their southern and quintessentially radical roots.

I
The "Reconstruction Syndrome" and the Calcification of Conservative Culture

> I will teach my children and they shall teach their children to hate the government.
>
> —An Alabama woman, 1866

The South began its move toward the modern Republican Party in 1865.

Is this too much to write? Does it sound too deterministic, too teleological, too . . . illogical? Does it dismiss too much Democratic dominance—decades of it, in fact?

Yes, probably so. Yet as outlandish as the statement is, as counterintuitive as it may at first seem, there is more than just a kernel of truth behind it.

To be sure, the realignment that eventually came to the South did not take a direct route but was fraught with fits and starts, turns and detours, potholes, congestion, delays, and even a breakdown or two. There were times when those guiding the journey wondered aloud whether they were even on the right track. Perhaps more fatefully, there were crossroads and routes to alternate destinations not taken. And yet, viewed from a distance, the southern journey toward the modern Republican Party can seem as ineluctable as it has been constant. For the journey has never been a one-sided affair. Like lovers, the GOP moved toward the South at least as fast as the region came toward it. And the implications, as much as anything else, have been truly national in scope and eminence.

To understand the nature of this curious statement, we must first travel back to the immediate moment after the great southern watershed of civil war—Reconstruction—and, in part, to that most elemental expression of southern white defiance: the Ku Klux Klan. For it was in the crucible of war and Reconstruction that the American South solidified its essential and enduring personality—a personality and culture that would dictate the path of partisan allegiance for the foreseeable future, and then some.

Chapter I
We Will Hate the Government

The history of the New South, the post-1865 South specifically, is of course influenced mightily by racial concerns. While race remains the most important key to understanding the region's history—and its political and social developments—the issue runs deeper and broader than that solely. In fact, much of the postwar South can be understood most clearly in terms of the chronic appearance of what may be termed a *Reconstruction Syndrome*—a set of powerful beliefs that have shaped southern history and culture for a century and a half. The attitudes that make up this syndrome, fortified by race, were originally born of the psychological trauma of military defeat, occupation, abolition, and the forcible imposition of a new political order. After the initial trauma, the syndrome has repeatedly manifested itself in the South—rising to the surface most clearly and violently in times of acute stress. As a result, for more than a century after Reconstruction, the dominant white, Anglo-Saxon, Protestant South was largely distinguished, and distinguishable, by the recurring component tendencies of the syndrome: very strong anti-black, anti–federal government, anti-liberal, anti-Yankee, anti-outsider/foreigner, and pro-militarily patriotic beliefs.

The Second Reconstruction cemented and personalized these convictions in the minds of a new generation of white southerners and their children. To a large extent, these unfortunate tendencies still persist at, or just beneath, the surface of much of the present-day South—shaping and coloring the region's approach to politics, economics, and social mores. Often these tendencies appear in softer, sanitized, more euphemistic forms. Yet appear they still do, as an almost manic concern for states' rights, local autonomy, hyperindividualism, an unfettered—almost fetishistic—view of freedom, political conservatism, sectional pride, traditional values, religion, and gender roles (in fact, reverence for all things traditional), pride in the white race's leadership and achievements, disdain for hyphenated Americanism in favor of ethnic, racial, and cultural homogeneity—in sum, for all of the things that "made this country great."

The southern reaction to war—replete with epidemic waves of violence—was a movement reflective of its time, to be sure—a desperate attempt not to conserve the society in which southerners had lived but to turn it back, back to the status quo antebellum. For the years immediately following the great conflict represented a chaos and anarchy of apocalyptic proportions. The events of 1861–65 literally ripped apart the world in which white southerners had lived. The South lost a war it fully expected to win. It was defeated, humiliated, and occupied by what it considered a foreign power. Slaves were set free, granted political rights, and called the equals of their former masters. Farms were destroyed, mules and implements lost, land pillaged, and towns laid to waste. One in every five southern males was killed, two-thirds of all southern shipping lost, and over nine thousand miles of railway destroyed.[1] It was within this crucible that the white southern people began to fashion their response to disaster.

An older school of historians excused the more violent and indefensible manifestations of southern response—such as the Klan—as the natural and understandable reaction of a defeated country and largely left it at that.[2] While this interpretation may account adequately for the birth of such resistance, it does little to justify the order's subsequent and bloody career. Nor is it of much use in explaining the group's metamorphosis from a convulsive social reaction to the paramilitary arm of southern political conservatism and a society dedicated to acts of terrorism. The early apologies for the Klan, of course, do not satisfactorily address why it failed to stop at targeting political rivals but grew instead to punish perceived social and economic enemies, eventually trespassed into the arena of personal morality,[3] and, most important, why the majority of white society in the Deep South supported, condoned, or tolerated it.

The Ku Klux Klan did not invent racism. It seems at once obvious, yet still necessary, to make this point. Nor did the KKK institute the practice of racially motivated violence and repression in the South. Alabama, much like its sister states, had a long and bloody antebellum tradition of violence aimed at keeping black men and women "in their place."[4] In the interim between Appomattox and the first appearance of the Klan, the Heart of Dixie erupted in a series of convulsive acts of brutality aimed at the newly freed blacks. What groups like the Klan did later was provide the basis for organized and sustained racial and political repression.

Because of the protestations of some that the Klan's actions were aimed only at "impudent Negroes" and that good "darkies" need not be concerned, it is worth defining the former term. In 1865 the insolent included former slaves who dared to leave the land on which they had lately been human chattel, visited town in a gesture of their newfound freedom, voted the Republican ticket, or refused to work for the miserable wages proffered by their former masters. All ran the chance of being called "uppity niggers" and incurring the risks and wrath associated with that dangerous label.[5]

White southerners who cooperated with the new Republican governments (scalawags) and northerners who came south after the war (Union League and Freedmen's Bureau carpetbaggers) also made up a good number of Reconstruction victims. The Union League was an overtly Republican organization that enjoyed initial support from hungry north Alabamians but lost white members roughly at the pace with which the freedmen joined. Northern teachers and social workers who came south to provide poor relief, education, and improvement for blacks in the wake of war and the carnage it bequeathed were primarily from the Freedmen's Bureau.[6] Of course, as in the aftermath of any disaster or dislocation on the order of war, profiteers came south as well. But most native whites viewed education for the freedmen as unacceptable, a threat that would make blacks insolent rather than self-assured, militant rather than devoted to their new liberty, and dangerous rather than dependent on, and subservient to, white people.[7]

The vitriol became almost immediately potent. Carpetbaggers were "the lowest, the meanest . . . vermin," actual "scavengers" who plundered a downtrodden region, as one pro-Klan newspaper assessed. Like Judas Iscariot, scalawags were the "vultures and carrion crows" of radical Republicanism, living only to thrust their disgusting beaks into the "vitals of the white people," a south Alabama paper offered; "a mongrel assemblage, reeking with African odors, and rank with the foul smell of the unwashed" who had rushed up to Washington to beg for the privilege of torturing the southern people as "Satan went up to ask to . . . afflict Job."[8]

In the summer of 1865 violence aimed at black people reached epidemic proportions in Alabama. Carl Schurz, a German-born Union general charged by Congress to assess conditions in the South, recorded that efforts to hold blacks in a state of subjection were of a "particularly atrocious nature" in Alabama. African Americans attempting to leave plantations for the first time were exposed to the most savage treatment. Whites of all types and ranks held the harshest sentiments toward blacks since they had been emancipated and lost their protective status as property. The maiming and killing of black people, Schurz reported, is accepted in Alabama as one of those "venial offenses which must be forgiven to the outraged feelings of a wronged and robbed people."[9]

A team of federal physicians stationed in Montgomery and Selma corroborated the harsh assessment. At one point they treated thirty-one assaulted freedmen (sixteen who died), three women who had had their ears cut off, two men with chins removed, and one man who somehow survived seven stab wounds, two pistol shots, and a third of his arm lopped off. The surgeons reported that the provocation for most of the attacks was the attempt of newly freed blacks to come to town. Similar reports poured into Congress from the port city of Mobile.[10]

Captain W. A. Poillon, assistant superintendent of Freedmen, Refugees, and Abandoned Lands in the south Alabama counties of Clarke, Choctaw,

Washington, and Marengo, and along the Alabama and Tombigbee rivers, further substantiated the wantonness and shocking nature of the brutality. Local police are "hostile to color," Poillon reported. Armed and marauding gangs of whites rob, insult, and assault "the helpless freedmen with impunity. . . . [P]rejudice and a vindictive hatred to color is universal here . . . and the only capacity in which the negro will be tolerated is that of slave." Blacks have "no right that the white man respects; all is anarchy and confusion; a reign of terror exists, and the life of the freedmen is at the mercy of any villain whose hatred or caprice incites to murder." Whites organized themselves into patrols, using dogs, to control the roads and pathways. The unfortunate who "attempts escape" from the dragnet or "he who returns for his wife or child, is . . . shot or hung." Blacks were still forced to stay and work on plantations without any pay. So many freedmen had been killed that the roads and rivers in south Alabama "stink with the dead bodies" of those who tried to flee. "Murder with his ghastly train stalks abroad at noonday and revels in undisputed carnage," the captain wrote, "while the bewildered and terrified freedmen know not what to do. To leave is death; to remain is to suffer the . . . cruel taskmaster, whose only interest is their labor *wrung* from them by every device an inhuman ingenuity can devise." The "lash and murder" were used to intimidate those whom "fear of an awful death alone causes to remain, while patrols, negro dogs, and spies (disguised as Yankees) keep *constant* guard over these unfortunate people."[11]

Violence was the blunt instrument by which white society preserved its privileges—political, social, economic.[12] The ties between all three were strong during Reconstruction—and amplified throughout Alabama by the dominant Conservative and Democratic press. Consider the attitudes of the *Southern Advertiser* out of Troy, urging its readers to arm every man for a civil struggle no less important than Chancellorsville or Chickamauga, to rout these "pestiferous Radicals and send them [back] . . . to the hellish dens that vomited them up."[13]

Though antebellum law prevented slaves from learning how to read and write under pain of death, once peace came illiteracy was used as the main pretext against their voting—though it was also tied to prejudices about black morality and the grim reality of subsistence wages. They are a "thoughtless, mindless and stupid people," the *Eufaula Tri-Weekly Times* opined, an "indolent and unambitious" race possessing only the lowest in moral and intellectual development, agreed the *Autauga Citizen*. Shall Alabama be placed at the mercy of "an indolent, ignorant, semi-barbarous black rabble?" the *Choctaw Herald* chorused.[14]

White supremacy was the one constant regardless of where in Alabama one looked—despite the volumes that have overstated the differences between Alabama's various regions. North Alabama or south, hill country or Black Belt, whites in the state were on the same page when it came to race. In some ways the north, populated by far fewer blacks, was worse. The Klan was certainly more powerful there. It was utterly repulsive, wrote the *Bluff City Times*, to be seated with "Sambo with all his filth and stench" in a railway coach or at a dinner table, or to be lodged under the same roof. Every feature of the white man differs from the black, a hill-country newspaper argued: "The nose is different. . . . The form and size of the mouth, the shape of the lips and cheeks . . . the apish chin." His skull is thicker than the white man's, the *Shelby County Guide* continued. "The middle part of the foot does not touch the ground. . . . [It is] the foot of the gorilla. The negro is a negro, and only a negro . . . an inferior race [who] should [never] govern . . . in America, a superior set of men."[15]

Of particular concern to Alabama's Conservative and Democratic majority —the representatives of business and wealth—was (as is common to nearly all times and places) the cost of labor. Specifically, the Conservative Democrats worried aloud over the prospect of carpetbaggers and scalawags convincing freedmen that they did not have to accept the execrable wages white planters were offering.

Such insolence flew in the face of everything sacred in southern society: caste, class, and social hierarchy. Blacks were being promised a "golden age of idleness and luxury," a south Alabama newspaper complained. African Americans were being played for the "ignorant dupes" they are and showing an unnatural and unattractive "contempt for the rights of property," a paper in north Alabama agreed. Others reminded the freed slaves that working for whatever was offered was an ineffable religious duty; it was part of "God's law" not to be idle. Such conservative, pro-business, and wealth cosmology found its antecedents, of course, in Calvinist and Puritan theology. Unleavened in the South by the New England commitment to education and the commons, the religious, ethnic, and reform diversity of the North, transcendentalism, abolition, women's suffrage, large populations of Quakers, Jews, or Catholics, or a diversified economy, the Calvinist connection between piety, material success, and God's favor mixed during the antebellum period to exacerbate a southern coolness toward social responsibility. The combination exploded when combined with the reflexive martial patriotism of war and Reconstruction and the region's subsequent "New South" desperation for industrial development at any cost. So was born "The Southern Religion." In its more extreme rightist forms, elements of nineteenth-century theologies like Christian Reconstruction would reappear under different monikers from

Social Darwinism to the Tea Party.[16] They had a long and special resonance in the South.

Whites promised jobs for blacks who voted the Conservative Democratic ticket and economic retribution for those who did not. "We have at present no less than 200 specimens of the genus African engaged in the interesting occupation of doing nothing," the *Union Springs Times* complained. "Young niggers, and old niggers, black, yeller, and streaked niggers, male and female niggers, niggers *ad nauseum* out of work, out of clothes, out of money," the Black Belt paper enumerated, "out of food, out of everything except filth and laziness." The *Eufaula News* in neighboring Barbour County placed blame on "a few white-skinned miscreants with black souls" for leading the freedmen astray. But the various editors made very clear the strong tie between the racial, the economic, and the violent in Alabama. Whenever the material interest of the employer was in question, he had every right to protect himself "by every means" necessary.[17]

By 1866 conditions had not improved. In fact, enmity toward the freedmen was becoming accompanied by a marked and rather violent attitude toward the federal government as well. A burning, implacable hatred and fear soon replaced whatever feelings of guilt or remorse had first existed among the defeated southern whites. White Alabamians committed hundreds, perhaps thousands, of unprovoked murders and outrages on black people while planters conspired to keep black wages at pitifully low levels. They want the freedman's labor, a Union officer explained, "but they want it their own way, and at their own prices."[18] Of all the offenses a black person could commit—owning firearms, "sassing" white people, voting—working for oneself or refusing to enter into a labor contract was perhaps the worst. White anger was commonly directed against the Freedmen's Bureau for supplying the former slaves with food and clothing, thus making it materially possible for them to resist entrance into coercive labor agreements.[19]

A Massachusetts cotton agent traveling extensively across the postbellum South found conditions in Alabama to be revolting, even in comparison with its southern neighbors. Whites there were "about the least civilized" of the whole region, he reported. "The life of the Negro is not worth much." He told of seeing a white man shoot a freed black riding a mule because, as the gunman explained to him, it was "more trouble to ask him to get off." General Wager Swayne, director of the Freedmen's Bureau in Alabama, said he could not name a single instance in which a state court had convicted a white person of a crime. In what was certainly one of the most lurid examples of these outrages, whites beheaded, skinned, and nailed the skin of a rural freedman to a barn as a ghoulish warning to other blacks. As important as the violence—and certainly more enduring—an implacable fear and suspicion of the federal government pervaded the state and promised to bequeath itself to whole generations of future white southerners. One Alabama woman, who swore the Civil War would never actually end, put it like this: "I will teach my children and they shall teach their children to hate the government."[20]

The Glory of All Conservatives

The Ku Klux Klan soon came into existence and harnessed what had previously been disparate currents of violence and hostility into an imperial structure.[21] In 1867 a state constitutional convention controlled by the new Republican electorate repeated provisions against enfranchising former Confederates while registering 105,000 black voters.[22] For all but the most exotic white Alabamians, this was simply too much. The nascent Klan, begun as a desultory order to provide amusement and mischief for a few young southerners who had missed out on the "excitement" of the war, quickly morphed into an organization that prowled the countryside at night dressed in sheets and terrorized black folk.

Begun just north of the Alabama line in Pulaski, Tennessee, in late 1866, the group soon took firmest root in the northern part of Alabama—a section most noted for its strong Unionist and Republican sentiment and heavy white population. In south Alabama the preservation of white supremacy had long been entrusted to other, proto-Klan strains such as the Knights of the White Camellia, the White Brotherhood, the Pale Faces, the White League, the White Caps, and the Men of Peace. Most estimates of Alabama's Reconstruction Klan put its number at around twelve thousand, or one in every nine white male voters. Some of the stronger counties, especially in north Alabama, boasted as many as eight hundred Klansmen. But far more important was the community support and encouragement the order, and others like it, received from white Alabama. According to one noted authority, the Klan enjoyed "almost universal support from conservative white Alabamians," including women and minors.[23]

For decades southern whites gazed back on these halcyon days with a kind of golden-age mythology on full display in such classics as *Gone with the Wind*. Swelled by honorable southern gentlemen and war heroes, the Klan brought back a measure of pride and stability to southern society by keeping carpetbaggers, scalawags, and freed blacks in their place. Usually this was accomplished with a minimum of violence. When violence was necessary, it was almost always justified, effective, and administered in doses strictly proportionate to individual indiscretions or the communal humiliation and outrage that southern society was experiencing in the form of black and Republican rule.

The secret to Klan success in Alabama, however, as in other southern states, during Reconstruction and its memory beyond was the massive quantity of societal support the organization enjoyed. Conservative Democratic newspapers throughout the state sang the praises of the KKK and printed its macabre warnings. Dunning-School historian Walter Fleming claimed that every white man, woman, and child in Alabama was in league with the Klan. Despite the hyperbole, the Klan's deepest reserves of strength did derive directly from its widespread acceptance and support from the greatest part of white Alabama. Scholars have confirmed that the Reconstruction KKK was the "glory of all conservatives," a thing of wonder and esoteric pride. Whether or not one was actually a member, he or she could bask in the reflected honor of the group. The secret order was standing up to the forces of alien and unwanted change: "Here [at least] was an organization that was doing *something*."[24]

As difficult as it is to imagine today, newspapers, particularly in north and west Alabama, openly supported the Klan, printed meeting notices, and published fawning editorials.[25] There were Klan parades, Klan songs, Klan dances, Klan ("nigger") jokes, and even Klan products to hawk. In April 1868 north Alabama's *Athens Weekly Post* celebrated the appearance of white hoods in the southern port city of Mobile: "The Ku Klux troops are very fond of nigger meat, and the Grand Beef Master has just issued ten days' rations of Union Leaguers." After a Reconstruction government order banning public announcements of Klan activity, the group turned to posters, handbills, and word of mouth. By fall, in what was a thin and reflexive defense, the same conservative editors who had publicly praised the KKK began to deny that it existed. By December 1868, the Klan went completely underground in response to the Republican state legislature's first law banning the organization.[26]

While the Klans of different eras were comprised of various classes and societal ranks, it is fairly clear that the Reconstruction incarnation was a top-down affair. General Carl Schurz blamed the "better" classes in Alabama, as well as poor whites, for the appalling mistreatment afforded to people of color after Appomattox. As one hill-country Kluxer remembered dryly, when south Alabama's Hale County wanted to organize their own Klan it was actually the "best citizens" who approached him for help.[27]

Alabama's most prominent military heroes buttressed the order, making the Klan something of an official, patriotic organization of honor. Former Confederate generals such as James H. Clanton, Edmund Pettus, and John H. Forney personified the connection between the Klan and elite Conservative Democratic white society, serving as public leaders for the "secret" order. Clanton, who doubled as chairman of the state Democratic and Conservative Party, drew water from the well of southern religious conservatism to explain that God had made the white man far superior to any white who acknowledged the rights of blacks, and "far superior to the African himself," as he pledged "our lives, our fortunes, and our sacred honor, never to cease our efforts until our State is rescued." So esteemed was Pettus in the aftermath of the war that many of his contemporaries regarded the general as the "greatest Alabamian" of them all.[28]

The 1868 election promised particular tumult.[29] Fortified by north Alabama newspapers that declared "Bayonets is Trumps. Niggers is Kings. Nastychusetts school marms is Queens," the Klan ran amok as the paramilitary arm of the Democratic and Conservative Party. Klansmen shot, threatened, lynched, raped, flogged, branded, mutilated, and terrorized both black and white Republicans. They burned black schools and churches, long perceived as centers for political action, and physically prevented the freed slaves from making it to the polls. Kluxers set up roadblocks on rural pikes, broke up Republican caucuses, and ran political opponents out of town. Planters threatened to slash the miserable wages of black laborers and tenants if they dared to vote anything but Conservative and Democratic.[30]

Nor was the call for social, economic, and political carnage subtle. "If this be treason, make the most of it," one Montgomery paper crowed. "God help you if the struggle comes, for [in] spite of your Rump [legislature], your Niggers, and all the remaining powers of hell at your command, white will win, and there will be such an outpouring of nigger blood, such a hanging of Radicals to 'sour apple trees' as was never known since the world emerged from chaos." Later a Sumter County freedman explained to Congress with a clarity defying dissent how—with murders going on day and night, civil authority suspended, and no one being brought to justice—some African Americans actually did vote the Conservative and Democratic ticket: "We [all] have to live until we die," he said, "and we all want to live as long as we can."[31]

Most of the violence took place at night or in out-the-way rural places. In Sumter, Klansmen burst into the cell of one black man jailed for horse theft, dragged him to a mill next to the river, and shot him at their leisure. "He was shot more than any piece of flesh I ever saw," the county sheriff remembered, "really, from the top of his head, plumb to the soles of his feet." After traveling Kluxers shot a black field worker for, apparently, nothing, an elderly Sumter County white challenged them, asking, "What in the name of God did you shoot that nigger for? He is one of the best niggers in this county."

The ringleader replied that "he didn't give a God-damn; he was a hundred miles from home; he was going to kill somebody; he didn't care who it was."[32]

In March 1869, the Confederate cavalry legend General Nathan Bedford Forrest severed his ties with the Klan and issued his now famous imperial decree of disbandment. But in Alabama, as in other southern states, the order continued to operate despite the signs of official disbandment. Dens went further underground but continued to function with the acquiescence and support of the cream of their local communities.[33]

The civil law in many Alabama counties was a farce, Republican sheriffs and officeholders complained. Authorities were overwhelmed with the sick and hungry, not to mention trying to provide protection against organized bands of armed vigilantes. Men who "care little for the rights or life of any man" populated large areas of the state, a Union soldier reported. The federals, like any occupying force, were confined mostly to town garrisons and tasked with defending against sniper fire aimed at even women carrying infants in their arms. Alabama was the "worst place" he had ever seen, one soldier concluded.[34]

The KKK continued to act as the paramilitary wing of Democratic and Conservative rule in the state throughout 1869 and into 1870. In July Klan and anti-Klan forces clashed in St. Clair County, with two hundred north Alabama Kluxers actually laying siege to the home of the Republican leader of its opposition. Later Klan assassins gunned him down from ambush and even opened fire on Union troops in a rare and brazen act of defiance against the federals. Shocked by the hill-country resistance, one soldier told his commanding officer that he had never heard of a "more complete subordination of the civil authorities . . . to the mob element." That same month, at nearby Cross Plains or Patona in Calhoun County, whites leaving Sunday morning services shot it out with a group of armed blacks. Enraged, north Alabama whites arrested William Luke, a Methodist preacher from Canada, and charged him with inciting the black community to violence. The white mob, which included a Baptist minister, shot the blacks and hanged the unfortunate Canadian. Although authorities arrested nine suspected Klansmen, no one was ever punished for the crime. Before they hung him, since he was white, his executioners allowed Luke ten minutes to write a farewell letter to his wife. The letter survived.

> My Dear Wife:
> I die tonight. It has been so determined by those who think I deserve it. God only knows I feel myself entirely innocent of the charge. I have only sought to educate the negro. I little thought when leaving

you that we should thus part forever so distant from each other. But God's will be done. He will be to you a husband better than I have been, and a father to our six little ones. . . .

Your loving husband,
William[35]

While north Alabama served as a Klan hub, its activity supplemented that of kindred groups in south Alabama's Black Belt. In Sumter County the Klan plotted the elimination of Gerard Chotteau, a Republican planter, physician, and organizer of area blacks. Despite extensive precautions, including hiring a team of bodyguards and moving his family to the relative safety of Livingston, the Klan eventually ran Chotteau out of Alabama, ambushing and wounding a black Republican legislator in the process. When snipers fired gunshots at Chotteau's children as they played in their front yard and burned his house to the ground in his absence, the local Conservative press responded by blaming the doctor for encouraging blacks to vote. A federal district attorney guessed that only fifty blacks remained alive in all of Sumter due to similar depredations. In nearby Greene County, Alexander Boyd, the white Republican prosecutor, announced that he intended to prefer charges against Klan members for terrorizing black people. At midnight forty Kluxers rode into Eutaw, broke into his hotel room, pulled Boyd from his bed, and riddled his head and body with bullets. But instead of fleeing the scene, the Klansmen regrouped outside and rode around the town square in morbid and defiant procession several times before disappearing into the night. Despite the fact that some five hundred people witnessed the Boyd killing and its aftermath, a subsequent case was dismissed.[36]

Episodes such as this illustrate that what is most material about the Reconstruction period is that vigilantes operated with the considerable support of their home communities—largely because they reflected the dominant political, social, economic, and racial attitudes of those areas. In the rare instances where community sentiment atrophied, the Klan quickly dried up and blew away.[37]

Still, some Kluxers rode during the whole period. Perhaps the most notorious of all, Ryland Randolph served as the leading Klan figure in Tuscaloosa County, a hotbed of activity, and the Conservative editor and publisher of the *Tuscaloosa Independent Monitor*. Close to Sipsey River whites made good on their threats by launching an organized campaign of brutal floggings and terror that drove virtually every black Republican from the area. The founder of this den, Randolph was also the darling of the white populace in Tuscaloosa, getting himself elected to the state legislature in 1868.

Randolph engaged in frequent street fights, had his newspaper temporarily muzzled by the federals, was arrested by the U.S. Army, and campaigned to have the University of Alabama closed until it could be reopened under Conservative auspices. His newspaper printed ghastly Klan warnings and, more than once, he wielded weapons in defense of white supremacy. In one street brawl, Randolph came to the assistance of a white man fighting a freedman by plunging a knife into the black man's back. The next day, in an editorial titled "Niggers-Radicals-Ghosts," Randolph gloated over the deed: "The cutting and beating of the insolent fellow . . . in [the] presence of crowds of his fellow niggers, has had a salutary influence over the whole of niggerdom hereabouts. They now feel their inferiority, in every particularity."[38]

John Hunnicut was so proud of his life as a Klansman in west Alabama's Pickens County that he left behind detailed accounts so that his grandchildren could be "amused." For Hunnicut the idea of being tried before a carpetbagger judge with a black jury was just "too much for a white man to swallow"—no matter what you had done. A man of modest means, Hunnicut took pride in relating that it was the most prominent citizens of a number of Alabama communities who stood back of the Klan and approached him for assistance in starting new dens.[39]

Ryland Randolph's sentiments were especially raw, but they, and his status as a folk hero, state lawmaker, and popular editor provide a window into what so many whites in Alabama saw as praiseworthy during Reconstruction. Like the cream of Alabama society as well as its more common components, Randolph invoked conservative religious beliefs ingrained in the region to justify his actions. Black, Republican rule is "unchristian . . . [and] hate-conceived," Randolph lectured. Anyone who would endorse black suffrage "deserves . . . death at the hands of the black savages." "No one has had more" chances to succeed than the slaves. "All fields of action, of wealth and renown have been alike open to him. . . . But no step forward has been taken [because] . . . Niggers are wooly 'nothings.'" "Look at him, smell of him, feel him, if you don't believe me. [H]ear him, and taste of him . . . and then tell me if he is a brother." "A brother?" Randolph wrote. "He may be a blotted copy of a Man, but never a brother." "Make him a citizen, and a voter and all that. Caligula made his horse a consul . . . [but] the Negro has no soul." He could not possibly be "the offspring of Adam. . . . [I]f the Negro was on the ark he went in a beast and he is a beast today."[40]

The Klan and other vigilante groups continued to wage their reign of terror in Alabama and the South with clear Conservative Democratic complicity. Indeed it was difficult to determine where the Klan began and the party left off. In the hill county of Blount, as in most others, the order's grip over the judicial process was so tight that when outrages occurred it was impossible to attain indictments much less convictions. A sample newspaper report from Shelby County in the hill country celebrating Klan activity in the Tennessee Valley suggests why:

> Florence, Alabama: About a week ago Saturday night the Ku Klux came into town to regulate matters. They were here from eleven P.M. to three o'clock A.M.—five hundred in all. They shot one very bad negro, putting six balls through his head.... They also hung three or four negroes nearly dead, and whipped others severely.... These Kuklux ... did not hesitate to unmask themselves.... Every one who saw them says their horses were ... beautiful.... They went to several stores; the doors were opened at once. They then called for rope [and] ... cut it to a suitable length to hang a man with. No one asked for money.... They did not disturb any one else, nor did they take any thing except for some few Enfield rifles ... found in the possession of some very bad negroes.... [I]t has made a great improvement ... [and] has been productive of much good and benefit to the community, though all regret such steps should have to be resorted to.[41]

Let Us Be Generous. . . . The Victory Has Been Won

Between 1870 and 1874 several critical events unfolded to culminate in the demise of the Klan in Reconstruction Alabama. Three Enforcement (or Klan) Acts, passed in 1870 and 1871, finally gave federal authorities the weapons to fight the order they so sorely lacked under state and local law. Using the new federal laws and the stricter federal courts, U.S. District Attorney John A. Minnis stunned Alabamians by achieving fourteen convictions by 1872. He continued his work against community-sponsored vigilantes until 1877 despite howls of protest from the Conservative press.[42]

From July to November 1871 a joint select congressional committee examined 154 witnesses in Alabama and documented at least 258 Klan outrages, including 109 killings (almost certainly a gross underestimation). South Carolina officials suspended habeas corpus in nine counties, arrested hundreds of Knights, and began legal proceedings that shook the order and its foundations throughout Dixie. In 1872 Congress passed the Amnesty Act, pardoning most of the remaining Rebels and leaving only 500 leading former Confederates in the South disfranchised.

As much as any single act could, the Amnesty Act heralded the imminent triumph of Democratic and Conservative politics in Alabama. Redemption from Reconstruction arrived in November 1874 as the Conservative Democrats swept state elections and retook control of Alabama. Gone was the need for—or the viability of—a secret, paramilitary order. Ku Kluxism died in Alabama because the federal government took effective action against it at the precise moment Conservative Democratic forces regained political power in the state and thus made its existence moot—even a possible liability. With the Bourbons back in the saddle, there was no reason for a continuation of the terror. Even Ryland Randolph called for an end to the violence.[43]

Everyone in Alabama knew the stakes involved before the first ballot was cast—or stolen—in 1874: white supremacy.[44] In this it was absolutely paramount for whites from the various physical sections and classes in Alabama to close ranks in order to reestablish the fundamental of white control over constituted government. The Tennessee Valley's *Florence Times-Journal* asked, will the white people of Lauderdale County lie on their backs and "permit the negroes, scalawags and adventurers [to] crawl like reptiles" into positions of official authority over whites? It is "false and suicidal" for anyone to deny that the race issue was *the* issue of 1874, came the call from Tuscaloosa, the "true and only issue" according to the *Jacksonville Republican* in north Alabama.[45]

Perhaps the most enduring lesson learned in Redemption was that black, Yankee, Republican, and federal rule could be smashed in the South if whites across class and sectional lines would only put aside their economic differences and cooperate with one another.[46] And so passion and pan-white solidarity resulted in north Alabama cooperating with south Alabama to elect George S. Houston governor in 1874.

Houston ran an intensely racial campaign as the Conservatives took advantage of Republican bickering to end Reconstruction in their state. Bourbon heavyweights Hilary Abner Herbert and John Tyler Morgan joined state Democratic and Conservative chairman W. L. Bragg to stump for essential white votes throughout the poorer north Alabama and hill country. Morgan again invoked the state's affinity for conservative religion by using a Bible as his main campaign prop. As a member of the Reconstruction Knights of the White Camellia and a later Populist leader put it, the appeal to the whites for united race action was "heard with the ardor of earnest men thoroughly aroused to meet the menaces of fanaticism precipitated from without." "South Alabama raises her manacled hands in mute appeal to the mountain counties," wrote Alabama's leading Black Belt newspaper. "The chains on the wrists of her sons, and the midnight shrieks of her women, sound continually in their ears. She lifts up her eyes, being tormented, and begs piteously for relief from the bondage. Is there a white man in North Alabama so lost to all his finer feelings of human nature as to slight her appeal?"[47] The answer was no. Whites from across north Alabama's Tennessee Valley and hill country responded to the appeals of the largely African American Black Belt for united political action and finally achieved Redemption from Republican rule.

It is insufficient to say simply that Redemption marked a sea change. After nine years of the most blatant and recalcitrant acts of oppression, repression, and outright violence, Conservative Democracy—with virtually one voice and overnight—called for prudence, forbearance, moderation, and solicitude toward Alabama's vanquished blacks and Republicans. Above all, they called for peace. Newspaper after newspaper, politician after politician took the exact same line and repeated the exact same message. Why? And why as soon as Redemption was accomplished in November 1874?

At stake was the holiest of holies: states' rights concerning domestic race relations and a cheap, regular, and plentiful supply of labor—black and white. With federal troops leaving Alabama, continued truculence beyond Redemption served no good or useful purpose; in fact it risked the state losing that which it prized most: to be left alone in its racial customs and to be revitalized economically with an infusion of docile labor, and northern capital and industrialization. With Redemption, the stage was set for the New South.

It really was quite remarkable. Here we have a civilization that had perpetrated, excused, apologized for, and tolerated one of the most systematic programs of violence and brutality in American history. It had refused to punish such acts even when they occurred in broad daylight and within the purview of all.[48] Now, suddenly, it called for a cessation of all of it—in fact, the society called for its utter opposite.

George S. Houston did not disappoint. In his inaugural address the new governor led the way in calling for peace, moderation, and protection for *all citizens* "without regard to race, color, or previous condition" of servitude, to safeguard everyone in Alabama and their property. His words echoed those of W. L. Bragg, chairman of the State Democratic Executive Committee, who, in the glow of victory, pledged a new "cheerful obedience" to the laws of the United States and a prompt assumption of Alabama's share of the nation's burdens in war and peace: "[We] will not throw away in rashness or folly, the splendid victory we have won," echoed the speaker of the state house.[49]

Alabama's Conservative and Democratic press followed the party line with one voice from every section of the state. "Let us be just and generous," called the *Union Springs Herald* from the Black Belt. The "battle has been fought and the victory won," answered the *Jacksonville Republican* in north

Alabama. Let there be "no excesses or vindictive retaliatory measures." "Your rights will be preserved inviolate," the *Opelika Times* assured black people in east Alabama. Conservative Democracy will "safeguard your interests and its own."[50]

The new era brought bountiful business prospects and, with them, a stress on the prerequisites of affluence: cheap labor, peace, security, and the attraction of northern capital and economic development. Our "greatest responsibility," adjudged the *Eutaw Whig and Observer,* is the task to "restore tranquility, peace, confidence, and prosperity." This way "industry will be encouraged, business will be fostered," and we will "show the world, that the white men of the State are able and willing to guarantee" and protect black laborers in all their rights of citizenship. "Retrenchment and reform . . . peace and prosperity," the *Southern Argus* cried in connecting tax cuts and fiscal conservatism to the resumption of white supremacy and right-thinking religion. The *Greenville Advocate* weighed in with "justice, peace, and prosperity" for all people.[51] Essential to all of these well-laid plans was the clear demonstration of Dixie's newfound suitability and reliability as a place for the profitable infusion of northern capital. Law and order, peace and tranquility, were essential to assure outside investors.

"[Let us] give the rest of the country an example of moderation and forbearance [that will leave no doubt in anyone's mind that] WHITE men are the true friends" of the Negro, and that productive blacks could expect assistance and protection at all times, chimed the *Choctaw Herald* of north Alabama. "Our most sacred duty [is] to vindicate by our actions the confidence reposed in us by our friends" in the Great North and West, reasoned the Black Belt's *Selma Echo*. "[We should be] particularly kind and forbearing to Negroes, these poor creatures." No abuses and no more outrages, called the *Troy Messenger* of central Alabama. "Hereafter the 'outrage' business will not be heard from," promised the Tennessee Valley's *Moulton Advertiser*. "The African people [will] enjoy all the advantages of liberty and law," magnanimously claimed the *Birmingham Iron Age*.[52]

Yet just as essential to the new order was a policy of northern and federal laissez-faire on race and the allowance of home rule, states' rights, and local adjustment of social customs by the South's "better" whites. Connected to this recognition of the wisdom and proper hegemony of privileged whites was also a budding regional defensiveness that would rapidly descend into a type of paranoia. The *Montgomery Daily Advertiser* vowed that people from across the country would learn that under "the rule of white men their interests . . . will be protected and their property greatly enhanced," and there will be a bright future for all classes. "Stop the cry of Ku-Klux," the paper continued in setting the template for regional hyperdefensiveness. "Show to the world at large and to the North in particular" that the South had been slandered and "misrepresented" about alleged abuses during the Reconstruction years. Then the credit of the state would be restored and capital and enterprise attracted. States' Rights and home rule were the way to go. The surest way to establish Dixie as a place where business could flourish was to "let the people" (meaning the whites) "adjust these matters for themselves." With the reaccession of native white men to power in Alabama, a "new era of peace and prosperity begins in the State," agreed the *Tuscaloosa Times*. Businesses of all kinds would revive, emigration would set in from other sections of the country, and people would be content to live and work in the sunny South.[53]

Because of his ultraviolent past perhaps no one had the bona fides of Tuscaloosa editor Ryland Randolph. Redemption and the corresponding decline of the Klan were intimately entwined with the dominance of capital, the seemingly eternal quest for cheaper and cheaper labor, the attraction of outside investment, and racial control of the ballot by economic means. It is with special interest, then, that we turn to Randolph's remarks in the wake of political victory:

> The State of Alabama is redeemed, perhaps forever. We say perhaps because it rests with the white people of the State to determine. . . . If [the Negro] must go through with the farce of voting, he must be made, by the controlling influence of capital, to vote with his employers. . . . The negro will resume his normal condition of undisputed inferiority; and both races will be happier and better off in every way. . . . [But] never forget or forgive those insidious [white] enemies who have . . . pulled with the negro hounds. . . . We, the white men of Alabama have just gained a signal victory, and it behooves us to conduct ourselves so that we may enjoy, fully, all the fruits. To this end, moderation and forbearance must be our motto [so that we may reverse] . . . this revulsion of political feeling created over the North. [If we are not careful] the tide of public opinion may yet be turned against us as suddenly and overwhelmingly as it has been moved in our favor. By proper precaution and obedience to the laws we will, in two more years, elect a Democratic President, and thus completely get our necks from under the yoke of Radical oppression. Let us prove to the world the blessings of the white man's government in Alabama under our Democratic Administration. . . . Our policy should be to invite, attract and welcome all capital and white labor to our great State; throwing no barrier in shape of insecurity to life, liberty or property. . . . We must treat

the African elephant in our midst kindly. . . . Let us white men, prove to the satisfaction of the misled masses of the North that a Southern State under our rule is freer from crime and outrage than it was under Radical misrule. Let us pocket all past insult and wrong . . . for our own sakes. Vulgarly speaking, we must not holler till we are clean out of the woods. . . . Discipline, prudence and moderation. . . . [R]estrain ourselves [and] . . . Alabama will be forever free from negro domination.[54]

In the wake of Redemption, southern whites got busy constructing a Myth of the Lost Cause and a New South Creed to rebuild their states along the lines of sectional reconciliation, local control of racial and social customs, the importation of industry and capital, a virulently pro-business, anti-union climate, and an acute defensiveness against regional slights. In this myth and creed, epidemic violence toward the freed slaves and the whites who aided them faded like an ancient mist before the new memory. Federal investigations were a needless, divisive, and partisan creature, inaugurated by Republicans only for the purpose of political intimidation before the next presidential election.

In this, the cynical view held, blacks are used as before without regard to their true interest and for the oppression of southern white men by "outsiders" posing as the false friends of the African, aliens who would prey upon the simple and ignorant nature of blacks to subvert the wise counsel and generosity of their real friends, the better whites. Rapacious outsiders would work to turn the black man against the very people upon whose prosperity depends his own well-being (as they had during Reconstruction and would again during the New Deal and modern civil rights movement). In the process these users would deny the socially separated, ineffaceable lines traced by God Himself. And so conservative religion, as it had before the Civil War, was again mobilized to buttress a pro-southern cause—this time business dominance, industrial development, and white supremacy.

Southerners had most assuredly lost the war. Just as surely, though, they had every intention of winning the peace. As in the aftermath of so many wars and dislocations came the rewriting of history. Things really hadn't been that bad down South, the *(Selma) Southern Argus* opined. Despite plenty of bad press up North, there had been no real antagonism between the races in Alabama during Reconstruction, only false and exaggerated reports of isolated instances that could have just as easily occurred in Michigan or Ohio. Indeed, the editor (a future Populist) wrote, we "know of no single case in Alabama in which a negro has suffered personal violence because of his color, or in which a republican has been maltreated or wronged because of his political opinions." So, now, wrote the editor, let us put all of this nonsense behind us for, in the end, "we . . . believe in the manhood of the northern people, in their sense of justice, in their love of truth."[55]

The flip side of the conservative myth and creed that supported it was something of equal and lasting power for the American South: resentment and bitterness toward all things federal, racial, and liberal. Along with it southerners cultivated a hyperdefensiveness and adopted a distinctly unattractive yet useful victimhood. The honest belief of the white southern people, wrote one astute Republican, is that they are "the most grossly wronged and outraged people on the face of the earth." Under the domination of the carpetbaggers and scalawags, a white resident of Sumter County remembered, Dixie had become "one vast cess-pool of political maggots, stenches, and corruptions," and remained so until all federal troops were withdrawn and federal interference with government and society ceased. So determined were white Alabamians to see that the federal government should remain a foreign and antagonistic threat in the minds of the white southerner that (not unlike in modern war-torn countries) local Conservative and Democratic officials hoarded food, medical supplies, and provisions sent as aid from the U.S. government. Then—in order to prevent the federals from receiving any credit in the minds of the masses—they redistributed the materiel to the people as something that had come from the South.[56]

And so began the South's strange and tortured relationship with the federal government, one climaxed in the New Deal. It was one of perpetual adolescent rebellion in which the region accepted—indeed supplicated with outstretched hands—federal bounty, only to take a perverse pride in what it liked to call its surly and stubborn independence and dislike of all things Yankee and federal: things which, by the way, were becoming increasingly conflated as one and the same in the southern mind.

Religion was scarcely an antidote. In fact conservative theology served as a firm pillar for such a society. As one pious Alabama woman confessed: "When I let my mind dwell on all of our wrongs, oh how wicked I get. . . . The Yankee Congress have filled the bitter cup of the Southern people to overflowing." Such sentiment permeated Alabama and the South. You could travel to any corner of Alabama, a Freedmen's Bureau agent agreed, and you will see "no signs . . . hear no words of nurturing" of black people or of loyalty to the national government. "No union is cherished; nothing *national* is cultivated."[57]

2
Elements of Democratic Solidarity *and* Discontent
Industry, Economics, Calvinist Religion, and Jim Crow

> Sentiment is all right . . . where your home is. But downtown, no. . . . [T]he dog that snaps the quickest gets the bone. Friendship is very nice for a Sunday afternoon . . . around the dinner table with your relations, talking about the sermon that morning. But nine o'clock Monday morning, [those] notions should be brushed aside like cobwebs. . . . [When doing] business . . . [a man] ought not to have a relation in the world—and least of all a poor relation.
> —Daniel Drew

Reconstruction was only the first major element that would serve as a glue and, later, *a solvent* of the Solid Democratic South. The era, with its attendant "syndrome," certainly left a set of powerful attitudes to serve as a basis for sectional ethos. But succeeding events only crystallized and hardened the original mold. The making of the New South, in terms of attracting industry after the war, went leagues in the direction of bequeathing Dixie with a stubborn set of uncompromising business values, economic shibboleths, and societal beliefs. The hardening of Jim Crow, with the simultaneous move to excise the African American from politics, dominated an era as disfranchisement and segregation helped snuff out sporadic labor insurgencies and the Populist movement. The result was, more than anything else, additional lessons in how race, religion, patriotism, and other issues could divide poor whites and blacks along an axis of emotion, to their mutual and seemingly perpetual detriment.

Making the New South: Industrialization and Societal Values

The Reconstruction Syndrome, along with its heavy attendant traits and predilections, was powerfully fortified in the South by the region's subsequent nineteenth-century experiences. The cataclysm of civil war ushered in profound and remarkable changes in the southern pattern of life—human, physical, political, legal, economic. The conflict settled the question of whether the eleven Confederate States would comprise a separate nation. Some were dragged kicking and screaming back into the Union, and the Union itself was preserved. A fifth of all southern white males did not emerge from the conflict; they were dead. Another tenth was maimed or without limbs. Only one in three southern white males survived the cataclysm intact—and that only in a purely physical sense. Shell shock, battle fatigue, and post-traumatic stress disorder were not yet part of the military lexicon. As with most wars, the lion's share of the fighting was done by the plain people who owned few if any slaves and little land. The Civil War was yet one more installment in the world's long history of a "rich man's war and a poor man's fight."

Dixie had been the clear military loser in the conflict and as such embarked upon a period unknown by any other group of American citizens before or since—occupation by a foreign military power. Although at most only 22,000 federal troops occupied the eleven former Confederate States (on average just 2,000 per state)—and the vast majority of those confined themselves to town garrisons—the psychological effect was devastating.[1] It was a blow from which the southern psyche has, perhaps even now, not yet fully recovered.

Yet the war brought other changes in the southern way of life, at least as profound and far-reaching as these, the most obvious. Culture, society, work, and the economy all changed dramatically. Prior to the hostilities, Dixie could best be described as an agrarian society comprised of large and small farms alike. Afterward wealthy planter elites were, to invoke perhaps a crude generalization, left with land but no labor, the freedmen with labor but no land.

After talk of "forty acres and a mule" faded and an economic reconstruction was ruled out, the southern states groped for some new arrangement to replace the slave-based, forced-labor system that had been abolished by, first, the Emancipation Proclamation and, then more completely, the Thirteenth Amendment. Now that the slaves had been, in a quick succession of constitutional amendments, granted their freedom (Thirteenth), civil rights, equal protection, and due process under the law (Fourteenth), and right to vote (Fifteenth), the slave-based agricultural system that had dominated the South since colonial times had to be replaced.

The predominant solution in the southern countryside, sharecropping and tenancy—while solving the riddle of planters with land but no labor, and freedmen and poor whites with labor but no land—was a prescription for disaster. Systemic debt, poverty, privation, and a precariousness of life that teetered on subsistence were the constant companions of the overwhelming mass of southern whites and blacks. Not least among their problems—apart from the usual agrarian threats of drought, flood, and pestilence—was fraud rife in the "crop-lien" or "furnish" system in which illiterate and semiliterate persons made their mark on contracts of debt with country-store merchants, some of whom had lately been masters under the slave system.

Nor could the freedmen and poor whites be overly blamed for their illiterate state. There were still former slaves walking the South minus a chin or nose or ear to mark their attempt at having learned to read and write under the chattel system. Spending for public education was not a priority for the southern taxpayer. Once the Great Depression finally reached the rural hinterland, many croppers and tenants did not know the difference—so steady was the downward economic spiral in which they were trapped, and so accustomed to cyclical poverty had they become.[2]

The solution that came to the southern city was, in many respects, no better. In the wake of war and Reconstruction, New South leaders largely prostituted their region in order to industrialize. In their exuberance to bewitch northern and English capital, boosters bragged of cheap, docile, black and Anglo-Saxon labor, gave away miles of the choicest real estate and tons of natural resources, and pledged their governments to guarantee tax incentives, subsidies, welfare for businesses, and undying opposition to organized labor.[3] After Reconstruction, Dixie's Redeemer leadership waged a calculated effort to transform the region by attracting northern capital, punctuated by the efforts of a cadre of the region's most prominent newspapermen: Richard Edmonds, Henry Watterson, Daniel Augustus Tompkins, and Henry W. Grady of the *Baltimore Manufacturers Record, Louisville Courier-Journal, Charlotte Observer,* and *Atlanta Constitution,* respectively.

In his famous 1886 message of sectional rapprochement to the New England Society of New York, Grady articulated the classic version of what has since become known as the New South Creed: sectional reconciliation and mutual improvement through an infusion of northern capital and manufacturing in a South brimming with raw materials, cheap labor, natural resources, and conservative, pro-business politicians.[4] In Alabama, as in other states, New South boosterism was institutionalized in chambers of commerce and state commissions that seduced outside capital by exploiting the region's poverty, desperation, low wages, and natural resources—and by cultivating a ferocious anti-union climate.[5]

Although such boosterism eventually led to a 450 percent increase in Birmingham's iron production over prewar standards (to 915,000 tons in 1892) and brought other industries to the state, progress did not occur without a cavalcade of sobering side effects. The infusion of northern capital into the South's fledgling industrial centers was closely linked to what can fairly be called "colonization" rather than a full and free economic development. A succession of predatory buyouts punctuated by J. P. Morgan's 1907 takeover of the Tennessee Coal, Iron and Railroad Company (TCI) on behalf of U.S. Steel epitomized such economic imperialism. U.S. Steel inflicted the prejudicial "Pittsburgh Plus" base-point system on Birmingham, artificially raising the price of southern iron so that it could not effectively compete with northern output. Absentee iron and steel entrepreneurs also restricted the Birmingham forges to the production of inferior forms of iron: pig, bar, and sheet. As a result the southern steel center reached only 40 percent of its potential iron output, and, from 1893 to 1913, the South's share of the national steel market fell by a full half.[6] Despite the artificially constrained production, Alabama boosters celebrated their chosen pattern of industrialization, flamboyantly borrowing names from the English steel towns for Birmingham and the satellite communities that dotted its perimeter: Leeds, Sheffield, Bessemer, Fairfield, and Pratt City.[7]

Industrialization brought technology, modernity, and some measure of nationalization to the South. But for southern workers it also meant the lowest wages and most wretched living standards in the entire country. The by-products of the New South factory system, to a large extent, crippled southern society: almost nonexistent unionization, pitiful health standards, hookworm, pellagra, illiteracy, a coercive and predatory alliance between big business and state and local governments, poverty, misery, despair. Sectional rapprochement, a staple of the New South movement, recast the political relationship between North and South in terms hardly favorable to Dixie. In stark contrast to the antebellum pattern of the Virginia Dynasty, Marshall, Jackson, Calhoun, Clay, and outsized southern congressional influence, the new arrangement virtually ignored the region. Economically, reconciliation meant colonization, with the South as a conquered possession, a reservoir of cheap raw materials, and a dumping ground for excess manufactured goods from the North. Economic historians studying New South cities like Birmingham invariably conclude with sad indictments: the city was inordinately influenced by a legacy of "slavery and peonage, the elites' clever manipulation of racial difference . . . [and] the ruthless exercise of local and police power to crush insurgency wherever it appeared."[8]

Southern industrial cities, in the estimation of scholars, were plagued by illiberal, retrograde political systems that forestalled attention to vital problems by exaggerating racial problems for political reasons. Such an environment was tailor-made for northern capital to flourish. The new industrialists were usually considered public benefactors "even when they made higher profits, paid lower wages, and maintained poorer working conditions" than did their competitors outside the region.[9]

The construction of a New South narrative with factory owner as hero was critical to the formation of a conservative political economy and the cultivation of a strong pro-business and anti-union culture. Such was not strictly a southern phenomenon. Far from it. This strain of thought could find its way back to at least Voltaire—although that iconoclast was mostly interested in the pacifying potential of commerce during an age of barbarous religious violence and fanaticism. Rather, the idea of proprietor as benefactor came south along with northern capital, but it took root in a soil far more desperate for the water of financial investment than that north of the Mason-Dixon Line, soil not leavened by the Yankee equivalent of a strong union movement, economic diversity, the New England commitment to public education and the commonweal, and wide-ranging ethnic, religious, and reform activities. As such, the New South entrepreneur—homegrown or imported—enjoyed an exalted status magnified by the desperation of the southern cause. This would be a prime factor in the more-or-less complete sway the business class held in the New South, a suzerainty only sporadically and partially challenged until the advent of the New Deal.[10]

In many ways the southern drive to remake the region along the North's industrial model promised the moon and more. Professional New South boosters, desperate for start-up cash and financial backing, appealed to northern and English investors and, in doing so, too often stepped over the line of enticement and seduction into outright solicitation. The southern industrial base, never very impressive, had been decimated by war.[11] Union generals destroyed over ten thousand miles of southern railway along with the region's few iron foundries, steel mills, and munitions plants. And, of course, Sherman burned Atlanta, marched to the sea, and engaged in "total war" tactics designed to break the Confederacy's will to fight. Southern currency, as befit a defeated military power, was worthless. All eleven state currencies, various town and city currencies, as well as Confederate money wasn't worth the paper it was printed on. Into this breach stepped the New South booster backed by Yankee capital and, to give the movement sectional veritas, fronted by former Confederate generals.

Within a few years the South's industrial cities were booming: Nashville, Atlanta, Richmond, Knoxville, Chattanooga, Louisville, Norfolk, Charlotte, New Orleans—and, of course, Birmingham. Of these the rise of Birmingham, the Magic City, was perhaps the most spectacular. The city gained its famous moniker because in 1870 it consisted of only a railroad crossing in a weed-covered pasture named Jones Valley. A year later it was, magically, Birmingham, a thriving metropolis—noisy, smoky, busy, and violent. Steel mills belched smoke and dirt into the air, coal mines ripped mineral wealth from the earth, and railroads hummed—and all because huge deposits of coal and iron ore had been found in the hills and mountains surrounding Jones Valley.[12]

The booster's job (attracting outside capital to finance the building of the New South's steel works, iron foundries, textile mills, and railroads and stocking them with workers) soon resulted in intense competition between and among the former Confederate States. Each sought to outdo the other in promising those things that made their state more attractive to Yankee mill owners and financiers. Taking out full-page ads in northern newspapers and magazines, the boosters promised (and delivered) goodies that exceeded any industrialist's wildest dreams—if they would just venture South: low or no taxation, bountiful natural resources, low spending on social services, abundant grants in the form of giant tracts of free land, government subsidies and incentives, a "favorable" social and political climate that would underwrite business success, cheap, plentiful, and docile workers (submissive blacks fresh from chattel servitude and dirt-poor whites without skills who were constantly reminded that they could be replaced in a moment with any of thirty "barefoot boys" waiting at the plant gate), and, perhaps most of all, no unions.

It was not strictly true that the South did not have unions—it did. But as a rule they were small, weak, broke, and thinly populated relative to their northern cousins and ensconced in a culture that stitched anti-union attitudes into its very fabric. The business owner, should he move south, would find himself blessed by the native populace—not just as a commercial actor but as a *public benefactor,* a savior even; a maker of payrolls, a provider of jobs, a supplier of sustenance—in a word, a hero. Labor unions, on the contrary, would be portrayed in the New South Creed as all that was bad and unproductive, selfish and detrimental—and these canted attitudes would be drummed into every schoolboy and girl that the newspapers (owned and operated to a large extent by the very industries leading the New South wave) could reach: the *Birmingham News, Birmingham Age-Herald, Atlanta Constitution, Louisville Courier-Journal.* All the major elements of the creed would endure in the South, including those that conflated piety, religious conservatism, and moralism with dislike for unions and other forms of collective or cooperative action.[13]

One Dies, Get Another

But, as anywhere else, the economic was not the economic alone. It was the political as well—and vice versa. Perhaps the defining problem confronting the South's old Bourbon elite and its new Redeemer industrial allies was the central problem that faces all economically conservative regimes: How do you maintain popular support, especially in a democratic political system that, ostensibly, requires majority rule? How do you curry mass electoral support for, at root, an economic agenda that stands to benefit very few? The usual methods of force and fraud were, of course, available. And it was not especially difficult to convince ordinary people that, despite reality, a program of conservative economics stood to benefit everyone, not just a few.[14] As a veteran labor organizer in Alabama would reflect years later: "Some poor people, bless their hearts, are the best people in the world. One of the reasons they are all poor is the fact that they ain't got much sense, they don't know enough to organize and don't know when people are using them."[15] But for the Redeemers, the problem ran deeper than that.

After the war the Bourbons who craved restoration looked on the South's mass of plain whites and black freedmen and collectively shuddered. What would be the electoral consequences if such a disparate and multitudinous force could ever weld themselves into a class alliance? The prospect haunted Bourbon dreams—as well it should have. As much as anything else, the New South's pro-business, anti-union climate merged with racial tensions—both natural and manufactured—to short-circuit the spasmodic, temporary, and largely unsuccessful attempts at biracial class insurgency that dotted the southern landscape: the Greenbackers, the Knights of Labor, the United Mine Workers, the Populists. Force and fraud found their uses, as did laissez-faire mythology about collective bootstraps and trickle-down profits. But perhaps the most effective armament in the Redeemer arsenal was emotion—racial loyalty, to be sure, but other high-caliber weapons like religious orthodoxy and right-thinking patriotism. Of course eventually there were material benefits to be derived from the factory for many in the South. Automobiles, refrigerators, and air conditioning would, in time, improve the quality of life. But as the masterful historian C. Vann Woodward recognized, the real tragedy bequeathed to the South by these times was more than material; it was one of enduring conservative values and attitudes that bordered on the pathologically callous and indifferent. "Measured in terms of ignorance and suffering," Woodward wrote, "the . . . neglect of social responsibilities [was] grave [but] . . . a more permanent injury was the set of values imposed upon the Southern mind by the rationalization of this negligence."[16]

To deal with the threat of organized labor, should it rear its ugly head, industrialists led the way in fomenting racial tension among the largely biracial membership of unions such as the mineworkers and the Knights of Labor. Upbraiding working-class whites for dishonoring their racial birthright to conspire with inferior blacks and whispering in the freedmen's ears that they could not trust the poor-white cracker who was interested in them only for the lynch knot, New South types did their best to snuff out any flicker of biracial cooperation.

If these tricks did not work, there was always brute force. City police, county sheriffs, indeed whole state militias were put at the disposal of mill owners and mine operators who used them to crush—quite literally—various labor insurgencies across the South. Harlan County, Kentucky, the Tennessee railroads, and the various hills and hollows of West Virginia all found their way into the bloody lore of labor history. In the coal industry alone, Alabama's soil ran red with blood (as did that of her sister states) in a succession of violent strikes that involved state militias, private armies, and special "deputies" (who were commonly recruited from the ranks of company guards and endowed with official police power) in 1894, 1904, 1908, from 1917–21, and several times during the 1930s.[17]

Meanwhile, New South boosters for the various southern states cut each other's throats to cast their state as the most ideal, business-friendly, tax-free, anti-union, docile workforce haven, Mississippi more than Georgia, Alabama more than both. Florida's legislature got so carried away that its leadership actually pledged more acres in free, public-land grants to prospective northern firms than actually existed in the state's entire land mass (22.4 million acres promised from a possible 15 million).[18]

The costs of industrialization for southern society were considerable. Illiteracy, urban tenancy, oppressive child, women, and convict labor systems, poor health, low wages, long hours, economic colonialism, squandered resources, and wretched standards of living all too often accompanied technology, modernity, and the factory. Tenancy reached epidemic proportions in the South's new industrial centers. In Birmingham, the city that led the nation in that category, nine out of every ten persons did not own their homes.[19] Six-year-old children toiled for eight cents a day in Huntsville's textile mills. In 1877 the Alabama legislature cut the maximum hours children could work to eight per day, but by 1895 the lobbying of a New England mill executive reversed the ceiling for child labor hours in Alabama.[20]

But arguably the crown jewel of the New South was the barbaric convict-lease system—a blight on the southern mind, soul, and psyche for over six decades. A purely southern phenomenon, a bona fide child of Reconstruction, the lease was born in 1865 and made its appearance in—and only in—the eleven former Confederate States. Alabama was the last state in the Union to abolish the practice, and that did not occur until 1928. But the lease—despite its barbarity, its obscenity, its pure capacity to conjure inhumanity toward other human beings—had one overwhelmingly redeeming quality that guaranteed its survival for over sixty years. It was profitable—fantastically profitable. And for that reason more than anything else, it came into existence and it thrived.

The lease involved the state's renting of prisoners to the burgeoning industries of the New South—coal mines, steel mills, iron foundries, turpentine camps, railroads, logging villages, textile mills. Arrangements for feeding, clothing, lodging, and disciplining the inmates were to be left in the hands of the leasers: the employers. And so the most appalling practices ensued—occasionally the perverse fruit of individual sadism or depravity, but more often from the more banal desire to fatten the bottom line.

Prisoners were scourged, sometimes to death, for minor infractions or failure to meet production quotas. Men and women were housed in the same cells, sometimes in rolling iron cages that resembled a crude traveling circus, moving from worksite to worksite as the southern sun beat down mercilessly and summer insects swarmed. The inevitable happened from housing inmates of different sexes in such close proximity; children were actually born into the lease. Employers used almost unimaginable forms of discipline for convicts who failed to meet work quotas or other petty offenses: beating, crucifixion, the rack. Bosses hung some convicts by their thumbs; survivors bore hands that resembled the paws of certain animals. Gangs of shackled men labored in ice-cold, waist-deep water in the mines. If just one failed to meet his quota, employers flogged all of them so viciously that skin was separated from bone. Foremen placed others into tiny wooden isolation boxes, no bigger than doghouses. Under the southern sun bodies swelled and burst before they were pried out days later, if still alive. Men, women, and children relieved themselves in the same filthy buckets of water from which they bathed and drank. Food was spoiled and filled with worms; bedding was vermin and lice infested. Mortality rates were appalling. At more than one railroad construction site they reached over 50 percent, the bodies simply buried in shallow graves dotting the railroad line.[21]

At construction projects inmates fell into concrete mixing vats and drowned or were suffocated while their supervisors made no attempt at rescue. It cost less to simply rent a replacement than halt the production process. "One dies, get another" became a macabre colloquialism with more than just a little validity.[22] In Alabama one inspecting prison board member found conditions so abhorrent that he wrote in his official report: "If the state wishes to execute its prisoners, it should do so directly."[23]

Paperwork was not a priority. Prison records went lost or missing, and inmates could easily get swept up for minor infractions and lost in the bowels of the lease only to wind up there decades later (if they survived at all), family members never learning their fate. By and large the convicts were not murderers or rapists either. At its heart the lease was a system of racial and class control—75 percent black, the rest mostly poor whites. Prisoners who found themselves in the system could get years for crimes as petty as stealing a chicken or taking a shirt from a clothesline, public drunkenness, or "vagrancy" (the act of being unemployed). At the county-fee level, sheriffs received the incentive of a dollar amount per convict added to the system. Not unlike the English naval impressment system, more than a few convicts found themselves living this nightmare because they looked physically able to do a "good day's work."

But the material benefits were simply too good to be outweighed by humanitarian details. More than one political dynasty, as one of the South's most eminent historians has noted, could trace the roots of its political and economic power to the lease.[24] Politically it was a bonanza to southern officeholders confronting the rage and hurt and seething resentment of a white electorate that felt itself violated in the most unspeakable ways during Reconstruction. Politicians could go to the people aggrieved at their own recent disfranchisement—and the *enfranchisement* of their former slaves—and promise them no new taxes for the construction of jails, penitentiaries, or schools for blacks. A prison population could be turned into a handsome revenue stream instead of a drain on the state's coffers. The disorder of crime and punishment could be replaced by the order of a terrorized black and poor-white populace confronted by the constant specter of the lease. Efficiency and conservative government would rule as food, clothing, and lodging would be born by the growing mills and factories of the New South rather than the taxpayer.

For southern conservatives this meant the substitution of form and structure for the just-lost slave system, a powerful mechanism to control the labor and lives of African Americans and whites of little means. For the bosses it meant cheap and, literally, captive labor. Not surprisingly, wherever it was found the lease depressed the wages of free workers—another boon to employers. The system also supplied a ready-made strikebreaking force at the disposal of state and corporate power should one of the region's few unions launch a strike, a fact not lost on leading entrepreneurs such as TCI's Arthur Colyar.[25]

And so, for all of these reasons, the women and religious reformers who confused theology with humanitarianism and clamored for an end to the lease could be patted on their heads and sent back to the kitchens or cloistered church by the all-knowing male decision makers. The bosses smiled to themselves at the innocence and quaint sentimentality of those unsuited by sex or demeanor for the hardscrabble world of business and politics.[26]

The Public Be Damned

All of this was possible only in a society where control was confused for authority, force for legitimacy. Perhaps more than any other region of the country, the southern states were smitten with the late nineteenth-century dogma of Social Darwinism—a perverse twist on Charles Darwin that attempted to apply his biological principles of "natural selection" and "survival of the fittest" to the *social* relations of human beings (in direct contradistinction to his explicit admonitions).[27]

Social Darwinism appealed to the pleasing self-image white southerners had constructed for themselves of rugged individualism, plucky frontier spirit, and stubborn independence. It is true; those elements *were* present in the southern makeup. But more often than not they combined with other, more silent characteristics, less pleasing to the psyche perhaps but just as powerful. The result was a kind of regional schizophrenia: rebels awed by social hierarchy and authority, individualists constantly looking over their shoulders to comply with convention, free spirits haunted by a reverential appreciation for order, and nonconformists tethered by conformist chains of their own making—a paralyzing and almost innate conservatism.

Pioneered by English philosopher Herbert Spencer and popularized by Americans such as William Graham Sumner, Social Darwinism badly misapplied Darwin's teachings but provided a powerful, nigh irresistible rationale for status quo and hierarchy in the relations between human beings. Nineteenth-century inequalities had a scientific explanation now. Men held sway over women, white over black, native over foreigner, employer over employee, and rich over poor because that is the way *nature* intended it. Science demanded it. Reason decreed it. And to tamper with that was to risk the progress of the entire human race.

Those who tried to interfere in this natural process were thus a threat to the whole species, to its survival and progress, to civilization itself: the do-gooder, the reformer, the liberal, the suffragette, the labor unionist—any who would try to subvert the inequalities and imbalances set down by nature. For these people were not merely going against nature. They were blaspheming against the Divine author of that nature. They were tampering with the very work of God Himself!

The Social Darwinists were not the first conservatives to invoke the power of God as rationalization for societal inequality. Edmund Burke, the eighteenth-century giant of conservatism, had lamented the fate of the "unhappy people" who toiled in poverty to make the free-market system run but concluded finally that it is "generally pernicious to disturb the natural course of things, and to impede in any degree the great wheel of circulation which is turned by [their] strangely directed labour." Burke warned against "breaking the laws of commerce, which are the laws of nature, and consequently the laws of God." In the nineteenth century Thorstein Veblen (in an echo of Adam Smith) would lampoon such tenets as "unjust legal fiction" propagated by the ruling classes and "sanctioned by the clergy" as the "torturous assumption that the wish of the aristocrats is the will of God."[28]

Still, this was powerful stuff in the late nineteenth century. Like most ideas that consume nations, Social Darwinism was not something that people necessarily repeated in a conscious sense. Few walked the streets with copies of Spencer's *Social Statics* tucked under their arms. But the ideas themselves, if not the wealth, trickled down into the very arteries of American life. And ordinary people did talk of "might makes right" and the "law of the jungle" and "personal responsibility" being the mother of all fortune and misfortune. The obvious problems inherent in the creed—emotion, morality, the difference between biology and social relations, inheritance, privilege, the human soul—would have to be addressed by others, but slowly and only over decades. In the late nineteenth through the early twentieth century, this conservative creed permeated society and, along with it, not-so-distant cousins: proto-libertarian economics, the "robber barons," lynching, "scientific racism," the "white man's burden" and its attendant impulse to colonize and dominate darker-skinned peoples, and, of course, the "scientific management" of industrial relations.

Proliferation of the creed found easy and natural alliance with the nineteenth-century worship of free markets popularly known as "neo-classicism" or laissez-faire. Nor was this conjoining found only among white industrialists. Historian Paul M. Gaston points out that conservative economics, anti-unionism, Social Darwinism, and the "Gospel of Wealth" was so pervasive that spokesmen for the black middle class such as Booker T. Washington accepted these ideas as givens.[29] Conservative propagation of libertarian economics—and uncritical acceptance of same—contributed powerfully to the rise of the "robber barons": giants of industry who bestrode the business world like Colossus, answerable to no one, responsible to no power but their own.

Theirs was a thoroughly revanchist society. Extortion, kidnaping, and violence were run-of-the-mill tactics in the barons' dealings with each other (not to mention employees or the consuming public), all of it mixed up with notions of free markets, right religion, and survival of the fittest. A. B. Stickney, president of the Chicago, St. Paul, and Kansas Railway, said that he trusted his brother rail men as gentlemen anywhere. But as rail executives he wouldn't leave his watch with them for a minute. Daniel Drew, New York steamship, brokerage, and railroad competitor of William H. Vanderbilt, found himself betrayed by partners Jim Fisk and Jay Gould after the trio had agreed to issue fraudulent stock to ruin Vanderbilt. Drew rebounded from the financial setback to concentrate on religion. He built churches and founded the famed Drew Theological Seminary. He also left an undiluted expression of Yankee materialism informed by Social Darwinism, laissez-faire, and religion—the very kind that was then coming south with the fervor and economic fundamentalism of northern investors as surely as Grant's armies once had. "Sentiment is all right . . . where your home is," Drew said. "But downtown, no. . . . [T]he dog that snaps the quickest gets the bone. Friendship is very nice for a Sunday afternoon . . . around the dinner table with your relations, talking about the sermon that morning. But nine o'clock Monday morning, [those] notions should be brushed aside like cobwebs. . . . [When doing] business . . . [a man] ought not to have a relation in the world—and least of all a poor relation."[30]

Such a materialist-based theology jelled perfectly with Calvinist traditions and tendencies already entrenched in a South dominated by Baptists, Methodists, and Southern Presbyterians. The result provided the perfect template for tying unbridled pursuit of wealth to God's plan for personal salvation and—consequently—a harsh view of those who failed to either achieve (or inherit) material wealth. The Calvinist theology so prevalent in the South was eminently conservative.[31] It clearly understood wealth as a badge of God's favor and election—and poverty as a sign of personal sloth, depravity, or other individual shortcoming. Poverty and gross inequalities—even those to the extent of the late nineteenth century—were not so much societal or systemic problems to be worked on as they were signposts of a godly, ordered society. While the Wesleyan alternative backing a more progressive cosmology certainly existed, it was a distinctly minority enterprise in Dixie. Social rank and the absence of real prospects for working oneself out of poverty were shouted down by loud exhortations as to the virtues of personal responsibility, divine ordered stratification, obedience to one's betters as a hallmark of Christian living, and the quest of the Holy Grail of becoming rich made open to every American by Horatio Alger's bootstraps.

Heated in the cauldron of the New South's desperation for outside investment, the economic consequences of Calvinism combined with Yankee materialism and reached a white-hot intensity not known in northern environs. Calvinism and Yankee materialism both came southward from the North of course (New England to be precise). But the southern version was exacerbated by the absence of the New England reverence for public education, the great university, and the commonwealth as much as it was by Dixie's conflation of reflexive martialism and a religious defense of slavery and states' rights with regional notions of patriotism. Northern religious, ethnic, economic, agricultural, and political diversity in the form of abolitionists, unions, suffragists, Transcendentalists, Unitarians, Quakers, Jews, Catholics with their concern for the common good, the Social Gospel of Protestant theologians like the German American Walter Rauschenbush, and larger and more numerous cities all mitigated the potential power that the fusion of Calvinism and economic materialism could evoke. Relatively unmolested by such factors, the fusion of Calvinism and economic fundamentalism took place in the unusually pressurized atmosphere of a desperate postwar South in frantic search of outside investment and industrial and urban development. The result was "The Southern Religion"—a cultural creation as much economic, martially patriotic, and socially irresponsible as it was *theological*. It was born and thrived in a relatively isolated, mostly rural and agricultural, ethnically and religiously homogenous, and economically desperate society, one reeling from military and material ruin, and united in its conception of victimhood and dedication to a certain "way of life."[32]

Less obvious but perhaps more important in all this was something that flowed naturally (if more darkly) from the fundamental tenets of undiluted Calvinism: an aversion to democratic institutions and processes. Southern religious conservatives valued political participation—but only from those who had, in their view, "earned" the privilege to exercise political voice (by virtue of their race, sex, rank, wealth, and property—all God ordained). Such an exclusive theology would, obviously, undergird efforts at disfranchisement in the 1890s and the turn-of-the-century era, but they would also persist well into the later battles over civil rights, including those over the poll tax, literacy tests, property qualifications, and gerrymandered districts.

Perhaps even more important, such religious-based aversion to democracy would serve as the mortar to glue the bricks of economic rightism to religious fundamentalism—first in the South—but eventually across an increasingly conservative America. This second Great Melding would come gradually, and later, but it is important to note that its roots lay in southern soil. In recent decades American journalists and pundits have reacted with horror to the exhortations of Religious Rightist figures prescribing the death penalty for gays, lesbians, and abortionists. They have recoiled at the ascription of hurricanes, floods, earthquakes, and acts of terror to divine retribution for the existence of secular liberals, gays, and other "demon-possessed" groups and individuals in America. Frank advocacy of anti-democratic behavior, voter suppression, hatred of government, and even defenses of inequality up to and including slavery from rightist religious and economic celebrities (not to mention figures of late Tea Party vintage) have elicited more disbelief and denial from mainstream journalists than alarm.[33] Yet it is critical to take note of the important developments that have been present in the southern experience since at least the Civil War.

Not surprisingly in the ascendant culture of the Gilded Age workers and consumers were damned (loudly and publicly), and the robber barons brooked little nonsense about the common good or the public weal. Price gouging, profiteering, bribery, price and supply collusion, pollution, the marketing of unsafe products—all of this—was business as usual for the barons. And it is difficult to tell which they were more proud of: their tactics or their ability to get away with them. "The public be damned," William Vanderbilt replied to a reporter who told him he had an affirmative social duty to the public. "I am working for my stockholders." J. P. Morgan concurred in stark terms: "I owe the public nothing."[34]

On other occasions, the barons displayed a chilling sociopathy and consequent disdain toward the law as a potential safeguard of the public interest. "What do I care about the law?" Commodore Cornelius Vanderbilt asked, revealing that his son had gained his disregard for the commonweal honestly. "Hain't I got the power?" When a close friend, Judge Elbert H. Gary, raised a rare legal objection, J. P. Morgan silenced him: "I don't . . . want a lawyer to tell me what I can not do" with technicalities like the law. "I hire him to tell me how to do what I want to do." But perhaps railroad magnate Jay Gould said it best: "I can [always] hire one half of the working class to kill the other."[35]

It did not take long for the barons of the New South to emulate their Yankee models. Theirs was a potentially chilling, virtually nihilistic, view of society, one that recognized no social responsibility beyond the making of profits, one that would not reemerge fully in American life until after the New Deal had run its course. Another irony, perhaps a fourth major one for our book, is that such social indifference to public, collective, and cooperative efforts to address social justice and social responsibility coexists in the South right alongside a regionally distinctive compassion for one's neighbors—one that is deep, warm, and genuine—as long as it takes the forms of private charity, individual help, or church-sponsored relief. Nothing public or government tinged is encouraged—as per the Reconstruction dictum. In too much of the South, that constitutes "socialism" despite the woeful inadequacy of private and individual relief efforts to begin to address the magnitude of the region's social problems and the glaring inconsistencies in millions of self-reliant southerners eagerly utilizing socialist things such as public schools, police and fire departments, college football stadiums, national and state parks, forests, seashores, libraries, roads, sewers, sidewalks, hospitals, playgrounds, bridges, tunnels, a military, radio and television airwaves, air traffic control, FHA loans, Pell Grants, and federally subsidized student loans—not to mention Social Security, Medicare, and the VA.

But the southern barons were clear about what they thought society meant. "Society," as Milton Hannibal Smith of the Louisville and Nashville Railroad explained it, was created to take "what the other fellow has . . . and keep out of the penitentiary." Henry Fairchild DeBardeleben, son-in-law of the New England coal tycoon Daniel Pratt, saw himself and his vast coal and iron holdings as the top of the Alabama food chain: "I was the eagle, and I wanted to eat up all the craw-fish I could,—swallow up all the little fellows, and I did it."[36]

Laissez-faire, market capitalism, neo-classical doctrine—whichever name it chose to go by—provided the intellectual power that was largely back of the reckless and socially irresponsible behavior of managers and executives. In a harshly conservative climate that worshiped "personal responsibility" and disparaged any notion of social responsibility, the late nineteenth-century dogma that called itself classical liberalism pressed the actual classical liberals into service of that which they never imagined—and utterly discarded the abundant arguments in favor of social justice, ethical behavior, a living wage, and environmental responsibility made by the original crop of conservative economists who birthed free market theory—Adam Smith front and center.

The chief irony is that the nineteenth-century free market advocates far outstripped in admiration the market and its "invisible hand" than the original classical liberal economists who had actually come up with the idea. Nineteenth-century disciples of market theory became exactly that—purveyors of a dogma that was every bit as religious as it was economic, one that exhibited an irrational, even spiritual faith in the magic of free markets and that routinely misquoted or employed in only the most truncated fashion the original classically liberal prophets while simultaneously appropriating their reputations for their own, relatively modern ends. When we witness robber barons arguing with straight faces that employers have no responsibility to society other than making profits at any expense, or denying that social justice should exist, or that considerations of morality or the common good have anything at all to do with economics, it is instructive for us to recall the actual words of giants such as Adam Smith, David Ricardo, Georg Hegel, and John Stuart Mill, for they were all classical advocates of free market capitalism who could by no gymnastic be painted as radicals.[37]

It may surprise many to learn that Adam Smith, the father of capitalism, was adamantly opposed to the ideas that liberty was always a good thing and the market the solution to every economic problem—as was Hegel. Smith rejected the notion that the public interest could not be served through state action and refused to believe that the pursuit of self-interest would always lead to socially positive outcomes. He especially disliked collusion among owners to set prices, bypass competitive markets, and lower wages; he recognized that the conflict between labor and management was not waged on a level playing field and demanded that capitalists leave the natural environment in at least as good a shape as they had found it. The Scotsman advocated an explicit moral philosophy as part of his political economy, designed to "make men better, not just better off," and he tirelessly championed public education and a living wage, what he called "a liberal reward for labour." "To complain of it," Smith lectured the capitalists of his day, "is to lament the necessary effect and cause of the greatest public prosperity." Not least, Smith was exceedingly suspicious of leaving matters of governance to capitalists for they were, as a rule, characterized by "mean rapacity" and "neither are, nor ought to be [the] rulers of mankind." He was especially disdainful of the sophistry employed by deep-pocketed elites who sought to delude lawmakers and the public into believing that whatever wealth wanted was somehow "identical to the general interest." French economist Frederic Bastiat ridiculed the same sleight-of-hand as a form of economic sophism.[38]

"The interests of the landlords," David Ricardo bluntly put, are "always opposed to the interests of every other class in the community." For his part, John Stuart Mill bitterly lamented the excesses of a capitalist system where the fruits of labor should be apportioned "almost in an inverse ratio" to the amount of work put in: the "largest portions to those who have never worked at all, the next largest to those whose work is almost nominal," and so on until those who do the dirtiest, dangerous, and most exhausting work "cannot count with certainty on being able to earn the necessaries of life." "If this or Communism were the [only] alternatives," Mill went on, "all of the difficulties, great or small, of Communism would be as dust in the balance."[39]

Adam Smith, in particular, has had his works bastardized to the point of posthumous conscription to the cause of the present-day version of extreme economic rightism termed neoliberalism, or Austrian or Chicago economics. Yet it might surprise many to learn that the Scottish moral philosopher was actually a hearty and pioneering exponent of humanity toward labor and public education, principally because this would, in his view, elevate the toiling masses from the cultural and moral degradation that so often accompanies grinding poverty. Public education, for Smith, held the potential to liberate the masses from the "delusions of enthusiasm and superstition" and "hence to being stirred up by priests and preachers." Education and rational information about public issues were, for the prescient Smith, the very lifeblood of a healthy democracy. The more educated the masses were, Smith believed, the "more capable" common folk would be of rising above the cultural torpor of their existence to "see through" such emotional appeals to become better citizens. Thomas Jefferson held similar views.[40]

While J. S. Mill opted for humanitarian reform to augment rather than replace the free enterprise system, the thrust of such efforts was lost on the late nineteenth-century booster of southern industry as well as most southerners. The result was a mentalité that accepted—with little or no question—the harshest and most unforgiving incarnation of a sociopolitical system that was something far beyond even free market economics.

Negroes Are Pure Animal.... I Give My Heart, My Hand, and Trust to the God That Made Us

As for race relations, they had, by the late nineteenth century, sunken to deplorable depths. The turn of the century brought more of the same. The 1906 Atlanta race riot was matched only two years later in the northern town of Springfield, Illinois. But lynching was, after 1900, reserved almost exclusively for blacks and confined almost solely to the South.[41] This was a signal change. During the 1890s, for example, in the leading lynch state in the country, white people had comprised a full third of Alabama's victims.[42]

"Scientific racism," together with Social Darwinism, was generally accepted as the prevailing wisdom. These intellectual creeds, along with Calvinist religion, acted as a positivist buttress that both reinforced and engendered common racist attitudes and behavior. Given this national context, southern violence against black people (considered by science to be something less than human anyway) was not surprising. Nor should it be considered all that surprising that whites, in the region where most African Americans lived, moved toward disfranchisement and segregation—especially once it became clear that the federal government meant to provide no obstacle.[43] The 1901 Alabama Constitution, the 1902 establishment of the "white primary," and the cementing of Jim Crow took place within the warm and nurturing climate of sympathetic national opinion.

The "best" opinion in the country took an exceedingly dim view of the African American and, at least implicitly, approved of measures to restrict and control the race. *Century Magazine, Scribner's,* and *Harper's* routinely lampooned blacks in the most stereotypical of ways. Leading intellectuals such as Henry Adams, Henry James, and John Fiske did not object morally to the rapidly deteriorating status of blacks in American law and society. James Ford Rhodes called blacks "innately inferior and incapable of citizenship." Harvard historian Alfred Bushnell Hart agreed that race by race "the negro is inferior, and his past history [implies] . . . that he will remain inferior." Princeton University's William Starr Myers concluded that the Negro must be treated as a "'grown-up child'—with justice, but with authority." Lloyd McKim Garrison, grandson of the famed abolitionist William Lloyd Garrison, declared that the Negro, "beyond his sweet disposition and courtesy, has not the qualifications for a very useful citizen."[44] White southerners were quick to pick up on the implications for disfranchisement and other forms of states' rights–sponsored control of blacks.[45]

Predominant opinion regarding blacks did not spring from thin air, though. The advent and ascendance of "scientific racism" (i.e., scientifically and medically "proven" conclusions regarding black biological inferiority) had much to do with the generally low opinion of black aptitudes held by America's best and brightest doctors, scientists, sociologists, and criminologists. Many of them subscribed to a view of irretrievable black inferiority—if not outright depravity. Numerous physicians and scientists wrote of blacks having "simple minds . . . smaller brain[s] . . . deficient judgment . . . [and a] lack of control in sexual matters." Dr. William Bevis's article in the *American Journal of Psychiatry* stressed the surge in black sexual passion and a simultaneous decline in mental development around the age of puberty. Sexual promiscuity, gambling, thievery, drinking, loafing, and all kinds of degradation and degeneracy consumed their energies thereafter. "Without proper guidance," he concluded, the African American would make a "complete wreck of his physical and mental life." Dr. R. W. Shufeldt's 1907 book, *The Negro: A Menace to Civilization,* concluded that blacks were "almost wholly subservient to the sexual instinct. . . . In other words, negroes are purely animal." White women, Shufeldt wrote, were at particular risk because of the black male's "savage lust." Black rapists might even "increase the size of the genital fissure by an ugly outward rip of his knife." Such was "their nature," Shufeldt and other scientists felt, "and they cannot possibly rid themselves of that, any more than skunks and polecats can cast away their abominable scent glands and the outrageous odor they emit."[46]

For almost a century after the Civil War, the Republican Party existed only on the periphery of southern society and its polity. The vast majority of white southerners viewed Republicans with the most intense dislike and suspicion—a revulsion so deep and so intense that it is impossible to state it too strongly. Southerners considered white Republicans to be an especially abhorrent lot, ranking them just above the freed blacks they occasionally tolerated as political partners. Some even regarded white Republicans—both the native scalawag and the northern carpetbagger—as the actual inferiors socially, politically, *and morally* of the South's large black population. As William Faulkner would write decades later, the South's past never died; in fact, it wasn't even the past.[47] Nowhere was this observation more telling than in the region's persistent bedevilment by the memory of war and Reconstruction—a twin recollection of the most intimate violation—both attributable, ultimately, to the hated GOP.

All of this eventually changed, of course. Today when we speak of the Solid South, we no longer speak of the Solid *Democratic* South. Today, and for the last several decades, the Solid South means the Solid *Republican* South—at least in terms of presidential elections and, increasingly, in downticket races as well. The white South is the place where we are able to see most clearly the GOP's rise from its leprous origins, through respectability and competitiveness, to ascendance and, finally, to consistently growing dominance.

Yet the trauma of civil war and Republican Reconstruction cannot be overstated. It left the South with an intense and abiding fear and hostility toward everything black, Republican, federal, and liberal—a burning memory that, it is not too much to write, was consuming and all-pervading. For the next eight decades, the Solid South was almost completely and exclusively Democratic in its politics and its political and associated moral culture. Anything even remotely connected to the Republican Party was inimical to the South and antithetical to its most sacred values. It was indelibly associated with the traumatic, caricatured, and largely inaccurate collective memory of corrupt and incompetent "black rule," backed by the bristling bayonets of an invading army of northern, federal aggression.[48] From Redemption on, Republican candidates, including presidential candidates, received only a handful of votes in the southern states.

3
For Blacks Only
The Perversion of Alabama Progressivism

> It is Christianity, but not orthodox. . . . It is wrong but right. . . . It is life instead of death.
>
> —Charles H. Greer

The Progressive Movement did not pass the South by. In fact there was a distinct, active, even flourishing movement in the southern states, and Alabama was front and center among them.

A great deal of reform was accomplished in the state, and a rich diversity of subjects tackled: health, education, child labor, voting, race relations, the regulation of corporations, trusts, and combinations (particularly the railroads), the treatment of prisoners and penal reform, social ills related to alcohol, the construction of roads, bridges, infrastructure, and a host of other important items.[1] Much good was accomplished.

But there was also a shadow Progressive Movement in Alabama and much of the Deep South, one whose "reforms" were far less savory, far less inclusive, and, it might be argued, even critically determinative of patterns that would afflict the state and region far after the era passed. Labor insurgency was crushed; women were kept "in their place"; barbaric and exploitative systems of profit making at the expense of human life and almost inconceivable levels of misery were protected (indeed expanded); whole populations were legally disfranchised and excluded from meaningful political participation; "reforms" widened rather than narrowed the already massive gulf between the races; other forms of discrimination, disfranchisement, and the hardening of lines of social demarcation and stratification were drawn more sharply. Even a populist terrorist group, the Ku Klux Klan, took on new life during this time and enforced a grotesque form of racial, religious, moral, gender, and nativist conformity in the most violent ways imaginable. All of this, too, was part of the reforms of the Progressive Era down South.

But the era left behind two overriding and enduring legacies in Alabama, both of which would have lasting and unfortunate consequences for the

South's development long after the period officially ended, on a number of fronts. The first was the institutionalization and public sanction of a powerful anti-democratic impulse, one that moved and had its being in the significant interrelationships between various types of political, economic, and religious conservatism—even variants of fundamentalism. The second was the establishment and deepening of a divide between what constituted acceptable forms of progressivism (or what was increasingly referred to as "liberalism") and those that did not.

When it was all said and done, new life would be breathed into the ugly impulse of anti-democratic behaviors (that should have been all the more galling) in a country whose founding ideology and mythology insisted on the basic requisite of popular participation. And the state's leading progressive figures—Emmett O'Neal, B. B. Comer, Thomas Kilby, and others—would personify a *whites-only economic* liberalism that would be enshrined in the state for decades to come in the work of Alabama's best-known representatives of liberalism: Lister Hill, John Sparkman, George Huddleston, and even the venerable Hugo Black to a degree, as well as lesser-known plebeian figures such as Horace Wilkinson and Bull Connor. The pattern would find its ultimate expression in George Wallace.

Discovery, and recognition, of this important binary would, with time, actually provide a critical missing link in understanding how Alabama (once considered the garden spot and great hope for the emergence of a liberal South) would, instead, choose a very different route. Instead of spearheading an awakened class-consciousness and willingness to engage in biracial liberalism, Alabama would choose to lead Dixie down another fork, a tragic fork: the region's embrace of an extreme racial, religious, and economic rightism that would eventually find enunciation in the Dixiecrat outburst, the independentism of George Wallace, and, given time, the rise of the modern GOP.

The Nature of Historical Inquiry and Making Sense of the Past

Allow me to begin with two premises. First, historians disagree. In some respects, it is one of the most basic and routine aspects of their calling. Not merely to record facts, provide chronology, or to learn, remember, recite, and regurgitate names, dates, and places but to interpret, then reinterpret, then interpret again—until the profession and then the public eventually gain an understanding of the past that resembles reality as closely as it is possible for such a humanistic inquiry to do. Of course several disclaimers are in order. Try as they might, historians can never know precisely, exactly, unquestionably what went on in the past—such are the inherent limitations of any inquiry into human affairs, especially those that took place in the past. Historians can only construct a rough re-creation of events. Nor can researchers in the social sciences ever be entirely free of bias, whim, caprice, or predisposition—no matter how mightily they may struggle toward absolute verity, objectivity, or even fairness.

These are the basic ground rules of social scientific research into the behavior of human beings. Such research differs—intrinsically, essentially—from that which is done in the physical or "hard" sciences. For example, it doesn't really matter what an astronomer or geologist thinks about a particular rock on Mars. The rock does not have a personality, bills, a mortgage, children, hopes, dreams, aspirations, fears—free will. But it does matter what a scholar studying civil rights thinks about African Americans and race relations. To ignore the difference is to proceed at peril. In the hard sciences one exception to a rule is catastrophic. An exception possesses the power to render a generally accepted—even long-venerated—axiom null and void. One apple refuses to fall to the ground and the concept of gravity must be rethought. A body of liquid doesn't displace when a solid substance is lowered into it, and Archimedes' principle is in serious jeopardy.

Not so in the social sciences. Exceptions to the rule will exist. More, because of the innately different subject matter (ones that have free will and human choice), those exceptions *must* exist. Even further, such exceptions—if they are exotic enough—may actually serve to *prove* the rule by their very rarity. Historians deal with innately different subject matter than that of the physical sciences—in fact subject matter that is "subjective": human actors with an unpredictable human will.[2] Those who do not appreciate the difference between scholarly inquiry in the social sciences and the hard sciences set a course for themselves (and their readers) that is bound for frustration, fruitlessness, and perhaps worst of all, self-deception.

Nuance is not a bad thing in and of itself. In fact, the search for nuance is praiseworthy. It enriches the final historical product, adds texture, layer, degree, complexity. Yet indulged in with a licentious rapacity, or even an undiscerning banality, the search for truth may deteriorate into an exercise in futility and even—if one is not careful—the magnificent irrelevance of infinite relativism.

It is not impossible, for example, for a determined scholar to eventually find a diary entry from a Confederate soldier who believed he was fighting for the betterment, indeed the freedom, of the African American slave. Does the discovery of such a document mean the South fought the Civil War to *free* the slaves? Does it mean even that the historian can conclude, with any degree of accuracy, that Confederate motives were mixed: some fought to free the slaves, some to preserve the chattel system? To ask the question is to answer it. If enough research is done, it is no doubt possible to come across evidence that "good Nazis" existed (à la the controversial 1958 movie *The Young Lions* with Marlon Brando). But even if the exception can be found, is the historian justified in concluding that overall Nazi motives were mixed? Some members of the Third Reich wanted to exterminate Jews, others did not? It just depends on who you talk to.

History's great strength, its great source of authority, is fact, detail, and documentation. Yet after such mining has been done, generalization and theory should be the goal. The great strength of scientific inquiry (even the social scientific kind) is the construction of elaborate models and theory. Yet too often such research neglects—or is just plain ignorant of—historical detail and primary sources, even when quite elegant data sets are produced. If a more complete understanding of what went on in the past—and its meaning—is our ultimate goal, then the utilization of the strengths of various disciplinary approaches is ideal.

The stubborn persistence by historians of searching for the one or the few exceptions to the neglect of the general rule can, taken too far, result in the emasculation of the discipline's ability to shed light on human behavior, to arrive at any meaningful consensus of what reality is—or was.[3] One can only hope that historians (usually those that end up concluding that liberalism, discontinuity, or a lack of regional distinctiveness defined the southern experience) will realize that detail without theory and generalization can be pointless, if not profoundly misleading.

Not only is the subject matter qualitatively different in a humanistic discipline such as history but also the nature of the *researcher*—replete with bias, whim, predisposition, and caprice. Researchers hold the capacity for influencing the course and result of historical inquiry in ways altogether unlike those of the hard sciences. Southern historian Charles Sydnor intuitively realized that the biases of historical researchers powerfully influenced choice of topic, evidence, character, and interpretation for all historians. The process by which the historian undertakes the study of history "needs to be sketched," he cautioned, "because whatever awakened his interest . . . may well have determined the nature and bent of that interest."[4] John Hope Franklin realized that this characteristic of historical inquiry held special relevance for those who studied the South.[5]

The answer to this conundrum, frankly, has much to do with whether one defines history as a form of the humanities or as a branch of the social sciences whose goal is to try to emulate the hard sciences. If history is understood *solely* as a social science, then it contains the attributes of the social sciences. On the plus side, this includes the strength of theory and conceptualization. But on the other, if care is not taken it can become afflicted with the same identity crisis that plagues a number of social sciences. Such disciplines retain the strength and vibrancy of theory and laws "governing" human behavior. But unleavened social science is also internally and irretrievably frustrated by the lack of objectivity that is inherent in all social sciences: that is, the fundamental *humanity* and, thus, the endemic and inviolable variability and unpredictability that is at the core of all of its questions, its subject matter—and, perhaps most important, its *investigators*.

History practiced solely as a social science in pursuit of the hard sciences cannot escape itself—no more than political science, sociology, or even economics can. It can aspire to transcendental law and immanent theorem, as the hard sciences do. It can mimic their methods, copy their jargon, generate reams of impressive data. It can wear their white lab coats, engage in observation, experimentation, and replication, and strive to achieve something amounting to "objective" inquiry. Yet in the end, history practiced exclusively as a social science on the pattern of the physical is fundamentally, if not fatally and futilely, flawed.

But history practiced as a mere form of the humanities is likely to be similarly delimited. This kind of history enjoys the strength of objective data: indisputable names, dates, places, and documents; wars, people, treaties, pounds sterling, and gold bullion shipped. But how to make sense of it all without the theoretical and conceptual frameworks provided by the social sciences? History practiced in this fashion—in a purely humanistic way—has the potential to, at its weakest points, devolve into a sterile and endless recitation of "one damn thing after another," with the discipline's inability to distinguish, differentiate, rank, order, or generalize between the thousands—even millions—of discrete names, dates, years, and places.

At its best history must be practiced as a hybrid that utilizes the strengths of both social science and humanity without, as far as it is able, being caught up in the respective snares of their mutually exclusive practice.

So what has this disquisition on the nature of historical inquiry got to do with anything currently at hand? Only this: first, how one answers the eventual question of whether the South is liberal or conservative, distinctive or not—and why—depends largely on how one practices and understands the craft and course of history itself. Second, and closely associated with the first, the Progressive Era is one of the most difficult on which to gain a clear grasp or understanding. The primary reason for this is that historians agree on so little about it.

Some argue the period represented a "liberal" break with the past that was notable for its increase in governmental activism in the polity and the economy, a willingness to experiment and change—means that allowed the pursuit of the "commonweal" or the "public interest." This concern with the general over specific interests stood in marked contrast to the narrow gestalt of the late nineteenth-century robber barons and their ever-larger trusts and combinations.[6]

Others argue, just as passionately, that the era really represented the triumph of "conservative" pro-business interests in American life, forces that tolerated, indeed sometimes facilitated, cosmetic changes in order to preserve their control over the country's political economy.[7] And still others maintain that the era had little to do with liberalism or conservatism, that its driving force may be found in a mania for organization, efficiency, standardization, professionalization, and functionality.[8]

Some say the middle-class Progressives marked a clear break from the Populist farmers that preceded them, that the two groups actually shared very little in common.[9] There are at least two subgroups within this school. One argues Progressivism's innate superiority as a bona fide reform movement as opposed to an agrarian radicalism that tended toward the paranoiac, conspiracy-minded, and even proto-fascist.[10] The other judges the farm rebels as more genuinely progressive reformers than their urban, middle-class counterparts.[11] Still others insist that there are strong, even physical, ties between the Populists and the Progressives.[12] Historians can't even agree on when Progressivism took place. Some say it was over by the time World War I broke out; others chart it well into the 1920s. One recent chronicler of its social reforms argues for 1880 to 1930. A pioneer dates southern progressivism back to 1870.[13]

Clearly, when all is said and done, historians agree on precious little about the subject. There are three things, though, on which almost all assent: (1) that a Progressive movement *did* occur, (2) that it took place sometime around the end of the nineteenth century and the beginning of the twentieth, and (3) that certain changes or "reforms" (admittedly of a debatable nature) were implemented.

For Whites Only

There is another, less-often cited aspect of the era that has managed to elicit a good deal of accord. In the words of C. Vann Woodward, perhaps the South's most celebrated historian, Progressivism was "for whites only."[14] While there has been significant historiographical agreement on this point, it has not gone entirely without challenge or refinement.[15]

"For whites only." Above all, the phrase implies exclusion. That is, African Americans were excluded, denied, cut out from the Progressive Era and its reforms—whatever their intrinsic nature or merit.

In one sense, nothing could be more accurate. Blacks, especially but not solely in the South, did not reap the dividends of the era's increases in governmental spending or social services—not nearly to the extent that whites did. Nor were they included as beneficiaries in myriad other reforms, especially those that tend to provide the strongest evidence for an interpretation of the era as liberal. In one sense, then, in a very clear sense, Progressivism was indeed for whites only.

But looked at in another way, perhaps an even more fundamental way, nothing could be less descriptive of the Progressive period. Parts of the era's reforms were not only for blacks *as well as* whites, they were solely, specifically, and especially designed with blacks in mind. They were changes or reforms, if you will, that had as their sole or primary impetus the desire to *do something* about the "Negro problem," the post-Reconstruction race question that was reaching crisis proportions as the turn of the century approached.

In fact, many of the most important reforms associated with the era were not accidents of exclusion; they were not simply oversights that neglected to take blacks into account as some unorganized, floundering, powerless interest group that could not compete in a game of pluralist politics. They were conscious changes in policy or programs made precisely and specifically *for blacks*, with blacks in mind—only not in the same way that additional streets, parks, sewers, lights, schools, hospitals, and libraries were for white citizens. They were deliberate changes effected in order to deal with a race question that had gained increasing importance since the abolition of slavery and the advent of two free races having to live side by side in the South.

In a very real way, the racism that pervaded the Progressive Era in the South also managed to pervert the movement as a whole. Combined with its genuine and unarguably beneficial reforms in a host of areas, the exclusion and white supremacy resulted in a weird, variegated, almost contradictory movement in the Deep South: the elevation of the white race (including some poor and many middle-class whites) with the simultaneous and increased concreteness of repression for blacks. Much of Alabama Progressivism, like much of the southern variant generally, was played as a zero-sum game in which whites believed progress was attainable only with a corresponding decline in black status—and the status of any poor whites who sought to make common cause with blacks.[16] A "win-win" strategy of mutual gains was not an option.

The influence of race during the Progressive Era continued what was rapidly solidifying into a tradition in the Deep South: a phenomenon in which race managed to twist and contort the course of history as it might have been practiced, as it was sometimes practiced elsewhere. The contortion repeatedly convinced poor whites to ally themselves with their economic betters against their own class interests and a potential biracial alliance with blacks. Or it led to a series of reforms that at once made life better for whites and worse (or, at best, neutral) for blacks.

The result was often a distortion more extreme than something we can term paradox, contradiction, or mere irony. Be it Populism, Progressivism, or a host of other developments, historians have disagreed endlessly, and with a resultant and concluding confusion, as to the very essence of these movements.[17]

In Alabama, race permeated virtually every aspect of the Progressive Era. Politically, the race question was resolved and reformed by removing the black man from active involvement in politics. This "reform" was enacted in the state's new disfranchising Constitution of 1901, a document that would eventually become infamous both for its antediluvian catalogue of disfranchisement mechanisms and because it would eventually be the longest constitution in the world.[18] It was consummated the next year by adopting the "reform" of an all-white (or direct) primary system. While poor whites and their Big Mule–industrialist/Black Belt adversaries disagreed on much, especially economic issues—especially the place of poor whites in Alabama's political economy—they generally agreed that politics should be reformed by eradicating black people from politics.

Alabama's Black Belt planter patricians had grown increasingly uneasy about their manipulation, by force and fraud, of the large black vote in their counties. So pervasive was the gentry's practice of "counting in" or "counting out" the black vote, as the occasion demanded, that it had become a recognized art form—although a ritual that for some compromised the moral and democratic bases of society itself. "Political morality demanded black disfranchisement," Wayne Flynt has written. "Accepted by many whites, this assertion enunciated the curious thought that white dishonesty . . . could only be stopped by denying the black man one of his civil rights."[19] Another leading scholar agreed that the result was "a bit like sweeping dirt under the rug in order to present a clean house . . . [or] closing banks to prevent bank robberies."[20]

Indeed, the suffrage committee at the 1901 constitutional convention felt no compunction about adopting the slogan "White supremacy, suffrage reform, and purity in elections."[21] Still, patricians like Thomas H. Watts, son of a Civil War Alabama governor, rationalized the practice. It was "less hurtful to the Negro [than shotguns] in the bodily sense." A Black Belt planter defended it with perhaps the quintessential definition of progressivism as perversion in Alabama. Disfranchisement of blacks was "a magnificent system that [unfortunately] cannot be . . . perpetuated" in its crude force and fraud form. "It is Christianity, but not orthodox. . . . It is wrong but right. . . . It is life instead of death."[22] New, more subtle methods were needed as reform.

More troubling to the oligarchy than the moral consequences of their fraud, though, was the threat the black vote posed in possible tandem with that of poor and working-class whites. The biracial possibility—democracy in action—implicit in Reconstruction Republicanism had grown steadily more present throughout a series of irritating independent uprisings during the 1880s. During these years there were several sporadic, and not inconsequential, challenges to the "Solid South"—Republicans, Independents of various stripes, farmers, and workers. Challenge became especially ominous in the Populist revolt of the 1890s.[23]

Yet 1901 was not to be the moment that biracial class-consciousness trumped emotionalism and white supremacy in Alabama. Actually, things worked out much closer to the reverse.

For their part, contrary to traditional writing on this subject, many plain whites welcomed the removal of blacks from politics for a variety of reasons. Black Belt voting irregularity had proven to be an insurmountable advantage to their patrician foes. Many common folk also welcomed disfranchisement because political alliance with African Americans had been temporary, expedient, and, for them, distasteful. It grated against a persistent and powerful poor-white racism.

At the turn of the century, southern whites of all kinds—Bourbon Democrats and Independents—agreed on the overriding goal of white supremacy, Jim Crow, and a whites-only politics. In Alabama, whites of various political persuasions, separated mainly by economic issues, temporarily subsumed them to disfranchise blacks in the state's new 1901 constitution and made certain they stayed excluded by legislating an all-white Democratic primary into effect the next year and by purging the Republican Party of black participation.[24] This was the Democratic Party, the Solid Democratic South, sometimes referred to by its proper and more accurate name in places like Alabama: the Democratic and Conservative Party.

Hill-country representatives such as J. Thomas "Cotton Tom" Heflin of Chambers County favored suffrage restriction because, as he put it, "I believe as truly as I believe that I am standing here, that God almighty intended the negro to be the servant of the white man." William H. Denson, congressman and a leading spokesman for the plain whites, initially favored a disfranchising convention because it would, in his words, "determine the question of whether or not the Anglo-Saxon race is to control Alabama . . . or shall it be a hybrid race hereafter?" "The plain English of it," Denson said, "is to eliminate the negro from the ballot box. . . . The rejection of the unfit is going on." Populist editor I. L. Brock was even more direct. A year after the constitution's passage he looked back and frankly confided his assessment to former Populist and new Republican patronage referee Oliver Day Street: "You know the populists always were willing and ready for the negro to be disfranchised if it could be done without disfranchising the white man."[25] Alabama's Redeemers, of course, were open about disfranchising blacks in the 1901 Alabama Constitution.[26]

In Alabama, whites of various strains on economic issues were of virtually one mind on race. The major sticking point in disfranchisement was the issue of whether whites of plain origins would also be caught up in the net of black disfranchisement. In the closing moments of the nineteenth century and the opening ones of the twentieth, many whites of all stations joined together to doom black voters in Alabama until the 1960s. It was the most notable occurrence yet of using race as a glue to bond whites of differing economic and cultural outlooks into common cause. And as such, after Reconstruction, it constituted another major germ of both Conservative Democratic solidarity and, paradoxically, a seed of eventual Democratic demise.

The passage of Alabama's infamous 1901 constitution sealed the fate of African Americans who aspired to vote. In one of history's greatest ironies, while the movement for black disfranchisement was led by the state's industrial and agrarian powers, the deed was accomplished with the vital complicity of many of the state's poorer whites. After a short grace period, guaranteed by provisions such as a grandfather clause, plain whites in Alabama lost the franchise in even greater numbers than did blacks. The 1901 constitution, along with passage of the all-white Democratic primary the following year, all but made meaningful black participation in politics in Alabama impossible. In addition to making the electorate whiter, the constitution also made it artificially *smaller and more affluent* than it would have been—in other words, less not more democratic.

While the argument over the 1901 constitution has traditionally been depicted among scholars as one between *south Alabama* and *north Alabama* (between the agrarian Black Belt of south Alabama, with its "Big Mule" industrial allies in Birmingham and Mobile, versus the state's poorer whites in north Alabama and the Wiregrass), the reality was considerably more complex.[27] As tables 3.1 and 3.2 make clear, support for calling the 1901 constitutional or "disfranchising" convention, and ratifying its work, was spread across the state—with considerable support for both coming from Alabama's hill country, Wiregrass, and the Tennessee Valley, all largely occupied by poor whites. The state would not experience a political event this momentous again, or representative of the importance of racial politics, until the presidential election of 1928.

The institution of a direct primary, touted by many scholars as a liberalizing, democratizing reform, was actually the anti-democratic antithesis of that when it came to black people. The direct primary condemned blacks to political oblivion because it was also an *all-white* mechanism.[28]

Momentum for the primary came mostly from a group of (again) "reform-wing" Democrats who had opposed the 1901 constitution because of the danger it represented to poor-white suffrage. They openly described their goal as "good government, white supremacy, and honest elections . . . white supremacy in fact."[29]

Patricians such as former governor William C. Oates went along with the direct primary because the reform meant racial exclusion—the overarching goal of the era. In his words the direct primary meant "a white primary . . . economy, wise government, [and] elimination of the negro." The *Birmingham Age-Herald*, which was dominated by Big Mule industrial, commercial, and financial interests, agreed that the primary was "the answer to Negro suffrage" and should work hand in hand with the new constitution so that white men could disagree in the primary and still present a unified front in the general election so that "the Negro vote would not count."[30]

Movement toward suffrage for women was intimately connected to the race issue as well. As with the direct primary, the suffocating nature of white supremacy twisted what should have been a democratizing reform into an anti-democratic move against black people.

Most southern proponents of women's suffrage favored a states' rights approach as opposed to federal law. For them, state control was a prerequisite because it was the only guarantee that the extension of the ballot to women would not let *black women* slip in to get the vote—or black males regain the franchise of which they had just been stripped. Progressive governor Emmett O'Neal amply demonstrated the limits of Alabama Progressivism by opposing the Nineteenth Amendment on exactly these states' rights grounds.[31]

Other southern women argued that female suffrage would actually help cement white supremacy because white women vastly outnumbered blacks and could be relied on to vote with their white brothers instead of their black sisters. The Selma-based Alabama Association Opposed to Woman Suffrage feared women's suffrage as a risky opening for blacks to regain the vote: "the most dangerous blow aimed at . . . white supremacy since the Civil War."[32]

Table 3.1 Vote by Alabama Section on April 1901 Referendum Calling the Convention

Counties For	(% For)	Counties Against	(% For)
I. Tennessee Valley (5–2)			
Colbert	(62)	Jackson	(44)
Lawrence	(69)	Lauderdale	(46)
Limestone	(53)		
Madison	(63)		
Morgan	(66)		
II. Hill Country (11–16)			
Bibb	(56)	Blount	(42)
Calhoun	(56)	Cherokee	(22)
Chambers	(87)	Chilton	(23)
Cleburne	(53)	Clay	(42)
Jefferson	(50)	Coosa	(43)
Lamar	(64)	Cullman	(27)
Randolph	(87)	DeKalb	(37)
Talladega	(75)	Elmore	(44)
Tallapoosa	(60)	Etowah	(45)
Tuscaloosa	(60)	Fayette	(33)
Walker	(56)	Franklin	(32)
		Marion	(46)
		Marshall	(22)
		Shelby	(37)
		St. Clair	(25)
		Winston	(35)
III. Wiregrass (5–5)			
Covington	(61)	Butler	(46)
Crenshaw	(50)	Coffee	(46)
Escambia	(68)	Conecuh	(37)
Henry	(57)	Dale	(36)
Pike	(54)	Geneva	(31)
IV. Gulf Coast Plain (2–1)			
Mobile	(65)	Baldwin	(35)
Washington	(82)		

Counties For	(% For)	Counties Against	(% For)
V. Black Belt (19–0)			
Autauga	(89)		
Barbour	(80)		
Bullock	(71)		
Choctaw	(59)		
Clarke	(68)		
Dallas	(97)		
Greene	(99)		
Hale	(97)		
Lee	(73)		
Lowndes	(91)		
Macon	(55)		
Marengo	(90)		
Monroe	(72)		
Montgomery	(83)		
Perry	(98)		
Pickens	(54)		
Russell	(92)		
Sumter	(95)		
Wilcox	(99)		

Source: Voting results compiled from returns in the *Alabama Official and Statistical Register* (Montgomery: Alabama Department of History and Archives, 1903), 141–42. Physiographic sections from the map located in Samuel L. Webb, *Two-Party Politics in the One-Party South* (Tuscaloosa: University of Alabama Press, 1997), xii.

Such arguments—steeped in the Reconstruction lore of racial apocalypse and federal invasion—were bound to carry weight. The Alabama Federation of Women's Clubs, founded in 1895, rejected national affiliation for twelve years because chapters in Illinois and Massachusetts permitted black women to be members. The Alabama women agreed to affiliate only after the national group assured them that black women would not be seated at the national convention.[33]

Nor was educational reform immune. It was also powerfully distorted by the obsession with race. The 1901 constitution famously accomplished the disfranchisement of Alabama blacks through myriad means: educational requirements, property qualifications, literacy tests, and character stipulations among them. Despite repeated assurances by Black Belt planters and their in-

Table 3.2. Vote by Section on November 1901 Ratification of the Constitution

Counties For	(% For)	Counties Against	(% For)
I. Tennessee Valley (4–3)			
Colbert	(73)	Jackson	(18)
Lawrence	(58)	Lauderdale	(35)
Limestone	(79)	Morgan*	(31)
Madison	(65)		
II. Hill Country (11–16)			
Bibb	(54)	Blount	(32)
Calhoun	(57)	Cherokee	(26)
Chambers	(89)	Chilton	(19)
Cleburne	(66)	Clay	(29)
Elmore*	(76)	Coosa	(41)
Jefferson	(57)	Cullman	(24)
Lamar	(50)	DeKalb	(34)
Randolph	(51)	Etowah	(36)
Talladega	(66)	Fayette	(34)
Tuscaloosa	(55)	Franklin	(30)
Walker	(51)	Marion	(26)
		Marshall	(15)
		Shelby	(20)
		St. Clair	(20)
		Tallapoosa*	(33)
		Winston	(30)
III. Wiregrass (4–6)			
Crenshaw	(60)	Butler	(38)
Escambia	(61)	Coffee	(48)
Henry	(54)	Conecuh	(42)
Pike	(68)	Covington*	(41)
		Dale	(31)
		Geneva	(34)
IV. Gulf Coast Plain (2–1)			
Baldwin*	(55)	Washington*	(48)
Mobile	(50)		

Counties For	(% For)	Counties Against	(% For)
V. Black Belt (16–3)			
Autauga	(50)	Choctaw*	(47)
Barbour	(72)	Lee*	(33)
Bullock	(63)	Lowndes*	(46)
Clarke	(77)		
Dallas	(97)		
Greene	(91)		
Hale	(98)		
Macon	(85)		
Marengo	(85)		
Monroe	(70)		
Montgomery	(78)		
Perry	(97)		
Pickens	(68)		
Russell	(74)		
Sumter	(95)		
Wilcox	(96)		

*Denotes a county that reversed its position from the April 1901 referendum on calling the constitutional convention. Eight counties in all did this. See table 3.1.

Source: Voting results compiled from returns in the *Alabama Official and Statistical Register* (Montgomery: Alabama Department of History and Archives, 1903), 141–42. Physiographic sections from the map located in Samuel L. Webb, *Two-Party Politics in the One-Party South* (Tuscaloosa: University of Alabama Press, 1997), xii.

dustrial allies that Confederate grandfather clauses and other devices would spare them, plenty of poor whites also lost the vote (an estimated 540,000 in Alabama by 1940).[34] Indeed, for the patricians, this was almost as urgent an anti-democratic goal of the reform as black disfranchisement.

Because of the literacy safeguard, after 1901 education took on more significance than ever for Alabama's people. Black Belt counties rigged a system in which they received state funds on the basis of their whole populations (including African Americans) but spent the vast bulk of the money on white schools. And they vehemently opposed additional local taxation.[35] As during Reconstruction, taxes were indelibly associated with racial liberalism.

In virtually every way, the disadvantages facing black schools were actually highlighted by the Progressive Era's reforms. Much of this was due to the 1896 "separate but equal" doctrine established by *Plessy v. Ferguson*. "Separate but equal" cost money. And in a section of the country that had never been particularly eager to fund public education, money for black schools (especially since the franchise was connected to literacy) was, to put it gently, not a priority. By 1909, 74 percent of Alabama's white children attended school compared to only 46 percent of blacks; the average white school year ran 131 days compared to only 90 for African Americans; the state had almost 2,500 more schools for whites than blacks although the populations of black and white school-age children were actually quite close; and black teachers received only half the pay of whites.[36]

As plain whites lobbied for increased educational expenditures in their counties, they were determined that better schooling should be a vehicle for *their* continued enfranchisement—not for people of color. Thomas L. Bulger, a spokesman for the hill folk of Tallapoosa County, put it this way: "What we would like to do in this county more than any other two things would be to disfranchise the darkeys and educate the white children."[37]

Perhaps the Progressive Era's most notable moral reform, the Temperance movement, was also twisted and turned by race. Alcohol was thought to be an especially dangerous passion inflamer. Dry forces zealously pushed temperance in order to protect "the white man and white woman from the violence of the liquor-crazed black."[38] Other prohibitionists couched their goals in terms designed to appeal to the state's industrial interests and employers—and with one eye toward attracting northern capital and investment. They promised that temperance would provide Alabama with a large pool of "sober and industrious blacks" who would make ideal, reliable, and docile employees. In 1907 the state legislature made local option the law and forty-five counties went dry, but the issue continued to be prominent in state and local politics.[39]

While some improvements were made in prison reform, convict lease continued to be a major source of racial control throughout the period. Blacks made up 80 percent of Alabama's state and county convicts and were often sentenced to years of indescribable hardship and suffering for petty or trumped-up offenses. The system, instituted before the Civil War, was a purely southern phenomenon and was practiced longer in Alabama than in any other state in the Union. The convict-lease system featured almost medieval type tortures, lice- and vermin-infested living conditions, and unimaginably high mortality rates.[40]

But the benefits of the system were simply too lucrative to be abandoned. The state saved thousands it would have spent building penitentiaries, made millions from leasing convicts, and allowed politicians to preach the anti-tax gospel with gusto.[41] The owners of Alabama's coal mines, steel plants, railroads, textile and saw mills, cotton plantations, and turpentine camps gained a plentiful and cheap source of literally captive labor. The existence of the convicts also depressed area wages and supplied a ready-made strike breaking force that seriously hindered the efforts of organized labor.[42] In 1905, 111 miners perished in an explosion at the Virginia Company's mines; six years later 132 (mostly black) convicts died at the Pratt Consolidated Company's Banner Mine. The state legislature passed a mine safety act, but convict lease survived in Alabama until its abolition in 1928.[43]

The Ape and the Tiger Sleep in Them

Lynching was similarly reformed during the Progressive period, but its reforms were just as curious as those in other sectors of the state's social and political life. After the turn of the century, lynching became much less common than it had been. But at the same time, it became a practice almost exclusively reserved for blacks.

In the 1890s, the decade when Alabamians lynched more people than any other state in the nation, a full third of the mob's victims had been white. During and after the Progressive Era, though, blacks made up virtually 100 percent of Alabama's lynch victims.[44] Several Alabama governors—including the patricians W. D. Jelks and Thomas Goode Jones and the progressives Edward O'Neal and his son, Emmett—used the various powers at their disposal, including the state militia, to crack down on the practice.[45] Prompted by worry about federal intervention in the form of the Dyer Anti-Lynching Bill (more on this below), progressive governor Thomas Kilby utilized the special legal talents of Horace Wilkinson to actually gain a few sensational convictions against lynch mobs. But the prosecutions came only in the rare instance when the mob chose a white victim. Mobs targeting blacks were virtually ignored. And politicos who posed as the tribunes of Alabama's plain people and their economic interests, such as the demagogue Tom Heflin, could still be found speaking in favor of the custom because "the ape and the tiger sleep [in blacks] and are very easily awakened."[46]

Perhaps the contradictory character of the era was best illustrated by the Progressive Era's most serious biracial class convulsion since Populism: the 1908 Alabama coal strike of the United Mine Workers (UMW). The strike, one over conditions and pay in perhaps the most repressive coalfields in America, was eventually crushed and the miners' union driven from the state for over a decade. While class and economic factors were certainly important, race, religion, and other cultural attitudes eventually dictated its outcome.[47]

Specifically, Alabama's coal operators, in tandem with sympathetic state and local officials as well as the mainstream press, were able to convince the bulk of whites that the strike of the predominantly black UMW represented a primal threat to race relations that was as serious and nightmarish as Reconstruction. Birmingham newspapers warned an increasingly nervous public that "idleness always begets crime and leads to . . . [the] criminal assault by negroes upon white women. [It has made] bomb throwers, midnight assassins, cutthroats, and murderers out of Booker T. Washington's race."[48] Dolly Dalrymple, a leading women's page editor, joined in: "White women and black women meeting on the basis of 'Social equality' indeed! White men holding umbrellas over negro speakers! Black men addressing white men as 'brother'! . . . white miners eating side by side with black men. . . . It is monstrous!"[49] During the strike a correspondent (secretly on the payroll of the mine owners) further scandalized whites both within and without the five-county Birmingham District by writing, "I have seen white men and white women, and fair and promising white girls closely mingling and listening to the false teachings . . . of ignorant and vicious blacks. . . . [Outside agitators], hellions . . . emissaries of the devil . . . have sought to teach the . . . negro miners . . . that they were as good as white men."[50]

While blacks made up three-quarters of the miners' union and held visible positions of leadership, racism and mutual distrust among the miners still impeded full biracial action. Slandered as race traitors, Alabama's white UMW leadership eventually repudiated their black allies, even agreeing to ship every black miner out of state and make the struggle "a white man's fight"—language darkly reminiscent of the 1901 disfranchising constitution.[51]

In a suitable irony, perhaps the state's leading progressive, Governor B. B. Comer, provided the coup de grâce to the strike by ordering the state militia to tear down the union's tents and temporary housing that had been providing shelter to an estimated thirty to forty thousand men, women, and children. In public Comer defended the move as one made to protect local health and sanitation from the open privies and latrines. But in private the governor admitted that race was at the heart of the matter: "You know what it means to have eight or nine thousand niggers idle in the state of Alabama and I am not going to stand for it."[52] During the next outbreak of labor insurgency in Alabama's coal mines, progressive governor Thomas E. Kilby was as hostile to unionism as Comer had been in his use of the state militia to crush the strike. Kilby publicly and unapologetically explained his intervention (and actual arbitration) on the side of capital over workers as a direct function of Reconstruction and the absolute imperative of keeping vicious white carpetbaggers and scalawags from poisoning the minds of ignorant, previously docile, and "easily manipulated" black people.[53]

To be sure, progressivism—in Alabama, the South, and elsewhere—included many instances of merit and genuine progress. But there was also a very real dark side to Progressive reform. In an astounding variety of ways the Progressive Era in Alabama was not "progressive" in any real sense for blacks or for whites who dared to make common cause with blacks. Like so many other types of reform, the era often made changes designed to consolidate the position of those already in power or to make slight concessions to a chosen few who would be allowed to share a portion of societal power.

Thomas E. Kilby, for example, is usually regarded as one of Alabama's most liberal, reform-minded political figures. A modern history of the state named Kilby, who served as governor from 1919 to 1923, as a shining example of Alabama progressivism. George Brown Tindall, in his classic *The Emergence of the New South*, described Kilby as the paragon of "business progressivism." And near the end of Kilby's term as governor, the Russell Sage Foundation credited him with moving Alabama "from the rear ranks to the front of . . . the union in her social progress."[54]

In many respects the praise is not undeserved. Kilby tapped new sources of tax revenue, raised property taxes to provide the state's highest level of public education spending to date, reorganized the prison system, created a child welfare department, helped pass a workman's compensation law, increased spending on social services, established the state docks in Mobile, and supported a twenty-five-million dollar bond issue for better roads that allowed the state to obtain federal matching funds.[55]

Nevertheless, Kilby was a creature as closely bound to the conservative pathways of his contemporaries as anyone. He won election as governor largely by exploiting Alabama's trenchant anti-Catholic bigotry, which overlapped closely with the state's pursuit of prohibition. He was very close to corporations and utilities, and once in office he served Birmingham's Big Mule industrial interests by using the National Guard to crush mining and railroad strikes four times from 1919 to 1922. And his racial views were completely conventional for Alabama.[56]

Even Kilby's postwar anti-lynching campaign, customarily lauded as one of his most progressive reforms, was in fact quite conservative. While Kilby and his white supporters certainly wished to eradicate the bane of mob rule, they were motivated by a desire to blunt the threat of renewed federal involvement in southern racial affairs that loomed after World War I. The overt threat materialized when Missouri congressman L. C. Dyer proposed a federal anti-lynching bill that, for many white southerners, evoked images of Thaddeus Stevens, military Reconstruction, and Henry Cabot Lodge's "Force Bill."[57]

The liberal veneer of Alabama's anti-vigilantism crusade concealed a conservative agenda directly related to race and xenophobia. Kilby and Alabama's conservative power structure embarked on a progressive policy (anti-lynching) in the short term to forestall federal intrusion into state affairs and maintain white, conservative, pro-business control of the state. Alarmed by postwar racial and economic dislocations, and imbued with the nativist impulses of the time, southern elites fought hard to quell vigilante violence and thus remove the most likely reason for Reconstruction-like federal interference into state affairs. A success in the short run, their strategy delayed the federal intrusion they so feared until the tumultuous Second Reconstruction decades later. But such measures were innately illiberal and not in the spirit of inclusive reform for all of the South's citizens.

Much of the progressive drive that characterized the era came to a jarring halt with America's entry into World War I.[58] Americans instinctively clutched at the familiar and conservative in the face of the uncertainty associated with massive global confrontation and the mind-blowing destruction wrought by modern killing machines perfected during the late industrial explosion. While Progressivism had its share of warts, defects, blind spots, hypocrisy, and racism, it had been essentially motivated by an economically liberal impulse to counter the rampant disregard for the commonweal that characterized so much of late nineteenth-century America and its "robber baron" mentality. Progressive reforms such as the direct election of U.S. senators, a national income tax, anti-trust legislation, pure food and drug acts, farm credit provisions, and child labor and safety regulations were aimed at preserving the common good at the expense of rapacious individuals inclined to take advantage of the vast liberties associated with the capitalist state.

The aftermath of America's involvement in war was so tumultuous that it accelerated the already present inclination toward conservatism. The year 1919 was especially convulsive, witnessing labor and racial unrest on an unprecedented scale and contributing to a decade of conservative dominance.

In Alabama, the conservative establishment used an ostensibly progressive vehicle to further an intrinsically conservative agenda. From 1919 to 1924, the state's power structure waged a determined campaign to end vigilante violence from within the Heart of Dixie. Though only partially successful, the campaign marked a dramatic reversal of longstanding policy and practice. But despite the apparent liberalism of the anti-vigilantism movement, conservative interests bankrolled, guided, controlled, and drove it—and made it part of a larger movement to replace extralegal methods of social control with legal ones.

Kilby and Alabama conservatives waged their campaign in the midst of a national climate of fear and reaction. Excess patriotism, unspent in brief wartime involvement, found expression at home in the persecution of blacks, immigrants, political outliers, and virtually any group that could be construed as "alien," including trade unions. Hate groups such as the revised KKK mushroomed to unprecedented size by feeding on a diet of national chauvinism and downright paranoia. Racial tensions boiled over in the "red summer" of 1919 as major race riots broke out in twenty-five cities across the country. Unions struck in record numbers as employers declared null and void the "business associationalism" compromises they had made with workers and the government during the war like union recognition and the legality of collective bargaining. Anti-foreign and anti-radical sentiment found its ultimate expression in the postwar Red Scare and witch hunts of Attorney General A. Mitchell Palmer and J. Edgar Hoover. Congress passed its restrictive Sedition Act in 1918 to stem the flow of undesirable "new immigrants," Jews, and Catholics from southern and eastern Europe. Two related laws followed, and domestic "patriotic" groups such as the American Protective League received government aid to encourage citizens to spy on, and report, any of their neighbors for un-American activities such as criticism of the war, union activity, or dissent. And businessmen openly linked arms with state militia to crush a wave of labor strikes.[59]

White Alabamians prepared for the postwar period with trepidation. Shortly after the Armistice was signed, a group of powerful Alabamians met in conference with conservatives from around the southern states in Washington in an extraordinary attempt to shape the nature of the postwar period in their respective states. Lloyd M. Hooper, a wealthy, conservative businessman from Selma, led the Alabama delegation on its self-described mission to control "the activities [of] . . . the negroes in Alabama." In one meeting, the Black Belt leader and his group met with elites from the other southern states to castigate the federal Labor Department, bemoan black "uppitiness," and discuss the various uses of state National Guard troops as instruments of social control. In another secretive meeting, the Alabama delegation met with their own senator Oscar W. Underwood and congressmen W. B. Oliver and John H. Bankhead II.

The assemblage agreed that "citizens of less stability" had to be controlled but that such control had to be accomplished by lawful means: the state militia, police, and criminal justice system. Reckless acts of mob violence (Alabama's old method of social control) had to go, for such behavior had the potential to attract unwanted federal attention to state customs and affairs. It was crucial, the group agreed, that state National Guard units be kept "independent of federal dominance and at all times under the exclusive control of the Governor.... No sympathy or support may be expected from 'Official Washington.' The whole question must be solved by us and in our own way." To that end, conservative white Alabama's best hopes lay in propaganda efforts and the strict adherence to legal and constitutional—not extralegal—methods. Favorable "public sentiment should be developed," Hooper and his group stressed. We should take "no steps nor . . . any action except as prescribed by law." For the group and its sympathetic congressional allies, it was all about race and conservatism. "No two races living together can survive upon equal terms, one must control." They noted that their position was not unlike that of whites on "the Pacific Coast with respect to the Chinese and Japanese and on the Texas border with the Mexicans. . . . The conservative citizens of the respective communities must organize . . . to render it impossible for citizens of less stability to administer affairs in their own way."[60]

Shortly after a race riot in Longview, Texas, such lobbying paid handsome dividends for nervous southern whites. Officials announced plans in July 1919 to reorganize the nation's army under a new national defense act. The plan called for a regular professional core, supplemented by two citizen-soldier components: organized reserves and state-controlled National Guard units. The southeastern states alone provided one-third of the 440,000-man National Guard contingent. Under the act Alabama added three new infantry companies, a regiment of infantry, a cavalry squadron, a machine-gun troop, and a huge supply of new artillery pieces, shells, and ammunition.[61]

The ominous specter of federal intervention into social customs motivated many white southerners to beef up efforts at social control through legal instead of the traditional extralegal channels—and to publicly crack down on extralegal mob violence. When Missouri congressman L. C. Dyer introduced his federal anti-lynching bill, it shook Dixie to the core and prompted scores of influential white southerners who had formerly winked at mob violence to declare war on vigilantism. Editors across the South—in places like Atlanta, Charleston, and Asheville—produced a flurry of editorials warning southerners that it was up to them to forestall federal intervention by proving that the region did not need outside assistance to get rid of lynching. James Weldon Johnson, national secretary of the NAACP, agreed that it was the Dyer Bill that finally awakened the white people of the South to the necessity of punishing and eradicating lynching themselves.[62]

In Alabama the postwar anti-lynching campaign led by Governor Kilby marked a clear break with the state's past. While several previous state executives such as Thomas Goode Jones and Emmett O'Neal had employed state troops to protect prisoners from lynch mobs, Kilby's efforts broke new ground by using state resources to aggressively pursue, prosecute, and convict the perpetrators of mob violence in an effort to deter the crime itself.

Three sensational convictions of Alabama lynch mobs followed in quick succession. But while Kilby employed the considerable legal talents of Horace Wilkinson to gain the convictions and national headlines in the three cases—all involving white victims—the lynch mobs of at least thirteen black victims went unpursued and unpunished.[63] One of the most notable aspects of Alabama's postwar anti-lynching campaign was that, like most public services of the long Progressive Era, it was for whites only. State authorities clearly followed a disturbing racial double standard in the prosecution of their anti-lynching campaign.

Prior to these cases it had been virtually unheard of for southern states to convict members of lynch mobs. Wholesale convictions were almost unthinkable. Editors around the country congratulated Governor Kilby and Alabama on some of the "most remarkable cases in the criminal annals of the state, and . . . the country." One newspaper dubbed Kilby the "AntiLynching Governor," and Alabama elites were overjoyed with their anti-vigilante work.[64]

Yet Alabama power structure's war on extralegal violence was also marked by a series of state-sponsored measures to ensure control of African Americans, foreigners, and labor unions. For example, Kilby used information from a spy ring in and around the five-county industrial Birmingham District that was surreptitiously run by Big Mule industrialist H. Key Milner, a scion of one of Birmingham's founding families. The goal of the espionage was to monitor segments of the population that were deemed to threaten elite control: "dangerous" blacks and members of labor unions. Milner's agents worked closely and secretly with law enforcement to dampen the prospects for biracial unionism and blunt vigilantism in favor of what some scholars have called "establishment violence."[65]

As in the other southern states, reorganization of the Alabama National Guard granted exclusive control to the governor, beefed up military manpower and firepower, and granted unprecedented legislative power to the adjutant general. The state legislature passed official resolutions condemning the "undesirable foreign population" in the United States; it was causing the "injury of Americans and their cherished institutions." The state senate blamed work-related disorders and public disturbances on "foreign immigration . . . anarchists, the Bolsheviks . . . and other undesirable people." And, to prevent the spread of alien-brushed union heresies among Alabama's impressionable black and poor-white workforce, the legislature established and funded a state patriotic society to inculcate Americanism in the state's residents and cultivate public support for conservative economic and social values. Alabama's lawmakers also acerbically resisted the Chamberlain-Kahn Bill's call for universal national military service, dubbing it "a Prussian system" that would cripple states' rights and the various states' essential control over their military capabilities by imposing a "dangerous . . . centralized Autocratic Military oligarchy."[66]

As white Alabamians moved decisively to forestall challenges from blacks, labor, and immigrants, the desire to prevent federal intrusion into state affairs remained strong.[67] By 1919 the machinery for "establishment violence" and social repression was firmly in place, but conservative elites worried about the rampant vigilante violence that was so traditional. Vigilantism not only stripped power away from the state government and made it susceptible to outside "help" from Washington, it also embarrassed a business leadership still trying desperately to attract northern capital to build an industrial South and southern profits. In short, Alabama's longstanding tradition of mob rule had to end. But an opposition to vigilantism grounded in states' rights and a racial double standard lacked the power to end the violence for good. Decades later the state still wrestled with the problems of vigilante violence and its fears of the federal leviathan.

At times progressivism in the Deep South was downright perverse. The rise of the so-called second Klan itself may be interpreted as a warped and distorted version of the Progressive Era. White, Anglo-Saxon, Protestant, middle-class, morally consumed, pro-conformity, militantly patriotic, even violent, the KKK may be understood as progressivism taken to its ultimate conclusion, its sometimes ugly and logical extreme. In Alabama, one of the nation's leading Klan states during the 1920s (along with a number in the South, Midwest, and West), the order also emphasized right religion, women "in their places," and, again, the sporadic appearance of a convulsion of economic populism.[68]

Two of the most important, if somewhat obscured, legacies of the Progressive Movement in Alabama are its official sanction of anti-democratic impulses of the state's ruling elite and its construction of a stark dichotomy between (acceptable) economic progressivism and (unacceptable) racial liberalism.

These two legacies would live on in Alabama and the South. They would color the region's reaction to the Depression and its ability to tolerate the New Deal. They would delineate what was possible during the crucible of a second world war. They would paint the boundaries of reform during all of these events—and more. Perhaps most important, the legacies would help sow the seeds for the two great meldings that the South would pioneer, and eventually export, as new paths to point the way for conservative regimes wherever they might be found and by whatever name, even "Republican."

Both meldings would solve the seemingly ancient riddle of how oligarchies gain enough popular support to rule. In Rome, bread and circuses had done the trick. But in the relatively new democratic experiment in America, it would, ironically, fall to the "backward" South to show the way.[69] And, with further irony, it would be the anti-democratic nature found in the political centerpieces of Progressive "reform" (disfranchisement and the direct primary) that would serve as the adhesive to bind religious fundamentalism to economic libertarianism—a second melding that would have particular resonance in modern American and Tea Party politics.

There would also be plenty of Progressive Era grist for the first Great Melding: a fusion of white supremacy and extreme laissez-faire that would rely on hatred and fear of the federal government for its mutual bond. Calvinist-sponsored, anti-democratic religious conservatism and Social Darwinism would buttress a combination of the meldings, fusing elements of anti-federalism (in the form of securing and cementing "home rule" on race) and, to a much more overt extent, the anti-democratic impulse that would serve as a linchpin of the modern American right.

The second obscured legacy of Alabama Progressivism, and its successor "conservative progressivism," would deeply tarnish the quality and nature of southern liberalism. Many of the era's reforms were undeniably progressive, activist reforms regarding corporations, railroad regulation, income taxes, direct election of U.S. senators, child labor, efforts at ending the convict lease, and so forth. But the way such reforms were constructed and implemented often established and continued the clear delineation between racial liberalism (which was anathema) and economic liberalism and governmental activism for it (which was not). The roles of leading progressives like B. B. Comer, Thomas Kilby, and even to some extent (while he was an elected official) Hugo Black are prime examples. Virginia Durr, a southern white liberal with impeccable credentials, insisted throughout her life that Hugo Black and his 1920s membership in the Klan was actually the function of class revolt against the well-heeled industrial, farm, utility, and banking elite that ruled Alabama.[70] Black's—not to mention Horace Wilkinson's, Tom Heflin's, and Bibb Graves's—Klan-sponsored challenge to the Big Mule/Bourbons contained undeniable and important elements of economic progressivism that would live on in the Deep South through the 1930s and beyond, a kind of recurring, plain-white populist tradition.

But this legacy would also clearly draw a line between acceptable economic liberalism and the unacceptable racial kind. It would set the stage for the emergence of the state's vaunted congressional liberals of the 1930s and 1940s, men like Hill, Sparkman, Huddleston, John McDuffie—and even for a time figures like Bull Connor. This is the missing link that helps explain how, once the Great Melding was accomplished, the path was paved for Alabama and other southern, especially Deep South, states to go Republican. The route became much clearer once the Dixiecrat path was hastily tried in 1948, then blocked for a 1952 repeat performance by savage intraparty warfare. The recapture by loyalists of the all-important state party machinery meant that subsequent battles between "liberals" and "conservatives" in the South would have to be fought out as Democrats and Republicans—not as loyalists and Dixiecrats—at least until George Wallace arrived to provide an interlude of national proportions.

4
Race over Rum, Romans, and Republicans

> Although Al Smith's skin may be white, his heart is as black as that of any African that roams the jungles. . . . Smith was raised with the negroes. He lived with the negroes. He moves and associates with the negroes now. He eats with the negroes. . . . He is [not] the equal of the negro, because the negro is better than he is. Any white man that makes the negro his equal is not as good as the negro. Yet—for what some hairbrained Democrats call "party loyalty" and "Southern tradition," they would ram an animal like this into the highest office. . . . [H]e is as black in his heart and soul as the blackest negro that roams the cotton fields of Alabama.
> —Alabama KKK newsletter, September 1928

The presidential election of 1928 was a powerful formative moment in the period between Reconstruction and the New Deal. It also solidified the southern personality characteristics of conservative culture forged in the crucible of Reconstruction—elements that would not only make the South solid for Conservative Democracy but foster a regional allegiance to these elements that was so strong it would eventually lead to the Solid South's undoing. In the 1928 clash white supremacy would be sought after as a trump card by both regular Democrats and proto-Republicans (or "Hoovercrats") in the South. Proper religion, patriotism, and ethnic purity become part of the mix of emotion and politics. But in the end, cultural conservatism would be dictated most decisively by which side white southerners believed could best preserve the racial status quo.

By the end of the 1920s the class and populist concerns of a "reform" movement (this time the second Klan) were evaporating—ironically—before the threat of *racial* cataclysm. It would be a harbinger of the post-1936 New Deal reform period, as well as the 1940s and 1950s. Underwritten by its devout adherence to the innately conservative cosmology of Calvinist theology, racial concerns would—for all but the most avant garde in the white South—trump class concerns. It would be another nail in the coffin of economic liberalism—another nail in the coffin of liberalism itself in the Deep South.

They Say We Are Intolerant

In 1928 the nomination of New York's Al Smith as the standard-bearer for the national Democratic Party exposed some of America's darkest prejudices in bold relief. His Catholicism, Tammany Hall connections, immigrant background, and political wetness promised the most divisive campaign since the Populist wars of the 1890s. Rum, Romanism, nativism, and Tammany became critical national issues, the topics of virtual hysteria, in 1928. Still, in Alabama, and much of the South, race managed to eclipse all of these.

The race question had always been of paramount importance for the South. Its centrality, in fact, has been one of Dixie's most enduring and essential features.[1] By the eve of the 1928 election in Alabama, the race issue would again prove triumphant over every other conceivable bone of contention. Alcohol, Catholicism, and Tammany, still hot topics, would all undergo fundamental changes in Alabama, transformations that would set them apart from similar issues elsewhere. In the Deep South, by November 1928 race would graft itself onto all of these issues—bending them, twisting them, contorting them into something decidedly and distinctly southern in flavor. Liquor was dangerous in Dixie, not just for its adhesion in the popular mind to domestic discord and sloth but because it threatened to send a savage race out of control. Catholicism was evil in Alabama, not merely because of its affiliation with foreign dominance and the odor of unwashed immigrants but because Romanists planned to use the African as a stooge, a foot soldier in the coming race war. Alliance with Republicans was ominous in the South because it recalled the dark specter of Reconstruction, Radical Republican politics, federal domination, and, worst of all, black rule. As Alabama senator Tom Heflin put it: there would "be no peace with liquor flowing and niggers full of rum." A new order had "come upon us—a great, big, fat, black nigger."[2]

Because of its primeval nature, race irretrievably altered the main issues of 1928.[3] By the midpoint of the presidential campaign, Alabama's regular Democrats and its Hoovercrats had largely forsaken talk of liquor, foreigners, and the pope in favor of the jugular issue: white supremacy. Both loyalists *and* bolters showed a seemingly insatiable appetite for race-baiting. In Alabama all other issues became peripheral or so altered by race that they were no longer independently distinguishable or even separate. The Ku Klux Klan rode again in this climate—a Klan of decidedly more middle-class orientation, yet one still transfixed by race.

In Houston, Alfonso Emmanuel Smith easily won nomination as the Democratic Party's national standard-bearer for 1928. In a transparent and rather pitiful attempt, in hindsight, party leaders selected Senator Joseph T. Robinson of Arkansas, a dry, southern Protestant and the Senate minority leader, to balance the ticket as Smith's running mate.[4]

But Smith's existence as the national party nominee posed a deep and delicate problem for the South. On the one hand, a vote against Smith was a vote against the Democratic Party. Since Reconstruction, southern whites had vested their most sacred and ineffable interests in a strong Democratic Party, known in states like Alabama by its full name, the Democratic and Conservative Party. The Solid South, to most post–Civil War southerners, represented the best chance of ensuring racial purity and guarding against the encroachment upon, and erosion of, white supremacy. In most southern states, including Alabama, Democratic solidarity was understood to be perhaps the most sacrosanct ideal of the day. Any deviation was regarded as a perversion, anathema, an act that threatened to subvert white supremacy, racial integrity, and the whole southern way of life.

Although the Democratic Party had weathered serious independent challenges in the 1880s and in the Populist revolt of the 1890s, Smith's candidacy presented entrenched Democracy with a far more urgent crisis. Al Smith personified almost all that was repugnant to southern Democrats in 1928. Besides being the governor of a "damn Yankee" state, southerners thought him part of corrupt, dirty, New York City machine politics. He was a Catholic, an ardent anti-prohibitionist, and, perhaps worst of all, a relative liberal on race. As one Protestant minister warned his flock, Smith's candidacy stood for "card playing, cocktail drinking, poodle dogs, divorces, novels, stuffy rooms, dancing, evolution, Clarence Darrow, overeating, nude art, prize fighting, actors, greyhound racing, and modernism." The Baltimore journalist H. L. Mencken prophesied that Smith's nomination would get "Methodist Ku Kluxers of every state south of the Potomac building forts along the coast to repel the Pope."[5]

Some southerners, in the interest of party unity, held their noses and voted for the papist anyway. But many simply could not bring themselves to commit the act. Fully realizing that their stance would be regarded as rank treason in the face of party solidarity, voting for the "man" still outweighed voting for the party.

In Houston, out of all the members of the Alabama delegation only one vote was cast for Al Smith.[6] Yet once he received the nomination, the state's oligarchy was locked into supporting him. Maintenance of the party standard was of supreme importance to these entrenched conservative Democrats, regardless of the identity of a particular nominee—even the presidential nominee. Most members of the State Democratic Executive Committee (SDEC) agreed that appealing beyond the boundaries of the party directly to the masses constituted a paean to democracy that was not worth the risk: a grave threat to stability in Alabama, especially to the hallowed system of white supremacy.

The South's "second" Klan responded to the Smith nomination as if its very life were in jeopardy. Klan leaders mobilized by declaring that their worst fears had finally come true: the Roman Catholic political machine had flung down the gauntlet in a life-and-death challenge to "Protestantism and Americanism."[7] From Atlanta, Hiram Evans promised to banish any member of the Invisible Empire who voted for Smith and vowed to use the Klan to spread the truth about the New Yorker: that his election would be tantamount to "bossism, nullification [of prohibition], alienism . . . [and] priest rule."[8]

Smelling an opportunity unlike anything since it had regrouped in 1915, Alabama's powerful and widespread Klan quickly mobilized. KKK senator Tom Heflin, the figure who would prove most prominent in the anti-Smith fight, soberly informed Alabamians that the Vatican was plotting to take over America through Al Smith and that Jesuit assassins—with "murder in their hearts and mean looks on their faces"—were plotting his own assassination.[9]

Heflin warned Alabamians that if Smith won, the pope would sail up Mobile Bay in a submarine. Atticus Mullin, political columnist for the *Montgomery Advertiser*, reacted harshly to such speech. "Heflin's hold on rural audiences [h]as never [been] more plainly shown," Mullin complained. "Eyes stuck out on stems as he related 'hellish Catholic plots'. . . and how he would keep on foiling the villain as long as his good tongue was not palsied." Mullin marveled that Heflin's emotional appeal resonated so powerfully that he elicited actual tears of rage from some listeners as he told Romanist atrocity stories and how Catholic assassins stalked him on the streets of Washington like "a wild beast." White Alabamians, especially simple, country folk, "fell for it," Mullin jeered about the emotional appeal, "hook, line, and sinker."[10]

Bourbon Democracy's response to the Smith nomination, while not openly hostile, was scarcely warmer than the Klan's. "No candidate other than a resurrected Thaddeus Stevens," historian Wayne Flynt accurately wrote, "could have worse offended Alabama Democrats." Privately, members of the oligarchy admitted that they were merely playing the game in order to protect the party and larger white supremacy. They cursed the national convention and found Smith's lineage and views obnoxious to the most essential principles of their venerable old party.[11]

So divisive was the Smith candidacy that many lifelong Democrats swore to vote for Republican Herbert Hoover and still not consider themselves Republicans. On August 13, 1928, a group met at Birmingham's plush Tutwiler Hotel to organize the Alabama Anti-Smith Democrats. Klansmen Horace Wilkinson and Hugh A. Locke assumed leadership of the bolters, working closely with the state's tiny GOP. A former Jefferson County Circuit judge, Wilkinson was also a deacon at the gigantic Woodlawn Baptist Church in Birmingham. Other Klan-backed speakers hurled vitriol at Victor Hanson's *Birmingham News, Birmingham Age-Herald,* and *Montgomery Advertiser,* all Bourbon supporters of the Smith candidacy.[12]

Women were conspicuous players at the rally and important in the bolt that followed. Women's Christian Temperance Union (WCTU) leaders made themselves quite visible, and one woman trolled the hall handing out copies of *The Rail Splitter,* a vulgar anti-Semitic and anti-Catholic tabloid from Illinois as "our little paper."[13] Also a Jefferson County judge and Methodist deacon, Hugh Locke attacked Alabama's patrician press as the "bloodhounds of the liquorcrats" and warned the assembled audience of men and women that Smith's election would mean a Victor Hanson dictatorship in Alabama.[14]

Other speakers contributed to the Klannish, anti-Catholic, and anti-black tone of the bolt. Members of the powerful Anti-Saloon League showed up; their female secretary cruised the hall soliciting donations. Montgomery evangelist Bob Jones crowed that Birmingham was the most typical Anglo-Saxon city in America and pointed out that large northern cities were made up mostly of unwashed foreigners. If Catholic Al Smith is elected, the preacher warned, "the gates to immigration will be thrown open. I had rather see a saloon on every corner . . . than to see the foreigners elect their candidate." The preacher closed by asserting that "God Almighty" had called southerners to be His chosen people and save the country from the wickedness of the big city. The Reverend A. J. Barton, a member of the Southern Baptist Convention's social service committee, preached against the pollution of American civilization by decadent European values. "They say we are intolerant," Barton reasoned, but "I have never been so happy in all my life as I am in supporting Herbert Hoover." At least "he is not a negro lover."[15]

Wilkinson, Locke, and Heflin—Klansmen all—comprised the ruling triumvirate of the Alabama bolters. All three understood and communicated race and politics in decidedly Calvinist terms. Both Wilkinson and Locke personified the combination of politics and religion as county judges and Baptist and Methodist deacons, respectively. Wilkinson played an especially important role in plotting strategy and legal angles for the bolters. Heflin himself came from a family with two brothers who were Methodist ministers.

Another prominent Klan figure, though, proved to be quietly uncooperative to either side. Heflin courted U.S. senator Hugo Black throughout 1928 but to no avail. While Black did not openly bolt, he and Governor Bibb Graves—perhaps the state's two leading progressives—were concerned enough about the bolt that they did refuse to campaign for Al Smith in Alabama.[16]

Of all the speakers who took the stump in 1928, no one was more visible, colorful, or outrageous than Tom Heflin. Dubbed "Cotton Tom" for his early and frequent support of the southern crop, Heflin hailed from the tiny town of Louina in east Alabama's Randolph County. One of seven brothers (two doctors, two judges, and two preachers), he had gotten his start in politics as mayor of Lafayette and later served as a state legislator and U.S. congressman. In 1920 he won office as a U.S. senator upon the death of John H. Bankhead.

Heflin had a special knack for mimicry, storytelling, and the absurd. He dressed in what has been described as "sartorial splendor": a black or cream-colored Prince Albert coat, a double-breasted vest, a broad-brimmed white hat, a high formal collar with a sash tie—and a corset. He owed much of his political success to the KKK but denied membership repeatedly until 1937 when his knighthood was revealed to the public. Heflin specialized in religious and racist prejudice and was the state's best-known demagogue. The Klan, in turn, hid his membership, campaigned for him, and celebrated his "magnificent and courageous fight[s]" against the evil forces of Rome.[17]

Nationally (and initially in Alabama), anti-Catholicism was the dominant issue of the campaign. Al Smith was the son of Catholic immigrants and the political product of Irish Catholic Tammany Hall. It is impossible to separate anti-Catholicism completely from nativism or the liquor issue, but the Hoovercrats in Alabama and elsewhere made much headway by speaking of dark popish plots, papal domination, Catholic immorality behind convent walls, stockpiles of arms, Roman corruption, and American subordination to a foreign potentate and his hellish designs. American politics had a long anti-Catholic tradition, but never before had the issue gained such widespread currency.[18]

From the outset, Alabama Knights urged voters to fight Smith because he was Catholic. Klan speakers warned voters to ignore the "nice sugar-coated pill of religious tolerance" in order to avoid the "iron-rule of Rome." The Hoovercrats missed no opportunity to amplify the nativism quotient of their appeal by consistently speaking of *Roman* Catholicism, not merely Catholicism. Asked why Alabama's KKK was fighting so hard for Republican Herbert Hoover, one Knight responded, "Because Mr. Hoover is a *Christian* American." The response spoke volumes.[19]

Not only did some Alabamians consider Catholics to be non-Christians, they also thought them un-American as well. Klansmen and other members of the anti-Smith faction worried that a vote for Smith would be a vote to subsume state to church, destroy democracy in favor of papal authoritarianism, and violate the most sacred and revered American principles.[20]

In 1928, Heflin's anti-Catholic attacks became obscene. He spared no method, adjective, invective, innuendo, or slur in an almost manic campaign. So ferocious were his attacks, so vulgar the accusations, so grossly was reality distorted, that it is possible the lines between fact and fiction became blurred even in Heflin's mind. American Catholics were agents of the pope of Rome, the pro-Smith press was "Romanized," Jesuits planned to take over every major city in the country, poison Heflin, plunge the United States into a series of foreign wars, and use brainwashing and genocide to convert every Protestant in America.[21]

On the floor of the U.S. Senate, Heflin claimed to have driven from cover "the most insidious . . . dangerous and deadly" political machine on earth, the Roman Catholic machine. Heflin announced that he had taken his stand for country against the invisible government of the pope of Rome "in spite of what the Jesuits may do with dagger or poison. . . . I bare my chest to all." "I defy these evil, un-American forces of Rome," he continued. "I do not fear them. I have not got time to consider what may happen to me. I am ready to accept whatever comes" from this "veiled, insidious monster" who had his lair in Tammany Hall.[22]

While Heflin led the charge, other members of the anti-Smith faction followed closely behind. The fact that Catholics made up only 3 percent of Alabama's population and were outnumbered by half a million Baptists alone made little difference. The only limit to the charges against the Catholics, it seemed, was the human imagination. "Having stopped the progress, withered the civilization, and destroyed the intelligence and culture of every people she has controlled," a Klan leaflet argued, Rome was now aiming her "brutal, arrogant and unholy propaganda at the sacred circle of the American . . . Protestant home." More typical charges referred to papal domination of the American government, the erosion of core American values, the use of American soldiers in Vatican wars, Roman control of the federal judiciary, repudiation of the U.S. Constitution, a new tidal wave of Catholic immigration, and state acknowledgment of papal infallibility. One of the wilder stories claimed that Smith's election signaled the military conquest of America and its Catholic colonization as "another Ireland." Another rumor threatened the genocide of all non-Catholics to be carried out by the Knights of Columbus, the Vatican's shock troops, who were, according to the KKK, sworn to kill all Protestants "by drugs and deadly poisons."[23]

Lynched with Good Christian Votes

Alabama's Bourbon oligarchy hardly took this lying down. It quickly mobilized to defend itself *and* the national Democratic standard-bearer against the Hoovercrats' bigotry. *Montgomery Advertiser* editor Grover Hall asserted that the same spirit of intolerance that would deny Al Smith the presidency could perform any other crime in the name of religion that fanatics had committed in the past. "Today the bodies of dissenters are safe from the flames but we burn the souls of men instead," Hall wrote. He said they must accept Smith and his Catholicism or "stop lying to our children about religious liberty in the Land of Opportunity for all." Montgomery judge Leon McCord reserved particular odium for reactionary evangelist Bob Jones. McCord compared the preacher to Judas Iscariot, accused him of selling out his party, perverting his religious mission, fomenting prejudice, and prostituting his frock for thirty pieces of Klan silver. "[N]o one asked the religion of the boys overseas when America needed her sons," McCord reminded the South's patriots.[24]

Although loyal Democrats fought hard against being tarred by the anti-Catholic brush, some of the venom invariably dripped onto them. Tom Heflin heard jeers and ridicule in the press and on the floor of the U.S. Senate, but Klansmen and Klanswomen in twenty-five other states flocked to rallies to hear his words.[25]

Because most American Catholics were of Irish, Italian, or southern and eastern European descent, the immigration issue was indelibly imprinted on the Catholic issue. Along with concern about papal domination came the worry that people only one generation removed from the old country would not harbor the same loyalties to American government, values, or society as the northern and western European stock that had migrated to the United States in earlier waves. The anxieties reflected the powerful insecurities of an earlier generation of immigrants who had remarkably short memories of their own odysseys to America. Several sensational events—not the least of which were the Red Scare of 1919–20 and the Sacco-Vanzetti trial—cemented the idea in the popular imagination that aliens lived for anarchy. Given any rein at all, they were likely to attempt a violent overthrow of the republic. In this respect, the second Klan shared important ideological space with the ubiquitous preparedness and patriotic societies spawned by World War I, groups that had no compunction in spying on their neighbors and crushing civil liberties in pursuit of conformity and patriotic support for the war.[26]

Anti-alien propaganda made up a large part of the 1928 campaign in the South. Klan circulars routinely referred to "wops [and] dagoes" and the "beggerly [and] illiterate" character of Catholic countries. The only way the Roman Catholic hierarchy can be maintained, an Alabama Klan leader announced, is by continually pouring on the "fuel of ignorance." And that could only be accomplished by opening the floodgates of immigration and inviting in the illiterate and criminal element of southern Europe who "know nothing but Rome." At a Hoovercrat rally, Klansman, Baptist deacon, and American Legion post leader Horace Wilkinson took the stump to denounce Smith, Catholics, Tammany Hall, Alabama's patrician press, and Democratic delegates at Houston with "foreign-sounding names."[27]

Yet Alabama's Democratic loyalists preyed on the same xenophobia the Klan used. The *Birmingham News* intimated that Klan-led anti-Smith politicians were actually bankrolled by forces "alien to this state's life." F. D. McArthur, a leading spokesman for the regular Democrats, refuted Wilkinson's nativist fire by using anti-alien fire of his own, pointing out that while six of his uncles died for the Confederacy, Wilkinson's Michigan grandfather had actually fought against Dixie.[28]

Reaction to the "new immigration" was not the only issue that amplified Al Smith's Catholicism. The battle over prohibition became virtually indistinguishable as well. Smith adhered to predominant Catholic culture on the issue. Traditionally far less concerned with issues of personal morality than evangelical Protestants, most Catholics regarded alcohol as a harmless vice, if a vice at all. While most responsible Catholics (and Episcopalians for that matter) considered drunkenness, spousal abuse, and excess with the same opprobrium as evangelicals, they hardly regarded social drinking with the same stigma.

This essential difference was largely the product of divergent views about theology and religious service. While Calvinist-influenced evangelicals emphasized faith, personal morality, and the narrow attendant monitoring of their neighbors' behavior, during this era Catholics concentrated on broader issues of social justice, social service, and ensuring one's salvation by performing good works. For many Protestants, though, the alcohol issue was one laced with profound social implications, sometimes regarding spousal and child abuse and the welfare of the family as a social unit.[29]

Most prominent Alabama evangelicals lined up with the Klan, the Anti-Saloon League, and women temperance activists on the liquor question.

Methodists argued that the 1928 election was not about Heflin, the Klan, Catholicism, or anything besides alcohol. The official state Methodist organ, the *Alabama Christian Advocate*, defended Heflin and embraced the KKK. Prominent Methodist minister Robert Shuler warned that if Smith were elected, the Democratic Party would become the "party of Rome and rum for the next hundred years." Other preachers urged their flocks to "vote as you pray" or "vote as Jesus our Captain would have us vote." Baptists sponsored speeches by the superintendent of the state Anti-Saloon League and railed against boss-ridden city masses, "largely foreign and thirsty." Eventually religious fundamentalist fervor bled over into outright demonization of political opponents. One Birmingham WCTU member, the wife of a Baptist preacher, believed that every woman who voted for Al Smith was actually an emissary of the Devil. "It is useless," she sobbed, "to pray that the wicked will change their votes." A Union Springs man agreed: "Satan hath dominion over all the liquor forces."[30]

But the bolters did more than just rail against demon rum. As part of their strategy for the election, Horace Wilkinson and Hugh Locke negotiated a pact with state Republicans to list twelve leading Democrats as presidential electors for Herbert Hoover. The move, endorsed by state Republican boss Oliver Street, was apparently designed to soothe the troubled consciences of Alabama Democrats who could now vote for twelve anti-Smith Democrats instead of actual Republicans. The GOP agreed not to run any candidates in order to free the bolters to vote Democratic locally and still be able to vote Hoover for president. Women, prohibitionists, and moral conservatives made up the bolt slate, including prominent Dothan Republican banker George H. Malone and Zue Musgrove Long, sister of perhaps the state's leading prohibitionist.[31]

Republican Masonic leader and former Populist Oliver Street was especially active in 1928. Although he opposed Alabama's entrenched conservative Democracy, his own perspective was a long way from one of enlightened tolerance. Street's anti-Catholic bigotry was so raw, in fact, that it earned him the official censure of the chairman of the national Republican Party. At least one Birmingham newspaper refused to accept his paid political advertisements against Smith, branding them "reprehensible . . . inaccurate propaganda." Undaunted, Street printed and distributed (most likely with Horace Wilkinson's help) two hundred thousand copies of a circular titled "Governor Smith's Membership in the Roman Catholic Church and Its Proper Place as an Issue in This Campaign." The Republican boss echoed Klan arguments by claiming that Catholics stood for state subordination to Rome and opposition to religious liberty, free thought, and virtually every other fundamental tenet of Americanism. Most objectionable, though, was a shocking imprint that accompanied the Street circular. The picture depicted a scene from the Spanish Inquisition in which Catholic priests were cutting off a Protestant woman's breasts under the caption, "She nursed a heretic child."[32]

While Street conspired with Klan strategists to fan the flames of intolerance, local klaverns took more concrete action. At a summer rally at Wahouma's middle-class Nathan Bedford Forrest den, Knights lynched the New Yorker in effigy. Before a crowd of some two hundred men, women, and children, a Klan leader held up a mannequin of Smith and asked them (Pontius Pilate style) what they wanted to do with it. "Lynch him! Lynch him!" the mob chorused. The Klansman then cut the dummy's throat with a long knife and mercurochrome spurted forth to simulate blood. As the macabre display went on, klavaliers tied a noose to the Smith mannequin and dragged it around the hall for spectators to kick and shoot with their firearms. When the crowd had been sufficiently worked into a frenzy, another Kluxer took the podium to swear that lynching was too good a fate for the New Yorker. In November, the hooded speaker promised, Smith would be lynched with "good Christian votes."[33]

He Has the Heart of a Black Man

Traditional Alabama Democracy did not sit still while the Hoovercrats took the political fight to them. The bolting forces had a distressing penchant for lowering the political debate to personality, creed, nationality, and mudslinging. Yet the oligarchy hardly worked to keep politics on an elevated plane.

In fact the 1928 campaign in Alabama degenerated to the very basest level of modern political discourse. Planters and industrialists matched their adversaries in intensity, viciousness, and the willingness to cater to the lowest common denominator. The oligarchy was somewhat hamstrung because it found itself pleading the case of a man it was every bit as repelled by as the Hoovercrats. Although the Big Mule/Black Belt coalition detested Smith in principle, he was, as the party's national standard-bearer, still the representative of all they cherished in 1928: party regularity and protection of the racial status quo.

The *Birmingham News* led off with the Reconstruction charge. The newspaper implied that the Klannish Hoovercrats were actually made up of Republicans in Democratic clothing. Comparing the bolters to Reconstruction scalawags for their disloyalty, the journal drew comparisons between the two threats to party solidarity, portraying the bolting triumvirate of Heflin, Locke, and Wilkinson as pawns on the chessboard of master Republican strategists.³⁴ *Birmingham Age-Herald* editor Charles Fell ridiculed the bolting faction's "lust for witch-burning" and denounced the group's "Christian appetite for hatred."³⁵

Patrician strategists trained many of their biggest guns on Klan darling Tom Heflin. As the state's senior senator, Heflin was a major embarrassment to Alabama's traditional Democrats. While Klan politicos and economic liberals Hugo Black and Bibb Graves did not win any points with the patricians by sitting out the 1928 schism, their silence effectively distanced them from Heflin's risky gambit.

The flamboyant Heflin was an extremely large man, a virulent racist, self-servingly inconsistent, and identified with prohibition, anti-Catholicism, Negrophobia, and political buffoonery.³⁶ Not every Methodist in Alabama was a fan. One expressed his thoughts about Heflin succinctly if crudely: "[S]ay listen, a yellow dog will piss against a post but would take one smell at you and run along. . . . Back to the shit from whence you sprung."³⁷

Despite its intensity, the patrician response to Heflin did not define Alabama politics. It was their own appeal to racial prejudice that ended up dominating the 1928 contest. Ultimately, in Alabama, the presidential campaign was reduced to a vulgar contest in race-baiting.³⁸ The Hoovercrats were, of course, quite adept at playing the race card. They countered by taking out full-page ads in Alabama's county newspapers slamming Al Smith for his racial liberalism. Bolting speakers railed that Smith "not only loved negroes but bootlicked 'em and admitted it." L. L. Gwaltney, a leading Baptist, editor of the state's denominational paper, the *Alabama Baptist,* and a man considered to be a progressive by some, pointed to ten million blacks in Dixie as reason enough for his opposition to the New Yorker. "To give [them] free access to liquor—to place this passion inflamer in the hands of a child race not far removed from their savage haunts in the jungles of Africa," Gwaltney wrote, "would be to court tragedy unspeakable." Introduced by Hugh Locke to a crowd of five thousand at Birmingham's Municipal Auditorium, Methodist preacher Bob Shuler thundered that Smith's only hope was to pander to "Harlem negroes." Meanwhile, Horace Wilkinson distributed thousands of hate sheets around the state with titles as restrained as "Al Smith, the Negro Bootlicker" and "Al Smith, the Negro Lover."³⁹

Race-baiting sprang naturally from the rump group's Klan roots. Their charter defended the bolt because, they reasoned, the Democratic Party had nominated a candidate who failed to represent the most fundamental principles of the party: namely the maintenance of white supremacy. Al Smith, the Hoovercrat leaders claimed, was a menace to the white race, an advocate of social equality, and a threat to racial integrity and the survival of white civilization.⁴⁰

Alabama Klan publications routinely referred to Smith's "love" for blacks, his appointment of over eight hundred blacks to public office in New York State, his association with Jack Johnson, the notorious miscegenist, integrationist, and former heavyweight boxing champion, rumored plans to name an African American to his cabinet, and the fact that Tammany Hall drew support from Harlem, the "Negro heaven . . . [and] black belt of New York City." The group printed and distributed racist leaflets about the New York governor under headings such as "Nigger, Nigger, Nigger," "Smith's Negro Babies," "Tammany and the Negro," and "More Nigger." A favorite Klan conspiracy theory held that Smith's election would initiate a Catholic overthrow of American government *and* white supremacy. Klan campaign workers in Alabama worked hard to tie Catholicism, liquor, and Tammany to the black race. One Kluxer wrote Tom Heflin to applaud his crusade against Smith and complain that in his "Romanized" hometown, he could watch the nuns line up to vote along with the "niggers, Dagoes, gamblers, macks, and pimps." Heflin responded by challenging Alabamians to "Choose ye this day whom ye shall serve, the God of white supremacy or the false god of Roman social equality."[41]

In September 1928 the Alabama Klan published its official position: Although Al Smith may have white skin, his "heart is as black as that of any African that roams the jungles." Yet because of what some "hair-brained Democrats call 'party loyalty' and 'Southern tradition,' they would ram an animal like this" into the nation's highest office. Smith "has the heart of a black man and . . . is as black . . . as the blackest negro that roams the cotton fields of Alabama."[42]

The planter-industrialist press howled against this kind of politics, but Alabama's entrenched Democracy had seniority compared to their upstart rivals when it came to race-baiting. While their appeals were usually more subtle and sophisticated, in the end they were no less lethal and certainly no more open-minded.[43]

At a rally in north Alabama, loyalist Democrats responded to bolting demagoguery with their own brand of Negrophobia. Republican Reconstruction was their best friend. "We have a white man's government in Alabama, and we are going to keep it unless federal bayonets again tear our heritage from us," F. D. McArthur announced. A mouthpiece for the oligarchs told horror stories about a giant black man heading a Herbert Hoover reception line in Washington, and another told of a Montgomery woman who quit her job in Secretary Hoover's Commerce Department because she could not abide working alongside black people.[44]

The scene repeated itself across the state as loyalists took the stump to appeal to white supremacy, anti-federalism, and the Reconstruction memory.

Former governor Thomas Samford of Opelika explained the patrician case simply: "It is a white man's party and we are white men." Major Frank Dixon—Klan opponent and future governor and Dixiecrat leader—cautioned that Hoover's election would reconstitute "Negro rule" and, as it had during Reconstruction, bring "the black heels of the ex-slaves down on the throats of Southern men and women." In Montgomery, regular Democrats strenuously preached the preservation of Anglo-Saxon civilization. Tyler Goodwyn, the author of a failed anti-KKK bill, demonstrated that in Alabama resistance to the hooded order in no way amounted to racial progressivism. "You ask what my party stands for, my answer it shall be," Goodwyn rhymed. "It stands for the rule of white men, white men like you and me." Goodwyn also pointed to fear and hatred of the federal government as reasons to stay true to the Democratic and Conservative Party. A Hoover victory, the lawmaker asserted, would light a spark and start a federal blaze more destructive than Sherman's march to the sea.[45]

Other loyalist Democrats followed the racial, Reconstruction, and antifederal line. Hugh Mallory, a confirmed Redeemer, used religion to buttress his argument for party regularity and white supremacy. "God meant Alabama to be a white man's state," he expounded to a Black Belt audience, "and the Democratic party has been His instrument in keeping it a white man's state." Congressman John McDuffie told a Wiregrass gathering that Herbert Hoover had achieved Republican nomination with the aid of 122 black delegates while not one single black face had "disgraced the Democratic convention." Benjamin Meek Miller, another future governor, agreed with McDuffie: "[T]here was not a seat for [one] nigger at Houston. . . . No nigger helped nominate Al Smith. He was nominated by more than 900 Anglo-Saxons." From his sickbed in Tuscaloosa, former governor Bill Brandon rose to appeal to white supremacy. Arguing that the Hoovercrats were Republicans in Democratic clothing, Brandon warned of "negro domination . . . Republican misrule . . . the slimy trail of the carpetbagger," and a second Reconstruction. "I believe in white supremacy and the rule of [the] white man," Brandon made clear in his support for the national party's candidate.[46]

Social Darwinism—replete with patriarchy and religious regularity—was appealed to, of course. The regular Democrats added the twist of throwing Tom Heflin's old words about Herbert Hoover and white supremacy back in the senator's face. Hoover's decision to desegregate the Commerce Department had "humiliated white girls" by dangling them as prey for "buck negroes," Heflin had charged in 1927. Again, conservative religion bolstered white supremacy. Such policies flew in the face of right religion, the Bourbons argued. "God Almighty has made [the] racial facts," and Herbert

Hoover had no business interfering with the "handiwork of the Almighty." Whites are the "superior race, the king of races, the climax and crowning glory of the four races of black, yellow, red, and white." If this was still too subtle, the publicity bureau of the Alabama Democratic Campaign Committee made it crystal clear. The Republican Party and Herbert Hoover were pledged to "insure the life of every Negro Rapist lynched in Alabama for Ten Thousand Dollars," it claimed in providing a remarkably convoluted interpretation of the recently defeated Dyer Anti-Lynching Bill. Could any "red-blooded white Southern man or woman place the stamp of . . . approval" on this outrage by voting on November 6 for Republican Herbert Hoover?[47]

Anti-federal sentiment was integral to the patrician appeal for regularity, much as it had been in the patrician war against the Klan itself. Because of Dixie's chronic bouts with a Reconstruction Syndrome, race could never be completely divorced from fear, hatred, and loathing of the federal government. The same aversion to the central government that fueled 1928 appeals for party regularity also shaped the resistance the oligarchy threw up against the Ku Klux Klan (as well as, for that matter, the pro-Klan bolters' rationale itself). When it came down to it an overwhelming anti-statist concern with federal intrusion and home rule eclipsed all other considerations in the Deep South. The 1928 campaign revealed that Alabama remained trapped in Reconstruction, consumed by thoughts and images of race and federal domination. The appeal, apparently, was irresistible.

Again and again in 1928, patricians referred to the specter of federal interference on race as reason enough to remain true to the Democratic Party. State chairman Buck Oliver made this appeal ad nauseum in a major Birmingham speech, reminding Alabamians that Tammany Hall had shielded the South from the 1890s "force bill," predicting that federal voting registrars would swoop down on the South if Herbert Hoover won, and pointing ominously to a Republican anti-lynching bill. Hoover's election, the Democratic chair assured his audience, would result in the Republican use of federal bayonets to "put the black heel on the white neck" just like during Reconstruction.[48]

While Birmingham editors praised Oliver's statement as "compelling . . . lucid . . . [and] an epochal utterance," they failed to acknowledge any connection between the patrician appeal to racial prejudice and the Klan's use of race and religion. In fact, despite Oliver's repeated calls to safeguard white supremacy and eschew federal intervention, these same journalists gushed and rhapsodized over the alleged enlightenment of the patrician's speech. "It is a carefully thought out passage that scorns to wave the red flag of prejudice," the Hanson editors wrote. Instead it "pleads like angels trumpet-tongued" against the lower-class "resort to witch-burning, and the hospitality to evil which the [bolting] malcontents are urging with such vociferousness."[49]

Following Buck Oliver's lead, other planter-industrialist leaders echoed the call for party regularity to avoid federal intrusion into southern race relations. Congressman George Huddleston made the anti-federal appeal in Birmingham. Victor Hanson's various news outlets repeated it, as did U.S. congressman Henry Steagall and Tuscumbia's Archie Carmichael. Anti-Hoover circulars habitually conjured the perils of black Republican misrule, Radical Reconstruction, and the searing imagery of federal bayonets. The effort thereby powerfully fed and fused conservative Democratic concerns with race and mistrust of the federal government.[50]

The racial nature of the 1928 conflict was amplified by an eleventh-hour appeal from Mabel Jones West, president of the Alabama Women's League for White Supremacy. Demonstrating that the Klan, Hoovercrats, and men in general had not cornered the market on racial prejudice, Mrs. West spectacularly repudiated the KKK, endorsed Al Smith, and chastised the secret order for its promotion of religious proscription. Declaring that the Klan, to which she had recently belonged, had allowed itself to be "prostituted," like other loyalist Democrats Mrs. West appealed to racial bigotry while criticizing the Hoovercrats for pandering to religious bias. When the time came to "choose between the Klan and . . . white supremacy," she said, "let the Ku Klux Klan go to the devil." In other words, in Alabama the Ku Klux Klan was insufficient to guard white supremacy if it insisted on doing so in collaboration with the hated GOP. The *Birmingham News* was so moved by West's actions that the state's leading newspaper compared her to sixteen-year-old Emma Sansom, the Civil War heroine who aided Nathan Bedford Forrest in preventing the Union capture of Alabama. The paper opined that Mrs. West's women's league was "one of the most significant developments" in preserving white supremacy since George Houston had been elected in 1874 and Redemption delivered Alabama from carpetbag, scalawag, and Negro rule.[51]

Other Alabama women were just as outspoken and involved in 1928. Dr. Marie Brauer provided right-hand assistance to Mabel West as secretary of the Women's Division of the Jefferson County Democratic Executive Committee. Future Dixiecrat and sister to an Alabama congressman and senator, Marie Bankhead Owen took active part in the loyalist campaign against Hoover. One Alabama woman working in the Commerce Department was so distraught over Hoover's desegregation of the agency that she appealed to South Carolina demagogue Cole Blease for assistance. Especially distasteful was the thought of having to use the same bathroom as black people. "Think of a Secretary of Commerce having to stoop to niggers . . . to win," she lamented. "I wonder how Mr. Hoover would like to have the women of his family use the same toilet that colored people use.... We call these colored people 'Hoover's chocolates' and all wish we could make him eat them."[52]

Perhaps the height of irony was reached when Bourbon leaders imported the notorious Theodore Bilbo to lecture the Hoovercrats on tolerance. Known simply as "the Man" in his native Mississippi, the diminutive Bilbo was one of the South's most consummate racists and a demagogue par excellence. Anticipating opposition from the Klan in Alabama, Bilbo boasted that he, himself, was "a charter member of the Ku Klux Klan—of Bilbo Klan No. 40." But the sheeted order was dead now, Bilbo stated, and if southerners wanted to keep white supremacy they had to move beyond loyalty to such groups. An expert at conjuring Lost Cause memory, Bilbo arranged for a contingent of Confederate veterans to dramatically ring the stage as he got to the heart of the matter: "The Republican party of the North is the negro party of the South..... If you ... desert to the Negro Republican party you will live to regret it. And there will be blood spilled—the blood of your children, some of them yet unborn."[53]

On the eve of the election, loyalists confidently predicted that the national Democratic candidate would carry Alabama as usual by an overwhelming margin, at least 50,000 votes. Shockingly, the election was almost too close to call with Smith barely edging out Hoover in Alabama, 127,796 votes to 120,725. Voter turnout was huge, over 83 percent, but the Black Belt made the difference by furnishing Smith with a 10,200 majority. Some pointed to the Black Belt's well-deserved reputation for vote fraud as the only reason the Democrat carried Alabama at all.[54]

Nationally, the Republican crushed Smith. In a result that illustrated the national complexion of religious prejudice, Smith fared worse than any Democrat in American history. He captured only eight states to Hoover's forty and actually lost five in the Outer South: Virginia, Florida, Texas, Tennessee, and North Carolina. Hoover snowed Smith under in the popular vote by six million votes and even won Smith's home state of New York. A jubilant Tom Heflin literally said, "I told you so."[55]

A Christian Lust for Witch Burning

The presidential election of 1928 foreshadowed future political developments in the United States by crystallizing the power of the race issue in southern politics. A huge number of white southern Democrats, furious over the choice of a New York racial and cultural liberal to represent the party, bolted the party of their fathers and committed the previously unheard-of heresy of voting for a Republican. In the 1928 South, though, these rebels could not yet call themselves "Republicans" without consigning themselves to the furthest fringes of society. And, truth be told, they were more anti-Democrats than actual Republicans as the GOP was constituted in the Roaring Twenties. So they took the euphemism Hoovercrats. Yet their support of the Republican Hoover marked the closest presidential election up until that time in the South.

Alcohol, Catholicism, urbanization, and ethnic purity were all major issues in the 1928 election. But in Alabama and the Deep South, race eclipsed them all as each side attempted to out-race-bait the other in what became a vicious internecine conflict. Klan rallies designed for the whole family lynched Al Smith dummies—replete with hanging, throat-slashing, spurting fake blood, and real gunshots—and promised to lynch the New Yorker, come November, "with good Christian votes." Loyalist Democrats fought back by invoking the emotional specter of Republican Reconstruction drummed into every southern schoolboy and girl by the age of ten. The caricature, which relied on the canted texts of the "Dunning School" of Reconstruction historiography, was replete with corruption, ignorant black rule, Yankee oppression, and antediluvian threats to white womanhood.

To a remarkable degree, the 1928 election represented a fierce family split among white southerners over the best way to preserve white supremacy and cultural authenticity. Although both sides agreed on the fundamental of preserving white supremacy in the South, they disagreed sharply over the best way to achieve that result. The bolters chose the GOP, but out of deference to (and wise recognition of) the region's Reconstruction memory, they called themselves "Hoovercrats" rather than Republicans. Alabama's loyalists, despite their serious misgivings, decided to remain inside the Democratic tent.

During the years leading up to and including the campaign, the state's Hoovercrats and nascent Republicans operated in very close physical and spiritual proximity to the state's powerful Ku Klux Klan, as well as the forces most clearly identified with prohibition, religious fundamentalism, traditional family values, nativism, xenophobia, religious, ethnic, and racial intolerance, and conventional white, Anglo-Saxon, Protestant notions of morality—enforced at the end of a whip or a gun, if necessary. In essence, for Alabama, the 1920s KKK provided another major component of what would one day become a major sectional political realignment. It is likely that it did so in much of the greater South as well.

By contrast, the loyalists were more cosmopolitan, business conservatives, concerned with preserving their favorable political and economic position, and not as likely to get worked up over issues like alcohol, Catholics, Jews, immigrants, or conventional forms of morality. Yet both factions were ultra-conservative on race. While the loyalists were determined opponents of the Klan, they fought the order as a *political* adversary and as an unsubtle police force against racial change—one that threatened to dry up northern capital and economic investment and bring down an unwanted federal invasion and real racial change on the heads of racially conservative white southerners.[56] The loyalists shared an interest with their fledgling Republican or Hoovercrat challengers, indeed a fixation on maintaining white supremacy.

The 1928 episode made clear that *if the two sides could ever be fused together*—using race or some equally emotional adhesive—*the product of such a union would be invincible in the Deep South*. Eventually, it would happen. As shocking and overheated as it might first seem, there is no way around it: a critical part of the mid-twentieth-century partisan realignment of the South may accurately be termed "neo-Kluxism."

The term "neo-Kluxism" denotes a focus redux on racial, cultural, ethnic, moral, religious, and even gender-relations homogeneity that bears striking parallels with the Ku Klux Klan of the 1920s and 1940s. That is, the "second KKK" and its 1940s incarnation posed as the self-conscious preservers of home and hearth in the South, a concept constituted by the interaction of several cardinal building blocks of conservative (read: predominant) southern culture: white supremacy, Anglo-Saxon, evangelical Protestantism, "dry," patriarchal, traditional family values, religious, ethnic, moral, and social conservatism, ethnic purity and nativism, patriotism, and "100 percent Americanism." The 1940s version did a very similar thing, with the exception of being poorer and more working class in membership than middle class and having that fact reflected in its de-emphasis on mainline Protestantism for more fringe, Pentecostal, charismatic, Church of God, and Holiness church support.

Tension between economic conservatives and social conservatives marked political reality in the South for a long time. The 1928 presidential election, in particular, signaled a deep and troubling divide in conservatism between the business and social types. Yet it also hinted at enormous possibilities. If a successful resolution between the conservative factions could ever be accomplished, the partisan beneficiary of its reconciliation would become an insurmountable entity in the majority white South.

Much had to be overcome if this were ever to take place, though, not least, elite disdain for the "priest-ridden ignorance to which our people now seem utterly lost," as Alabama newspaper mogul Victor Hanson put it. Other representatives of the southern commercial class exhibited similar unease with the moral and religious attitudes of the plain folk: their disturbing propensity to be moved to irrationality by "intolerance, hatred . . . [and] religious bigotry . . . [a] lust for witch-burning . . . [and a] Christian appetite for hatred."[57] In the modern United States, the Republican genius has proven to be the amicable resolution of this tension by putting the emotionalism to use in uniting various conservatives instead of allowing it to feed conservative disunion. But all of this happened in the South first.

Anti-federalism and anti-democratic impulses served as the essential glues of the two great meldings pioneered in the nineteenth- and early twentieth-century South and then exported nationwide to drive conservative Republican ascendance. The first melding, dependent on the most intense sort of enmity toward the federal government, allowed southern oligarchs to eventually appropriate completely the sacred cow of white supremacy from their class antagonists, adversaries who had mounted occasional and bothersome insurgencies and who, as long as they could lay a co-claim to the mantle of white supremacy, remained a dangerous, if not substantial, threat. The successful patrician coup would be perfected in the South's opposition to the second New Deal.

The second Great Melding would rely on racial orthodoxy and anti-federalism as well but would powerfully supplement the adhesive mixture with a blatant antipathy toward democratic processes, institutions, and a liberal understanding of suffrage. This anti-democratic mortar would serve as a powerful substance to cement economic fundamentalism to its religious cousin. During the three decades after 1980 this melding would come into its own, bringing strange bedfellows together—libertarians and Christian Dominionists, Grover Norquist and Jerry Falwell, James Dobson and Sarah Palin—to find perhaps its most unadulterated expression in the Tea Party of Michelle Bachmann and Rick Perry as well as the slightly less extreme new rightism of Ronald Reagan and George W. Bush. But again, as with the first melding, this second variant—potent as it is—could locate its roots in the South of the late nineteenth and early twentieth centuries.

5
Placing Culture on Hold
The New Deal Coalition, Its First Cracks, and the "Great Melding" Takes Shape

> I do everything I can [to make ends meet]. I've even gone out and competed with Niggers to get jobs mowing lawns.
> —Lorena Hickok

Although no one could know it at the time, the New Deal held within it the seeds of its own destruction. While the program would eventually develop into a coalition of unparalleled strength and effectiveness, it would also harbor tensions and contradictions that made it, from the beginning, temporary and ephemeral—doomed to do anything but last. Nowhere would this be truer or more apparent than in the Deep South, in places like Alabama.

For the New Deal in its complete sense was not one singular program or even a set of closely related goals. It was, far more accurately, a patchwork quilt of policies, initiatives, people, and agencies—schemes to do something, *anything,* to alleviate the unprecedented crisis that confronted the country. Its goals and personalities—sometimes pacific, sometimes contradictory and competing, often confusing because of the sheer immenseness of the task that lay ahead—reached out to and subsumed a bewildering array of different Americans.

By March 1933, the New Deal offered sanctuary for the weary and beleaguered from all walks of life: people of conservative nature and those with a more liberal bent; people beset by the revolutionary economic tempests of the age who had found little or no relief elsewhere. By the time Franklin Roosevelt took the oath of office as the country's thirty-second president, most of them had nowhere else to go. So the New Deal became one and the same entity that responded to the plight of the rural inhabitant and the urban dweller; of actors, artists, authors, and playwrights; of bricklayers, iron molders, steel rollers, and textile workers; of unskilled teens who had never spent a night away from home; of country people accustomed to generations of poverty, debt, and no electricity or indoor plumbing; of widows; of the starving, educated and uneducated; of the farmer and the city worker; of those who worked with their hands and those who worked with their minds; of the small town, the big city, and the sparsely dotted countryside.

The unprecedented exigency that became known as the Great Depression eventually made all of these—and more—partners in the great experiment called the New Deal. For a while it also made them allies in the political expression and engine that drove the experiment: the Democratic Party of Franklin Roosevelt. Yet the New Deal could not—nor did it even attempt to, in most cases—reconcile the wildly divergent worldviews, philosophies, and beliefs that the kaleidoscope who called themselves "New Dealers" or New Deal supporters brought with them.

The participants themselves looked on one another at best with curiosity, in some instances with downright suspicion and dislike. The New Deal contained the seeds of its own destruction because it brought together so many people with so little in common for a goal that so many of them understood to be only temporary. It brought together people who viewed the culture, religion, folkways, and even the languages of other constituent members as alien, foreign, even dangerous. It could not last. In fact, it is a testament to the political will and ability of its designers that the coalition managed to hold itself mostly together for nearly four decades.

The break was apparent even before there was a New Deal. It was there at least as early as 1924 at the Democratic National Convention in New York. Alabama broke regional ranks to vote for a formal anti-Klan plank, laying bare the deep and seemingly insoluble differences between the two major wings that made up the Democratic Party.[1]

One was urban, industrial, and unionist, largely ethnic, wet, Catholic and Jewish, identified with the political machines of the great cities of the Northeast and Midwest; many of the allegiant could trace their roots to southern and eastern Europe, some to liberalism, others even to radicalism. The other wing was dry, southern, Protestant, rural, and conservative, sometimes even fundamentalist, indifferent or unfriendly to big-city machines and unions, and staunchly, even overwhelmingly, Anglo-Saxon. These were people, Democrats all, animated by the most profoundly different ideologies; people who found the other side's culture alien, bewildering, and sometimes repugnant. Yet the New Deal, which pasted this Democratic coalition together—and added millions of Americans who went along out of desperation more than anything else—meant, at its very core, *inclusiveness*: including all who needed help in the cataclysmic days of the Great Depression. Most important, for the South, this inclusiveness would after 1935 extend to both races, meaning in essence that either the South or the Democratic Party would eventually have to change if the affair were to have any chance of flowering into a lifelong partnership.

The New Deal was not perfect, in this or any other way. It was beset by fits and starts and false starts and backtracking, by contradictions and half-measures, by ego, shortsightedness, even hypocrisy. The Agricultural Adjustment Act (AAA) hit black tenants and croppers first and hardest. The National Recovery Act (NRA) was so bound to local customs that blacks called it the "Negro Removal Act"—or worse.[2] Yet taken as a whole, the New Deal far outstripped the head-in-the-sand paralysis associated with Herbert Hoover and the three successive Republican administrations of the 1920s. Together they had presided over a breathtaking fall in mass consumption demand resulting from the decoupling of wages from a fantastic rise in corporate profits, thus contributing so much to the infrastructure of Depression-era economics. Republican intransigence on the tariff and the forgiveness, or adjustment, of foreign debts did little to strengthen the underlying buttresses of the 1920s global economy. And although the new measures for blacks were more imperfect than those for whites, the New Deal did something no program in American history had done since Reconstruction: it included them. At an imperfect and substandard level, to be sure, but it included them. And they knew it.

It was there in hundreds of gestures large and small. It was there every time Eleanor Roosevelt spoke at a black university or had African Americans to the White House for tea; when Aubrey Williams created an office for his New Deal agencies to address Negro affairs; whenever Harold Ickes would actually say it—out loud—that under FDR blacks had "a special New Deal of their own." Or when Roosevelt himself, so often criticized for being cautious, even indifferent, to black concerns, would declare that in America "there should be no forgotten men and no forgotten races." In private the president could even be more forthcoming, confiding to the NAACP's Walter White that he had to tread carefully where senior southern congressmen were concerned (because "I did not choose the tools with which I must work") but assuring Mary McLeod Bethune that "People like you and me are fighting ... for the day when a man will be regarded as a man regardless of his race." And because of Roosevelt's longevity and unmatched election to four terms, black identification transcended mere identification with the man to become mass identification with the party itself. "My friends, go home and turn Lincoln's picture to the wall," the editor of the *Pittsburgh Courier* advised other blacks in 1938. "That debt has been paid in full."[3]

Chapter 5
I Will Steal for What I Have to Have

Today there is no way to accurately convey the depths of heartache, misery, despair, and panic that accompanied the Great Depression. We are simply too far removed in time and plenty. But the crisis had no precedent that approached it in severity—at least in the American past.

Millions were thrown out of work. Banks and farms failed on a massive scale. Life savings were lost on Wall Street or at the town bank. Those fortunate enough to have work toiled for only a few hours, for pennies at that. Proud men and women, accustomed to providing for their families, paying their taxes, and obeying the law, found themselves brawling on street corners over the rubbish that fell from garbage trucks so they could have something they could call food to put on the table that night. Many resorted to hoboing, crime, or hitching the rails.

Most of us are familiar now with the raw numbers: real GDP down by a third, unemployment of 25 percent (50 percent in some cities), underemployment at another 25 percent, personal income slashed by 44 percent. In some countries, unemployment reached 33 percent. Between 1929 and 1932 the stock market lost 90 percent of its value. In just two months the market lost all of its gains from the previous two years put together: nearly $40 billion. There are other numbers: 10,800 bank failures, 9 million savings accounts lost, residential construction down by 95 percent, wages by 60 percent, dividends by 56 percent, crop and livestock prices by 75 percent, 85,000 businesses gone, record farm failures and home foreclosures.[4]

Alabama was hit hard. Farm families endured a seemingly inexorable downward shift in mobility, as they had for over half a century. The federal government actually singled out Birmingham for distinction—as the hardest-hit city in America. By summer 1932, a staggering 85 percent of the eligible working adults in Birmingham were jobless or forced to work only part-time.[5]

Yet the statistics, as appalling as they are, tell only half the story. True desperation is present in the supplications for help—*any help from anybody*—that poured out of formerly proud Alabamians suckled on the cultural ideals of independence, rugged individualism, and personal responsibility. Driven to their knees in the 1930s, many reached out for whatever hand they could grasp—even the federal government's. One woman, caring for five children with a husband and his paycheck in prison, asked authorities for anything they could spare. Another, in Huntsville, her man in Atmore Prison and a three-year-old to feed, also begged for relief. "[M]y folks is just poor honest working folks" with no means of helping, she explained. Her husband could not be counted on; she realized that now. "I prayed and begged him to change and be a better man and stay out of the pen, but he was never satisfied until he got [sent] back down there." A Daphne woman with children seven, five, three, and one—all sick, with no warm clothes—and a house about to "fall down" pleaded for help from the government. A one-armed Ashby man with a disabled wife and seven children also wrote the state: "Please help. If I don't get some help and some work . . . we all will starve in a pile." Others, disabled by service in World War I, were reduced to begging. "If I don't get some help I don't know what I am going to do," J. J. Henderson of Dothan said about his wife and three starving children. Another confessed in 1934 that he had walked over three thousand miles in the previous year trying to find work.[6]

Many southerners were so desperate that they were ready to cast off the cultural folkways of centuries—at least temporarily—in the cataclysm that was the Great Depression. "I will steal for what I have to have," Belle Ogle of Birmingham announced. "I will join any Communist . . . and just as soon shoot to kill and get killed as to breathe." By the winter of 1934, one Birmingham man had seen enough, starving slowly and freezing to death with his family, "without food, water, shoes, coal, or a house." If "[we] cannot get some help," he threatened, "[we are] going to raise hell." Others put cultural traditions and mores—even sacred racial ones—on hold in order to deal with an economic emergency that was simply overwhelming. "I do everything I can," one woman confessed with obvious shame. "I've even gone out and competed with Niggers to get jobs mowing lawns."[7]

Across the South civic-minded men and women stepped into the breach, determined to do something about the tragedy that confronted their people, a people ordained by destiny or history to bear a heavier burden than most other Americans—who were themselves being pressed harder than they ever had been before. In doing so, southerners became a central part of the New Deal and assumed a national prominence they had not felt since Woodrow Wilson was in office.

Grateful for the relief, most inhabitants of the South felt a deeply personal sense of loyalty and affection toward the New York patrician in a wheelchair who led the nation. FDR was somehow "of" them. Despite the pedigree of a northern aristocrat, southerners felt Roosevelt understood them—and they responded warmly and in kind. It didn't hurt that he kept a "Little White House" in Warm Springs, Georgia, where he traveled frequently to take the region's healing baths. Polls routinely put his approval in Dixie as higher than that in any other section of the nation. Before 1935 scholars and pundits agreed that to oppose Roosevelt in the South was to "court political suicide."[8]

White southerners loomed large in the New Deal, especially in the early days of relief and recovery before the program began to metastasize into an actual kind of reform. They leaned on Roosevelt and he, in turn, relied on them. A succession of southern sons led the New Deal charge in Congress, some as majority leaders in the Senate, others as Speakers of the House, while Bibb Graves functioned as a model New Deal governor in Alabama. Graves's vigorous advocacy of FDR, the New Deal, tax reform, labor unions, and spending on schools, roads, and hospitals earned him a deep and abiding affection from the poor and desperate of the 1930s—and, in equal part, hostility from the state's most entrenched interests of wealth and privilege.[9]

The Tennessee Valley Authority (TVA) was an especial sore spot. The TVA was a truly transformative plan for what was previously the poorest region in America, a huge river valley that drained parts of seven southeastern states. The federal project and its intricate series of dams and reservoirs on the Tennessee River brought electric power to thousands of rural inhabitants for the first time, as well as flood control, navigation, and recreational opportunities. And it absolutely infuriated private utilities such as the powerful Alabama Power Company. As a high-profile advocate of the TVA, Alabama senator Lister Hill added utilities to the list of private coal and railroad enemies he made by backing New Deal legislation on bank regulation, public works, and industrial recovery.[10]

Still, it was Bibb Graves who served as the lightning rod for critics of the New Deal in Alabama, and it was his flouting of a long historical precedent of using the governor's mansion to mobilize the state militia as violent strikebreakers that earned him the most enmity from the chambers of commerce. In fact, Graves created the state's first Department of Labor, appointed a Bricklayers' Union member to head it, and named Mollie Dowd, a well-known suffragist and union organizer, to be state labor mediator.[11]

In these early years, critics of the New Deal in Alabama were confined to the most hidebound and reactionary representatives of industrial interest, persons who had chained their destinies to those of the corporation and big business to the exclusion of virtually anything else in life—even society, legality, or the common good. Foremost among these was Benjamin Meek Miller, a large landowning product of the Black Belt who served as governor of Alabama from 1930 to 1934, sandwiched between two Bibb Graves terms. Hubert Baughn of the newly created *Alabama: News Magazine of the Deep South* was a vociferous editorial ally. Selma real estate man Sidney J. Smyer, Montgomery banker General Robert E. Steiner, and Black Belt solicitor James Hare joined Frank M. Dixon, a World War I amputee who assumed the governorship in 1938, as Graves's (and Roosevelt's) principal opposition in Alabama. Their resistance centered on animus to Graves's reform bills and federal involvement in the economy, what they felt was a grave threat to free enterprise and liberty in America—a creed to which they demanded unwavering allegiance.

But when Miller momentarily hesitated to send state troops to crush striking textile workers, his corporate sponsors turned on him with a vengeance. When he went back on a "no new taxes" pledge to dare the heresy of an increase to fund state programs during the darkest days of the Depression, well-heeled backers blasted Miller's treason and swore that "hell was too good" for him or any lawmaker that would go along. At this point actual Republican opposition in the South was anemic. The GOP failed to win even one Alabama county in the 1932 presidential election, and its 1934 gubernatorial candidate received a paltry 13 percent of the vote.[12]

Still, New Deal forces were not all light and harmony in Alabama even if the opposition was principally of the antediluvian kind. The "New Deal" was so broad and so all-inclusive during these early years of recovery that it shielded many under its broad umbrella who held the most conservative views on social and cultural issues—particularly on race. Many people counted themselves "New Dealers" or New Deal adherents who did little more than extend their hands in a time of great need, who were interested in little more than survival during the darkest days the country had known. And it was this element of the New Deal—plain whites who were habitually fearful of economic leveling with blacks—that would soon break away to follow the elite vanguard of opposition to Roosevelt and the Democratic Party itself in the South.

In this respect much of the New Deal liberalism that could be found in southern environs was "soft." At its heart it was more concerned with recovery than reform—and elementally opposed in the most intense fashion to a fundamental restructuring of regional patterns of societal power, prestige, and privilege, particularly on matters of race. In Alabama the New Deal was Horace Wilkinson and Hugh Locke—in addition to true liberals like Aubrey Williams, Gould Beech, and Clifford and Virginia Durr. A 1920s Klan leader and stalwart champion of the 1928 Hoovercrat "bolt" in Alabama, Wilkinson reemerged in the 1930s as one of Bibb Graves's top lieutenants and the chief dispenser of New Deal patronage in economically ravaged Birmingham. In doing so "Boss" Wilkinson supported Graves, Hugo Black, FDR, and the New Deal on the radio airwaves and from the pages of his *Alabama Herald*. But he also built a political machine that controlled politics through the placement of a network of clients in key locations in city and county government.

For most of the Depression decade Wilkinson's clients included two of the three Birmingham city commissioners, and hence control of city government itself. The machine ran, like most urban machines, on patronage and almost certainly graft and was built largely on the remnants of a grassroots base of artisans, clerks, and shopkeepers who had swelled the ranks of the 1920s KKK. Yet Wilkinson's machine offered expanded municipal services that garnered significant support from a desperate populace in contrast to a Big Mule menu of fiscal retrenchment and austerity that offered to slash the city budget by firing workers and cutting badly needed services.[13]

Rivalry between the Graves/Wilkinson version of the New Deal and planter-industrialist opposition finally erupted in a war over civil service. Placing their cause in the hands of James A. Simpson, a Vanderbilt attorney who defended corporations with, in the words of one contemporary, the "fervor that most men can find only for individuals in appealing straits" (and assisted by two former Wilkinson protégés—Theophilus Eugene "Bull" Connor and Jimmie Jones), the Big Mule/Black Belt clique fought the urban New Deal by backing a civil service bill designed to choke off the patronage that was the lifeblood of the machine. Yet the battle revealed that in the Deep South, forces intimately aligned with the New Deal were not necessarily liberal, particularly on matters of race.

Horace Wilkinson and Hugh Locke relied heavily on the racist imagery that would soon propel them to be considered among the South's top race-baiters. While it is not necessary to expound on the racial shortcomings of the planter-industrialist clique—or representatives such as Bull Connor, Jim Simpson, and Hubert Baughn—the most reactionary racial attitudes could be found on both sides of the New Deal in 1930s Alabama. In fact, in one of the choicest ironies of southern politics, Wilkinson mercilessly race-baited former pupil Bull Connor over the civil service bill, venturing that, in due time, the NAACP would recognize his distinguished service to make blacks the masters of whites and, "if intelligent tests are not too high," Connor would be awarded the "Senegambian Service medal and the Caucasian Double Cross." Wilkinson fanned the flames of Negrophobia on the issue by publishing claims that civil service "Makes Life Easy for the Negro" and railing against it as "a Republican measure, devised by Republicans to keep Republicans in office" and to fill public offices with "a nigger or a communist."[14]

CIO: Christ Is Out

Yet it was New Deal initiatives themselves that most often undermined the racial status quo—Wilkinson's protestations notwithstanding. Chief among these was the origin and ascendance of the concept of industrial unionism as put forth in the advent of the Congress of Industrial Organizations (CIO). While the New Deal did not establish the CIO, it did create the *conditions* that gave rise to the CIO. And the race-class threat that New Deal progeny posed also worked in reverse, portending the shape conservative backlash would take. Structural improvements in the fortunes of labor, consonant with a rise in concern over the possibility of radical economic upheaval, allowed liberal New Dealers to push pro-labor legislation that guaranteed the most elementary rights to unions: the legal right to exist, for individuals to join without retaliation or termination, to engage in collective bargaining, and to set minimal standards of employer behavior that constituted fair labor practices.[15] Capitalizing on these rudimentary safeguards, John L. Lewis of the United Mineworkers of America (UMW) along with a handful of others led the movement for industrial unionism that, in 1935, became the CIO.[16]

By definition industrial unionism challenged the racial status quo because it organized all workers in an industry regardless of race, sex, ethnic origin, or skill level. Prior to the CIO the craft unionism of the American Federation of Labor (AFL) offered little if any impediment to established racial custom.[17] In places like the Deep South, challenging these conventions—linking race and class change with a kind of New Deal sponsorship—was emotional dynamite.[18]

For the public mind the effect was lasting, if difficult to disentangle completely. Southern employers objected to the changes whether they stemmed from federally mandated wage increases for blacks due to NRA "blue eagle" codes or whether the higher black wages came as a result of new CIO contracts. The CIO was part of an amorphous threat that recalled earlier attempts at biracial class action in the South (Independents, the Greenback-Labor movement, the Populists) and with them conjured the old intense emotions against racial mixing and social change encouraged by "outside agitators," passions skillfully and purposely aroused by those with the most vested in preserving the race/class/political status quo. "We never thought we'd have to fight the Ku Klux Klan," a textile organizer sent to 1930s Alabama said. "But no sooner had we stepped into the field than [out] they came with the Night Shirts and the fiery crosses."[19]

The new industrial organization sometimes functioned at less than an ideal standard, especially at the local level. Yet southern hostility to the CIO reacted to the *perception* of CIO revolution rather than the *reality* of measured reform. By far the most racially inclusive of the unions was the UMW. Coal miners had led the way on biracial cooperation in the South for decades, yet even the mine worker brand was not without some racial blemish.[20]

The steelworkers were "worse than lukewarm" on race, remembered black communist Hosea Hudson. The CIO constitution "didn't mean nothing in Alabama," he recalled. It was like "pouring water on a duck's back. They wont listening." While Hudson's reminiscence was surely the relative disappointment of a confirmed radical who desired revolution, he did have a point. There *was* an appreciable gap between national race rhetoric and local reality—even for the CIO. Even the new industrial unions preserved white privileges via a narrowly conceived "job seniority" that protected "white jobs" as opposed to departmental, plant, or company seniority that would have better leveled the economic playing field between the races. African Americans were also hit harder by a seemingly endless cycle of layoffs and recalls during the 1930s. By 1939 black employment in the Birmingham steel mills had fallen by a full third. Similar trends occurred even in the coal mines.[21] When a northern unionist pointed out the obvious gap between national and Alabama CIO policies on race, a state union leader admitted that biracial solidarity was not perfect in the industrial locals but reminded the critic of southern cultural realities and the boundaries within which southern unions operated: "The men won't work under Negroes. Don't forget no one down here can afford to be called a nigger lover."[22]

Despite the racial limitations of even industrial unionism, cultural folkways ran so deep in the Heart of Dixie that any attempt at economic amelioration for blacks raised serious suspicions that quickly bled over into the taboo of social equality. While Depression-era blacks like Perry Thompson fully recognized the racial limitations of unionism, they also knew full well that organized labor was a quantum leap ahead of business and industry in matters of racial progressivism. Labor in Alabama "has done more to help the colored man than any organization in the world, even the church," Thompson decreed. "It has brought both races closer together. You know, a hungry man growls the same kind of way . . . white or . . . black."[23]

And that was enough for southern whites as well. The massive majority greeted news of the CIO by battening down the hatches of white supremacy, aided of course by the panicked calls of white employers who recognized that the new unionism threatened their regional advantage of dirt-cheap labor. Nor did management shy away from using the violent and coercive forces of the state that were at their disposal. "[B]ack in those days," remembered a leading union organizer in Alabama, police "thought nothing about going out and beating people up or shooting people, killing people, they didn't care." Chief among their targets were William Mitch and William Dalrymple, two midwestern imports brought in by John L. Lewis to breathe new life into the moribund District 20 of the UMW.[24]

An Indiana socialist, Mitch immediately bruised local sensibilities by supporting black civil rights and the NAACP and by continuing the UMW tradition of placing African Americans in visible leadership positions. In 1933 he went too far, though, launching the first major coal strike in Alabama in over a decade. The act earned him the burning enmity of the most mossback of the coal operators, Charles and Henry F. DeBardeleben, and incurred the wrath of Governor B. M. Miller, who promptly sent in the National Guard. The DeBardeleben version of union busting included dynamited booby traps set in the roads leading to DeBardeleben Coal and the Alabama Fuel and Iron companies, armored blockhouses, barbed-wire fences, machine-gun nests, company unions, and absolute resistance to the NRA wage mandates—even though Big Business dominated the crafting of the codes. In August 1934, when workers voted in the UMW at his Overton mine, Charles DeBardeleben responded by closing it down. Two months later 1,500 striking miners clashed in a pitched battle with an army of company guards at brother Henry's Margaret and Acmar mines, resulting in the bloodshed of eleven people.[25]

Things were just as rough in the Great Textile Strike of 1934, the largest industrial work stoppage in America up to that time. The strike began in north Alabama and engulfed thirty mills across the state before going national. "Flying Squads" of striking workers, traveling by jalopy to pickets around the state, soon found the highways to south Alabama blocked by giant cotton bales and mounted company men brandishing shotguns, machine guns, high-powered rifles, tear gas, and clubs. At the "Battle of Battle Street" in Talladega, two people lost their lives and sixteen others were wounded. Despite the paucity of blacks in the mills, race reared its ugly head as critics of the CIO's Textile Workers Organizing Committee (TWOC) branded the insurgency a race revolution. "Radical Union leaders . . . have even organized negro labor, and caused negroes to insult white women," a scandalized lawyer representing a Mobile mill charged in broadening the conflict to the wider community. State Democratic notable and corporation attorney Gessner T. McCorvey involved himself wherever he could, imagining the pillar of white supremacy coming under attack and black people rising en masse "against the white people"—scenarios with no small part in the southern imagination left over from slavery days.[26]

In late 1933 McCorvey found a sympathetic ear in Governor Miller, but after Bibb Graves's election in 1934, the industrialists got a chilly reception in Montgomery. The textile companies had not kept "one single part of their bargain," state labor commissioner R. R. Moore reported to Graves. Instead they had threatened to "mow every striking worker and their family down like sheep" if they did not return to work. "I wonder why we have the nerve to talk about Hitler." Graves responded by breaking with plutocratic tradition and refusing to send in the militia to crush the strikes, earning the enduring thanks of working people in Alabama and the searing rancor of business interests.[27]

The roughness, despite the presence of few actual blacks in the textile mills, indicated that CIO work stoppages—properly framed—cut to the very quick of southern culture. White supremacy, of course, was central, but the challenge extended to regional understandings of God, family, home, and civilization itself. Hence the intensity of the response. "You people in New York," wrote Virginia textile organizer Lucy Randolph Mason in a state of exasperation, "don't know what it means to have the politicians, the local and state administrations, the press and the public lined up with the employers against the workers." Southern preachers sermonized to their mill flocks that CIO actually meant "Christ Is Out." More than one minister preached obedience, complacency, docility, and servitude to society's betters as part of God's plan. "In the beginning of the Bible," a South Carolina cleric told the mill workers, "it tells us to be satisfied with our wages." Fundamentalist religion emphasized fatalism, hierarchy, and submission to authority—including employer authority—no matter how oppressive that might become.[28]

Regional xenophobia extended to "outside agitators" from as close as the next *county*, and civil liberties were not held at a premium. A Birmingham law allowed police to hold people indefinitely without charges; a state statute outlawed picketing completely. Press, pulpit, and community coalesced to make union activity akin to treason and religious heresy. Beatings and floggings of the most brutal nature were not uncommon. Southern employers hoarded munitions and employed professional spy agencies and armies of company guards in numbers that broke records. Local jurisdictions allowed companies to deputize entire private security forces, imbuing company guards with the full official power of the state.[29]

Things got very rough in the north Alabama hill-country burg of Gadsden, reputed to be the toughest anti-union town in the country and home to three major plants that were struck during the 1930s: Goodyear Tire and Rubber, Dwight Textiles, and Republic Steel. Perhaps nowhere, with the possible exceptions of Harlan County, Kentucky, and Gastonia, North Carolina, did the forces of community conformity and authority come together so thoroughly and completely against organized labor. Mobilized by chamber of commerce types to keep business running, opposition to the union tapped the most powerful and primal of southern emotions to the service of private profit: white supremacy, religious piety, patriotic fervor, nativist paranoia, and gender convention. Press, politician, pulpit, and police joined conservative hands to preserve the most sacred of the cultural shibboleths, which everyone was sure were in danger of extinction if the union got recognized or workers got a raise. And industry looked on in satisfaction.

In such a climate, company thugs ran wild. When the rubber union's national president visited Gadsden to calm things, a howling mob of hundreds beat him within an inch of his life, inflicting broken bones, bloody contusions, and grotesque lacerations. Law enforcement looked on and did nothing, except give him a ride to the county line afterward and dump his limp body from a patrol car. Workers who joined the union or *even expressed the opinion* that others had a right to join were mobbed, knifed, clubbed, or terrorized into silence or flight. The state labor department, U.S. Department of Labor, the National Labor Relations Board (NLRB), and a congressional committee all looked into Gadsden. But instead of slowing down the mayhem, the investigations only stiffened community resolve against unions and "outside" government involvement. Etowah County officials passed laws outlawing communism, union meetings, and biracial gatherings—all three equal in the eyes of the law as threats to the cultural pillars of society. "We are a God-fearing, proud, Anglo-Saxon citizenry," a Gadsden resident explained, "determined to keep the wheels of industry turning. All we ask is to be let alone." Company executives and bogus company unions damned the "outside agitators," "troublemakers," and "outsiders . . . stirring up strife and unrest" in a litany of rhetorical exposition that would receive an international forum a generation later in the modern civil rights movement.[30]

Like that freedom struggle, the community response to 1930s labor insurgency was not merely racial *or* economic. It was broader and deeper, a response that understood change on a racial or class level to mean the obliteration of culture and civilization as it was known.

Ordinary citizens of Etowah County who wanted a union recoiled at the notion that they were somehow part of an alien conspiracy simply because they wanted to put food on the table for their families. "We are not labor agitators," insisted one grocer whose store came under surveillance and threats because he sold food to the striking workers. If constituted authority did not provide some form of protection soon, he predicted, people would be forced to resort to "other methods" and "then there will be some killing done."[31]

Yet it was clear that such individuals were swimming against a tide that was far too strong. When a UMW miner from Coleanor traveled to Gadsden to support the strikers, two police officers met him at the county line and told him to turn around and leave. "I am going to kill you if you don't," one said as he brandished a gun. "I'm a good mind to kill you anyway." Birmingham journalist and prominent New Dealer John Temple Graves II condemned mob action as wrong in his syndicated column but regretted that the Gadsden labor troubles had damaged Alabama's national image as an attractive place for capital investment and made martyrs out of the union organizers—not exactly a ringing endorsement for freedom of speech and association in the Deep South.[32]

In the country's consciousness, the New Deal and rising fortunes for plain working people—black and white—were part and parcel. As one southern mill worker put it, Franklin Roosevelt is "the first man in the White House to understand that my boss is a son of a bitch."[33]

White resistance to the CIO increasingly took on the tone of a culture war, one in which the New Deal as an idea was on the wrong side—hopelessly bound up in the southern mind with the new industrial organization and the erasing of caste demarcations. Denunciation of the CIO as communist and foreign—un-American and unconstitutional—came, of course, from the Klan and others stringently devoted to maintaining white supremacy. But it came in equal parts, volume, and frequency from the Bourbon defenders of business and free enterprise who increasingly found themselves in common cause with their old Klan adversaries as the New Deal challenged established racial and economic customs in equal measure. "The CIO is infested with Communists," bellowed Imperial Wizard Hiram Evans. In Birmingham, leaflets blanketed the city with the words "CIO is Communism. . . . Ku Klux Klan Rides Again." Klan leaders denounced "alien" CIO leaders and the imminent "industrial war" they were trying to foment.[34]

At the same time, the pages of Hubert Baughn's quintessential business-boosting *Alabama Magazine* sounded virtually the same as the Klan. CIO leadership was made up of left-wing professionals and "hate makers"; it was "vicious and stupid . . . communistic and un-American." Nothing federal was wanted or needed in the area of industrial relations, according to the southern conservatives. Baughn was in rare agreement with homegrown New Dealer John Temple Graves on the point. Graves wrote bitterly that southern employers should pay the best wages they can and "not one damn cent more."[35]

The clash was clearly taking on cultural connotations as the racial fused with the economic. FDR's New Deal administration was infested with Catholics, Jews, communists, and other "very dangerous . . . sinister influences," those who "preach class hatred," the forces of unrestrained laissez-faire complained. The upshot was that John L. Lewis and his band of "Communists . . . foreigners . . . [and] Aliens" were being given undue aid and comfort by the New Deal, especially from "German Jews" like New York senator Robert F.

Wagner.[36] The country's soul was at risk. Actual "Americanism" and "constitutional rights" were on trial against this "hell howling band of communists and Jews," the economic royalists thundered, further fusing race with economic rightism and a closed, xenophobic culture. New Deal–backed unions were bent on ripping the South wide open by sending "white Jew prostitutes" into Dixie to win the votes of twelve million blacks with a social equality slogan minted in Moscow.[37]

I Am Just as Good a Liberal as Any

Confronted by an opposition that skillfully, if imaginatively, equated industrial unionism with racial, religious, and cultural Armageddon, the leaders of the new CIO reacted with disbelief. Steve Nance, a native Georgian and the first regional director of the TWOC, was stunned. One thing that could not be said about them, he naively maintained about the business forces aligned against the unions, is "that we are foreigners, Reds, outside agitators or damn Yankees." "My great-great-grandfather fought in the Revolutionary War," Nance stipulated. "My grandfather and my father [both] fought in the Confederate Army.... This is strictly an American and a southern movement."[38]

Yet for all his southern pride and lineage, Nance did not understand the most basic thing about the South. *Nativity* and *patriotism* meant allegiance to a culture, not bloodlines or battle formations—a cultural creed that bound together mutually reinforcing conservative orthodoxies on race, class, gender, ethnicity, *and religion*. Franz Daniel, another southern textile organizer, bitterly recalled what the CIO was up against during the New Deal. Every newspaper in the South repeated time after time that "all of us" were communists and foreign agitators destroying the peaceful arrangements the bosses had so painstakingly made in Dixie. "We had no more stepped into the field than the churches came after us like locusts," pitching revivalist tents, paid for by the owners, and preaching to the workers that we were "agents of the devil and that the mark of the beast was on our foreheads." It worked. "Time after time the[y] were able to destroy our majorities."[39]

Nor was the communist/race traitor charge limited to being levied by just the bosses and professional Kluxers. It permeated every crevice of southern culture. Conservative southern AFL unions leveled it at the new CIO. Later even the CIO would use it against more heavily black unions such as the International Mine Mill and Smelter Workers. John Altman—Pickens County attorney, twenty-year general counsel for the state AFL, and a Conservative Democratic ally of Horace Wilkinson—publicly denounced UMW and SWOC organizer William Mitch for spreading racial heresy: exactly "what the Communists preach" on social equality. If unionists didn't watch out, racial liberalism would eventually ruin organized labor, he warned.[40]

There were real live communists in Alabama during the Great Depression, but precious few could be found in the ranks of the CIO unions. In fact, not many could be found in the state.[41] There were a few lone wolves—Hosea Hudson, Andy Brown, Eb Cox, and Henry O. Mayfield—all blacks who held membership in the CIO and the Communist Party. But their Red inclinations increasingly marginalized them in the ranks of organized labor, and Hudson was eventually drummed out of the CIO.[42] Yet for those determined to marginalize the CIO itself, their existence—not their rarity—was the nugget of gold that could be multiplied in the public imagination many times over.

During the Great Depression no more than eight thousand people "joined" the Communist Party in the entire state of Alabama, a remarkably small number given the depths of the economic abyss that lay before them.[43] Still, the vast majority of these individuals were African Americans, lending more credence to the fear that the Reds were bent on economic revolution using the black man as their stooge. The existence of relatively few actual communists legitimized the entire fable—so flimsy was the threshold needed to sustain the legend.[44]

It was far easier for the average white to believe that the only blacks who wanted civil and political rights—and social equality—had to be godless revolutionaries who had sold their souls to the communist devil or were being brainwashed and used by unscrupulous radicals bent on the overthrow of the republic. As emotional as such a tale was, it was still preferable to whites than the alternative: admitting that some black people were just not content with their station in life—economic or political—and did not, after all, consider the white southerner their best friend. It was Reconstruction again.

Without question much of the communist threat was bound up in southern white anxieties about race and sex, in addition to class. The communists espoused racial equality, which meant, in most white minds, interracial sex and the eventual eradication of a separate white race and, with it, white patriarchal privilege. All of this was bound up in the infamous Scottsboro Boys case that loomed over the state like a pall during the 1930s: young black males accused of rape who accepted communist defense counsel. An isolated 1931 incident in which a deranged black radical kidnaped and shot three young, white, affluent, Mountain Brook women also gave strength to the story. Birmingham whites responded to the tragedy with a campaign of wanton and indiscriminate violence (bombings, burnings, random shootings of blacks) and a 10:00 P.M. curfew in African American neighborhoods facilitated by the city electric company turning off the power.[45] A business executive at the Alabama Mineral Land Company applauded Bibb Graves's refusal to pardon the Scottsboro Boys because, he thought, the danger of rape was so high that it was not safe for white women to drive alone in daylight. They are "much safer in some portions of the African jungle" than in the streets of Birmingham, the businessman contended. He recommended public hangings to deter black crime because the electric chair was too civilized.[46]

At the outside three thousand of the state's eight thousand communists lived in Birmingham. The majority knew little of the difference between Lenin, Stalin, or Trotsky—nor did they care. They were starving. The Reds showed compassion and promised relief. At a minimum they represented hope.

Birmingham city government, dominated by New Dealers, mobilized to meet the threat as if it were St. Petersburg in 1917. After police and a white mob fought a pitched street battle against three thousand hunger protesters on May Day 1933, the city passed the notorious Downs Sedition Ordinance. Named for its sponsor, city commissioner William O. Downs—a former Klan cyclops and county sheriff who owed his political career to Horace Wilkinson—the law was a product of true paranoia, if a model of legislative dexterity. It allowed the arrest and imprisonment of any person possessing more than one copy of a "radical publication" as defined by local law enforcement, including magazines and newspapers as incendiary as the *Nation* and the *New Republic*. In effect, the ordinance allowed police to arrest anyone for anything, which they set about doing especially through a notorious "Red Squad," headed by private detective Milt McDuff, brother of the city's police chief. The squad also defined "radicals" as anyone protesting an employer's treatment.[47]

When more force was needed Birmingham authorities called on the KKK and the White Legion, a true vigilante order that operated with utter impunity and apparent official sanction (it held its meetings in the county courthouse). The legion meted out some of the most brutal assaults recorded on suspected radicals, black and white, throughout the 1930s, employing rawhide whips, blackjacks, and revolvers, and often working in concert with local law enforcement. In 1933 actual hysteria was reached when a Tuscaloosa mob lynched three black males charged with rape who had agreed to be represented by communist attorneys. Determined not to allow Tuscaloosa to become a second Scottsboro, white vigilantes ran wild with apparent police approbation, shooting, bombing, and terrorizing the area's black population for weeks.[48]

So abject was southern farm poverty, so complete the system of subjugation under which tenants lived, and so dismal their prospects for change that some five thousand rural Alabamians actually turned to the Communist Party. Most were attracted by the radicals' determination to abolish hunger rather than capitalism, yet the response that greeted them in Alabama's countryside at least equaled in ferocity the urban example.

A full-fledged race riot broke out in Tallapoosa County in July 1931 when eight hundred black sharecroppers affiliated with the communist Share Croppers Union (SCU) struck white landowners for cash wages for cotton, a nine-month school year for their children, and a school bus. Constituted authority took a holiday as landlord, police, and vigilante mobs ran wild beating sharecroppers, burning their homes, assaulting their wives, and firing indiscriminately into their cabins. When militant blacks fought back with shotguns, whites quickly recruited reinforcements from surrounding counties. The scene, to a somewhat lesser extent, was repeated throughout the Black Belt during the 1930s. Similar terror campaigns erupted against black farm "radicals" striking for better wages in Dallas, Hale, Lowndes, Macon, Montgomery, Sumter, Randolph, and Lee counties—and repeatedly in Tallapoosa. Vigilantes beat, jailed, kidnaped, and burned alive white communist labor organizers. Some bodies wearing cement boots were found at the bottom of Alabama's rivers.[49]

Black Belt communism was a revolt against the inherently oppressive—some would even say medieval—circumstances of agrarian life in the South. Communism was a function more of hunger than of ideology, but it was also an attempt to defeat the racism, bigotry, and inequity endemic to tenant life. Violence bolstered black solidarity, but it also raised the stakes. In Alabama, economic insurgency could mean death.

Perhaps most important, communism revealed that, at its core, much of what passed for New Deal liberalism in the South was soft. Where race was concerned, the attitudes and behavior of early New Deal supporters were often not that much better than the stultifying bigotry of FDR's most bitter business and industrial enemies. And it gave portents of what might happen in the South if the New Deal continued to veer toward the dangerous curve of racial inclusiveness.

Official sympathy for radicals who espoused social equality was not forthcoming even from Bibb Graves. As governor, Graves consistently disappointed Joseph Gelders, a Jewish communist and physics professor at the University of Alabama who had been brutalized with a baseball bat after being abducted from the streets of Birmingham. Anti-black and anti-labor vigilantes later carried Gelders to Chilton County for a grotesque, if more leisurely, beating that left him nearly dead with two black eyes, a broken nose, swelling of the head, a ruptured heart muscle, several missing teeth, a concussion, and assorted contusions and lacerations. After noisily voicing the state's indignation at the incident, Governor Graves repeatedly failed to follow up and allowed the case to fizzle when the chief prosecutor showed himself determined not to convict the floggers.[50] Unfortunately, it was a performance reminiscent of Graves's blind spot toward his base of Klan supporters during the 1920s. Graves also steadfastly refused to pardon the Scottsboro Boys, instead lambasting their attorneys as outsiders and radicals.[51]

At the local level, many New Dealers were not much better. Horace Wilkinson's Birmingham machine was anything but enlightened on race. When a delegation of prominent national radicals visited the city, Police Commissioner William Downs assured the group that he was "just as good a liberal as any [of] them" but that "every time a nigger comes back here from up North we have to give him a dose of castor oil to rid him of bad ideas and bring him back to his senses." He advised the radicals to go back north and "leave the 'niggers' to the South which has taken care of them since the Civil War."[52]

Generals without an Army

"Liberalism" was an extremely popular word during the New Deal, something that is perhaps almost impossible to comprehend today. Instead of running from the sobriquet, the L-word was the "word everyone claimed." Bill Downs claimed it, just before he explained to visiting radicals how blacks who got out of line were treated in Alabama. Herbert Hoover claimed it. Individuals as diverse as Grover Hall, Handy Ellis, John Temple Graves, and Donald Comer were called liberals simply for supporting the notion of New Deal recovery in the darkest days of the Depression. Some New Dealers received the designation for doing nothing more than being willing to receive checks from Washington. "The most bewildered and ardent claimants," wrote the grandson of an Alabama congressman who was routinely labeled a liberal, "were men today"—including his grandfather—"who would be called conservatives."[53] Yet a great many historians have interpreted the era in the South as one of general liberalism, a "golden age." Alabama, in particular, has been singled out as "a liberal oasis" during the 1930s and 1940s, a place where liberalism was the predominant and prevailing pattern of thought and behavior.[54]

In reality, though, the vaunted liberalism of the New Deal era was soft in the middle. Its outer layers—comprised of desperation at the economic plight of the southern people matched by a willingness to temporarily subsume regional proclivities to accept federal aid—were indeed intact, even hard in some places. But at center much of the New Deal in the South remained distinctly illiberal: exclusive in nature, temporary in outlook, self-interested in conception, and suspect by design. The Alabamians most deserving of the liberal label were imports from the North, pariahs at home, or émigrés who took refuge in the university departments of other states or in the cloistered offices of Washington, D.C.[55] In any event they predominantly relied for sustenance on sources outside the region—northern philanthropic groups such as the Rosenwald Fund or the New Deal government itself. George Tindall was undoubtedly correct when he wrote that during the 1930s southern liberals remained a small, literate, group, in effect, "generals without an army."[56]

In Alabama all sorts of people with ideological outlooks that are difficult to really call liberal participated in the New Deal. Among those administering New Deal relief in Alabama were conservative newspaper editor Grover C. Hall, textile magnate Donald Comer, fiercely anti-union DeBardeleben Coal vice president Milton H. Fies, and Montgomery real estate man Algernon Blair. John H. Bankhead II, an essentially conservative man, authored the 1937 Bankhead-Jones Farm Act that provided long-term, low-interest loans to struggling farm tenants courtesy of the federal government. Along with tenants he included unionists among his staunchest supporters. Yet Bankhead and younger brother William, who served Roosevelt as Speaker of the House, increasingly soured on the New Deal, opposing FDR's 1937 "court-packing" scheme and fully breaking with the president over his choice of Henry Wallace for second place on the 1940 ticket.[57]

Other Alabama New Dealers did not wait for court-packing or other excuses. John McDuffie, an Alabama congressman who performed as a reluctant New Dealer, came clean in 1935 as soon as FDR appointed him to life tenure on the federal bench: New Dealers were "a cross between Socialists and Communists," he announced. John Temple Graves II—a syndicated Birmingham columnist with degrees from Princeton and George Washington universities—managed to hold on until 1937. George Huddleston is routinely cited as a liberal New Dealer, but his grandson points out correctly that the congressman broke early and often with FDR and was virulently conservative in his beliefs. In Birmingham, Horace Wilkinson, Hugh Locke, Bill Downs, and Lewey V. Robinson were also closely identified with the New Deal.[58]

By 1948, Huddleston, Comer, Wilkinson, Locke, and J. T. Graves would all be nestled snuggly in the warm embrace of the Dixiecrats. Those who remained loyal Democrats during the trials of the 1940s—Bibb Graves, Lister Hill, and Charlie Dobbins—would trim their sails significantly on race.[59]

For those who would turn away from FDR, the New Deal, and eventually even the Democratic Party, race was the problem. By and large white Alabamians, like white southerners themselves, loved Franklin Roosevelt, especially during the early days of the decade. Yet theirs was a tumultuous romance and a conditional love. White southerners were genuinely grateful for what Roosevelt had done for them in their darkest hours, but they were also increasingly disturbed by the undeniably inclusive bent of the New Deal. "You put more stress on your African jungle friends than you do on your white friends," a frustrated Baptist minister from Mobile impugned the president. Such folly could only lead to communism and interracial marriage, the preacher warned as he recommended the forced expulsion of all blacks back to Africa. Planters in Alabama's Black Belt ridiculed the federal government for spending so much time and money on "poor white trash and Niggers." Middle-class relief recipients resented "lazy blacks and poor whites" for receiving money and doing no useful work. Even some spokesmen for the working class, such as Noel R. Beddow, agreed that blacks were on relief because they did not want to work and declared that the New Deal was producing Bolsheviks in Alabama faster than even "Russian envoys" could.[60]

For many white southerners who avoided open conflict with the administration during the first phase of the New Deal, the strategy was one of wait and see, and federal action as temporary salve. Once the emergency was over, as North Carolina senator Josiah W. Bailey intoned, we "will return to reliance upon private profit and individual initiative. . . . This, as I understand [it], is the essence of the New Deal."[61]

Perhaps nowhere were southern New Deal deficiencies more apparent than on the question of a federal anti-lynching bill. Anti-lynch law had been proposed, steadily, since the 1910s and just as steadily and vehemently resisted in Dixie. Time after time when the issue came up, southerners relied on the clarion call to arms of Reconstruction remembered and placed their trust in senior southern senators to form a firewall of sectional resistance. And repeatedly the strategy proved successful. Yet the horrific, by any standard, 1934 lynching of Claude Neal revived the issue and, in doing so, again supplied the South with incontrovertible evidence that the Democratic Party was colluding with blacks to do it in.

After breaking the accused black rapist from an Alabama jail, a white mob transported Neal just over the Florida line where a carnival of sadism ensued that featured a mob numbered in the thousands, official compliance, public festivities, and newspapers advertising the event for days in advance. A frenzied mob that included children tortured Neal with red-hot pokers and homemade spears in a number of unspeakable ways, at one point castrating him and forcing him to eat his own genitals. Finally they killed him and dragged his corpse behind a car for hours. Neither Alabama governor Benjamin Meek Miller nor his Florida counterpart sent the militia to prevent the lynching, yet Miller did send in the National Guard to quash black protests after the killing took place.[62]

For the first time in its existence Will W. Alexander's Commission on Interracial Cooperation (CIC) endorsed a federal anti-lynching law, and Democratic senators Robert F. Wagner of New York and Edward P. Costigan of Colorado agreed to sponsor a bill authored by the NAACP.[63]

White southerners—with the exception of a very few like Alexander's commission and Jesse Daniel Ames's Association of Southern Women—walked in lockstep against the bill. Although the Wagner-Costigan bill twice passed muster in the House, it faced a southern filibuster in the Senate where New Dealers Tom Connally of Texas, Pat Harrison and Theodore Bilbo of Mississippi, James F. Byrnes of South Carolina, and Joseph T. Robinson of Arkansas resisted. They were joined by Richard Russell of Georgia, Carter Glass of North Carolina, and Ellison D. "Cotton Ed" Smith of South Carolina—who invoked precisely the argument Jesse Ames was fighting against: that the virtue of southern white womanhood was a legitimate rationale for lynching. North Carolina's Josiah Bailey channeled Reconstruction memory as reason enough to oppose the measure by declaring that allowing the federal government to enforce a law against lynching was "the forerunner of a policy studiously cultivated by agitators"—not for preventing lynching but to introduce federal interference in local affairs and "a civil rights bill [like that] which Thad Stevens tried to put upon the South."[64]

The stance of Jimmy Byrnes—a South Carolinian who, in his legendary career, served as congressman, senator, governor, Supreme Court justice, and U.S. secretary of state—was especially telling. Byrnes was a New Dealer and had actually gone to Washington during the dark days of the Depression with his hand out, saying, "I admit I am a New Dealer, and if [the New Deal] takes money from the few who have controlled the country and gives it back to the average man, I am going to . . . help the President work for the people of South Carolina and the country." Byrnes's economic populism, as did his early defeat for the Senate at the hands of Cole Blease, confirmed him in most minds as a leading southern liberal—or at the very least a moderate.[65]

Yet as the New Deal moved from recovery to reform, Byrnes became increasingly uncomfortable with the whole thing. When anti-lynching came up again in the Senate, Byrnes bitterly blamed the defection of northern Democrats (who had backed the South against the 1921 Dyer Anti-Lynching Bill) squarely on race: because "90 percent of the Negroes in the North . . . are voting for Democratic candidates." A devout segregationist, Byrnes was so incensed that as early as 1938 he suggested the South might actually have to go Republican. Although he "had never voted for a Republican candidate" himself, he said, Dixie might have to consider doing so. In supporting the national Democratic Party, white southerners had always rested firmly in the belief that when problems affecting the "Negro and the very soul of the South arose," they could depend on the Democrats of the North. Now the New Deal and its consequent legislation—here regarding lynching—had changed things.[66]

Eventually Byrnes would make good on his threat, flirting with the Dixiecrats before formally becoming one, throwing his considerable weight behind several Republican presidential candidates, blessing Strom Thurmond's move to the GOP, and eventually defecting entirely to the GOP while working mightily to get South Carolina and the South to go Republican.

Meanwhile, Alabamians did more than their share to defeat the bill. And when it came to such a life-and-death issue as opposition to the federal government on racial questions, they found that little separated New Deal *proponents from opponents,* or other erstwhile Alabama adversaries from each other—even Ku Kluxers and Bourbons. The state branch of the KKK predictably blamed lynching on the incitement of "Northern and New York liberals." Grover Hall blasted federal intrusion, and future Alabama governor Frank Dixon called the measure "dangerous ... disastrous ... unwarranted ... [and] unwise." Alabama senator John Bankhead participated in the filibuster and even Hugo Black spoke against it, suggesting that the bill was somehow anti-labor. When Black vacated his Senate seat for the Supreme Court, Dixie Bibb Graves, wife of the New Deal Alabama governor, reliably opposed the bill. Even leading Alabama editors for a Scottsboro pardon—and anti-Klan politico Forney Johnston—defended southern opposition to the anti-lynching law as a sound example of states' rights and no part of some alleged "indifference to the negro in his long road to enlightenment."[67]

Finding Forney Johnston and Grover Hall (whom many considered to be liberals for their 1920s opposition to the Klan) on the same side *against* a federal anti-lynch law would be a paradox perhaps anywhere else but the Deep South. The "liberalism" of Alabamians like Johnston and Hall had never retained in it a place for racial progressivism or federal attempts to rectify southern shortcomings on race relations. The son of a former Alabama governor, Johnston was hostile toward the Klan because of political turf jealousy, not racial enlightenment. He was a major player in Alabama's planter-industrial oligarchy as a key corporation attorney and political operative. Johnston's advocacy of a pardon in the Scottsboro case was, likewise, generated by concern for Alabama's public image and retention of allure for outside economic investment, not sympathy for the accused. Although he actually thought the accused "boys" might be innocent, Johnston nonetheless disparaged them in his private correspondence as "gorillas . . . coons . . . African cro-magnons . . . scum . . . tramps . . . transient trash . . . convicted morons . . . [and] chimpanzees [with] . . . sordid jungle reactions."[68]

Grover Hall, who had won a Pulitzer Prize for his editorials against the 1920s Klan, was little better. In his private appeals for a Scottsboro pardon, Hall explained that he did not care if the accused were innocent or guilty of the rape of "two cut-rate prostitutes," nor whether the "moronic beasts" who stood accused would kill and "eat one another without benefit of pepper sauce." What was at stake was Alabama's image (unfairly sullied by "agitators"), the specter of federal intervention in her racial affairs, and the state's attractiveness to northern investors—not the "'honor' and 'dignity' of two hookwormy Magdalenes."[69] After six uninterrupted days of southern haranguing against the anti-lynching bill, the Senate moved on to other business.[70]

The Southern Way of Life

Southern whites were not hallucinating in their estimation of the New Deal as a departure from the predominant pattern of racial exclusivity that had marked the federal posture since the end of Reconstruction. "No Negro born and raised in the South as I was relishes this running to Washington for remedies that lie at home," a leading black educator said, but he stressed that federal involvement was the only alternative left to blacks who had systematically been deprived of their rights by southern states like his home of North Carolina.[71]

This was true whether the issue was lynching or disfranchisement or Jim Crow itself. While it cannot be claimed that Franklin Roosevelt was an enthusiastic, open proponent of increased black rights, his administrations did mark a clear and fundamental change for the better than what had come before. He was receptive to entreaties on behalf of blacks and friends of the race in a way no president had ever been.[72]

Of course, the New Deal was not completely without racial discrimination, but the double standards became harder for both blacks and whites to see as the decade wore on. As exclusive programs like the AAA, NRA, and TVA were replaced by the inclusive Works Progress Administration (WPA), National Labor Relations Act (NLRA), Fair Labor Standards Act (FLSA), and Social Security, white southerners became increasingly alarmed and disenchanted.[73]

The gradual absorption of racial parity into the New Deal program struck at the very core of southern culture. This was so because white supremacy was not something that floated above and apart from the rest of the South. On the contrary it was the *central underpinning* of a whole southern culture that was predicated at its most basic level on a strict and hierarchical order of things, a society in which blacks were subordinate to whites in much the same way that women were supposed to be submissive to men, workers to employers, children to adults, immigrants to natives, and flocks to their ministers. This was civilization itself as most southerners understood it, blessed by nature and ordained by God. It was the "Southern way of life," something precious to keep and preserve and protect.[74]

And as with other societies founded on the intellectual mound of Social Darwinism, to tamper with any part of its foundation was to challenge the handiwork of God Himself. To question the authority of any one of its pillars was to threaten the whole natural order of things that they supported. Race was one—the most crucial one, but still just one—of these foundational pillars on which a whole southern civilization rested. To question the innate superiority of white over black was to threaten to bring down the whole culture that relied on such premises. To have a political view in such a society, one did not need an extensive understanding of the ins and outs of policy, an appreciation of nuance or shades of gray, a patience for detailed explication, or even a grasp on what actually constituted history or reality. One needed only to have a cultural IQ—an instinctive understanding as to what was held most precious and dear and inviolable by the dominant society.

In this way, southern politics is not now—nor has it ever been, predominantly—about politics. It's about culture. This is the Great Irony of southern politics and, as the twentieth century wore on, it would increasingly become the Great Irony of American politics as well.

Essentially, this is what the father of progressive journalist Charlie Dobbins was complaining to him about when he said, "We don't have politics in Alabama based on issues. All our politics is race."[75] As the New Deal became increasingly about reform rather than recovery, and as blacks were included as participants rather than recipients, things looked dim for an extended love affair with the South.

Opponents of the New Deal, where they cropped up, began talking more and more in terms of those things that southerners held dear—not politics per se but *objects de cultur:* Americanism, the Constitution, patriotism, a way of life. Alabama's stigmatized and anemic Republican Party showed some brief flickers of life when a young attorney named Claude O. Vardaman expressed resistance to FDR by urging the GOP to "rally to the party of constitutional government." In 1938, Alabama Republicans imported Missouri congressman Dewey Short to give the keynote address at their Constitutional Day Rally. A leading opponent of Roosevelt, Short had won national attention by charging that FDR had deliberately prolonged the Great Depression and blasphemed Americanism.[76] When conservative governor B. M. Miller proposed a tax hike to pay for Alabama's miserably supported state government, a Troy physician informed him that "We are taxed to death" and accused the governor of betraying the whole Democratic Party. The Thirteenth, Fourteenth, Fifteenth, and Eighteenth amendments to the U.S. Constitution, the doctor said, while quoting Bible verses, "all violate the immutable laws of God, and are the causes of all this trouble we are having. The Negro and Yellow Races shall be Driven from *our Country!*"[77]

After a while it would not even be necessary to say anything explicitly about race. One could just say something about the South or southern culture, and southerners would know by the code words what was meant: "That kind of thinking doesn't represent the true South," Gould Beech recalled. "Meaning, he's not right on the race issue." As if on cue the *Alabama Magazine* simply announced that Aubrey Williams "doesn't talk like an Alabamian any more," and its conservative readership knew exactly what it meant.[78]

In mass, the southern mind was not dependent for its opinions on the wisdom or learning of academics or the literati. In fact, generally speaking, there was a broad gulf, even a deep well, of suspicion and disdain for such book learning and schoolmarmishness, such an overpowering current of anti-intellectual sentiment that a Wiregrass judge named George Corley Wallace would one day exploit it like no other and, in doing so, provide a template for recent American Republicanism. It was an anti-intellectualism that ran even to what constituted the political elites. "If the Southern people of the ruling orders read the Southern novelists but little," W. J. Cash wrote in *The Mind of the South*, "they read the studies which were concerned with the questions directly involved . . . hardly at all," and they dismissed them as "the work of busy-body theorists bent on raising disturbing issues."[79]

Cash could have just as easily added that a chasm existed between elites and masses in the South on every level, perhaps most tellingly in places where there *were* actual stirrings of liberalism: organized labor and religion. Such a yawning gap, though, isolated the southern people and made it easier for them to be taken in by demagogues who would oppose programs like the New Deal based on a conception that tied racial orthodoxy to the centrality of southern culture itself. In such things, the fallen New Dealer Theodore G. Bilbo was expert. "If our buildings, our highways, our railroads should be wrecked," Bilbo declared, "we could rebuild them." "If our cities should be destroyed . . . we could erect newer and greater ones. Even if our armed might should be crushed, we could rear sons who would redeem our power," he went on. "But if the . . . white man's blood . . . should become corrupted and mingled with the blood of Africa, then the present greatness of . . . America would be destroyed . . . by a Negroid [nation] . . . and all hope for the future would be forever gone."[80]

They Learned They Were No More than Negroes

In such a culture, true patriotism and bona fide religion were closely bound up with what constituted socially acceptable thought and behavior on questions of race, class, and gender, behavior that fell within the parameters of conduct that did not threaten the status quo. Such expectations extended to blacks as well who sometimes played along and adopted the submissive role in order to get along and, in notable instances, receive praise as "good Negroes" who "knew their place."

The message was not lost on African Americans like Clinton L. McKinney, who appealed to the State Democratic Executive Committee for help in registering "all worthy Negroes" to vote. The plan—McKinney reassured Alabama's white power structure while trying to enlist their aid in subverting white supremacy—was to cooperate with whites to perpetuate their rule, an "inheritance that was handed down from the fathers," not the foreign-born, communist element that was trying to drive a wedge between the southern Negro and white man.[81]

While blacks like McKinney trudged uphill trying to make inroads on elite-controlled voter registration, African Americans who attempted to forge bonds with poor whites faced at least as steep a climb. So high was the fortress of white supremacy in southern culture that some blacks thought all such projects doomed. "[T]hese God damn white folks ain't going to get with you all like these northerners do," an ancient black physician lectured younger black radicals in Alabama. Hosea Hudson, who never stopped trying to organize the races in common radical causes, despaired that most plain whites "had a lot of hang-ups." They just "could not turn that racist sugartit aloose." Still Hudson and others held out hope that in the depths of the Great Depression poor whites would realize how much they held in common with blacks.[82]

At some elusive moments, it looked like a meaningful alliance might be forged. When plain-white bystanders were shoved and beaten along with black hunger protesters in the streets of Birmingham, they were shocked. Whites had been socialized to believe they were "better than the niggers," a black radical observed, but "they learnt their lesson.... [T]hey were no more than Negroes in the eyes of the ruling class ... and their police."[83]

Still, cultural prohibitions went broader and deeper than just race and rendered black-white cooperation a sin that made obvious the fact that the sinner must be a nut bent on overthrowing the republic and the American way of life. Aubrey Williams was no communist, a close friend remembered.[84] Neither were the Durrs. Yet in such a rigid culture anybody who dissented on the central issues could easily be branded a Red and removed to the farthest fringes of society—marginalizing, along with them, their political and economic arguments no matter how solid. Even demonstrating sympathy for poor and starving blacks automatically made whites Red in the repressive climate of the Deep South.

Whenever the races cooperated, a black Alabama radical remembered, "that was 'them Reds.'" Hosea Hudson grew disgusted with poor-white reluctance to join the CIO, and later the Communist Party itself, and laid the whole reason to race prejudice among the impoverished. They just did not want to "come sit down with a bunch of niggers, that's what they were saying."[85]

Yet this observation is only a partial understanding. To be sure, racial orthodoxy was the core component of the predominant culture. But the outer layers were made up of other types of cultural orthodoxy, the violation of which meant apostasy. Two of the most pivotal were religion and patriotism—both directly challenged by communism. Communist identification with irreligion and revolution made it easy for white southerners to dismiss its economic critique as godless nonsense subversive of the most hallowed freedoms and American way of life. This, along with the obvious threat to racial supremacy, severely damaged prospects for white recruitment to radical or even liberal causes.

As the recipients of far less justice and equity from this culture, and thus with less emotionally invested in it, blacks were easier to recruit than whites. But they were not *easy* by a long shot. All told very few African Americans came over to communism even during the abyss of the 1930s. So strong was the pull of cultural conformity, especially for members of the black middle class, that many refused to join the radicals or even allow a legitimate space within which the liberal industrial unions could operate. This was an obstacle that bowed implicitly to prevailing white supremacy, but it also included strong acceptance of the allied religious, civic, and economic buttresses of the wider society. And it drove black radicals crazy. "Don't think everybody was with us" in Alabama "cause it was a lot of them . . . 'niggers' . . . was against us," remembered one black radical. The black middle class was hopeless. Many complained that Reds from the North were coming down to agitate "lower class . . . ignorant niggers" and ruining the peace and happiness that "good white friends" had designed. "And now these crazy, ignorant niggers are turning their back on those who had been their friends all the time."[86]

Nor did it take a black communist to recognize the cultural constraints even among African Americans. "You've got more 'Uncle Toms' in Alabama than there is anywhere in the country," a leading black railroad unionist claimed, "plenty of them" that made the work of biracial union organizing very difficult. A frustrated Emory O. Jackson, an African American editor who consistently stood on the front lines of early civil rights actions, concurred with the glum assessment. "[T]hese niggers don't want to be anything but second-class citizens," he despaired. "I've lost money fooling with these niggers. . . . From here on in, I'm going to . . . make me some money." Near the end of his life a despondent Hosea Hudson agreed: "I been let down so many times by Negroes, I ought not to *never, never* do nothing but set down in the chair and read the paper and watch the TV."[87]

He's as Black as Melted Midnight

All of this came to a head at the 1936 Democratic National Convention in Philadelphia. FDR and the New Deal had enjoyed a full three-and-a-half years in which millions of white people, North and South, had been helped and, for that, they were deeply grateful. Yet the interim had also made clear that the New Deal meant to include blacks as an integral part of American government and society, if only by mere inclusion in government programs.

By 1935 the Second New Deal was well under way, and the shift in emphasis from recovery to reform boded ill for whites committed to the old ways on race relations.[88] John L. Lewis had arranged for the political action arm of his CIO to give a massive $600,000 toward the reelection of Franklin Roosevelt, and, within the Democratic Party of its fathers, the white South found itself in increasingly uncomfortable proximity to elements it considered beneath it: blacks, unionists, northern ethnics, big-city machines, and Catholics and Jews from outside Dixie.

The 1936 convention marked a turning point for the South, if not in deed yet then at least in word. Perhaps as important as the CIO and the massive shift of blacks from the party of Lincoln to the party of Roosevelt, the South lost its beloved "two-thirds rule" at the convention: the perennial southern safeguard that stipulated a national party nominee had to have the support of at least two-thirds of the delegates to the convention—a firewall the South had long relied on to bargain for candidates amenable to its sectional interests. The convention also saw the inaugural seating of thirty African American delegates and alternates, as well as the prominent participation of Arthur W. Mitchell of Chicago, the first black Democrat to sit in Congress.

When a black minister rose to give an opening convocation, "Cotton Ed" Smith of South Carolina exploded—"My God, he's as black as melted midnight!"—and stormed out of the hall.[89] In South Carolina, Smith later used the celebrated walkout to highlight the differences between himself and a Roosevelt-supported challenger in the Democratic primary:

> [W]hen I came out on the floor of that great hall, bless God, it looked like a checkerboard—a spot of white here, and a spot of black there. But I kept going, down that long aisle, and finally I found the great standard of South Carolina—and, praise God, it was in a spot of white! I had no sooner than taken my seat when a newspaperman came down the aisle and squatted by me and said, "Senator, do you know a nigger is going to come out up yonder in a minute and offer the invocation?" I told him, I said, "Now don't be joking me, I'm upset enough the way it is." But then, bless God, out on that platform walked a slew-footed, blue-gummed, kinky-headed Senegambian! And he started praying and I started walking. And as I pushed through those great doors, and walked across that vast rotunda, it seemed to me that old John Calhoun leaned down from his mansion in the sky and whispered in my ear, "You did right, Ed."[90]

Reaction to the convention took the form of a fledgling first attempt at rallying anti–New Deal Democrats into a cohesive front. Like most first attempts—from bike riding to kite flying—it floundered briefly, then crashed. But it set a signal precedent of opposition that would find full expression in the not-so-distant future.

Perhaps most important, the 1936 movement was a harbinger of the Great Melding that would find full fruition in the next decade: a meeting of the minds between longtime adversaries habitually separated by class issues. Confronted by the emergency of the Great Depression, the white South temporarily resurrected class issues to a place of prime importance. But for many, the medicine of the New Deal was beginning to seem worse than the illness itself. Because the New Deal meant the activism of the *federal* government, opposition in the South called upon the Reconstruction legend to meld together two crucial strains of sentiment that had previously been held somewhat apart by class antagonisms: opposition to the federal government on *race issues* that usually involved all ranks of southern whites and resistance to the central government on matters of *the economy* that more regularly concerned just the Bourbons.

Businesses and corporations in the South had long been expert at whipping up racial unrest. It served their interests by keeping the workforce divided along the most emotional and heartfelt fault line that existed.[91] And they showed little compunction in squeezing every drop possible from the method.

Yet the race-baiting that had served the planter-industrialist cabal so well for decades in Alabama usually amounted to encouraging feelings of white supremacy among poor whites, and racial suspicion and distrust among black workers. Here, in the New Deal, was an unprecedented threat that could be transformed into a golden new opportunity, a chance to do something the business conservatives had been trying to accomplish for decades: make absolutely indistinct the health of their enterprises from the wider health of southern civilization. Here at last was a federal program that melded class and race together as a unified threat.[92]

If this could be turned on its head, it represented a chance to make the Bourbon *economic* program synonymous in the southern mind with the maintenance of *white supremacy* by hammering on the fundamental common denominator of the threat: *unwanted federal encroachment* on local customs and states' rights. If the Big Mule/Black Belt alliance could persuade ordinary whites that their most sacred racial and social interests were inherently bound up with fortifying laissez-faire for business interests, their position—both economic and racial—would only be that much more impenetrable. It was something they had managed in certain times and places in the South, but here was the chance to do it on a systematic, region-wide level. An educated, well-informed, rational, literate electorate, difficult to move with purely emotional considerations, could pose a problem for such a strategy. But, tragically, in the Deep South this was not a general impediment.

The anti–New Deal movement began formally in January 1936 with a decidedly southern flavor, and it hit upon cultural themes as both substitutes and additions to the purely racial theme, taking the opportunity to disparage the New Deal whenever it could as something that was decidedly un-American, unconstitutional, unpatriotic, and immoral. Texas oil and lumber man John H. Kirby got the ball rolling by organizing a Grass Roots Convention in Macon, Georgia, that, at this point, had very little to do with genuine grassroots. Rather, the convention was designed to bring together various anti-Roosevelt forces and launch a presidential campaign for the notorious Georgia governor Eugene Talmadge. Needing more than just local backing, though, the new southern Committee to Uphold the Constitution called upon Vance Muse, the Texas head of the reactionary Christian Americans, to arrange financing and propaganda. In short order Muse lined up big-time support from northern *Republican* industrialist interests in the form of John J. Raskob and General Motors' president Alfred P. Sloan. Muse also secured cash from Henry du Pont, patriarch of the paint and chemical dynasty that was no stranger to such causes, contributing generously to the most obscurantist of groups, including the Liberty League, the Sentinels of the Republic, the Minute Men, the Crusaders, the National Economy League, and the American Taxpayers League—along with the GOP. At the convention rabid Louisiana bigot Gerald L. K. Smith appeared alongside Talmadge, as did the aristocratic Virginia white supremacist and renowned novelist, the Rev. Thomas W. Dixon. Muse made certain every delegate's seat had a fresh copy of the *Georgia Woman's World* that featured a picture of (in his words) the First Lady "going to some nigger meeting, with two escorts, niggers, on each arm."[93]

But Talmadge was the biggest draw. Known colloquially as Old Gene, Talmadge was the walking-talking personification of the melding thesis in the South. Beginning political life as a glowering, red-gallused agriculture commissioner who acted as the populist successor to Tom Watson, Talmadge the governor soon evolved into a dream for the Georgia Power Company and other large business interests and utilities, yet still claimed a fanatical following among the state's rustics. From 1933 to 1937 Talmadge augmented his virulent version of white supremacy by slashing public expenditures on old-age pensions, free textbooks, and the length of the school year while he lowered property taxes and damned the "combination of wet nursin', frenzied finance, downright Communism an' plain dam-foolishness" called the New Deal. Apart, and in addition to, Talmadge and Muse, various anti–New Deal forces, calling themselves Jeffersonian Democrats, actually fielded alternative electoral tickets in a few states in 1936, doing best in Texas as the "Constitutional Democrats" and stressing similar anti-black and anti-Red themes.[94]

The opposition soon bled over into targeting Franklin Roosevelt himself as suspect on a personal level: a traitor who imperiled the very fate of the American republic. A leading anti-Roosevelt journal complained that he had no respect for the constitutional system and had taken upon himself unprecedented economic powers that "no constitutional President" would ever try to claim. The mask of the "benevolent Dr. Jekyll" was slipping further from the "ominous visage of Mr. Hyde Park." Others charged that the president should stop picking communists and sympathizers for sensitive government posts. Some simply derided him for the "Roosevelt Depression." He was "stupid and blundering . . . the greatest spender of all times," and he blamed the failure of his economic nostrums on the country's valiant businessmen who were trying gallantly to keep the nation's economy afloat.[95]

By 1936 Roosevelt was largely fed up with walking on eggshells to appease the interests of capital. His early programs, especially the National Industrial Recovery Act (NIRA) and AAA, had allowed big business and big farm interests to dominate the shaping of policy only for Roosevelt to hear unprecedented criticism from wealth and privilege. To a large extent, the president felt he had saved capitalism from the capitalists only to be villainized as a traitor to his class, as a communist, as insane—rather than thanked. So, for his part in 1936, FDR did little to quell the anger of what he termed the economic royalists: "Never before in all our history have these forces been so united against one candidate as they stand today. They are unanimous in their hate for me—and I welcome their hatred."[96]

The Bourbon strategy of spending money and energy to convince plain-white people that their most essential racial and cultural interests lay in doing everything to boost business hit its stride in the movement against the New Deal. Alabama's industrialists poured their resources into at least two major publications to reach this end: one was the *Southern Outlook*, which specialized in anti-black, anti-Semitic, and anti-union invective, and the other was *Alabama Magazine*, which announced a drive to encourage respect and appreciation for business and businessmen in the face of FDR's diatribes against "those who provide employment and create payrolls" and in order to stem the New Deal's attacks on business and Roosevelt's "hatred of business." Its goal was to enlighten the people to the simple idea (the magazine frankly editorialized) that "what helps business helps them and what hurts business hurts them."[97]

To that end the leading business-boosting journal published ceaseless editorials that could have doubled as advertisements from various corporations. Throwing subtlety to the wind, they sought to indoctrinate the masses with notions like "What Hurts Business Hurts You" and "Industry seeks no special favors," only to realize a "fair return" on its investment.[98] When New Deal legislation came up that affected race and economics, such as Hugo Black's Wage and Hour Bill, the Bourbon journal was there to denounce it in racial *and* cultural terms ("carpet-bag . . . revolutionary") and provide a forum for hide-bound coal barons like Charles DeBardeleben to damn it as

"Un-American . . . Russianized . . . Dictatorship" that would "Enslave . . . the working man." DeBardeleben would become a Dixiecrat and, later, a pioneering modern southern Republican.[99]

In fact, the planter-industrialist elite missed no trick in melding together racial and economic anti-federalism into a potent witch's brew that would harm the health of the thousands of plain whites in Alabama who gulped it down. The potion called for one part white supremacy mixed with one part laissez-faire stirred into a froth and seasoned with a hearty dose of canted Reconstruction antipathy to the federal government. The New Deal, therefore, revealed the "social and economic asininities" of the Rooseveltian era that betrayed the president's lack of sympathy for the South, his "obstinate class mind," and his actual goal of holding the Democratic Party hostage to the balance of power in the northern states: "the Negro vote." His ultimate goal, an industrialist journal charged, was to return to the 1860s through "the reconstruction of racial and political relations in the South on an equalitarian basis"—a nightmare scenario that obviously would not help him or the South.[100]

When FDR backed the NRA, he displayed "bad manners and bad temper" toward the South. When he supported the Wage and Hour Bill, he again demonstrated a "lack of sympathy for Southern conditions." Since Roosevelt had taken office, the South's "shackles have been multiplied, not removed or lessened," Hubert Baughn of the *Alabama Magazine* railed. A conservative white Birmingham Democrat agreed that it was heartbreaking for the South after all those decades of loyalty to see itself being traded off completely for the votes of Negroes and labor unions in the North.[101]

While the racial component of the appeal was sometimes lightly camouflaged by code-wording as to true "Southerness" or "sympathy" and "loyalty" toward the South, often in this period race was there in its unvarnished form along with the anti–New Deal conservatism. For example, Bruce Shelton of the *Tuscaloosa News* publicly ridiculed a Roosevelt visit to Alabama's famed Tuskegee Institute by writing that "We hears dat de president am visitin' in de state today."[102] The dyed-in-the-wool conservatives at the *Alabama Magazine* predicted that FDR could win the black vote over even Abraham Lincoln and criticized the First Lady for allowing herself to be photographed between "a pair of cullud New Dealers." Joking acridly about the Supreme Court's decision canceling "a Texas darkey's" conviction because blacks had been systematically excluded from the jury, another editorialist stressed that the majority opinion had been written by "Mr. Justice Black of Alabama, suh."[103]

A particularly salient part of the business-driven opposition to the New

Deal was the Klan-like quality of its rhetoric and ideology. This was an apparent contradiction since the Big Mule/Black Belt elite had formed the heart of opposition to the KKK during the 1920s in places like Alabama. Yet the business sector's Depression-era revival of the Kluxist spirit was no paradox.

After 1930 Ku Kluxism served the interests of capital—and it also revealed two important things. First, it showed that the opposition to the Klan that the South produced during the 1920s was, for all practical intents and purposes, flawed. Alabama's "better sorts" had fought the Klan as a *political* rival that could appeal to the common people to win congressional seats, governors' mansions, and local posts, but it did not challenge the hooded order's narrow and fundamental spirit of racial, gender, and ethnic proscription. In fact, it more regularly found common ground with the secret society in this intolerance, objecting only if and when violent means became so blatant that they threatened to damage prospects for outside investment or bring down a real racial threat in the form of unwanted federal attention. Second, the Klan itself changed during the Depression decade to function as a smaller but decidedly more militant wing of a capitalism that felt itself under siege by unionists and radicals.[104]

The anti–New Deal movement marked a further rapprochement on the common basis of racial conservatism that would emerge into a full-blown romance in the next decade between erstwhile neo-Kluxist and neo-Bourbon adversaries. Eventually the romance would give rise to the Dixiecrats, various independents, and a modern Republican Party in the South. B. M. Miller had made opposition to the 1920s Klan the marquee issue in his successful 1930 bid for the governorship, deriding opponents for "sucking the biggest teat at the Klan-ridden capitol." Yet Miller fought the New Deal with gusto during the 1930s. Other 1920s Klan opponents like Frank Dixon also made up the inner sanctum of Alabama Bourbonism, but Dixon held membership in Vance Muse's Christian Americans, derided as an "anti-labor K.K.K.," and shared much of that outfit's extreme animus to organized labor and anything remotely liberal.[105] In 1936 the SDEC forestalled an independent elector movement against FDR by naming a slate of loyal New Dealers such as Bibb Graves and Hugo Black, both of whom had been Klan-backed politicians during the 1920s. Yet the opposition to FDR was led by former Klan powers Mabel Jones West and W. Cooper Green in concert with Borden Burr, perhaps the leading union-busting attorney in Alabama. Gould Beech admitted that opposition to the Roosevelt version of Democracy was financed by the deep pockets of the Bourbons but pointed out simply that they were drawing on an abundant "reservoir of racism . . . built up with the Klan ideas."[106]

In 1936 the rank racist and pro-business sentiment that formed the bulk of opposition to the New Deal was still considered extreme by most Americans and most southerners. But as the New Deal moved along and as racial hostility to the program increased, it would become easier for many plain southerners to forget their class differences, yet again, and make common cause with economic elites. Race and anti-federalism would furnish the common bond. And beliefs that seemed extreme in opposition to the Democratic New Deal in the 1930s would eventually come to be considered a pedestrian part of mainstream conservatism.

6
Splitting the New Deal Coalition Open

> You ask any nigger in the street who's the greatest man in the world. Nine out of ten will tell you Franklin Roosevelt. That's why I think he's so dangerous.
>
> —A white southerner

Liberals in the Deep South could push and pull the electorate along on economic issues. Although they encountered fierce resistance from conservative industrial and planting interests, and often disinterest from the plain electorate, they could get away with such behavior—especially when times were hard and people were starving—as long as they did not challenge the sacred conventions on race. Clearly in Alabama liberalism began and ended with economics. But whenever "liberalism" bled over into matters that did involve race and the broader but related question of culture, the most liberal-minded Alabamians of the age ran for the hills. They knew very well that they could go only so far. If they were interested in remaining elected officials in the state of Alabama, they had to steer clear of the all-important racial taboo.

A precious few liberals did cross the line—Gould Beech, Aubrey Williams, Clifford and Virginia Durr, Herman Clarence Nixon—but they were the exceptions that prove the rule. They were not representatives who had to stand for reelection in the state of Alabama. For the most part they were insulated bureaucrats and academics in other states, or outcasts and pariahs who encountered the fiercest and deepest kinds of social ostracism in their home communities.

As long as racial and economic issues were held apart, the seats and positions of public-office liberals were safe. But when the two melded together they were increasingly in trouble. And, of course, the two could not be held artificially apart forever—even in Alabama. What the New Deal did, at its most fundamental level, was begin the process of coalescing the two on a national level by including African Americans in relief and recovery in significant and visible ways, by giving aid and comfort to the rising industrial unionism that would organize blacks along with whites, in a hundred different ways. In effect, the New Deal was the beginning of the end for Deep South liberals connected to the Democratic Party who pushed economic progressivism while remaining true blue southerners on race. The New Deal forebode the day when economic liberalism and racial liberalism would be blended so thoroughly, even in the South, that "liberalism" itself would become an untenable position for a southern white politician to hold. And when class-based conservatism and racial conservatism finally met to marry in solemn ceremonial backlash, anointing the States' Rights Party into existence, it did so almost ten years to the day—and, ironically, in the same Birmingham hall that had hosted the first Southern Conference for Human Welfare. The New Deal hastened the day in Alabama when it would become impossible to keep "economic liberalism" and "racial liberalism" separate in the public mind—the same day the Democratic Party began to die in the South.

Not Only a Mistake But a Disgrace

In 1936 three-quarters of American blacks abandoned the party of Lincoln for Franklin Roosevelt and the New Deal—a genuine watershed. The shift was primarily a function of Roosevelt's massive popularity and his administration's willingness to include African Americans as Americans, yet some small black discontent with the GOP had been brewing throughout the 1920s. Herbert Hoover's forces had openly appealed for Klan support in 1928 and his administration was so racially exclusive that Walter White of the NAACP tagged him the "man in the Lily-White House." Demographic and cultural shifts also played a role: growing assertiveness associated with the "New Negro" movement, the NAACP, the undermining of "scientific racism" by sociologists Franz Boas and others, the outflowing of culture and art known as the Harlem Renaissance, and the Great Migration from the South that had, by 1930, moved a fifth of all black Americans north of the Mason-Dixon Line.[1]

The southern reaction to first the New Deal and then the Democratic Party as a whole was without question orchestrated from above. Yet it was eventually received and echoed with a full throat at the common level. Like the most notable instances in the southern past when plain whites and blacks pooled their efforts only to watch their alliances come apart because of racial suspicion and mutual distrust, the New Deal itself was broken apart on the anvil of race by the hammer of wealth—a development lustily cheered by those who controlled commerce in the region.

Like the Populist storms that swept the South during the 1890s, the New

Deal movement was born of economic desperation—a desperation so intense that plain people put aside their racial differences if but for a moment. And like the 1890s, the economic crisis would eventually pass, giving plain whites room to return to an indulgence of racial and cultural superiority at the expense of all else. Like the Reconstruction efforts of Republican blacks and whites, the New Deal eventually found itself touched with the poison pen of federal encroachment. And like all things federal since Reconstruction, white southerners would tolerate the intervention of the central government only if it came in the form of federal dollars, disaster relief, or grants and aid for corporations.

Quite ironically, in the new climate of the Great Depression, resurrection of the Reconstruction profanity boded ill for uninterrupted allegiance to the Democratic Party. "My father was an old Confederate soldier and a lifelong Democrat," explained one wavering Alabama Democrat, "but I can't swallow this 'New Deal.'" Other southern critics were more direct about the unsavory nature of the party under FDR. "You ask any nigger in the street who's the greatest man in the world," one said. "Nine out of ten will tell you Franklin Roosevelt. That's why I think he's so dangerous."[2]

Of course, the racial liberalism of the New Deal that made it antithetical to the overwhelming majority of white southerners was linked to a trove of allied cultural orthodoxies. And it did not take long for opponents of the New Deal to mix them by tapping into the almost limitless regional reserve of anxiety over cultural regularity.

At first the carping was limited to extreme right-wing critics of the administration, but before long the critique would trickle down to poison the more general well of southern opinion. The New Deal was not only "a mistake," Carter Glass of Virginia declared, but an actual "disgrace." Fellow Virginia powerhouse Harry Flood Byrd teamed up with conservative editor Douglas Southall Freeman of the *Richmond News-Leader* to worry over the meaning of increased centralization of authority in Washington. North Carolina's Josiah Bailey called it "un-American" to specify by law what a farmer could sell, a manufacturer could make, or a consumer could pay. "It denies Liberty," Bailey declared in invoking the slippery slope. "We will stick to Liberty or go over to Communism." Other congressional skeptics and sometime critics like Walter George of Georgia, Tom Connolly of Texas, and "Cotton Ed" Smith of South Carolina joined in. Wholehearted adversary Thomas P. Gore of Oklahoma, though, hit upon what would become a mantra for the economic royalists aligned against FDR. The National Recovery Act and old-age pensions were the handiwork of a leviathan set out to destroy the self-reliance and self-respect of the people: "[T]he dole spoils the soul."[3]

Yet what might have remained unadulterated economic conservatism in other environs did not stay quite so pure in the Deep South. Leading planter and Bourbon organ the *Alabama Magazine* flatly damned the New Deal by showing the slip of bigotry it habitually wore. The TVA, for example, was the creation of "modern Shylocks" while the private firms that opposed it, such as Alabama Power, were "Christian, Aryan, and Constitutional."[4] Other economic conservatives in Alabama opposed FDR's "Raw Deal" by stoking the chords of regional orthodoxies on morality and character, long a favorite theme of conservatives from the southern Bourbons to Andrew Mellon. The New Deal and its programs undermined the honor and morality of the people with "monstrously immoral" edicts that are "vicious and rotten." Labor laws were a favorite target. The Wagner Act existed only so that unions could assault, insult, intimidate, and murder. The act's National Labor Relations Board insulted, harnessed, and, perhaps most unforgivable of all, "disbelieved" the employer. Its unfair labor practice charges resulted in needless and costly delays. Worse, in what would become a routine critique of any policy that challenged the predominant conservatism, the New Deal took taxpayer money for vicious laws and customs that were "horribly immoral."[5]

These Alabama opponents of the New Deal had a ready conception of what they viewed as the proper relationship between government and private enterprise, one that would have made Adam Smith blush: "The fundamental is that the management should reduce wages. Any workmen that does not want to accept the new terms are privileged to quit, and the Government should have an adequate army ready to enforce law and order." The New Deal was a "Raw Deal" and socialist to boot—and it was high time the government used its power to shrink wages instead of boosting relief efforts and labor laws. If a strike occurred, government (the non-socialist kind) had an affirmative duty to send troops with "the right mental attitude" to crush such insolence. This, of course, was not seen as socialist. And the soldiers to be sent should be men who hated those who challenged property rights "as they would hate thieves." Deviation from this ideal was a New Deal abomination of right-thinking "moral principles."[6]

As opposition to the New Deal burbled and frothed, it mixed together a number of related ingredients of the southern status quo to form a potent antidote to the liberal idea. The elements were racial, economic, religious, and regional—but all were supremely cultural in makeup. And the effect was to tie the economic argument against the New Deal to wholesale discontent with the entire social and cultural drift of the Democratic Party.

Shortly after the 1936 election, in which blacks left the party of Lincoln en masse, Arkansan J. C. Sheffield released a treatise titled "The Second Secession" that found wide distribution and sympathy throughout the South. Sheffield called for the establishment of a southern Democratic Party, and his statement skillfully tied together moral, religious, economic, sectional, racial, ethnic, and Reconstruction reasons for the birthing of a new party. For Sheffield the treason of the Democratic Party in taking the Negro to its bosom besmirched the legacy of the party's southern fathers, degraded it beyond rehabilitation, and justified the breaking of "family ties" from a party that had become "prodigal with no hope of return." As envisioned, the new southern Democratic Party would rest on four essential, related, and inviolable principles: free enterprise, Jim Crow, industrial development, and the "rededication of our social and political economic order to the . . . Christian civilization" (a harbinger of things to come).[7]

At root, the appeal tapped into the most powerful conservative southern emotions regarding home and hearth, religion, sex, and civilization—and fused them with an extreme version of economic rightism. Particularly galling for the aggrieved southerners, the Democratic Party had been "conceived in southern minds, and hearts, born and . . . cradled in the South." It had "walked in southern ways, breathed the southern air and spoke with a Southern accent." When a people give birth to a party, "love it, cradle it, nurse it [and] . . . hold it close," it is only fitting that the reasons for withdrawing family ties be set down for posterity:

> The Democratic Party [has always stood for] . . . segregation of the white and colored races, [government] by white people . . . free enterprise . . . without unnecessary interference or competition from the government [and] . . . the . . . Christian principle that . . government is the servant and not the master of the Citizen. . . . [But now an] unholy alliance of Northern Democrats and Republicans [have poisoned its] . . . blood stream . . . with alien ideas. [The Party has] . . . abandoned the simple family life, and eschewed the religion of its fathers. . . . It walks not in Southern ways. . . . It is spendthrift, profligate, . . . and makes illicit love to dusky hewed damsels of the roadside . . . fornicates with Republicans, and dwells in the house of the ungodly . . . joined with the Republicans to demand that white people and colored people . . . eat, sleep and travel together . . . humiliate white Southerners . . . [and return to the] "carpet bag" days . . . [to] fawn at the feet of Northern negro radicals and [w]hore for the Northern negro vote. . . . [National New Deal Democrats] have forced . . . alien schemes of government and economics . . . down the throats of the people . . . socialized and

governmental ownership . . . of . . . business and public services, aiming utterly to destroy the American idea of economics and free enterprise, upon which this Nation was built. They have adopted non-Christian policies . . . to compel the individual to [bow] to . . . bureaucrats and make the Citizen a vassal of the Government. . . . So, with an old Rebel Yell . . . worthy of Lee, Jackson and Davis and Forrest . . . and all of our grandfathers who wore the grey . . . we launch the Second Secession Movement which will free us from 20th Century White Slavery . . . and licking the boots of political mongrels.[8]

The combination was masterful and would win increasing approbation from a South captivated by emotional imagery grounded in white supremacy. Here was a radical mutation of classical economics, predicated on racial custom and amplified by passionate appeal to religious, moral, familial, sexual, and ethnic regularity—all bound up with the powerful thread of the Reconstruction Syndrome. It was 1874 all over again—or 1901 or 1928. Whenever the South found itself threatened, especially on the economic front, the old reliable race and Reconstruction bogey could be rolled out by elites to compel obedience from plain whites who might momentarily think about wandering off the conservative reservation.

The process of melding together economic and racial rightism so that they became scarcely distinguishable from an all-encompassing and smothering cultural conservatism was gradual. Attempts at making a regional shibboleth of the two had been tried before, but the relationship had a stormy and checkered past. Challenges in the form of a working-class suitor had periodically appeared and threatened to woo white supremacy away from its privileged rival. But those attempts had failed repeatedly.

Still, the melding together of unhinged market values and white supremacy was helped along inestimably by the budding courtship the two experienced in common resistance to the New Deal. In fact, the maturation of their relationship was marked by a critical reconciliation between two former warring factions: neo-Kluxist and neo-Bourbon.

In the 1930s what can only be termed "neo-Kluxism" became a signal part of the Bourbon program. Neo-Kluxism would do much of the spadework for what would one day become Republican ascendance in the South. The Klan actually had two major reasons to dislike the New Deal, racial *and* economic, for its Depression-era incarnation often took form as the shock troops of industry besieged. In Florida, for example, robed Knights acting as strikebreakers for a company kidnaped union organizer Joseph Shoemaker, castrated him, and immersed him in a vat of boiling tar. He died from his wounds.⁹ In Alabama, Kluxers upset by the mid-decade shift of blacks away from the GOP complained bitterly that "a Darkey Drives the Donkey Now." The Klan's imperial wizard railed about "that nigger-lover Roosevelt," and Klan editorials tapped into much of the anti-Semitism underlying southern opposition to the New Deal by lambasting the "Jew Morgenthau" and the "Jew Ickes." One popular Klan cartoon of the president and the First Lady had them singing a bit of doggerel: "You kiss the niggers and I'll kiss the Jews. And we'll stay in the White House as long as we choose."[10]

Klan rhetoric could become extreme. A nation's citizens must be "ONE PEOPLE," Alabamian and national Imperial Wizard Hiram W. Evans thundered in 1937, in tying together racial, civic, moral, and patriotic themes about the Negro race being inassimilable. For Evans and other Klansmen, blacks were a race even more different from whites than the Chinese, "with inferior intellect, inferior honesty, and greatly inferior industry . . . childish, lethargic, superstitious, mentally arrested . . . hardly removed from a savagery . . . a group *unable* to be part of the American people." No matter how intelligent or well educated a handful of blacks might become, they would always "remain an *alien race*," unable to share in our national purpose, animated by "interests hostile to ours and a ready ally" for the enemies of America. The only possible escape would be unthinkable: an amalgamation of the races that would make America a "nation of mulattoes!"[11]

As extreme and even pathological as such rhetoric could be, it was only one degree removed—if removed at all—from the views of the New Deal's more mainstream southern critics. Klan ideology, as repulsive and crude as it was, shared an immanent kinship with what was increasingly passing for respectable conservative opposition to New Deal liberalism. Vance Muse, the Texas conservative who directed the union-busting Christian Americans and helped organize the 1936 anti–New Deal convention in Macon, Georgia, predicted that white women and white men would be "forced into organizations with black African apes whom they will have to call 'brother' or lose their jobs." "No niggah's good as a white man because the niggah's only a few shawt yere-ahs from cannibalism," Georgia governor Gene Talmadge said. "For thousands of yere-ahs the niggah sat on the wealth of the world. Gold and diamonds and rubies and emeralds. And wha'd he do? Filed his teeth and ate his fellow man."[12]

All of this seemed to come together in an explosive mix whenever the topic of sex was added. Interracial sex jeopardized not only racial hierarchy but also white patriarchal control. "Man has nothing against the gorilla," William Blanchard of the south Florida White Front explained, "but if he entrusts his fruitful garden to such a beast he is a very great fool." White women were the bridge over which the white race must pass. If it fell, white supremacy would be "but the rotting memory of a dead age." Black lust "is precisely what knots the lynching rope." In his filibuster against a federal anti-lynching law, anti–New Deal Louisiana senator Allen J. Ellender said as much: "I believe in white supremacy, and . . . if amalgamation . . . is permitted, there will be a mongrel race . . . [an] identical condition under which Egypt, India, and other civilizations decayed." In Alabama, Bourbon opponents of the 1920s Klan waxed nostalgic about the Reconstruction KKK while wailing about the racial carnage wrought by New Deal liberals.[13]

We Must Wake Up the Roosevelt Worshipers

At this point Republicanism was largely inimical in the South because it still meant the party of Lincoln and Reconstruction. But in its struggle against New Deal liberalism, southern Republicans began to construct a nascent, if infant, respectability. Like the conservative Democratic critique, Republican complaints castigated the New Deal in broad cultural terms that tapped into regional sensibilities and encompassed not only race but also ethnic purity, patriotism, civic virtue, the Protestant work ethic, and preservation of a constitutional form of government.

In Alabama, Oliver Day Street led the Republican opposition. Scion of a hill-country Populist and Republican family, Street had spoken out against Klan violence during the 1920s. Yet by 1928 he had buried his distaste and made common cause with the Klan to help lead the Hoovercrat "bolt" against Al Smith that nearly won Alabama. During the campaign, Street's anti-Catholic bigotry became so raw that it earned him the censure of the national Republican Party.[14] In that episode, and again during the 1930s, Street demonstrated that as a public opponent of the Klan he needed no lessons in intolerance from the sheeted order.

Like Street, Hubert Baughn, the racist and reactionary editor of *Alabama Magazine*, insisted that he was anti-Klan—a claim that did have some validity since he had functioned as a Big Mule/Black Belt stalwart who opposed the 1920s incarnation. Yet the style of his political critique against anything liberal contained all of the strongest precepts of Ku Kluxism itself and marked, perhaps, the most telling example of the growing reconciliation between neo-Bourbon and neo-Kluxist forces in Alabama.[15] The shrinking distance between Republican resistance to FDR and conservative Democratic opposition to New Deal liberalism boded well for growing GOP respectability.

A favorite way to disparage New Deal liberalism was to characterize it as something hailing from the utter fringes of the political spectrum—"socialistic, communistic . . . anarchistic . . . and Nihilistic"—evidence of a dangerous "Socialistic drift," according to Oliver Street.[16] J. G. Bass, a leading Alabama Republican, warned that the New Deal would lead directly to the socialist and communist takeover of America. O. R. Hood, a disgruntled hill-country Democrat flirting with Republicanism, feared the other extreme of the political spectrum. He described FDR as a fascist dictator and likened him to Adolf Hitler.[17]

Either way—in the tortured logic of a critique that was still considered extreme at this point—the liberalism of the Democratic Party under the New Deal imperiled the very existence of the constitutional republic and threatened *true Americanism*: the rallying cry of the 1920s Klan and the repressive World War I patriotic and civic societies. The New Deal was trying to destroy "[our] constitutional form of government," Republican state campaign chair J. G. Bass informed Alabama voters. Democratic economic and social relief amounted to a sacrifice of "our constitutional rights," agreed a white county Republican, while another from Epps's Penala Plantation in the Sumter County Black Belt proposed a new party of "Constitutionalists" to kill the New Deal.[18] "Shall the howl of a Red New Dealer" in America count more than twice the voice of an American who "respects the constitution of the United States?" asked Oliver Street.[19]

Closely related was a view of the New Deal as something that would do irretrievable harm to the natural American tendency to industry and thrift. New Deal reform would, instead, instill the bad habits of sloth and indolence in the masses and jeopardize the worker-bee base that the country relied on. Withholding relief aid and public works jobs, in such a mind-set, was a form of tough love that could only strengthen the backbone and fortify the moral character of the people. Of course, this criticism usually emanated from those with such abundance (inherited and not) that they did not carry the burden of Depression impoverishment, live with the despair of long-term joblessness, or feel the sting of the era's hunger, privation, and want. The Democratic solution to the Great Depression was "character destroying," according to one Alabama Republican. Liberals were simply dreaming of a destructive Eden in which no one, "not even father, works" and in which one "plucks all the comforts and luxuries off the trees."[20]

Appropriating tax money to subsidize such indolence was a curse and blight on a formerly great republic. It was dishonest for government to take from its people anything more in hard-earned dollars than was absolutely necessary to discharge only the most meager functions of government, which certainly did not include feeding the shiftless masses and undeserving poor. When government went beyond this and robbed "at the point of a gun" the industrious and thrifty to subsidize the bad habits of the "lazy, trifling, [and] shiftless," then tyranny was afoot—a despotism that usurped the natural and God-given rights of a free and democratic people.[21]

New-style Democrats like Franklin Roosevelt and Harry Hopkins had given birth to an American Leviathan, according to the old hill-country Populist-turned-Republican Street, a "Frankenstein" monster state in which "every idler, loafer, tramp, bum and hobo" was certain he would be fed, clothed, and lodged. In words that would gain a frequent and imponderable resonance in later decades, food for the starving and relief to the jobless were the worst forms of "class hatred."[22]

Especially repellent was the New Deal's embrace of the worthless and undeserving poor, especially those who sought to break free from their assigned places in the social order—shades of Calvinism and Social Darwinism. Foremost culprits among these types were blacks, Jews, union members, and nonsubmissive women. Labor unions were nothing more than "criminal organizations" that were "as subservient to the ignorant proletariat" as they ever had been in Russia, complained a leading Alabama Republican. Yet they had been given carte blanche by "cowardly" New Deal officials from Franklin Roosevelt on down. Union labor dictators were just as "hateful as . . . Hitler," Oliver Street agreed in throwing fascism into the gumbo with communism.[23]

Street, who corresponded with the most virulent bigots of the day (including people like Elizabeth Dilling of Chicago), summed up his opposition to the New Deal by stressing racial anarchy: "We must wake up the Roosevelt worshippers," he screeched, "to what the New Deal . . . is doing to torpedo the Southern doctrine of White Supremacy." The Democratic Party's New Deal was deliberately sacrificing southern white people for the northern black vote, a course that could only lead the southern states back to the "awful conditions prior to 1901" when African Americans actually voted.[24] Street leveled blame at the usual suspect: the Jew. Why was it that "so many Jews occupy high and controlling positions" in the New Deal, Street mused: the "Morgenthaus, Lehmans, Frankfurters and Cohens that serve the wheel chair."[25]

This was racial, religious, and ethnic intolerance in a raw form and—it is important to recognize—formed much of the basis for Alabama's Republican opposition to New Deal liberalism. In later decades, an ascendant GOP (chastened by "political correctness") would seek to elevate its critique to the higher planes of philosophical departure. Yet it is worth noting that, at its core, the growing Republican and conservative Democratic dissent from New Deal liberalism—in the South—was openly and unapologetically little more than glorified racism and bigotry.

Eventually much of the Alabama Republican critique of the New Deal deteriorated to a personal level aimed at Franklin Roosevelt as a criminal, thief, communist, and even a traitor to his country—a tack that would be revived with gusto against future liberal figures. "Don't trust Roosevelt," Street urged anyone who would listen, as he called for the president's impeachment.[26] Other Alabama Republicans echoed the damnation of the morally degenerate Democrats who pushed the New Deal. Bennie L. Noonjin, a rising power in state GOP circles, reproached the Jewish editor of the *Birmingham News* and the *Birmingham Age-Herald* for supporting the New Deal, which "borders on a type of treason." Alabama Republicans pointed to a kind of patriotism mixed with Protestant religion as reason enough to oppose New Deal liberalism. "The so-called Democratic presidents" the American electorate had put in office had just about "destroyed the political morals of our people," went the lament. "All honest patriotic people" were morally and spiritually bound to fight against the leftward drift of FDR and the Democratic Party.[27]

Despite the convoluted nature of the critique, Oliver Day Street was dexterous enough to tie most of the disparate elements together. The "absurdities" of the New Deal constituted an "undermining" of the Constitution, "a war" on the Supreme Court and on the individual, a "criminal waste" of taxpayer money, an open and avowed effort to "destroy business," state coddling of "beggars and vagrants and tramps and bums," and Washington bureaus increasingly staffed by "socialists, pinks, reds, and communists" who were busy executing the "Socialist platform" under the name of Democratic liberalism.[28]

It is somewhat remarkable to pause to consider that this critique emanated from a man who had once been Alabama's leading Populist figure. While this kind of critique still remained in 1936 an extreme version of opposition to FDR's Democratic Party, it would soon qualify as a more mainstream conservative protest against the liberal state. Integral in this important transformation—which, in essence, would bespeak a quantum shift to the right for the American electorate—was the adoption by both Republicans and conservative Democrats of virtually the same language, symbols, and rhetoric of opposition. According to Street's perhaps inflated estimate, by 1940 almost all Democrats in Alabama agreed with his critique—as virulent as it was—yet were careful not to voice their unhappiness too openly lest they suffer the lash of party discipline.[29]

Before they became Dixiecrats—and long before they actually turned to the GOP—most southern whites were disgruntled conservative Democrats distressed by the liberal drift of the New Deal Party. During this period, southern conservatism mastered a sophistic approach to the ever-present question of race relations and federal intervention. The argument called for states' rights by default if alleviation of the most conspicuous and heinous forms of prejudice could be demonstrated. During the 1930s battles over a federal anti-lynching statute, for example, various southerners pointed to the relative decline of lynching as proof positive that nothing should be done to tamper with what were obviously peaceful and harmonious relations between the races. Later, as more and more white southerners fled Democracy for the safer confines of the GOP, a similar specious logic would be used to justify an insistence on local control over race and other matters.

If the most egregious forms of abuse had been dealt with (e.g., lynching, the Klan, de jure segregation), then there must be no legitimate role left for the central government to play in the whole area of race relations—no matter the de facto reality in realms such as voting rights, criminal justice, job fairness, poverty, economic opportunity, or even Jim Crow. If the federal government dared to legislate in such areas then the action would automatically constitute unwanted, unnecessary, and "unconstitutional" meddling—a trespass on states' rights.

In fact once civil rights legislation passed over rabid conservative opposition, these very same conservatives could claim that a level racial playing field had been achieved as mandated by the federal government. Thus, the race issue was a dead letter. The argument could then be turned on its head. In a newly perverse form of the sophistry, conservative southerners could insulate themselves from federal action concerned with racial fairness by casting the whole race issue as already solved. Any additional race-related measures—or even the mention of civil or voting rights—would constitute an attempt to persecute and humiliate the South, try to enforce "reverse discrimination" against white people, and actually *dishonor* the color-blind ideal that pioneers like Martin Luther King had fought for.

In 1940 Alabama governor Frank M. Dixon provided a classic preview of this powerful sophistry. "We do not have lynchings in Alabama," Dixon proclaimed. Thus a federal bill along these lines constituted a direct threat to state sovereignty and the right of a free people to conduct their own affairs. The increasing liberalism of the New Deal government represented an ominous portent of a grasping central state trying to assume more and more power in the local affairs of the people. Left unchecked, it would result in a Washington totalitarianism that would intrude upon and eventually control the "personal, private and daily affairs of every citizen" in the country.[30]

After taking the New Deal and liberalism to an irrational extreme, Dixon argued that on all subjects, race included, government was supposed to function as the absolute and reflexive servant of the people. The state must remain ever-malleable to the wisdom and will of the people, the logic went. So extreme and uncompromising was the particular articulation of this rightist position that no provision for exception was included—even in the event that the popular will violated the Constitution or even the bounds of common decency. For southern conservatives like Dixon this was the genius of democracy and a free people: that the state would serve as a knee-jerk instrument reflexive of the public will regardless of any universal or enduring notions of equity or fairness.[31]

"The people of this state are unanimous against" the federal government legislating on lynching or other race-related topics, Dixon claimed in defining *the people* as conservative, white Alabamians who shared his view. To pass such a bill, therefore, would thwart the will of the people "whose servants" the government is supposed to be. It would strike at the foundational cultural pillars of the republic itself and be "disastrous to our American way of life" and offensive to the white taxpayers who paid the freight for all of society. Because lynching rates had recently decreased in most of the old Confederate states, there was no reason for the central government to concern itself with the whole galaxy of southern race relations. Such agitation could only disturb the steady "progress" that southern whites had been making for black people and hurt, far more than it could help, the "very people who are its supposed beneficiaries"—an argument that would be mined relentlessly in later decades. Southern whites were already bearing a "tremendous" tax burden to provide for the health, education, and welfare of black people. Northern hypocrites who sponsored such laws did so only for the crass reason of winning black votes and didn't have to pay a dime in taxes to prop up the black race. Yet these same Yankees had more than enough of their own social problems to occupy them without intruding upon the peaceful and contented race relations of Dixie.[32]

Boys, Here's Where I Cash In

What had been contained until this point as extreme and even fringe discontent against the New Deal burst forth after 1936 in a series of high-profile conflicts that pitted Franklin Roosevelt in direct contravention to the most serious of his southern detractors. The result was to lend significant impetus to the right-wing movement against New Deal liberalism on both race and the economy. By 1940, when FDR would stand for reelection to an unprecedented third term, the forces of southern conservatism would mass in considerably more impressive array—and the pull away from the Democratic Party toward something else would be even that much stronger.

In a significant way Roosevelt loaded and cocked the gun his antagonists pointed at his head. In February 1937, shortly after his second inauguration, FDR announced what soon became known and widely derided as his "court-packing scheme" to name fifty new federal judges to the bench including possibly six new Supreme Court justices. The move sprang, of course, from the president's growing frustration with a Court that had struck down the NIRA and AAA, among other pet pieces of legislation.[33]

Southerners, in particular, rallied against the plan on the basis of states' rights, constitutionalism, and white supremacy. Some took the occasion to disown the New Deal itself. Hatton W. Sumners, a New Deal congressman from Texas, spoke for many when he announced simply, "Boys, here's where I cash in."[34] Carter Glass of Virginia held up Harold Ickes as the type of "visionary incendiary" who would likely play a large role in selecting new "judicial sycophants" and reminded his southern colleagues that Ickes had recently castigated the South for school segregation. Glass charged that Ickes had practically committed the administration to "a new Force Bill" that threatened the intrinsic civilization of the South with another "tragic era of reconstruction." Speaker of the House William Bankhead of Alabama supported the plan but without his usual enthusiasm; in private, Bankhead expressed doubts. North Carolina's Josiah W. Bailey spearheaded a move among southern Democrats that took a written form known as the "Southern Manifesto." The document rebuked the New Deal itself as contradictory to the bedrock principles of states' rights and the "American system of private enterprise and initiative."[35]

Strike two occurred on the issue of the economy. FDR commissioned a National Emergency Council packed with southern representatives of industry and labor to craft a study released in August 1938 titled "Report on Economic Conditions in the South." While the study had been designed as an administration indictment against continued economic colonialism, it was received as a slap in the face by an ever-defensive region. Roosevelt described Dixie as "the Nation's No. 1 economic problem," intending empathy but instead evoking deep resentment.[36]

The economic report struck a number of nerves, most of them accurate, which was part of the reason it was received with such hostility by the intended southern beneficiary. It pointed out that much of the region's profits were siphoned off by outside financiers, that the region's tax burden fell most heavily on those least able to pay, and that efforts toward more progressive taxation were fought most ferociously by outside investors, industries accustomed to paying low wages, and large landholding corporations, utilities, and mega-farm and timber interests.[37]

Nowhere was this state of affairs more pronounced than in the Heart of Dixie. Alabama's infamous 1901 constitution had ensured that its tax structure would be the most malformed of any state in the Union for at least the following century.[38] Nor did it help much when the director of the U.S. Public Health Service dubbed the South "the No. 1 health problem of the nation" or when the economic report pointed out that homes in the rural South were the "oldest, have the lowest value, and have the greatest need of repairs" of any farmhouses in the country: half of them were unpainted, a third had no screens to keep out insects and mosquitoes, and six in seven did not have inside water. Alabama took the dubious distinction of having the highest percentage of farmhouses lacking running water (97), with Mississippi, Georgia, and Tennessee close behind. The South also had markedly lower industrial wages and farm income than other regions. Yet the profits of the South's textile mills easily exceeded those of the North.[39]

A likely source of the backlash sprung from the tendency of New Dealers to describe southern conditions as medieval. No matter how accurate the comparison, nobody—especially southerners—wanted to hear what the report had to say on that score. Nor did they want to hear Clark Foreman praise Roosevelt's efforts to help the people of the South escape "feudal economic conditions" or Florida senator Claude Pepper envisage a South where "the feudal system" would remain a romantic legend but democracy would be the reality. Nothing was so bad as when the president himself added his voice to this chorus of stating the obvious but uncomfortable truth. In March 1938 at Gainesville, Georgia, FDR lectured the South in uncharacteristically harsh terms, telling its people that they "may just as well face the facts": the consumption power of millions of people was inadequate because of the region's famously low wages—and improvement would never come if Dixie believed that "the feudal system is still the best."[40]

General discontent continued to mount over a number of economic grievances. The powerful southern farm bureaus were angry at the New Deal tenant law. Crop controls aggravated the cotton trade. NRA codes enraged commerce even though businessmen had taken a leading hand in their crafting. And federal relief threatened the regional wage differential. Economic dissatisfaction and the report became factors in Roosevelt's third major controversy, the "purge" elections of 1938. In a calculated gambit the president insinuated himself against several handpicked southern conservative Democratic opponents of the New Deal in their home state reelection campaigns.

The result was a disaster. If FDR thought the South had circled wagons and evoked the Reconstruction memory to thwart "court-packing," he had seen nothing yet. In Alabama, New Deal ally John Temple Graves II broke so publicly and so fiercely with Roosevelt that he went over to join hands with the reactionary industrial organ *Alabama Magazine*. Senator Walter George won big in his reelection bid, sniggering that FDR's involvement against him was "a second march through Georgia." In South Carolina, "Cotton Ed" Smith and Olin D. Johnston's primary race degenerated into a contest in race-baiting that the incumbent won. After his victory Smith thumbed his nose in fine sectional style at Roosevelt: "No man dares to come to South Carolina and try to dictate to the sons of those men who held the hands of Lee and Hampton."[41]

In the November 1938 midterm elections, Franklin Roosevelt and the New Deal got a major comeuppance as the president's Democratic margin fell precipitously in the House by 61 percent (from 223 to 136 seats) and 25 percent in the Senate (from 56 to 42 seats). Surveying the disaster later, historian George Tindall accurately pointed out that the southern congressional leadership on which FDR leaned so heavily had become by 1938 "undependable and some of it hostile." Furthermore, the senators who did stick with him—Maury Maverick of Texas, Claude Pepper of Florida, and Lister Hill of Alabama—were the "exceptions that proved the rule."[42]

I Would Like to Be a Liberal But the Damn Fool Liberals Will Not Let Me

November 1938 also marked a critical turning point in Deep South estimations of what the New Deal was all about when the Southern Conference for Human Welfare (SCHW) selected Birmingham, Alabama—the citadel of Bourbon strength—to hold its inaugural meeting. The brainchild of Jewish communist Joseph Gelders, and brought about in part by Virginian Lucy Randolph Mason's entreaties to Franklin and Eleanor Roosevelt, the SCHW constituted an impressive gathering of liberal-minded southerners by any estimation. Yet its first meeting in such an inhospitable clime probably did as much to stimulate conservative backlash against New Deal liberalism in the Deep South as it did to actually further the group's progressive agenda of black voting rights and economic reform.

Still, the roster of 1,200 delegates who attended on that Thanksgiving weekend read like a who's who of progressive thought in the South. Herman Clarence Nixon served as field secretary, University of North Carolina Press director W. T. Couch was program chair, UNC president Frank Porter Graham became the group's first chairman, CIO organizers William Mitch and

Yel Cowherd and native Alabama communist Rob Hall made the local arrangements, and Supreme Court justice Hugo Black addressed the gathering. Blacks and whites, men and women, attended: Mary McLeod Bethune, Eleanor Roosevelt, regional editors Ralph McGill, Mark Etheridge, Virginius Dabney, George Fort Milton, and Clarence Poe, Florida senator Claude Pepper, Arkansas Democrat Brooks Hays, historian C. Vann Woodward, and Swedish sociologist and economist Gunnar Myrdal. In addition to Gelders, Nixon, Hall, and Black, a host of important liberal Alabamians attended: Aubrey Williams, Clifford and Virginia Durr, Justice Department lawyer Helen Fuller, U.S. judge Louise Charlton, and the Women's Trade Union League's Mollie Dowd—as well as U.S. senators John Bankhead and Lister Hill, Congressman Luther Patrick, and Governor Bibb Graves.

Yet at least two omens of things to come appeared during the convention proceedings. First, conservative New Dealers such as Horace Wilkinson were conspicuously absent. Second, in perhaps the most dramatic moment of the proceedings, another New Dealer, Birmingham police commissioner Bull Connor, appeared with a phalanx of officers to enforce the city's segregated seating ordinance. Mrs. Roosevelt defied Connor by moving her chair into the center aisle in silent protest, registering an indignity even the police commissioner endured to avoid arresting the First Lady. Yet if Eleanor's message was clear, so was Connor's, despite the mangled syntax of his famous declaration that "Negroes and whites would not segregate together" in Alabama.[43]

The involvement of communists in the SCHW was a double-edged sword and a matter of some complexity. There is no question that the vision and energy of radicals like Joseph Gelders, Rob Hall, and Hosea Hudson were absolutely essential to the successes that liberalism did achieve in the South. But there can also be little question that they came at a price. The region was so essentially conservative that, in a salient way, the involvement of communists also made more difficult the SCHW's and other organizations' chances for survival in Dixie—much less their effectiveness.

The presence of even one communist painted a large red X on the backs of all the liberals involved and made mass denunciation that much easier for the opponents of liberalism because of the Communist Party's popular identification with two things that made it absolutely unacceptable in the South: godlessness and advocacy of the radical overthrow of the American government. Even if the overwhelming majority of liberals involved in the SCHW were not actual subversives or irreligious (quite the reverse), guilt by association in the South could easily resolve the difference and stretch to include anyone who consorted with such folk. The resulting perception was the same regardless of the reality. The SCHW was a seedbed of godless radicals bent on the defilement of patriotism and overthrow of the republic. The indictment, however unfair or inaccurate, propelled the group and many of its participants to the utter fringes of the culture in which they lived.[44]

Joseph Gelders had dreamed the idea up and he was a homegrown Alabama communist. By 1947 the House Committee on Un-American Activities (HUAC) would brand the SCHW a communist front organization in a report that one historian called "a masterpiece of logical fallacies, quotations out of context, and guilt-by-association techniques." Other liberal Alabama members such as Aubrey Williams and the Durrs would be hounded unmercifully by HUAC and see their liberalism inaccurately but effectively marginalized as radicalist subversion and communism. Within ten years the group would go defunct, its death knell assured by the withdrawal of CIO money to pay for its "Operation Dixie" offensive.[45]

Yet the anti-radical rejection of the SCHW was only part of a broad cultural reaction that found the group and its goals obnoxious in virtually every way that buttressed the prevailing status quo: racially, morally, ethnically, religiously, civically, and in relation to prescribed gender roles and class relations. The SCHW's advocacy of voting rights for blacks was enough to send it beyond the pale for most white southerners. But combined with the involvement of a communist or two among the 1,200 attendees, the product was cultural dynamite. In Alabama, plain whites did not need to know much about the actual issues discussed at the municipal auditorium to know that they were fervently against the SCHW. All they had to do was have a cultural reflex that worked in order to respond to the massive stimuli rained down on them by the planter-industrialist machine.

Hubert Baughn's journal of hidebound conservatism dutifully led the way. The *Alabama Magazine* deplored the gathering (with some truth) as a foreign enterprise that was not representative of the Deep South. "[W]hointhehell invited" the SCHW to Alabama, Baughn asked. Certainly it was "neither spontaneous nor Southern."[46] Yet after accurately establishing the unrepresentativeness of the group, Baughn went the whole neo-Kluxist nine yards to race-bait and Red-bait the group and its goals, quickly falling back on the tried-and-true reasoning of Social Darwinism.

Race as usual came first, and the ritual summoning of the Social Darwinist intellectual creed necessarily brought religious, sexual, and economic orthodoxies into the picture. Nothing fundamental was kept separate. The basic purpose of the "long-haired men and short-haired women" who made up the SCHW was "off with the poll tax and votes for the darkies." It could all only lead to the abomination of "free love," the business journal charged.[47]

The goal was to equalize the economic, social, and political condition of blacks and whites, "a task in which nature and God Almighty [had obviously] failed for a million years." Nothing good could be gained by tampering with the natural hierarchy, the business boosters charged. It was antithetical to God and nature. Segregation was the immutable precondition to "racial tolerance" and sympathy in the South: there could be neither unless Jim Crow remained intact. Segregation was timeless, changeless, and instinctive for both races, a relationship that had been settled and would stand regardless of the machinations of godless agitators and their "crackpot schemes" to lead the South away from white control.[48]

The heretics were laboring under the false belief that economic reform could undo racial certainties. Still reacting to the insulting economic report, the forces of business charged that the New Dealers were actually deluded enough to believe that legislating higher wages and shorter hours could work some kind of magic in the South and "change the I.Q. of the darkey." It was the same kind of arrogant misjudgment that thought a federal anti-lynch law could stop just retribution against rape and that if the "average darkey is given a vote" he might take a genuine interest in government and himself.[49]

The interests behind the SCHW, according to the Bourbon opposition, were not just uncharacteristic of the South but were dangerously foreign and betrayed the inherent depravity of the New Deal. The Roosevelts themselves had sponsored the "piebald, unwashed, long-haired movement" infested with communists and facilitated by left-wing allies in the New Deal administration: "radical groups" and "pink Alabamians" bent on forcing a left-wing program "spawned [by] . . . radical eggs" in the South. The SCHW was packed with radicals, black and white, and had an "extreme left-wing complexion." The whole thing smacked of Reconstruction—Moscow style—with an approbating nod from the man in the White House.[50]

At root, the SCHW represented northern hatred of the South and was the worst design launched at Dixie in decades. Its intent was to place the South on the defensive, "flout Southern ideals and traditions, fan racial unrest, and jam through federal domination" of southern affairs—including universal manhood suffrage and its ugly by-products. The program was anything but southern, yet the president was sympathetic to it because he "hate[d] the South" and "never understood" anything about it except for the "darkey vote." Naturally the offense should have aroused the ire of the great rank and file of all southerners as "nothing else . . . since Reconstruction days."[51] In short, the SCHW was made up mostly of scalawags: southerners who had betrayed the Democratic Party and their homeland.[52]

Thus suitably instructed by the foremost barometer of conservative Alabama opinion—one that was skilled in tying together the most sacred regional shibboleths on an allied array of topics in the most narrow manner possible—other individuals and groups in the culture fell into lockstep. Mabel Jones West, leader of the women's auxiliary of the 1920s Klan, responded to the clarion call first, making clear that Bourbon and Kluxer had, in the tempests of the 1930s, drifted into lying down together.[53] West summoned an emergency meeting of the Alabama Council of Women's Democratic Clubs and oversaw the drafting of resolutions that echoed the Bourbon line and made sure the SCHW represented a serious cultural affront predicated on the violation of race norms, one that extended to encompass the whole of southern society. "[L]eft-wing agitators" tied to the Roosevelt administration and "professional radical agitators" were responsible for the assault, the women's groups resolved. At one meeting they formally expelled one of their members for taking part in the SCHW: federal Judge Louise Charlton.[54]

Once the anti–New Deal genie had been let out of the bottle it was as if all the pent-up southern Democratic frustration with Roosevelt liberalism came flooding forth. To be sure, at this point the *Alabama Magazine* and Mabel Jones West still represented the far end of the neo-Bourbon and neo-Kluxer spectrum. But once they equated opposition to the SCHW to opposition with New Deal liberalism *itself*, disgruntled Democrats around Alabama needed no further encouragement. Former Birmingham mayor George B. Ward echoed the Democratic women's clubs and added that he hoped the city would never again play host to the SCHW—a wish that was requited. The Birmingham City Commission, comprised at this point of Big Mule representatives Bull Connor, Jimmie Jones, and Jimmy Morgan, called for HUAC to investigate the SCHW from top to bottom looking for communist infiltration. Editorial opinion across the state reflected this mass outpouring of sentiment against the New Deal's liberal excesses. From the Black Belt, the *Selma Times-Journal* lamented the SCHW's advocacy of abolishing segregation and the poll tax and agitating for passage of a federal anti-lynch law. The *Montgomery Journal* was more forceful, denouncing the making of the federal government into a "policeman" with "federal bayonets" and the "scrap[ping] of every vestige of state rights in the regulation of internal affairs."[55]

Considered one of Alabama's leading liberals, Grover C. Hall of Old Grandma, the *Montgomery Advertiser*, expressed sorrow and regret at having initially supported the conference as something that could ameliorate regional ills and damned it as a "gratuitous insult" and "spit in the faces" of the southern people and their "way of life." For Hall and other southerners of essentially conservative principles that were deeply rooted in the Social Darwinistic conventions of their age, New Deal liberalism was acceptable so long as the federal government provided relief checks and did not tamper with established social hierarchies. Taken too far, Hall warned, this "reform" held the potential to undo the good work of "moderating journals such, if we may say it, as The Advertiser."[56]

Although scholars have too starkly bisected Alabama into a progressive north and a reactionary south, the response from Alabama's hill country was no better. Although New Deal programs such as the TVA did much to make north Alabama the most Democratic region in the state, racially liberal events such as the SCHW meeting tore at the bonds between the region and the national party—bonds that would eventually come undone. Instead of helping race relations, the meeting had actually hurt them, concluded the *Huntsville Times*. It was nothing more than a collection of "parlor pinks, left-wingers and social uplifters." The *Decatur Daily* agreed that the SCHW was a worthless meeting of "crackpots." Perhaps the group considered itself liberal, the Morgan County journal mused, but not like anything approaching the Alabama definition of liberalism: "'Liberalism—what sins are committed in thy name!'" But the *Tuscaloosa News*'s take on the meeting was perhaps the most telling for the future of the Democratic Party in the Deep South:

> [A] dyed-in-the-wool New Dealer, . . . Bibb Graves is not the only person who is shocked. . . . He is not the only Alabama man who, regarding himself as a New Dealer, is shocked and surprised by this revelation of what the REAL New Dealers—Eleanor Roosevelt, Aubrey Williams, and others of that stripe—are trying to do to the South. It is distressing that these people who are not forced to live in the South must destroy the harmony which it has taken us so many years to achieve . . . distressing that our peace and happiness must be sacrificed to these agitators who pose as socially-minded intellectuals . . . high-minded "liberals" [yet are actually] . . . people on the federal payroll, living sumptuously off our taxes [coming] . . . down here among us to stir us to discord and strife. . . . [S]ome day [the SCHW will] be recognized as one of the most important events of its kind [because] . . . at last it opened the eyes of the South to the fact which the South had long refused to recognize. . . . [The SCHW] was not Democratic. It was New Deal, pure and simply, and the left-wing variety of the New Deal at that. . . . [It was] a direct slap at the Democratic Party—the White Supremacy party as it has been constituted for years in the South—and an open revelation that the New Dealers are more concerned with the negro than with anybody else. . . . [They] do not see their folly. They do not realize they are in the process of transplanting Germany to the

American South; they do not reckon what the white man of the South will do when his back has been pushed to the wall. . . . [It] was a valuable eye-opening shock . . . [and] it stank.[57]

Hostility to the SCHW quickly resonated with ordinary Alabamians whose racial sensibilities had been irretrievably offended. But like the elite and editorial version, their critique extended to a wholesale cultural denunciation of the group—its plans, origins, program, and any of its ideas—and the ritual summoning of the most inviolate cultural tenets in defense. Key among these were religion and Reconstruction but also a regional form of patriotism cum xenophobia that clearly viewed the South as something separate and distinct from the rest of the United States.

White southerners had to wake up, an outraged hill-country man from Etowah exhorted. There has not been a "more dangerous meeting . . . of alien influences . . . *in our Southern country* in the past one hundred years." Southerners should atone with a week of prayer to ask God for the spirit that animated "our forefathers" during the 1860s, agreed W. P. Gordon of Blount County. Then Aubrey Williams and others of "that tribe [of] . . . young Hitlers" would be put on notice. A Birmingham resident, whose "blood is still boiling," called the meeting outrageous and recommended that the Dies Committee investigate immediately.[58] Perhaps more ominous for the prospects of continued Democratic solidarity was the complaint of an ordinary southern schoolteacher. She said her long-held and treasured form of liberalism had been shaken to the core: "I would like to be a liberal but I begin to believe that the damn fool liberals will not let me do so."[59]

While conference attendees such as Montgomery liberal Virginia Durr thought the whole communist charge a diversion from "the real issues" and "absolutely insane," Republicans sensed a crack in Alabama's culture wall and dove in.[60] B. Lonnie Noonjin—an ambitious north Alabama businessman, real estate operator, and former University of Alabama and professional baseball star—hit on the tried-and-true morality, patriotism, and southern culture themes to bash the New Deal. Noonjin, who was emerging as a leader in the new Alabama Republicanism, deplored the SCHW as dangerous, something that made "real Southerners shudder," and denounced the New Deal as an "orgy" and a departure from sanity. The decline in "moral values . . . Americanism and patriotism," Noonjin informed the people of Alabama, far outweighed any material benefits that might accrue from government programs. The New Deal was no mere partisan difference of opinion. Its designs were now clear. The South had been "sold out" by the Democrats.[61] Sensing, perhaps for the first time, that Republicans were gaining traction on the race issue, Alabama Democrats complained that a publicity agent working for the GOP had convinced Bull Connor to show up at the SCHW meeting with a riot squad and then tried to sell the Republican *Chicago Tribune* a story about communists.[62]

The High Tide of Regional Reform?

Often the SCHW is cited as the high tide of regional reform, accompanied by a roster of liberal attendees, and pretty much left at that.[63] But in reality the SCHW marked instead the "softness" of much of Alabama's variant of New Deal liberalism. Its aftermath makes clear just how incredibly fragile and vulnerable to instant dissolution much of southern liberalism actually was.

Before the ink had even dried on the SCHW's resolutions many Alabama New Dealers realized they had made a horrible mistake. Southern economic liberals knew that as long as they paid ritual homage to the god of white supremacy, they could indulge their progressive tendencies on other issues. But so powerful were the regional conventions on that subject—and so hopelessly interwound with the mainstays of the culture itself—that stepping over the color line could only incur the wrath of an electorate that would shut its ears to a progressive message on economics or anything else. While observation of the cultural bounds of racial decorum did extend the lives of economic liberals in the Deep South, as well as the progress they made on that score, their periodic gratification of the god's hunger for at least rhetorical racial sacrifice also gave sustenance to the whole cultural belief system behind it. And it did so in a way that contributed to their own demise once the economic and the racial had been completely fused in the South. Paying ritual tribute to white supremacy, even if done for the noble reason of preserving the viability of economic liberalism, also led to the monster growing so large and so strong that eventually it could not be controlled—by anyone.

Even before the SCHW was Red-baited, economic liberals who had attended the meeting ran from the group as if it were a house on fire. And, indeed, in Alabama it was. The anti–poll tax, anti–Jim Crow, and pro-federal anti-lynching themes taken up by the conference alienated even southerners understood to be liberals who did not have to run for elective office. The *Raleigh News and Observer* spoke for many moderates and liberals around the region by pointing out that the conference began with the one thing certain to provoke the South.[64] Bibb Graves said he was "profoundly shocked" by what had transpired at the Birmingham meeting, "shocked and surprised." Congressman Luther Patrick promptly resigned from the conference steering committee and claimed he did not have the "slightest knowledge" of the background or goals of some of the meeting's attendees. Lister Hill fled the scene of the crime, resolving to have nothing more to do with the heretics. John H. Bankhead wired former Klan maven Mabel Jones West to get his resentment of the proceedings on record. Birmingham postmaster Cooper Green (an actual planner of the event) denied that he had served as a delegate and declared his allegiance to Jim Crow. F. D. Patterson, the black president of the Tuskegee Institute, earned large bonus points with scandalized white Alabamians when he condemned the proceedings as the work of insurrectionaries from afar. John Temple Graves, who attended the meeting and expressed high hopes for it beforehand, immediately denounced the affair in strident terms.[65]

The mass exodus continued. Congressman Joseph Starnes, a New Deal supporter from north Alabama and a member of the Dies Committee, helped persuade the HUAC to send a subcommittee to Birmingham to investigate.[66] Of course, HUAC did not require much encouragement. The committee operated under the obscurantist chairmanship of Texas congressman Martin Dies Jr., an early opponent of aliens and international Jewish bankers, who had graduated to target Reds and, soon after, New Dealers, whom he charged with being the dupes of communists.[67] Confronting the contemporaneous Wagner-Costigan federal anti-lynching bill, Alabama's two U.S. senators, both prominent attendees at the SCHW, locked arms and toed the regional line. Bankhead said he resented the "visionary, shallow thinkers" and "self-handpicked would-be racial uplifters" at the SCHW who had demonstrated so little understanding of fundamental southern conditions. Just before his appointment to the U.S. Supreme Court, where he would make history by pushing the high court left on civil liberties and civil rights, Hugo Black's behavior testified to the power of electoral shackles in the Deep South.[68]

As dramatic as any reaction to the SCHW was that of George Huddleston—Alabama congressman, friend to labor, and a politician perennially described as a liberal New Dealer.[69] Yet Huddleston's behavior after the conference and his career as a whole make clear the softness that formed much of the core of New Deal liberalism in the Deep South. It was a liberalism that did not extend to race. It was also a liberalism that embraced—and in some cases merely tolerated—the New Deal as a temporary stopgap measure to deal with an unprecedented economic emergency. It was a political bent of mind that actually could be quite conservative, one that relished a return to ante-Depression days and a relationship between state and central government marked most notably by a pro-business laissez-faire and proto-libertarianism. Like Bibb Graves, Luther Patrick, Lister Hill, John Bankhead—and even journalist John Temple Graves and black college president F. D. Patterson—

U. S. congressman George Huddleston could not get away from the SCHW fast enough after its final gavel. The Alabamians who stayed with the conference and its resolutions—Aubrey Williams, the Durrs, William Mitch—were the ultimate exceptions. They were imported northerners foreign to Deep South cultural traditions or the most exotic of native southerners regarded by the bulk of Alabamians to be as strange as they were exceptional.

In truth, George Huddleston's racial conservatism was nothing new. As early as 1912 he had made the mistake of publicly defending blacks in the most paternalistic of terms yet had felt his hand stung by the hard slap of his home state's social conventions. "We have the negro here with us," the then-young Birmingham alderman had said in a speech to the Alabama Bar Association. "[W]e cannot kill him, we cannot deport him, we have got to make him a citizen." "The right of suffrage should be extended regardless of race and sex," Huddleston recommended in sounding not unlike the foremost scions of Black Belt privilege at the state's 1901 constitutional convention. Yet a mere decade after the codification, the post-disfranchisement color line had stiffened considerably. Huddleston found himself confronted with his comments a year later when he announced for the vacant congressional seat of the venerable Oscar W. Underwood. A rival for the open seat informed the good people of his district that the young alderman had publicly recommended the "kinky-headed Sambo and thick-lipped Dinah to vote and each to count as much as your vote, or yours, or yours."[70]

Shaken, Huddleston did, in the words of his grandson, "What politicians have always done: backtracked, claimed he was quoted out of context, changed the subject." He even said the bar association's stenographer had taken down his 1912 speech inaccurately. But he never made the same mistake again. In a 1929 speech to the Birmingham Women's Democratic Club, Huddleston went far in his defense of white supremacy, telling the assembled women that "we battle against social equality between the races and for the purity of the blood that flows in our veins. The real issue is whether the people of the South shall be degraded mongrels of mixed and polluted blood." Two years later the congressman rose up out of his chair and "nearly hit the ceiling," remembered a female American Civil Liberties Union envoy who asked Huddleston (as a leading liberal friend of labor) to represent the accused Scottsboro Boys. "I don't care whether they are innocent or guilty," Huddleston yelled at the startled woman. "They were found riding on the same freight car with two white women, and that's enough for me."[71]

What is interesting is just how temporary support for the New Deal was for southern liberals like George Huddleston. In 1933, the Alabama congressman supported the First Hundred Days of relief so energetically that he earned a personal note of gratitude from FDR's top lieutenant, Postmaster General Jim Farley. Yet before the year was out, Huddleston told the Birmingham real estate community that Roosevelt's recovery plans were actually "steps toward collectivism." The open break came just two years later. "My grandfather voted for the TVA," George Packer remembered, "but he never said a good word about it." For his grandfather and the people he represented, Washington became "something alien . . . a burden on them, a threat to freedom and custom." In 1935, Huddleston invoked states' rights to oppose the Social Security Act. A year later Huddleston learned about party discipline. He found himself opposed for reelection by the Roosevelt administration, John L. Lewis, William Mitch, and upstart Alabama Democrat Luther Patrick. During the 1936 campaign, Huddleston called Mitch a "carpetbagger" and stood by while a supporter race-baited and Red-baited the union leader for consorting with black UMW organizer Walter Jones. "I am opposed to centralization of authority in Washington, and . . . the robbery of our states," Huddleston assured his Alabama constituents. Then, carried away by the moment, Huddleston claimed a Confederate heritage for his father that existed only in his mind. "My father fought for the rights of these states to live their lives, and to be free from a central autocracy in Washington. . . . I would bare my thin and ancient breast to die for these principles."[72] Instead of baring his breast at a set of neo-Confederate ramparts, Huddleston did the next best thing. In an impromptu election-eve restaurant encounter, he brained his opponent over the head with a heavy glass ketchup bottle.

For Huddleston and other southerners who supported the early Roosevelt years their break with the New Deal version of liberalism occurred because, they believed, liberalism had left them—not because they had left liberalism. The rhetoric and the sentiment would be repeated decades later as white southerners would leave the Democratic Party en masse for the GOP, claiming the same thing. "Men have called me a liberal, and I was glad," Huddleston told his House colleagues. But principles that were liberal now are called conservative. "My principles and myself remain unchanged," Huddleston claimed, "it is the definition of 'liberalism' which has been changed."[73]

In 1940 the former Alabama congressman went whole hog and supported Republican Wendell Willkie for president against FDR. In 1948 he joined the Dixiecrats. As Huddleston's grandson perceptively understood, the southern liberal allegiance to New Deal liberalism was the ephemeral product of the calamity and cataclysm of the Great Depression. It was inherently temporary and contained within it the seeds of its own destruction. As George Packer put it: "By 1948 the South's brief love affair with the federal government was over. Depression had begun the affair, and war had sustained it beyond its natural end.... Race became the lever with which conservatives pried the South out of the New Deal coalition, and they did it in the name of Americanism."[74]

We Were Just Brought Up to Believe It Was Not Proper to Vote Republican

Central to the successful resistance against black incursion on voting was the solid front presented by the forces of planter and industrialist conservatism. As early as 1933 leading conservative politico Gessner McCorvey had insinuated himself in a Mobile cotton mill strike because he feared labor "agitators" (if successful on the shop floor) would stir up blacks against whites across society. Bourbons decried any attempt at increasing the black voter rolls, saying that the vote already extends to "the gutter and the cesspool. It blankets the mob. Every so-and-so a king!"[75] State Democrats increasingly found fault with the New Deal liberalism of FDR for stimulating black efforts to register.[76]

To resist the stirrings of blacks and progressive whites on this score, the Bourbons relied primarily on Reconstruction and Red-baiting. A black Birmingham communist remembered that everyone involved in the area's Right-to-Vote Club, even people who were not radicals, got Red-baited: "Here's the communists. This here's a communist outfit." Other conservative Democrats invoked the memory of the 1860s to work its magic: "Who would have expected the carpet-bagger to spring to life after two generations of merited oblivion within the Democratic Party and at the bidding of a nominal Democratic President?... The mind staggers at the prospect."[77]

The 1940 presidential campaign thus provided more avenues for expression of disgust with the New Deal than four years earlier. For one, Franklin Roosevelt was seeking an unprecedented third term as president. For the Bourbon press, the novelty opened his campaign to comparisons with "Il Duce" and "Der Fuehrer."[78] Opponents of the New Deal had also had four years in which to gestate their resistance to the growing liberal drift of the Democratic Party.

Still, the Republican Party was not yet a viable possibility in the South. Southern Republicans by and large favored Ohio senator Robert H. Taft, "Mr. Republican," for his severe anti–New Deal rhetoric. In Alabama the Taft-ites lined up behind Lonnie Noonjin while Claude O. Vardaman led a younger, urban Republican wing that favored the New Yorker Thomas E. Dewey. When the Republican schism at the national convention led to the surprise nomination of compromise candidate Wendell Willkie, Alabama Republican leader Oliver Street advised him not to dare mention black rights in the South. The Negro question down South, Street expounded, "has more lives than the proverbial cat." If Willkie had to talk about race he should stick to mumbling innocuous things about justice and do nothing to aggravate the enduring "prejudices of the Civil War and the Negro," which would, in any event, be conjured against any Republican in Alabama.[79]

While conservative Democratic opposition to the New Deal in 1936 had led only to a symbolic gathering of dissident forces, 1940 saw the independent elector movement actually raise its head. The dream recalled another Wormley House bargain like that of 1876 when southern bloc intransigence threw a presidential election into the House of Representatives where Dixie sought to win regional concessions. In 1940 dissenters in Mississippi and Texas chose the unpledged elector route while some South Carolina Democrats supported the favorite-son candidacy of Virginia neighbor Harry Byrd. Other disgruntled forces in Texas and South Carolina actually backed Republican Wendell Willkie as the only "real Democrat." Yet many southerners were turned off by his internationalism and relative progressivism, not to mention the hated Republican label.[80] While the 1940 separate elector movement attracted only negligible support, like the anti–New Deal summit in Macon four years before, it was an important point—one that presaged a powerful rump movement that loomed on the horizon for the Democratic Party.

Alabama flirted with the independent elector movement and organized several "Willkie Democratic" clubs before the fledgling insurgency was snuffed out by the powerful state Democratic Party. Again it was reactionary planter and business interests that led the anti-Democrats. Coal baron Charles DeBardeleben bankrolled large advertisements damning Roosevelt liberalism and New Deal manipulation and pushed Republican Willkie's candidacy as "the 'American Way' . . . to keep America free," something for workers who were "truly loyal."[81] *Alabama Magazine* editor Hubert Baughn also demonstrated that conservative business interests in Alabama were already prepared to go Republican as he chimed in for Willkie. Baughn charged that the "New Deal dictatorship" of the racially and economically liberal "Raw Deal" had made an abomination out of the Democratic Party in the eyes of lifelong southern Democrats.[82] But perhaps the most far-reaching dissent was voiced by Walker County small businessman and lifelong Democrat Robert H. Carr, who announced his support for Willkie by echoing the melding of social conservatism with free-market economics. He especially decried the New Deal's "gilded theories" and "totalitarian government with [a] . . . hatred toward industry and business."[83]

The unhappy Alabama oligarchs took full advantage of hurt feelings in the state when FDR passed over Speaker of the House Will Bankhead for second spot on the 1940 Democratic ticket. For the Bankheads it was the final straw; for white southerners it was yet another example of the New Deal deserting whites for "radical and Negro elements . . . the darkey vote . . . [and] dusky Democrats."[84] Democrats from all over the state returned from the national convention in Chicago in a dark mood over the South's treatment. "We have been sold down the river," Brewton's Ed Leigh McMillan said. Wiregrass delegates Will Lee and Robert Malone voted against a third term for Roosevelt at Chicago. Both the Black Belt *Selma Times-Journal* and the hill-country's *Talladega Daily Home* spoke ill of Chicago. "My God!" exclaimed Birmingham attorney R. DuPont Thompson, repelled by the diversity he saw in Chicago. "As a life-long Democrat I [ask] . . . is this the democracy of the Fathers?" The state Democratic Women's Clubs, represented by Mabel Jones West and Democratic national committeewoman Laura Sharp, deplored in strident terms what they termed the surrender of the national party.[85]

Democratic Willkie Clubs formed in Jefferson, Walker, and Mobile counties as a "patriotic duty" under Robert H. Carr, R. DuPont Thompson, and insurance man Fred H. White. Near Birmingham a number of Democratic veterans including Henry R. Howze, O. G. "Pap" Gresham, F. M. Jackson, and bakery owner William P. McGough joined the Willkie-Republican movement. In Mobile, George H. Denniston, a leader of the Alabama State League of Young Democrats, resigned his post and announced his support of Willkie. Remarkably, even the mildest type of reform associated with exercise of a First Amendment right of association could send conservative white southerners beyond the pale. For example, a Mobile native singled out the NLRB as evidence that the New Deal was breeding "communistic employees" and concluded that the Democratic Party had been "taken over by foreign philosophies" the same way France had been taken over by Nazi Germany.[86]

But in 1940 the state Democratic Party was easily strong enough to snap the whip of party discipline and compel obedience to the regular standard regardless of Roosevelt's increasing distastefulness. Wiregrass committeeman Robert Malone, who had openly opposed FDR at Chicago, relented and publicly announced that he would vote for the president. E. C. "Bud" Boswell— a Wiregrass politico who had played a large role in quelling the 1928 "bolt" and would render yeoman service to the disfranchisement of blacks after World War II—cracked the whip for the regular Democratic Party. Still, the state's most ardent business interests chafed under the party discipline. *Alabama Magazine* cried foul and the *Selma Times-Journal* declared that in bolting the Democrats were courageously putting country above party.

Arch-conservative industrialists such as Charles DeBardeleben cursed party discipline as a "stench in the nostrils of millions of . . . patriotic . . . [and] free Americans" despite the Strum und Drang.[87]

But the ground was not yet ready to nurture the independent seed—mostly because the regular Democratic Party still owned the trump card of white supremacy. Gessner McCorvey, now state Democratic chairman, spoke to people by statewide radio and urged them to resist the bolting impulse just because the Roosevelt administration had done some unsavory things that were now "water over the dam." Bolting was anathema, McCorvey instructed the home folks, because the preservation of white supremacy depended precisely upon Democratic regularity. Alabama had gone Democratic ever since 1874 when the great Democratic leader George S. Houston had led the "white men of Alabama . . . to redeem our State from [the] Carpetbag misrule of the Reconstruction era." As a consequence, McCorvey concluded, "we were just brought up to believe that it was not the proper thing for a southern white man to vote the Republican ticket." Responding to the pulling of its Reconstruction chords, crowds of regular Democrats booed, jeered, hooted down, and egged the pro-Willkie "Caravan of Democracy" at a dozen sites across the state.[88]

Although the most reactionary part of the Big Mule/Black Belt oligarchy was on the losing side in 1940, its forces were picking up steam. Roosevelt's personal popularity, looming American involvement in World War II, lingering gratitude for the economic resuscitations of the New Deal, and party loyalty and patronage prevented any serious rupture in the 1940 South. But it was also clear that the growing racial and economic liberalism of the Democratic Party was resulting in more and more powerful and vocal enemies in the South. Given time, money, and a few high-profile sectional grievances, a strong independent or even third-party challenge might become a reality. National Democratic committeeman Marion Rushton as well as Governor Frank Dixon and state legislator Bud Boswell all assisted Gessner McCorvey in holding the regular Democratic line in 1940. By 1948 they would all be Dixiecrats.

As legendary political scientist V. O. Key Jr. noted, the greatest asset of the southern Bourbons was their highly developed political skill.[89] It was an acumen that tapped into the cultural fabric of the South to repeatedly turn their numerical minority into a ruling majority. Central in this transformation was the ability of the privileged to define *southern* interests as *their* interests, to make *cultural* survival synonymous with their survival, and to wrap the whole package with a red, white, and blue stars-and-bars bow that equated patriotism to the southern nation with the health and even ennoblement of capital. To this end, the Bourbons shrilly derided "class warfare" whenever they could, this "business baiting and setting class against class" that was becoming so much a part of the new national Democratic Party under the New Deal. Increasingly in their rhetoric, they tied together social legislation and labor unrest, white supremacy and an extreme form of laissez-faire.[90] For maximum popular resonance the critical component was race:

> In seven years Roosevelt . . . has drawn to himself the city gang, the hoodlum and the bum . . . New York negro[es] . . . [and] Jew[s]. . . . All right, Southerners, if that is the thing you like, then vote for your Roosevelt. . . . The Democratic Party in the South . . . limit[ed] . . . to the white race . . . the right of selective association as . . . constitutional right . . . is doomed. It can not survive a third term. . . . Franklin D. Roosevelt sent Jr. to Chicago to be photographed arm in arm with negroes . . . sent Mrs. Roosevelt to dine with the Pullman porters [and] to invite . . . over 400 negro housewives to the White House for afternoon tea. . . . What chance has the frail boundary of tradition when this dominant family demands that it be abolished and the South is filled with Lister Hills . . . [and other] Benedict Arnolds . . . to rubber stamp his wishes; . . . [when] pinks and radicals [are] in high place and favor in Washington, [and] public and private morals have suffered the fate of the Supreme Court and the Democratic Party? . . . God pity the South for the failure of its Democratic leaders in the crisis.[91]

Send Every Damn One of Them Back to Africa

For hurt and disillusioned white southerners, the most powerful symbol of all that was wrong with the New Deal became, curiously enough, a single woman. While black Americans regarded Franklin Roosevelt as a fair and compassionate man who included them in his plans to get the country moving again, they viewed the First Lady in categorically different terms. She was a friend and an advocate. Eleanor became, increasingly throughout her husband's four terms, *the symbol* of white liberal sympathy on racial matters. Through countless acts of racial equality—large and small—Eleanor Roosevelt won an admiration and affection from black Americans that had previously been shown to perhaps only Abraham Lincoln.

In the South, though, Eleanor's predilections toward racial equality made her the ultimate symbol of the debasement of what had begun as a noble and necessary effort to relieve titanic economic disaster. A Civilian Conservation Corps and National Youth Administration in which blacks played visible roles were bad enough.[92] The industrial unionism associated with a communist-inspired and un-Christian CIO, given aid and comfort by New Deal labor laws, was even worse. But a First Lady consorting with black women at White House teas, allowing herself to be escorted by black male ROTC cadets, and resigning membership in the Daughters of the American Revolution (DAR) because a black singer was denied entrance to their national concert hall—it was all just too much.[93]

As white southerners found themselves drifting further and further away from FDR and the New Deal, they increasingly located the source of their unease as Eleanor. By the time her husband died, Mrs. Roosevelt had become the very personification of southern white cultural estrangement from the New Deal and, increasingly, from the Democratic Party itself. She was the ultimate defiler—a modern-day carpetbagger in a suffragette's dress—a rather grotesque combination. Her misuse of the highest unelective office in the land was a scandal headed toward outrage destined for disaster. It was a violently offensive and perverse attempt at coup: the pollution of the nation's morals, the abolition of its most cherished ideals, and the desecration of its most sacred customs. It was colossal, and it was a debauch. It could all end only in rot and ruin.

Accordingly, white southerners attacked Eleanor on a number of different but related fronts corresponding, roughly, to the areas in which her activities most clearly challenged regional norms: race, politics, religion, patriotism, morality, ethnicity, and gender relations. In doing so, socially conservative southerners fostered the growing sectional rapprochement between neo-Kluxer and neo-Bourbon—a union that would eventually lead toward partisan realignment for the South—because Eleanor Roosevelt's impieties themselves straddled the line between the racial and the economic.

For some, Eleanor represented an American "Eve," leading a good and pure Adam away from his natural inclination to do the right thing. In the process, she was working a profound disservice not only to her husband but to the whole Democratic Party, which had always stood for the preservation of the tabernacle of white supremacy.

For others, Eleanor herself was the source of black impudence and unrest. As black males returned home from war only to find themselves thrust back into a second-class status—and as black females increasingly felt their oats as needed members of the home front's working class—African Americans showed increased assertiveness and a newfound resistance to the old harness of racial inferiority. For a huge number of southern whites, Eleanor was the cause. The sexual aspect of this liberation—growing independence among black domestic help to be specific—was a sign of things to come. It could only mean the complete rollback of southern racial and sexual ways, as well as the corruption of traditional economic arrangements between the races. Again, Eleanor was to blame. All the more because she was an "unruly woman" herself who embarrassed her husband, did not know "her place," refused to defer to his authority as the God-ordained head of the household, and obviously had complete disregard for the gravity and sanctity of the wall between white women and black men. All of this—defiance of segregation, female submissiveness, class hierarchy, and traditional morality—meant that the First Lady embodied a grave challenge to the accepted forms of Calvinist religion and patriotism that undergirded the southern status quo itself.

In sum, Eleanor Roosevelt represented the ultimate threat to southern culture. Her meddling was no mere irritant, no simple legal, political, or policy matter, and it was not to be confronted as such. It was a clear and present danger to the dominant and conservative status quo so deeply entwined with the South itself—hence the intensity of the cultural reflex against her. Eleanor Roosevelt was repugnant because, at root, she was a cultural enemy, a threat to the continued existence of civilization—of a whole "southern way of life."

Some southerners tried to rein in the First Lady by appealing to the continued health and vitality of the Democratic Party in Dixie. "I have been a Democrat all of my life," one lawyer apprised the president, "but your and Mrs. Roosevelt's 'nigger' activities . . . have set me wholeheartedly against you." "I could never vote for Mr. Roosevelt," another southerner agreed, "because I cannot tolerate *Mrs. Roosevelt*" (italics added).[94] Folks were for Roosevelt in Alabama, a Lister Hill constituent warned the senator, "but not for Mrs. R." Her endorsement of black rights was a "disgusting . . . affront to Alabama folks, women especially." Indeed, Eleanor's racially liberal activities were a "costly price to pay for your good husband," a disenchanted Florida woman warned the First Lady. A woman from Quinton, Alabama, wrote simply: "You are hurting him very much by what you are doing."[95]

The irony was considerable as concerns gender. Eleanor—the very embodiment of strong, independent womanhood—was resented by southern white women for being too liberal, too outspoken, and too much of a threat to established ways. Race and sex were central to this reaction. Eleanor, by her unhidden advocacy of black equality, frightened white women (and men) in the South, people who had been reared on the milk of indelible regional myths associated with male supremacy, black uppitiness, black rape, and the necessity of the lynch knot.

Nor was this paradox exceptionally new. While the South had its Jesse Daniel Ameses and its Julia Tutwilers and Hallie Farmers, it also had multitudes of women who conformed totally to the Social Darwinist tenets of female (and black) submissiveness and the maintenance of rigid and interrelated social hierarchies.[96] Calvinist and conservative theology underlay much of this—and gave it so much of its power. And while women like Jesse Daniel Ames fought against the popular excuse of protecting white womanhood as a pretext for mob violence, women Klan leaders of the 1920s like Mabel Jones West morphed into the most virulent critics of the New Deal. Because, for them, race trumped class—or anything else. White supremacy meant the protection of women meant social order. Any threat to this arrangement—even economic and governmental reform that crossed the line into the land of racial egalitarianism (no matter how modestly)—meant cultural oblivion.

Some creative Alabama whites tried to combine criticism of the First Lady with education and partisan warnings. What people in Dixie think of the way the president and his wife "[are trying to] force the negro on the Southerner, your social reforms," an outraged Alabamian explained, was causing more disunity and race hatred in the South than ever before. "You both seem to have forgotten" that the South votes solidly Democratic, "but I don't think you will find it that way in future elections . . . unless you change your attitude and stick up for us for a change."[97]

Eleanor Roosevelt's many activities as First Lady clearly challenged southern racial conventions. During the 1930s she accepted invitations to speak to the Urban League and numerous black conferences, lunched with NAACP executive secretary Walter White on the White House patio, and posed for photos with African Americans all over the country. She supported a federal anti-lynch law and repeal of the poll tax, and worked tirelessly with black activists and white liberals to chip away at the walls of racial apartheid in the South. The First Lady counted among her friends in Alabama alone white Montgomery liberals Aubrey Williams and Clifford and Virginia Durr, black Pullman porter and civil rights leader E. D. Nixon, and Jewish communist Joseph Gelders. In 1938, she played a leading role in helping Gelders and Virginia's Lucy Randolph Mason get the SCHW off the ground by arranging an audience with the president and support from among her vast network of like-minded racial and economic liberals. And at the conference she defied Bull Connor's enforcement of Birmingham's Jim Crow ordinance by dramatically moving her chair into the center aisle between blacks and whites, an act one delegate remembered as "a glorious moment."[98]

In doing so, the First Lady exposed herself as public enemy no. 1 to the forces of reaction wherever they resided, even in the U.S. Congress. In 1939 Mississippi senator Theodore Bilbo, an early supporter of the New Deal, advocated a bill to expatriate every black person in America to Africa and later suggested on the floor of the Senate that the First Lady be sent along with them as their "queen." "I am a real friend of the Negro," Bilbo quipped. "I am making arrangements to send every damn one of them back to Africa."[99]

As early as 1936, the conglomeration of business and racial rightists that met at Macon, Georgia, in opposition to the New Deal made sure to provide every delegate with an issue of *Georgia Women's World* featuring (in the words of publicity director Vance Muse) the First Lady "going to some nigger meeting, with two escorts, niggers, on each arm."[100] To be sure an ugly racial prejudice seethed at the core of much of the South's conservative resentment toward Mrs. Roosevelt. Many whites considered blacks to be children. A Selma woman objected to Eleanor because African Americans "[are] like a mule, [they] can't stand good treatment and behave." Still others found Roosevelt liberalism repellent because, as one Texan explained, blacks "are not two jumps ahead of an ape."[101]

African Americans who exhibited behavior that was not suitably deferential, according to the dictates of the southern caste system, came in for much attention—their "misbehavior" often being laid to the First Lady. For southern whites, poor manners ranged from refusing to step aside for whites on sidewalks and streetcars, addressing blacks as "Mr." or "Mrs.," looking white people in the eye—all the way to black GIs asking white coeds for dates and throwing them kisses.[102] Some blacks mocked white preachers and threatened to attack white people, a Black Belt Alabama woman complained. "They are nasty where before" Eleanor "they were so nice.... Now they run [around] like a bunch of wild animals."[103]

While bad manners could no doubt be found among black people, as they could among every race and region, white response constituted a kind of "blackification" of bad behavior that would have enduring resonance and momentous consequences. In such a mind-set, if an instance of poor behavior occurred involving white people, it was denounced simply as bad behavior. But if the perpetrators happened to be black, the same conduct found denunciation as bad *black* behavior. The tendency generated in many southern whites a fear that African Americans had somehow gotten out of control, out of their place, thanks to racial liberals like Eleanor Roosevelt, and were preparing to run roughshod over regional folkways. Yet at root, much of the discontent fused anxieties with the southern economic status quo as well as the racial and cultural. "Bad behavior" among blacks included the refusal to work on farms or in domestic service for the pittance customarily offered when alternative work existed at higher wages in businesses and factories once World War II began. A 1942 internal FBI report confirmed the severity of the situation: the race situation is "on the lips of every businessman" in

Birmingham. If Mrs. Roosevelt were not curbed, the FBI report continued, "the [U]nion [itself] is imperiled."[104]

The Most Dangerous Woman in America

If such alarmism could be found in the calm confines of J. Edgar Hoover's bureau, there is little wonder why the disquiet descended into a kind of regional paranoia. Perhaps the best example of this development was the conviction among many otherwise rational southerners that the South was being taken over by "Eleanor Clubs."

According to legend, the clubs—also known as the Daughters, Sisters, and Royal House of Eleanor—were directly traceable to the First Lady. Born out of the creation of wartime employment opportunities that took black domestics out of white homes, the clubs allegedly proposed installing a white woman in every kitchen by Christmas. Southern white women might not understand the gravity of Adolf Hitler, Commission on Interracial Cooperation (CIC) director Will Alexander remarked with evident chauvinism, but they "certainly recognized what a crisis the loss of a cook is." Rumors about the clubs dictated that the black maid perform some act of interracial intimacy, such as bathing in the family tub or eating with the family. Women across the South felt worried enough to write the Roosevelts directly.[105]

Frank Daniels, editor of the *Raleigh News and Observer,* was so alarmed that he asked his brother Jonathan, the North Carolina New Dealer, for help: "I know you are in with all of the pinkeys and liberals tied up with advancement for the Negro race, but people are frightened." Despite widespread belief in the clubs, a flat denial by the First Lady, and even an investigation by Hoover's FBI, the only evidence ever produced about the clubs resided in the imagination of the white South.[106]

The "uppitiness" of black domestics was symptomatic of Eleanor Roosevelt's swimming against the racial tide that, for the white South, represented a real danger to the accepted norms of moral, economic, religious, and sexual behavior—all of which were entangled. Of these, sex was perhaps the most sensitive. Demagogues such as the Mississippi New Dealer Theodore Bilbo put the issue in terms any white southerner could understand: "I am willing to take the negro as a Christian brother, but damned if I can take him as a son-in-law." When Eleanor appeared at a war canteen's interracial dance, the white South went into paroxysms. Condemning the First Lady's behavior with "all the intensity of my soul," outraged Louisiana congressman Charles McKenzie feared the act would "mongrelize the white race." "You are the most dangerous woman in America today," an enraged woman declared.

Mixing black males and white females in any capacity "always leads to intermarriage" and litters of mulattoes. A young southern girl branded the First Lady a "negro lover" and a "mighty sorry" one at that.[107]

Southern whites tried different tacks. Some took the pedantic approach, explaining things from their point of view and expressing their confidence that—if she only knew the real situation—Mrs. Roosevelt would stay in Washington, bake cookies, and host tours of the White House. "[I am] a great admirer of both you and the President," one wrote, but "believe me, you are playing with fire."[108] Others around the South (mostly women) earnestly instructed the First Lady that white people were the best friends blacks had, making painstaking efforts to uplift blacks "mentally and morally" and giving them plenty of food. There is little question that a good deal of such sentiment was sincere, if patently misguided. "We do not mistreat the negro down here," one elaborated, "but we have to keep them in their place else they will rule us."[109]

Others tried harsher methods. Some appealed to the men in Eleanor's life to rein her back in to her proper place. For whites in the South, the First Lady's activities were so alarming precisely because they cut across the pillars of traditional society that were themselves closely connected. The First Lady was an open and vocal advocate of economic reforms, but her racial message was obvious. In speaking out so boldly, Eleanor, by word and deed, furnished a strong alternative to traditional female submissiveness, acceptance of supposed inferiority, and gender roles. A Georgia couple actually asked the president to "confine" the First Lady to the White House while a Florida editor suggested she should "have her tongue tied for the duration." Frank Daniels proposed that Eleanor be "kept at home and made to shut her mouth" while another distressed white southerner appealed to the ultimate male authority figure of the time, J. Edgar Hoover: "Can't the F.B.I. shut her up?"[110]

Some compared the First Lady's unorthodox views to treason, impugning her sense of patriotism during a time of war. Whites urged FDR to check the "fifth-column activities" of the First Lady and ventured that the Founding Fathers would be shocked she had resigned her DAR membership over segregation. For a great many in the white South, issues of race and patriotism had been intimately bound up for centuries in a manner that powerfully reinforced the tenet of white supremacy. Black people "[want us] to hand over what the white man has fought and bled for," a woman explained, but this was impossible. The country had been discovered and settled by white men and women. The framers had decided that white men should run the country, she continued, "not negro, Japanese, Chinese, Indian, or any other color."[111] "Who are you for, anyway," an Alabama woman brazenly asked. "If you cared anything about your country you would leave well enough alone on race" during the war. Eleanor's persistent efforts to "choke the Negro race down our throats" scandalized everyone who hewed to tradition and patriotism, that is, "all true Southerners."[112]

Religion had, perhaps, the strongest emotional pull of any subject in the South. While recent scholarship has claimed that the post-1954 religious reaction to *Brown v. Board of Education* was more enlightened than has been traditionally portrayed, it is clear that—as with organized labor—this interpretation must be tempered with the realization that there was a yawning chasm between the real and rhetorical tolerance of southern church leaders and much of their flocks.[113]

For a great many plain whites, folk concepts of religion actually buttressed rather than challenged regional conventions on racial supremacy. "No power on earth can change us," a sixty-eight-year-old Selma woman informed Eleanor, but "We are praying for you" to see the light, which could only be revealed "thru our savior if tis Gods will." A Mobile man was certain there was no way racial integration would work in the South: "You know the Bible says [blacks] are cursed, on account of Ham's looking on his father's nakedness, to be wood choppers and water carriers . . . servants" for the white race. Another woman was even more patient with the troublesome First Lady. Black people were brought over from Africa to be drawers of water and hewers of wood for whites, she repeated the biblical lesson. To this same "African savage, God gave them the richest country in the world and they never had sense enough to develop" it. During antebellum slavery blacks "got the best of food and plenty of it," and since that time whites in the South had taken blacks to their bosom, "into our homes as servants." There they continued to profit by association with whites and get the "benefit of the culture and refinement" of the white race. Blacks "really ought to be glad and thankful to God that the white man brought him over here and lifted him out of savagery," she informed the First Lady, instead of being ungrateful and challenging Dixie's established racial customs and patterns—including the old one of slavery.[114]

Mrs. Roosevelt's conduct was so shocking to the great majority of the South that it actually represented a deep cultural affront. Some refused to believe that a good person or a *white person* could be capable of such sacrilege. "I don't mean to be rude," one southern woman asked the First Lady, "but do you have colored blood in your family, as you seem to derive so much pleasure from associating with colored folks." For those who stopped short of questioning the racial lineage of the First Lady, there was no question about the effect her behavior was having. It was more than a bad example or inconvenience. It was a towering threat to the South's very "way of life."[115]

The white South, renowned for the formality of its manners, responded to the cultural threat of Eleanor Roosevelt by turning her into a leper. From an otherwise warm and congenial people, known the world over for the depth of their graciousness and hospitality, spewed a hostility and venom toward the First Lady unmatched in the era in its intensity or viciousness. "Honorable men and women, who in their personal lives are true to the rules of decency and character," recorded one startled southerner, "spread slanderous jokes and lies about her with icy malice." Many of the punch-lines, of course, involved interracial sex with the First Lady as a participant. Among well-to-do white people, on the steps of fashionable churches on Sunday mornings, one correspondent reported, a listener can commonly hear "a most callous and un-Christlike kind of talk" about Eleanor and black people. When the First Lady traveled to Salisbury, North Carolina, to speak at a black AME church she had to book a room at a motel because "no 'nice' home" would put her up.[116]

Because the First Lady's challenge was so foreign to their culture, white southerners understood it intuitively as an attack on that *culture* itself rather than a legalistic or policy challenge on discrete subjects such as voting, lynching, education, recreation, or the poll tax. The effect of this cultural conceptualization was at least threefold: it turned Eleanor Roosevelt into a modern-day damn Yankee and carpetbagger; it ratcheted up the intensity of the regional response to the interloper; and it provided justification for demanding sectional isolation and home rule on a virtual smorgasbord of topics—directly related to race and not. "You are the most poorly informed person I know of," a female critic informed Eleanor. "[W]e do not like meddling." First Lady or not, Eleanor had "no right to intrude upon the southern peoples rights and their freedom," another woman complained. No question about it, Eleanor should keep her "Nose out of Dixie Problems," agreed Hamner Cobbs of the *Greensboro Watchman* in Alabama's Black Belt.[117]

Proper morality and the economic expression of societal values loomed close by. "[Have these people] no regard for the traditions of the south or the culture of the white race?" an enraged Louisiana congressman asked. Did they "honestly believe that the white people of this nation have reached such a low point of moral and social decadence that they . . . are willing to accept all comers?"[118] The problems of the South should be "solved by southerners and not by people in Washington who know nothing of the problems," an Arkansan remarked in sounding the reasoning for racial laissez-faire that would soon be conjoined with southern laissez-faire on virtually any topic, particularly economics.[119]

Of course, if reason and calm entreaty did not do the trick, white southerners were prepared to take matters into their own hands—as they had since before 1861. "If these people have to," an Alabama woman warned Eleanor, they will "kill every negro in the South and any one who trys to stop them." The mayor of Eufaula, deep in Alabama's poor Wiregrass, wrote to likewise caution the First Lady that messing with southern racial customs would have only one result: bloodshed. In an afterthought the mayor assured her that "We people down here KNOW the Negro, his aspirations, prejudices and limitations. The GOOD negro . . . has no difficulty . . . from his white friends. . . . The BAD negro [does]."[120] A sixty-seven-year-old lifelong Democrat in the Alabama Black Belt damned the First Lady's activities as a slap in the face that would only lead to race riots and killings.[121]

New Deal columnist John Temple Graves—urbane and educated—agreed about the gravity of the Eleanor situation. Birmingham's most prominent families were all saying they were "going to have to get their guns out again," he reported. Much of the upset revolved around the absence of white male protection during the war. "When our soldier boys return home," a disconcerted young woman consoled herself, "the negroes will get the daylights knocked out of them. . . . We can always count on our boys."[122]

Eleanor Roosevelt engendered such intense emotions from southern whites because she represented an assault on cultural autonomy and a threat to the potential for its survival. Her transgressions were taken so seriously because the conservative culture itself and all that it represented were held in the most sacred esteem.

Yet the imposition to southern culture did not begin or end with the First Lady. She was a lightning rod; there can be no doubt about that. But once struck by the bolt of racial disaffection, the whole temple of southern Democracy was in trouble of catching fire and burning down. An Alabama woman explained the matter well to a president she longed to continue to support. "Now, my husband and I love you and believe you have done more than any President for our country," she wrote FDR, but on racial matters "we disagree with you and are deeply grieved" about it. The actions of both FDR and Eleanor on race would be "the sole reason" the South stepped away from the Democratic Party, she predicted. Some people in the South, she warned, "hate you and your wife as . . . they would a rattlesnake."[123]

7
The "Liberal South" and the Central Tragedy of Southern Politics

> The Democratic party in Alabama has as its motto "White Supremacy."...
> [N]othing will wreck [it] quicker in this State than any effort... to abolish segregation.
>
> —Frank M. Dixon

Scholars have been almost uniformly optimistic, even sanguine, in their estimations of the innate liberalism of the New Deal and World War II South. Some of this sentiment is the function of rational estimates of genuine and deeply held liberalism in spots. Yet much of it is also the product of wishful thinking. In fact, a good deal is the result of the rather uncritical acceptance of contemporary evaluations (and in some cases the momentary hopes) of the most complete, and thus unrepresentative, of the region's liberals. What is even more remarkable is that of all the southern states, Alabama has been most consistently pointed to by both historians and activists as *the most liberal* state of the liberal South during the period.

Some awfully good scholars have taken this tack. Consider the estimation of Wayne Flynt, an excellent historian who has so often been correct about so much in his varied writings:

> By the 1960s Alabama had become a state that seemed to epitomize opposition to the federal government. But in the 1940s and 1950s no state congressional delegation did more to expand federal powers to assist the nation's weakest and most vulnerable people.... Several informal polls of House members voted the Alabama delegation the best of any state. The state's congressional delegation was also one of the South's most liberal.... The answer lay in the long tradition of political dissent and populist protest, especially in north Alabama.... The New Deal encouraged the formation of unionism and produced strong popular loyalties among [Alabama's] small farmers, workers, even small businessmen. Federal patronage... further solidified reformers.... The

class-based liberalism of the 1930s and 1940s united black and white unionists who were experiencing common economic problems.[1]

Other very skilled historians have rendered similar judgments. Patricia Sullivan wisely acknowledged that the novel developments of the New Deal–World War II era "did not make the liberalization of the region's *political structure* inevitable." The analysis did, though, exhibit considerable empathy with the optimistic view of the most committed wartime southern liberals and their reality of an essentially "liberal South." It was a South replete with a genuine "liberal-labor realignment initiated by the New Deal."[2]

A number of contemporary observers, the most thorough liberals the region had to offer, voiced optimism about the South's liberalism during the 1940s. In retrospect it has been tempting for historians to interpret these moments of unguarded optimism as blanket statements as to the essential, enduring, and untapped liberalism of the region. For example, during the 1940s Alabama native Aubrey W. Williams, one of the most complete liberals to be found anywhere in the South, thought he saw a "bottom deep awakening . . . an unmistakable assertion of decency and a turning on people who live by exploiting hatred, religious bigotry, by trading in people's prejudices and fears." Fellow Alabamian Clifford Durr enunciated similar sentiments as did, briefly, the Florida novelist Lillian Smith.[3] Iowa native, U.S. vice president, and perhaps the age's most prophetic liberal Henry A. Wallace went further by declaring a "spirit of liberalism is abroad in the South." His tour of the region as a presidential candidate four years later would do much to correct this misplaced optimism. In 1944 the CIO's executive board under Philip Murray approved support of the Southern Conference for Human Welfare as engaged in work to expose and express "the true liberalism of our great southern states." Even black sociologist Ralph Bunche thought that southern whites were "slowly awakening to . . . the Negro diversion" and realizing that there are "more pressing [problems] than the black one."[4]

But no one went further than Clark Foreman and James Dombrowski of the SCHW in their report on the South submitted to Sidney Hillman's newly powerful CIO-PAC. For Foreman and Dombrowski, the reactionary South—the South of demagogy, conscience-free laissez-faire, and hidebound conservatism—was an illusion. "It spoke the loudest" because it had "the heaviest financial backing" and, thanks to a severely constricted ballot, "the advantage of a Congressional forum." But this reactionary echo chamber was not real. It reflected perhaps 20 percent of the true South while the vastly more populous "silent South" remained quiet largely because of the disfranchising mechanisms of the poll tax and the white primary.[5] Thus if the poll tax could be abolished, poor whites and blacks could formalize a natural alliance and join hands for the majority's liberal and progressive causes.

One of the leading historians of the period evaluated the report and its claims in positive terms, estimating that the growing unionization of the region, its generous bounty of federal monies from New Deal programs and war production, national CIO liberalism on race, and a poor white and black electorate disfranchised by the poll tax added up to a scenario that was bursting with possibilities for the liberation and ascendance of the South's true liberalism:

> The report explored the combination of developments that had created a window of opportunity in the South, an opening toward liberalism and political democratization. The nationalizing trends of the previous decade and the "logic of the South's economic development" drove it in a liberal direction. No other region had benefited more from the New Deal or from the infusion of federal dollars during the war. Industrial growth and federal activism supported the rapid growth of the labor movement, creating possibilities for new political alliances and constituencies. By 1944, union membership in the South reached 400,000 for the CIO and 1.8 million for the American Federation of Labor [AFL]. Beyond expanding the ranks of industrial unionism, the national CIO's firm stand against racial discrimination had created an arena for interracial action and had won the respect and support of black southerners, who composed one-third of the South's population. The efforts of organized labor and the progressivism of the New Deal also reinforced and complemented the growth of southern liberalism. By 1944 indigenous groups of progressive ministers, editors, educators, and writers were evident in communities throughout the region. . . . An organized campaign to enfranchise the disfranchised was essential to reaping the changes of the previous decade and resisting the . . . forces of economic and political reaction [that] remained entrenched.[6]

For activists of the time, and historians later, Alabama's inherent liberalism was the most impressive to be found anywhere in the region. Positive evaluation of the extent and character of the state's liberalism appeared on many fronts. Bibb Graves's Depression-era gubernatorial success was, according to historian William D. Barnard, proof that "the majority of the people of Alabama had placed progressive government first." According to this rather unquestioned view the state was neatly split between a liberal, class-based, north Alabama that was a "breeding ground for political dissidence" and a reactionary Black Belt that had been "the mainstay of political, economic, *and racial* conservatism since Reconstruction" (italics added).[7] The state's massive love affair with the 1920s Klan was explained away as a mistake—quickly corrected when the most "prominent politicians" broke with the order because of its violence and "call[ed] for measures to curb its activities." Bibb Graves, perhaps, did not "take as strong a stand against the Klan as many would have liked," but he did come to his senses and "act to end the 'reign of terror' that existed in some counties, and . . . resigned from the organization in 1928 for the good of the state."[8] For J. Mills Thornton III, Alabama's 1920s experience with the KKK was—rather than something to be embarrassed about—actually the nursery that incubated the state's liberalism of the 1930s and 1940s.[9] The gubernatorial administration of Chauncey Sparks, elected in 1942, "disappointed many anti–New Dealers" because he sponsored tax reform that "placed much of the burden on corporations, particularly utilities, and expanded social services," Wayne Flynt wrote. "Some liberals such as Charlie Dobbins liked Sparks and considered him [to be] a genuine progressive."[10]

Liberal journalists of the time gushed over the Alabama example. Helen Fuller of the *New Republic* asked: "Why is it that Alabama in the last generation has produced so many more liberally minded men than any of her neighboring states?"[11] Washington, D.C., columnist Stewart Alsop flatly declared Alabama "a liberal oasis"—an estimation that has been repeated with pride many times since by scholars and others understandably a little defensive about the shellacking the state has taken in a national press far more diligent in cataloguing the South's shortcomings than its own.[12] In response Wayne Flynt titled his chapter on 1940s and 1950s politics and society in a popular Alabama history text "The Flowering of Alabama Liberalism." Mills Thornton, an equally skilled historian, called the period "a golden age" of liberalism.[13] John Egerton regarded Alabama as "progressive, forward-looking, essentially liberal" during the 1940s and puzzled over the 1960s image of the state: "[W]hat in the world happened? . . . What happened there?"[14]

In an important sense, everything these academics and columnists wrote was true. Lister Hill *was* a liberal beacon who did much to win federal aid to the state. So did John Sparkman. The Senate duo successfully fought for federal programs that constructed hospitals, public housing, provided antipolio vaccine, and fostered medical research. Alabama's House delegation, particularly north Alabama's Bob Jones, Carl Elliott, and Kenneth Roberts, along with Hill's (and their own) political mentor, Marc Ray "Foots" Clement, supported the New Deal, the TVA, and federal programs for the small farmers and workers that made up their constituencies. So did north Alabama congressman Albert Rains and Governor Bibb Graves. Sparkman himself came from a modest farm background that did much to acquaint him with the plight of the South's poor working people. He had shoveled coal to get through law school.[15] Alabama *did* vote for the New Deal and the Democratic Party. The idea of a kind of federal activism *was* accepted and even embraced among much of the state's population. All of that was true.

But certain crucial questions remain, questions that should be kept in mind throughout these several chapters on the New Deal and World War II. What was the quality of Alabama's liberalism? Was it a fundamentally liberal worldview, or was it more a manifestation of the most human, yet staggering, form of hypocrisy: a willingness to accept federal monies and aid and "programs" only when the majority of the state's people were in dire economic straits or when the assistance found its way into the hands of corporate recipients? Was this liberalism really found among "the people," or was there a deep and massive gulf between the progressive outlook of the state's congressional delegation and the increasingly restive masses that were happy with economic goodies but certainly not social change? How important was the fact that this population increasingly began to look askance at the delegation as proficient in attracting appropriations but weak and ineffective in safeguarding the integrity of sectional customs? Was the apparent acceptance of federal activism a true cultural attribute, or was it a temporary expedient that would not carry over into anything remotely impinging on reform for the broader status quo? Was the "liberalism" one that had true staying power, or was it a narrow economic variant that would crumble quickly and from within as soon as the term became more associated with the deeply rooted beliefs of the people on race rather than economics?[16]

Was the liberalism one that could last—or was in any sense innate—or was it a fleeting, ephemeral kind that would blow away the moment it became identified in the popular imagination as a threat to the culture's deep-seated conservative shibboleths on a host of matters tightly interwound with race: patriarchy, ethnic purity, proper religion, patriotism and civic virtue, the federal relationship and, yes, class hierarchies? Was it a deep and abiding progressive outlook, or was it a shallow strain, narrowly defined as the temporary willingness to accept federal aid, disaster relief, or business boosterism courtesy of Uncle Sam? Was the South, itself, a region that would continue to give logical allegiance to a federal government that had provided massive New Deal and wartime investment, or was it a place where less rational, emotional considerations would eventually hold sway?

Chapter 7

The Great Arsenal of the South

World War II brought massive change to the home front, and perhaps no region was more affected than the South. Of the enormous military production expenditures that found their way South, over half went to just three states: Alabama, Texas, and Louisiana. Aircraft manufacturing plants sprang up in Birmingham, Dallas, New Orleans, Tulsa, Nashville, and Miami. Navy and private shipyards crackled to life in Newport News, Norfolk, Charleston, Houston, and Orange, Texas. New or expanded yards sprang up in Mobile and Chickasaw, Alabama, Houston, Brunswick, Orange, and Beaumont, Texas, New Orleans, Tampa, Jacksonville, Panama City, Pascagoula, and Wilmington. The world's largest ordnance, explosives, and powder plant, a du Pont facility, opened its doors in Childersburg, just forty-five minutes south of Birmingham. The world's largest chemical warfare plant began production two hours north of Birmingham in the rapidly growing hamlet of Huntsville. The uranium for "Fat Man" and "Little Boy," the atomic bombs used in 1945, was produced just slightly to the north, at the Oak Ridge nuclear facility in Tennessee.[17]

Satellite industries and manufacturing facilities grew by leaps and bounds. The Tennessee Coal and Iron Company (TCI, a subsidiary of U.S. Steel) operated mostly in Jefferson County, Alabama's most populous county, and alone increased its workforce from 7,000 to 30,000. By contrast, the whole iron and steel workforce of Houston, Texas, a distant second, was only 18,600. About half of them black, these and other steelworkers labored in a catalogue of Alabama mills—including Republic Steel, Sloss-Sheffield, Woodward Iron, Connors Steel, O'Neal Steel, J. I. Case Company, and Alabama Cast Iron and Pipe Company. Donald Comer's Avondale Mills used one-fifth of the state's cotton crop, employed 7,000 men and women, and ran ten textile mills in Alabama's northern and east-central counties. Alabama's Benjamin Russell Mills became the number-one producer of military and athletic uniforms in America. By 1943 Mobile's Alabama Dry Dock and Shipbuilding Company and Chickasaw's Gulf Shipbuilding Corporation employed 40,000 people and produced, on average, a ship a week for the U.S. Navy.[18]

War production stretched and tore at the capacities of Alabama's towns and cities and created new boundaries. Birmingham, the hardest-hit city in America during the Great Depression, took the new name the "great arsenal of the South" and watched as its factories belched smoke around the clock. TCI opened new tin-plating, sheet-forging, and coal mine facilities in Ensley, Fairfield, and Short Creek. O'Neal Steel specialized in steel fabrications for bombs, Bechtel-McCone Aircraft Modification Company outfitted half of the B-29 bombers used in the war, and Birmingham's Robert I. Ingalls started a huge cargo ship building plant just across the Mississippi line in Pascagoula. Massive military installations employed thousands of civilians: the Anniston Ordnance Depot and Fort McClellan in north Alabama, Montgomery's Gunter and Maxwell Air Force bases, Mobile's Brookley Army Air Corps Field, and Selma's Craig Air Force Base.[19] Just past the Alabama border, on the Florida Panhandle, were Eglin—the largest air force installation in the world—and the massive Pensacola Naval Works.

Along with such rapid expansion came deep changes in southern society and its workforce. With so many men overseas, women responded to the patriotic call to enter the factory. Half the workforce at Mobile's Brookley Air Field was female, as was half the du Pont explosives plant at Childersburg. The 500-person village struggled to cope with the sudden influx of 14,000 new workers, while 300 families lost their farms as the federal government appropriated 32,000 acres of land. At Birmingham's Bechtel-McCone, and at the Huntsville and Redstone arsenals to the north, women made up 25 to 40 percent of the labor force. Union density jumped from 16 to 25 percent in Alabama during the 1940s (meaning that one in every four Alabama workers was a member of a labor union), and the state's absolute number of union workers leaped 263 percent, from 64,000 to 168,000. Mobile County was swamped by an estimated 90,000 new residents in just three years as its municipal, housing, street, and sanitation facilities were overflowed. Between 1940 and 1944, Mobile's population virtually tripled to 201,000 as a *Washington Post* writer reported that the easy-going, French- and Spanish-influenced city was flooded with thousands of "primitive, illiterate backwoods people . . . hostile, defiant, suspicious, and terrified." Mobile's black population also grew by 17,000. Novelist John Dos Passos described the port city as a wreck, with gutters, garbage cans, and sidewalks overrun, youth gangs on robbing sprees, teenage girls, young sailors, and war workers cavorting freely, a local high school built for 2,200 students housing almost 3,700 in two shifts, and the city's police force of just nineteen officers completely at a loss.[20]

Yet perhaps the most critical change that accompanied the dislocations was the growing number of black faces in what had traditionally been white male jobs. The increased presence of white women, along with blacks and labor unions on Deep South shop floors, provided the kindling for what had the potential to combust into a conflagration of revolutionary proportions. Participation in the New Deal and military service, increased educational opportunities provided by the GI Bill, and expanded horizons from overseas travel contributed—along with black factory work—to a new attitude among many African Americans, especially toward the federal government. A leading black Tuskegee attorney remembered that blacks began to look to the federal government when local and state officials failed to provide the basic services they believed all American citizens should have.[21]

Key among the wartime changes was upward pressure on southern wages—including black agricultural wages. Labor shortages, the 1936 and 1938 federal minimum-wage laws, growing unionization, and the absorption of southern workers into an increasingly national labor market all tended to push wages up in a region that prided itself on low wages, worker docility, and muted labor activism.[22]

No sector of the southern economy was more radically affected during World War II than agriculture. New Deal farm policies pushed tenants off the land while wartime industrial opportunities in northern and southern cities exercised a powerful pull. Mechanization, crop diversification, and land consolidation resulted. Alabama produced nearly a tenth of the nation's cotton in 1940 while the war years saw sizable increases in livestock, poultry, dairy, pulpwood, peanut, and soybean production. The number of farms declined, but their size grew dramatically as people left the countryside for the city, and large planters gobbled up the remains.[23]

In the countryside, though, tensions simmered as large planters coming out of economic depression increasingly chafed under New Deal agricultural policies and bitterly resented the growing mobility of, and upward wage pressure on, black and poor-white farm labor. Once a Negro left the state for the greener pastures of northern labor, "the Yankees should be made to keep him up there and take care of him," white Alabamians felt. "If we can get along without him now, we can damn sure . . . do without him then."[24]

The "Great Melding" and the Scourge of the FEPC

Just as the competition, crowding, and smoldering tensions of the 1920s had contributed to a rejuvenated Ku Klux Klan, the new wartime period also nurtured an internal traditionalist reaction to the fast pace of changes imposed from without. The increasingly charged atmosphere lent itself to the fortunes of several key individuals who would come to play leading roles in the state's postwar political wars—three in particular who would eventually serve as the ruling triumvirate of Alabama's powerful Dixiecrat Party: Frank M. Dixon, Gessner T. McCorvey, and Horace C. Wilkinson.

Even more important than their individual careers, the conservative Alabama backlash to wartime change prompted by national and international expedients would highlight in bold relief the "Great Melding" of economic conservatives and racial conservatives into an irresistible alliance that crossed class lines and threatened to redefine the way politics was done in the South. Of course, this trend had already appeared in reaction to the New Deal, and even to some extent earlier, but in the wartime period it would accelerate and gather significant mass. Old class-based differences would fade into the background and a pan-southern white unity that crossed socioeconomic lines would come into its own—one with clear portents for the future political direction of the region into third-party protest movements and, ultimately, a new Republican ascendance.

The melding process was evident in the factional rapprochement that grouped Dixon and McCorvey, consummate representatives of planter-industrialist privilege, with their old plain-white nemesis, Horace Wilkinson. But it was, perhaps, most evident in the region's reaction to Executive Order 8802 and the 1941 establishment of the Fair Employment Practices Committee (FEPC).

Won from a reluctant Franklin Roosevelt by A. Philip Randolph and other black activists as the price of calling off a wartime march on Washington, the compromise was not without blemish. But what the FEPC lacked in teeth it more than made up for in symbolic meaning. The new law called for federal intervention in private businesses to ensure racially fair employment and included the cancellation of federal contracts as a possible enforcement power. As much as any New Deal program, the FEPC put the lie to the age-old southern paternalist fiction of being concerned about the economic advancement of blacks but opposed only to their political and social equality. Here was an opportunity for the self-proclaimed "best friends" of the black race to make good on their legion of contentions that they wanted to see African Americans advance economically while remaining in a separate caste channel.[25]

More, though, the failure of southern moderates (not to mention conservatives) to get behind the FEPC underlined the *impossibility* of severing race and social equality in any clean sense from economic advancement and class issues. That is, if southern blacks were to ever truly advance *economically* out of the rut to which they had been consigned there had to be access to what had been reserved as white-only jobs. There could not be true economic improvement without some measure of social equality. Race and class were endlessly and intimately entwined in the South—with each other—and with the other most notable pillars of a society dedicated to upholding a deeply conservative and stratified status quo: religious orthodoxy, patriarchal gender relations, narrow moral conventions, ethnic purity, and an unquestioning patriotic creed. White paternalists and moderates could not hold the economic apart from the racial in the past any more than historians can do in the present.

The mixed racial and economic nature of the FEPC threat was obvious in the reaction it engendered. Industrialists and businessmen took the lead. The Southern States Industrial Council (SSIC), representing six thousand smaller industrial councils and large agricultural interests across the South, furiously fought the FEPC in order to—as they put it—preserve the "traditions . . . principles of living, and . . . philosophies of life . . . of the Southland." The response of the SSIC, which had been founded in 1933 by Alabamian Robert Rast Cole—a virulent anti–New Dealer, president of Monsanto Chemicals, and a director of the Associated Industries of Alabama—revealed the industrialist affinity for cheap black labor, but it also demonstrated a rapidly maturing awareness of the benefits of winning over poor-white support for its economic program by stoking fears about the debasement of white supremacy. New Orleans businessman and National Association of Manufacturers director John U. Barr—soon to be a regional leader of the third-party "Byrd for President" movement, the Dixiecrats, and later the White Citizens Councils—served as vice president of the SSIC. As part of its campaign against the FEPC, the SSIC widely distributed the pamphlet "Shall We Be Ruled by Whites or Blacks?"—a diatribe by Mississippi congressman and fallen New Dealer John E. Rankin.[26] On the floor of the U.S. House, Rankin spoke about the FEPC: "Oh! This is the beginning of a communistic dictatorship. . . . Mr. Speaker, we never reduced the Negro to slavery. We elevated him from the position of savage to that of servant." In fact, the SSIC had even more immediately been a reaction to the 1933 National Recovery Act. Tennessee's John Edgerton, president of the SSIC and the NAM, openly lauded the South's competitive advantage in having a segregated labor system that kept wages depressed for all workers but especially praised the system's effectiveness in preserving "labor's racial purity" in Dixie. An SSIC member and Alabama Paper Company representative elaborated: "Colored labor has always been paid less than whites and for good reason."[27]

In Alabama, Governor Frank Dixon seized on the FEPC as an issue to catapult himself into the state's brightest political spotlight. In doing so, Dixon did much to contribute to a quickening tradition of Alabama governors adopting the panoply of regional champion against outside assaults on southern cultural traditions.

In July 1942, in a dramatic announcement, Dixon rejected a lucrative contract with the federal government to have Alabama convicts produce 1.75 million yards of osnaburg cloth for the U.S. Army. In a letter that was reproduced in nearly every newspaper in the South, Dixon spelled out the class basis behind much of the racial circling of wagons in his state and buttressed the melding logic with emotional reasons of patriotic necessity. In the war emergency, Dixon explained, every American desired maximum production, and the only way to achieve this was to allow those experienced in manufacturing to "run their plants in the way they have found best," to rely on the captains of industry, their ability, and their judgment. Failure to hew to the most sacred postulates of business omniscience—to elect instead to intrude in a racial way in employment in the South, with social issues and attempted reforms—could only result in resentment and "confusion" and in slowing down wartime production at a critical moment.[28] In other words, as conservatives had long argued, unrepressed laissez-faire equaled patriotism and progress. Governmental oversight undermined the national interest.

Big Mules and the Black Belt Bourbons responded with an avalanche of praise for the Alabama governor. Fed up with federal "economic dictatorship" and "bureaucratic creature[s]" such as the War Labor Board, planters and industrialists feted Dixon's southern revolt in the most unrepressed fashion.[29] Heartfelt congratulations flowed into the governor's office from nearly every heavyweight business figure in the state, and many from Alabama's sister states. Much of it came from those of wealth who would soon form the vanguard of opposition to both the federal government *and* the Democratic Party because of its growing racial and economic liberalism. A number would become pivotal figures in Alabama's participation in the Dixiecrat Revolt: Frank P. Samford, president of Liberty National Life, Donald Comer of the Avondale Mills, Dothan banker Wallace D. Malone, Hamner Cobbs of the *Greensboro Southern Watchman*, Horace Hall of the *Dothan Eagle*, materials magnate Winton Blount, union-busting attorney Borden Burr, and constitutional lawyer Horace Wilkinson. Third-party leader R. DuPont Thompson and University of Alabama scientist and advanced white supremacist Roland M. Harper added their enthusiastic approval. A good number of those most pleased by Dixon's stand against what they perceived as the racial *and* economic encroachment of the federal government would eventually gravitate to a new Republican Party grounded on the melding of the race/class concern for its power in the South, notable among them: Wallace Malone, Winton Blount, Frank Samford, Hamner Cobbs, Horace Hall, SSIC director Thomas McGough, Fred D. Renneker, the Munger family, Birmingham auto salesman Don Drennen, and Marshall County's former Populist and GOP leader Oliver Day Street. In the tidal wave of approbation for Dixon's stand, it was easy to lose sight of the fading class lines in deference to the racial imperative: the close familiarity with which oligarchs such as Montgomery banker

General R. E. Steiner and Geneva's Bud Boswell moved together with former plain-white tribunes like Horace Wilkinson and W. A. Sanford, as well as the moderate Birmingham journalist James A. Chappell.[30]

As the prevailing orthodoxy on regional mores went, the class concerns of plain Alabamians, while not being purged completely, were to be suppressed and pushed down to a muted level—and in many cases replaced with an economic conservatism that included racial overtones about proper black conduct in employment and the economy. At the same time, ironically, the class interests of Alabama's biggest movers were only fortified by the willingness of plain whites and their representatives to bury their economic grievances in sectional, moral, and cultural allegiance to the god of white supremacy.

Little or no attempt was made to hide the racial essence of the appeal to a cultural closing of white ranks. In later decades, after the modern civil rights movement made headway, much would be done in response by economic conservatives to create a system of code words and dog whistles to insulate their message from public denunciation on the grounds of bigotry and intolerance. In 1942 and 1943, such exigencies did not exist.

Rotary clubs, Lions dens, Kiwanis clubs, and chambers of commerce around the state—wherever businessmen gathered—openly rejoiced in the race-based defense of commerce's prerogative to run their companies as they saw fit, without the federal government having a word to say. Organized labor was not perfect in its racial record, but its shortcomings were a far cry from the blatant manipulation of racial prejudice by southern industrialists and businessmen. "[Dixie will take a] decidedly backward step if it does not do everything possible to maintain the 'supremacy of the white race,'" the executive committee of the Mobile Chamber of Commerce resolved in support of Governor Dixon.[31] The Talladega Chamber of Commerce also unanimously approved Dixon's defiance of the federal government. A Birmingham electric company businessman estimated that Dixon had performed one of the most outstanding acts on behalf of white supremacy "since Reconstruction days." Another businessman tied government intervention on employment to the steady decline of the spirit of individualism and self-reliance in America on display since the New Deal, marked by the disgrace of farmers, workers, and dairymen seeking (and accepting) government assistance. "All of this... can be borne... however [except]... abolition of the color line."[32]

In order to bolster their cause with plain-white support, the economically conservative and privileged tapped into a key psychological factor: the very human desire to feel superior to *someone* about *something*. In the South the tendency was particularly pronounced due to the difficult heritage of privation and suffering among much of the region's poor and working-class people.

But in giving way to this weakness in a racial sense, poor whites also signed up to support a whole raft of interrelated conservative cultural orthodoxy, not only on race but also on gender, religion, morality, patriotism, and especially economics (much of which they did not fully understand). In effect, indulging white supremacy undermined the plain-white capacity to engage in class dissent in the South, something that would cripple the long-term prospects for a viable economic liberalism to flourish, or even exist, in the region.

The elite strategy was not new. It had been used to divide poor whites in Alabama during Reconstruction, the independent wars of the 1880s, the Populist moment, and in 1901. Nor would it end with World War II. The Dixiecrats, George Wallace, and eventually the modern Republican Party would all profit handsomely in the South by exploiting the racial—and moral—chauvinism of plain whites and by employing a "divide and conquer" strategy to impede the possibility and potency of biracial class cooperation.

Some of the South's most highly developed liberals realized that the poor-white inferiority complex could work as a distinct liability. Virginia Durr blamed Alabama's racial violence on "poor white rednecks" who were incredibly "ignorant, pitiful, stupid and dangerous." Yet she also felt for them: "I feel so sorry for them for I know the long background of poverty, disease, ignorance, oppression and lack of any cultural enrichment in their lives."[33] Many poor whites, or "rednecks" as they were more commonly called, engaged in violence against blacks and others foreign to Alabama's prevailing culture because they were "so low down themselves they need[ed] someone to kick."[34] After World War II (as after World War I) a rejuvenated KKK would spring up in the South to torment blacks, "uppity" women, and moral nonconformists. *Newsweek* accurately described the bulk of their members as the "backward and the frustrated, the poor and the disappointed of the Deep South." A Greenville, Alabama, observer agreed, linking the violence to the state's grinding poverty and illiteracy. Others were less diplomatic. They preferred the term poor "white trash, the kind . . . that feels the need to assert its supremacy by means other than superiority."[35]

All the White People Have to Be on the Same Side

Stimulated by the massive elite approval of Frank Dixon's stand against the federal government, plain-white Alabamians circled the wagons of cultural solidarity. Sixty-four West Blocton whites sent a homemade petition to the governor to express their support. A rural, hill-country woman encouraged Dixon not to let "those Hitlerites and would-be negro-loving critics . . . get you down." A Birmingham woman assured the governor that she and the overwhelming majority of "ordinary people of the South are backing you"—an assessment affirmed by a poor woman in Bessemer and by *Birmingham News* editor James A. Chappell, who put the level of support among white Alabamians of every rank at "everyone who I have talked to."[36]

Nor was this any surprise to Dixon and his business backers. The business-boosting president of the Bessemer Lions Club rejoiced that the racial outpouring of support for Dixon's FEPC stand expresses the views of "every Alabamian of white extraction."[37] Dixon agreed. "There is only one side in this matter . . . [and] all the white people . . . have to be on the same side."[38] For journalist Gould Beech, one of the most fully formed liberals in the state, it was maddening. Watching poor whites subsume the possibility of interracial class cooperation and instead parrot the economically rightist talking points of insulated wealth was almost too much to bear. That whole race business of the 1940s was "just as it had been at the turn of the century. . . . It was just used and misused and used and used and used."[39]

Recognizing that the Dixon letter was rapidly developing into a cause célèbre and acknowledging that a state champion on white supremacy could not be challenged, Alabama's politicians dutifully got their approval of the governor's stance on record. Congratulations poured into Dixon's office from congressmen Joseph Starnes, H. B. Steagall, Pete Jarman, Frank Boykin, and (tellingly) John Sparkman. George Grant outdid his colleagues by informing Dixon that "You are absolutely right. . . . We are all with you 100%." Sam Hobbs one-upped Grant by telling the governor he was "of course, 110% right!" Carter Manasco went them one better and had Dixon's letter read into the *Congressional Record*. But John H. Bankhead II, member of the Walker County political dynasty and a U.S. senator, outdid them all. Describing his request as emanating from the "best friends" of the Negro (but actually writing only after Dothan banker Wallace Malone prodded him), Bankhead wrote the U.S. chief of staff, General George C. Marshall, asking the U.S. government to remove all black troops from being billeted in the South.[40]

Northern blacks responded in kind. The other side of Dixon's growing celebrity was that he was also rapidly becoming a magnet for outside criticism of the South. A New Jersey critic claimed that America was not engaged in battle against a triple Axis but really had four enemies of state: "Hitler, Mussolini, Hirohito,"—and Dixon. "You and your kind are a perfect example of what Adolf Hitler is trying to do." An irate New York woman agreed that Dixon's act stamped him down in history as a traitor, a fascist, and "a stooge to Hitler" for spreading the doctrine of white supremacy and recommended

"Liberal South" and the Central Tragedy of Southern Politics / 177

that he be hung by the neck until dead. A Cleveland critic was even more direct in pointing out one of the South's oldest and dirtiest little secrets. Stop killing Negroes, he ordered. "You FUCK Negroes."[41]

Other northern criticism was less pointed but no less emotional. The *Philadelphia Inquirer* declared Dixon "a disgrace" and New York's *PM Magazine* agreed. A young New Jersey man informed Dixon that he was soon to be inducted into the army but did not feel "half as patriotic as I did before reading about you." Another young northerner told the Alabama governor that the Third Reich was built on fascism and racial superiority: "You are either in the wrong country or I am . . . drafted to fight the wrong enemy." A Chicago native who had resided briefly in Alabama warned that using blacks as scapegoats would eventually result in Alabama becoming a "cultural and economic scapegoat" for the nation.[42]

Criticism from black southerners was less voluminous but no less pungent. Perhaps more familiar with the regional folkways of the Deep South, including the region's Reconstruction experience and its strong religious convictions, some southerners focused on the un-Christlike nature of the governor's act. Alabama had stayed out of the Union too long during the Civil War, the secretary of the Dallas NAACP remarked. "You really ought to move back into the Union now instead of rebelling against civilization." Racial discrimination, he held, was neither Christian nor civilized; it was a sabotage of the war effort: "May God have mercy on [your] soul." Other southern black criticism took note of the troubling white working-class and patrician rapprochement that was increasingly apparent in the Alabama reaction. "It is just such dam, low brow, half-casts as . . . that dog of a [Horace] Wilkinson," worried one North Carolinian, who would abuse blacks so much they might eventually sell state secrets to the Axis.[43]

In the often Orwellian world of southern politics, though, outside criticism was actually a good thing. Damnation and abuse at the hands of Yankees—black Yankees no less—could win for an astute politician a hallowed place in the pantheon of the white South's "national" heroes and, if played correctly, life tenure in office. Frank Dixon emerged from the torrent of northern abuse geometrically strengthened at home. And in one of the deepest ironies, Alabama whites rewarded Dixon for his "courage" and manliness in standing up to the meddling, smart-aleck Yankees—even though taking such a stand incurred absolutely no real political risk at home where the overwhelming number of whites were in perfect concert with his position.

Still, Dixon was rewarded—and rewarded handsomely by the appreciative natives. And he rode a personal wave of popularity based on a kind of masculine politics that gloried in his bravery and toughness in standing up to outside agitators—a style of machismo politics that would be perfected in the next generation by an obscure Barbour County judge named George Wallace. In an editorial aptly titled "A Southern Champion Arises," Ed Field's Black Belt *Selma Times-Journal* lauded Dixon's "strength and wisdom" and called for more of the same to replace the "weakness and compromise" that characterized much of the South's congressional delegation of "weaklings." The Black Belt *Sumter County Journal* announced that it was bursting with pride in Dixon because he "has the courage and . . . 'the guts' to tell these Yankee social reformers where to go." From the hill country, the *Pell City News* applauded the Alabama governor for having the gumption to "stand on his 'hind legs' to defend the beliefs" of the southern people. A flurry of editorials from around the state—north and south, Black Belt, hill country, Tennessee Valley, and the Wiregrass—praised Dixon as the emerging knight-errant of southern culture, the panoplied champion of white supremacy and white southern traditions versus the monster of northern usurpers and their cousin, the federal leviathan.[44]

Former Klan member and Jefferson County court reporter A. B. Hale, anticipating George Wallace's future campaign slogan, commended Dixon for having enough backbone to "stand up" for white supremacy. A friend of aspiring politico Chauncey Sparks (who was himself busy taking note of the state's response to Dixon) denounced the "spineless puppets" who formed the South's congressional delegations for allowing abominations like the FEPC in the first place. Other whites, male and female, from all corners of the state lauded Dixon's manhood and courage against the "odds so heavy against him."[45]

Cockeyed Reformers and Scheming Rabble-Rousers

The broad reaction was the function of the cultural essence of Dixon's stand—for it was far more than just racial. In standing up to the federal government on a racial issue, Frank Dixon purposefully tapped into, or blundered upon, a cultural defense of the white South and its sacrosanct "way of life" on a host of interrelated mores—gender, civic, religious, and economic. In defending the racial status quo, Dixon elevated himself to the role of Cromwellian protector of the white South and—in the minds of virtually all white southerners of the time—what constituted the "Southland." For African Americans were in no way considered *of the South* in the same way white southerners understood their own nativity. Blacks were a part of the South, to be sure, but one with alien roots and only a legitimate part of the Southland when kept firmly "in their place" of subservience, quietude, and dutiful physical labor.

Southern views on federal involvement in business and employment matters as a *cultural* question had been evident for some time. Former New Dealer John Rankin had denounced the appearance of the FEPC on the floor of the U.S. House in decidedly cultural terms as the product of "alien influences . . . using the Negro as a smoke screen." A leading journal of Bourbon opinion in Alabama deplored the FEPC as the effort of "pink-minded social equality advocates" to move into Dixie and break down the region's segregation codes. This race agitation was not of the South's making but was instead "thrust upon us—in wartime—by cock-eyed reformers and scheming trouble rousers from way off yonder." When an African American member of the FEPC from Chicago blurted out that he believed a committee order "supersedes the South's traditions," the region's economic conservatives became apoplectic and trotted out the offending quotation whenever and wherever they thought it might be of use.[46]

Accordingly Frank Dixon's defiance of the War Manpower Board (WMB) was understood in broad cultural terms. A former Ku Klux Klan member recommended that the governor's letter of defiance to the WMB be made required reading in every southern school and college for its regional acculturation value.[47] Others, in Alabama and the surrounding southern states, similarly applauded the Dixon letter as one to be cherished by "every red-blooded Southerner" as a classic defense of the southern people's "way of living" and as a stand to keep the South, "our homeland . . . fit for Southerners to live in."[48] As a corollary, patriotism became defined as fealty to the Southland's (read: white South's) way of thinking on race. A writer who described herself as a "loyal southern woman" commended the governor's action as just good citizenship. Horace Hall of the *Dothan Eagle* said it plainly, too. Denouncing as laurel seekers the few Alabama newspapers that criticized Dixon for his stand, Hall castigated their editors for siding *against* Alabama and the South and with the "left-wing radicals of the North." The leftist Yankees sought only to tear down Dixie's social barriers and interfere with state sovereignty.[49]

Much of the cultural reaction was the fruit of the ever-present Reconstruction Syndrome and the deeply bitter memories of the days when Yankee troops walked Alabama. A Florida admirer congratulated the Alabama governor for having the intestinal fortitude to "tell Yankee social reformers where to go" while an Alabamian characterized the racial policies of the federal government as northern zealots trying to "stab us in the back."[50]

For most of the white South, the black legend of Reconstruction—retold ad nauseum and with greater liberality each time—was real, vivid, remarkable, and painful. Decades of the most mind-numbing inculcation of this creed had concluded in the result that, for the overwhelming number of white southerners, the federal government was not some organic whole of which they felt an active and vital part along with the other peoples and sections of the United States. The federal government was not something of which all but the rarest southern whites felt membership or pride in—or even something from which they could expect any measure of amity or assistance. On the contrary, the most persistent product of the Reconstruction trauma was a lasting southern conception of the central government as something strange, powerful, menacing, and foreign, a voraciously tax-hungry alien force prone to meddlesomeness, never to be trusted, and only rarely to be complied with.

So pervasive, so deeply rooted, and so common was this mind-set in the South that the seemingly impossible was possible. In Alabama even *Republicans*—the *villains* in the original Reconstruction drama—repeated the black legend of Reconstruction precepts in opposition to federal interference on southern racial customs. It really was remarkable. Oliver Day Street, former Populist and Alabama's leading *Republican* for the first half of the twentieth century, applauded Dixon in explicitly Reconstruction terms: this was not the first time that federal officials had tried to "set the Negro astride the necks of the white people of the South." Selfish, national "outsiders" had tried it seventy-five years earlier and, as a result, southern Republicans had "suffered all these years."[51]

The sentiment infested the South and, eight decades removed from the Civil War, Frank Dixon did all he could to stoke the flame of simmering resentment against the central government. For the businessmen of the Bessemer Lions Club, their reasons for backing Dixon, along with the obvious economic motive, were pure Reconstruction memory. Its members saw the federal contract for war cloth as just another federal bureau's attempt to annul "states' rights . . . [and] home rule," time-honored principles under the Constitution.[52]

Dixon agreed that the FEPC was the greatest threat to the South since Reconstruction. Instead of quelling the brewing rebellion, the governor did all he could to encourage it. For in the memory of Reconstruction and race hurt lay the best possible chance for Alabama's privileged to win the support of the state's plainer whites.

To this end, Dixon ventured into Yankeeland to follow up on his smash hit of defiance by delivering a Christmas season speech to the Southern Society of New York that openly broached the possibility of another southern secession—this time from the Democratic Party. While floating the trial balloon of a third party for the South, Dixon told the assemblage that all true southerners were manning the ramparts of white supremacy as they did in the days following the Civil War. "True patriots of the South," Dixon thundered, "will drive out . . . negro using and [negro] loving Southerners . . . just as they did sixty-odd years ago" so that all decent southern people could be left alone.[53]

There should be no confusion that race was at the heart of the Reconstruction proposition and thus at the heart of the whole southern "way of life." The hill-country *Cullman Democrat*, for example, supported Dixon's defiance of the federal government as a brave stand against a movement whose ultimate aim was a "mongrel race." The FEPC was only the fruit of trying to appease a few radical groups and the growing black vote up North. Frank Dixon readily assented that race was at the heart of the segregation matter—and, in fact, the prerequisite for continued fidelity to the national Democratic Party. "The Democratic party in Alabama," Dixon said in reference to the New Deal's FEPC, "has as its motto 'White Supremacy.' I know of nothing which will wreck the Democratic party quicker in this State than any effort . . . to abolish segregation." Once before the federal government had taken on an experiment of "forcing negro domination on the Southern people," Dixon warned in conjuring the Reconstruction nightmare. The results had been unhappy.[54]

Alabama newspapers—largely owned and financed by planters and Big Mules and functioning in their interest—did much to encourage cultural solidarity across class lines against any issue that challenged the prevailing racial status quo. In doing so, they repeated and legitimized the cultural shorthand that was fast developing in the region. It was a shorthand that denoted responsible southern behavior on race, the Reconstruction memory and lingering aversion to "outsiders," a narrow and skewed construction of what constituted "friendly" relations between the races, a strong animus toward federal bureaus as agents of racial change, and a masculine conception of defending the regional status quo. Frank Dixon had spoken "with courage," the Tennessee Valley's *Decatur Daily* celebrated. Thomas Abernethy's *Talladega Daily Home* in the hill country preferred to emphasize that Dixon had thwarted the radical fools who would "force a second reconstruction upon us." Ed Field's *Selma Times-Journal* agreed that the fault was that of New Deal radicals "mothered by Eleanor Roosevelt, whose genius for meddling into affairs which do not concern her is almost unprecedented." North Alabama's *Cherokee County Herald* concurred that "outsiders . . . and . . .

white-collared snakes" were to blame, while Horace Hall's *Dothan Eagle* and the *Gadsden Times* elected to stress the masculine greatness of Dixon's stand and his refusal to let the state be bullied and "bull-dozed" by the proponents of social equality.[55] Within just a few years Abernethy, Field, Horace Hall, and Hamner Cobbs would all lead the vanguard of disgust with the national Democratic Party over racial liberalism into the Dixiecrat Party and, thereafter, into the modern GOP.

Alabama's news media did much to solidify the regional status quo and its cultural canon in the way it dealt with wayward native newspapers that dared to find fault with the newly crowned state champion. The methods of compelling cultural conformity, developed during World War II, would be put to extensive use in succeeding decades. *Alabama Magazine* lumped the *Montgomery Advertiser* in with regional lepers like the NAACP, the CIO, and the largely communist Alabama Farmers' Educational and Cooperative Union because Grover C. Hall Jr. criticized Dixon's *approach* (not his purpose) in handling the federal war cloth contract. The CIO "isn't Southern and never will be. It [is] . . . a trouble maker," Barrett Shelton's *Decatur Daily* said in dismissing labor leaders' criticism of Dixon. Horace Hall of the *Dothan Eagle* took scorching aim at his nephew, Grover Jr., for comparing Dixon to Georgia's Gene Talmadge and issuing a plea for the Alabama governor to decline to take the state down the sorry path of the demagogue. Junior was apparently taking his stand against the South in a fit of "palpable self-hypnosis" and delusion that a Pulitzer Prize could be won by demonstrating naked sycophancy to the New Deal and "the pinkos." In doing so, Grover Jr. was writing "down to Southern readers and . . . up to Northern critics" and, as such, was certainly not representative of the people of Alabama in challenging the right of the white man to choose his own associates—or the white businessman to hire his own employees.[56]

So suffocating and complete was the enforced conformity that scores of the *Advertiser*'s employees felt compelled to send a telegram to the governor disowning their editor's mild criticism. Grover Jr. himself, inundated by attacks, rapidly retreated and wrote a "clarifying editorial" less than a week later that emphasized his complete agreement with Dixon's segregationist *goals* and tried to stress that he had taken issue only on the basis of *methods*.[57] Col. Harry M. Ayers's *Anniston Star* found itself accused of being a hotbed of left-wing northern radicalism and South hating because it fell just inches short of full cultural approbation of the episode. Ayers's newspaper applauded Dixon's stand "heartily" and blamed "outside agitation" for provoking the incident. So far, so good. But then Ayers broke ranks to disagree with Horace

Wilkinson's suggestion that a league to protect white supremacy should be formed.[58]

One upshot of the tidal wave of enforced conformity on this host of allied issues was that many Alabamians developed an enlarged and distorted sense of what constituted true and proper representation in a democracy. Differing concepts of representation had certainly long existed: models ranging from officeholders serving as valued and knowledgeable trustees for the electorate to those functioning as public servants. In Alabama, and much of the South, the chilling atmosphere of mass conformity did much to retard the development of the trustee model and endowed the public servant model with widespread and virtually unbridled acceptance. Elected representatives, in such a society, were "hired" to enact the public will—period. No thinking, no discussion, no interjection of moderation, discretion, or the fruit of learnedness or principle was wanted or needed: just reflexive personification of the popular will—no matter how unenlightened, uninformed, or unjust it might be.

Dissent, therefore, was invalid—especially dissent that emanated from within the predominant culture. In the few places that it did sprout up, it was quickly stamped out as the "hysterical yappings" of the so-called liberals of the South and sentiment that was "completely out of step" with southern opinion.[59]

On this second point there was actually a good deal of truth, Dixon explained. The FEPC cloth contract, including federal language against employment discrimination, was jaundiced and "extremely dangerous." More, it was being forced on the southern people without their consent. Dixon had merely stood up as "a trustee" of the people and the majority's will. In a perfectly titled editorial, "Dixon Registers with the People," the *Opp Weekly Journal*, in the state's poor Wiregrass region, expressed its belief that he had as well.[60]

8
Cheap Labor, the FEPC, and Frank Dixon as Knight-Errant of the South

> We will not stand for . . . social equality. "White supremacy" is the motto of our party in Alabama.
>
> —Gessner T. McCorvey

For Alabama's privileged planter-industrialist clique, Frank Dixon's resonance with the people was a bonanza. Alabama politics had long been riven by tensions between those who had little and those with plenty. In the domestic storms of the New Deal and World War II, though, wealth and privilege glimpsed a way for class healing to occur, a soothing of economic differences that would allow the masses of plain people to align themselves behind the Bourbon program—even if they did not fully comprehend the details or implications. The melding of economic conservatism and white supremacy into one allied and sacrosanct strain could, if handled properly, indemnify the conservative cause and compel widespread acceptance of the privileged program—acceptance that cut sharply across previously important class lines. And if the national Democratic Party came along, so be it. If not, there were other options.

Throw Down Your Shovels and Sit on Your Asses

The Bourbons had found their long-awaited hero in Frank Dixon. In the War Manpower Board (WMB) controversy Dixon emerged as a champion of white supremacy and a national figure, Hubert Baughn rejoiced. Leading conservative and coal magnate Henry DeBardeleben saw in Dixon an emerging sectional champion of white supremacy and the preservation of states' rights. The logical conclusion was that the Democratic Party that had sponsored the FEPC must be either reformed or abandoned. According to DeBardeleben, practically everyone in his social circle, all "'old fashioned'" southern Democrats and states' rights enthusiasts, felt the same way.[1]

I. W. "Ike" Rouzer, president of the Alabama Mining Institute, agreed.

Rouzer, a devout apostle of unsanctioned economic fundamentalism, thought of himself as a leading friend of the black race. He often argued that white supremacy was in the best interest of blacks—a redux of the self-serving self-deception in such evidence at the 1901 Alabama constitutional convention. This step-by-step national Democratic retreat on white supremacy as a part of the New Deal could have but one result, Rouzer pontificated: "disaster."[2]

Joe Starnes, former-New Dealer from the hill country and vice-chair of the House Un-American Activities Committee, greeted the exhortations of his new Bourbon handlers by echoing the call for the preservation of a conservative Democratic Party based on the cornerstones of states' rights, white supremacy, and opposition to the New Deal. He further lamented the obvious declension of the old party into a sordid collection of undesirables. The Guntersville congressman heartily commended Dixon for his defense against the unwarranted imposition of federal power and the erosion of states' rights and individual rights under the New Deal war effort. The "'planned economy' group" was to blame, Starnes mused in revealing the close interplay of class hierarchy, anti-Semitism, and white supremacy. In other words, it was the "negro group; the Jewish group; the CIO; and every pink and radical group" in this country that was the cause of such bothersome programs such as the WMB. The solution, though, was national, not merely regional: a coalescence of conservatives from across the country predicated on the bedrock of the South. "This is a white man's country," Starnes proclaimed, and for him the time had long been at hand when those who believed in our system of government and "our way of life and . . . racial integrity as well as states' rights and individual liberty" should organize throughout the country to resist the tide of an increasingly liberal national Democratic Party.[3]

During the summer of 1942 the ruckus over Frank Dixon and his stand against the WMB was but the individual expression of the more generally felt FEPC threat of the time. For Alabama's business interests, the FEPC marked a low point in federal-state relations—something that far exceeded the threats of the NRA, the Wagner Act, and even the WMB. In their view the FEPC was clear encroachment on holy ground: the unfettered right of managers and owners to run their business affairs as they saw fit—including (perhaps especially) the *racial* aspects of hiring, firing, promoting, and paying. Further, the FEPC embodied an even more obnoxious threat to southerners of wealth and privilege. In the most fundamental of ways it called into question what had never really been systematically questioned before in such a sharply stratified society: the God-given right of owners and managers to make decisions and exercise authority without regard for what they felt were trifles (or worse) such as racial fairness. The FEPC threat, therefore, was no pure racial threat—as if something could exist in the South that was purely racial in nature. It encapsulated the deepest, broadest, and most profound challenge to the authority of those who occupied the rarified air of the highest echelons in the South's pyramid of social and economic power.

To wage war on such an inherently offensive statute, the planter-industrialist clique invoked the most powerful levers of cultural solidarity. And in the summer of 1942, when the national FEPC chose four major regional cities in which to hold high-profile investigations and hearings (New York, Chicago, Los Angeles, and Birmingham), it meant war.

Hubert Baughn's *Alabama Magazine,* long the focal point for planter-industrialist conservatism, led the way for the Bourbons by connecting the dots between Reconstruction memory and the new threat. Of all the "halo-wearing missionaries of New Deal socialism" that had sought to "reconstruct" the long-suffering South, the FEPC was the "gravest threat yet" to the time-honored right of the southern people to "direct the social development" of their region. FDR's racial experts and even the "most starry-eyed of Washington dreamers should have the sanity to desist from juggling his dynamite in [Birmingham,] one of the nation's principal war production powerhouses," Baughn editorialized. Labor board tribunals, wage-hour enforcers, and other "houndings" were part of the enormous and "cold-blooded campaign for all-out regimentation." The disciples of New Dealism would be sure to send their agents into the Heart of Dixie to stir up the "delicate issue of [racial] equality . . . absolute regimentation and . . . an outside attempt at reconstruction . . . and . . . carpetbagging."[4]

A favorite theme of the Bourbons soon became the issue of timing—as if consistent, significant progress was already being made in Dixie, and doing anything to improve fairness on the American job front would only empower the Third Reich. Outside groups agitating on racial questions would undo many years of progressive work, Horace Hall warned. "Blindly zealous social reformers" needed to cease their assaults on white supremacy during the war. And then the contradiction: it was time for America to win the war instead of seeking goals that are *unattainable.*[5] If only the "crackpots, professional reformers and trouble-stirrers from afar . . . will stop rocking the boat," a business-boosting conservative opined, Dixie could devote the necessary time and energy to military victory. Besides, the South had already made substantial progress on race relations—even in the face of considerable outside interference.[6]

A good deal of the elite-directed Reconstruction-like resentment against the "return of . . . carpetbagging and exploitation" was aimed at the Democratic Party—Franklin and Eleanor Roosevelt and the New Deal to be precise. The state's business interests took intense pleasure in pointing out that the FEPC's chief investigator for the state of Alabama was John Beecher. A thirty-eight-year-old native of Birmingham, Beecher was a graduate of the University of Alabama and had worked as a writer for the *Birmingham Age-Herald*, an English professor at Dartmouth and the University of Wisconsin, and a New Deal veteran of the Resettlement Administration and the Farm Security Administration. But he was the worst kind of scalawag incarnate for conservative Alabamians. Beecher was an actual physical descendant of the infamous abolitionist Harriet Beecher Stowe of *Uncle Tom's Cabin* fame. Mrs. Roosevelt could have her social equality, an irate Alabamian who was soon to bolt the party fumed, "but she damn well can't ram it down the South's throat, war or no war!" "While the world burned last week," another unhappy Alabama Democrat fumed, southern shipbuilders and plane makers were called to apologize to Mrs. Roosevelt's Pullman porter friends for not hiring their "untrained brothers! . . . Is this the reward of the South for . . . sending the first and most volunteers to the guns?"[7]

While patriotism, convenience, paternalist fiction, and Reconstruction were all important weapons in combating the FEPC, the central issue revolved around the right and ability of the "better sorts" and payroll makers to make and determine racial and economic decisions. And in the climate of World War II Alabama, the racial ugliness was thinly, if ever, disguised. As national committee members arrived in Birmingham for the last of the FEPC's four regional meetings, economic conservatives sympathized with employers who had "carefully nurtured race relations" in their plants for decades and now wondered whether "bureaucratic meddling" would destroy proven arrangements. Columnist Major Squirm, the alter ego of *Alabama Magazine* editor Hubert Baughn, was more direct. He flatly denounced the New Deal's "committee to Put More Darkies on the payroll" and lamented that employers would have to suffer the indignity of the FEPC "jerkin' them up before . . . Dat committee fer de purteckshun uv Rastus & Sambo" that showcased "a cullud committee member from Chicago."[8] In a patent admission of the race-based nature of the employer resentment, Alabama's leading mouthpiece of planter and industrialist opinion scoffed that if an employer came out and admitted that "negroes were not hired in certain places in the South because they are negroes," this perfectly reasonable explanation would be rejected by the FEPC as some sort of obsolete provincialism.[9]

Anxious to placate such criticism, *Louisville Courier-Journal* publisher Mark Ethridge, a noted southern progressive and chairman of the FEPC, famously announced that his committee had no intention whatever of undermining Jim Crow: "there is no power in the world—not even in all the mechanized armies of the earth, Allied and Axis—which could now force the Southern white people to the abandonment of the principle of segregation."[10] Yet the hue and cry from the South was so fierce that the FEPC canceled a fifth and final regional hearing scheduled for El Paso.

Within two months of the Birmingham meeting, Governor Frank Dixon undercut the federal committee by establishing a State War Manpower Commission to oversee much of the function originally ascribed to the federal bureau. He unabashedly stacked the commission with the most devout segregationists, free-market apostles, and anti-federal types that could be found in Alabama: *Greensboro Watchman* editor Hamner Cobbs served as director, Montgomery judge Walter B. Jones as chair, and Horace Hall of the *Dothan Eagle*, Barrett Shelton of the *Decatur Daily*, and Frank P. Samford, president of the Associated Industries of Alabama, all served as members.[11]

Its elite solidarity intact against such federal incursions on race and economy, Alabama's oligarchs realized that race was *the* signal issue on which a broad, anti-federal and pro-business alliance could be formed—and perhaps eventually exported.[12] As such, race and anti-statism together made up the cultural glue and common denominator that could hold together various classes of whites in a solid front against outside incursions that might ultimately threaten the hegemony of the planter-industrialist cabal. There was nothing to worry about on the Big Mule/Black Belt score. The intense white supremacy and economic conservatism of the planters and industrialists were virtually undiluted. The place for worry was Alabama's plain whites, a number of whom had demonstrated a disturbing propensity for attempting periodic coalitions with African Americans against the state's "better sorts."

Yet the record on this front was itself decidedly mixed. Along with the occasional transcendent class-consciousness, the plain folk had also exhibited a strong recurring indulgence of their own racism—a tragic proclivity to cut off their nose in order to spite their face. White supremacy was a suffocating concept, though. If the privileged could meld their economic conservatism as a package deal together with parochial conventions on white supremacy as part of a region-wide stand against federal intrusions, there would be a good chance to fashion a pan-white alliance that could eclipse even party lines—and prove virtually unassailable in the South.

Vital in the resonance of white supremacist tendencies with the folk was the conception of Dixie as a region with frontier origins. The frontier mentality was alive and well in Alabama, even during World War II. It was woefully evident just in the way so many plain whites spoke about blacks (reminiscent of the way early settlers had spoken about Indians)—as half-civilized savages who, given an ounce of freedom, threatened to bring down the entire established order, particularly the sexual order. Yankees may have emancipated the blacks, a woman from Marengo County reasoned, but it was the South that had "Christianized them." "I don't know what we will do," one Birmingham woman wailed, claiming that the army had taken her boyfriend and that black men were going around saying that "'when all these white men are gone [we] will get all these white women.'" The New York and Washington correspondent for the United Press wire service stationed in Alabama agreed: the attitude of the average white southerner toward black people was the same as that of "the Nazis against non-Aryans."[13]

Accordingly, Alabama whites attracted from other whites both expressions of "scientific racism" and more popular stereotypes of black sloth and unfitness for labor or citizenship. Blacks were innately inferior, according to one Virginia correspondent, because of synostosis or a "premature locking of the coronal and sagittal sutures of the skull" that halted black brain growth at puberty and left the Negro "racially, a moron." In effect, the genetic affliction condemned blacks alone among the races of men to "a sub-adult status bordering on the sub-human." Deportation to some thinly inhabited portion of Africa was the only reasonable course. Even then, superior white engineering could only make blacks secure for a generation or two until they reverted to savagery.[14]

Such criticism found its expression in anti–New Deal doggerel:

4000 years ago Moses said to his people:
"Pick up your shovels, mount your asses, load your camels and ride with me into the Promised Land."

4000 years later Roosevelt said to his people:
"Throw down your shovels, sit on your asses, light up a Camel, this IS the Promised Land."[15]

We Simply Have to Maintain White Supremacy

Such reasoning portended an important reconciliation that was taking place in the Deep South between erstwhile antagonists: the Kluxer and the Bourbon. While the South's aristocracy had furnished the most intense and virulent opposition to the 1920s Klan, it was based primarily on privileged anxiety over federal intrusion into race relations, an abiding desire to keep the region attractive for the investment of outside capital, and pure political competition. Yet no appreciable difference existed between Kluxer and Bourbon on the cardinal issues of white supremacy and nativism.[16]

Still, despite its lack of a principled basis, the break between the Klan and the oligarchy had been bitter. During the New Deal–World War II era, though, the increasing melding together of racial and economic conservatism into one alloyed juggernaut offered the possibility of reconciliation between Kluxer and Bourbon. It was a healing that, if it took place on the basis of shared affinity for white supremacy and local rule, could herald the beginning of an invincible political alliance between whites of various social ranks in the Deep South.

Key in this reconciliation process was the adoption by the Bourbons of the most basic tenets of "neo-Kluxism"—that is, an echoing of Klan-minded ideas of native white supremacy and 100 percent Americanism without necessarily praising the KKK by name. In return, the Klan-minded would have to suppress their occasional concern for class differentiations and adopt allegiance to the stark economic conservatism of neo-Bourbon laissez-faire. In a pivotal way, the almost unconscious rapprochement between neo-Kluxer and neo-Bourbon during these years anticipated the predominant buttoned-down Klan-like organization of the post-*Brown* period: the White Citizens Councils.

In Alabama, the unification of neo-Kluxist and neo-Bourbon strains took on flesh and bone in alliances such as that between former Klan leader Horace Wilkinson and noted Klan opponent Frank Dixon. Mabel Jones West, the 1920s leader of Alabama's Women of the KKK and the Women's White Supremacy League, apprised Dixon of her "one hundred per cent" support of his racial stand and damned newspapers such as the *Birmingham News* for questioning the governor's wisdom in defying the federal government. A self-described "100% American" let Dixon know that she was supportive of any economic effort for "keeping the niggers under our feet." A Eufaula native who also cited "100% American[ism]"—the motto of the 1920s Klan—praised the Big Mules' efforts to "keep the Nigra down" and "pay them as less as possible." A self-described "True Son of the South" agreed that God had never intended blacks to have more than a place to eat and drink, and maybe a pair of overalls. Patricians such as South Carolina's poet laureate agreed with the plain-folk assessment of black ambitions. What snooping northerners just didn't get was that black people had a "dim infallible genius . . . to get along without money." Far from wanting Social Security, all they desired was a little "rustic security": a few cows, a little land, and a hand-to-mouth existence in which they could rely on a "better white" person to loan them a coin or two if things got too tough. The welfare of black people had "always been close to my heart," the poet explained. But anything else—especially anything remotely connected to government relief or programs—threatened to rot from within the African's capacity for moral action, which was fragile at best.[17]

The rapid fusing of neo-Kluxist and neo-Bourbon thought into one synthetic strain was also evident in the reaction of the few racially and economically liberal forces in Alabama. The Alabama *CIO News Digest* damned consummate Bourbon Frank Dixon as "suffering from hallucinations" that made him think he was "carrying the 'flaming sword'" of his famous kinsman, the Baptist Rev. Thomas W. Dixon of Virginia. The Tidewater Dixon was the noted author of several best-selling pro-Klan, white supremacist novels—one of which had been used as the basis for the first silent movie, the explicitly white supremacist *Birth of a Nation*. The elder Dixon had already turned to the Republican Party in disgust over the New Deal's racial liberalism, shortly after the 1936 Macon meeting. As a modern-day race leader, Frank Dixon made a sorry spectacle compared to the Virginian, the labor journal wrote tastelessly, because he was "a peg-legged bigot whose creaking cork leg is moved to take each step at the command of Birmingham's industrial barons." National CIO leaders asked the federal government to investigate civil rights violations against blacks and union leaders by the Klan and other "white supremacy terrorists," especially Dixon and Horace Wilkinson.[18]

While Klan types were able to adopt extremely conservative economic ideas along with their racism, Bourbons also showed themselves willing to express the most representative Klan ideas while retaining their rank's traditional distaste for the order's name. A Mobile attorney pushed for a league of white supremacy yet managed to retain an exquisite form of self-deception to insist that the group not be connected to the Klan: it had to remain "on a high plane." Monroe Stephens of east Alabama proposed the establishment of a Society to Maintain White Gentile Supremacy, writing to Wilkinson that the white race was the only race that had "any real merit" yet demanded that the group have no dealings with the KKK or like organizations but should instead "appeal [only] to the intellect." Overt association with the Klan could only debase and embarrass the organization, Stephens felt, although he himself was convinced it was "a Nigger trick to take advantage of the war," that "'No Kinky haired race' has ever done anything worthwhile in this world," and that the fall of France—Egypt, India, Persia, Greece, and Rome—were all directly traceable to the "admixture of negro blood . . . [and racial] amalgamation."[19]

These formative years witnessed in the new Bourbon-Kluxer understanding the emergence of the leading figures of what would soon be the ultimate expression of the Great Melding of racial and economic conservatism: the Dixiecrat movement. Along with Dixon, state Democratic Party chair

Gessner McCorvey also came into his own about this time. He sent a highly publicized 1942 missive to the treasurer of the national Democratic Party warning that it would not receive one dime from Alabama's Democrats until the party reformed its left-leaning racial policies. Southern whites were "almost up in arms over what the Federal Government is doing" on race, McCorvey cautioned. "This is a rising tide that knows no bounds and cannot be expressed in words."[20]

If McCorvey knew anything, he knew southern white people. His ancestors had served on the SDEC for over half a century and were among the leading patricians in Alabama. His father, a student of William H. Dunning at the University of Chicago, taught history at the University of Alabama for half a century. "We will not stand for anything remotely resembling social equality," McCorvey flatly informed the national party. "'White supremacy' is the motto of our party in Alabama. We simply have to maintain white supremacy . . . we are going to maintain white supremacy . . . and there is just no rhyme or reason in the federal government, especially during a Democratic administration [and] . . . war times . . . trying to work out a social revolution."[21]

Birmingham police commissioner Theophilus Eugene "Bull" Connor, who would win lasting infamy in the 1960s civil rights wars, also got into the act during the war by sending a racial warning—in his official capacity—to Franklin Roosevelt (a letter that, to Connor's lasting chagrin, went unanswered). Although Connor made certain to denounce the Klan by name, the letter was actually a model of neo-Kluxist thought and a harbinger of the mixture of paternalism, super-patriotism, and Reconstruction hurt that would become central to the States' Rights cause.

After informing the president that "Half of our Negroes have venereal diseases" and reminding Roosevelt that he had been a faithful New Dealer for years, Connor got to the point. Unless something was done quickly by FDR on race, "[we are] going to face a crisis in the South . . . the annihilation of the Democratic Party." Worse, a refusal to turn the handling of race issues back over to the states and localities would "see a revival" of organizations such as the KKK that would shatter the "progress made by law abiding white people, who have conscientiously labored to aid Negroes." There was a war to be won, Connor reminded the president, "and the South is doing its part." But the "downfall of white supremacy [and] . . . segregation and [the] . . . amalgamation of the races" could not be a part of the effort. Such things were poison imported into Dixie by "agitators" teaching blacks how to become "impudent, unruly, arrogant, law breaking, violent and insolent." If the national Democratic Party did not backtrack on its headlong rush into racial liberalism, Roosevelt and the other party fathers could expect the "Ku Klux Klan, which I never joined," to revive and grow strong again, along with considerable "bloodshed." "You have made us a fine President," Connor wrote, and "I have always voted for you . . . [but] don't you think one war in the South . . . is enough?"[22]

Perhaps no other Alabama politico emerged from the wartime racial tumult with a higher profile than Horace Wilkinson. A former 1920s Klan leader as well as New Deal patronage dispenser under Bibb Graves, urban machine boss, and spokesman for the white working class, Wilkinson had long been a thorn in the side of Bourbon leaders like Dixon, McCorvey, James Simpson, and Bull Connor (one of his many former pupils). Yet in the wartime crisis of the 1940s Wilkinson's race ideology dovetailed perfectly with his limitless ambition. And his prickly and curmudgeon-like personality famously preceded him. New allies such as John Bankhead, Chauncey Sparks, and Gessner McCorvey—whenever they disagreed with him on political issues—walked on eggshells to avoid provoking Wilkinson's vaunted ire and hellish personal wrath.

In the summer of 1942, as Dixon, McCorvey, and Connor were staking their claims to leadership of Alabama's white supremacist forces, Wilkinson worked closely with the Alabama governor to distribute a scatter sheet across the state on race relations titled "A Battle to Death against the Black Dragon." But it was Horace Wilkinson alone who produced a masterpiece of race relations logic that found itself reproduced across the entire South. The virtuoso performance came in a July speech to a group of businessmen gathered at the Bessemer Kiwanis Club, and both its content and audience represented perfectly the new alliance between privileged economic conservatives and plain racial conservatives along the shared axis of white supremacy and anti-federalism.

Levie Shelley, a close friend of Chauncey Sparks's and, along with the next governor a longtime privileged opponent of Wilkinson, acknowledged that—despite their past class differences—the Birmingham boss had sounded an alarm that "deserves [the] most serious consideration by all who love Alabama, the South, and their traditions." A disgruntled working-class Democrat from Ensley agreed with Wilkinson that the time had come for an anti-NAACP: a society to uphold white supremacy. And, perhaps best of all for Wilkinson's rising fortunes, a Jewish writer for New York's *PM Magazine* decried the Alabamian's call for a League to Maintain White Supremacy in a feature article: "the swastika is no prettier when entwined with magnolia blossoms."[23]

Yet the inspired performance, while primarily racial in nature was not exclusively so. Wilkinson skillfully hit upon paternalist conceptions of friendship for the black race, a regional definition of patriotism, moral degeneracy and criminal depravity, cultural orthodoxy, gender, and of course economic considerations—all of which were tied closely to the staples of white supremacy and conservatism.

First, the lawyer laid out his case by cataloguing a series of racial horror stories: insolence on buses and streetcars, blacks working "white jobs" at Republic Steel, "taking over" a Dothan liquor store, throwing kisses to Montevallo coeds, and clashing with military police and white civilians in Tuskegee. Wilkinson lingered over the melding outrage of the FEPC and the U.S. Employment Service, with blacks seated at desks next to white people and white employers having their "right to operate [their] plant in the most efficient way" stripped away from them.[24] Nor were working-class whites safe from the rapacious appetite of the federal leviathan and its socially corrosive effects. No longer could white labor unions segregate their locals or lines of seniority and promotion with impunity, as in the good old days. So we were all—poor and privileged whites—in this together.

The unbridled aggression of an insatiable central government had destroyed the old plain-versus-privileged order of southern politics. And while disgust with the New Deal Democratic administration was perfectly understandable, the national GOP was no place to go for succor—yet. On race the Republicans were virtually indistinguishable from the national Democrats—"tweedledee and tweedledum"—Wilkinson argued in anticipating George Wallace. The Supreme Court, rather than providing a calming influence, had disturbed the thinking of the Negro and "furnished fuel for flames that bid fair to become hotter than some sections of our country can stand." The black "criminal element" interpreted these liberal judicial decisions as "a license to murder and ravish and rob." In seeking survival, Alabama and the South had a duty to provide an example for the rest of nation:

> About ten per cent of the population of this country are negroes. The whites being in the majority, it is their right and responsibility to work out the problem within the law and by a law that all whites and blacks must obey. . . . Extra-legal methods, however necessary or effective they may have been in the days of yore, are not to be resorted to now. . . . [A] Herculean effort is being made to break down and destroy segregation and with it many of the most cherished institutions in the south. . . . The white men of the south who oppose dragging the white man down to the level of a negro must organize. If there is room in this country for a National Association for the Advancement of Colored People, there

is need of a League to Maintain White Supremacy.... [I]t is tragic for the white people ... to sit idly by and allow these negroes to misguidedly place their selfish interests ahead of an all out war effort [and] ... our national security and our local way of life [to] rapidly disappear.... Mr. President, I am willing to sacrifice to save the British. I am willing to serve "from Greenland's Icy Mountains to India's coral strands."... I am willing to sacrifice to save France.... I would do even more to save America, for in saving America we save the world. But it will be difficult to save America if the best and most patriotic part of America is to be denied the right to live its own way of life. That is the reason Alabama ... must lead.[25]

No One Down Here Can Afford to Be Called a Negro Lover

While the shortcomings of working-class whites on issues of racial enlightenment were serious, they were fewer and less expertly orchestrated than the naked exploitation of race tensions from above. Still, the frenzied manipulation of fears and jealousies by the South's bosses paid a growing dividend in elevating race issues among the plain folk to a higher pitch than their traditional class resentments.

Few iron laws are extant when commenting on the social and psychological impulses of human beings possessed of a free will, but it does seem clear that a certain pragmatism was at work in southern labor's approach to white supremacy: that is, a greater degree of biracial cooperation could be found in unions that had a large black membership (e.g., coal, iron, steel) and, by corollary, a lesser degree in those that had few minorities (railroads, textiles, carpentry, painting, the building trades). While some of this was no doubt the product of sincere feelings of cooperation—especially in the mines where workers had to rely on each other in life and death situations—there was also a strongly pragmatic current of self-interest running through the calculations of white unionists. Failure to organize African American workers could only assist management in depressing wages and readying a supply of non-union labor for strikebreaking duty. As a result, whites organized blacks in coal, steel, iron, and rubber but often consigned them to segregated locals, shut them out of white-only jobs through restrictive seniority and promotion rules (agreed to by management *and* unions), abandoned them first when layoffs occurred, and allowed only minority status in union leadership and representation on grievance committees, federated labor councils, and state boards.[26]

Perhaps another iron law was present in this regard—iron not in an immutable sense but only in that, like the mineral, it was strong and could be breached only in the most dramatic and exceptional cases. That is, the greater the amount of external/federal pressure in working for change in the South, the greater the possibility of that change occurring. Again, in a corollary sense, where such pressure was not found, the chances for voluntary, unilateral change on southern social customs was decidedly more remote.

Internal reform had never been a particular hallmark of the region—nor was it during the 1940s. When change did come, it was usually the product of the most intense outside pressure and/or an internal realization that "reform" could be shaped to advance the interests of the parties in control. Yet organized labor presented an interesting situation in this regard, for southern unions were bombarded with racially liberal messages from their national parent bodies during these years—and a sharp rift soon developed between national rhetoric and provincial reality on race matters. A further divide was present between state labor leadership (which tended to embrace the national message of inclusion) and a southern rank and file that followed the national union line on economics but—like other white southerners—balked when it came to social matters.

While the predominant perception of wartime economic changes was one in which federal directives turned southern racial conventions on their heads, the reality was more modest. In fact at the end of 1942 leading Birmingham blacks complained that only 606 African Americans had received job training as opposed to more than 6,000 whites as a result of the War Manpower Commission programs—strictly "a token opportunity."[27]

Token or not, the change itself posed a potentially lethal threat to deeply engraved cultural folkways. Even border-state whites wondered if the time would ever come when blacks would be relieved of their "present lofty employments" and housemaids would return to the work they knew best. Many working-class whites thought in mutually exclusive, zero-sum terms that understood black gains to mean white losses. In the working-class hub of Ensley, a manual laborer who found it distasteful to work alongside blacks (and unacceptable to work under them) believed that any increase in the African American standard of living would "definitely lower the standard for the white man."[28]

While national union leaders such as the Steelworkers' Philip Murray were vocal exponents of black civil rights during the 1940s, there was a virtual canyon between national rhetoric and local practice in the South. The results were similar in the other CIO unions. Local union officers, drafted from the rank and file, and subject to electoral retribution, "often stood with their constituents against progress." The AFL unions were light years behind the CIO on race.[29]

Despite the national rhetoric, the reality on the ground in the Deep South was often ugly. A TCI machinist from Pleasant Grove said that despite the succession of racially liberal messages from the CIO's national and state leadership, most of Birmingham's mill workers easily backed Frank Dixon in his stand for segregation. CIO member Virgil Powell of Republic Steel's Rainbow Mines announced that he and the mill's other white miners were behind Dixon and white supremacy "100%," while CIO worker Neal Carroll reported similar results among the white union men in Bessemer. Hugh DuBose, a close ally of arch-segregationist Horace Wilkinson and publisher of his various white supremacist scatter sheets, was, himself, an ardent supporter of the labor movement. Alabama *CIO News Digest* editor Ed O'Connell angrily denied the patrician charge that the state CIO was interested in breaking down segregation as "a plain, unvarnished lie." "You don't know the pressure we're under here," an exasperated O'Connell told a visiting New York journalist—both from management *and* the workers. "The men won't work under negroes. Don't forget that down here no one can afford to be called a negro lover."[30]

Of course, practices varied by union and from plant to plant within the same industry. The Steelworkers represented a mixed bag. While national rhetoric was impressive, local custom could be antediluvian. Black Birmingham furnace men complained openly that the union was "not doing its part for the black man." African American unionists objected to racially restrictive work rules, class and departmental seniority practices, and other covenants in which the white union majority cooperated with management to keep blacks out of white jobs. At TCI's tin mill, where the local union was "a well-known haven" for the Klan, fifteen blacks saw their vacation pay and seniority bargained away by the union. Reuben Farr, the white, southern director of the United Steelworkers (USW), chafed under what he called the "bigotry" of the three international reps who serviced the Birmingham locals.[31]

Some rubber and steel locals in Alabama served as recruiting centers for the KKK; some Kluxers/union members would become infamous during the 1960s. Hosea Hudson, a black communist and the CIO president of a predominantly black foundry local, deeply resented "them racists down there" at the Steelworkers district office who forbade him from signing up white members or negotiating contracts that covered white workers. Eventually Hudson saw himself purged from the USW in what he weighed as a purely racial move. At Ensley's U.S. Steel works black jobs were confined to the hottest, heaviest, and most difficult tasks such as pick and shovel work and helpers to white millwrights, brick masons, and mechanics. But blacks found a way to cope with the treatment. "It wasn't perfect," one remembered of the 1940s. "We weren't working in the Garden of Eden.... We were all out there [just] trying to make a living."[32]

Indeed they were, and, with a white working class torn by their racial fears and anxieties, Alabama's industrialists had strong weapons at their disposal. TCI executives remained impervious to black requests for job equality until the federal government threatened to cancel the company's lucrative contracts. That is, the racial status quo had a definite inertia to remain fixed until change was demonstrated to be in the monetary self-interest of the companies themselves—what historian Numan Bartley has referred to as "pocket-book ethics."[33]

Things got particularly nasty at TCI's Red Mountain iron ore mines where the company hired a large batch of whites to try to lighten the majority black Mine, Mill and Smelter Workers local. In 1943 the white union members decided to leave Mine, Mill for a white Steelworker local, one complaining that Reid Robinson, the national Mine, Mill president, was trying to "change our way of living—the segregation policy that we have been raised ... under." By the end of the decade the CIO-sponsored USW had "raided" the black and radical Mine, Mill locals atop Red Mountain in a series of turf wars that featured mudslinging, physical threats, intimidation, shootouts, and an election-eve brawl in which Klansmen took part, resulting in the loss of an eye for one Mine, Mill officer.[34]

The Devil's Workshop

Still, if potential for biracial activism in the South existed, it could usually be found in the CIO unions, not the AFL. Racial restrictions within unions could be found throughout the country but, as a rule, they were more rigid and common in the South and in the craft locals. Auxiliary locals were often employed to insulate white wages from the depression associated with unorganized black labor but also to keep black workers segregated and marginalized on the periphery of the labor movement. Boilermakers, machinists, carpenters, longshoremen, paper makers, bricklayers, painters, pulp sulfite workers, brotherhoods of railway clerks, railway car men, tobacco workers, and musicians used the auxiliaries. In jobs where black males might come into contact with white women—plumbing, milk delivery, electrical work, and building trades like painting, bricklaying, and plastering—outright exclusion was more commonly followed. In 1943 fourteen unions, eight of which were in the AFL, as well as seven unaffiliated railroad brotherhoods, had racial bars. In 1944 a controversial Alabama railroad case resulted in a landmark U.S. Supreme Court ruling that unions had to represent all members of a bargaining unit fairly, regardless of race. During the Depression and the war railroads laid off black shopmen and mechanics, or eliminated their jobs, only to turn around and hire whites to replace them. Almost 80 percent of all African Americans employed on the roads were confined to laborer or service positions until the 1960s. Blacks who tried to work as brakemen, firemen, or ticket collectors—regardless of their experience or skill—were usually driven from their posts by the most caustic resistance of the railroad brotherhoods.[35]

Even in the 1940s the three largest rubber-making plants in the South—at Natchez, Memphis, and Gadsden, Alabama—strictly adhered to a Jim Crow policy of segregated showers, locker rooms, water fountains, toilets, cafeterias, and lines of progression for seniority and job bidding. Blacks worked in skilled and unskilled positions at the Gulf Shipbuilding Corporation in Mobile during World War I. But during World War II only a miniscule twenty-two blacks (all of them porters) worked among Gulf's ten thousand employees, even though the yard was organized by the AFL's Metal Trades with a specific resolution barring racial discrimination. Close by, at the Alabama Dry Dock and Shipbuilding Company, national CIO rhetoric failed to translate into reality. Although African Americans had overwhelmingly supported the CIO's Marine and Shipbuilding Workers Union against two raiding attempts by their AFL rivals, they were rewarded by being confined to unskilled positions as a result of union *and* management complicity, and saw their participation in the workforce plunge by 50 percent. Mobile blacks at the International Paper plant organized into a racially separate Hod Carriers local that later became a segregated Pulp, Sulphite Workers local. In Mobile, where black and white carpenters' locals had not cooperated since 1921, the war era saw a white union business agent actually call a strike at a bakery *to prevent blacks* from working there, white carpenters refuse to work with black carpenters at Brookley Air Field, and a white carpenters' official issue public statements that his members were "strictly white and only seek employment where white carpenters are employed and do not mix."[36] Obviously, during the war, conditions even in labor unions—possibly the most progressive formal organization in Dixie—left a lot to be desired when it came to race.

Perhaps it was too much to ask that working-class whites would resist the Bourbons' melding entreaties along the lines of racial exclusion and caste solidarity, given the reality of southern life. While limited biracial unionism did occur during these years in industries such as steel, rubber, and autos, it was usually in segregated auxiliaries or with stringent limitations (observed by both unions and management) on job classifications, seniority, and promotions. Ploys such as class and departmental seniority, which limited seniority to separate job classes and departments, prevented blacks from competing for open jobs plant-wide and kept them tethered to the most menial and labor-intensive occupations. Mine work was a notable exception. Although it was no nirvana (segregated locals and minority representation on committees and boards were the rule), the coal mines still represented the closest thing in the South to a true biracial workplace. Considerable cooperation was present in some mines and in others laudable attempts were periodically made.

Still, even in the mines, it was not difficult to find entrenched racial views. A sample Bessemer miner admitted that he was "a union man, and believe[d] in a negro having his rights" but that those rights should be exercised "in his place" and should not extend to the "injustice" of blacks taking jobs "that have always been ours." More precipitously, fewer and fewer black faces were seen during these years. Between 1930 and 1960 the African American presence in southern coal mines fell from 44,000 to 7,000, or from 20 percent of the total workforce to just 6.8. Mechanization was the main reason, but many critics also blamed the union for not aggressively protecting black jobs from the upgrades.[37]

The war did impinge sharply on the freedom unions had to engage in vigorous forms of collective bargaining. Industry accused labor, and labor accused industry, of putting narrow self-interest above winning the war—a marketing and public relations fight that capital clearly won. Businesses lambasted unions for striking industries as critical to the national defense as the steel mills and railroads, and unions charged businesses with price gouging, war profiteering, and using the war as a pretext to stymie the most modest types of economic reform. Truth be told, both sides had a point. For all the volumes written about "the greatest generation" and its undeniable sacrifices to win the war and the peace, human self-interest, expedience, and the shrewdest kind of timing did not take a holiday during the war. Despite historian Robert H. Zieger's later celebration of the CIO's refusal to allow the war to dictate when and where workers would strike, such praise four decades later does not begin to touch the damage in the southern cultural fabric done to the popular conception of labor's patriotism (or lack thereof) energetically played up by the Bourbons (while ignoring their own efforts to use the war as a pretext to get ahead).[38]

Strategically, the decision to wage strikes during the war was a horrible blunder—at least in a southern sense. Unions had never been *of the South* in the same way that organized labor was in the North. Labor was already perceived as a subversive force in southern society, almost as threatening to hierarchical class relations as it was to race customs. Strikes during wartime only provided grist against unions for the Bourbon propaganda mill and confirmation of the worst suspicions southerners harbored about the radical, foreign-dominated, northern, and Jewish "agitatin'... trouble-makin'" unions.[39] The strikes—especially in industries as sensitive to national war production as coal, iron, steel, and railroad transportation—furnished made-to-order ammunition for southern economic conservatives to use in blasting *the whole* labor movement and everything it stood for as something selfish, unpatriotic, and un-American. They could point to the strikes and argue that unions were something beyond the pale of southern culture—and always had been. They were intrinsically foreign and dangerous to the culture itself.

This wartime charge was a blow in the emotional South not soon to be forgiven and never to be forgotten. *In reality*, labor unions may have been perfectly justified in striking and putting forth strike demands, but their actions did not take place in a vacuum—politically, socially, or culturally. And within the culture, *perception* of labor union disloyalty far exceeded the reality of valid economic grievance. War was not the time to strike if a union had any interest in keeping a future reservoir of public sympathy from which to draw in an already arid and ultraconservative region. More, since unions were seen by many southerners as the fair-haired progeny of the New Deal, the strikes did much to burden the New Deal Democratic administration that was supposed to be aiding the Allies in a war against fascism and tyranny. Even some southerners sympathetic to labor felt alienated and turned off by the timing of the strikes.

Alabama's forces of privilege were, of course, expert at whipping up popular emotions against labor based on race. It was not particularly difficult to transfer the tactic to a cultural creed of hyper-patriotism that damned the strikes but said nary a word about price gouging or war profiteering. And with its toehold secure on the subject of strikes, the Bourbons were soon able to denounce virtually any union-related bargaining demand on wages, conditions, or hours as unpatriotic and un-American, no matter what their endemic merit. Alabama governor Frank Dixon denounced the 1941 Sloss-Sheffield and Iron Company strike as "simple lawlessness and anarchy brought on by irresponsibility and [a] lack of patriotism" and laid responsibility squarely on the shoulders of the federal government. *Alabama Magazine* scored a direct cultural hit by ridiculing the bargaining demands of ten thousand CIO shipbuilders in Mobile as "a nice way to treat our Marines who are crawlin' on their bellies through jungles to hold off the Jap."[40]

The state's planters and industrialists detested hard-fought New Deal victories such as a forty-hour work week, Social Security, a minimum wage, and the concept of overtime pay. Now they took advantage of the war to deplore such standards as "peacetime leisures" and "pet social projects" from out-of-touch Washington bureaucrats. And they lampooned FDR's "platitudinous generalities about labor's patriotism" as having fooled no one. The oligarchs denounced the work week and overtime as the same kind of cultural sacrilege as the Works Project Administration: an abhorrent and divisive attempt to create social equality between the races in the South and "make us over, to pour our democracy into strange and unnatural moulds" that strike at native southern "patriotism" as would a snake.[41]

The *Dothan Eagle* weighed in with an editorial that could easily have been interpreted as a call for violence. "There has been too much delay, too much pampering . . . too many crocodile tears for the long-haired social revolutionists," editor Horace Hall expounded. "Loyal, liberty-loving Americans must rise up in righteous wrath and strike down these monsters [and] . . . unprincipled scoundrels . . . who are throttling the national defense . . . and endangering the lives of our people. . . . America has had enough! These [are] enemies within our own borders . . . [with] selfish ends, . . . shameless monster[s] . . . irresponsible and criminal . . . [with] rule or ruin . . . demands [from] . . . the lash of masters who are but criminal leaders of organized labor . . . more dangerous than all of Hitler's submarines!"[42]

Piqued by such stimuli, Alabamians of all ranks responded by absorbing and repeating the elite cultural creed against labor unions. One Mobile native described lawmakers who voted for a forty-hour work week as "bigger traitors . . . than Judas Iscariot." The irate Alabamian would sooner trust Hitler or Mussolini than he would any of the country's foreign labor bosses and agitators. Even some southerners who had previously been sympathetic toward organized labor now counted themselves among the disaffected. In a section of the country where the status quo wrapped racial custom together with social and class hierarchy, gender conformity, unbridled patriotism, and religious orthodoxy, the Big Mules were clearly gaining ground by condemning programs like the FEPC as the "Devil's Workshop."[43]

By using patriotic symbols, religious imagery, and hostility toward the federal government, the Bourbons augmented their briefs for white supremacy and unquestioned business control of society. They also went a long way toward perfecting their wartime melding of racial conservatism and economic conservatism into one and virtually the same thing: conservatism.

This Situation Is Unthinkable to Me

While segregationists routinely charged that black soldiers ran away under fire, actually there was a good deal of evidence that blacks in combat acquitted themselves quite well. The black Tuskegee pursuit squadron, for instance, was so renowned overseas that white bomber pilots requested their protective escort on their riskiest missions.[44] And for those dedicated to the precept of white supremacy, this was part of the problem. During World War II almost one million African Americans served in the U.S. Armed Forces, precipitating a crisis in how to deal with such a social dislocation and still preserve regional traditions. For many southern whites the outrage did not lie in black military service per se but in the billeting of black troops with whites and the presence of northern black soldiers on southern soil, replete with their dangerous and disrespectful ideas about social equality.

The mixing of black and white troops in southern environs—housing, eating, bathing, and training—was "the most damnable outrage" ever perpetrated on Dixie and a "senseless social experiment" that was just outrageous, according to leading southern segregationists.[45] White Alabamians forced to bivouac with black troops in military posts blamed the "G. D. Yankees" for the mess.[46] Other southerners said much in reasoning that federal troops should be required to respect southern racial customs the same way they would overseas.

For many the verdict of the Civil War in annulling the southern nation had not completely taken root. The *reality* that the South was not a separate nation along the lines of England or Italy did little to impinge on the widespread *perception* that, actually, it was. And truth be told, in a *cultural* sense these critics of the military's domestic policies had an argument—the South was different. Why was the U.S. government so insistent about troops observing the peculiar laws and customs of countries overseas and "so flagrantly inconsiderate" of the laws and customs of the South, an irate white spokesman articulated the angst. The effort to use war exigency as an excuse for destroying the things that made the South different was disgraceful and appalling.[47]

The open espousal by black leaders of a Double-V campaign to win victory, first against Hitler and then against racism at home, rubbed southern feelings raw. White southerners have always been renowned as patriots, an angry woman answered, and "we need Patriots just now." A Mobile black responded that African Americans, too, were the most loyal of Americans, whose integrity needed no questioning. They should be allowed to do their part in war production and military service. A black minister from Sheffield, in northwest Alabama, mused that he had heard a great deal of talk about democracy, especially during the war, but had yet to actually encounter it in Alabama: "where does he live? I would sure love to meet him." He asked for no special favors, just justice, decency, and a job where he could fit in. Still, many Alabama whites of all social stations recommended drafting more black men—not to fight but to relieve social tensions on the home front. Charles B. Crow, nephew of patrician matriarch Marie Bankhead Owen, was more direct than some about his hopes to stem social equality during the war: "Maybe they will hurry up and get those [black] troops over [to] the southwest Pacific and let the Japs get them!"[48]

Rational black pleas for legal and economic justice often fell on deaf ears because white fears were quite emotional and frequently revolved around sexual and social equality. During wartime such fears were exacerbated as large numbers of white males left home; women felt vulnerable and men insecure. Some blacks could not resist the temptation to vent their frustrations with the South's closed society by taunting white women about a new sexual order—although doing so only added fuel to the growing bonfire of sectional neurosis.

For the privileged architects of the racial and economic melding into a new regional orthodoxy, the tension was a godsend. Plain and working-class whites such as Willis Pace Estis, a Pleasant Grove machinist who worked for TCI, admitted that whites like himself were confused and anxious over the racial uncertainty. A UMW coal miner at Piper worried that with the white men away, the "young bucks" had to be attended to. Young black males were "really getting bad," bragging that they would have dates with white girls every night. "No red blooded American," he explained, especially southerners, was going to tolerate this. "One pure white girl is worth more than all the riches known to Man." With the white boys gone, black women were getting just as bad, a Birmingham woman complained. "You wouldn't want your sister or your wife or your daughter talked to like that by a negro," she complained to a public official.[49]

The acceleration in race worries only made the plain-white position more vulnerable vis-à-vis the planters and industrialists. Eventually Alabama would come to be known the world over as the home of George Wallace, master manipulator of a whole gallery of southern emotions. He was the sculptor of southern white anger and fear, which, as his insightful biographer Dan T. Carter understood, has been perhaps unsurpassed in the history of American politics.[50] But it is important to realize that for all of his political virtuosity, Wallace was not an original artist. He molded his grotesque but magnificent works out of clay that had been lying in Alabama's soil for at least a hundred years, and at certain times and places it had already been well worked before Wallace set his tragically gifted hands upon it.

To a large extent sex was the hot-button issue of the explosive payload of social equality. In the furnace that was the 1940s, whites across the South worried that demagogues like Mississippi's Theodore Bilbo might be right: Americans were going to have to choose between a mass exportation of blacks or becoming "an octoroon nation." The "curse of mongrelization" hung heavy and acrid in the air. Yet miscegenation and interracial offspring was only one concern in the gamut of social equality offenses. Scandalized Tuscaloosa whites vehemently objected to race mixing because blacks and whites used the same dining rooms, barbershops, even some wards of a local federal hospital. Congressman John Rankin, also of Mississippi, made racial labels on Red Cross blood vials a national issue.[51]

Many were convinced that mass violence was to follow as wild rumors swirled around the South that the March on Washington movement really aimed at taking over the top jobs in D.C. and leading to a "rule the whites, or kill them!" policy. "Believe it or not," more than one white southerner declared, "this is the *truth*!" Blacks are "preparing for War if necessary to win their Power over the whites."[52]

Alabama novelist William Bradford Huie poignantly captured the insidious fear that working people in his home state lived in with a best-selling novel, *Mud on the Stars*. "Birmingham is a smoke-belching automaton standing in an Alabama cotton patch and manipulated by wires from the Northern offices of Steel," Huie wrote. "A hundred thousand men and women. Working in the mines. Working in the mills. Working in the offices. Jammed together. Afraid. Afraid of the Shut-Down. Afraid of the bosses. Afraid of the union racketeers. Praying for more capacity and more security. Praying for smoke and more smoke. Praying for dirtier collars and dirtier dresses."[53]

Confronted by a flood of their own emotions—fear, rage, envy, worry, insecurity—white Alabamians of various social and economic ranks locked arms in a pan-white alliance against change—any kind of change. Among the most threatening was what they perceived to be the New Deal–sponsored fruit of social and sexual amalgamation. Franklin and Eleanor Roosevelt had coddled and egged on the black man to "claim a place at our table and a share in white women, his mad dream," and now chickens were coming home to roost. Some felt the First Lady was such a threat to southern mores that she should be banished from speaking anywhere in the South and should be, instead, "declared QUEEN OF LIBERIA." Alabama's Democratic Party chairman did much to stir popular passions when he accused Franklin and Eleanor of having done more to upset the "friendly relations heretofore existing" between the races than "all other presidents and their wives put together." Such agitation, Gessner McCorvey warned, was only going to lead to bloodshed. McCorvey's chief rival for chair of the state Democratic Party agreed that the agitation of national Democrats was only the latest act in an ongoing Reconstruction play. "This situation is unthinkable to me, and to all true Southerners," John D. McQueen said in defining suitable civic behavior. "[We will] simply never accept" social equality.[54]

During the war, southern whites began to worry that noises about public school integration might go far toward breaking down the whole Jim Crow line in the region. Education had long been seen as a particular corrosive of subservient black attitudes—and, as such, a distinct threat to the preservation of the status quo. By World War II it was almost gospel in the white South that educated blacks were "the ones that give us all the trouble."[55]

As liberalism increasingly came to be defined as being more about race than economics, blame for this unhappy state of affairs was laid at the doorstep of "liberal educators" who were doing their best to "break down the Southern door" of white supremacy through the public schools. The critique was not unlike the Reconstruction version aimed at carpetbag and scalawag teachers of the freedmen. Disgruntled Democrat and soon-to-be Dixiecrat Hamner Cobbs of the *Greensboro Watchman* grouched that southern students had to get their history from texts written by "Northern men, for Northern schools, and published by Northern firms" that were the most blatantly anti-southern tracts that could be found. Conservative whites like Cobbs worried that school—the most important vehicle for the inculcation of societal values next to the home—was becoming a place where conformity on the South's cultural precepts was fast rotting away. The editor grieved that students were beginning to believe that Abraham Lincoln was the greatest American, Jeff Davis the worst, and Robert E. Lee great, but "only through the back door." "What we need now," Cobbs lobbied, was "Southern history written by Southern men," or at least by those who had shown some sympathy to the South.[56]

While the actual explosion over public schools would wait for the 1950s, the issue of black voter registration picked up considerable steam during the war. This was due, principally, to the obvious incongruities in having African Americans go overseas with whites to risk their lives only to return home to pick up their mantle of second-class citizenship and queue back into separate lines. While America and her allies easily won the battle of global opinion over the war, this inconsistency was a notable point of hypocrisy in the record of the foremost defender of the free world—and would be picked up aggressively by communist powers even before the war ended.

Still, in much of the southern white mind there was little difference between Jim Crow, disfranchisement, and interracial purity. An assault on one was an assault on all, and retention of white supremacy was a slippery slope. "What's coming next?" a hill-country state senator from Calhoun asked plaintively when learning that segregation had been breached on military bases, "the poll tax eliminated?"[57]

The intertwined and regional understanding of the threat did not bode well for the future of the Democratic Party in the South. As the war dragged on, the party's viability in the South was increasingly compromised because whites correctly identified the national Democratic Party with northern and federal assaults on Jim Crow, voter registration, social and sexual equality, and all sundry matters—tensions that strained at the bonds of New Deal southern loyalty. An exasperated South Carolina legislature met to pass a resolution denouncing every group seeking amalgamation of races and to reaffirm its unwavering belief in white supremacy—and to demand that henceforth the "damned agitators of the North leave the South alone." Still a New Deal Democrat and Roosevelt supporter, perhaps Theodore Bilbo most clearly represented the looming and inherent contradiction within the Democratic Party. "We will tell our negro-loving Yankee friends to 'go straight to hell,'" the senator told the Mississippi legislature. Dixie will never consent to having integration in our schools and colleges, he said, not so long as "Anglo-Saxon blood flows in our veins!"[58] It was a contradiction whose resolution could not be postponed forever.

9
Racial Challenge, White Reaction, and Chauncey Sparks as the New Champion

[T]he only compromise that will suit . . . American negroes is the abolition of segregation, which in turn means the abolition of laws against miscegenation, which . . . means amalgamation . . . which . . . means the self-destruction of this nation by a mongrelized people.
—Hamner Cobbs

I have always voted the Democratic ticket, but by God I am through. And thousands of . . . American[s] are [too because the New Deal Democratic Party has failed miserably at keeping America] a good Christian nation . . . [and] preserving States' rights.
—C. L. Vance

"Kill the body, and the head will fall." This advice is one of the best-known nuggets of wisdom derived from the sweet science of prize fighting. The proverb refers, of course, to the value of doing groundwork in any endeavor before attempting a coup de grâce. To a large extent race relations on the southern home front during World War II bear a suitable relation. Whether viewed from the ramparts of defending white supremacy or the beachhead of assaulting it, the war pounded at the solid edifice of regional convention. By the end the defenses were still upright but several gaping holes were now present.

Votes for Soldiers

Much of the hope for the political liberation of the South and the emergence of its latent and (what some liberals felt was) its predominant liberalism lay in voter registration. The most optimistic assessments proclaimed that a largely silent majority liberal South lay waiting to emerge if only it could be freed from the oppressive yoke of suffrage restriction strapped onto it at the turn of the century. Remove the poll tax, fertilize the region with the ample seed of poor-white and black votes, and the South would bear the fruit of an enlightened liberal majority based on shared ground among plain folk—black and white. Evidence existed to suggest that at least half the equation was correct. According to more than one southern voting registrar, as soon as blacks enrolled, they pledged to vote for Franklin Roosevelt because he had saved them from starving.[1]

Led by Virginia Durr's SCHW anti–poll tax committee, various wartime liberals made abolition of the tax their chief goal. Durr's committee garnered support from the AFL, CIO, YWCA, the National Farmers Union, leading black organizations, and a host of other groups predisposed to liberal ideas. At least on the face of it, the liberal hope seemed more than just another pipe dream. Eight southern states featured various poll taxes, cumulative and not, ranging from one dollar to twenty-five dollars.[2]

Other mechanisms worked hand in hand with the tax to suppress participation: literacy tests, character clauses, property qualifications, and de facto subterfuges such as scheduling voter registration in intervals or in the parlors of white women where only the most intrepid of black men would venture. The sum resulted in a dramatically malformed and restricted electorate. During World War II, only 19 percent of the South's 14.5 million potential voters actually voted. In Alabama, the figures were 14 percent for the general election and only 8 percent in the all-important Democratic primary.[3]

Yet the liberal dream held within it several questionable assumptions. First, it presumed that the disfranchising mechanisms of the turn of the century had been imposed on the poor—black and white—by southern elites without aid and comfort from plain whites. Despite its widespread currency, that notion was actually more myth than fact.[4] Second, and perhaps most naively, the liberal focus on the poll tax conceived of politics as a strictly rational endeavor. That is, once poor whites and blacks could vote freely, without de jure and de facto restrictions, they would recognize common ground and gravitate naturally to a biracial alliance based on mutual class concerns. An allowance for the power of emotional appeals and race prejudice did not factor into what was a somewhat antiseptic and unrealistic view of politics and human behavior.

Nevertheless, World War II brought war on southern racial conventions at home just as surely as it brought war to the door of the Axis. Sponsored by liberal Florida senator Claude Pepper and widely supported by African Americans who felt poll tax annulment was the least a grateful nation could do for blacks in uniform, the Soldier Vote Bill of 1942 constituted the opening salvo against restrictive registration laws.[5]

The heart of southern white privilege led the fight against the bill, lending additional credence to liberal images of conservative elites trying to keep the lid on a congenitally liberal region. In any event, there was little question that southern white elites stood poised to lose the most from a sudden and massive registration of black and poor-white soldiers. Alabama governor Frank Dixon declared the bill "disastrous." Hubert Baughn continued yeoman service to the cause of Bourbon conservatism by terming it another assault hidden in the "Trojan horse of 'patriotism'" against the South's "way of life," a section that easily led the country in military support.[6] The *Gadsden Times* said the measure threatened white supremacy while the *Anniston Times*, also in the hill country, and the *Selma Times-Journal*, from the Black Belt, thought the threat Reconstruction-like. Respectively, they branded the bill "another form of force bill" and "a new reconstruction" designed to leave the South floundering helplessly "in a flood of colored votes."[7]

Confronted by the privileged stance, only Luther Patrick and John Sparkman among Alabama's vaunted congressional delegation had the resolve to favor passage of the bill. Pete Jarman called for a Senate filibuster while George Grant and Governor Dixon railed about "pseudo-reformers" and "social reformers" taking advantage of blacks for their own selfish purposes.[8] Even Lister Hill opposed the Soldier Vote Bill as unconstitutional, taking great pains to demonstrate his sympathy with Birmingham auto dealer and later Republican Don Drennen, who asserted that if the bill passed it meant "our southern democracy is gone." For his efforts Hill gained only the backhanded praise of a Bourbon press that realized he was feeding the monster of white supremacy not out of conviction but only from a desire to keep it at bay.[9]

Despite talk of a filibuster, few public figures wanted to be perceived as against the troops in any form or fashion in 1942. The bill passed, but the episode signaled the hammering of yet another nail into the coffin of the New Deal coalition that had temporarily elevated class concerns to a place of distinction in the South. For an increasingly restive region, it drew a line in the sand.

Former New Dealers such as John Temple Graves and patronage boss Horace Wilkinson spoke loudly against the bill on the basis of cultural integrity—and economics. Graves blamed "radical outsiders" and urged the governor to allow the state's congressional delegation to take the lead in fighting it. Wilkinson recommended a Senate filibuster and provided an advanced lesson in melding white supremacy to economic conservatism in opposing the law. For Wilkinson and other cultural conservatives in revolt against the New Deal, the bill was part of the same "foolish and destructive notion" of entitlement then taking root: the crippling idea that everybody deserves to "eat whether they work or not." Opposition to it was a question of cultural survival. If the mind-set of public indulgence then in vogue was allowed to proceed unchallenged, it would mean the end of "the American way of life."[10]

A Federal Monstrosity

All of this was but an undercard for the fight over abolition of the actual poll tax. Anti–poll tax bills passed the House of Representatives only to fall prey to filibusters and other forms of resistance in the Senate in 1943, 1945, 1947, and 1949. In Alabama the forces of privilege congealed against this measure, led by *Alabama Magazine* and its cache of corporate sponsors like Alabama Power, DeBardeleben Coke and Coal, Monsanto Chemicals, and Birmingham Trust and Savings. The first attempt at overturning the poll tax, a 1942 Claude Pepper bill, passed muster in the House but faltered in the Senate when Mississippi's Theodore Bilbo and Texas's Tom Connally—both New Dealers—led a nine-day filibuster. Birmingham mine executive Hugh Morrow fought the bill because he had "never lined up against the white people of the Black Belt" and never expected to. Mobile's S. Palmer Galliard, another future defector from the Democratic Party, said that the real goal of the anti–poll taxers was social equality and interracial marriage.[11]

The fight again pointed up how far former class foes had closed ranks during the war. Gessner McCorvey wanted to retain the poll tax in order to keep blacks *and poorer whites* shut out of politics, arguing that its abolition would allow "all kinds of rabble . . . thriftless, shiftless, worthless . . . people" into politics. Horace Wilkinson, former tribune of the white working class, was scarcely less elitist in the new melding equation of state politics. He suggested that instead of abolition the tax should actually be *raised* from $1.50 a year to $5.00 because it was the best protection against people who "[have] no more business voting than a jackass, be they white or black." And Grover Hall Sr., commonly mistaken by scholars and contemporaries as a liberal for his opposition to the KKK, was already on record as favoring the poll tax as insurance for the rule of the "responsible citizens" against the "pauperized thousands" and the "dispossessed."[12]

For his part, Frank Dixon used the poll tax controversy to piggyback on the FEPC cause célèbre to solidify his rapidly growing reputation as a champion of sectional culture. The governor complained that southern whites, the most patriotic people in the country, were being put upon at a time when they were bending every knee for the war effort. Only disunity and disaster could result from this "vicious misguided . . . danger[ous] . . . unconstitutional . . . invasion of states rights," a vile outrage crammed "down the throats" of the freedom-loving southern people.[13]

Harry Flood Byrd, jockeying with Dixon for sectional leadership, echoed the Alabamian. It was a slippery slope the federals were following, the Virginia apple magnate averred, and if they were successful, then every other registration protection was in jeopardy. Alabama congressman Henry Steagall agreed with the catastrophic consequences of the slippery slope assessment: if the bill passed it meant the end of representative government in America.[14] As he had with the FEPC, Mississippi congressman John Rankin painted the poll tax bill as a communist device to punish the South. Dixon's Bourbon backers chorused that the bill was only a thinly veiled attempt by crusaders trying to exploit the war emergency. It was the creature of "congressional zealots . . . professional reformers, rabble-rousing agitators and social equality advocates." It was a "fedrel monstrosity" and a "shameless rape of the Constitution"—nothing less.[15]

In the face of a withering assault that cast opposition to repeal as a litmus test of southern patriotism, only Luther Patrick stood by it among the famed Alabama congressional delegation. One reason Alabama had such an extraordinarily liberal reputation was that its congressional delegation *was* expert at winning government largesse during the New Deal and World War II and in this respect really was quite progressive. Many people in the South, and elsewhere (and later scholars), just assumed the liberalism carried over to racial and cultural areas. But it rarely did. Every one of Alabama's other congressmen and senators—those from north Alabama and south, even Lister Hill and John Sparkman—fought the poll tax bill. And all made certain to communicate their congratulations to Frank Dixon for serving as their leader in the struggle to defeat it.[16]

Perhaps most alarming were the emotional estimations of non-Bourbons and those thought to be moderate and even liberal. *Anniston Star* editor Col. Harry M. Ayers swallowed the slippery slope argument whole and wrote—almost hysterically—that should the bill pass, the United States would be on its way toward "totalitarian government." Others thanked the Bourbon champions for standing up for "our Southland" in protecting mechanisms such as the poll tax, which was Dixie's salvation in preventing "the worthless and ignorant class who don't know anything . . . and who don't give a damn" from controlling politics.[17]

For many, the poll tax fight was another battle in the war over race and Reconstruction memory. "I . . . well remember how they voted . . . in the 1870s," a Barbour County man recalled about the state's blacks. "I shall never forget." Republican patronage boss Oliver Day Street echoed the sentiment, shuddering at his recollection of blacks voting before 1901. The poll tax was needed to keep control of government in the hands of people "[who are not] mere children in intelligence," an Alabama woman explained. She suggested a solution: the government should let blacks choose one state and then relocate all of them there—kind of like Indian removal.[18]

Resistance to the bill won virulent criticism from northern sources as wartime politics took on an increasingly sectional tone. A New York theater producer condemned the "white trash bloc" of southern congressmen for obstructing the bill and argued that taking such stands were a form of job security down South. He echoed the prevailing liberal view that the poll tax was the silver bullet to conservative domination of Dixie. Many of the southern representatives had spent their lives protecting "white womanhood and public utility companies," the New Yorker wrote tartly, pointing out the close connection between race, class, and gender in southern politics. "Do you think it's going to be any fun" for defeated southern congressmen to "go back to . . . some Coca Cola town with . . . nothing to break the monotony but an occasional lynching party?"[19]

Direct assaults on the poll tax were not successful during the war and white subterfuge was common, but that did not prevent African Americans from trying to increase their number on the existing rolls. Registrars around the South asked blacks seeking the vote questions like how many windows there were in the courthouse or the number of steps between city hall and the post office. Blacks could still be required to write out the whole Constitution, a Georgia registrar chortled, and then be disqualified if they "leave out a comma."[20]

In 1942 black attorney Charles Gomillion of the Tuskegee Civic Association persuaded a young black man to register to vote in Macon County, Alabama. After seventeen attempts, he finally succeeded. Gomillion filed a voter registration suit against the county charging, in part, that the board had put off meeting for a year and a half only to convene in secret and register two hundred whites. An Alabama Republican appointed to the federal bench threw the suit out, but black activists Arthur D. Shores in Birmingham and John L. LeFlore in Mobile continued to push the NAACP cause of black voter registration. Shores even ran for the Alabama state legislature to encourage African Americans to register. Staunch segregationists met a mass attempt to register blacks in Montgomery by denouncing professional meddlers, imported agitators, and social reformers—along with the federal government—for stirring them up. Continued attempts to press white southerners to move faster than they wanted, they explained in passive-aggressive style, could only antagonize the "real friends" of blacks among white people.[21]

Despite the counsel of patience for "one day" when black goals would be met, it was clear that white intransigence was most fundamentally about power and control.[22] Despite constant assurances that progress was being made in the South, it was clear that things were not going to change in any meaningful way any time soon—or strictly on their own.

For southern whites the poll tax was the key to black voting, and black voting was the key to a whole Pandora's box full of racial and political trouble. Reacting to a question about abolition of the poll tax, a Tennessee election commissioner asked, "Why? And have some big, black son-of-a-bitch sitting up in the courthouse sending white men to jail?" If blacks started voting in large numbers they would soon elect black officials. At city hall there would be "some sporting black reared back like God Almighty! No, Sir! Son, I'm not for that! I'm a Southerner and a Democrat." The white female chair of the Montgomery, Alabama, County Board of Registrars explicated further. "All niggers—uneducated and educated—have one idea in their mind—they want equality," she said. "But look on them for yourself. You don't mean that we could have them in our churches . . . our cemeteries . . . our schools and . . . our homes any more than we have apes or other animals." Voting will "lead to social equality. The niggers are in the majority in this county and in Alabama. They would take over the power in the state. The white people are never going to give them this power."[23]

For God's Mercy! What Is Going Wrong in Alabama?

Frank Dixon's masculine stand against the FEPC in 1942 had done more than enunciate his own personal battle against federal involvement in employment discrimination. It furnished a blueprint for future Alabama governors to follow that would find its ultimate fruition in the career of George Wallace. In the FEPC matter, in numberless speeches and public appearances, and in his leadership against abolition of the poll tax, Dixon served as the personification of states' rights and white supremacist opposition to the federal government—not only for Alabama but for the entire region. To a large extent, Chauncey Sparks would follow in his footsteps.

This was actually something of a surprise, since Sparks was regarded by some contemporaries and later historians as a progressive political figure and because he had been, in a real way, the accidental winner of the 1942 gubernatorial election.[24] By virtually all informed estimates, the election was Bibb Graves's to lose. Graves did not win, but only because he died midway through the campaign.

The "little colonel's" untimely demise left the field wide open, a development that eventually benefited Sparks more than anyone. James E. "Big Jim" Folsom, a virtual unknown from Cullman County, ran a surprisingly close second on a shoestring campaign and was one of the most colorful personalities in southern politics. Yet Folsom and his brand of progressivism would have to wait four more years. Alabama's privileged forces coalesced around Sparks, the "Bourbon from Barbour," and he received the eventual endorsement of outgoing governor Frank Dixon and emerging powers such as real estate entrepreneur Sidney Smyer. In fact, it was largely Smyer who advised Sparks to pose as the anti-labor candidate against Folsom and the Graves remnants in a year of emotional work stoppages. Alabamians are "mighty sore about these strikes," Sparks confidante Robin Swift agreed. And they are "going to get sorer, for organized labor has no patriotism, no sense of responsibility, and in its greed would wreck this country. . . . Here is the issue [that will put you]" in the governor's mansion.[25] Sparks's victory in the Democratic primary marked a triumph for Alabama's economically conservative forces, one that was echoed nationally in 1942 as the GOP gained forty-six seats in the U.S. House and nine in the Senate, and vocal New Deal opponents Josiah Bailey, Carter Glass, and Pappy O'Daniel won reelection.[26]

As tensions mounted, the South moved closer to the outbreak of actual violence. For many, the issues of black "uppitiness" and *patriotism* during a time of war seemed to be on a collision course. Fed up with expressions of black assertiveness and the various threats to Jim Crow, white Alabamians talked more often of resorting to the old methods of Ku Kluxism and vigilante control. Many were convinced that sooner or later racial violence would break out. The presence of northern black soldiers in Dixie was doing nothing but aggravating the southern Negro to boldness, the mayor of Eufaula complained. It was an outrage that the white people of the South—the most patriotic in the country mind you—should have to be burdened with the fear of racial trouble breaking out. "Draft them all [and] put them in Labor Battalions," an angry Mobilian suggested. All the Negroes, even the southern born, were "getting out of line," another Alabama man agreed.[27]

But "getting out of line" varied immensely in the South. To be sure, there was too much smoke during these years for there to be no fire. Some blacks took distinct pleasure in acting the part of what one African American scholar has termed "baaad niggers"—taunting and provoking older whites and females who felt vulnerable from the absence of large numbers of young white males off to war.[28] For some, the bad behavior was no doubt an expression of freedom, an "acting out" by behaving in ways that were deliberately annoying, even confrontational, to those who had traditionally dominated society. In this way, wartime behavior bore a certain kinship to the much later expressions of "ghangsta" rap and hip-hop culture—rude, crude, loud, and purposefully offensive. For some, according to black sociologist

Ralph Bunche, these years saw the altogether predictable overcompensation of people who generally felt powerless. To cope, they engaged in "exhibitionism, raucousness, flashiness in dress . . . exaggerated self-assertion [and] an air of belligerency."[29]

Southern whites worried that wartime conditions had sent blacks out of control. A Bessemer grand jury estimated that 90 percent of its cases involved African Americans: "They have not only plundered and robbed, but have killed, slashed and ravished each other." Even in "northern" cities such as Washington, D.C., southerners reported that whites were being "daily, almost hourly insulted" by blacks, pushed around, "slapped, cursed and knocked down by their overbearing, superior attitudes." Black people were not satisfied with equality, white southerners feared; they were demanding superiority and even the Yankees were fed up.[30]

Still, much of what was termed bad black behavior consisted of merely a refusal to bow to the traditional sacred cow of white supremacy. In most of the South it didn't take much to get branded a "bad nigger," or get arrested, or worse—only a small breach of the color line. Buses and streetcars were particular centers of conflict, arenas of shifting race relations in which drivers—guardians of the status quo—were licensed to wear sidearms and endowed with a kind of semi-police status.

Armed segregationists, a strict color line, shifting definitions of custom, more assertive blacks—it all added up to the inevitable in the Deep South. In 1942 a Birmingham bus driver shot a black man six times in a dispute over three cents *after* he stepped off a bus. In Montgomery police beat and robbed a black army lieutenant following an argument between the soldier and a white driver. In August, a Mobile bus driver shot and killed an African American soldier on his way back to base. Wartime violence spilled over into other challenges to the status quo. Interracial brawls broke out on passenger trains, ironically enough, near Scottsboro in north Alabama. In Tuscaloosa County weeks of flogging and terror climaxed with fiery crosses in front of a CIO/Steelworkers' hall on the eve of a NLRB representation election.[31]

There is little question that violence was the ultimate cornerstone of white supremacist society. It had been for a long time. While many have pinned white supremacist violence on the South's poorer whites, and in fact their hands were as bloody as other whites, quite often it was the "better sorts" that winked at the violence, condoned it, and even encouraged and organized vigilantism when push came to shove. The antebellum slave patrols and vigilante groups had functioned this way—as had, to a large extent, the Reconstruction Klan, the whitecaps and the lynch mobs of the 1890s, and various other groups.

Elites knew that at its most basic level, violence formed the underpinning of their strict societal status quo. And violence could be the only result of all these wartime challenges to Jim Crow, concluded many, including a leading Birmingham car dealer. If the apostles of social equality persist in their madness, the *Gadsden Times* warned, they were "going to start something they won't be able to finish," a society "soaked in blood."[32]

In 1943 tensions boiled over when a two-day riot erupted at the Mobile shipyards of the Alabama Dry Dock and Shipbuilding Company (ADDSCO). The violence was an especially good example of the intersection between challenges to the racial *and* economic status quo—as well as the ongoing melding process that was making privileged-white lions and plain-white lambs lie down together. The strike featured two days of violence from pipe- and club-wielding whites, many of them union members, aimed at the few blacks who worked at ADDSCO. But it also featured regional revolt against the federal government and the considerable agitation of race feelings by a company resentful of federal involvement in matters of employment discrimination.

The violence erupted in response to a six-month-old FEPC directive calling for the promotion of twelve blacks to the position of welder. For whites, the federal character of the incident was compounded when U.S. Army troops and Coast Guardsmen assisted state and local police and the National Guard in restoring order.[33] But mostly the episode supplied Chauncey Sparks with an ideal opportunity to follow in Frank Dixon's footsteps as an Alabama governor who would be willing to thumb his nose at Yankees, "outside agitators," and the federal government.

Thought by some to be a progressive, Sparks lost no time in stoking the chords of Reconstruction hurt, southern white cultural resentment, narrow conceptions of morality, and acceptable black ambition by crafting very public answers to criticisms of Alabama emanating from national sources.

> We would not have any [racial problems] but for influence over which we have no control. If self-seeking politicians, misguided philanthropists and outside influences would quit trying to regulate matters which are entirely local, we would have no future difficulty . . . if we can be let alone and zoot-minded propagandists do not misinform. . . . [F]uture race rioting . . . will have its roots buried in inflammatory negro newspapers . . . ambitious politicians and misguided and emotional missionaries who place shibboleths above reality. The South does not need to be taught morality by prosecutions, by . . . committee [or] by [the] preachments . . . [of] some unreasonable agitator. . . . [W]hen the negro quits chasing rainbow ends and butterflies, such as social equality

and the abolition of segregation and confines his attention to fundamentals, such as industry, education . . . economic security, and those things which go to make a civilization, the better off he will be and the less successful the agitators will be.³⁴

Northerners and some southerners reacted with horror. Not only had Alabama erupted in race riot but the state's chief executive was seemingly providing if not outright justification then at least a heavy covering fire for those responsible. A Boston-born journalist writing for the *Mobile Press-Register* blamed the violence on the rank-and-file "pea pickers" who refused to work with blacks, while an African American rebuked the company's white managers for telling blacks that no matter how many federal directives came down, they would never hire "Nigger welders and electrician[s]." A Mobile labor journal pointed to the Klan and anti-Roosevelt forces as culpable while Alabama's *CIO News Digest* blamed the "stupidity" of the company as well as outside "agitators . . . [and] troublemakers." An investigator from Sparks's office laid the mess to the inability of the company to offset the "vicious propaganda" of the federal government and national labor unions.³⁵

A white South Carolinian living in New York, embarrassed by Sparks's defiance, urged him to work for a better South instead of one that recedes to the days of 1860 and wondered aloud "just what the historians will say." A native New Yorker lived up to regional stereotypes by being more direct. "For God's mercy! What is going wrong in Alabama?" he asked. "Alabama must not be allowed to out-Hitler Adolf."³⁶

The Business Community Is Firmly behind You

Still reeling from Frank Dixon's departure, Alabama's forces of business and wealth were overjoyed with their newfound hero in Chauncey Sparks. From the beginning there had been some reluctance on the subject of Sparks. He had shown a few tentative progressive inclinations on economic matters—not much really but certainly enough to give the most devout adherents of privilege pause. Dixon himself had delayed his all-important endorsement of Sparks, feeding to some degree doubts about the new governor. But Sparks's aggressiveness in taking up the racial and sectional cudgel left by Dixon cheered the planter and industrialist forces. There would be no interruption after all in the ineluctable march toward the melding of racial and economic conservatism.

In fact, Sparks looked to possibly be a mighty aid to the ongoing Bourbon project of appropriating completely the white supremacy issue from their economically progressive adversaries. For a seeming eternity they had been forced to share the hallowed ground of white supremacy with the region's economic liberals. But finally all of that was changing.

The business community "[is] firmly behind you . . . on your stand relative to the supremacy of the white man," an Alabama Power Company manager congratulated Sparks. Business types were especially impressed by Sparks's manly posture in following Dixon's lead in taking a "fearless . . . stand" against the forces that would corrode white supremacy. A Randolph County banker blamed Yankee labor interference. He actually liked Negroes, he explained; he never wanted to live "where there *ain't* no negro, no mule and no possum."[37]

Whenever criticism arose, planter and industrialist press figures instinctively provided cover to ward it off and to consolidate popular support for their sectional champions. To be sure, they believed in the slippery-slope logic they employed, but they were also acutely aware that it was the kind of thing that could be understood and parroted at the folk level—and indeed the kind of thing that was so threatening it could prevent other, more mundane economic issues from even gaining air.

If politicians like Chauncey Sparks had any ideas about retaining their mildly progressive edges, they would soon be disabused of such naiveté. For they would have considerable trouble prevailing over the oligarchs who were determined to erase such impulses. The slippery-slope strategy reduced any unorthodoxy on race customs to a level that resonated with the masses— the level of a cultural threat that imperiled the survival of a civilization. On the slippery slope, the smallest snowball could quickly become an avalanche. So it was all the same in terms of danger: an inch was a mile. The only compromise that would suit the large body of American Negroes, Greensboro's Hamner Cobbs wrote, "is the abolition of segregation, which in turn means the abolition of laws against miscegenation, which in turn means the ultimate amalgamation of the races, which in turn means the self-destruction of this nation by a mongrelized people."[38]

Alabama's press, regardless of section, got overwhelmingly behind Sparks. The *Tuscaloosa News* praised the governor for his strong reply to PM *Magazine*, that "pinko New York daily" that had been poking its nose into southern race relations. Grover Hall Jr., obviously chastened for ever-so-slightly questioning Frank Dixon's methods in the army cloth matter, resolved not to make the same mistake with his successor. Junior dutifully crept back onto the reservation of white supremacy by characterizing the whole to-do as the product of sensationalistic Yankee reporting—and not even a race riot at all. Despite the penance, the Bourbons showed themselves quick to anger but slow to forgive by dismissing Hall's *Montgomery Advertiser* as not competent to discuss the race issue in Alabama.[39]

Only in the Deep South could the position of Chauncey Sparks be confused for that of a moderate. Yet in Alabama, Sparks—through his firm insistence on racial and economic laissez-faire and paeans to Negroes making gains through the proper channels of approved behaviors—won for himself a reputation as a moderate and in some corners even a "liberal." The gulf between this view—and the more realistic assessment of Sparks as a slightly more polished preserver of business privilege and white supremacy than his predecessors—lay bare an even larger divide that was rapidly developing North and South on the whole question of race and politics. Near the time of the Mobile riot, Chauncey Sparks agreed to give the Founder's Day speech at the famed Tuskegee Institute and chose race relations as his topic.

While the address only enhanced Sparks's developing reputation for moderation, again, it was actually a model of sectional and racial rigidity. Its seizure by white southerners as evidence of some kind of good faith and racial moderation only pointed up how far the white South was drifting away from the mainland of American democracy, pulled by a tide of unwavering conviction to a cultural creed.

Sparks began his address by, in effect, providing an apologia for slavery—not as a tragedy but as a providential opportunity for blacks. Bondage had, contrary to some people's estimations, actually afforded a civilizing and cultural kindergarten for a people with "no historic or racial background of education, of culture, or of achievement." Pioneers like Booker T. Washington worked hard to help "this primitive people" improve themselves so that they might show themselves worthy of their new country, so that they might develop into "an asset" to their states and "an aid to the civilization of a [free] nation" that offered them such bountiful opportunities. Then Sparks publicly asked questions that only a white person of privilege could ask: "Does it make any difference whether I ride in the front or in the rear of a bus? Does it make any difference whether I attend a school for whites alone? . . . Are we not wasting time, generating friction and antagonism, by striving for . . . rainbows' ends . . . unattainable and unnecessary?" "Outside agitation" had been nothing but harmful to blacks, the governor said as he lectured against interference from "misguided agitators" trying to construct laboratories for the propagation of "false ideas."[40]

The ground rules of goodwill and white friendship set, Sparks turned to the carrot of his message. A large burden rested on the white man of the South. "Ignorance is a burden. Poverty is an economic disease," Sparks said in striking the notes that would win him praise for liberalism. "What makes you poor makes me also poor," he told the black audience in sounding like one of the 1901 paternalists. "You cannot remain down without, at the same time, dragging me with you." But help from the white benefactor would come at a price. Although Tuskegee had long operated semi-autonomously, the time had come when the state's best whites should take a more active role in the school's purpose and program. "We owe it an obligation," Sparks said, but at the same time we have to participate in the "control of its activities."[41]

Almost without exception, whites in Alabama and throughout Dixie hailed Sparks as a newfound southern leader on race relations. Because the Alabama governor had spoken of black progress and education—albeit within strictly confined parameters—and had not recommended the lyncher's knot or the Kluxer's whip, whites saw in him a wise but firm figure, a visionary, in fact, who spoke the no-nonsense truth about what was possible in the realm of southern race relations. Desegregation and social equality were impossible. They were not to be spoken of or even thought about. To do so was a waste of time and energy and could only sow division. Whites were to work to lift up the black race, but only within strictly separate spheres and in ways that would profit the whites who controlled the region's business and commerce.

Sparks was developing into a regional defender of white supremacy—Frank Dixon with a little more polish but not one ounce less resolve. Grateful planters and industrialists responded with an outpouring of warmth. For many, Sparks's speech marked the emergence of a true and tolerant southern progressive, and it marked an occasion when Bourbons and more moderate Alabamians could sit down and agree on race. The *Birmingham News*, which had expressed some mild criticism of Dixon's recalcitrance, praised Sparks. The *Jacksonville News* lauded his "sane, progressive" course while the *Alabama Journal* called it "sound and progressive," and Thomas Abernethy's *Talladega Daily Home* said Sparks had exhibited the "deep wisdom of a statesman." Even moderate Harry Ayers of the *Anniston Star* applauded it as "perfectly stated."[42]

Yet this was a "progressivism" built firmly on the shifting sands of states' rights. "The negro does not get justice down here and we all know he does not," wrote a textile mill owner. But in the next sentence he blasted Yankee agitation and forced social equality as twin demons. A Birmingham attorney extolled Sparks. He predicted that northern and eastern Yankees, convinced the South was home to a primitive people and jaundiced by the past, would not be able to understand or appreciate the "intelligent southern white man's view point on the so-called race 'problem.'"[43]

Indeed, the speech elicited a similar reaction from some black accommodationist voices, lending more credence to the growing belief that Chauncey Sparks was in fact a liberal. F. D. Patterson, principal of the Tuskegee Institute and fast becoming a hero to white supremacists in Alabama, endorsed Sparks's words and implicitly rebuked northern "agitators" by saying that this was not the time for a resumption of Civil War hostilities. The acting chaplain and black librarian at Kilby Prison wrote the governor with warm congratulations. Still other voices of black accommodationism chimed in. "We do not need any outsiders coming in telling us what we should do," the Rev. E. M. Wilson stated. Segregation was the best system for all concerned, and the southern white people "[are] our best friends," Wilson said in repeating the mantra that white southerners thrilled to hear from blacks. Wilson's stance probably derived somewhat from his position on the state payroll as chaplain at Atmore Prison, but he was a leading voice of accommodation during this period, consistently extolling the southern white man for his help and blasting black leaders who rejected Jim Crow as "agitating race hatred among our people" and deserving of forced exile from the South.[44]

As in the various Frank Dixon cause célèbres, the Tuskegee speech highlighted the ongoing healing process taking place among erstwhile Bourbon and Kluxer adversaries. Oliver Street made common cause with Chauncey Sparks in 1943. So did Tom-Tom Heflin.[45] In doing so the former Populist and the former poster boy for the Klan and dirt farmers lay down with mortgage bankers, mega-farmers, and coal, textile, and real-estate operators. They carefully defined what would constitute the ground rules for white friendship with the black race and suitable black endeavors. It was a narrow set of rules and conventions that, if dutifully adhered to by the inferior race, could preserve comity between the races. It would also (it almost goes without saying) guarantee perpetual black subservience. Yet for declaring lynch parties, public hangings, and race riots out-of-bounds, the neo-Kluxer and neo-Bourbon were able to join hands and call themselves "moderates"—and sometimes even "liberals."

Southern whites of various stations met the onslaught against racial and cultural norms by building a bubble to protect themselves from the outside world. It was an artificial universe in which conservatives were moderates, moderates were liberals, and liberals were wild-eyed radicals. In such a society, right-wing extremists were considered mere conservatives, sometimes even mainstream. Part of this mountainous self-delusion was the belief that criticism emanated only from foreigners and the North—intrusive Yankees, uppity blacks, and alien agitators—all sources with no credibility or standing. Southern blacks were well satisfied with the status quo.

Despite the pervasiveness of the self-deception in the white South, the rest of the world did not go along so easily. "For God's sake!" a Tuskegee graduate moved to New York lectured Sparks, "You insulted our dead, Sir. . . . Stop helping Hitler!" Sparks's Founder's Day address was almost perfect, the black *Birmingham Weekly Review* jibed. It had succeeded in insulting 95 percent of those in attendance.[46]

Yet most of the strongest criticism came from black northerners. The *Baltimore Afro-American,* a leading journal of black opinion, observed that Sparks's address told blacks to "Love Jim Crow" and was the same speech Booker T. Washington might have given thirty years earlier—revealing that the South remained inert on matters of race. A columnist for the *Chicago Defender* focused on the appeal of the speech to common southern whites. Sparks' address had been overseasoned with the kind of prejudice that appealed to the "uninformed white man in the hills and swamps. They have no education and are easy victims of this type of political mass psychology." If Sparks succeeded, racial prejudice and misunderstanding would block any real attempts at biracial cooperation.[47]

But no one exceeded the *Pittsburgh Courier's* George S. Schuyler, who speculated that the Alabama governor might win the Nazi Iron Cross and ridiculed Sparks's insistence on absolute segregation as something that would be "an incalculable boon to the colored folk, freed from the incubus of ignorant, arrogant, exploiting racism," although bad for white southerners. "It would not work, of course, because white people will not stay away from colored people. They starve and pine away without them as a flea shrinks without a dog. Colored labor and . . . lands are vitally necessary to them." "What was Europe before it found colored people to fleece?" Schuyler asked. "What was Anglo-America before the African slave trade got into its stride? What enriched the Belgians, the Dutch, the Spanish and the Portuguese, to say nothing of the French? What is Germany and Italy after, if not colored people to enslave? Segregation, indeed!"[48]

Yet Alabama's *status quo society* was so thoroughly skewed to the right that Sparks's defense of segregation, back-seat bus riding, and white supremacy actually received criticism from the right as *too liberal*. The *Greensboro Watchman's* Hamner Cobbs, a personal friend of Sparks and his closest aide, was highly disappointed. Now southern blacks were going to take Sparks for a racial progressive relative to Frank Dixon and be further encouraged to press for change. "Appeasement Doesn't Pay," an angry Cobbs warned in print in projecting the war effort against the Nazis to blacks at home. Reforms instituted by southern liberals would be as dangerous to the South as the "appeasement of Chamberlain" was to Europe.[49]

A more vulgar expression of such criticism that emanated from parts of Alabama actually did make Sparks look, relatively speaking, like a moderate. Conjuring the gravitas of Civil War and Reconstruction heroism, the Robert E. Lee Club of Reeltown in Tallapoosa's hill country let the governor know that they did not like his speech one "little bit." The "stuck up negroes in Tuskegee . . . already think they are as good as white people," the angry group of plain whites grumbled, "and such folks as you is the cause of it." "If you are such a negro lover," the club advised, "go to the North where the negro lovers belong. . . . [Y]ou are as yellow as a negro."[50]

They Are Forcing the White Man to Become More Conservative

Chauncey Sparks soon provided additional evidence that 1940s Alabama was a society tilted almost irretrievably to the right. Devoted to the preservation of an interrelated and hierarchical status quo, the state's culture produced a conservative polity that understood anything short of the most rabid and militant racism to be enlightenment, tolerance, and wise understanding.

In May 1944 Sparks gave another of his high-profile statements on race relations, this time seizing the opportunity to address seven hundred black churchmen attending a Colored Methodist Episcopal conference in Birmingham. Whites—both those defined as conservatives and the more moderate variety—praised the governor's speech as the epitome of wise and tolerant southern statesmanship. Victor Hanson's newspapers, which had frequently been on difficult terms with the state's most devout anti–New Dealers—and had been damned as liberal and even radical for their independence—demonstrated that whites of various persuasions were drawing their wagons closer in the face of the perceived onslaught against southern custom. The Hanson papers agreed with their sometime adversaries that Sparks's words were "very wise . . . [and] progressive" and demonstrated a humane approach "toward understanding." The mossbacks at the *Alabama Magazine* described the talk as full of neighborly advice, and the *Birmingham Post* revealed that Alabama Republicans were also in concert with Sparks's message.[51]

In light of the white consensus, it bears examining exactly what Sparks said. The governor divided his remarks into four major sections: the Negro press, northern leaders, the FEPC, and white supremacy. On at least four occasions he used the word "nigger"—a term he had been booed for at Tuskegee. He dismissed the FEPC as a "foolish gesture" that was undermining the sacred right of employers to reward ability, fitness, experience, and character—an argument that would anticipate those used most energetically against the concept of employment discrimination and workplace seniority in later decades. Federal intrusion into the time-tested patterns of peaceful southern life was an experiment in "regimentation and . . . personal control." He whipped out the ever-reliable slippery slope argument. If society were going to continue down this sorry path it might just as well make people go to "a certain church, dress according to a given style and pray thus," Sparks said in striking the chords of hyperindividualism and antibureaucracy that were held so dear in the conservative South. The black press and the North—black and white—were doing nothing but a disservice to southern blacks by butting in and making unworkable demands à la Reconstruction. "I should like to see the South let alone," the governor closed. "All they are doing is . . . forcing the white man to become more conservative and to agitate the Negro."[52] Within the guise of helping blacks, in truth Sparks did his best to buttress the society that kept the race in an utterly subservient position—and he was rewarded for it by being called a liberal and an enlightened statesman.

Yet Chauncey Sparks's next service to the cause of white supremacy as its sectional champion would leave no doubt that he was far from liberal on any matter that involved race. A July 8, 1944, army order prohibiting racial discrimination at post exchanges, theaters, and other recreational amusements went relatively unnoticed until the August implementation of the directive in the cradle of the Confederacy: Montgomery's Maxwell Air Force Base. This assault on regional customs provided Sparks a made-to-order opportunity to solidify his growing reputation as regional defender of the status quo, and he did not falter. Sparks immediately fired off a strongly worded telegram of protest to President Roosevelt that played in almost every newspaper in Dixie.[53] Grasping the initiative, Sparks also cabled every member of Alabama's congressional delegation to lead the state's response, setting in motion a chain of events that further consolidated the governor's role as race leader and allowed white Alabamians to further suppress class differences in support of the overriding cultural cause.

Perhaps most alarmingly for the future of the Democratic Party, the coordinated response sharpened the focus of sectional discontent on the party as little more than an appendage of a hostile northern aggressor bent upon destroying the southern "way of life." A cultural split was increasingly being defined in the South as a *sectional* split that would eventually have serious repercussions for the country's partisan alignments. In southern eyes the Democratic Party was fast developing into a party of, by, and for the North, while whites were being pushed out of the party of their fathers. Here, yet again, was a northern-dominated party playing politics with a matter of life and death.

The governor's leadership bore fruit. Alabama's full congressional delegation responded to the "crisis" by convening an emergency meeting in the office of its senior U.S. senator, John H. Bankhead. They agreed that the military order was completely unacceptable and politically motivated, designed only to reap dividends in terms of the northern black vote. Every single Alabama senator and congressman pledged to do everything in his power to resist the growing tide of federal encroachment on southern race relations and praised Sparks's reply as so definitive as to be "unanswerable."[54] Beyond that, though, they did not come up with a coordinated plan, leaving individuals free to focus on the aspects of the situation they viewed as most offensive.

For many southerners the preservation of cultural perquisites was paramount. Mobile congressman Frank Boykin flew into a frenzy, declaring the army order "the worst thing that's ever happened to us" and urging his colleagues to stop the bleeding or "our way of life in the South is ruined." "Where . . . segregation goes, our whole social structure crumbles," a leading Bourbon organ echoed. The South had no choice but to fight to "preserve the civilization" in which it was vested. In speaking to the issue of mass indignation, a plain-white Montgomery woman agreed that every white person she knew was thoroughly disgusted by the ridiculous and repulsive order.[55]

Closely related to the cultural response was the view that the whole thing was a political and sectional assault, a kind of Civil War and Reconstruction redux—this time spearheaded by the national Democratic Party. A hill-country newspaper blamed "South-prejudiced malcontents" for goading FDR to plunge "a dagger . . . into the heart of a section of his own country." Others pledged support for the cause from all true "Sons of the South" because the order was so obviously an abomination, the seed of influences completely "foreign" to the South.[56] Both the cultural as well as the war and Reconstruction interpretation of the event fed growing sectional definition of the outrage.

But there was also the personal. White Alabamians became additionally distraught that the president had snubbed their governor by not even deigning to answer his wire—reinforcing the unmistakable idea that the situation was not significant to anyone outside the South.[57]

Others held out the fear (or hope) of violence as the result of all the turmoil. Birmingham police commissioner Bull Connor issued repeated warnings that there would be blood in the streets if the army desegregation order was not rescinded. And he became beside himself when the president refused to answer *his* letters, those of a fellow New Dealer. The *Birmingham Age-Herald* mused philosophically that social customs "rooted in ancient emotions" could never be changed by government fiat, and attempting to do so was a mistake that would arouse the masses to violence. Such policies absolutely and positively would not work in the South, a Birmingham realtor announced, and any attempt by the central government to "ram this policy down the South's throat will result in only one thing."[58]

Whites of various social ranks praised Sparks and pledged their undying fealty to the cause of white supremacy. Big Mules, Little Mules, planters, clerks, and common workers expressed admiration for and pleasure with the governor and especially praised his manliness in being willing to "stand up and fight" for states' rights. The blue-collar *Ensley Industrial Press* convinced itself that in "standing his ground" against the northern hordes, Sparks was somehow facing terrific odds and deserved the acclaim due a cultural hero. White Alabama Republicans liked Sparks's stand against the "agitation from the outside by vicious meddlers, well intentioned reformers and irresponsible self-seekers." Blacks and whites in the South had come far together, and no minority group in world history had made as much progress in such a short time as the American Negro, the Republicans said in parroting the regional Democratic folklore. Yet all of this was in jeopardy of being lost if the Yankee reformers insisted on pressing too far too fast. Inspired, Gadsden's mayor (another New Deal loyalist) soberly prepared to batten down the hatches in his north Alabama burg in response to trouble brewing half a state away on a federal military reservation outside Montgomery.[59]

Sparks and other Alabama leaders did much to cultivate the reaction to outside involvement by touring the state to speak to various business groups, warning outsiders not to meddle in southern domestic affairs, and watching as the "best opinion" trickled down to the common folk. Just because outsiders invested money in the South, that did not give them the right to dictate matters of internal control. They "are not going to give us a little salt and then come down here and tell us how to run our internal affairs," Sparks assured the assembled members of the Alabama Cotton Manufacturing Association. Besides, once they came to the South, the whole world would be astounded by the extent of Alabama's economic progress and per capita income and expansion of wealth.[60]

Much of the frustration emanated from a general conviction that all was well on the racial front and that nothing really needed fixing. The state's leadership both articulated and reinforced this prevailing belief. With Jim Crow and white supremacy at its core, this was of course a reality for whites and they decided that the arrangement was best for everyone. Senator John Bankhead argued this in response to the War Department order and warned that the consequences of tampering with established customs would be "unhappy" for both races. The Negro is "happiest being just himself," a sympathetic Texan weighed in, "living his simple life" content in his God-assigned place. He would never have "wanted to rule the white man" had it not been for some misguided whites starting a movement to put blacks in the white man's place. They did not have the "slightest desire to mix with the white people," an Anniston attorney agreed. "If everyone would just leave us alone, white supremacy would continue to reign," an elderly Montgomery woman lamented, and "our Southern negroes would continue to be happy."[61]

The cultural fable was derived no doubt from wishful thinking, some of it in response to blacks "playing the game" of servility and quietude in order to survive in the Jim Crow South. But such was the power and strength of the figment that it continued to persist even in the face of obvious black resistance. A group of 250 black Alabama Baptist ministers, representing 50,000 members of the black Baptist church and an estimated 150,000 people in Jefferson County alone, passed a resolution in response to the Maxwell order denying the statement "made by anybody, anywhere, at any time, that we are satisfied with the evils of segregation." Some of Alabama's most rigid segregationists like Bull Connor and Hamner Cobbs recoiled at the effrontery and wrung their hands about what this could mean for future events.[62]

But the bulk of white Alabamians blissfully continued to believe that "the better class of our colored people" would always appreciate white supremacy and took comfort in the knowledge that the South's whites "have, and always will be their genuine friends." Meanwhile, Hubert Baughn and the Bourbons at the *Alabama Magazine* scoured the bushes for "good Negroes" who would publicly endorse segregation. Whenever they found one, they gave prominent coverage and then concluded that "the average negro" did not want social equality any more than whites did.[63]

A common theme running through much of the southern discontent was the feeling that the whole thing was the result of crass political calculations made by the national Democratic Party rather than true resolve on the part of the would-be reformers. In a real way this belief both cheapened the quality of the attempted reform from afar and provided comfort in those moments when white southerners might have had second thoughts about their customs. In any event, this resentment hastened the day when a formal break from the Democratic Party would become more than just a fantastic threat.

Before the body blows of the war period many white southerners had thought, with some good reason, of the Democratic and Republican parties as tweedledee and tweedledum on race. But no more. The anti–New Dealers who would soon form the vanguard of the Dixiecrat movement took the lead in blaming the national Democrats for all that was wrong. The whole thing was the fault of the New Deal pandering to "Negro politicians," hill-country editor Thomas Abernethy fumed. Actually, it was the NAACP, the CIO, the Communist Party, and other "Left Wing and radical groups," former New Deal congressman Joseph Starnes of Guntersville said. For a decade the southern people had sat blind and apathetic to the determination of the New Deal to "destroy our white civilization." Hamner Cobbs of the *Greensboro Southern Watchman* agreed. There was no denying that the "black and tan elements" that controlled the Democratic Party were dead set on torching the customs of the South.[64]

Talladega's Tom Abernethy captured the essence of what many frustrated southern Democrats were trying to say. A budding Dixiecrat, and then Republican after that, Abernethy had a knack for keeping his finger on the pulse of the people—especially the state's ordinary whites: "The so-called democratic party of today holds the South in contempt . . . proceeding with contemptuous assurance that Southern votes are in the bag, regardless of how this section is treated. . . . So long as we are spineless lickers of the new deal boots," the northern black vote would be far more important to national party leaders than the southern white vote, Abernethy concluded. "If we ever get the guts down in Dixie to kick over the traces and demand consideration, we'll be the most important section of the nation." Until then, he said, we "might as well keep our mouths shut." Southern protests commanded no attention from those who were willing to "stab the South in the back for temporary political gain—knowing full well we will not resist."[65]

I Always Thought the Democratic Party in the South Meant White Supremacy

The nature of the looming break was, almost above all, sectional. Frustrated white southerners were increasingly coming to believe that the Democratic Party, so long their home and the guardian of white supremacy, was changing—and the change was emanating from north of the Mason-Dixon Line. More and more white southerners began to have the sinking feeling that the Democratic Party, for so long the party *of the South*, was that no longer. Somehow it had turned. Somewhere during the tumult and confusion of the Depression and world war, when southerners were busy doing something else, the party had become the party *of the North*—including northern blacks to boot. Now "'smart-alecky'" blacks from up North were going out of their way to offend southern white women and poison the feeble minds of southern blacks. And it did not help that Yankees kept pointing out that blacks were dying alongside whites on the fields of Europe to keep the "tenets of Hitler" alive back home. The North had never understood the attitude of the southern people concerning blacks, despaired a Birmingham resident: "[O]ur resentment has [always] been against the North and never toward the Negro. . . . The South cannot forget the destruction brought upon it by the Union Army in the War Between the States."⁶⁶

Others connected the dots between the northern propensity to pursue black votes during Reconstruction and their willingness to do so again in the 1940s. "It reminds me of the carpetbagger days," lamented a Montgomerian. Such sentiments were given official sanction when Governor Sparks publicly warned that if southerners learned there were political reasons for the War Department's desegregation order, it would be "difficult to hold the South within its traditional Democratic allegiance." "I . . . always thought that the Democratic Party in the South meant white supremacy," Congressman Frank Boykin concurred. Any "decent southerner" would think the same, said a Birmingham accountant, adding public morality to the indictment. "But I guess that is the thanks the South gets for its past perfect support of the Democratic Party."⁶⁷

Some were so truculent in their reaction to the sectional assault that they furnished a sneak preview of the bonfire of southern conservatism that would blaze forth in the next few years. Long a member of the ultra-right HUAC along with Martin Dies of Texas, Joe Starnes painted with a broad brush in condemning the gumbo of the CIO, the Communist Party, left-wing radicals, and the New Deal Democratic administration of Franklin Roosevelt as the leading actors in a new Reconstruction tragedy. Despite the fact that the South's sons volunteered in greater numbers than any other section of the country, the north Alabama congressman acidly remarked, white people were just going to have to face the fact that "a so-called democratic administration" has been playing to the Negro vote, organized labor, and "other left-wing and radical elements": groups that "[hate the] real . . . democrats" who wanted to preserve the "constitutional system."⁶⁸

Victor Hanson, with a good deal of accuracy, was called the "biggest mule" in Alabama.⁶⁹ He owned three of the state's largest and oldest newspapers: the *Birmingham News*, *Birmingham Post-Herald*, and "Old Grandma," the *Montgomery Advertiser*. Hanson and his newspapers had always represented the pinnacle of old, respectable, business-oriented conservatism in Alabama. They had provided the most intense and unrelenting hostility to organized labor, for example. It is thus somewhat of an anomaly that Hanson's papers toed the New Deal line fairly consistently during these years, although it is clear that the shrewd publisher realized there was much for Alabama's business community to gain from the centrist-liberalism of the federal government—especially from congressional appropriations and skilled ministrations and personal favors of Lister Hill and John Bankhead in the U.S. Senate. Hanson's editors, no doubt, also exercised a moderating influence on him: James G. Chappell at the *Birmingham News*, Charles N. Fiedelson at the *Birmingham Age-Herald*, and Grover C. Hall Jr. at the *Advertiser*.

For their collective support of parts of the New Deal these editors and papers had incurred the most violent wrath of Alabama's planter and industrialist combination. Yet of late there had been a noticeable lessening of their once-even-mild criticism of the state's leading opponents of the New Deal. When, in 1942, Grover Jr. dared to criticize Frank Dixon's methods for directly challenging the War Production Board, the state's Bourbons nearly ran him out on a rail. A mutiny erupted at the *Advertiser* with ninety of its employees announcing that they abhorred the editorial policy of their paper on the matter—and Grover Jr. beat a hasty retreat six days later. A year later a pointedly contrite Junior and the *Montgomery Advertiser* tried to do penance by backing Chauncey Sparks and his fighting posture against northern criticism of the Mobile shipyard riot. The response from the planters and industrialists had been cool at best.[70] But in 1944 a third opportunity presented itself, and "Old Grandma" proved that it was still the most venerable part of Alabama conservatism. In fact, in doing so, the newspaper acted in perfect concert with its two sister Hanson papers in Birmingham.[71]

Faced with the Maxwell order and the mass mobilization of white Alabamians of all ranks (and with the memory of its ill-received attempts at moderation still fresh), the *Advertiser* cut loose with both barrels. Montgomery was a tolerant, liberal, and intensely patriotic city, the newspaper prefaced, but it was "profoundly disturbed" by the federal government's attempts to break down its cherished segregation customs. Even "armies and bayonets . . . cannot force impossible and unnatural social race relationships upon us," Grover Jr. said in ringing the Reconstruction tocsin. It had been tried before and failed: "It will fail . . . again." This latest trouble, no doubt, emanated from some "academic or idealistic impulse" of a group of northern "troublemakers . . . a puny majority," the *Advertiser* said in checking off the requisite anti-intellectual box in the creed of cultural conformity. But domination by white people, owing to their superior qualifications, would be maintained "at all costs," the *Advertiser* warned. This rather naked admonition revealed that the newspaper's curious "liberal" creed included a place for violent coercion if confronted with the prospect of part of the citizenry refusing to conform to the status quo. Quickly recovering, lest its liberal reputation be completely lost, the *Advertiser* stipulated that, of course, "[t]his is said kindly and firmly and in the utmost friendship for the members of the Negro race."[72]

It was the perfect enunciation of an intrinsically conservative creed wrapped in the mantle of a liberalism and enlightened tolerance that even the most hidebound reactionary could take pride in. Newspapers around the state eagerly reprinted the wisdom of the state's oldest and most venerable newspaper. Antediluvian conservatives welcomed the *Advertiser* back into the fold of southern civilization. Its exposition on the sanctity and centrality of southern cultural and racial orthodoxy could not be topped. It had demonstrated yet again that New Dealism in the South too often held no place for racial liberalism. George Grant was so happy that he had the editorial read into the *Congressional Record*. The *Advertiser* was well-known as a "progressive paper," the congressman chortled, and "stands for the fair treatment of all races." Thus, there was no way anyone could "find fault" with its righteous indignation. Hubert Baughn and Hamner Cobbs, previously the most unforgiving of the *Advertiser*'s anti–New Deal critics, signaled that the Hanson-Hall contrition was acceptable to Alabama's business elite. They publicly welcomed the newspaper back into "the family . . . of a decent Southern civilization."[73]

The *Advertiser*'s rapid self-reformation was only part of a larger pattern of southern liberals seeing their liberalism come apart at the seams as the racial crosstie of southern civilization was exposed. Vaunted liberal John Temple Graves, now writing his syndicated column for the Republican *Birmingham Post*, joined the *Advertiser* in coming unhinged over the army order. This was exactly the kind of thing that could result in a full-blown southern revolt replete with electoral vote withholding, he screeched. Jim Crow was not going to be abolished. "Sensible people on both sides of the line know it," Graves wrote, quickly putting the shawl of liberalism back on at least one of his shoulders. "What we need is an improvement in the Negro's lot on his side of the line."[74]

Facing reelection in 1944, progressive Lister Hill again decided to feed the monster of white supremacy. Hill attended the emergency congressional delegation meeting in John Bankhead's office and dutifully pledged to "do everything in my power" to thwart the order and block desegregation. "I deplore the order," the progressive senator assured the home folks. When skeptical conservatives responded that Hill's defense of white supremacy had been suspect in the past and that a single weak "record protest" was just political expedience, a frantic Hill responded in shriller terms. "I deplore the War Department's action just as much as you do," he fairly yelled at his Alabama constituents; he had been busy doing "everything in my power to get the Maxwell order rescinded!"[75]

All Americans Should Get Down on Their Knees and Give Thanks to Business

As reward (and penalty) for his growing racial leadership, Chauncey Sparks became a magnet for regional and even national discontent over race relations. Much as Frank Dixon had before (and George Wallace would two decades later), Sparks began to receive entreaties from people around the South and the country overwrought about challenges to white supremacy. In Sparks, these individuals saw the physical embodiment of their distress, and they appealed to him for help as champion of an as-of-yet amorphous and largely undefined cause. It had a lot to do with a feeling of general malaise when it came to growing national Democratic liberalism. Yet their disillusionment was in no sense a pure or unadulterated worry over racial changes alone.

As economic and racial conservatism became increasingly understood simply as "conservatism" in the public mind, those attracted to an Alabama governor as champion of the general status quo articulated their unease in this compound form. White supremacy was certainly the most fundamental building block of the combination. It was the common component of the budding neo-Kluxer and neo-Bourbon pairing. But it was hardly an isolated or wholly independent element. A devout belief in the efficacy—and indeed, the sanctity—of strict laissez-faire economics, social Darwinism and survival of the fittest, ethnic purity and the relative supremacy of different species, and a conviction that this symbiotic status quo was blessed by the Creator anchored the new conservative creed in a broad and deep cultural milieu.

Much of the discontent was very ugly and, in the context of the 1940s, still stood apart as something extreme. A lot of this had to do with the simple fact that much of the most unvarnished sentiment remained underground. Many expressed political opinions in private correspondence to elected officials instead of the various talk-radio, Internet, and social media modes that revolutions in technology would one day make available. In time, though, the twin seeds of anti–New Dealism and discontent with the Democratic Party would grow to fruition in a conservative alliance of southern and western states that would energize alternatives to the modern Democratic Party—including Wallace independentism and, later, an ascendant national GOP. To be sure, what follows is very ugly stuff at a vulgar and base level. But it contains all of the ingredients that would, in time, be absorbed, echoed, accepted, preached, believed, and propagated by a modern Republican Party as, eventually, mainstream doctrine: a callous libertarian creed, rank social irresponsibility, an exaggerated individualist dogma, and, of course, white supremacy. While the critical racial component would, in time, be more expertly camouflaged, it would persist as an important if more subtle undercurrent to the ostensibly "color-blind" issues of conservative ideology such as economics, taxes, and suburbia—not only in the South but in the nation as well.

Conservatives from around the country sent Chauncey Sparks assorted materials outlining their credo. Many expressed a desire for solidarity with the southern governor. And Americans from all sections paid homage to the canon of white supremacy and unrestricted free enterprise based on the common cement of animus to the central government.

A good deal of the unhappiness centered around the conservative antipathy to labor unions as the usurpers of a divinely inspired order of things that had whites over blacks, men over women, natives over foreigners, and employers over workers in a timeless and God-given design. Conservatives complained to Sparks about the malformed children of the New Deal: the minimum wage, overtime pay, Social Security, labor laws, disability insurance, protections against employment discrimination, safety regulations, and prevailing wage rates—and suggested that public acceptance of such meant that America was on its way to breeding a "race of loafers." Unions under the "Labor Barons, and alien grafters" were an import from fascist Europe, they claimed, and would lead the masses to revolution. Swift and decisive government action was required—not to protect workers but to draft John L. Lewis and "all his communistic union officials" and "professional agitators" into the army. Mass conscription would also prevent labor from controlling all the dangerous "alien born, alien races within our Country."[76]

The flip side to the demonization of labor was veneration of big business. "Every American should get down on their knees and give thanks" that business had persevered in face of the terrific handicaps brought on them by FDR and his alliance with the "labor gangsters. . . . Thank God for our business leaders who have made good in the face of appalling odds."[77]

Despite the later polished protestations of more coded appeals, the ugly underside of such a philosophy was never far from the surface and threatened to bubble up with the slightest provocation. Jews and immigrants were the root of the labor evil. America's Jewish problem had to be addressed and solved. One way was to bar Jews and "the city of Brooklyn and the fur and garment trade" from any connection to politics, schools, press, or stage, the same conservatives advised. It was well-known that the Jews "contaminate our national life," a charge with clear antecedents in Europe's long history of anti-Semitism. Of course this suggestion was not made "with hatred" but in the simple realization that "the Jewish nation is a parasitic race." There was no greater gap in any race known to man, an anti-labor author wrote, than between brilliant and honest Jewish leaders and the "dirty, crooked, aggressive Kikes that clutter our subways."[78]

Not far removed from the Jewish problem, for this breed of conservative, was of course the elementary but towering problem of white supremacy. After the unions, the immigrants, and the Jews were taken care of, free-enterprise enthusiasts advised Sparks, "[we should] get after our tremendous negro problem" and sharply redefine black duties, privileges, place, and work. Repeal of voting and the Fifteenth Amendment was a must because of the simple fact of black sexual promiscuity: black people were "multiplying much faster than our white race." "We respect the Negro," the conservative stipulated, "but nobody wants black children mixing with white in schools, opening the way for mixed marriages."[79]

These were not mere sociological or economic problems, though. They were also political and held the potential to imperil the very survival of the republic. This is key. The first Great Melding fused libertarian—even corporatist—economics with white supremacy. In the cauldron of the Great Depression, southern Bourbons appropriated away the race issue, virtually in toto, from their economically liberal rivals, thus dooming the fate of "liberalism" itself in the South. To do this, the forces of privilege capitalized on the anti-federal animus they held in common with white supremacists as glue to fuse their program (replete with Chicago School economics) to that of the average southern white opposed to racial integration and civil rights.

But something else was afoot at the same time: the second Great Melding that would largely succeed the first, taking up where it left off. It would fortify and augment the first as the public face of modern conservatism and, eventually, find full fruition in the modern GOP, the Reagan-Bush years, and the radical-right Tea Party wing. Instead of just using race and hostility to the federal government, this second melding would conjoin economic fundamentalism to the religious kind by catering to a deep anti-democratic impulse as well, one common to both Austrian economics and the Religious Right. Just below the surface of both the neoliberal economic creed and fundamentalist religion—clothed by constant paeans to freedom, liberty, and the individual—lay a dark, powerful, and pungent dislike of democracy. Both economic and religious fundamentalists wanted people to vote—only they wanted "their kind" of people to vote, not just the indiscriminate masses.

The intellectual and ideological lineage of both meldings could be traced—quite clearly—from the Reconstruction Redeemers to "New South" boosters to the leading exponents of southern disfranchisement to the most rabid opponents of the New Deal to the Dixiecrats and, finally, to the modern Republican Party and its Frankensteinian Tea Party.

Democracy is a system of government fitted "only for the extremely intelligent and thinking races of the temperate zones whose actions are governed by reason," one conservative correspondent explained to Sparks. It was never meant for people whose actions are governed by impulse, like "Latins, Negroes, etc." Only native-born Americans should be allowed to vote as "[a]lien influences" already had a toehold in national life. "ALL the Alien Races," according to the correspondent, all the "darker skinned peoples . . . have not the slightest conception of Democracy . . . are not fitted for [it] and . . . don't want Democracy." Besides, they were all under the control and influence of John L. Lewis and the other labor bosses who were directly antagonistic to "[our] American Way of Life."[80]

Nothing was left, really, but to recognize the handwriting on the wall and leave the Democratic Party for a new home in the GOP, the manifestos concluded. The Solid South had always voted Democratic, but it was time to realize that the GOP was the only place for real useful, productive, and deserving Americans: the makers, not the takers.

The Democratic Party was rapidly descending into a repository of "takers," not "givers," the parasites of society, the critique (obviously influenced by Ayn Rand) went on. The mathematics of the 1940 election made the future clear. The Republican candidate had received 90 percent of the "thinking vote" of the country, representative American citizens, homeowners, businessmen, farmers, managers, and professionals—"in short about everyone who has worked hard to get anywhere." Meanwhile, the Democrats attracted only the lazy and undeserving "'Have nots.'" FDR and the Democrats were bent on the ruination of the country, transforming it from the land of the free to a "land run by organized minorities" and interest groups who had descended "[upon us] like an insidious disease." Their ranks were made up of the "foreign born, south Europeans, Jews, Negroes . . . communist organization[s] . . . and others who have little conception of liberty or Democracy and who don't know what they are voting for."[81]

This was not mere partisan politics. It was economic corporatism—something approaching quasi-fascism—grounded on the most holy type of patriotism and fidelity to our nation's founders and, ultimately, the religion that upheld civilization itself. The Founding Fathers were hardheaded, practical men, the creed held. They would be spinning in their graves at the sight of modern, liberal, New Deal America in which "all our negroes and alien races mill around with the unthinking and dissatisfied elements, at the mercy of alien leaders and propagandists, who are telling them they are free and equal and entitled to everything anyone else has, without doing anything to earn it." The proper portion of the masses—their destiny—whether they recognized it or not, was one of hard labor and low wages. It was only common sense and the genius of our American system that the "least deserving, the least competent, the least desirable of our people will always have to do the Heavy Lifting," one conservative wrote in unconscious repetition of one of the eighteenth century's coldest economic thinkers, Bernard Mandeville. Such is the essence of freedom and democracy, and to challenge that Social Darwinistic status quo is to tamper with the handiwork of God Himself.[82]

And it all went back to the moral fiber of society based on conservative, Calvinist religion, perhaps even Puritanism. "Liquidate labor, liquidate stocks, liquidate the farmer, liquidate real estate," billionaire and Republican secretary of commerce Andrew Mellon had famously advised on the eve of the Great Depression. "It will purge the rottenness out of the system. People will work harder, lead a more moral life."[83] Liberalism (now meaning moral as well as racial laxity) was running amok. Religion was losing its grip on public life. The American family had degenerated and national sovereignty was being undermined by foolish subservience to a world court with a bunch of "silk hated Diplomats making speeches all day" and trying to commit us to global, one-world schemes and squandered national sovereignty. Birth control and contraception were two of the most "vicious evils in our time."[84] A form of insidious moral authoritarianism, consequently, trailed close behind such a worldview. Liberalism, unionism, racial integration, internationalism, and moral turpitude were all allied evils of the New Deal and the Democratic Party—a party now clearly beyond the hope of rehabilitation.

They Say Christ Was a Jew

As far out as such a creed might seem, it was only one step removed from much of the discontent that was seething among millions of disenchanted southern Democrats. Given time this frustration would ferment and become virtually unrecognizable from Dixiecrat, Wallace Democrat, and, eventually, modern Republican grievances.

Such frustration not only congealed during the war, it also took on a "pan-southern" character. The Second Reconstruction did not spring forth wholly formed, Athena-like, in the 1960s. It was well ensconced in the southern mind far before then. At root it was a cultural rebellion, but, as before, the coming revolt expressed itself in markedly partisan terms. This time the uprising would target the Democratic Party instead of the party of Lincoln.

The Roosevelts provided a simple and stationary target for southern discontent: fish in a barrel. Again Chauncey Sparks thrust himself and the office of the governor of Alabama into the coachman's seat and seized the reins of regional unease with a fairly sensational announcement: he planned to formally condemn Eleanor Roosevelt at the 1944 Democratic National Convention.

Put the blame for the insidious racial liberalism "right where it belongs," a Mississippi supporter urged Sparks on. Relishing the national showdown, disaffected southern whites rallied to Sparks. South Carolina union members sent word of their solidarity with Sparks's plan as did one of Alabama's best-known native sons, J. Frank Norris, pastor of the gigantic First Baptist Church in Fort Worth, Texas. "Here's strength to your arm!" the minister blessed Sparks, as the regional champion prepared to sally forth to battle once more against the forces of liberalism, secularism, and racial equality. Mrs. Roosevelt had forced her ideas about race on the whole South, a Texas woman and lifelong Democrat complained, and "[we are] pretty well fed up" with her trying to ram blacks "down the throats" of Dixie. Eleanor would be the "one reason why F.D.R. can't carry the Solid South again."[85]

Other whites around the South enunciated their dissatisfaction in markedly cultural, patriotic, and religious terms—at once demonstrating the complex interrelationships of southern conservatism and invoking the authority of Scripture and cultural standards to legitimate their cause. Invariably, though, the religious and cultural argument soon slipped into narrow moral proscription and a bigoted intolerance. It was time for the Southland to wake up and do some fighting back against "the evil doers," a South Carolina attorney suggested in Old Testament terms. The New Deal had run roughshod over every single tenet that had made the country great. Yet what was expected of a wing of the party that was dominated by foreigners? "I know who my political forbears are," the lawyer crowed; the New Dealers could not say as much, "if you get what I mean."[86]

An Oklahoma woman was more direct in her support of Sparks, grounded at root on the splicing together of folk religion, white supremacy, and anti-Semitism. To her, Roosevelt's New Deal was directly connected to the Negroes and the Jews "taking control of the United States." The country's "Asiatic Exclusion law" excluded blacks and Jews from becoming U.S. citizens because "their way of life is not our way of life. . . . If that law was followed . . . even Roosevelt could not be a citizen of the U.S. because he is a Jew," she charged. Now, in World War II, we are "fightin on the side of . . . two condemned races . . . the Negro and the Jew [both] condemned by God and His Son." And the "Bible says for us not ever to say our prayers for them because those prayers will not be answered." If we in this country do not wake up to this fact real soon, the United States will become "as barren a land as the African Desert." "I don't ever go to church" anymore, she explained, because "they don't tell us the truth. They say Christ was a Jew and the Jews were the Chosen Race and That Absolutely Is Not in the Bible Anywhere." "I've a notion that God was not a Jew. . . . How . . . the Jews . . . get over the idea that they were the Chosen People when they do not believe there ever was a Christ, is beyond me," she iterated. "I'll send you Biblical proof," she offered Sparks, that "the Jews are Negro and . . . it's the Jews themselves that are stirring up the Negro against us. . . . I am 100% behind you on this white supremacy business. We are the superior race."[87]

Other white southerners were somewhat more rational in their expositions against the national Democratic liberal drift but no less convicted. A Georgian explained to Sparks that it was all about another Reconstruction. In a prophetic passage, the Georgia Democrat held out hope for an alliance between the southern and western states that could keep "outsiders" from the North from "meddling in our affairs."[88]

Of course unhappiness with Rooseveltian racial liberalism ran very strong in Alabama and boded ill for the 1944 election. "[There is a] whale of a political mess [brewing in Alabama right now]" for FDR and those identified with him, a leading Alabama columnist pointed out. Even if Alabama were to end up voting for FDR again, according to others, it would not be with the same gusto or open pocketbooks. Until the New Deal ceased its "starry-eyed . . . agitation and . . . 'sasiety reform' expeditions," a Bourbon jibed, there was no sense in national Democrats trying to "shake the plum tree" for money.[89] Whites complained bitterly of black and labor influence in the party, New Deal social equality efforts, and a general miasma of despair that apparently we can "expect nothing" from FDR in stemming the tide of racial liberalism.[90]

At root the discontent really signaled the deep-seated belief of many white southerners in the immutability and sanctity of white supremacy, ethnic purity, and religious exclusion. When, for example, a white Chicago woman running WPA seminars addressed blacks as "Mr." and "Mrs.," white Alabamians were scandalized. When the Chicago woman held a black baby in her arms a white Bessemer woman vomited. The New Deal Democrats were doing their best to lower the whole South down to "a Negroid level," a Mobile lawyer and future Dixiecrat complained. A Birmingham man charged that the New Deal under the "DIMMIEKRATS" just "smells of NIGGER and POLL TAX." Southerners spent the whole year raising the crops, coal, iron, lumber, tobacco, and cotton that fed and clothed the North, he explained. "Hell . . . you would go NAKED and Hungry if it were not for [us]."

But "DAM YANKEEDOM" could not leave well enough alone. Its missionaries just had to come down to "GOD'S CHOSEN SPOT" and tamper with white supremacy: the "children of Moses" versus the "gentiles" of the South, the "sons of Abraham" that dominated the northern Democratic Party. "I can roll off their names . . . Cohens, Moses (Noses), Baruchs, Frankfurters, Lehmans, Rosenwalds, Bearmans . . . Frankfurterites" and, locally, the "Jew department Stores."[91]

As disappointment with the New Deal Democratic Party grew, liberalism itself began to tack away from its position of respectability—and even, once, *desirability*—in the South toward a place of disgrace and association with racial heresy. In a region resplendent with admiration for the concept of rugged individualism, strength and manliness increasingly came to be identified with conservatism while weakness, evasion, and even treason were attached to liberalism. This was possible, of course, only because liberalism itself was moving at warp speed toward being identified with race rather than just economics.

Bourbons began denouncing "liberals" and "left wingers" more often in their diatribes against assaults on Jim Crow and white supremacy. Others concluded that, while perhaps noble in theory, liberalism was naïve in practice, perilously so. Idealism is great, a Montgomery schoolteacher mused, but "[b]eauty and sweetness" were not enough. "[We need] firm courage" and "common sense" (and hardheaded dollars-and-sense practicality had long been associated with the economic variant of conservatism).[92]

During World War II this notion was largely transferred to the racial variety as well. Nor was this sentiment limited solely to the South. Around the country sympathetic conservatives gave their support to the embattled Alabama front because "liberals" pandering to "special interests and fanatics" were advocating a violent assault on states' rights and obliteration of "the American way of life," "weird ethnological horrors" designed to force people to associate with different types of people.[93]

White southerners complained with more frequency of congressmen being asleep when it came to race. With a few honorable exceptions, a Black Belt Alabamian felt, the state's vaunted congressional delegation has "sold us . . . out." In Ensley a working-class family enunciated their disgust. The family had always voted Democratic—but no more: "We are sick and tired of" Democratic programs that led to their having to ride buses and elevators "Jammed with Negroes."[94]

As they had for decades, Alabama's Bourbons fed racial dissatisfaction among workers in a patently divide-and-conquer strategy. A divided working class meant weaker labor, less oversight, a more dangerous workplace, the wanton expulsion of industrial waste into the environment—but more profits. Planters and industrialists heaped abuse on labor for having grossly violated "white supremacy"—a doctrine that had been the crowning jewel of the Democratic Party long before the abomination of the CIO had come along.[95]

A constant barrage of blame and opprobrium for labor on the racial score provided a serious obstacle to meaningful biracial class action. But more, it caused a schism within the southern labor movement—a clear demarcation between *economic issues,* which resonated with the rank and file, and social and racial issues on which the membership was much more resistant to dictation from above or beyond. Further, an unrelenting propaganda blitz did much to compromise the position of unions themselves within the culture. Barely tolerated, sometimes not even that, unions found themselves marked as engines of an unpatriotic, subversive, racially dangerous, irreligious, even treasonous kind of selfishness. The stigma—however unfair—has been lasting in the South.

A fierce aversion to federal involvement in the economy accompanied the anti-unionism *if* the involvement happened to be workplace safety regulations instead of the dispensation of grants, favors, tax breaks, subsidies, and low-interest loans to businesses. For the Bourbons, white supremacy was another cog in the wheel of a conservative society dominated by capital. Nor was much of this hidden or even muted during the 1940s. The editor of *Alabama Magazine* wrote that the "radical" New York *PM Magazine* had accused his magazine of being "fer segregation [and] . . . friendly to industry. . . . I . . . enter a plea of guilty as hell on all counts."[96]

Apart from government oversight—derided as unnecessary, unpatriotic, and even *un-American* bureaucratic regimentation—taxes probably absorbed the most time and energy of the Bourbons. On this score, as on the subject of regulation, the privileged profited handsomely from the state's unhappy memory of race and Reconstruction. Like Reconstruction and federal involvement in employment discrimination, the tax issue also had a powerful racial subtext. At its base level, the concept was Robin Hood in reverse: a complaint against taking from the deserving rich to give to the lazy and degenerate poor (whose skins were usually not white).

Because of the strength with which the Social Darwinist creed resonated in the Deep South, even plain folk who benefited significantly from federal programs funded by taxes preferred to think of themselves as "rugged individualists" who had pulled themselves up completely by their bootstraps, were self-made, God-blessed, and stood squarely on their feet without the need or desire for a character-crippling federal wet-nurse. Left alone, they were just one step away from a Rockefellerian fortune. The Roosevelt administration had "done more to destroy our democracy than could be done by all the armies of Europe," the vice president and manager of a Montgomery plant proclaimed. Private industry was being taxed out of existence by the New Deal Democrats. Another disgruntled Democrat confessed that she no longer wore the "Mongrel collar" of the New Deal because of the national Democrats' determination to "intermix the negro with the white" and, during war, give work to blacks that was above their station. She looked forward to the day when blacks returned to "their work" and people like her would be relieved of the "atrocious" burden of paying taxes for the worthless part of humanity.[97]

As befit a new Reconstruction era (and so often in the state's history), extralegal violence was not out-of-bounds. In fact, as with the first Reconstruction, vigilantism could actually be called upon by the "best sorts"—according to the dictates of the charter marking the new merger of the neo-Bourbons and the neo-Kluxers.

Labor unions and the blacks were getting entirely out of hand, Alabama's most privileged believed, and, what with so many white boys overseas, social control might have to be enforced by a new vigilantism. "It is rare indeed," admitted Horace Hall of the *Dothan Eagle*, "when the citizens of a nation are justified in taking the law into their own hands," but that situation is "rapidly approaching." Brother of the famed *Montgomery Advertiser* editor Grover Hall (who had, ironically, won the Pulitzer Prize in 1928 for his editorials *against* the KKK), Horace argued for, in effect, a Bourbon-controlled alliance with the hood of vigilantism. "Nearly three-quarters of a century ago," he reminisced, the South found a way to "rid itself of the carpetbaggers the Federal Government encouraged." Dixie could point the way again—and without the aid of fiery crosses and sheets, "with machine gun fire if need be." Ed Field's *Selma Times-Journal* reprinted and endorsed the piece. In just a few years both Hall and Field would help lead Alabama's bolt out of the Democratic Party to the Dixiecrats and then the GOP. "If this be treason," Field encouraged Hall, "let [the] pusillanimous 'liberals' and New Dealers make the most of it."[98]

No Man Living Was a Stronger Roosevelt Man than I

Much of the angst came from realization of the extraordinary role the South had played in making the region solid for Democracy in the first place. Poisonous resentment oozed through the region about it having been the South to, first, anchor the New Deal and then spearhead support for American involvement in World War II. Whites displeased about the racial drift of the party thus approached the 1944 presidential election with high hopes. If the Solid South showed discipline and held itself together, some thought, "[we could] pretty near get anything we want" in terms of racial concessions.[99]

Others were not so optimistic. As the election year drew near Chauncey Sparks planned to handpick an anti–New Deal delegation from Alabama and formally propose a plank at the Democratic National Convention disowning Eleanor Roosevelt and endorsing white supremacy. Alabama "liberals" the stripe of Col. Harry Ayers tried to block Sparks in the hope of working things out within the Democratic tent and preventing millions of new black votes from going back to the party of Lincoln. State party chair Gessner McCorvey laid quieter yet potentially far more damaging plans. He resolved to hit the national party where it hurt most: in the pocketbook.[100]

This much should be clear. The modern Republican Party in the South was eventually the beneficiary of this conservative Democratic malaise. It became predominantly the spiritual, physical, and logical heir to the Dixiecrats, George Wallace, and the white supremacy wing of the old southern Democratic Party. The ascendant GOP—so powerful in the South that it would eventually grow to be an actual Solid *Republican* South in national elections—harvested the seed plowed by Dixiecrats and disgruntled southern Democrats—and in this the 1930s and 1940s were critical.

By 1943 the ground was already being prepared. "I have always voted the Democratic ticket, but by God I am through," spat Birmingham druggist C. L. Vance. And thousands of others were too: "I . . . I HEAR THEM TALK." For Vance and the others it was all about culture and religion with race at its epicenter. Since 1932 the Democratic Party had failed miserably at keeping America "a good Christian nation . . . [and] preserving States' rights." Another unhappy Democrat agreed that it was clear the party had turned into something freakish and deformed that was going to end in "negro rule."[101]

The 1944 election was thus the moment of truth for "every Anglo-Saxon Southerner," a disgusted southern Democrat declared. The party was no longer home. Dixie had been insulted and embarrassed too long by Mrs. Roosevelt, the New Deal, "niggers and nigger-loving Yankees. . . . [T]he vast majority of Southerners feel as I do." The handwriting was on the wall. Whichever party or faction could most make white southerners feel like it was the party of the South through its racial and allied cultural policies would command its allegiance. "No man living was a stronger Roosevelt man than I," an attorney agreed, but "[nobody is] more strongly in opposition than I. . . . The above is virtually my religion."[102]

Religion, morality, class, patriotism, sectionalism, Reconstruction, xenophobia, patriarchy—all of it—was so thoroughly interwound with racial discontent that there was no untangling it for a culture in the throes of crisis. The South—the voting, white South—had gone with the Democratic Party much earlier, not because of any endemic need or affection for that particular label but because of what it offered in stark contrast to the Republican Party of Abraham Lincoln: because it was a *cultural* match for the South's underlying devotion to conservatism, hierarchy, and status quo, not necessarily a partisan match. Now it was all coming undone. And—as much angst as it would entail—it was starting to look more and more like a partisan shift was going to have to take place.

As with the first Reconstruction and the partisan birth of the Democratic Solid South, race was at the center of things for psychologically devastated white southerners. "Are these Africans *worth* dying for" and ravishing "our Southland for, a *second* time?" one asked. "Are we going to let foreigners usurp *our* rights in our own native land, especially an inferior race whom God himself cursed! God forbid—if we have men in the South." "These low brow, inferior Africans who are being coddled" by the New Deal Democrats in Washington are "ignorant, overbearing, foreigners who ought to be in Africa where they *belong!*" The angry southerner continued: if Dixie voted a fourth term for FDR and his wife, "who are the *sole* cause of this tragic situation," then the "ghosts of our dead Confederate fathers should haunt us all for they will have died in vain, in their fight with the Yankees."[103]

Yet even as the tide was turning in the South to favor third parties, rump factions, and serious consideration of other partisan alternatives, a timeless warning stood atop politics in the region. It was a warning that many plain whites understood intuitively but that politicians would have to learn through the difficult tuition of experience. In the South, politics was about culture more than anything else. So long as a particular party could get across that it safeguarded the predominant culture of the whites who voted (and even those who did not), it would retain the allegiance of the region and it would flourish. Political parties would challenge utter servitude to the cultural dogma at their peril. Parties would come and parties would go, but the southern "way of life" was here to stay.

For example, an Autauga County man praised Frank Dixon for his wartime defense of the state's racial customs because it would have made the old folks proud. But over and above the praise, the constituent communicated a more important message—one that some loyalist Democrats were slow to discern. He warned that the fidelity of the state's white voters was the ultimate example of conditional love—utterly dependent on political figures adhering to the most deeply rooted and enduring cultural norms. "If I ever find you going contrary to the rules," he warned the politico, "I will . . . rebuke you." The rules, of course, were the most rigid cultural dictates on white supremacy and its allied religious, economic, and patriotic buttresses. It was the same sentiment that viewed sectional allegiance to the New Deal as a stopgap, temporary expedient. "We expect Washington to return Alabama to us at the end of the present emergency," as one resident had put it in 1942.[104]

The culture was so strong, even suffocating, that it overwhelmed not only partisan allegiances but, given time, the cultural dictates of other sections that were not as homogeneous as the South. Born in Maine, Roland M. Harper worked in Alabama for almost forty years before he became involved in politics. When he did, the science professor at the University of Alabama, now an adopted southerner, articulated the prevailing sentiment of the South rather than his Yankee culture. After four decades, he did so with the eloquence of erudition that many of his more common southern brothers did not possess, combined with the same degree of intensity.

Dixon's and Sparks's racial work was the spiritual heir to Reconstruction. The central government had been trespassing on the domain of state and local governments for a long time, he wrote. For Harper, the assault adhered to the new conservative thesis of economic and racial conservatism melded into one. In the eyes of the regional defenders against federal incursion, the minimum wage and maximum hour legislation ranked alongside anti-lynching and anti–poll tax strictures and black jury service as the most obnoxious affronts to cultural regularity. Taxes were a special abomination— even "unconstitutional" for some in the developing conservative ethos. And, combined with the latest attempts to mix the races in the workplace, in the jury box, on buses and streetcars, "trouble-makers in the South" and New Deal Democrats were doing their best to destroy southern civilization and its culture. The New Deal "sob-sisters" and their "'Quislings'" in the South were not really working to help blacks but to foment another Civil War. Later, kindred rightists would make similar claims about a modern Democratic Party using the smokescreen of civil rights to keep blacks on a plantation of dependency. Some native southerners helped the new abolitionists betray their neighbors, Harper charged, not to help blacks but to "win northern approval, and . . . handsome profits."[105]

For the Yankees it was simpler. Their efforts brought "smug satisfaction" that they were irretrievably better than the "barbarous southerners." African Americans needed no help, Harper parroted the comforting regional mythology. Segregation "does not necessarily mean discrimination" and even during slavery southern blacks had it better than the average European peasant. Exhibit A: northern agitation had made blacks so unhappy that "they rarely if ever sing at their work now. . . . Why?" The new abolitionists were looking for the South to evolve into a "mongrel community, unfit to govern itself," like Latin America. Then it could be permanently dominated by the superior North, "much as England dominates its dusky colonies."[106]

For Harper and many other white southerners, native and adopted, at root it was all about a kind of *cultural colonialism*, a sectional threat from the North aimed at the southern culture. Politics then was most fundamentally about defense—a bulwark for white supremacy, of course, but also a defense of sectional solidarity, cultural allegiance, and intrinsic mores.

The Civil War was not over yet. In fact it was just beginning again. This time, instead of the fields of Shiloh and Antietam, it would be waged in the arena of partisan politics and realignment. And before it was all over, perhaps a good number of Yankees could be persuaded to cross the old lines.

10
Race, Religion, and the "Status Quo Society"

[The South is] the only place in the western world where a man could become a liberal simply by urging obedience to the law.

—Hodding Carter

Well, around here communism's anything we don't like. Isn't it that way everywhere else?

—An Alabama dairy farmer

The limitations of the liberalism of Alabama progressives like Chauncey Sparks and Lister Hill revealed at an individual level the same kind of softness that afflicted much of what constituted New Deal liberalism in the South. If it in some way involved race, the liberalism could not be sustained. And with almost every issue that presented itself, a tie to racial traditions, perquisites, and mores eventually manifested itself—no matter how hard the historical actors, or historians, have tried to keep the issues apart. Matters of economics and religion and gender could no more be held separate from racial considerations than they could be divorced from each other.

A Giant Step to the Right

Interaction between these factors, substantial in any society, were particularly acute in Deep South settings. Alabama, in particular, was a place that can be described as a "status quo society." Dedicated to the preservation of an interrelated conservative orthodoxy on matters of race, class, gender, religion, patriotism, and ethnicity, these stanchions of the prevailing status quo also worked to mutually support one another. Predicated on the most basic understanding of the Social Darwinist creed, society was organized hierarchically by design. Men enjoyed sway over women, natives over foreigners, bosses over workers, preachers over flocks, and, at its most primal level, whites over blacks.

Because society itself was designed by a divine Creator, tampering with the status quo implied a rejection of His handiwork—and was thus akin to cultural sacrilege. In such a society stratification not only *was*, it was the way it *should be*. More, in such a society the conventional spectrum of political attitudes was skewed noticeably to the right. Because protection of the prevailing status quo and its hierarchies was the fundamental value of the society, conservatism itself took on a normative quality. Everything took one giant step to the right.

Thus those who would most commonly be defined as liberals in mainstream America were classified as radicals in the 1940s South—and so on: centrists were liberals, conservatives were moderates or mainstream, and quasi-fascists were regarded as mere conservatives. Sometimes, if the subject were sufficiently polished, the society would even skip a category and a thoroughly conservative individual like Grover Hall Sr. could roundly be considered a liberal. In such a society, as Pulitzer Prize–winning Mississippi editor Hodding Carter would later observe, the South was "the only place in the western world where a man could become a liberal simply by urging obedience to the law." Esteemed southern historian C. Vann Woodward recognized that in the civil rights South moderates were thought of as "liberals" and integrationists were considered "radicals." In 1944 Swedish sociologist Gunnar Myrdal, in his famous study of the South and race relations, *An American Dilemma*, made essentially the same point: "In the South . . . a person may be ranked as liberal . . . merely by insisting that the law shall be adhered to in practice."[1]

Despite significant evidence as to the spotty nature of Chauncey Sparks's brand of progressivism, many in Alabama continued to insist that he was a genuine liberal. *Montgomery Examiner* editor Charles G. Dobbins Jr. considered Sparks a bona fide progressive because of his willingness to expand social services and tax corporations and utilities at a higher level than their absurdly low levy. Yet the assessment of Sparks as liberal carried over to racial matters as well. James Chappell, the moderate president of the *Birmingham News*, felt Sparks was essentially "a liberal spirit" because of the racial views the governor had articulated in his Founder's Day speech at Tuskegee—views that were strictly segregationist and even laudatory of white supremacy in nature. Sparks himself was well satisfied that he was an enlightened progressive on race issues, even after the same and other statements.[2]

Public commentators who dared find fault, no matter how qualified, with the "moderate" guardians of white supremacy such as Sparks found themselves damned as radicals in the status quo society that was the Deep South. This phenomenon was actually quite remarkable because for decades all three newspapers owned by Victor Hanson had performed as the most faithful servants of wealth, commerce, and industry in Alabama. Yet for his measured criticism of tactics, *Montgomery Advertiser* editor Grover C. Hall Jr. was a "starry-eyed Pink," according to the mossback Bourbon publication *Alabama Magazine*. "[Y]oung Pinkie" and the few others who would criticize Sparks "[have] got some strange notions in their cocoanuts" and "[are] plum out of step" with prevailing Alabama sentiment on race—which, of course, was "the fundamental issue involved." The "young squirt is so far over on the left," its editor charged, that he was behaving like one of those "drumbeater[s]" for the SCHW. While it was headquartered in Birmingham, the *Alabama Magazine* served at this time as one of the flagships for conservative, white sentiment throughout the South.[3]

Despite the *Montgomery Advertiser's* storied career as the oldest and most prestigious newspaper in Alabama, one dedicated to the maintenance of Bourbon and planter programs since antebellum times, it came under fire as a liberal sheet by arch-conservatives such as Hamner Cobbs of the *Greensboro Watchman*. And it was not mere political liberalism, for such a thing was increasingly impossible in the eyes of the South's conservative guardians. The political was the moral and the moral was the political, and any newspaper that would refuse to blindly and silently toe the most extreme line on race was "wallowing in a . . . filthy muck" and "stench" that Alabama could not tolerate.[4] Ed Field's *Selma Times-Journal* denounced as liberal, and even radical, newspapers that took a moderate stand on the racial antics of Dixon and Sparks.[5]

To be precise the junior Hall's inflammatory editorial had criticized Frank Dixon's methods, not his purposes or goals, in presenting such a defiant face toward the federals. Yet in the eyes of the most conscientious guardians of the status quo, it still qualified as blasphemy. In an editorial passage misinterpreted as a celebration of Alabama's alleged political "liberalism" of the 1940s, Grover Jr. actually penned a stinging admonition to Dixon *not* to follow in the footsteps of southern demagogues who—through the crassness of their racial oratory—had worked injury to "the South's pattern of living" by antagonizing both races, drawing unwanted national attention to the South's racial customs, and risking another Reconstruction. Hall wrote that "Alabama to date has had incompetent governors, greedy governors, good, bad, and indifferent governors. But it has been spared the shame of having a vicious governor or one willing to exploit the Negro issue." He warned Dixon against following the lead of neighboring demagogic governors: Blease, Bilbo, Tillman, and Talmadge. The *Advertiser* hoped that Dixon would see the wisdom of examining "calmly and dispassionately this most vital issue" instead of indulging a "sincere obsession" with white supremacy. Although Grover

Jr. was careful in the editorial to stipulate that there was "no division," nor should there be, among southerners as to the "folly of attempting to establish desegregation or impose social equality" (and quoted approvingly Louisville editor Mark Etheridge's well-known caveat about the immutability of southern segregation), he still came under a hailstorm of criticism.[6]

The fallout was so intense from within and without that the editor actually backtracked with an apologia six days after the original editorial. Ninety of the *Advertiser*'s employees publicly disowned the editorial, and a tumult of criticism descended on the paper from around the state. He had not "attacked segregation by either word or implication," Hall pleaded desperately, or "advocated . . . 'social reform' in race relations [or] defended any individual . . . who had agitated the question of race segregation." "This restatement," a chastened Hall stressed, "is made for the benefit of those who have some regard for the truth, or who have been misled by those who do not."[7]

In keeping with the characterization of the mildest kind of self-criticism as some kind of liberalism or radicalism, the status quo society hewed to other curious definitions. The most extreme white supremacists and economic reactionaries actually saw themselves in the cleansing light of moderation. Hubert Baughn objected to being called an "extremist" by progressive Alabamians and described himself as mainstream and friendly toward the Negro even though his political commentary bordered on the fascist. Ed Field offered "unqualified support" to Dixon's and Sparks's high-profile acts of defiance to the federal government, damned Franklin and Eleanor Roosevelt and other "New Deal radicals" for their racial agitation, and painted blacks who sought improvements as treasonous. By no mental gymnastic, no matter how dexterous, could Victor Hanson's newspapers be evaluated as liberal. Yet Field insisted that they were. Still, for all of this, Field described himself and his Selma newspaper as moderate.[8]

In the status quo society nonconformists took their chances at their peril and many suffered severe social ostracism. "Good Negroes" embraced the racial status quo without complaint, and Jim Crow was in the best interest of all Alabamians, black and white. Segregation was "not only desired" by the white race but was actually an essential protection for blacks, numberless individuals and civic groups argued.[9]

Before long white southerners developed a kind of shorthand to denote conformity to the cultural orthodoxy. In later years it would develop into a full-fledged code. In such a society it was not necessary for those who subscribed to its fundamental tenets to go on at length about what they meant. All they had to do was talk in generalities and everyone knew what they meant. Thus coal mine magnate Ike Rouzer could say north Alabama congressman Joseph Starnes spoke "the same language that I do" and everyone knew he was talking about dedication to white supremacy without his having to say so explicitly. When Governors Dixon and Sparks took their stands for the white South, plain Alabamians lauded them by saying, "You certainly speak the Southern language." They have "spoken like an American," the *Sumter County Journal* noted admiringly, and "[we are] proud of [them] for it."[10]

The Southern People Will Not Swallow Mr. Nigger

The more it was pushed on race, the more the South began to view itself as not only a separate culture but, in fact, a separate *nation*, for all intents and purposes. White southerners saw themselves as a section that, in effect, was its own country, with its own culture and customs, and, like other nation-states, its own *sovereignty*—blissfully unaffected by the results of the conflict that began in 1861. Good citizenship meant allegiance to "our Southland" first and foremost and to the broader nation only second. White southerners spoke incessantly of the "Southland" and the southern "way of life," especially when confronting federal directives on race. The most virulent defenders of white supremacy and economic conservatism advertised their efforts as uniquely *southern* in nature.[11] No matter how mild their criticism of the southern status quo, the southern economic liberal first had to demonstrate his bona fides by emphasizing "strongly his local and regional patriotism."[12]

Yet this was only an insurance policy. In no way did it guarantee a receptive hearing or even an agreement that the messenger was still a patriot once the progressive message had been delivered. Those most commonly referred to as paternalists shared in this view. "This is the South, brother. You spell it with a capital 'S,'" as the *Opp Weekly Journal* explained. "We understand the Southern Negro and he understands us, and no pet social reforms [and] . . . brain-children of some antagonistic northern organization . . . is going to change it." Even native southerners who moved North were slow to give up their conviction that Dixie was still a separate country. "These Yankees up here are truly 'negro lovers,'" a white southerner transplanted to Philadelphia complained. The South "[will] never swallow . . . smart-allec nigger[s] . . . as equal if it takes another Civil War."[13]

While white southerners no doubt knew *mentally* that the Civil War had ended, there is little question that many still believed in their hearts that hostilities could erupt at any moment. Some even believed they had never entirely ceased. Thus the all-important race issue (on whose primacy southern conservatives, moderates, and liberals all agreed) was of such import that it constantly threatened to initiate a new round of hostilities between the states—if only in the minds of all but the most heretical white southerners.[14]

As political scientist Marian D. Irish wrote in 1942: "The elementary determinant in Southern politics is an intense Negro phobia which has scarcely abated since Reconstruction."[15] Yet per the requisites of the Reconstruction Syndrome the trauma afflicted not only race relations but also taxes, education, social spending, the federal relationship, fear of outsiders, and all other matters of liberalism that were connected to race. Surveying the South in 1944, Nobel economist and sociologist Gunnar Myrdal observed: "The issue of 'white supremacy vs. Negro domination' . . . has for more than a hundred years stifled freedom of thought and speech and affected all other civic rights and liberties of both Negroes and whites in the South. It has retarded its economic, social and cultural advance. On this point there is virtual agreement among all competent observers."[16]

Thus federal agencies were routinely disparaged as neo-carpetbaggers, consistently intruding where they were not wanted on racial and economic matters, working all kinds of mischief to the white supremacy and privileged business dominance of the status quo society. "[R]enegade white men" from the South who helped in any way qualified as neo-scalawags. Southern industrialists became specialists in remonstrating about the "unwarranted meddling" of the central government—echoes of Reconstruction. So ingrained was the cultural animus against the federal government that even *Republicans* in Alabama spoke the Reconstruction language and, remarkably, backed Democratic governors who stood up to the federal leviathan.[17] The American Civil Liberties Union was nothing more than a group of modern-day carpetbaggers and a "New York abomination," an older Marengo woman charged. She recalled the "dark days of Reconstruction" that had made the South solid for Democracy and deplored the immorality of the new racial liberals who "always side with [the] wrong-doers."[18]

Bourbon editors helped things along during the 1940s by salvaging and re-running Reconstruction copy in their papers waxing nostalgic about murders, mayhem, and social chaos. Giving flesh to the most prevalent regional stereotypes about crime, the 1860s-vintage copy mused that violent crime was the province of black people—"fruits of the poisonous seeds that have been sown by the carpet-bag adventurers with whom the South has been cursed." Other planter and industrialist types made the connection between the new carpetbaggers and the racial turmoil agitated by New Deal liberals and mothered by Eleanor Roosevelt, "whose genius for meddling into affairs that do not concern her is almost unprecedented."[19]

Yet the same voices that moaned and groaned about nefarious federal intervention in employment matters showed little compunction in calling for federal action when southern owners wanted tax breaks, land grants, corporate subsidies, job creation, disaster relief, research and development support, and the removal of freight-rate differentials. Whether calling for federal aid and generous incentives or (more commonly) demanding that Washington keep its hands off regional customs, white southerners viewed things through the Reconstruction lens of "our Southland" versus a foreign and diabolical central government. It had been that way ever since southern whites—frustrated by the military action over slavery and preservation of the Union—had reenvisioned themselves as the noble heirs of an old tradition of colonial revolt against tyranny, oppression, and the British Crown. This theme would reappear in the modern GOP incarnation of the Tea Party revolt. The leading citizens of the South, concluded one, need to form a "WHITE LEAGUE" and declare that "this is a white man's country." "[We will never assent to having] niggers [placed] in the same" workplaces as whites. The southern people "[will just not] swallow Mr. Nigger."[20]

In the status quo society all things were tilted a full degree to the right so that even common words and concepts became imbued with conservative norms. During World War II, for example, across the white South "patriotism" actually meant support for the war effort *and* white supremacy and business domination. Any suggestion of economic reform was instantly branded as the highest expression of unpatriotic behavior and decidedly counter-productive during a time of war.

Of course, the suffusion of the patriotic idea with such normative baggage involved the most direct kinds of dissembling and duplicity—even to oneself. Southern conservatives were not interested in racial advancements before or after the war, so their posture had little to do with the poor timing or selfishness of the reformers. Whites dedicated to the preservation of the southern status quo were not putting anything on hold during the war years. There was no significant racial progress to put on hold.

But besides its disingenuity, the redefining of "patriotism" as a rhetorical preserve of the Right actually served as a smokescreen to protect the status quo before, during, and after the war. Exploitation of wartime panic and fear only distracted southern voters from less emotional issues having to do with persistent class inequalities. To this end, the disruption of reform was exaggerated for political effect—as an excuse *not* to engage in, or even address, exactly the kinds of grievances most energetically condemned. Thus "the right kind of American thinking people" believed wholeheartedly in white supremacy, as a Birmingham man phrased it. All patriotic Americans should be busy asking, "'What am I doing to keep America a good Christian nation . . . [and] preserving states' rights?'" another said, tying in proper religion.[21]

Southern politicians insisted that Dixie could not afford to have "race troubles . . . [just] now"—as if the matter would be taken up with vigor as soon as the bullets stopped flying. "Millions of folks" feel this way, Frank Dixon announced.[22] Every man and woman pushing the cause of racial liberalism, the *Gadsden Times* charged, was giving aid and comfort to the nation's enemies by "promoting disunity" at home. Nor was there seemingly any limit to how melodramatic the accusations against economic reform could get. The "disgusting attempt" of the reformers to use the war to push their untimely demands "while the Cream of the Crop of American youth" are fighting in the "oil-burning, shark-infested waters" of the South Pacific, an Alabama pharmacist charged, was nothing less than a communist plot to demoralize the home front.[23]

Much of the lament was a commercially driven one that made little if any distinction between agitation on the issue of white supremacy and agitation on the issue of the economy, and, truth be told, the connections between the two were intricate. Bourbon mouthpieces for industry denounced any labor activity as disruptive to the war cause, especially that which involved the CIO and its attempts at biracial unionism.

When labor representative Noel Beddow brought up labor's sacrifices on behalf of patriotism, business spokesmen responded in worshipful tones toward the entrepreneurial class. Unions did nothing but drive a wedge between "payroll makers and their employees," they insisted. Despite all the workers' noise about the Germans and Japanese, business boosters argued, America's private enterprise system was in reality "the Number One target of the left-wing legions of Washington in spite of hell, high water, Hirohito and Hitler."[24]

The issue was sectional and disquietingly reminiscent of Reconstruction—as were all threats to the solidity of Dixie's interwound caste and class system. Patriots of both races were deeply offended by the noxious efforts of Washington's "'pinks' and left-wingers" to pass legislation about employment discrimination, a leading Alabama industrialist complained. Only the most "subversive influences of the North" could possibly enjoy such a scenario.[25] This was the worst time to bring up racial equality, a DeKalb County judge worried. It was "simply no time for pet social reforms," economic and racial conservatives chorused.[26]

The South Is Crazy

The maddening part for the few white southerners whose liberalism had matured past the point of a kind of narrow economic progressivism was that it all worked so well. Poor and working-class whites routinely and almost uniformly subsumed their class interests when faced with the prospect of a threat to the status quo—whether it was racial, economic, sexual, religious/moral, or patriotic in nature—because there was so much interplay between and among all the pillars. Wrapping up his wartime tour of the South, Gunnar Myrdal glumly concluded that, apparently, poor-white southerners were still content to "pay the price of their own distress in order to keep the Negro still lower."[27]

Yet the Swede rejected red herrings and false consciousness as a complete explanation. For, as Myrdal realized, there was truth to the view that social reforms involved an element of economic equalization that could not wholly set blacks apart. So, *racial* conservatism made some degree of economic sense. Despite the cataclysmic harm economic conservatism inflicted on the status of plain whites, there was also overlap between white supremacy and keeping the economic status of blacks low. Thus, once the elites were able to appropriate completely white supremacy from the economic progressives—and make "liberalism" mean both the racial *and* the economic—their appeal for the political support of unsuspecting white folk was that much more powerful. Myrdal acknowledged that there was "a measure of logic in the political correlation between the anti-Negro attitude and the traditional [economic] conservatism . . . [the] conservative laissez-faire society . . . of the South."[28] Thus the emotional power of the South's Reconstruction-based *politics of emotion* was amplified because the economic reality of modest white perquisites in the status quo society might be imperiled if social change came to Dixie.[29]

In actuality the war furnished a golden opportunity for conservative opponents of the New Deal to take deep swipes at the Roosevelt program—and they displayed little bashfulness about doing so. The alleged racial emergency during wartime exigency was an excuse to end the experiment that had been on going since the old economic emergency of the 1930s. But it was not simply economic conservatives the stripe of Frank Dixon and Gessner McCorvey who pronounced the death of the New Deal and pleaded for a moratorium on race issues (as if they could be held apart or in abeyance from other concerns). Erstwhile supporters like Joe Starnes and J. T. Graves rejoiced that the New Deal was "necessary, successful and is finished."[30]

Neo-Bourbons seconded such New Deal buyers' remorse, underlining the developing rapprochement between former economic foes. Federal control meant "centralization . . . dictatorship and the loss of democracy and . . . [of] *souls*," Hubert Baughn announced. The New Deal had been a disaster for states' rights, and now in the war emergency state powers should never be surrendered unless absolutely necessary to win the war, and only with the clear understanding that the end of hostilities would mean the immediate return of that power to their rightful owners. Any type of dissension on the home front, especially the kind that questioned the all-knowing and all-powerful role of the business leader in southern society, automatically meant that "Hitler must be cheered," reasoned a north Alabama editor. The only "sound and patriotic thing" for southern whites to do was to maintain the racial and economic "status quo" until the Axis had been defeated.[31] It was as if the corporate-dominated "business associationalism" that had characterized America's involvement in World War I—replete with government mediation between labor and capital—had been ratcheted up several notches after the New Deal to now require full and total business domination if any victory were to be won.

Whatever the specific rationale, there was no question that a concern with maintaining white supremacy underwrote the calls for unity and patriotism—a patriotism that meant a regional creed as much as it did a national one. "As true Southerners," the Ensley Kiwanis Club asserted, "we know that the only peaceful way the two races could ever exist in the South is by segregation and white supremacy." The former chairman of the SDEC agreed: the South "simply will never accept social equality between the races." Businessmen, civic clubs, and state Democratic and Conservative Party notables thought any change in white supremacy simply unthinkable—and resented the federal government for aiding and abetting any carpetbagger attempt to chip away during the war.[32]

But there was really little need for concern. Poor whites in Alabama had long since buried their class concerns in the rush toward white solidarity with their "betters" on the central issue. An agitated Montgomery woman explained: "We will never accept social equality. We demand that blacks be kept in their place" during the hostilities. Perpetuation of white supremacy through the war was the least the powers-that-be could guarantee the plain folk. After all, a Walker County man whose son was stationed in Hawaii stated, when the great battles come, it would be "the underprivileged white boys of Alabama who will gladly give their lives" for America.[33] The concept, and the sentiment, proved enduring.

In the status quo society, loyalty that deviated in some way from the conventional forms of patriotism qualified as basically worthless. Narrow mutual exclusion was a recurring feature of the ultraconservative mind in the South—and it appeared during the 1940s much as it would in later decades. Racial conservatives believed that blacks could not possibly support efforts to bring about racial reform and still qualify as patriotic Americans. If African Americans believed the reformers, then the "inevitable conclusion is that they owe this country no devotion and no loyalty and that the hand of every white man is against them," a Tennessee columnist explained it. Are the New Dealers advising blacks in the midst of war that this is, in effect, their chance to trade loyalty for social concessions? The danger on the home front from racial agitation was just as serious as that coming from overseas, wrote an Alabama politico, a cancer "just as fatal as a Jap or German bomb."[34]

While there was no doubt a kernel of truth in the assertion that oppressed people might look at the nation of their oppression as undeserving of blind loyalty in all situations, at all times, to take the slippery-slope approach and condemn an entire race as treasonous for desiring some measure of liberty— even during war—was an obvious either/or distortion. And blacks intuitively sensed the inconsistency, turning the tables on those who would impugn their patriotism for believing in America's founding creed. Alabama's rejection of a federal war contract because of Jim Crow could do more harm than "a hundred Nazi spies and saboteurs," a Philadelphia editor charged. Americans were sending their boys off to fight foreign enemies for the profit of domestic ones, a New Yorker lectured. "The South is crazy if it thinks this war can change the rest of the world save itself."[35]

In a society so dedicated to protecting and perpetuating a stratified status quo, threats to the stasis were often expressed in the most simplified yet stunningly powerful ways. There was no particular arch-conservative mandate that epithets and labels bear direct relevance to truth or reality, only that they be strong enough to stick and to generate a visceral reaction. Simplicity and emotionalism lent themselves to the ease with which epithets could be parroted by the masses with very little critical analysis being necessary. As European fascism became more commonly known, southern conservatives increasingly referred to any kind of federal rule they did not like as the "federal police" and the actions of a "federal Gestapo"—communicating profound cultural disapproval. On the other end of the political spectrum, communism became a catchall phrase to tar any southerner who would dare challenge the status quo. Sometimes the old standby of Reconstruction rhetoric was fused with newer wartime realities so the modern-day carpetbagger and scalawag might also (however difficult it was) find time to be communists.

At the first meeting of the Texas branch of the Civil Rights Congress, which did have a few communists in it, Col. Roscoe Simmons warned attendees interested in racial equality that before it was all over, they might be tarred with a red brush: "If you believe in liberty, they call you a communist." An Alabama dairy farmer was even more frank. "Well, around here communism's anything we don't like," he told writer John Dos Passos. "Isn't it that way everywhere else?" Sometimes, in the rapidly changing crucible of geopolitics, the status quo defenders did not know exactly which epithet would fit to do the most cultural damage—so they used both. One particularly racist, xenophobic, economically Darwinian diatribe concluded by imploring God to "deliver us from our present headlong plunge towards Communism—Fascism—or whatever you want to call it."[36]

It worked the opposite way as well. Anything that qualified as a buttress of conservative, hierarchical society received blessing as exactly the type of thing that had made this country great or "upon which this Nation was built."[37] Patriotism. Americanism. Enough said. Members of the dominant culture understood that the example supplied was a good thing, something to be cherished and defended—even if they did not know exactly why.

Drowned in the Veins of the Negro

Of course, simple definitions of good and bad tended to bleed over into inconsistency and even hypocrisy, something the status quo society learned to deal with very well—usually by ignoring it. Perhaps the most glaring example concerned the southern attitude toward interracial sex—the unholy grail of civil rights and social equality.

If white southerners were to be believed, there was nothing else that could possibly happen that was quite so bad. It was *the* reason not to allow blacks to vote or work with whites, or little white girls to go to school with little black boys, because it could all end—*would all end*—in sex, interracial marriage, the amalgamation of the races, and the mongrelization and eventual destruction of the white race (and, with it, all of its race-based privileges). It had been the favorite excuse for lynching.

There was only one problem. White southerners got a whole lot more worked up over sex that involved white women and black men than they did when white men had sex with black women—consensual or otherwise.[38] Why the double standard? Interracial offspring could, potentially, result from both kinds of intercourse, could they not? Interracial sex was interracial sex. Only in the white-dominated conservative South it wasn't, principally because the type of interracial sex involving white men was a privilege of caste *and* gender—a masculine indiscretion to be winked at, even joked about, one that could result in a Founding Father having black descendants or a white supremacist icon like Strom Thurmond siring black children on the side.[39]

Interracial sex involving white women, though, was another matter altogether. It was no mere racial matter or some white supremacy problem that could be conveniently compartmentalized, even artificially. For it threatened the intrinsic and cross-stitched fabric of the whole society—one that valued and relied on male dominance almost as much as it revered white supremacy. And the twain could not be kept apart.

Thus the sex issue insinuated itself into virtually every aspect of the southern situation and was impossible to keep completely separate from racial and economic issues—and vice versa. When a shipbuilding operation on Pinto Island near Mobile erupted in near riot, authorities considered quarantining the whole island and its racially disparate workforce until order could be restored. But eventually they rejected the idea: "We can't shut them up because they have innocent girls over their [sic] and no telling what would happen." Federal anti-lynching legislation was deeply resented in the South for several reasons. As a federal idea, it smacked of Reconstruction, federal encroachment onto state sovereignty, and a sop to black voters up North. Yet again, interracial sex was also at heart of the issue. "How many senators who have lived in the midst of an ungovernable, lustful crowd, and had their womenfolk outraged, would sit down and say, 'Let the law take its course'?" asked "Cotton Ed" Smith of South Carolina. "Let the law take its course? No! . . . We would lynch some white people if they would go down [South]—and I think I would join in."[40]

Yet the idea of racial intimacy extended well beyond sexual relations proper. While the southern ethos dictated that interracial sex was to be avoided at all costs, there were a host of behaviors that risked social equality and interracial intimacy that were seen as but preludes to the inevitable fact of miscegenation and the destruction of white integrity. In the status quo society all sorts of acts were viewed as on a virtual par with the taboo of interracial sex—risky conduct just one step removed.

These behaviors by whites constituted the most aberrant kind of race infidelity, while black participation implied the worst kind of offense. For example, when white and black patients ate and slept in the same public spaces at a Tuscaloosa army hospital it scandalized hill-country whites. When white nurses bathed black soldiers, they went into paroxysms.[41] Yet the conduct did not need to be so close to sexual as assisted bath-giving to invoke white ire. Sitting in adjacent desks or using the same coatrack, dining hall, water fountain, toilet, or hotel bed could also send whites into orbit.[42]

While some of the behavior whites complained about was no doubt the result of blacks purposely pushing white buttons during the war, racial "rudeness" also extended to trying to vote, refusing to work for low wages, and challenging segregated seating aboard public transportation. Southern whites who ventured north invariably returned home chastened by the bitter tuition of experience: witnessing African Americans with "their outright impudence, their pure unadulterated laziness and their ignorant air of superiority." Blacks were "going out of their way to be impolite" in the chaos of the war and "forgetting" their manners in the rush to assert their "'rights,'" contended budding Dixiecrat and Republican John Temple Graves.[43]

To be sure, some of the animus stemmed from more rational objections having to do with things such as the fear of declining property values if blacks moved into previously all-white neighborhoods.[44] Economic loss of one's primary investment would hardly do much to improve relations between any two groups of people, no matter what the origin. Yet central to the low status of blacks were more emotional considerations. One was the widespread conviction that African Americans were something less than human in a full sense—something more akin to animal than man. To remain consistent, white southerners often denied the most common forms of humanity and human characteristics to blacks or exaggerated other characteristics to imply that they were somehow subhuman. How could blacks vote intelligently, one woman asked, when "they don't know one office from another and *care less* . . . don't know what has caused [World War II] and . . . *care less.*" Alabama congressman Pete Jarman objected vehemently to the War Department's contention that its desegregation policy was the result of blacks feeling the same obligations and dislocations as whites because of their service. Black soldiers do not suffer the same way whites do, the congressman explained. "They are simply not so constituted and their lives are simply not on a sufficiently high level."[45]

For others, the determination to see blacks as less than human extended to the point of projecting onto the race the characteristics of animals—notably a stench regardless of bathing habits. A Mobile man objected to being crowded together with blacks on streetcars because "Frankly, it is not pleasant . . . to have some negro hanging over you; the '*Negro Odor*' . . . [is] almost more than a person can stand." Southern white colloquialisms about the "Negro Smell" were so common that even U.S. senators could publicly joke about black "outstinks" as well as instincts.[46] The segregation peril was also commonly referred to in animalistic terms. Reese Adamson (a prosperous Birmingham auto salesman who would convert to the Dixiecrats and then the GOP over frustration with national Democratic racial liberalism) urged railroad officials to do whatever necessary to enforce Jim Crow laws against what he called the "black creeping octopus."[47]

Religion was, in the most basic sense, the rope that bound together the somewhat disparate elements of the status quo society into a cultural creed that compelled obedience in the face of cosmic consequences. Conventional theology demanded allegiance both to the foundations of the society as well as to itself. Deviation was not to be countenanced by anyone who wished to remain a citizen, a neighbor, or even a resident in good standing. Religion—especially the predominant Calvinist kind—strengthened (and was strengthened by) the rigid stratification that characterized the Deep South: white supremacy, patriarchy, lopsided class relations, the most unquestioning kind of patriotism, and ethnic purity. While a Wesleyan tradition of reform did exist in the white South, it remained a decidedly minority current—as did the sometimes more reform-minded Catholic, Jewish, and black Protestant denominations.[48]

In such a society, religion meant, in most cases, submission to the hierarchical status quo. Lida Bestor Robinson, an elderly Baptist woman in Marengo County, provided a good example. She fortified white supremacy champions like Frank Dixon by informing him that she was routinely praising him "in my talks to Almighty God" and asked that he remain firm in his defiance to the federal government on the issue of job discrimination. Unbeknownst to Dixon, his ability to "act straight" was actually an answer to one of *her* prayers. The North might have freed the Negroes, she allowed, but the South had "Christianized them" and thus knew them best. Any public figure who would stand up forthrightly against the Yankee and federal infidel to defend southern culture was worthy of praise and support (a lesson not lost on a school of young, aspiring Alabama politicos). "God bless you in your fight [for] . . . white supremacy," a married couple praised Chauncey Sparks for his various stands. "God made [blacks] different . . . [and] the mark of Cain is on them."[49] A north Alabama resident in the nearly all-white county of Marion believed that if the white civilization of the South was to survive and not degenerate into a "country of mongrels," the nation needed strong leaders to stand up at home and in Washington. "I pray that God will . . . help all of us" in this holy mission. A Birmingham man echoed the prayer. White supremacy and racial purity were divine blessings. If ever the "zeal with which we guard and defend this gift of God" should flag, "[our race will be] drowned in the veins of the Negro" and "our dear Southland" lost forever.[50]

God Segregates the Races

Like race, religion was another of the great emotional levelers in southern society—a force that encouraged elite lions and plain lambs to lie down together. Big-business interests were gung ho in favor of propagating a culturally sound, standard version of religious belief that preached black submission and the Divine Right of owners and managers. It also defined proper patriotism and xenophobia toward cultural aliens as societal "goods" that served the twin gods of white supremacy and elite dominance.

The theological belief was certainly genuine but it was also incredibly self-serving. Both stratified racial and economic orthodoxies bound by religious doctrine were critical to the stability of southern society—a society to be cherished and defended in the face of assaults by outsiders. Big Mules like Ike Rouzer of the Alabama Mining Institute and Donald Comer of the Avondale Mills damned the "evil . . . interference of extremists, . . . outsiders" and the federal government in local problems of race and economics. Corporate attorneys and other future Dixiecrats, such as S. Palmer Galliard of Mobile, condemned the involvement of "prejudiced outsiders" like, increasingly, those of the northern-dominated national Democratic Party. Afflicted by the myopia that naturally accompanies self-interest, the Bourbons fully believed that the paternalism they had propagated for years was best for all involved.[51]

Melding white supremacy with the leadership of the South's business sector and making the product sacred through its absorption into a prevailing religious creed suppressed nascent class differences of opinion wherever they might be found. Plain-white folk followed along because, in part, race and religion were both so vital to their daily lives. And if white supremacy and conventional piety both said that business domination was good, who were they to question the creed? People just needed to "turn to God for Guidance" and away from the racial "Hitlerism known as C.I.O.," as a rural hill-country woman explained, or America would find itself worshiping false idols and "bowing at the feet of union overLords."[52]

Part of the society's cultural creed was the projection of standards of proper behavior onto even the dissenting minority in the South—regardless of the existence of some small dissent. All "Christian people . . . both white and black" felt nothing but loathing for the "outsiders" stirring up racial trouble, a plain north Alabama woman believed. Only the very wicked could feel otherwise. Just a small minority of southern ministers were agitating for social equality, a Tuscaloosa insurance salesman worried, but most of the people were in full agreement that "Our Southland is the last stand of our pure Caucasian race. May God preserve it!"[53]

White southerners had no problem divining the intentions of God Almighty to inform agitators like Eleanor Roosevelt that she was "at variance with God's wishes" in insisting upon an infraction of "God's Divine Law of

Race Segregation." Nor did they shy away from lamenting that any sign of racial liberalism in the South meant that "[our once beautiful country has] gone so deep in sin [and] trampled God's laws so low . . . it makes me shudder," as a Virginia man put it.[54] A Tuscaloosa native agreed there were certain principles that southerners cherished more than any ideas about national unity. If push came to shove, it would be "worse than foolish" for the federals to force the South to choose.[55]

This kind of moral certainty came from someplace very deep in the well of southern cultural norms. White supremacy served as the most fundamental building block of the South as a status quo society, yet it did not have to exist alone. It was part of the hierarchical structure of the good society made clear in the Social Darwinist creed that held sway in Dixie and did so much to inform the region's pervasive conservatism. White supremacy was part of the natural order of things: an order based on inviolable distinctions and hierarchies; an order created, blessed, nurtured, and ordained by a higher power.

No matter what the northern infidel and the federal interloper might say, white southerners rested firmly and securely in the knowledge that their cultural system was made by God. It also happened to be one tied very closely to the other major southern stratifications on class, gender, patriotism, and ethnicity. Integration is "against the laws of nature," a white Texan delineated things. "Nature or God segregates the races. . . . Reason this out. . . . Did you ever see a black bird associating itself with the doves?" Importing Africans to North America in the first place, a white Virginian chimed in, had been a "horrible violation of God's Divine Law of Race Segregation."[56]

In Alabama, the creed was so common that public figures felt comfortable enough to enunciate it without hesitation. In fact they connected it to continued fealty to a particular political party. Mobile's Frank Boykin characterized his defense of white supremacy as in ineffable concert with his holy duty as a public servant: "The good Lord started segregation when he put negroes on earth and I am [just] going along with Him." "I . . . always thought that the Democratic party in the South meant white supremacy," he said with some resentment. It is no coincidence that the most fervent apostles of white supremacy and black inferiority were also committed to other forms of stratification based on the most rigid kinds of economic and gender hierarchies. When Dothan's Wallace Malone presented a loving cup to Alabama Power president Thomas W. Martin, recognizing him as Alabama's Most Useful Citizen for 1944, toastmaster Horace Hall of the *Dothan Eagle* celebrated the event with distinctly religious language and imagery: "we love you best for your high Christian character." Martin accepted the award by expounding on a fourfold platform of essentials, one that placed unfettered "private enterprise" on par with "Christianity." Indeed, he maintained, business was such an innately good thing that there was not a single activity the government should be involved in if it could be done by private enterprise.[57]

Despite the basically accurate self-assurances as to the near unanimity of allegiance to white supremacy, there were in fact a few southern religionists who spoke out in dissent. Dorothy Tilly, a respectable white Methodist from Georgia, launched a South-wide group called the Fellowship of the Concerned to work in local communities against racial injustice. A devoutly religious woman, Tilly countered death threats by playing telephone callers a recorded version of the Lord's Prayer. Blacks, such as James T. Mason of the Easonian Seminary, appealed to Birmingham's white ministers to use their spiritual voices against the evil of racism because there was no other "that God depends upon to stamp down wrong" as He did the cleric.[58]

The unhappy experience of those who spoke against white supremacy on the basis of religion was predictable in the South. Betty Carter, wife of liberal Mississippi journalist Hodding Carter, described the fate of a young Baptist preacher who got "ahead of [his] troops" on the race issue and tried to lead them to liberalism: "He was gone in three months." Events like these led to stinging resentments among many blacks who simply could not reconcile the repressive nature of white supremacy with Christ's message in the Gospels or the loud and continuous southern white proclamations of self-righteousness and religious piety. "[T]hroughout my lifetime," famed black pastor and educator Benjamin E. Mays concluded sadly, "the local white church has been society's most conservative and hypocritical institution in the area of White-Negro relations." Secular organizations did not have a record to be proud of either, the South Carolina and Georgia minister wrote, but at least they did not prate on and on about a "brotherhood among men and a gospel of redemption and salvation."[59]

When criticism from within the society arose it was not only muted, it was dismissed as fiendish. Charles Fiedelson, the Jewish editor of the *Birmingham News*, supplied a moderate and occasional critique of the most unrestrained Bourbon excesses. For his trouble, Fiedelson found himself denounced as a supreme "baiter of business" whose attacks must cause "great delight among all leftists, parlor pinks and downright reds."[60] Consummate conservative publisher Victor Hanson watched nervously as rightists dismissed his newspapers for their relative moderation as "journals of Eastern opinion" that only criticized things southern in order to seek applause from the North. When Fiedelson censured HUAC as "a stench in the nostrils of intelligent Americans," an outraged hill-country newspaper claimed that the Jew might be an authority on the "political perfumes issuing from Moscow" but he knew nothing about American noses.[61]

Devout liberals came in for the same sort of dismissive treatment. When the SCHW aimed at the enforced white supremacist/patriotic creed by purchasing a full-page ad in the *Birmingham News* connecting southern racism to Aryan supremacy, the reaction was almost certain. Alabama's business interests struck back at the SCHW as a "meddling, rabble-rousing, star-gazing" outfit going straight down a "pink-tinted alley."[62]

The unceasing hammering that anyone in Alabama took who exhibited the mildest of reform impulses had real effects at squashing dissent. It was remarkable that a man as conservative as Victor Hanson could be pilloried along with his *Birmingham News* as the state's "foremost apostle of socialistic reform" simply for writing nice things about New Deal recovery from time to time.[63] Yet so close and so suffocating was the conformist climate of status quo Alabama that this was precisely what was possible. The most vocal racial and economic conservatives railed against the *News* as the home of "Vick's pinks," a "stable of left-handed typewriter jockeys," and a mouthpiece for "federal papa-ism, handouts, [and] interference . . . against local independence, states' rights and the initiative and industry of the individual"—the trifecta of southern conservatism.[64] When the newspaper objected to a congressional committee blocking a full House vote on a permanent FEPC, critics lambasted the *News* and its "crew of . . . radical [and] . . . left-handed editorialists" for not possessing a single "corpuscle of Dixie blood in their veins." By August 1944 Hanson was so beat down by the criticism that he issued an order to his editors suspending all mention of the race question from his newspapers.[65]

Sadly, the link in the southern white mind between liberalism and suspect patriotism—so carefully cultivated by wartime cultural conservatives—far outlasted the existence of de jure segregation itself. It was one that the national Democratic Party would have to confront over and over again.

11
Liberals, Friends of the Negro, and Charging Hell with a Toothpick

> The body-odor of Negroes, irrespective of physical cleanliness . . . is repugnant to the 100-percent-white, but is tolerated by those whose blood is tainted with the Negro strain. To guard against mixed breeds, The Creator attached to the lower grade of those types possible to intermix, an odor that is offensive to the higher type—notably the horse and the camel. The odor of the Negro is sickening to full-blooded white people; but is less offensive to those alleged whites whose blood is tainted, even in faint degree, with Negro blood. (This may account for the enthusiasm with which some white (?) people promote the "interracial" gatherings!).
>
> —D. Alexander

Saying that southern liberals were "liberal" except on matters of race is a well-meaning non sequitur. This is so because white supremacy was tied together, part and parcel, with the other main pillars that supported the status quo society of the South: patriarchy, bourgeois domination, religious and moral chauvinism, xenophobia, hyper-patriotism. Race did not—could not—float above and beyond the other buttresses of southern society like some disconnected thing, separate yet real. To speak of race (or class for that matter) in those kinds of terms is to speak of an artificial construct, partial and contrived, and real only in the imagination of the historian. For paternalists and Negrophobes—economic liberals and conservatives—arguing that a white southerner was liberal on everything but race was like asking Mrs. Lincoln if she enjoyed the play—aside from the shooting.

In addition to the united nature of the society's principal bulwarks, the ongoing and successful laissez-faire project of "melding" economic conservatism and racial conservatism into one and the same orthodox mould (on the basis of their shared antipathy to federal intervention) made it increasingly difficult to be southern *and* be liberal. In effect, the melding process magnified and solidified economic conservatism by making the inviolate subject of white supremacy an essential part of it. In the Deep South the process would eventually make it extraordinarily difficult—even unbearable—to be both white and a liberal Democrat. While "liberalism" meant, predominantly, a respectable economic version when the New Deal began, by the time it ended the word implied, in the South, a blasphemous position favoring the federal reformation of both the economy *and* white supremacy. By the time World War II was over, it was increasingly hard for white southerners to consider being liberals because to do so meant cultural apostasy and disloyalty to one's race, region, family, and friends—in effect, to oneself. To be "liberal" meant to be a *racial liberal*—and that meant losing friends, status, identity, and position.[1]

The battle to insist that southern liberalism was an honorable tradition, one worthy of continued allegiance—or to keep Alabama Democracy separate and somehow different from the increasingly liberal national variant— was an uphill fight. It was a frustrating path to follow, one filled with ever more frequent and resonant charges of sectional disloyalty and weakness. Rare was the political figure that clung as tightly to the liberal label in the South after World War II. Such a person risked being painted not only as heretic, traitor, and communist but also as unmanly—yet another kiss of death in the machismo politics of the region.

Despite these realities it has been possible for some to argue that the South was liberal during the 1940s and Alabama even an oasis of sorts. At an electoral level, southern liberalism *did* exist during the 1940s and, in a congressional sense, Alabama *was* an oasis.[2] Alabama's congressional delegation and many of its constituents were New Deal "liberals" in the sense that they had grown addicted to the fruits that fell from the federal tree under FDR: cheap and abundant TVA electricity, federal spending and military installations, satellite industries related to the war effort, federally sponsored employment, and the like. The implicit assumption for many, then and later, was that such liberalism extended to race and cultural matters.

Yet at a far more fundamental level Alabama was anything but liberal. Conservative cultural values were so deeply rooted, so ingrained, that often they did not require formal enunciation. Like the air and the water of the place, they were always present yet taken for granted—and sometimes not even discernable to visitors. Yet they were far stronger and more primeval than even congressmen seeking federal dollars for pet projects and home districts. If whites in some places in the South did not go around obsessing about race it is largely because, for them, the issue was settled—*not* because it was unimportant. Like the water of a placid lake, the basic waves and currents of the culture—race, class, gender, religious, and ethnic hierarchies— only rose to the surface when the culture itself was disturbed by a rock hurled from outside. Then there was considerable splashing and upset.

We Are the Best Friends of the Negro

In the face of the coming racial change, thousands of white southerners insisted that they were the true friends of black people—that, in fact, white southerners were the *best friends* African Americans ever had; that southern blacks were perfectly aware of this fact; and that Jim Crow was the cornerstone of peaceful, contented, mutually harmonious relations between the races. Thus the perpetuation of segregation was necessary for the continuation of positive, amicable race relations in the region.

The claims—both in frequency and in decibel level—were simply too high to be completely false. Obviously the argument was self-serving, self-deluding, even prejudicial. But it was not without some seed of truth. From the perspective of all but the rarest of white southerners, there was little about race relations that actually needed changing in 1943. In their world, race relations *were* peaceful and the races *were* content—whites certainly were. From atop their lofty place in the social pecking order, all looked well far below. Vantage point was everything. Blacks too cowed to openly disparage Jim Crow were the ones whose voices they most often heard. The rest—black, northern, and even a few southern white voices—were easy to lose in the cacophony of racial, religious, and patriotic adherence to the status quo, easy to write off as the mere carping of an always unhappy yet small and irrelevant minority.

Much has been made of the difference between Negrophobes and paternalists in the southern experience.[3] In different times and places paternalists have even been considered progressives and liberals on the race question—and possibly in a culture as skewed as far to the right as the status quo society of the Deep South, this argument has some modest measure of validity. On the intake side of the equation, the difference between paternalists and Negrophobes is relevant and certainly present. The distinction is ostensibly one of moderation. Both were white supremacists, of course, but the paternalist mitigated by a sincere compassion for African Americans, the historians tell us. Negrophobes, on the other hand, were moderated only by a sincere hatred and fear of black people.

But even if we accept this argument on its face, it does not hold for the other side of the equation, one more concerned with results than motivations. Here there is far less of a distinction between the two positions. All but the most radical in the white South were segregationists and racial supremacists. All but the most exotic opposed social equality. In truth, the intentions and motivations of the paternalist position have been embellished through time—and no doubt look more progressive than they truly were when placed next to the irretrievable reaction of much of the status quo society. True enough, paternalists felt themselves the real friends of blacks, the protectors of a weaker race from the misguided notions of meddling aliens from the North, and a sense of noblesse oblige did exist. Yet it was a "friendship" based, at root, upon the crassest kind of profit motive and the singular condition that blacks remain in their place—a place of distinct subordination in every way.

No matter how it is sliced, utter black subservience was the substratal precondition for the friendship. Economic reality dictated that African Americans labor for pennies only in those narrow channels of industry or agriculture prescribed by the dominant caste. Any hint of political action was suspect. Social equality was off-limits. If the relationship qualified as a friendship at all, it was only the most perverse kind. It was actually more of an acquaintance. And in the status quo society that was the Deep South, it was tilted so far to the white side that it recalled the alleged quip of Louis XII: that agriculture supported the peasant the same way the rope supports a hanged man.

More, though, the relationship was predicated at its most basic level on the perpetual docility of the dominated partner. The major benefit of the friendship for the African American, apart from the gradual uplift he would experience by being around a superior race, was a negative commodity—the promise that he *not* be subjected to violence. For paternalism, at root, was an expensive protection racket not unlike organized crime. Violence may have been costly to business, but it was still endemic, its ultimate basis. The benefit for black people was the *absence* of the bloodshed that would invariably occur if they ever opted out of the arrangement.

There was a clear connection here to the indigenous character of the intense opposition mounted against the 1920s version of the Klan by the South's elites and "better sorts." No matter how effete the paternalist might sound, and even believe himself to be, one way or another the cornerstone of white supremacy was going to be maintained in the status quo society. There was no question about *that*. Of course, paternalists preferred that the arrangement proceed by consent. Peaceful surrender by blacks in the face of overwhelming odds was better for business, better for attracting capital investment, the better to keep the hated federal government at bay on matters of both race and commerce.[4]

Yet the silent but ever-present potential for violence was powerful. "Physical coercion," one of the most astute observers of the wartime South wrote, "is not so often practiced against the Negro, but the mere fact that it can be used with impunity and that it is devastating in its consequences creates a psychic coercion that exists nearly everywhere in the South."[5] Northern attempts to alter the "mutually beneficial" friendship between the races in the South disturbed the status quo and recalled the shrill and bitter emotions of civil war and Reconstruction. The ultimate result of paternalism was one of perpetual black inferiority, enforced by the club or by sweet entreaty, but achieved nonetheless. Southern white people, as they promised again and again, were just not going to accept the demise of white supremacy no matter how it was put across. "You know as well as I do" that white southerners would rather fight than switch, a hill-country attorney explained. The southern people are taught from infancy that white supremacy is "our *right* by *birth*," a St. Clair hill-country resident waxed nostalgic. Southern soldiers, "when they would play 'Dixie' would charge Hell with a toothpick." "Now we are sitting again on a Powder keg . . . a Civil War."[6]

In 1942 *Montgomery Advertiser* editor Grover C. Hall Jr. wrote that "Alabama has had incompetent governors, greedy governors, good, bad, and indifferent governors. But it has been spared the shame of having a vicious governor or one willing to exploit the Negro issue." Very good historians have interpreted the remark in far too sanguine a way—as a celebration of Alabama's preponderant and essential liberalism during the age.[7] But the positive estimation misses the point that, far from a commendation, the editorial was actually a warning to Frank Dixon to avoid taking the path of the crass demagogue in protecting white supremacy: governors like Talmadge, Tillman, and Blease. White supremacy itself was never questioned. Indeed, segregation and federal noninterference were expressly demanded by Hall both in the original editorial and a week later in his clarifying remarks.[8]

The remark was about methods; a direct warning to paternalist Dixon that he was drifting dangerously close to the reef of demagogy inhabited by Bilbo and his ilk. The deeper point missed—sometimes by the actors themselves as manifested by the editorial's hot reception—was that the gulf between paternalist and Negrophobe has long been overestimated. Tactics varied. Paternalists were far more concerned about matters such as outside investment and economic development than the plain whites who followed the siren call of the demagogue. Business demanded that they be concerned about the commercial effects of grown men running around in sheets and flogging the life out of people. It is likely, too, that many a public paternalist was a private Negrophobe. But ultimately, the results for black people were the same: enforced subservience, submission, and second-class status. Like the fate of a condemned prisoner, execution by hanging, electrocution, or some more humane method still resulted in death. And for blacks, the ends mattered more than the means.

Racial traditionalist Benjamin F. Neal supplied a fitting example of how little space really existed between the paternalist and the Negrophobe. During a biracial teachers' conference in Milledgeville, Georgia, whites marred the proceedings by shouting "Nigger" from the audience, painting Nazi symbols on the building, and even stalking black attendees. Judge Neal denounced the vulgar tactics in a stern public lecture as "not unlike those used by Hitler to subjugate the races." Yet just two months earlier the jurist had penned a think-piece on race in the state's official Methodist organ defending segregation in religious life as logical because of the emotional black nature, and disfranchisement because of the corrupting influence blacks brought to political life. African Americans were "utterly incompetent to intelligently exercise the right of franchise and totally unfitted for jury duty," the judge wrote. Southern whites had given "a pretty good home to Negroes" and there was no rhyme or reason for black discontent. This is "a white man's economy, a white man's civilization, and we in the South are unwilling for our standards of morality . . . social status . . . the future of our children and grandchildren to have its moral standards crushed and our ideals of common decency . . . destroyed," Neal explained. If Jim Crow were abolished, southern culture would be "destroyed; the morals of our people would degenerate beyond description, the religious life of both races would be demoralized."[9]

The "true friend of the Negro" argument was seductive to southern whites, some northern whites, and even some later scholars. Yet wiped clean and examined in its unvarnished state, it is exposed for what it was: a sugarcoated obscenity.

Consider D. Alexander of Childersburg, Alabama. Forty-five minutes southeast of Birmingham, Alexander described himself as a true son of the southern soil. His father had owned slaves. He had been born and reared in the South and weaned on the ethos of "paternalistic dealings" with the race; he was proud to be one of the Negro's "real friends." Misunderstood southern whites, almost all like himself, were the "best and truest friends" of the race and only had the "sincere[st] regard for the material welfare of their charges . . . for their spiritual, moral and physical welfare." Southern whites liked the Negro and were themselves descended from slave owners who had held more than just a passing and proprietary interest in black people.

If only the "fanatical . . . interracial meddlers" of the North would go back to "their dens" and leave southern whites and blacks alone in their friendship, all would be peace and light in the South. Chief among the villains were neo-carpetbaggers like the "home-hating mistress" Eleanor Roosevelt, whose unwise ministrations only undermined the positive uplift of "the Negro's best friend . . . the Southern whites." The Reconstruction motif was everywhere for disaffected southern Democrats of Alexander's stripe, for it was the New Deal version of Democracy that was bent on destroying southern culture and morality by "[having us now] drain the dregs [of] . . . that bitter cup, Reconstruction . . . in the form of social intermixture between white and Negro."

Yet there were certain religious, moral, racial, and cultural ground rules to observe before blacks could even think about associating with white people, as in antebellum times. And this is where, for many whites not unlike Alexander, the wheels came off the paternalist wagon:

> Of the five races with which the Earth is peopled, only one the Negro, is ashamed of his race and tries to be something other than what GOD made him. . . . [D]uring the preceding 5850 years of recorded history [before American slavery] . . . the Negro [had not progressed] . . . one *iota* beyond savagery . . . [and] barbarism. . . . [His] advances . . . are not due to his independent efforts but to tutelage by the Superior Race . . . and he reverts to savagery, even cannibalism, when the . . . protecting arm of the white race is withdrawn. . . . [Advancement] of the Negro as a race in America, is due chiefly to the civilizing influence of the Southern whites during the years when he was nominally a slave, actually a ward of the Christian element in the slave-holding States. . . . With the Puritanical example of slave-holding before them, the Southern whites . . . put them to work on plantations in a climate suited to their experience and at an occupation the most natural, the most congenial to mankind—agriculture. For one *Simon Legree* . . . there were a thousand kind-hearted Christian masters whose training made human beings out of the brutal savages dumped on American shores. . . . Good food in abundance; clothing suited to the climate, and reasonable hours of labor was the slave's lot. The Biblical seventh day of rest was universally observed . . . church attendance was an accepted institution. . . . Bible teaching . . . was carried on by the mistress and her adult daughters every Sunday morning. The effects of that training for the unlettered savages is seen today. . . . [Yet today the South's] critics . . . forget that a man may love his dog and provide him with food and shelter, without desiring the animal as a bed-fellow; or . . . [love] his horse, without stabling it in his parlor. . . . That policy of the Southern whites, to refuse racial intermixture with the lower races is due to pride in the superiority of their own race . . . not to hatred toward the inferior race. . . . [T]he downfall of every ancient civilization is traceable to racial contamination that weakens intellectual, moral

and, eventually, physical power. . . . GOD made the Negro black; the southern whites did not do it, and all the race-hatred spewed upon them will not change HIS mark![10]

Lest anyone confuse the paternalist position for unbridled belief in the advancement of black people, Alexander stipulated that education—literal and figurative—should be limited to the elementary subjects suited for the African. "The Negro has a long road—many centuries long—to travel . . . and he makes a grave mistake in demanding a college degree while still in grade school." No matter how friendly or polite the white friend of the Negro might be, if blacks tried to harm themselves or white society by rejecting southern culture, that "courtesy" would instantly be replaced by the most basic underpinning of the status quo society: violence.

Whites would not hesitate to employ the "brute force of the jungle type," which was the only thing blacks truly understood. It could not be any other way because the forces in question were immutable. Even if whites somehow wanted to change the God-given animal nature of black people, they were powerless to do so. One indicator of the timeless inherence of Negro inferiority was, according to Alexander, the body odor of blacks, which "irrespective of physical cleanliness . . . is repugnant to the 100-percent-white, but is tolerated by those whose blood is tainted with the Negro strain. To guard against mixed breeds, The Creator attached to the lower grade . . . an odor that is offensive to the higher type—notably the horse and the camel. The odor of the Negro is sickening to full-blooded white people; but is less offensive to those alleged whites whose blood is tainted, even in faint degree, with Negro blood."[11]

Goodwill . . . and My Very Loyal Friends among the Negroes

Above the exaggerated distinction between paternalists and Negrophobes, the sanguine interpretation ignores an even larger point about the deep popular well of white supremacy that provided the lifeblood for the society itself. Segregation and white supremacy and social inequality and racial purity were the unquestioned ground rules of the culture. When and if the racial status quo was threatened by outsiders, then race would eclipse all else in the society. Above the overt actions of specific governors, issues of race were omnipresent in the society on a daily basis. At home, in the workplace, in their churches and schools and civic clubs, plain-white southerners were ever-susceptible to the demagogic impulse, which the privileged were only too happy to use if it could be applied to their advantage.

A similar overly optimistic outlook judged the appearance of the *Southern Farmer* in 1940s Alabama as additional evidence of the endemic liberalism of the state and the South. "New Dealer Aubrey Williams could return to Montgomery and publish a journal liberal by the standards of any region," one assessment held.[12]

The *Southern Farmer* was an extraordinarily liberal publication. Between its advice on tractors, feed, agricultural techniques, and farm products, it *did* aggressively defend the causes of racial, social, and economic justice for all people, blacks and whites alike. Yet it was actually representative of very little in Alabama. Publisher Aubrey W. Williams, a native Alabamian, was a pariah—denounced at home as a communist, a "nigger lover," and a menace, and by Texas congressman Martin Dies as "the most dangerous man in America."[13] Like most prophets, Williams was not honored at home. His editor, Gould Beech, another white Alabamian, demonstrated the rarest of racial and economic liberalism as well. Yet neither was embraced, much less even accepted, in his native culture.

What made the *Southern Farmer* possible was that it was bankrolled and published from the outside—by J. P. Warburg and wealthy socialist patron Marshall Field of Chicago—and thus had no dependence on regional acceptance or financial support. Field was absolutely loathed in Alabama as a "cog in the advancement of the negro plan" and the financier of New York's *PM Magazine,* "the most consistent half-tearing anti-Southern sheet in America," completely committed to overturning the entire sociopolitical structure of the South "as quickly as possible."[14]

Like interracial friendship, the concept of "goodwill" was also overrated in the southern experience. Virtually all southern whites, even the most reactionary, saw themselves as ambassadors of goodwill toward the black masses. Yet scholars must be careful not to confuse self-deception for reality. Horace Wilkinson, Frank Dixon, Gessner McCorvey, Hamner Cobbs, Ed Field, William Downs, even Hubert Baughn—*all of them*—argued that their virulent brands of white supremacy were based on friendship and goodwill toward the black race.[15] And at some level, these individuals probably believed it was. Paternalists, moderates, and even some so-called liberals described their racial views as the products of goodwill. Yet despite the variations in emphasis, all were devoutly wedded to the concept of perpetual white supremacy.

Grover Hall Jr., denounced by the most conservative white Alabamians as a Judas for his racial "liberalism," actually explained his criticism of Frank Dixon's rabble-rousing approach to employment discrimination as the function of his desire to see white supremacy *preserved*—not abolished. Hall

Liberals, Friends of the Negro, and Charging Hell with a Toothpick / 275

counted himself among those who looked at white supremacy as consistent with "democracy and Christianity." Most white southerners had a genuine affection for Negroes, a small-town Black Belt inhabitant agreed, as long as they were kept "in their place."[16]

And here is where taxes and jobs came in. Others put it more simply. The white South "looks at the Negro kindly like he is a brute," explained a hill-country resident. African Americans were "mere children in intelligence," an Alabama woman clarified. Since Reconstruction, southerners had done everything they could for the "coloreds," especially considering the perennial millstone of their prostrate economy.[17]

White southerners from all social ranks viewed taxes as a sacrifice they had made since Reconstruction, principally for the advancement of their inferior wards—the black race. And many resented it bitterly, or at least kept a close scorecard. Ninety-five percent of the monies needed to carry on the "excellent system of public education" for blacks was contributed "voluntarily and willingly" by the whites, expounded one, as he lectured against amalgamation with "the weaker race." The whole point of taxes and schooling was to elevate the African race and was consonant with altruism in other areas—the generosity of white people who "*give* the colored employment" (italics added).[18]

The white South, in sum, had done black people a huge favor in bringing them over in shackles from Africa. The Negro's white benefactors (including plain whites) had continued this pattern of noblesse oblige with every new tax assessment. One of the region's most impeccable liberals, Virginia Durr, described an upbringing that was typical in the South, where she both "loved" black household servants and still, into young adulthood, insisted on following the strictest conventions of Jim Crow. She would reject such social schizophrenia only when northern friends at Wellesley pointed out the paradox to her.[19]

The survival of the paternalist system was tied closely to cultural integrity, business domination, chamber-of-commerce preeminence, and keeping the civilization impregnable from external assault and reform. White people were determined to educate the Negro, Chauncey Sparks said frankly, but only "as a matter of aiding our economy." Yankees just could not understand the southern point of view, another white said in sounding like an old-time slave owner: "we are fond of our negroes who know where their place is and keep it." But Dixie would "never swallow the negro as an equal," he insisted, even if it took another Civil War. A probate judge in north Alabama's Tennessee Valley related that both of his grandfathers had fought for the Confederacy, yet he had never hated black people. In fact, "Thug" Almon echoed the cliché, "I have some very sincere and loyal friends among the negroes." But the number-one problem of the South, he maintained, was still controlling them.[20]

Evidence of goodwill was valuable to white southerners. It could be a precious commodity. If enough goodwill could be demonstrated it could serve as a potential firewall to prevent Yankee and federal intrusion into southern race relations. In 1943 Champ Pickens, founder of the Blue and Gray Football Game between college all-stars from the North and South, covertly suggested to Governor Sparks that Alabama commemorate Tuskegee scientist George Washington Carver with a memorial coin in order to stave off northern meddling. National magazines like *Time* and *Readers Digest*, he predicted, would "eat it up." Then, should real race trouble arise, southerners could draw upon their reserves of demonstrated goodwill and counter charges that the white South was "narrow-minded" in putting the trouble down. Of course, goodwill would only be extended to the black if "he stayed in his place."[21]

Whites were so intent on convincing themselves and northern critics that Dixie was the land of milk, honey, and flowing over with goodwill for blacks that they actually began to believe their own press. Everybody knows that whites in the South are "respected and . . . loved by the colored people," a Birmingham man assured himself. In fact, there was actually "no prejudice or hatred" toward black people that could be found anywhere in the South.[22]

Another common yet self-soothing fiction was that southern whites were determined to lift up their black brothers, but would do so if only they were left alone by the ignorant Yankee and the unfeeling federal leviathan. In the southern white mind the Yankee do-gooder and the federal usurper were becoming virtually indistinguishable from each other. Thus northern critics should stop exaggerating alleged inequalities and minor warts. After all, southern blacks under white tutelage had made more progress in less time than any other race in the history of the world. As a result, the related fable went, most blacks in the South liked the racial status quo—replete with Jim Crow. The fiction was persistent and pervasive.[23]

The remarkable thing about this type of friendship for blacks was that it was so flexible. Virtually any kind of white supremacist could claim the mantle of friend and repeat the mantra of goodwill toward the inferior race. "We love the South and all that is in it. We like our Southern negro and God knows we will do more for him than any other race of people," a Mobile pilot boasted. But in the next sentence, he added that he was a big fan of the Eugene Talmadge approach to race relations. "We were always brought up to be kind to Negroes but to keep them in their places," a Bessemer woman elaborated. "No knocking on the front door."[24] Talmadge himself parroted the goodwill language. African Americans who did not like segregation had simple recourse: "Stay out of Georgia." Outside influences, ignorant of traditions and customs, should butt out. Even white supremacists as raw and unrepentant as Hamner Cobbs and Hubert Baughn talked the goodwill talk.[25]

The fiction was so intoxicating that it became part and parcel of the developing rapprochement between Kluxer and Bourbon—and boilerplate for the emerging States' Rights movement. As Frank Dixon warned, southern blacks attracted to nonsense from the North had to get a hold of themselves before it was too late. Otherwise the Negro would "lose his friends" among the southern whites. During the Dixiecrat phase, paternalist insistence on goodwill toward African Americans would allow rump Democrats to construct a largely illusory wall between race prejudice and opposition to things like desegregation and abolition of the poll tax based on, ostensibly, higher considerations having to do with arcane states' rights philosophy.[26]

The argument gained mass during the war. Dixon tried to soothe the fears of poor and working-class whites (and upped the sectional ante) by insisting that southern goodwill could only continue with Washington's official acknowledgment of southern sovereignty. "No right-thinking Southern man is unjust to the colored race," Gessner McCorvey seconded in true paternalist style. "The negroes are our problem and we [will] care for them properly if we are just left alone . . . [but] we will not stand for anything even remotely resembling *social equality*."[27]

The southern fear of Yankees, "outside agitators," and the federal government was really quite logical in one respect. Clearly Alabama whites committed to the perpetuation of the racial status quo were growing paranoid. But it was a paranoia with some reason. Despite the cavalcade of rhetorical protests of concern for the advancement of the race and friendship with it, southern whites had actually done precious little to give substance to their claims of goodwill—and planned on doing even less. Regardless of the rhetoric, as the Supreme Court would eventually rule, separate but equal itself was inherently unequal.[28] The easy majority of white southerners knew (and they were right) that change, if it came at all, would only come when it was imposed from the outside—from the enemies of their world from outside of it.

Liberalism . . . Is Radicalism

Perhaps the most far-reaching domestic change during the war was that liberalism was slowly but surely dying in the South. Contrary to being some kind of golden age for liberalism or the salad days of progressivism, actually the 1940s were years when the internal contradictions and inconsistencies indigenous to the New Deal became impossible to contain any longer. Historian Patricia Sullivan was undoubtedly correct when she wrote, "Confined by racial and sectional identity, traditional white southern liberals had become apologists for . . . segregation."[29]

We should remember, though, that the result was not preordained; there was some choice involved in the matter. Southern liberals were "confined by racial and sectional identity" because they chose to be. They might well have found themselves in an unenviable and increasingly untenable position, but a resolution of the problem was still theirs to make. And the path that all but the tiniest minority of them took boded ill for the survival of a viable liberalism in the region. Liberalism had never been more than a minority current in the South—but at least up until these years it had been a respectable and, once in a while, formidable well of economic progressivism. Yet the melding process that had been going on since at least 1933 had, by the war years, enough time to begin to work its magic. The effect was to *racialize liberalism* and thus send it beyond the pale of acceptable southern culture.

Melding made the strictly economic liberalism that had passed in the South impossible to sustain. It made painfully evident to all the connection to white supremacy that had always been an inherent part of southern economics—a relation that had been hidden very well by traditional liberals, by choice and by practical design, for so long. Brought into the open by the most pro-business white southerners, the result was to obliterate liberalism as a viable and respectable haven for those who wished to reform the South even on a principally *economic* basis. And as disappointing as this result might have been, it should not have been all that surprising. It was the logical and perhaps even the irresistible end point for a society dedicated to, most fundamentally, preserving a stratified and interlocked rightist status quo.

The most fully liberal outposts realized what was happening: an attempt to win, with white supremacy, plain-white support for a program of racial *and* economic conservatism. The SCHW warned that anti-labor corporations were using the speeches of Frank Dixon and Horace Wilkinson to "incite racial feeling in the unions" in a conspiracy to "exploit racial differences . . . [and] drive a wedge between the South" and the national Democrats. The SCHW denounced the ploy as unpatriotic but to no avail; the conservatives had already cornered the patriotism market in the South. Dixon himself was delighted to have the opposition of a group as culturally leprous as the SCHW. "As long as I am condemned by [people like] th[em]," he chortled to his attorney general, "I am satisfied."[30]

Uniting to preserve white supremacy went far toward patching up any other differences that might have existed between the social and economic classes in Alabama.[31] And since the national Democratic Party was the chief offender on the score, the future was not bright for the prospects of continued southern fealty to Democrats at any level.

Segregation was the deal breaker for the southern liberal. A refusal to let go of that bone, with an extravagant tendency to craft the most convoluted defenses of the institution as beneficial to both races, inestimably helped the melding process along. While southern conservatives were busy making economic liberalism and racial liberalism one and the same thing, southern *liberals* were choosing sides and coming down, ultimately, on the side of segregation and the status quo. During the war years the traditional southern liberals that historians have sometimes also referred to as moderates were actually in transition. In another society that was not as dedicated to an interlocking status quo or not quite so predicated on the fundamental of white supremacy, the "liberalism" of these individuals would have been more modestly (and accurately) appraised. They would have been considered, *at best*, enlightened conservatives or conservatives with some progressive leanings.

Yet it was the refusal to challenge—or even recognize—the second-class economic, gender, religious, social, and patriotic consequences of Jim Crow that blinded southern liberals to the impossibility of retaining any kind of meaningful liberal position. As a member of their rank, John Temple Graves, said so succinctly: segregation "is not an argument in the South. It is a major premise."[32] Indeed it was for so many of the southern liberals represented by Graves. And as the New Deal and its Democratic Party became more and more racially liberal, a southern liberalism that remained committed to white supremacy could do nothing else but atrophy.

Nor was Temple Graves alone. *Louisville Courier-Journal* editor Mark Ethridge had already made his truncated view of race relations known in a widely quoted estimation of the FEPC, for which he served as chair.[33] Col. Harry Mell Ayers, editor of the *Anniston Star* and an Alabamian usually described as a liberal, or at least moderate, opposed abolition of the poll tax as a slippery slope that would result in America "surrender[ing] all states' rights" and acquiescing to an all-powerful, "totalitarian government" in Washington. Ayers also praised Chauncey Sparks's insulting defense of the racial status quo in his Tuskegee speech as "perfectly stated" and repeatedly counseled against desegregation and the too-rapid elevation of the African American. Yet many have insisted on describing Ayers as a liberal because he rejected trial balloons floated by Sparks and others about leaving the regular Democratic Party to retain southern social customs. Other moderate Alabama editors found themselves vehemently denounced for racially moderate positions but stopped well short of challenging Jim Crow.[34]

Alabama moderates considered Sparks (as did the governor himself) to be a "liberal spirit" and an enlightened voice on matters of race relations.[35] Yet like others of his cloth, Sparks was dedicated to upholding the multilayered status quo when it came to race and other matters. Sparks proudly counted himself among Alabama's "best people," progressives, and "thinkers and forward looking people." Yet he insisted that "white supremacy has been helpful to both races" and that it would be sheer folly to discard it. In doing so Sparks demonstrated a strong allegiance to the xenophobic strain of the cultural orthodoxy, one that could trace its deep and stubborn roots to at least Reconstruction. Reasonable and enlightened people could talk about incremental improvements in certain areas of life for blacks, but to cast the benefits of white supremacy away would only satisfy a fetish demanded by "certain misguided and misunderstanding disturbers from the North (and some in our own Southland)."[36]

To be sure, the issue was a difficult one, and it ripped and tore at the bonds of liberalism across the South. Along with Ethridge and John Temple Graves, liberal editors like Virginius Dabney, Jonathan Daniels, and even Ralph McGill (of Virginia, North Carolina, and Tennessee, respectively) issued pronouncements that varied in degree but which all stipulated that racial segregation had to be maintained as a precondition to improvement in black life. Because they espoused desegregation, the SCHW and the NAACP were stigmatized as alien and radical even by traditional southern progressives. Howard W. Odum, of Chapel Hill's sociology department, looked to follow the Commission on Interracial Cooperation route with a new Southern Regional Council to avoid another (in his view) unproductive and licentious period of Reconstruction and proceed toward a more orderly kind of reform from the prerequisite of Jim Crow. To this end the liberals held a succession of meetings during World War II (Atlanta, Durham, Richmond), yet black reformers and the few liberals who were open to desegregation grew increasingly disillusioned with the narrow parameters set by traditional southern liberals. John Temple Graves declared that segregation was never going to be eliminated in the South: "This is a fact to be faced, but it does not preclude a constant improvement in the Negro side of jim crow." "Anyone with an ounce of common sense must see . . . that separation of the two races must be maintained in the South," *Atlanta Constitution* editor Ralph McGill stipulated. "We thought we had to give them a little justice" to keep the blacks "in line . . . [t]hrow a little meat to the lions," Jonathan Daniels remembered patronizingly—but still avoid striking at the wall of segregation. Militant Yankees, an impatient northern black press and black leaders, and insensitive, outside agitators like Eleanor Roosevelt, according to Daniels, were on the "extreme left on the racial thing." University of North

Carolina Press director W. T. Couch was so alarmed by demands for desegregation in the 1944 volume *What the Negro Wants* that he insisted on writing a special publisher's introduction in which he declared that the end of Jim Crow "would be disastrous for everyone and more so for the Negro than the white man."[37]

Only a very select few southern liberals pointed out the impossibility of keeping liberalism both viable and Jim Crowed. "Do we want the tangled race skein completely unraveled? Or don't we?" the Florida novelist Lillian Smith asked her fellow liberals. "Are we merely trying to avoid . . . more 'tensions' which embarrass white folks or are we trying to secure for the Negro his full human rights?"[38]

These were confusing times of confusing change, and many of the southern liberals themselves got confused. John Temple Graves, who cherished his reputation as regional liberal and an enlightened and rational thinker, issued so many contradictory statements on race during these years that it is almost impossible to keep up. In fact Graves was so inconsistent that he functioned as a kind of southern Talleyrand, desperately trying to have it both ways as he straddled the most controversial of fences. By the war years, though, Graves had already disowned the New Deal he had once embraced as a tune that was clanging discordantly with the most dominant theme songs of southern culture. He had given up defending a Rooseveltian program that he saw as slipping hopelessly into a deeper racial liberalism that rendered it a sectional profanity. He had given up writing his syndicated column for the *Birmingham Age-Herald* and was instead writing for the Republican *Birmingham Post*. By 1948 Graves would become a full-fledged Dixiecrat in revolt against the racial and economic liberalism of the national Democratic Party. Soon after he would turn formally to the GOP. Perhaps Alabama's most respected labor leader later remembered him as being "as bad as any Klansman in the state or nation, and very capable with his writing. He inflamed the public."[39]

Yet during World War II Graves was reluctant to completely give up his cloak of detached and cerebral enlightenment. After all, he was a product of both Princeton and George Washington universities and had spent years studiously cultivating the image of thoughtful progressive. Graves and others of his type may be forgiven their confusion, for the times themselves were somewhat muddled and even more complex because of their own vacillations. The traditional southern liberal does deserve some credit for trying to ameliorate a tense situation during a taut time. Yet it is clear that figures such as John Temple Graves and Chauncey Sparks have been given far too much credit as "liberals" by contemporaries, by scholars—and by themselves.[40]

Perhaps they did appear genuinely liberal when weighed against a society that was skewed so far toward maintenance of the status quo. Drowning in an unending sea of reaction, southerners with a hint of progressive inclination (then and now) latched onto any piece of moderate flotsam going by and called it "liberal." Yet the dissent of the traditional liberals was much more a matter of style over substance, language and rhetoric over reality. At root these moderates were as committed to the principle of white supremacy as the Ku Kluxer or the most self-possessed paternalist. They insisted on "fairness" for blacks, but it was actually a rather grotesque type of fairness predicated on the most elemental kinds of inequity: a fundamental unfairness to which they were no doubt blind but which was still so central to its formation that the product could not rest upon any intrinsic or recognizable form of equity or justice for black people. They lauded goodwill, but it was a goodwill that was so narrowly conscribed as to be little more than the most pleasant affirmation of the status quo. A decade later the Supreme Court would have to spell part of it out: separate but equal is unequal.

The Temple Graves record on race and class was almost a study in contradiction. He initially favored the FEPC but quickly turned on it when the committee came to Birmingham to hold regional hearings. Later he damned it as a "monstrosity."[41] He spoke often of improving life for blacks but was an unwavering opponent of desegregation in any form. The whole thing was "a matter of states' rights," Graves propounded, and should be left to the states—where of course the status quo would be in no danger of changing. At times Graves the reasonable progressive sounded dangerously like an anarchist in his insistence on sectional and cultural sovereignty. "Not all the laws this Nation can pass, not all the excitement this Nation's race leaders can create, not all the federal bureaus laid end to end, can force 30 million white people in the South to do what they are deeply and passionately resolved not to do in race relationships," he wrote in imitation of Mark Ethridge.[42] Graves insisted that he was a great friend of the Negro, but it was the kind of friendship in which one party was so eminently superior that he could lecture them in print—and did: "You claim that you are not treated right. I do not agree . . . but if so, it's because so many of you are lazy and wasteful . . . say[ing] 'Aunt Eleanor will take care of you.'"[43]

Improvement for blacks could proceed at full steam but would take place only on that side of life reserved for blacks. Shortly after he rejected the FEPC, Graves illustrated how by echoing John Bankhead's call for every black soldier to be removed from the South.[44] He deplored anti-labor violence but condemned union organizers as outside agitators who created turmoil in the first place, gave the state a black eye, and hurt Alabama's chances to attract outside capital. Organized labor was permissible but could succeed only if waged with a more "southern point of view": one that displayed a healthy suspicion of outsiders and exhibited proper respect for the vast wisdom and authority of southern employers.[45]

There was more. Graves initially viewed the SCHW as a good thing but almost immediately turned on it as a group of vile outside agitators. The southern freight rate differential had to be addressed because the improvement of southern society rested on the ability of bosses to retain the regional wage advantage—that is, to "pay the best wage they possibly can; and . . . not one damn cent more."[46] Sometimes he spoke of mob violence as revolting; other times he agreed that white southerners might have to "get their guns out again" if blacks persisted in pushing the bounds of racial custom.[47] Graves condemned the 1942 Soldier Vote Bill as a dangerous scheme hatched by "radical outsiders" and suggested that assaults against segregation could spark a regional revolt that would lead the South out of the Democratic Party.[48] In fact, anyone who challenged segregation was by definition a radical.

Perhaps struggling for some form of consistency that could allow himself to retain the liberal title he had claimed for so long, a frustrated Graves attempted to redefine liberalism as something committed to the polite retention of the southern status quo. In doing so Graves revealed that he was as committed to the status quo society and its skewed definitions as anyone else in it. What the country needed, he riffed off of the NAACP, is "a society for the protection of the name 'liberal' against unlawful use by statists who look to the state for all progress, all goodness, wisdom and contriving. . . . Liberalism is not the word. The word is radicalism."[49]

Graves's inconsistency drove the Bourbons crazy, for they desperately wanted to count the fallen New Dealer with the writer's gift as one of their own. "Jawn" has "a knack for playin' both sides of the street," the *Alabama Magazine*'s Major Squirm jabbed accurately. He is the "self-appointed guardian of everybody else's business." Freshly recruited to the new, melded conservatism by the Bourbons, former Kluxer Horace Wilkinson grew exasperated with Graves's vacillation and erraticism. "Why not state definitely whether you favor social equality now or in the future . . . instead of apparently talking on all sides of a question," the gruff Birmingham politico demanded.[50]

I Am Not Aware of Any Discrimination

Beyond confusion (and perhaps as the progenitor of a fair amount of it as a columnist syndicated throughout the South), Temple Graves and other southern liberals hewed to certain basic assumptions of how government should work in a democratic society that, it is not too much to write, were flawed on at least three points. First, Graves energetically subscribed to the popular notion of his section that—while not solely a southern predilection—still enjoyed virtual ubiquity in the region. It demanded complete reflexive mimicry of the popular will from elected officials—even if that will involved caprice born of the most narrow-minded intolerance or unleavened ignorance. None of this relieved the elected official of being a *servant* of the public in every sense of the word, replete with the responsibility to mirror unquestioningly the public's will on any given issue, especially those that most closely touched the central nerves of the prevailing culture. The few outlying southern liberals who insisted that segregation was something the South was "moving away" from and was "an admitted wrong," Graves said, did not represent virtually any segment of southern white society or valid "public opinion."[51]

Second, Graves and other southern liberals hewed to an insistence that segregation could somehow be held separate from other issues, even other *racial* issues. This was a fantasy that at once allowed the southern liberal to retain the positive conception of himself as "exceptionally enlightened" and flowing over with "goodwill" toward the Negro, as they described themselves, yet still a stickler for Jim Crow. This willful mental gymnastic was a compartmentalization of Jim Crow that artificially divorced segregation from matters of "economic opportunity and legal justice" for blacks. It functioned much as the broader fiction tried to keep race separate from issues of class, gender, law, religion, ethnicity, and civic duty.[52]

Third, many of the traditional southern liberals were imbued with such an inherent sense of race superiority themselves that they, like Graves, perceived that the whole complex problem of race relations in the South could be resolved by simple gubernatorial pronouncements and conventions of moderates—"with or without Negroes in attendance." Of course, segregation would first have to be declared immutable and inviolable, whether blacks understood that or not. The decent white had to be assured that whatever favors he did blacks did not encourage a "breakdown of segregation." Only then could southern whites of "just plain decency and enlightenment, . . . and southern good will," act. The South is "full of decent white people," Graves reminded blacks as much as he did the North, people who would gladly "go the limit to improve the Negro's lot" if only these ground rules would be acknowledged and acceded to up front.[53]

Contemporary whites and, later, historians themselves have frequently overstated the nature of the South's "goodwill" of these years.[54] Far too often goodwill is confused for the polite but firm racial control and economic exploitation of paternalistic white southerners—a velvet-gloved white supremacy rather than an iron fist.

Fitzgerald Hall provided a good example. President of the Nashville, Chattanooga, and St. Louis Railway that sliced through the railroad hub of Birmingham, Hall was closely tied to a number of powerful Alabamians. He spoke of friendship between blacks and whites, goodwill and the like, and firmly believed that he was among the most enlightened persons in the South on racial matters. "We have undertaken to treat them with every consideration . . . not only fairness, but with kindness . . . with great intelligence and great tolerance . . . [with] real interest and genuine affection," he declared. "I doubt if any racial minority in any country at any time has ever been treated in as excellent and friendly a way. . . . The fact is that the real Southerner is and has been the colored man's best friend."[55]

Yet for all that, it was a type of friendship that rested, ultimately, on control of a race that was presumed to be immutably inferior, one that should be suspended in an ether of timeless and indissoluble subservience. Blacks should aspire to do only the work for which whites determined they were "best qualified." After all, whites were kind to blacks because they were a generous people who *chose* to be kind. African Americans made up only a tenth of the population of the South and, thus being in the majority, whites had every "legal and moral right to control." And with that control came certain racial and labor-related lines beyond which "our colored friends . . . would be ill advised" to cross, "undue demands" they would be well counseled not to make. This was not just for the benefit of whites, the railroad magnate explained, but for the benefit of the whole society. There is a line "*for the interest of all*, beyond which neither race must go."[56]

Liberalism increasingly meant a racial *and* economic variety, and union challenges to matters as mundane as job promotions and seniority constituted a crisis that threatened the foundations of civilization. Self-deception, and even an Orwellian type of reverse reality, marked the worldview of paternalists like Hall and his position on federally mandated employment fairness or the requests of black unionists. Southern whites were committed to justice and fair play, but opening up white jobs to black people was out of the question.[57] Besides, "I am not aware of any discrimination against our colored workers," Hall informed a black dining car employees' representative with a straight face, but if there were, he told the rep, "I want to know about it." In any event, he did not need anyone's advice on discrimination because "there is and has been none so far as this Company is concerned."[58]

The contradiction in insisting on separate job lines for blacks and whites while simultaneously maintaining that no job discrimination was occurring was, admittedly, one of Herculean proportions. Yet it was not unusual. It was the kind of alternate reality that would become an essential part of the new melded, inchoate conservatism then being formulated in the white South.

Even seven decades removed, Reconstruction was a constant theme for paternalists like Hall—a fear and loathing of federal involvement in economic and racial matters unless it brought with it goodies like large land grants, tax exemptions, research and development monies, bonuses, incentives, and government funds for economic development. Xenophobia was a hallmark of the paternalism because it was outsiders who most commonly carried the germ of discontent that threatened to contaminate the peaceful, happy, and docile black worker. The railway president's correspondence fairly crackled with admonitions against "outsiders" who wanted to "stir up trouble" and the "carpetbaggers and agitators and a selfish few who want to exploit our colored friends for their own selfish purposes." "I hope and pray that extremists on both sides will keep their mouths shut," Hall said in hewing to a conception of himself as an enlightened centrist, "that the carpetbaggers and . . . self-appointed reformers will . . . go home."[59]

The Reconstruction reference was more than just a metaphor, however. For paternalists and self-proclaimed moderates such as Fitzgerald Hall, it accurately described the meaning of the later New Deal for the South—and the declension of the Democratic Party in the South. He spoke of "New Deal meddlers" as "carpetbaggers" and—in an almost unconscious inversion of reality—lamented New Deal attempts at racial liberalism as an "effort . . . to revive race prejudice." "I feel very bitter" about the national Democratic effort on race, he confided to a fellow anti–New Dealer, and said, "This time I think that we of the South must and should control the reconstruction, peaceable, if possible, but control." Frank Dixon was key in firming up maturing intrasectional ties by agreeing with Hall that the efforts of a few "Northern fanatics" connected to the New Deal to use the war to effect a "social revolution" boded ill for continued allegiance to the Democratic Party. The threat was not just racial; it was broader and more complex. The whole social and economic structure was in danger, Dixon confided to the railroad executive. The New Deal sellout jeopardized the very "control" of southern whites over their section.[60]

The status quo was sacred, interlocked, and mutually reinforcing. Political implications loomed, for it was increasingly evident that the Democratic Party was drifting away from its heritage as the guardian of states' rights and white supremacy toward social equality and a new kind of abolitionism. Because Hall was a Tennessean with close connections to like-minded paternalists in Alabama, North Carolina, and the other southern states, he exemplified the pan-southern nature of the worldview. It was one that would take more definite shape in its growing discontent with the national party and a determination to save southern civilization and culture at all costs—even if that meant leaving the party of their fathers for a new home.

It Must Be Obvious to a Congenital Idiot

In Alabama perhaps no one represented the looming disaster for the Democratic Party more clearly than Forney Johnston of the old and prestigious Cabaniss & Johnston law firm. Recipient of a powerful intellect and the educational advantages that came from being the son of an Alabama governor, Johnston was generally viewed as one of the most articulate and enlightened white people in the South.

A well-connected attorney who represented big business and heavy industry, Johnston first made his name as a southern liberal by chairing Senator Oscar W. Underwood's campaign for the U.S. presidency. At the 1924 national Democratic convention, Johnston put Underwood's name into favorite-son nomination with a dramatic attack on the Ku Klux Klan, punctuated by a call for the party to adopt a plank in its official platform repudiating the secret society by name. Pandemonium erupted in Madison Square Garden and the plank missed inclusion by just one vote out of some 1,100 cast. Yet despite the prevailing perception of Johnston as a tolerant liberal, he was actually the proprietor of the most restrictive, discriminatory, and illiberal views on matters of race, culture, economics, and the kind of narrow religion that buttressed them all.

Johnston's growing unease with the Democratic New Deal provides a window into the intellectual roots of what emerged as the origins of a powerful cultural conservatism that would eventually find expression in George Wallacism and a modern and ascendant Republican Party in the South. Johnston's outlook on race and the allied pillars of southern society, his definition of what constituted friendship between the races, and his growing disenchantment with both major parties (and especially the New Deal) spoke volumes about which way the white South would go after World War II.

The racial problem had confronted southerners since birth. "[We should retain] our friendly cooperation and understanding" to blacks marked by a "kindly insistence on segregation . . . [b]ut . . . racial intermixture—never." The Big Mule attorney found this stance to be in perfect concert with the philosophy of Thomas Jefferson and Christian doctrine, indeed so self-evident as to be universally embraced by the "genuine negro" of the South. Only the "mulatto negro of the North" resented such a civilized status quo. For

Johnston, the issue of accepting one's racial inferiority was a simple matter of morality. The northern mulatto was "congenitally immoral on both sides," mistakenly ashamed of his Negro ancestry, and thus bent on amalgamation. Johnston praised the "true Negro" of the South. But he spoke in such primordial terms that it was difficult to tell if he was lauding a human being or enumerating the qualities necessary for an ideal pet. The "true negro" of the South had been "richly endowed by God with patience, adaptability, simplicity, essential loyalty and kindliness." "We like the black man for he has a constitutional incapacity for serious worry and the most extraordinary talent for contentment found in any of the races [which] . . . make the true negro the [most] appealing companion."[61] In other words, the good Negro was a lot like man's best friend: cheerful, obedient, and just happy to tag along.

Southern whites had to maintain the status quo in all respects. To sanction abolition of the poll tax would be to approve of social equality, and thus racial intermarriage and amalgamation—for none of it could be kept apart. They were all "inter-related and inter-dependent. They stand or fall together," Johnston explained. "Down goes one and down go all." Thus the New Deal, labor unions, and the "professional negro" were pushing the South to wreck their economy and to the edge of the abyss where "the African and his descendants [would] . . . inter-marry."[62] Labor unions, hoping for dues money, membership, and power, were ready to sacrifice southern civilization on the altar of their selfishness. Working-class whites and even blacks were making wages "beyond anything in experience," Johnston argued, a sinister development of upward mobility that would only encourage interracial marriage. And in a most fantastic declaration (reminiscent of Fitzgerald Hall's various flights of fantasy): "There has never been discrimination in [the South] as to employment of negroes."[63]

The result of looming social and economic equality was the abomination of sexual mixing that meant "a war of annihilation" that rested on the most abhorrent disrespect for self-determination and local self-government. For Johnston the Republican Party, as presently constituted, offered little solace, for the parties were virtually indistinguishable on race. If, and until, this changed, there was no reason to consider the GOP a safe haven. The federal government was acting as if it were Reconstruction all over again, another "tragic era," subject to the whims and caprices of "carpetbaggers and . . . meddlers" who refused to leave Dixie alone. Instead, they took an almost perverse pleasure in pushing southerners ever closer to becoming "a mongrel people." Even the Supreme Court could not be relied on to protect "our constitutional system." Homegrown scalawags, "eager to be known as liberals," Johnston despaired, were bent on selling out the South.[64]

Yet it had to be obvious that certain inalienable differences between the races could not be simply legislated away. Introducing the "African tribes into the life of a race so vastly" superior in self-government, civilization, and the "Christian ideal," had been a tragic mistake, Johnston felt. But to compound that error with "racial hybridizing" now would be unspeakable. Jim Crow was a given, Johnston iterated—a fundamental axiom, a basic tenet of nature. He went further in fumbling with the various Social Darwinistic strands of racial, religious, and economic supremacy, trying to tie them all neatly together with a deep (if even barely hidden) contempt for democracy. Despite his erudition, the product was quite ugly. Segregation was "good enough as a basic and common-place mandate in breeding swine," Johnston explained, and, even though it is "contrary to current neo-christian and pseudo-democratic concepts when it concerns the purity of races . . . [this] must be obvious to a congenital idiot . . . [and] implies nothing unfriendly or derogatory to the negro."[65]

Still the simplicity of the Negro, his "obvious and primitive reactions and . . . impulses," could not just be ignored. Greater predilection for crime and moral degradation were only two of the race's demerits. The "primitive or reflex tendency of the negro calls for a firm hand," Johnston continued on criminal jurisprudence. It was "no injustice to the negro"; in fact, it was "an enormous aid" to him for whites to use tough love to keep him from drifting out-of-bounds—criminally and morally. No method, *even lynching,* should be outlawed—hence Johnston's aversion to a federal anti-lynching statute. The lynch knot was necessary to "make even the most primitive negro intelligence understand that response to the [sexual] impulse when directed toward a woman of the white race means death."[66]

Everything depended on how friendship itself was defined. And in the status quo society that was the American South the kind of friendship that reigned between the races was actually the most impoverished kind— regardless of the protestations of those who most benefited socially and economically from the arrangement. The logic that sustained it, and the whole host of related buttresses of a culture and society skewed so sharply to the right, rose from the darkest part of the human soul—that part dedicated to keeping people different and poorer suspended in a state of perpetual subjugation. And, what's more, those ramparts were defended by maintaining a well of popular support with the most powerful emotions that were possible to ferment from the caricatured elements of what constituted proper religion, morality, and patriotism.

For the vast majority of white Alabamians, dedication to the conservative culture far outstripped loyalty to any one party. As ugly as they are to gaze on directly, these are the roots from which sectional and cultural disgust with the national Democratic Party would sprout so powerfully. And they are the same roots that would one day nourish the large and powerful tree of Dixiecrat rebellion, Wallace independentism, and Republican domination in the South—a South that would eventually form the centerpiece of modern national Republican ascendance.

Epilogue: Since 1944

The difference between people like John Temple Graves, W. T. Couch, and Forney Johnston as opposed to Theodore Bilbo, Gene Talmadge, and Bull Connor has been overestimated. To be sure, real differences existed. But they were more cosmetic and incidental than fundamental and intrinsic.

Next to the raw racism of people like Bilbo, Eastland, and Gerald L. K. Smith, the paternalist brand of racism and the progressive type of Graves, Couch, and Grover Hall Jr. might indeed appear "liberal." Yet this difference was more one of language and degree than content and substance. Racial segregation and its presumed consequences—racial amalgamation and the destruction of white civilization—was *the fundamental* agreed on by *all* but the strangest and most aberrant of white southerners, even among economic liberals. Culture and civilization—the South's "way of life"—was the most important thing in the South itself. It *was* the South.

There were differences in delivery, no doubt, between polished patricians like Frank Dixon and Gessner McCorvey and those who spoke for the more common sorts, men like George Huddleston and Horace Wilkinson and even John Temple Graves; between oligarchs and puppet masters like Wallace Malone and Donald Comer and Frank P. Samford and their mere mouthpieces in Bull Connor, Jim Simpson, and Hubert Baughn. Yet despite the quality of their vehicles or the circuitousness of their routes, they all wound up in the same place by 1948—mostly because they had nowhere else to go.

The variances in accent, emphasis, language, and degree on a state level mattered not nearly as much as what the Democratic Party would do about these issues on a *national* level. And when first FDR, and then Harry Truman, advocated a permanent FEPC, and then anti-lynching, anti–poll tax, and anti-segregation legislation, the national Democratic Party sealed its fate in the South. The party signed its own death warrant because segregation was the linchpin of southern white unity regardless of rank, class, type, or intelligence. And because segregation could not be held separate from economics, religion, cultural health, or even other aspects of white supremacy, incursions on Jim Crow risked all. As Temple Graves put it, segregation "is not an argument in the South. It is a major premise." The only real question that remained was *if* and *when* another party would step up to capitalize on the South's estrangement from the Democratic Party. By 1944 it was clear that once a party (even the formerly reviled Republican Party) could resolve, and then learn how, to distinguish itself from the liberal national Democrats on the point of white supremacy, *it*—not the old Democratic Party "of our fathers"—would be on its way to becoming the new party of the South: the party of southern white culture and the southern way of life.

Many have pointed to 1964 as the critical moment the South became Republican—when Barry Goldwater's presidential candidacy and opposition to the Civil Rights Act began to swing the South toward the GOP. Richard Nixon, in his characteristically earthy fashion, called that idea so much "bullshit." He thought he saw the origins in 1952.[1] Generally speaking, Nixon was more right than wrong. The true foundations for the South to go Republican were actually set far earlier than 1964, in the twin cataclysm that was the Great Depression and World War II, perhaps even before, in the trauma of Reconstruction and its New South–boosterism past.

The irony of all of this is that the very things that made the South solid for Democracy in the first place were the same things that—once threatened by the national party—presaged the end of Democratic solidarity in the South. The other great irony is that this took place not in the cauldron of Goldwater's 1964, or the 1968 and 1972 struggles between Richard Nixon and George Wallace for the white vote, or even in the 1980s rise of Ronald Reagan and the Religious Right. It took place simultaneously and parallel with and actually *within* the salad days of the New Deal. Nor were these the only two ironies with which to reckon.

Steadily, quietly, silently in some quarters, the acidic solvent of cultural dissonance would seep alongside the New Deal triumphs and alphabet soup almost undetected. Once it fermented, actual rebellion, dissolution, and realignment lay in store for the once Solid South. This realignment would lay the basis for a modern Republican ascendance nationally that would become extreme. It would envision—indeed lust after—a revocation of the New Deal and the Progressive Era, a virtual return to the Gilded Age and its nineteenth-century robber barons. Only now are some of the more astute political observers beginning to recognize a connection. Political scientist and

Washington Post editorialist E. J. Dionne recently wrote (somewhat shocked by his own words) that today's Republican Party "actually imagines a return to the times prior to the New Deal and Teddy Roosevelt's Square Deal, the heady days before there were laws on wages and hours, environmental concerns, and undue economic concentration."[2]

Yet the roots of all this were southern. As long as the sacred ground of white supremacy remained contested terrain between oligarchs and economic progressives in the South, economic liberalism could remain a viable enterprise. The first genius of southern conservatism was to take advantage of the more inclusive aspects of the national New Deal and, by doing so, achieve a decades-long—even an ancient—wish. The southern plutocracy's appropriation of the Holy Grail of white supremacy from their class foes would cut the legs from under economic liberalism. It was an act that would render economic liberalism an idea without an acceptable cultural pedigree. Exposed thus, it crumbled.

Without its white-supremacist basis—taken for granted or not, mouthed mechanically and half-heartedly at times, or not—economic liberalism, once so promising in places like Alabama, could not survive in the South in any long-term or meaningful way. Neither could (presently) "liberalism" itself—which ceased to mean a pure economic and class critique with acceptable cultural bona fides on race. Instead, the conservative offensive emasculated the intermittent populist challenge by snatching its white-supremacist props from under it and tarring the whole liberal enterprise with the poison northern and national brush of racial heresy. It was an act of thievery and manipulation so brash and so thorough that it eventually cast the whole liberal project far from the clouds of the Dixie Olympus, way beyond the bounds of acceptable southern culture. To be sure it did not occur without a struggle, a contest, or some dissent. But once gelded, liberalism was effectively transformed into a mildly interesting, perhaps even quaintly exotic critique, securely harnessed by the albatross of anathematic racial views that served as its Achilles' heel.

In this coup the Reconstruction memory in the South proved itself indispensable for the Bourbons. For the essential glue of the new melding that joined economic royalism with white supremacy was the seemingly bottomless reservoir of hatred, fear, and hostility toward the federal government left over in the South from the Civil War and its caustic aftermath.

More, though, such animosity held within it the potential for limitless national expansion and alliance. The Dixiecrat dream, the longing to take the movement beyond just the borders of the South, would have to wait for a second great melding to occur: one that also had its roots in the South. But the foundation had been set. It lay in expertly fomenting fear and suspicion of the central government in the giant ironical face of New Deal relief for millions of southerners. For this was an animus that held the potential to win over important white allies outside Dixie (especially in the rural Midwest, the Plains States, and the Rocky Mountain West) based on the ferocious power anti-statism was capable of generating. So was born Red America.

The key glue of antipathy toward the federal government powerfully united economic conservatives (even fundamentalists) and white supremacists in the South: Dixiecrats like Dixon and McCorvey, and the Talmadges, Byrds, and John U. Barrs of Georgia, Virginia, and Louisiana. But the adhesive also worked on a good number who were much more economically progressive—even loyalists or regular Democrats: Lister Hill, Sparkman, Huddleston, A. A. Carmichael, and South Carolina's Jimmy Byrnes and others. It worked on others, too—men who had long served as economic liberals and New Dealers while simultaneously enunciating the crudest types of intolerance imaginable: Wilkinson, Bull Connor, Joe Starnes, and Strom Thurmond, Leander Perez, and John Rankin and Theodore Bilbo of South Carolina, Louisiana, and Mississippi. The fusion took commonplace, seemingly innocuous euphemisms such as "states' rights," "freedom," "constitutionalism," and "Americanism"—a particularly slippery term that had long been tied to the sheeted intolerance of groups like the Ku Klux Klan and the American Protective League. Later, in the second Great Melding (that between religious and economic fundamentalists fused by an antipathy toward democracy) terms like "freedom" and "liberty" would find increasing power, currency, and resonance—as in Jerry Falwell's Liberty University, Harding College's Freedom Forums, Sean Hannity's *Let Freedom Ring*, and the Catholic bishops' religious liberty campaign.[3]

The dogma would trickle down to the street level in mantras such as "Get the government off my back"—especially the central government. It wed the laissez-faire Bourbons with the anti–civil rights crowd and allowed patrician lion and plebian lamb to lie down together. It suppressed—indeed removed in many cases—the erratic and problematic insurgencies against capital once organized by the Knights of Labor, the UMW, the Populists, and others of independent mind. It united patrician, Big Mule/Bourbon Dixiecrats like Dixon, McCorvey, Frank Samford, Donald Comer, John U. Barr, and so forth to the plebian element of Wilkinson, Connor, and John Altman—with the economic liberals giving up their economic liberalism to become junior partners in a winning combination. The alliance would feature a libertarian or even quasi-fascist economic agenda of no taxation or tax bonuses for the wealthy, no regulation, and anti-unionism (the Redeemer program, essentially) accepted by all (tacitly at first, then more enthusiastically)—and the expert employment of white supremacy to get the white vote. George Wallace was, essentially, the *last* of the old-time southern economic populists who was sufficiently racist. A special kind of political animal, he held on in the Deep South bailiwick of Alabama and used that governorship as a platform for successive national runs for president. But Wallacism only delayed and retarded full-fledged Republicanism in Alabama and the South until his near assassination in 1972.

The conservative approach here, when it came again, was to cope with growing numbers of black voters and democratizing federal voting laws by camouflaging the most unvarnished appeals to white supremacy while retaining the essential message in coded forms. The genius of this approach eventually included the perfection of a second great melding: one that would weld the extreme concepts of Austrian economics to extreme religious fundamentalism based upon (in addition to the old reliables of white supremacy and anti-federalism) the almost irresistible impulse to deny large amounts of people the franchise. Left out of the equation of religious and economic fundamentalism, these disfranchised would be labeled the undesirables, the unfit, the unworthy. Increasingly, they would be pushed off on (and accepted by) the national Democratic Party, giving even more heft to the argument that the national Democrats had allowed themselves to become the party of the "undesirables," the "takers," the "losers"—a conservative critique that has even been taken up by some liberals frustrated by lack of success at the polls.[4]

Thus the noxious yet powerful aphrodisiac of anti-democratic thought popularized in the fantasies of Ayn Rand and others would serve as a love potion to unite economic fundamentalists with their Calvinist religious cousins.[5] The union, a second great melding, would eventually bring the radical rightist and oligarchical brand of southern politics into unprecedented national vogue and repackage its Social Darwinistic essence in—among other names—the Reagan Revolution, Grover Norquist's "starve the beast," and the Tea Party Express. The consequences for the democratic experiment called America have been considerable, and they have been unhappy.

Actually, though, this trajectory should not have been all that surprising. What *has* been surprising has been the speed, intensity, and extremity of the modern Republican ascendancy and the corresponding ineptitude, timidity, and cravenness of the modern Democratic response. But the general "realignment" of the South to the GOP really should have shocked no one. The fact that white southerners increasingly conflated the racially and culturally liberal national Democratic Party with state and local Democrats, beginning in the 1930s, led to the severe weakening of prospects for continued Democratic vitality in Dixie. In part this provides a crucial missing link in the story of how the South—once the bastion of solid Democracy—went Republican.

In short, southern liberalism was never what it was cracked up to be—either by its adherents, admirers, the hopeful, or later scholars. It was "soft" on the inside. Its apparently solid outer crust was economic (and white) in nature. But its center, its essential being, was depressingly vulnerable in its stubborn adherence to racial conventions such as segregation, white supremacy, and various other forms of cultural conservatism. This was a fatal and regionally distinctive flaw that led, repeatedly, to the primacy of race and other emotional issues over class concerns for the whites who made up the majority of the South. It was a foundation that was waiting to reemerge when racial crisis and a return to prosperity pushed the material and temporary cataclysm of the economic Depression into the background of daily life.

Sadly this was true for all rank and manner of southern whites—Democratic loyalists and New Dealers, Dixiecrats and southern rebels, those from the hill country, Black Belt, Wiregrass, and Piney Woods. And it was especially (if most tragically true) of even the most celebrated southern liberals of the time: men such as Lister Hill, John Sparkman, and George Huddleston.

Another (and related) missing link in the story of how the South became Republican involves a simple but important lapse in popular and collective memory. In Alabama and other parts of the Deep South, the Democratic Party was never simply the Democratic Party—not until the New Deal anyway. It was founded and named—formally and far more accurately—the Democratic *and* Conservative Party.[6] Thus when sectional realignment to the modern GOP finally came (after the national Democratic Party embraced economic *and* racial liberalism), the South's adoption of Republicanism (and its contrasting conservatism) should not have been as surprising as it has been to so many.

Their Numbers Are Negligible and They Are Stupid

While events after 1944 are beyond the scope of this study, their massive import does bear at least some brief remark. In some ways 1944 is not the end of the story but only the beginning. Subsequent political and social developments only magnified and accelerated the tendencies and themes already elucidated here. The forces that first formed and then tore apart the Solid South only picked up steam after World War II.

The one, most notable exception occurred just after the war when, for a brief moment, it appeared that a coalition of labor unionists, returning war veterans, dirt farmers, and others might resurrect a Populist movement on the broad shoulders of the boy-giant, James E. Folsom of Alabama.[7] While Folsomism represented the most advanced liberal alternative—economically *and* racially—that Alabama has ever seen, it was not to last, or even to be recognized for some time. Folsom's surprise election as governor in 1946 ushered in a period of intense conflict at the state legislature, where economic conservatives circled wagons and appealed to race to derail Folsom's revolutionary program to provide universal health care, old-age pensions, reapportionment, and a new state constitution to replace the infamous 1901 Alabama document. Blocked by powerful industrial, anti-labor, and big-farm interests, and increasingly viewed as a traitor by plain whites who had not fully understood the depths of Folsom's commitment to cultural liberalism (or his racially liberal proclivities), the potential was never reached. While scholars have often blamed the big boy's personal shortcomings (he was a giant at six feet, eight inches)—including alcoholism, a penchant for womanizing, and the scandal of fathering a child out of wedlock—Folsom's real Achilles' heel was that his outsized personality and carnival-like campaigning at the state's remotest crossroads and branch heads could not cover up forever what amounted to an economic (and, more important, a racial) rejection of the region's most sacred tenets.

The 1948 "Dixiecrat Revolt," long seen by scholars and others as a failure, was, actually nothing of the sort. With just a few months, limited resources, little organization, huge potential negative retribution awaiting them, and the weight of decades of Democratic Party regularity, the Dixiecrats mounted an impressive rebellion, by any measure, against Harry Truman and his civil rights program of federally sponsored desegregation, anti-lynch laws, abolition of the poll tax, and fair employment through a permanent FEPC. When Truman's civil rights planks became part of the national Democratic platform at Philadelphia's 1948 national convention, Alabama and Mississippi delegates staged an historic walkout. Meeting in Birmingham, Alabama, the insurgents quickly organized a States' Rights Party that threw up a scary challenge to the incumbent president—especially since the party was also split to the left by Henry Wallace's candidacy on the Progressive Democratic ticket. In November 1948, South Carolina governor Strom Thurmond won four states outright (Alabama, Mississippi, Louisiana, and South Carolina) and showed well in various counties, districts, and bands across Florida, Georgia, Tennessee, and Texas—polling over one million votes and garnering thirty-nine valuable electoral votes. Due to the Dixiecrats, Harry Truman nearly lost the 1948 presidential election.

The revolt "failed" in the sense that its candidate did not become president, nor did the States' Righters achieve their dream of throwing the election into the House of Representatives à la 1876, where they could use the southern presence to wrangle for a more palatable compromise. Because of these shortcomings, the revolt has often been dismissed as a failure—or worse, seen as the vindication of some kind of economically rational, liberal, bottom-deep awakening in the South. It is an error of the largest sort to understand the Dixiecrat episode as either.

The Dixiecrat rebellion actually provided the most perfect enunciation of the Great Melding between economic reactionaries and white supremacists yet, one that had been brewing since at least 1933. It also presaged the future. Although the Dixiecrats did not "win," in a clean or technical sense, they did lay vital groundwork for an appeal to economic conservatives and white supremacists far beyond the borders of the former Confederacy—one bound by the powerful cord of hatred and fear of the federal government. As Jim Martin would accurately remark fifty years later, the 1948 revolt formed the "nucleus" of modern Republican ascendance in the South.[8] And Martin was one person who knew what he was talking about. A lifelong north Alabama Democrat and oil man, Martin joined the GOP, opposed the Civil Rights Act, and won election to Congress in 1964 on the coattails of Barry Goldwater. Two years later he came within a whisker of out-race-baiting Lurleen (read: George) Wallace for the 1966 Alabama gubernatorial election *as a Republican*. Martin made his observation about the historic partisan realignment of the Solid South from what amounted to ringside.

While the present study deals with the making—and then the breaking—of the Solid South through World War II, a fitting epitaph (and future clarion call) was issued soon after the Dixiecrat Revolt. In the spring of 1949, attempting to regroup and chart a new direction after their November 1948 loss, a Dixiecrat "appreciation dinner" was held in Dothan, Alabama, for leading States' Righters from across the South: a resounding show of defiance to the forces still calling for loyalism to the national party. And at that dinner the future was made prophetically clear.

In the South, party would always remain secondary to essential conservative ideology, partisan affiliation subordinate to enduring cultural verities. The keynote speaker for the dinner was none other than John Temple Graves, and he understood this perfectly. Disgusted by what he considered the racial and economically liberal excesses of the New Deal, Graves had, after World War II, become a vocal and eloquent leader of the Dixiecrats. In a few years more he became an actual Republican. And in the heart of Alabama's poor Wiregrass, Graves dared to enunciate the heretical prophecy in public. "Gentlemen," he told the gathering of Dixiecrat notables, "let us not wince any more when we hear the word Republican."[9]

Salvation was in sight. The core of a new and powerful political party is already in existence, Graves suggested, one in which southern Democrats and conservative Republicans around the country would join hands in an epic struggle against civil rights, the federal government, labor laws, and unwanted regulations and interference in the market economy. Angry, fearful, and feeling betrayed by their own sacred Democratic Party, the most influential states' rights adherents in Dixie took the former New Dealer's words to heart. By the end of the conference they passed a formal resolution to cross party lines, even state and regional lines, to build a new, conservative party founded on the bedrock of racial and business conservative melding: of white supremacy and an untethered laissez-faire. The future demanded it. Party would (as it ever had) remain secondary to conservative culture and ideology in the South.

Before the conference adjourned, the attendees made it official and, indeed, gazed around the corners of time to see a future of national rightism that would be based on, but not bottled up in, the South. The meeting formally resolved that "we will join hands with any national group or party, who sincerely embraces states' rights and constitutional government. *We declare that principle is above any party.* We invite all Americans to work with us" (italics added).[10]

The 1950s brought a sort of Republican respectability, finally, to the South in the candidacies of the wildly popular war hero Dwight Eisenhower. Republicans scored ever-increasing vote tallies in 1952 and 1956 in the South, and former Dixiecrat editor Tom Abernethy actually ran a scintillatingly close campaign for Alabama governor in 1954 *as a Republican* based on little more than naked racial prejudice linked with laissez-faire dogma and a poisonous view of the federal government. All of it nearly came unglued for the Republicans in 1957, though, when the essentially moderate Eisenhower decided that enforcement of federal court decrees outweighed southern devotion to hallowed customs such as Jim Crow and sent federal troops to Arkansas to ensure that Little Rock's Central High School would be desegregated. Dixie's apoplectic reaction to Ike's treason underscored just how essential it was for the GOP to hew to conservative southern customs if it stood any chance at all of one day making the South Republican.

Before it was all over, a shaken Eisenhower and his brother, Milton, would be accused of being Communist agents by reactionary groups such as the John Birch Society. And even before his prophetic exit warning about the dangers of the "military-industrial complex," Ike would privately express considerable disgust with what he was up against in what was then still considered the "extreme" right wing of the GOP. In a letter to his brother, Edgar, President Eisenhower expressed revulsion for the small-minded right-wing extremism that, had he lived long enough, he would have seen ascend to the level of mainstream Republican conservatism in groups such as the Religious Right and the Tea Party of Jerry Falwell, Pat Robertson, Paul Weyrich, Grover Norquist, Jude Wanniski, Newt Gingrich, Sarah Palin, Rick Perry, Rick Santorum, and of course George W. Bush. If a *"rule of reason* is not applied" to the political processes of our country, Ike lectured his brother, "we will lose everything—even to a possible and drastic change in the Constitution. This is what I mean by my constant insistence upon 'moderation' in government. Should any political party attempt to abolish social security, unemployment insurance, and eliminate labor laws and farm programs, you would not hear of that party again in our political history. There is a tiny splinter group, of course, that believes you can do these things. Among them are H. L. Hunt (you possibly know his background), a few other Texas oil millionaires, and an occasional politician or business man from other areas. Their number is negligible and they are stupid."[11]

In the next few decades Eisenhower's low estimation of the extremists who were willing to actually attempt what he saw as a disastrous shredding of the safety net and the social compact would share a kindred disdain from that of several of the party's leading strategists. But the numbers of rank and file who could be swayed in this way to vote Republican would not remain negligible. What is much worse, perhaps, is that things did not have to be this way. The Holy Grail of the southern white vote, fought so furiously over by George Wallace and Richard Nixon in 1968 and 1972, would lead the GOP to cynically turn its back completely on its once-proud heritage of liberalism and racial tolerance associated with Abraham Lincoln, Teddy Roosevelt, and Bob La Follette. Instead of those progressive-minded figures the GOP got, at its 1964 national convention in Miami, the virtual expulsion of its Old Guard moderate element in the form of Everitt Dirksen, George Romney, William Scranton, Jacob Javits, and Nelson Rockefeller. In its place the party adopted the "extremism is no vice" extremism and anti–civil rights posture of Barry Goldwater and a disastrous election in which the Republican won only six states: the former Dixiecrat states plus Georgia and Goldwater's home state of Arizona.

In 1988, George H. W. Bush's advisors, Lee Atwater and Roger Ailes, would cynically employ the infamous Willie Horton ad to sink Democratic candidate Michael Dukakis and provide the quintessential Republican demonstration of race to carry Dixie and use the South as the most reliable bedrock of national GOP strength.[12] But, actually, John Mitchell, Richard Nixon, Pat Buchanan, Kevin Phillips, and Lee Atwater finished what had been started much earlier by the South Carolina tandem of Strom Thurmond and Harry Dent: building Republican dominance in the South on the foundation of white supremacy and racism and using that solid southern bedrock of GOP dominance as the launching point for the emergence of a national Republican majority.

Nixon, as astute a politician as any, recognized the folly of removing a gnat with a sledgehammer and advocated for a more velvet-glove approach. He believed Goldwater had actually blundered in 1964 by being too transparent on race. By appealing to the "foam-at-the-mouth segregationists," Nixon reasoned, Goldwater had "won the wrong [Southern] states" (Alabama, Mississippi, Louisiana, South Carolina, and Georgia) and in the process alienated much of the rest of the country. Nixon and his advisors were after a much more subtle racial appeal. They "scrupulously avoided explicit references to race" in developing a "racial policy conservative enough to entice the South from Wallace, but not so radical as to repel" the vital swing states of Ohio, Illinois, Pennsylvania, California, and New Jersey. Harry Dent, a South Carolinian who cut his political teeth helping Strom Thurmond, advised Nixon to "follow [Kevin] Phillips' plan" although to "disavow it publicly." Nixon ordered chief aide-de-camp H. R. Haldeman to "use Phillips . . . study his strategy . . . go for Poles, Italians, Irish . . . learn to understand the Silent Majority . . . don't go for Jews & Blacks." Haldeman's partner, John Ehrlichman, would confirm that that is exactly what the Nixon White House did.[13]

Kevin Phillips, the boy wonder of Republican strategy, would eventually live long enough to find himself so repelled by the extremism of the party he helped put in ascendance that he would leave it in spectacular disgust—cursing especially the two George Bushes, the Religious Right, and the even more extreme figures of the Tea Party. But in 1969 Phillips was the toast of the GOP when he published *The Emerging Republican Majority,* a book that became, in effect, the bible of the "Southern Strategy." The young GOP wunderkind based his calculations and projections, as hauntingly accurate as a Nostradamus quatrain was supposed to be, on large-scale demographic shifts that favored what he called the conservative "Sunbelt" of the South and West as opposed to shrinking liberal population centers in the old industrial Northeast. "Substantial Negro support is not necessary to national Republican victory," Phillips concluded bluntly. "[T]he GOP can build a winning coalition without Negro votes." In a particularly Machiavellian passage Phillips recommended that although Republicans did not need black votes, the GOP should work to *maintain* black voting rights in the South because of the salutary effect it would have in pushing angry white southerners further into the arms of the GOP. "[F]ar from contrary to GOP interests," Phillips explained, black voting "is essential if Southern conservatives are to be pressured into switching to the Republican Party—for Negroes are beginning to seize control of the national Democratic Party." In an even more candid moment Phillips distilled his strategy down to a simple, if disturbing, formula: "Who hates whom: 'That is the secret.'" "The trick was," as historian Dan Carter, perhaps the closest student of the "Southern Strategy," has written, "to use the emotional issues of culture and race to achieve what . . . John Mitchell had," more euphemistically, "called a 'positive polarization' of American politics."[14]

For decades race was the most reliable fodder of a politics that ran on emotion. In the Jim Crow South, even through the early 1960s it was perfectly acceptable, even beneficial, for the region's political figures to race-bait opponents openly and directly. With the 1965 Voting Rights Act and federal intervention in voting, a growing black electorate, and the maturation of a post-*Brown* generation of white southerners who rejected segregation—at least in public and in principle—it became no longer acceptable to do this. More subtle, coded race appeals filled the void, clever and thinly disguised dog whistles about "law and order," welfare, quotas, taxes for "social programs," food stamps, "states' rights and local government," urban decay, "big government," crime, and "personal responsibility"—the allegedly "color-blind" issues that are anything but. To a large extent, conventional race-baiting became supplanted and supplemented by what may be termed the "New Racism": a baiting of political opponents on the basis of religion, morality, "character," "values," "terror," "patriotism," "tax fury," and the like. No longer could southern pols call a political opponent a "nigger lover." It did become acceptable, even commonplace and shrewd, to paint political opponents as moral reprobates, of flawed character, inferior values, suspect religious orientation, and questionable integrity and patriotism—basically, of being morally and religiously inferior human beings: in other words, "New Negroes."

The result of the new racism was essentially the same as the old. That is, in a South once compelled by notions of racial orthodoxy and now equally as enthralled by conceptions of moral, religious, and patriotic orthodoxy, political figures could gain ground by questioning an opponent's moral fiber in much the same way they once did by impugning a person's commitment to white supremacy. Waged in this way, elite politics could tap into mass support for an economic agenda of low taxation, corporate welfare, anti-unionism, gutted social services, austerity and fiscal retrenchment, taxpayer bailouts of Wall Street, inadequate funding of the public sector (particularly public education), massive privatization, decreased worker safety, lower environmental standards, the weakening of public- and private-sector collective bargaining rights, and other ostensibly "color-blind" issues by using morality or patriotism or militarism or tax fury in the same way they once had used race alone.[15] And race would still be present just beneath the surface of most of these issues.

And in the most private councils of conservative strategists, there was euphoria over the ability to tap into a southern white conservative base—and go national—in this way. "We can elect Mickey Mouse to the Senate," the late Terry Dolan, head of the National Conservative Political Action Committee, boasted in 1982. "People will vote against the liberal candidate and not [even] remember why." The key to raising funds from Christian conservatives, Dolan lectured, was to "make them angry and stir up hostilities. The shriller you are, the easier it is to raise funds. That's the nature of the beast." Catholic Religious Right pioneer Paul Weyrich agreed. "In the past we conservatives paraded all those Chamber of Commerce candidates with Mobil Oil strapped to their backs. It doesn't work." There are "rural people in West Virginia who don't understand Reaganomics and who are being hurt by Reaganomics and who wouldn't like it if they did understand it." The way to reach that mass of people is through emotional issues like "the issue of prayer in the schools."[16] Gay-bashing and feminist-bashing conservative Catholic activist Terry Dolan would say much the same thing: making people angry and stirring up their hatreds was the name of the game in Republican fundraising. "We are *trying* to be divisive," stressed Dolan.[17]

These are as open avowals as it is possible to find of how the "politics of emotion," especially hate, has been manipulated. With it, the modern Republican Party worked to capture the white South from the Solid Democratic column and turn it into a bastion of support from which to launch a national ascendance. Kevin Phillips saw the candidacy of George Wallace and his race politics as a halfway house or mere "way station" for disenchanted southern Democrats in transit to a more permanent home in the GOP.[18] Harry Dent, the godfather of "compassionate conservatism," agreed but cautioned that, for national consumption, the racial messages had to be coded and then denied in public.[19] Defending such GOP appeals—and expressing the same disdain for the Republican base that Dwight Eisenhower had once applied only to H. L. Hunt and a few southern millionaires—Phillips explained that John

Wayne "might sound bad to people in New York. . . . But he sounds great to the schmucks we're trying to reach through John Wayne. The people down there along the Yahoo Belt" in rural America.[20]

Perhaps no one realized the potential of emotional issues predicated on moral chauvinism for modern Republican fortunes more than Lee Atwater, the most influential GOP strategist in the modern era—until perhaps Karl Rove. Atwater was the South Carolina pupil of Strom Thurmond and Harry Dent and would raise emotional politics to an art form for Republican presidents Ronald Reagan and George H. W. Bush. Throughout his brief but glory-filled career, Atwater worked closely with Roger Ailes, a leading advisor to Presidents Nixon, Reagan, and Bush I, and later the creator and director of the Fox News ("fair and balanced") cable news network. As chairman of the Republican National Committee, Atwater schooled an entire generation of conservative political operatives. A native southerner, Atwater forthrightly acknowledged that "Republicans in the South could not win elections by talking about issues"—that the party's economic insulation of the privileged classes held little intrinsic appeal for the common southerner. Instead, character assassination on racial, moral, and religious grounds was the key: "You had to make the case that the other candidate was a bad guy."[21] Issues were not important for this newer politics—vague perception of especially religious and moral character was. Atwater took pride in not knowing the ins and outs of actual political issues: "I don't know 'em. I don't want to know 'em." Instead he viewed himself as a "Machiavellian political warrior," especially adept at using "ad hominem strategies characterized by personal attacks, dirty tricks, and accentuating the negative."[22]

Atwater specialized at implanting negative emotional images in the minds of voters so powerful that the perception could not be "busted up" even with the reality of the candidates' stands on different issues. Echoing Dwight Eisenhower and Kevin Phillips to some extent, Atwater took it further. He believed the average voter could absorb only a limited amount of information about candidates and should never be bewildered with specifics. According to his biographer, Atwater believed the average voter was kind of slow, actually—would "perceive facts as ideas. . . . So you could throw fact after fact at a voter . . . who might never be able to connect the dots." For the mass of average voters, perception was greater than reality. In fact, perception *was* reality. "The *National Enquirer* readership is the exact voter I'm talking about," Atwater quipped. "I've learned a lot about politics simply by going to wrestling matches." Atwater saw his job as tapping into the voters' "emotions instead of their brains," finding the one specific example, the one "outrageous abuse, the easy-to-digest tale," say, about fraud in the welfare system or food stamps, "that made listeners *feel*—usually repulsion—rather than think."[23]

But like George Wallace, Atwater was not an originator or a pioneer, only the most influential and seminal of American political strategists in the modern era. A South Carolina native, Atwater was a neo-Confederate student of Sun Tzu, Niccolo Machiavelli, and several Confederate generals, who learned his racial politics at the knee of fellow South Carolinians Strom Thurmond and Harry Dent, and who ended up leaving his legacy to protégés who would number among the GOP's top strategists: Mary Matalin, Tucker Eskew, and Karl Rove. Manic, obsessive, and a remarkably charismatic individual, Atwater had a passion for junk food, running, Tabasco sauce, and playing the guitar. He poured his considerable talent and energy into manipulating perceptions over reality and emotion over thought, and preying on the most divisive and intense passions he could arouse in the electorate—and was unapologetic about working to make average voters look at liberal candidates as bad people. Doing field research on what he affectionately called "swing voters," Atwater concentrated on feelings and negative images as he frequented bars, Waffle Houses, and massage parlors to find out what average folk wanted to hear and to make politics "more consumer driven, in touch with the customer/voter." For Atwater and the new Republican politics, it was all about perception over reality and using mass media to manipulate those perceptions. "[I]t's not what happens to us that matters," Atwater concluded, according to his biographer, "it's how we *interpret* what happens to us. The interpretation establishes an attitude, which can then be catered to emotionally. Therefore, the political goal was to get in front of the interpretation—mental crowd control: *When we want your opinion, we'll give it to you!*" A master at using impressionistic images and symbols, Atwater was steadfast in his belief that once a perception was established, it "can't be busted up even with opinion changes on specific issues that my opponent might accomplish."[24]

Along with Kevin Phillips, Lee Atwater tapped into southern conservative religious symbols and black/white images to lay the groundwork for the transition of emotional politics from overt race-baiting to a combination of subtle racism and explicit moral chauvinism. While Atwater lay on his deathbed apologizing for the infamous Willie Horton ad that was used so effectively on behalf of George H. W. Bush, another southerner, a congressman from Georgia, was overseeing the full transition of this politics to conservative morality and religion. Newt Gingrich, who in 1994 would spearhead the capture of both houses of Congress with a sitting president from the opposition party (a feat last accomplished in 1947), talked about welfare and subtle race messages and perfected the art of the "New Racism." Central to his strategy was exploiting the deep religiosity of southerners, especially white southerners, to brand partisan differences based on perception and religious/moral messages into the psyches of millions of voters. His project, Gingrich privately told a gathering of Republican lobbyists just a week before the historic 1994 congressional elections, was to paint Democrats as the enemy of "normal Americans" and the proponents of "Stalinist" policies. To this end, Gingrich relentlessly created perceptions based on notions of traditional morality and conservative religion. He sought, with wild success, to transform the political landscape into a religious "battleground" between the Republican Party as the party of God and the "secular anti-religious view of the left" on the other. Democrats were not simply wrong, he announced. "These people are sick." To provide the GOP with a uniformity, concerted action, and consistency of message that has since become legend, the House Speaker distributed a vocabulary list to be strictly followed by Republicans when talking to any member of the press about any Democrat—buzzwords that would allow the poison of emotional politics to seep into the very subconscious of voters and take root: "sick, traitors, corrupt, bizarre, cheat, steal, devour, self-serving, and criminal rights." The strategy itself knew no bounds because it was the end that justified the means—as in any holy war. Just two days before the 1994 election, Gingrich attempted to exploit a tragic South Carolina incident in which a mentally deranged young mother named Susan Smith drowned two of her children in a car. Pouncing on the event, Gingrich laid the incident directly at the doorstep of Bill Clinton and the Democratic Party—despite the fact that Smith's father was a member of the Religious Right. The double-child murder "vividly reminds every American how sick their society is getting and how much we have to change," Gingrich intoned. The "only way you get change," he went on, "is to vote Republican." Religious Right fund-raiser and strategist Paul Weyrich gushed that Gingrich was "the first conservative I have ever known who knows how to use power."[25]

The use of a new politics based on moral and religious venom, divisiveness, and the darker angels of human nature to build the Republican Party in the South was not unlike the old race-based strategy of white supremacy used so long ago by the Conservative Democratic Party to control the Solid South. In this important way, the modern Republican legacy in the South is, essentially, equivalent to its old George Wallace/Dixiecrat legacy—a reality that made Trent Lott's 2002 racial gaffe particularly embarrassing and potentially damaging on the national level. The essential kinship between the old racist politics of the southern Democrats and the religious, moral, patriotic, and tax bigotry of the new Republican politics was hardly lost on one of the region's most astute political observers—George Wallace himself. "It sounds to me like when I hear all this talk," Wallace said in surveying the 1990s political landscape, "that the Republicans have stolen a lot of their thoughts and words and principles from old George Wallace." "You know I should have copyrighted all of my speeches," Wallace said wistfully. "If I had, the Republicans in Alabama, throughout the South, and all over the nation would be paying me hundreds of thousands of dollars. They owe everything to my kind of Democratic thinking." Before he died Wallace identified himself as a Republican.[26]

Today, in the post–Voting Rights Act South, individuals like Ralph Reed, Richard Land, Trent Lott, and (previously) Jerry Falwell profess to be great racial progressives and admirers of Martin Luther King. But there remains fusionism's core commitment to economically conservative values among these Religious Rightists—as well as Pat Robertson, James Dobson, "Pastor Ted" Ted Haggard, and the kindred Catholic rightists who also portray themselves as civil rights champions: George Weigel, Robert P. George, and the late Richard John Neuhaus.[27] How did this happen? Did it simply occur in the natural order of things?

In large part the answer lies in the civil rights acts that liberals wrote into law during the 1960s: the 1964 Civil Rights Act, John Kennedy's executive orders banning racial and gender discrimination in federal employment, and the 1965 Voting Rights Act. The 1965 law, in particular, rendered the first racial and economic melding, in its unvarnished mode, untenable. Court decisions like *Engel v. Vitale* and *Roe v. Wade* hinted at morality and religion as the new American flashpoint.[28] Gradually the old racism was replaced with the new. While racial appeals in conservative politics were recalibrated away from George Wallace's bluster about segregation now and forever and schoolhouse doors to more muted and implicit Nixonian code about busing, quotas, and affirmative action, right-wing notions of religion and morality largely replaced conservative racism as the public face of the Great Melding. Lee Atwater actually announced the sea change: "You start out in 1954 by saying 'Nigger, nigger, nigger.' By 1968, you can't say 'nigger'—that hurts you. Backfires. So you say stuff like forced busing, states' rights, and all that stuff." Allegiance to extreme-rightist economic conservatism, heroically personified by newly popular libertarians who had long been considered fringe figures (Milton Friedman, F. A. Hayek, Ayn Rand), remained a constant in the alliance. The New Racism or the second Great Melding combined Religious Right moral chauvinism, and even a morality-based hatred, with neoliberal rightist economic extremism and callousness built on a foundation of deep-seated anti-democratic tendencies. People like M. E. Bradford, James Dobson, Jerry Falwell, Pat Robertson, Murray Rothbard, Ted Haggard, and Tim LaHaye (not to mention Ronald Reagan and George W. Bush) personified the alliance, even as some country-club types held their noses.[29]

More recently moralism and militaristic nationalism have increasingly played the public role that white supremacy used to play for the meld. Reliance on focus-group-tested topics such as abortion, gay marriage, school prayer, the Ten Commandments, war, terror, and taxes bring in the votes and the checks of plain-white folk who have little idea of the neoliberal agenda behind the meld.[30] Plain-folk Christians continue to buy into the whole meld and thus find themselves supporting an economic agenda of tax cuts, free trade, anti-unionism, and privatization that is not only hostile to their own interests but also embarrassingly difficult to reconcile with the New Testament message of Jesus Christ. Thus the reliance by Religious Right figures in their public pronouncements on Old Testament staples like Exodus and Leviticus rather than the Beatitudes in the Sermon on the Mount, Mary's Magnificat, Luke, or the overtly socialistic Acts of the Apostles.[31]

Like the old racism, the new kind also uses the primacy of emotion-based politics over the rational to further an economically conservative agenda. It is the old marriage of neo-Kluxism and neo-Bourbonism that originally birthed the GOP into power in the modern South. While a growing number of evangelicals struggle to make sense of economic, trade, and environmental policies that seem at odds with Christ's message in the Gospels, there remains the flawed assumption that the apparently oxymoronic alliance between religion and right-wing economics just kind of "happened."[32] Yet nothing just happens—especially in the world of politics. This melding—like the one in the infamous 1901 Alabama Constitution, like the 1948 Dixiecrats, like the 1964 Goldwater win in the South—happened because elite economic conservatives *wanted* it to happen and they worked very hard and effectively to exploit powerful emotional issues (race and white supremacy and law and order, or evangelical religion and moralism and abortion and gay marriage, or Tea Party tax revolt) to encourage plain people to forget their economic interests.

Nor is this mere speculation, polemic, propaganda, or liberal exaggeration. While pundits like resident *New York Times* conservative David Brooks continue to write editorials celebrating the penchant of ordinary people to put social and emotional issues ahead of economics, the plain, unvarnished facts are that at least three former national chairmen of the Republican Party have publicly acknowledged and apologized for the modern GOP's use of race-baiting to build the party in the South: Lee Atwater, Ken Mehlman, and Michael Steele—along with various conservative writers and Christian Coalition pioneer Ralph Reed. In 2003 a conservative *Wall Street Journal* editorialist publicly advised President George W. Bush and other Republicans to "work to retire the Southern strategy." "Don't make excuses for it. Don't euphemize it. Say it was wrong and now it's over. End the pit stops at Bob Jones University, the strained defenses of the Confederate flag, the coded references to states' rights."[33] The advice has not exactly been heeded, nor has the modern right's penchant for using the emotional to short-circuit the rational. But, as we have seen, this is a rather timeless story, with very deep southern roots.

If anyone still persists in believing that the American South is not distinctive, or that most whites there put the economic ahead of the emotional, or that the conservatism of the region did not long ago morph into an extremism, or that the Religious Right-technological-communications-think tank revolution of recent decades and almost unlimited campaign cash has not rendered reality largely irrelevant, and even polluted and jaundiced our two major parties, they need only consider the spectacle that was the 2012 Republican primaries.[34] A March 2012 poll of Republican voters in Alabama and Mississippi was especially telling. Almost three-and-a-half years after Barack Obama was elected president of the United States—after countless confirmations that there "is not a shred of truth to the rumor that President Obama is not really an American citizen, or that he's secretly a Muslim"—on the eve of the GOP presidential primaries there, only 12 percent of Mississippi Republicans and 14 percent of Alabama Republicans believed that Obama was a Christian. In fact, a full 45 percent of Alabama Republicans and 52 percent of Mississippi Republicans insisted on believing that Obama was actually a Muslim—percentages dramatically higher than in the non-South.[35]

The voters that made up the Republican primaries in Alabama and Mississippi were white, evangelical or born-again Christians—a crushing majority of them—at least 80 percent. Six in ten were defined as "blue collar" or not having a college degree. Two in three identified themselves as members of the Tea Party. But like its previous incarnations, this is a movement that is in no appreciable way constrained by class or societal ranks. While the spectacle of watching whites of modest means repeatedly act to their material detriment is unquestionably maddening, the cultural pathology is much deeper than just "false consciousness" on their part. Perhaps it cannot be said any better than by a south Alabama financial consultant (whose views were heartily endorsed by a Birmingham radiologist) as he tried to explain the extreme vacillations on policy matters by Mitt Romney evident during the 2012 presidential campaign.

> As you have mentioned to me on previous occasions, it is almost impossible to know exactly how politicians feel at any given moment on various subjects, because sometimes they lie, sometimes they change their minds and sometimes they misunderstand the question. Personally, I'd rather gamble on Romney. My important issue is I know Romney is a Christian and I know Obama is NOT a Christian. Obama lies about this important point. He has never lived and practiced the Christian faith. Everything he does indicates he is Not a Christian. I believe Obama's heart over flows with the Muslim faith. Romney may not be as good a Christian as many of us would like, but he has lived and practiced his Christian faith all of his life. None of us are perfect, but Romney provides me more peace of mind on more issues than Obama. I don't even believe Obama likes America. I believe he wants to destroy everything about America that has set us apart from most of the world. There are more black millionaires and more black college graduates in America than the rest of the world combined. I believe Obama is an ungrateful racist. Staying in Jeremiah Wright's church 20 years and after all the ugly and racist things Wright said about white people and America proves Obama doesn't like us. He tells us in his own books that he doesn't like us. I don't like the way he has done Israel. I don't like his apologetic attitude to the middle east. Obama's ideas have ruined our economy. He is divisive and fuels class warfare. I resent Obama trying to ruin the relationship of Christians with their churches. He encourages people to reject the Bible. He encourages all kinds of SIN. So, I just don't believe Romney could make enough flip flops or mistakes to ever lead me to vote for Obama. I'm just praying the most voters will agree with me in November. I pray that many people who voted for Obama in 08 will vote against him in November.[36]

Despite the fact that a slew of the nation's most distinguished historians have already consigned George W. Bush to the cellar of American presidents for the smorgasbord of disasters that marked his terms, voters such as these in Alabama, Mississippi, and increasingly elsewhere were absolutely certain that it was, in fact, Barack Obama who was responsible for America's mountain of problems, especially its daunting economic woes. Worse, in his efforts to "fix" them Obama—despite his serial reluctance to offend Wall

Street, oil companies, corporate polluters, war profiteers, high tax brackets, the gun lobby *and* the profound disappointment he has been to so many on the Left—was somehow a socialist trampling on the Constitution, waging a "war on religion," an ungrateful racist (whatever that means exactly), and determined to ruin their way of life.[37] Most whites in the South, and increasingly in the Mountain and Plains states, suburban enclaves, and gated communities everywhere, planned to vote accordingly.

Notes

Preface

1. See, e.g., Jason DeParle and Sabrina Tavernese, "Poor Are Still Getting Poorer," *New York Times*, 15 September 2011; Hope Yen, "Census: US Poverty Rate Swells to Nearly 1 in 6," Associated Press, 13 September 2011; Paul Waldman, "Glory Days," *American Prospect*, 7 September 2011; Amy Goodman, "Noam Chomsky on Why the Right Hates Social Security," http://www.readersupportednews.org, 13 September 2011 (accessed 14 September 2011); and Sam Hananel, "House to Vote on Bill Targeting Boeing Labor Case," Associated Press, 15 September 2011 (on a Republican congressional assault on the enforcement powers of the National Labor Relations Board [NLRB]).

2. Various scholars and journalists have discussed the importance of "fusionism" but have not recognized its important southern and much earlier roots, which go back to at least Reconstruction and the turn-of-the-twentieth-century disfranchising movement. See Glenn Feldman, ed., *Painting Dixie Red: When, Where, Why, and How the South Became Republican* (Gainesville: University Press of Florida, 2011), 330. A former protégé of conservative icon William F. Buckley, Michael Lind dates the origins of national fusionism to the mid-1950s and attributes it to conservative theorist Frank S. Meyer. See *Up from Conservatism: Why the Right Is Wrong for America* (New York: Free Press, 1996), 53–54. Lind, more than others, understands the more general importance of southern history and politics for the American pattern. See, e.g., *Made in Texas: George W. Bush and the Southern Takeover of American Politics* (New York: Basic Books, 2001). Libertarians Brink Lindsey, Ryan Sager, and John Tierney also date conservative fusionism to the mid-1950s. See Lindsey, "Liberaltarians," *New Republic*, http://www.tnr.com/, 4 December 2006 (accessed 5 December 2006); Shawn Macomber, "Save the Elephant," *American Spectator*, http://www.spectator.org/, 15 September 2006 (accessed 16 September 2006); an interview with Ryan Sager on his book, *The Elephant in the Room: Evangelicals, Libertarians, and the Battle to Control the Republican Party* (New York: John Wiley, 2006); and Tierney, "Can This Party Be Saved?" *New York Times*, 2 September 2006. Liberal Princeton economist Paul Krugman puts the origins of this "movement conservatism" even later, in the 1960s and 1970s. See "The Great Revulsion," *New York Times*, 10 November 2006.

Leftist political scientist and founder of Political Research Associates, Jean Hardisty, traces it to the early 1970s in *Mobilizing Resentment: Conservative Resurgence from the John Birch Society to the Promise Keepers* (Boston: Beacon Press, 2000). Salon.com writer Andrew O'Hehir described it as a post-1980 coalition in the "The Know-Nothings," 14 September 2005 (accessed 15 September 2005). Yet fusionism's actual roots date to the latter part of the nineteenth-century South.

3. Sara Diamond, *Roads to Dominion: Right-Wing Movements and Political Power in the United States* (New York: Guilford Press, 1995); Frederick Clarkson, *Eternal Hostility: The Struggle between Theocracy and Democracy* (Monroe, ME: Common Courage Press, 1997); Frank Schaeffer, *Crazy for God: How I Grew Up as One of the Elect, Helped Found the Religious Right, and Lived to Take All (or Almost All) of It Back* (Cambridge, MA: Da Capo Press, 2008); Max Blumenthal, *Republican Gomorrah: Inside the Movement That Shattered the Party* (New York: Nation Books, 2009); Gary North and Gary Demar, *Christian Reconstruction: What It Is, What It Isn't* (Deland, FL: Institute for Christian Economics, 1991); and H. Wayne House and Thomas Ice, *Dominion Theology: Blessing or Curse? An Analysis of Christian Reconstructionism* (Sisters, OR: Multnomah, 1988).

4. Glenn Feldman, "Putting Uncle Milton to Bed: Reexamining Milton Friedman's Essay on the Social Responsibility of Business," *Labor Studies Journal* 32 (June 2007): 125–42; Fred Arthur Bailey, "M. E. Bradford, the Reagan Right, and the Resurgence of Confederate Nationalism," in Feldman, *Painting Dixie Red*, 291–313.

5. On Ayn Rand receiving Social Security checks and Medicare under the name Ann O'Connor (her husband was Frank O'Connor), see Michael Ford, "Ayn Rand and the VIP-DIPers," *Huffington Post*, 5 December 2010. Rand began life as a Russian Jew before turning to atheism, and her real name was Alisa Zinovievna Rosenbaum. See also Joshua Holland, "Ayn Rand Railed against Government Benefits, But Grabbed Social Security and Medicare When She Needed Them," http://www.alternet.org/, 29 January 2011 (accessed 3 March 2012). "If you think Paul Ryan and his Ayn Rand–worshipping colleagues aren't after your Social Security and Medicare, I am here to disabuse you of your naiveté," wrote longtime Republican staffer Mike Lofgren in "Confessions of a GOP Operative Who Left 'the Cult': 3 Things Everyone Must Know about the Lunatic-Filled Republican Party," http://www.truthout.org, 5 September 2011 (accessed 6 September 2012). Habitual Republican and Libertarian presidential candidate Ron Paul, like Ayn Rand, has no problem accepting and cashing Social Security checks. See Thomas Mullen, "Morning Joe Wrong on Ron Paul and Social Security," *Washington Times*, 21 June 2012. Although Paul's libertarianism is so extreme that he is on record as opposed to hurricane, tornado, and disaster relief and has argued that Social Security and Medicare are unconstitutional, he still cashes the checks. When asked if he should set an example for the younger generation by declining a government benefit he has railed against for years, Paul said "No. . . . Just as I use the Post office, too, I use government highways, you do that too, I use the banks. I use the Federal Reserve system, but that doesn't mean that you can't work to remove this. In the same way on Social Security, I am trying to make a transition." Chris Good, "Ron Paul Collects Social Security," http://abcnews.go.com/blogs/politics, 21 June 2012 (accessed 24 June 2012).

6. See, e.g., John Aloysius Farrell, "Ron Paul: No Federal Financial Aid for Tornado Victims," *National Journal* and Yahoo News, 5 March 2012; Catherine Dodge and Elise Young, "Christie Contradicting Cantor on Disaster Budget," Bloomberg News, 2 September 2011; Lucy Madison, "Foster Friess: In My Day Women Used Bayer Aspirin for Con-

traceptives," http://www.cbsnews.com/, 16 February 2012 (accessed 18 February 2012); "Senate Defeats Republican Bid to Reverse Obama's Contraception Ruling," Associated Press and http://www.guardian.co.uk, 1 March 2012 (accessed 4 March 2012); Greg McCune, "Republican Candidates 'Mishandled' Contraception Issue, Daniels Says," Reuters, 16 March 2012; Julie Herschfeld Davis, "Republicans Losing on Birth Control as 77% in Poll Spurn Debate," Bloomberg News, 14 March 2012.

7. For more on the proper name of the Democratic Party in Alabama as the Democratic and Conservative Party, see Glenn Feldman, *The Disfranchisement Myth: Poor Whites and Suffrage Restriction in Alabama* (Athens: University of Georgia Press, 2004), 222n62.

8. For a fuller explanation of what may be called "The Southern Religion" and its chronological and regional development, see Glenn Feldman, "Exporting 'The Southern Religion' and Shaping the Election of 2012," in the Chauncey DeVega blog "We Are Respectable Negroes" (WARN), 30 January 2012, http://wearerespectablenegroes.blogspot.com/2012/01/fear-of-black-president-love-of.html (accessed 2 February 2012).

Chapter 1

1. On the southern carnage, see, e.g., William J. Cooper and Thomas E. Terrill Jr., *The American South: A History* (New York: McGraw-Hill, 1991), 2:384–85.

2. For Alabama, see the Dunning-School rendition of Radical-black Reconstruction in Walter L. Fleming, *Civil War and Reconstruction in Alabama* (Gloucester, MA: Peter Smith, 1949), 653–709 and John W. DuBose, a member of the Knights of the White Camellia, in *Alabama's Tragic Decade: Ten Years of Alabama, 1865–1874* (Birmingham: Webb Book Company, 1940).

3. The Klan also targeted alleged wife-beaters, drunks, slackers, loafers, adulterers, and those of both colors who neglected their families. *Athens Weekly Post*, 20 August 1868.

4. See, e.g., the Reminiscences of Julius C. Greene, ca. 1935, Auburn University Archives (hereafter AU), Ralph B. Draughon Library, Auburn University, Auburn, AL.

5. U.S. Congress, Joint Select Committee on the Condition of Affairs in the Late Insurrectionary States, *Report of the Joint Select Committee to Inquire in to the Condition of Affairs in the Late Insurrectionary States So Far As Regards the Execution of the Laws, And Safety of the Lives and Property of the Citizens of the United States and Testimony Taken: Alabama, Volume III (or Volumes 8, 9, and 10)*, 42nd Cong., 2nd Sess. (Washington: GPO, 1872) (hereafter cited as *Report of the Joint Select Committee*). See, e.g., the testimony of C. L. Stickney, 28 October 1871, p. 1530. See also Duke University, Trinity College Historical Society, *Historical Papers, Reconstruction and State Biography*, ser. 1 (New York: AMS Press, 1897), the Reminiscences of Sanders Dent (hereafter referred to as Sanders Dent Reminiscences).

6. For a recent study that emphasizes the diverse makeup of those who came south to educate the freed people, see Ronald E. Butchart, *Schooling the Freed People: Teaching, Learning, and the Struggle for Black Freedom, 1861–1876* (Chapel Hill: University of North Carolina Press, 2010).

7. William Dudley Bell, "The Reconstruction Ku Klux Klan: A Survey of the Writings on the Klan with a Profile and Analysis of the Alabama Klan Episode, 1866–1874" (Ph.D. diss., Louisiana State University, 1973), 152–65. The words "carpetbagger" and

"scalawag" were, of course, terms of opprobrium. See also Mary Farmer-Kaiser, *Freedwomen and the Freedmen's Bureau: Race, Gender, and Public Policy in the Age of Emancipation* (New York: Fordham University Press, 2010).

8. *Athens Weekly Post*, 30 July 1868 (first quotation); *Moulton Advertiser*, 31 July 1868 (first quotation repeated); *(Selma) Southern Argus*, 8 May 1874 (second quotation); *Tuskaloosa Blade*, 21 November 1872 and 20 August 1874.

9. United States, *Report on the Condition of the South by Carl Schurz, 1865*, 39th Cong., 1st Sess. (New York: Arno Press and the *New York Times*, 1969), 18, 20. See also Cooper and Terrill, *The American South*, 2:397.

10. Reports of J. M. Phipps and J. E. Harvey, 21 August 1865, 70–71; Captain W. A. Poillon to General Wager Swayne, 29 September 1865, and Poillon to Carl Schurz, 9 September 1865, 72–74, all in the *Report on the Condition of the South by Carl Schurz, 1865*.

11. Poillon to Schurz, 9 September 1865 and Poillon to Brigadier General Wager Swayne, 29 July 1865, in *Report on the Condition of the South by Carl Schurz, 1865*, 72–74.

12. For various accounts of Reconstruction-era violence in Alabama, see series I: Correspondence, Family Correspondence, box 35, folders 10, 13–16, and box 40, folder 5, Luther Ely Smith Family Papers, Missouri Historical Society, St. Louis; marker in Mesopotamia Cemetery, Sibyl D. Banks to author, 30 March 1993, Greene County Historical Society, Eutaw, AL; "Ku Klux Klan Was Important Factor in Shaping State's Destiny," clipping in folder: KKK thru 1979, Mobile Public Library Archives, Mobile, AL; Y. Y. Story to Dear Brother Gravath, 14 August 1871, nos. 863–66, American Missionary Association Archives, Fisk University, Nashville, TN; *Mobile Nationalist*, 2 August 1869, clipping, folder: Interesting Transcriptions from the *Mobile Nationalist*, Mobile Municipal Archives, Mobile, AL; and J.A.S. to Robert B. Lindsay, 12 August 1871 and Your Friend to Hon. Charles Hays, 8 April 1871, both in folder: General Correspondence, April 1871, Alabama Governors Papers, Robert B. Lindsay Papers, Alabama Department of Archives and History (hereafter ADAH), Montgomery, AL. See also Allen W. Trelease, *White Terror: The Ku Klux Klan Conspiracy and Southern Reconstruction* (New York: Harper and Row, 1971); Michael W. Fitzgerald, "The Ku Klux Klan: Property Crime and the Plantation System in Reconstruction Alabama," *Agricultural History* 71 (Spring 1998): 186–206; and George Rable, *But There Was No Peace: The Role of Violence in the Politics of Reconstruction* (Athens: University of Georgia Press, 1984).

13. *(Troy) Southern Advertiser*, 5 July 1867. See also the *Opelika Weekly Era and Whig*, 17 February 1871; *(Greensboro) Alabama Beacon*, 18 May 1867; and *Livingston Journal*, 2 October 1868. Republicans were astonished that, faced with the prospect of blacks voting, some Alabama whites actually "prayed to hear the sound of the Cannon again." And "he was a Christian! What a prayer to go up." *(Moulton) Union*, 4 November 1867. Others found the sudden emancipation of African Americans the most abhorrent reality of their time. See *Tuskegee News*, 27 September 1866.

14. *Eufaula Tri-Weekly Times*, 27 November 1874; *Autauga Citizen*, 1 November 1866; *(Butler) Choctaw Herald*, 16 March 1868.

15. H.J.Y. Mays to Gen. Haydin or Brev. Maj. W. J. Hart, 25 July 1868, folder: Freedmen's Bureau, Disturbed Conditions in Demopolis, 1868, RC2: G9, Alabama Governors Papers, Robert M. Patton Papers, ADAH; *(Eufaula) Bluff City Times*, 9 December 1869; *Shelby County Guide*, 30 April 1868; the *Montgomery Mail* quoted in the *Monroeville Journal*, 12 February 1870; *Troy Messenger*, 1 September 1870; *(Talladega) Alabama Reporter*, 16 February 1870; (Perry County) *Marion Commonwealth*, 20 July 1871; *Mobile Repub-*

lican, 20 October 1870; *Eufaula News,* 14 February 1874; *(Claiborne) Monroe Journal,* 19 October 1867; *Clarke County Democrat,* 9 January 1868.

16. For a fuller explanation of what may be termed "The Southern Religion" and its chronological and regional development, see Feldman, "Exporting 'The Southern Religion' and Shaping the Election of 2012." Selma *Daily Messenger,* 4 January 1868 (first quotation); *(Talladega) Democratic Watchtower,* 29 May 1867 (second quotation); *(Greensboro) Alabama Beacon,* 8 January 1870. See the discussion of Christian Reconstruction and Dominionism in chapter 2.

17. *Jacksonville Republican,* 14 November 1874; *Eutaw Whig and Observer,* 3 December 1874; *Union Springs Times,* 16 January 1867; *Eufaula News,* 7 November 1874. See also the *Greenville Advocate,* 2 January 1868 and *Autauga Citizen,* 3 January 1867.

18. The labor element of interracial violence was a constant throughout the Reconstruction era. See, e.g., Testimony of Judge William S. Mudd, 4 November 1871, *Report of the Joint Select Committee,* p. 2008. United States, *Report of the Joint Committee on Reconstruction at the 1st Session, 39th Congress* (Westport, CT: Negro Universities Press, 1969). Testimony of the following witnesses: A. W. Kelsey, 22 January 1866, 1–4, Brev. Maj. Gen. Edward Hatch, 25 January 1866, 4–8, quotation on p. 7, Brev. Brig. Gen. G. E. Spencer, Judge William H. Smith, and J. J. Gries, 26 January 1866, 8–15, Maj. Gen. George H. Thomas and Maj. Gen. C. B. Fisk, 30 January 1866, 26–32, M. J. Stafford, 3 February 1866, 59–63; D. C. Humphreys, 7 February 1866, 63–67, Brev. Lt. Col. Hunter Brook, 1 March 1866, 113–16, Gen. B. H. Grierson, 2 March 1866, 121–24, Brev. Gen. Wager Swayne, 9 March 1866, 138–41, Capt. J. H. Matthews, 10 March 1866, 141–47, and Gen. A. L. Chetlain, 14 March 1866, 149–51. A Huntsville booster, sanguine about attracting Yankee farmers and investment South, advised them to "keep out of cotton and niggers. . . . The curse of this county is cotton and niggers." In effect, work the land yourself. *(Wetumpka) Elmore Standard,* 15 May 1867.

19. Affidavit of Hesikia Bush, 16 May 1870, Affidavit of Simon Bush, 16 May 1870, and Deposition of Emmeline Burns, 13 June 1870, all in Series: Administrative Files, folder: Ku Klux Klan, Alabama Governors Papers, William H. Smith Papers, ADAH (hereafter Smith Papers). Burns reported that Klansmen threatened her by informing her that they had just "killed a damn nigger down the road as dead as hell." "Report of the Assistant Commissioner of Alabama, 1866," Records of the Assistant Commissioner for the State of Alabama, Bureau of Refugees, Freedmen, and Abandoned Lands, 1865–1870 (Freedmen's Bureau), Wager Swayne, Maj. Gen. and Asst. Commissioner, box 5, folder 77, Alabama Pamphlets Collection, ADAH. See, e.g., the Testimony of Daniel Taylor, 1132 (p. 47) and Testimony of Mr. Sayre, 357–71 (pp. 49–50), both in Ku Klux Report, Alabama Testimony, box 5, folders 74 and 79, Alabama Pamphlets Collection, ADAH. See also C. W. Buckley to Brev. Col. C. Cadle Jr., 27 January 1866, reel 19 (see also reel 18), Records of the Assistant Commissioner for the State of Alabama, Bureau of Refugees, Freedmen, and Abandoned Lands, 1865–1870, Record Group 105, Microcopy 809, National Archives (hereafter NA), Washington, DC (hereafter Freedmen's Bureau Records). Also see "A Proclamation," 1865, box 1582, folder 19, Robert Jemison Jr. Papers, W. Stanley Hoole Special Collections Library, University of Alabama, Tuscaloosa, AL (hereafter UA), and Jennifer Kaye Speirs, "Educating Blacks in Reconstruction Alabama: John Silsby, the American Missionary Association, and the Freedmen's Bureau" (M.A. thesis, Auburn University, 1991), 39–40.

20. See the testimony of A. W. Kelsey, 22 January 1866, 2, 4 (first quotation); an Ala-

bama woman, 7 (second quotation); Brev. Maj. Gen. Edward Hatch, 25 January 1866, 7; Brev. Gen. Wager Swayne, 9 March 1866, 141; and Capt. J. H. Matthews, 10 March 1866, 146, all in *Report of the Joint Committee on Reconstruction*.

21. Item No. 3, folder: Ku Klux Klan, Rec. #5714-4, ca. 1867, Museum of the City of Mobile, Mobile, AL; "Revised and Amended Precept of Ku Klux Klan," box 4, folders 19 and 20, Alabama Pamphlets Collection, ADAH; John Clayton to General [no last name], 13 April 1868, box 1, folder 7, Ira Roe Foster Papers, ADAH; Ms. Tommie H. Clack to W. S. Allen, 17 July 1964, Record Group 161, Ward Sykes Allen Papers, AU; Sanders Dent, "The Origin and Development of the Ku Klux Clan," unpublished typescript in the Duke University Historical Society Papers, Trinity College Historical Society, Duke University, Durham, NC.

22. Bell, "The Reconstruction Ku Klux Klan," 167–76.

23. Knights of the White Camellia Notebook, ca. 1867, SPR 84, folder 1, ADAH; "The Constitution and Ritual of the Knights of the White Camellia," box 4, folder 18, Alabama Pamphlets Collection, ADAH; Bell, "The Reconstruction Ku Klux Klan," 206–9, 234, 266, 274; Fleming, *Civil War and Reconstruction in Alabama*, 661; Virginia Van der Veer Hamilton, *Alabama: A Bicentennial History* (Nashville: American Association for State and Local History, 1977), 46; Kimberly Bess Cantrell, "A Voice for the Freedmen: The *Mobile Nationalist*, 1865–1869" (M.A. thesis, Auburn University, 1989), 73; David M. Chalmers, *Hooded Americanism: The History of the Ku Klux Klan* (Durham: Duke University Press, 1987), 9 (quotation); William Stanley Hoole, ed., *Reconstruction in West Alabama: The Memoirs of John L. Hunnicut* (Tuscaloosa: Confederate Publishing,1959), 21, 27, 72; Oliver Otis Howard, *Autobiography of Oliver Otis Howard, Major General, United States Army* (1907; reprint, Freeport, NY: Books for Libraries Press, 1971), 380–81.

24. Sanders Dent Reminiscences, 10–27, esp. 12, 16–18; "Grandfather Talks about His Life under Two Flags: Reminiscences of Hilary A. Herbert," 1903, SPR 4, Hilary Abner Herbert Papers, ADAH; "The Ku Klux Klan: A Brief Story, Alabama Reunion Edition of the Heritage of Blount County," 1989, pp. 194–95, Blount County Historical Society, Oneonta, AL. See also Claude G. Bowers, *The Tragic Era: The Revolution after Lincoln* (Boston: Houghton Mifflin, 1920), 306–11; Joel C. DuBose, *Alabama History* (Richmond, VA: Johnson Publishing, 1915), 185–86, 188, 286; Lucille Griffith, *History of Alabama, 1540–1900* (Northport, AL: Colonial Press, 1962), 340–44; Fleming, *Civil War and Reconstruction in Alabama*, 668; Bell, "The Reconstruction Ku Klux Klan," 211, 218 (quotations).

25. For cooperation between Klan groups in west Alabama and Mississippi, see James L. Alcorn Diary, James L. Alcorn and Family Collection, Mississippi Department of Archives and History, Jackson, MS.

26. For sample "nigger" and "coon" jokes printed in newspapers, see the *(Notasulga) Universalist Herald*, 15 January 1869; *(Butler County) Choctaw Herald*, 29 February 1868; and *(Eufaula) Bluff City Times*, 29 February 1872. *Athens Weekly Post*, 2 April 1868; *Selma Southern Argus*, 7 July 1869. In north Alabama the *Moulton Advertiser* and *Florence Journal*, along with the *Athens Weekly Post*, were especially energetic boosters of the Klan. See, e.g., *Athens Weekly Post*, 19 March 1868; *Moulton Advertiser*, 27 March 1868; and Bell, "The Reconstruction Ku Klux Klan," 212–17, 253–54, esp. 212. For more on Mobile, see Michael W. Fitzgerald, *Urban Emancipation: Popular Politics in Reconstruction Mobile, 1860–1890* (Baton Rouge: Louisiana State University Press, 2002)

and Billy G. Hinson, "The Beginning of Military Reconstruction in Mobile, Alabama, May–November 1867," *Gulf Coast Historical Review* 9 (Fall 1993): 65–83.

27. *Report on the Condition of the South by Carl Schurz, 1865*, 20 (first quotation); Hoole, *The Memoirs of John L. Hunnicut*, 56; Bell, "The Reconstruction Ku Klux Klan," 221 (second quotation), 222–23.

28. *East Alabama Monitor*, 12 February 1869 (first quotation, Clanton) and *Montgomery Daily Advertiser*, 20 July 1870 (second quotation). For more on Clanton, see the *Opelika Weekly Era and Whig*, 23 June 1871; *(Opelika) Union Republican*, 16 October 1869; *Henry County Register*, 27 August 1870; and the James Holt Clanton Folder, p. 2, box 22, 7N, Unprocessed Manuscripts Collection, ADAH, and news clipping (about ten thousand people turning out for Clanton's funeral) in box 2, folder 30, Matthew P. Blue Papers, ADAH. On Pettus, see the *Troy Messenger*, 10 November 1870 and the *Selma Journal*, 2 August 1907 (third quotation), clipping, box 182, folder 10, Edmund Winston Pettus Papers, ADAH. For more on both, see Michael Newton and Judy Ann Newton, *The Ku Klux Klan: An Encyclopedia* (New York: Garland Press, 1991), 116, 462. See also the *Mobile Republican*, 17 August 1872. Other former Confederate generals besides Nathan Bedford Forrest served as grand dragons of the Klan in the southern states: Wade Hampton in South Carolina, John Brown Gordon in Georgia, and John H. Forney in Alabama. See the *(Atlanta Imperial) Knighthawk*, 23 April 1924, 3.

29. Lt. L. E. Campbell to Lt. H. Dodt, 7 November 1868, Collection No. VFM-174, Special Collections, Morris Library, Southern Illinois University at Carbondale (hereafter SIU), Carbondale, IL; Virginia Durr interview, Oral History Project, Columbia University, New York.

30. *(Montgomery) Alabama State Journal*, 16 January 1869; Bell, "The Reconstruction Ku Klux Klan," 179–80 (quotation), 253–65.

31. Testimony of Granville Bennett, 1 November 1871, 1738 (second quotation), *Report of the Joint Select Committee*; *(Montgomery) Daily State Sentinel*, 27 and 31 January 1868 (first quotation), also 12 and 13 February 1868. See also Sarah Woolfolk Wiggins, *The Scalawag in Alabama Politics, 1865–1881* (Tuscaloosa: The University of Alabama Press, 1997), 40; Newton and Newton, *The Ku Klux Klan*, 48; William Loren Katz, *The Invisible Empire: The Ku Klux Klan Impact on History* (Washington, DC: Open Hand Publishing, 1986), 36; Hamilton, *Alabama*, 46; and Herbert D. Shapiro, *White Violence and Black Response: From Reconstruction to Montgomery* (Amherst: University of Massachusetts Press, 1988), 5, 10, 14. A subsequent state legislative committee reported on the 1868 election violence: "Not a few have been savagely murdered, being shot down, or cut with knives, or hung upon the trees, or in the bridges upon the highway, railroad trains have been thrown from the track . . . officers of justice have been killed, or violently assaulted. . . . Some of those crimes have been committed not by disguised men, but openly, and boldly, and by daylight. Such is the depravity of public sentiment, in some places, that assassins and felons need no masks or darkness to shield them from arrest. . . . [T]hey are safe enough without disguise or concealment." *State Senate Committee Report*, 14 December 1868, reprinted in the *Moulton Advertiser*, 15 January 1869.

32. Testimony of Allen E. Moore, sheriff, Sumter County, 30 October 1871, 1566, 1567, and 1581 (quotations), *Report of the Joint Select Committee*. Forcible resistance to the Klan was not unusual in Alabama. See, e.g., *(Montgomery) Daily State Sentinel*, 13 April 1868. A black Republican in Sumter County supplied a window into such resistance by pleading to the governor for help before taking up arms.

The Sheriff can not stop these things unless aided by some strong force and even then it would have to be a permanent thing here. The Sheriff says he is utterly unable to put a stop to this thing as most of the whites concerned . . . are in the Klan or sit still and wink at their doings. How long shall this continue? We have tried peaceful means and they have failed, must we sit still and allow ourselves to be shot like brutes for the fear of offending the law. . . . [I]f our State and National Governments are not able to stop these scoundrels let us know it and we will at least die like men with *arms* of some kind in our hands. What is the use of the white man telling us to respect the laws, when such things are being carried out in our midst by white men. Now, Governor, with all due respect, I want protection for myself and family as well as the balance of my oppressed people. . . . If you can't send soldiers here *permanently* and a good strong force, for God's sake don't say anything about it at all, for . . . sending proclamations to the Sheriff, isn't worth the paper on which you write them. Send protection and send [it] quickly in the name of God.

George W. Houston to Gov. William Smith, 13 August 1869, Series: Administrative Files, folder: Ku Klux Klan, Smith Papers.

33. *(Montgomery) Alabama State Journal*, 7 November 1868; Testimony of William S. Mudd, 1 November 1871, 1745–71, *Report of the Joint Select Committee*; Bell, "The Reconstruction Ku Klux Klan," 267–71, 282–87; Chalmers, *Hooded Americanism*, 19; J. H. Rogers, *The Ku Klux Spirit* (Baltimore: Black Classic Press, 1980), 30.

34. C. W. Buckley to Brev. Col. C. Cadle Jr., 27 January 1866 (quotation), reel 19, Major A.A.A.G. to Captain W. A. Poillon, 24 August 1865, reel 1, Brev. Lt. Col. Edwin Beecher to Major General Oliver Otis Howard, 20 October and 15 December 1868, both in reel 2; see also reels 18 and 19, Record Group 105, Microcopy 809, Freedmen's Bureau Records, NA; R. A. Goodloe to Dear Sister, 9 March 1868, box 1, folder 13, Goodloe Family Papers, UA. Sheriff J. M. Treadway to William H. Smith, 31 October 1870, John H. Myer to Smith, 13 June 1871, W. L. Ginn to Smith, 26 April 1870, T. H. White to Smith, 8 June 1870, John A. Mayer to Smith, 19 May 1870, and Dr. Gerard Chotteau to Smith, 14 November 1868 and 1 June 1869, all in Series: Administrative Files, folder: Ku Klux Klan, Smith Papers.

35. "From *Advertiser* Files," *Montgomery Advertiser*, 12 February 1972; "100 Years Ago (1872)," Rev. Arad S. Lakin File, Huntingdon College Archives and Special Collections, Montgomery, AL. Alabama newspapers often blamed "carpetbaggers" for the violence perpetrated against them. See news clippings, Collection No. VFM-175, SIU. *Jacksonville Republican*, 16 July 1870 (second quotation) and *(Demopolis) Southern Republican*, 27 July 1870 (second quotation repeated); *(Carrollton) West Alabamian*, 7 September 1870; Bell, "The Reconstruction Ku Klux Klan," 300–301, 302 (first quotation), 303; Testimony of Francis Lyon, 27 October 1871, 1408–28, *Report of the Joint Select Committee*; Wayne Flynt, *Mine, Mill, and Microchip: A Chronicle of Alabama Enterprise* (Northridge, CA: Windsor Publishers, 1987), 75; Gene L. Howard, *Death at Cross Plains: An Alabama Reconstruction Tragedy* (Tuscaloosa: The University of Alabama Press, 1984), 91. See also Loren Schweninger, "The American Missionary Association and Northern Philanthropy in Reconstruction Alabama," *Alabama Historical Quarterly* 32 (Fall and Winter 1970): 129–56.

36. E. P. Chambers to Dear Chuck, 22 November 1874, M. L. Patterson Papers,

#579, Southern Historical Collection, University of North Carolina at Chapel Hill (hereafter SHC); Testimony of A. E. Moore and J. C. Gillespie, 30 October 1871, 1565–87, 1602, B. F. Herr, 31 October 1871, 1668–75, S. A. Hale, 2 November 1871, 1812–35, Francis Lyon and William B. Jones, both 27 October 1871, 1408–28 and 1458, all in *Report of the Joint Select Committee; (Demopolis) Southern Republican*, 7 July 1869 and 6 April 1870; *(Carrollton) West Alabamian*, 17 January 1872; Newton and Newton, *The Ku Klux Klan*, 109; Bell, "The Reconstruction Ku Klux Klan," 308–11, 312, 313–20; William Warren Rogers Jr., "Scalawag Congressman Charles Hays and Reconstruction in Alabama" (Ph.D. diss., Auburn University, 1983), 49–50; Melinda Meek Hennessey, "Political Terrorism in the Black Belt: The Eutaw Riot," *Alabama Review* 33 (January 1980): 35–48; William Warren Rogers, "The Boyd Incident: Black-Belt Violence during Reconstruction," *Civil War History* 21 (December 1975): 309–29.

37. In Limestone, Madison, and Monroe counties, local communities finally joined hands to fight the Klan and it soon evaporated. Limestone whites finally turned against the order when Kluxers robbed a local white planter of the proceeds of his cotton crop sale and, on another occasion, united to break three white friends out of jail who were accused of killing a resident of white Lawrence County. *Talladega Sun*, 25 March 1869; Bell, "The Reconstruction Ku Klux Klan," 288, 293–94. See also *The Memoirs of John L. Hunnicut*, 56. For more on Klan-like groups breaking people, friend and foe, out of jail, see Thomas Worthington, typescript memoir, 6 November 1931, William R. Erwin Jr. Personal Files; Henry Boardman to Dear Sister, 26 July 1870, James Locke Boardman Papers; and William W. Belknap to Hon. George E. Spencer, 15 October 1872, William Worth Belknap Papers, all three in Special Collections Library, William R. Perkins Library, Duke University, Durham, NC.

38. A street duel with a white university student hired as a gunman by a University of Alabama professor led to an amputated leg for Randolph, which only served to add to his gravitas and local fame. See *The Memoirs of John L. Hunnicut*, 26; Testimony of N. L. Whitfield, 11 November 1871, 1978–79, *Report of the Joint Select Committee; Weekly Huntsville Advocate*, 28 January 1870; Bell, "The Reconstruction Ku Klux Klan," 191, 215–16, 228, 229, 318; DuBose, *Alabama's Tragic Decade*, 201; Stanley F. Horn, *Invisible Empire: The Story of the Ku Klux Klan, 1866–1871* (Boston: Riverside Press, 1939), 119 (quotation). See also Ryland Randolph to Walter L. Fleming, 21, 23, and 27 August and 15 October 1901, and the *Alabama Daily State Journal*, 18 October 1874 clipping, all in the Walter L. Fleming Collection, Special Collections, New York Public Library; *Montgomery Advertiser*, 1868 clipping, box 89, 7N, Nannie Randolph Taylor Henley Papers, Unprocessed Manuscripts Collection, ADAH. Randolph called Reconstruction "a motley thing, half military and half nigger." *Tuscaloosa Independent Monitor*, 9 and 30 October 1867.

39. *The Memoirs of John L. Hunnicut*, 26, 51–58, 97–103, 48 and 104 (quotations); Testimony of Henry Low, 11 November 1871, 1996–99, *Report of the Joint Select Committee*.

40. Editorials in the *Tuscaloosa Independent Monitor*, 9 and 30 October, 13, 20, and 27 November 1867, and 4 March 1868.

41. *Shelby County Guide*, 3 December 1868; Testimony of William B. Jones, 27 October 1871, 1471–72 and M. A. McNeil and C. S. Drake, 28 October 1871, 1537–50, *Report of the Joint Select Committee*.

42. For a sampling, see the *Shelby County Guide*, 7 May 1868; *Bladen Springs Herald*,

19 January 1872; *(Tuscumbia) North Alabamian and Times*, 18 April 1872; *Opelika Weekly Locomotive*, 16 June 1871; *Tuscaloosa Times*, 14 October 1874; *(Perry County) Marion Commonwealth*, 20 April 1871; and *(Florence) Lauderdale Times*, 19 March 1872. Diary of Solomon Palmer, 1852–1893, entry for n.d., November 1872, SPR 263, folder 3, Palmer Family Papers, ADAH. See also the address of John A. Minnis, "Ku-Klux in Alabama: Charges of Hon. Richard Busteed," 1 July 1872, typescript, Library of Congress (hereafter LC), Washington, DC, address also located in box 4, folder 21, Alabama Pamphlets Collection, ADAH. The following cases were prosecuted in Alabama under the Enforcement Acts: *U.S. v. Elisha Eustis, John J. Jolly, and Edwin Reese*, 26 April 1871, Case #75 A, B, C, *U.S. v. John Perkins*, 20 April 1871, Case #78, *U.S. v. John Pettygrew, Hugh L. White, and William Harper*, 6 January 1871, Case #79 A, B, C, *U.S. v. Allen Alexander and Charles Smith*, 6 April 1874, Case #127 A, B, and *U.S. v. Frank Jackson*, 15 January 1874, Case #157, all at the National Archives, Southeast Region (hereafter NA-SE), East Point, GA. See also U.S. Congress, *Affairs in Alabama*, H. Rept. 262, 43rd Cong., 2nd Sess., 1875; U.S. Congress, *Civil Rights in Alabama*, Ex. Doc. 46, 43rd Cong., 2nd sess., 1874; and U.S. Congress, *United States Troops in Alabama*, H. Ex. Doc. 110, 43rd Cong., 2nd sess., 1875.

43. The figure of 109 Klan killings in Alabama is most probably a low-end estimate. The chief justice of Alabama's Supreme Court said that at least 50 such killings had occurred in Tuscaloosa County alone from 1865 to 1871. Testimony of E. Woolsey Peck, 3 November 1871, p. 1852. See also *Report of the Joint Select Committee*, 1408–2008. For Alabama opposition to the Klan Acts, see the *Florence Lauderdale Times*, 18 April 1871; *Mobile Daily Register*, 18 March 1870; and *Huntsville Weekly Democrat*, 15 April 1875. See also the *Mobile Daily Tribune*, 31 December 1871, clipping, Historic Mobile Preservation Society, Mobile, AL. United States, *Proceedings in the Ku Klux Trials at Columbia, S.C., in the United States Circuit Court, November Term, 1871* (New York: Negro Universities Press, 1969); Everette Swinney, "Suppressing the Ku Klux Klan: The Enforcement of the Reconstruction Amendments, 1870–1874" (Ph.D. diss., University of Texas, 1966), 298–307; Bell, "The Reconstruction Ku Klux Klan," 204, 324–57; Mary Beth Norton et al., *A People and a Nation: A History of the United States*, vol. 2, *Since 1865* (Boston: Houghton Mifflin, 1986), 443; Ray Granade, "Violence: An Instrument of Policy in Reconstruction Alabama," *Alabama Historical Quarterly* 30 (Fall and Winter 1968): 201.

44. For an unabashed account of Reconstruction-era ballot-box stuffing and counting out, see the Reminiscences of Julius C. Greene, p. 19, ca. 1935, AU, also found in box 1, 7N, Unprocessed Manuscripts Collection, ADAH.

45. *Florence Times-Journal*, 27 May 1874; *Tuskaloosa Blade*, 14 May 1874 (second quotation); *Jacksonville Republican* quoted in the *Eufaula News*, 19 February 1874 (third quotation); *Eufaula News*, 7 March 1874. "The aim was to array all the whites on one side, and all the blacks on the other," the Republican press realized. "And every white man that . . . [was] a traitor to the government of his fathers . . . by [refusing to] vote the Democratic ticket, was to be regarded as no better than a negro!" *(Montgomery) Alabama State Journal*, 3 November 1874. See also the *Daily Selma Times*, 7 January 1874; *(Talladega) Our Mountain Home*, 18 November 1874; and *(Jefferson County) Southern Argus*, 6 and 13 November 1874. See also J. B. Moore Diary, 12 September 1874, box 166, 7N, Unprocessed Manuscript Collection, ADAH.

46. "We must 'agree to disagree' on every issue except putting the corruptionists out of power," a Tuscaloosa lawyer advised. "Quarreling among ourselves will only lead to a

Radical triumph." H. M. Somerville to Robert McKee, 27 May 1872, box 1, folder 11, Robert McKee Papers, ADAH. See also the Dallas County Political Scrapbooks, 1860s–1890s, box 13, folder 15, August 1876, ADAH.

47. John Witherspoon DuBose, "Forty Years in Alabama: A History of the Lapse and Recovery of Civil Government," unpublished manuscript, chapter 32, pp. 1018, 1020 (first quotation), box 3, folder 22, John Witherspoon DuBose Papers, ADAH; *Montgomery Advertiser*, 1 November 1874 (second quotation); Bell, "The Reconstruction Ku Klux Klan," 200–204. There was evidence of plenty of fraud and violence in the election, too (some of it Klan sponsored), including the shooting to pieces of Willie Keils, a fourteen-year-old boy caught in the cross-fire of snipers firing at a Republican judge in Eufaula. See, e.g., *(Montgomery) Alabama State Journal*, 3–7 November 1874; *(Talladega) Our Mountain Home*, 11 November 1874; and *Eufaula Times*, 3 November 1874. E. M. Keils to George S. Houston, 1 December 1874, box SG 6410, folder 1, Alabama Governors Papers, George S. Houston Papers, ADAH. See also Allen Johnston Going, *Bourbon Democracy in Alabama, 1874–1890* (1951; reprint, Tuscaloosa: The University of Alabama Press, 1992), 14, 17. On Houston's business background, see the *Tuscaloosa Times*, 18 November 1874.

48. Even in the William Luke killing at Cross Plains and the notorious Pig-Iron Kelley Riot in Mobile, the mouthpieces of Conservative Democracy had blamed Radical Republican "agitation" for the carnage. They did the same in regard to the Eufaula election riot of 1874 when a mere boy was killed by Klan shooters. See, e.g., *Montgomery Daily Advertiser*, 22 July 1870; *(Troy) Southern Advertiser*, 14 June 1867 (quotation in note); and *Weekly Huntsville Advocate*, 2 September 1870. On Eufaula, see the *Eufaula Times*, 3 November 1874. The *Union Springs Herald*, 4 November 1874, admitted there had been plenty of violence and outrages but excused such "bloody revenge" to the "just indignation of the Southern people." On the withdrawal of U.S. troops, see the *(Butler) Choctaw Herald*, 25 November 1874.

49. W. L. Bragg address, 22 October 1874, box 14, 7N, W. L. Bragg Speeches, ADAH; "Address of the State Exec. Committee, Democratic and Conservative Party," also with the *Shelby Guide*, 22 October 1874, clipping, both in Walter Lawrence Bragg Papers, box 14, 7N, ADAH. Houston also called for northern investment in the South to aid in its economic development. See the following: *(Prattville) Autauga Citizen*, 26 November 1874; *Eufaula Times*, 27 November 1874 (first quotation); *Montgomery Daily Advertiser*, 10 November 1874 (second quotation); *Tuscaloosa Times*, 18 November 1874 (second quotation repeated); *Mobile Register* quoted in the *(Grove Hill) Clarke County Democrat*, 24 November 1874 (third quotation). See also Bragg's speeches prior to the election as to its signal importance.

50. The closest thing to a discordant note was sounded by the *Moulton Advertiser*: "The haughty, imperious, dictatorial leaders of the Black cohorts of Ham in Alabama will now leave the State, and the poor nigger until the next election. The nigger will live off the democrats until he gets another chance to vote his best friends rights and privileges away" (13 November 1874). *Union Springs Herald*, 11 November 1874 and reprinted in the *Tuscaloosa Times*, 18 November 1874; *Jacksonville Republican* (a Democratic newspaper), 7 November 1874; *Opelika Times* reprinted in the *Tuscaloosa Times*, 18 November 1874 (second quotation).

51. *Eutaw Whig and Observer*, 19 November 1874; *(Selma) Southern Argus*, 6 November 1874; *Greenville Advocate*, 12 November 1874.

52. *(Butler County) Choctaw Herald*, 18 November 1874; *Selma Echo* reprinted in the *Eufaula News*, 10 November 1874; *Troy Messenger*, 2 November 1874; *Moulton Advertiser*, 13 November 1874; *Birmingham Iron Age*, 19 November 1874.

53. *Montgomery Daily Advertiser*, 6 November 1874 and Meyer Lehman, Esq. to Henry C. Semple, Esq., ed. of the *Montgomery Daily Advertiser*, 11 November 1874 (first quotation); *(Perry County) Marion Commonwealth*, 12 November 1874; *Tuscaloosa Times*, 18 November and 2 December 1874 (second quotation). *Marengo News-Journal*, 21 November 1874 and *(Greensboro) Alabama Beacon*, 14 November 1874. Republican sentiment was less effusive. The Negro is "told that he shall be 'protected' and all that," wrote the *(Montgomery) Alabama State Journal* on 8 November 1874. "But from whom does he need 'protection?' Certainly no 'Carpet-bagger' and Republican. . . . The Negro is useful as a laborer. . . . It is therefore important that he be kept in Alabama. But he is to be kept as a 'negro only!' . . . never to enjoy any other of the rights and privileges which belong to the white. . . . [L]et the Negro think wisely and well over the dark future that looms up before him, and his race." See also the *(Talladega) Our Mountain Home*, 18 November 1874. For somewhat naïve northern appreciation of the "remarkable coincidence" of declined violence and Conservative Democratic recapture of power, see the *Rochester Union* reprinted in the *Tuscaloosa Times*, 25 November 1874.

54. *Tuskaloosa Blade*, 12, 19, and 26 November 1874 (block quotation).

55. Of course, the Myth of the Lost Cause and Creed of the New South have been written about in many places before, perhaps most famously in W. J. Cash, *The Mind of the South* (New York: Alfred A. Knopf, 1941); C. Vann Woodward, *Origins of the New South, 1877–1913* (Baton Rouge: Louisiana State University Press, 1951); and Paul M. Gaston, *The New South Creed: A Study in Southern Mythmaking* (New York: Alfred A. Knopf, 1970). *(Selma) Southern Argus*, 5 February 1875 (quotations). The *Southern Argus* was edited in this period by Robert McKee, who supported the Populist ticket in 1892. On McKee, see Going, *Bourbon Democracy in Alabama*, 13. As education reformer J.L.M. Curry enunciated the myth: "For years suffrage has been as free here as it is possible for it to be anywhere. But while the whites have not sought or desired to intimidate the negro at elections, they have not been, nor are they now, favorable to negro suffrage. Not that they would deprive the negroes of any right secured to them by the Constitution or the laws." Editorial for A. Broadus, 10 November 1879, box 1, folder 5, Curry Family Papers, Jabez L. M. Curry Papers, ADAH.

56. The disturbing tendency of white Alabamians to take credit for federal munificence, along with the state's "odorous" press, judged Brevet General J. McArthur, were not "harbingers of a very speedy withdrawal of the Federal bayonets for if such be the sentiments of the people of Alabama (and I believe that they are) then the placing of power in the hands of such a people will result in baneful influences upon the Country." Brev. Gen. J. McArthur to Gov. Lewis E. Parsons, 30 July 1865, Correspondence: General, RC2: G6, Alabama Governors Papers, Lewis E. Parsons Papers, ADAH. S. F. Rice in Lucille Griffith, *Alabama: A Documentary History to 1900* (Tuscaloosa: The University of Alabama Press, 1987), 477 (first quotation); Frank Herr, "Reconstruction Times in Sumter County," unpublished typescript, Series 7, folder G-5, Alabama Collection, Julia Tutwiler Library, University of West Alabama (formerly Livingston University), Livingston, AL (second quotation); John B. Callis, Brev. Col. to Wager Swayne, 7 June 1866, folder: Alabama Reconstruction Correspondence, Wager Swayne, Wager Swayne Papers, ADAH. See also "First Semi-Annual Report on Schools and Finances of Freedmen,"

1 January 1866 (1868), Freedmen's Bureau, J. W. Alvord, Inspector of Schools and Finances, pp. 4–5, box 5, folder 71, Alabama Pamphlets Collection, ADAH; Testimony of Daniel Taylor, Ku Klux Report, Alabama Testimony, 1132 (p. 47), box 5, folder 74, Freedmen's Bureau Documents, Alabama Pamphlets Collection, ADAH. For more on northern aid to the South, see Richard H. Wilmer, Bishop of Alabama, to Mrs. Algernon S. Sullivan, 7 February 1867, J. F. Dowell to Mrs. Algernon S. Sullivan, 21 March 1867, J.L.M. Curry to Mrs. A. S. Sullivan, 18 April 1867, all three in the Southern Relief Association of New York City, 1866–1867, documents, box 5, folder 78, Alabama Pamphlets Collection, ADAH.

57. Kate Cummings Diary, 24 March 1867, box 2, folder 25A, ADAH (first quotation); C. W. Buckley to Brev. Col. C. Cadle Jr., 27 January 1866, Microcopy M-809, reel 19, Record Group 105, Freedmen's Bureau Records (second quotation), NA. See also no name, Brooklyn, New York, to My dear Friend Mr. Lull, 1 May 1865, box II, folder 67, Cabot Lull Collection, UA.

Chapter 2

Epigraph. Robert Bartels, ed., *Ethics in Business* (Columbus: Bureau of Business Research, Ohio State University, 1963), 35.

1. There is a wealth of excellent historical work in this area. See, e.g., James M. McPherson, *Ordeal by Fire: The Civil War and Reconstruction* (New York: Alfred A. Knopf, 1982). See also John B. Boles, *The South through Time: A History of an American Region* (Englewood Cliffs, NJ: Prentice Hall, 1995), 299–336, and George C. Rable, *God's Almost Chosen Peoples: A Religious History of the American Civil War* (Chapel Hill: University of North Carolina Press, 2010).

2. Wayne Flynt, *Poor but Proud: Alabama's Poor Whites* (Tuscaloosa: The University of Alabama Press, 1989), 281.

3. *Baltimore Manufacturers Record*, 12 March 1914, 4, 18 October and 6 December 1923. Of course, the classic treatment of this is found in Woodward, *Origins of the New South*. See also George Brown Tindall, *The Emergence of the New South, 1913–1945* (Baton Rouge: Louisiana State University Press, 1967), 318–20; Blaine A. Brownell and David R. Goldfield, *The City in Southern History: The Growth of Urban Civilization in the South* (Port Washington, NY: Kennikat Press, 1977); and Raymond A. Mohl, *Searching for the Sunbelt: Historical Perspectives on a Region* (Knoxville: University of Tennessee Press, 1990).

4. See the classic work on this subject: Gaston, *The New South Creed*, 17, 48–53, 69–74, 203.

5. James C. Cobb, *Industrialization and Southern Society, 1877–1984* (Lexington: University Press of Kentucky, 1984), 19, 31.

6. Ibid., 19–20. Historian Jonathan Wiener has argued that Alabama's strong planter elite retarded industrial growth that it saw as anathema to its interests, primarily the removal of a black labor class from the plantation. According to Wiener, planter opposition led to repeated false starts for Birmingham industrialists and delayed viable iron production in the city until the 1890s. See Jonathan M. Wiener, *Social Origins of the New South: Alabama, 1860–1885* (Baton Rouge: Louisiana State University Press, 1978). Wiener's study is one of several that offer an alternative to C. Vann Woodward's discontinuity thesis of economic development and his conception of the "New Men" who led industrialization

in the South. See Woodward, *Origins of the New South*. Wiener used Harvard Marxist sociologist Barrington Moore's concept of the "Prussian Road" to industrialization to argue that Alabama's planter elite retarded growth. Dwight Billings, in *Planters and the Making of a "New South": Class, Politics, and Development in North Carolina* (Chapel Hill: University of North Carolina Press, 1979), asserted that planters actually took the lead in shaping and hence molding North Carolina's industrialization to fit their needs. Lewis N. Wynne's study, *The Continuity of Cotton: Planter Politics in Georgia, 1865–1892* (Macon, GA: Mercer University Press, 1986), made the case for a planter-industrialist alliance that preserved the privileged position of Georgia planters in the new economic order. David L. Carlton, in *Mill and Town in South Carolina, 1880–1920* (Baton Rouge: Louisiana State University Press, 1982), provided some support for Woodward's embattled thesis. In an insightful piece, James C. Cobb called for a cease-fire to the planter-industrialist debate by pointing out that both planter and industrial elites shared the common goal of socioeconomic control over the working and poorer classes. Cobb, "Beyond Planters and Industrialists: A New Perspective on the New South," *Journal of Southern History* 54 (February 1988): 45–68.

7. Woodward, *Origins of the New South*, 236. See also Philip Taft, *Organizing Dixie: Alabama Workers in the Industrial Era*, ed. Leon Fink (Westport, CT: Greenwood Press, 1981), 5.

8. Taft, *Organizing Dixie*, 183.

9. F. Ray Marshall, *Labor in the South* (Cambridge, MA: Harvard University Press, 1967), vii–viii. See, as one of the latest installments in this long story, Diane McWhorter, *Carry Me Home: Birmingham, Alabama: The Climactic Battle of the Civil Rights Revolution* (New York: Simon and Schuster, 2002).

10. On Voltaire's conception of merchant as hero, see Jerry Z. Muller, *The Mind and the Market: Capitalism in Modern European Thought* (New York: Alfred A. Knopf, 2002), 25–30, 36–37. The idea of capitalism as panacea would be popularized in the twentieth century by proto-libertarian, rightist economic thinkers such as Joseph Schumpeter. See pp. 310–11.

11. See Susan Delfino and Michelle Gillespie, eds., *Global Perspectives on Industrial Transformation in the American South* (Columbia: University of Missouri Press, 2005); David L. Carlton and Peter Coclanis, *The South, the Nation, and the World: Perspectives on Southern Economic Development* (Charlottesville: University Press of Virginia, 2003); Roger L. Ransom and Richard Sutch, *One Kind of Freedom: The Economic Consequences of Emancipation*, 2nd ed. (Cambridge: Cambridge University Press, 2001); and Gavin Wright, *Old South, New South: Revolutions in Southern Economy since the Civil War* (New York: Basic Books, 1986).

12. Ethel Armes, *The Story of Coal and Iron in Alabama* (Birmingham: Chamber of Commerce, 1910). For studies of Alabama industrialism, see W. David Lewis, *Sloss Furnaces and the Rise of the Birmingham District: An Industrial Epic* (Tuscaloosa: The University of Alabama Press, 1994) and Henry M. McKiven Jr., *Iron and Steel: Class, Race, and Community in Birmingham, Alabama, 1875–1920* (Chapel Hill: University of North Carolina Press, 1995).

13. The moralistic component of the economic setup was particularly important and pervasive, as it had been during slave times. While the Social Darwinistic impulse was perhaps more concentrated and unmitigated in the South, it was by no means restricted

to conservatives in Dixie. "Liquidate labor, liquidate stocks, liquidate the farmer, liquidate real estate," billionaire and Republican secretary of commerce Andrew Mellon advised Herbert Hoover on the eve of the Great Depression. "It will purge the rottenness out of the system. People will work harder, lead a more moral life." Robert Reich, "Republican Politics as Social Darwinism," *Huffington Post*, 26 September 2010.

14. The work of Voltaire, the Reverend Robert Thomas "Parson" Malthus, Edmund Burke, Bernard Mandeville, and even Adam Smith (crudely removed from its complete context), propagated the idea of the positive "trickle-down" effects that would accrue to broader society from the concentrated wealth of the few. See, e.g., Muller, *The Mind and the Market*, 42–43 and Robert L. Heilbroner, *The Worldly Philosophers: The Lives, Times, and Ideas of the Great Economic Thinkers*, rev. 7th ed. (New York: Touchstone Books, Simon and Schuster, 1999), 98.

15. Howard Strevel in E. B. Rich and Howard Strevel, interview by Edwin L. Brown, Glenn Cole, and Ralph A. Johnson, Birmingham, Alabama, 9 June 1988, p. 3, Oral History Collection, Center for Labor Education and Research (hereafter CLEAR), University of Alabama at Birmingham.

16. Woodward, *Origins of the New South*, 61. See also Joseph Gerteis, *Class and the Color Line: Interracial Class Coalition in the Knights of Labor and the Populist Movement* (Durham: Duke University Press, 2007) and Melton A. McLaurin, *The Knights of Labor in the South* (New York: Greenwood Press, 1978).

17. On this subject, see particularly Brian Kelly's very good *Race, Class, and Power in the Alabama Coalfields, 1908–21* (Urbana: University of Illinois Press, 2001); Edwin L. Brown and Colin J. Davis, eds., *It Is Union and Liberty: Alabama Coal Miners and the UMW* (Tuscaloosa: The University of Alabama Press, 1999); and Daniel Letwin, *Alabama Coal Miners, 1878–1921* (Chapel Hill: University of North Carolina Press, 1998).

18. Woodward, *Origins of the New South*, 117.

19. Ibid., 227–28.

20. Cobb, *Industrialization and Southern Society*, 72, 87.

21. This discussion on convict lease owes much to the fine treatment in David M. Oshinsky, *"Worse than Slavery": Parchman Farm and the Ordeal of Jim Crow Justice* (New York: Free Press, 1996), 55–80, as well as Edward L. Ayers, *The Promise of the New South: Life after Reconstruction* (New York: Oxford University Press, 1992), 11, 22.

22. Matthew J. Mancini aptly titled his excellent book on the subject *One Dies, Get Another: Convict Leasing in the American South* (Columbia: University of South Carolina Press, 1996). See especially pp. 99–116 on Alabama. See also Alex Lichtenstein, *Twice the Work of Free Labor: The Political Economy of Convict Labor in the New South* (London: Verso, 1996). A recent related work is Douglas A. Blackmon, *Slavery by Another Name: The Re-Enslavement of Black Americans from the Civil War to World War II* (New York: Anchor, 2009).

23. Dr. Shirley Bragg, "Report to the Governor, Alabama," January 1907, quoted in Clarissa Olds Keeler, "The Crime of Crimes, or The Convict System Unmasked," pamphlet in *From Slavery to Freedom: The African-American Pamphlet Collection, 1824–1909*, Alabama, American Memory project, LC, http://learning.loc.gov/cgi-bin/query /r?ammem/rbaapc:@field(DOCID+@lit(rbaapc15100div5) (accessed 17 February 2012).

24. Woodward, *Origins of the New South*, 215. Woodward discusses the Bankhead political dynasty of Alabama, which made its fortune in the coal mines.

25. Oshinsky, "*Worse than Slavery,*" 81.

26. Wayne Flynt, *Alabama in the Twentieth Century* (Tuscaloosa: The University of Alabama Press, 2004), 38, 48.

27. On Social Darwinism, see Richard Hofstadter's classic, *Social Darwinism in American Thought* (Boston: Beacon Press, 1955). See also Carl N. Degler, *In Search of Human Nature: The Decline and Revival of Darwinism in American Social Thought* (New York: Oxford University Press, 1991).

28. Edmund Burke, *Reflections on the Revolution in France,* in R. B. McDowell, ed., *The Writings and Speeches of Edmund Burke* (Oxford: Oxford University Press, 1991), 8:209 (first quotation) and Burke, "Thoughts and Details," 9:137 (second quotation). See also Muller, *The Mind and the Market,* 118, 119. Heilbroner, *The Worldly Philosophers,* 227 (third quotation).

29. Gaston, *The New South Creed,* 209.

30. The Stickney remark is from Heilbroner, *The Worldly Philosophers,* 217. Robert Bartels, ed., *Ethics in Business* (Columbus: Bureau of Business Research, Ohio State University, 1963), 35 (Drew quotation).

31. Scholars of southern religion have, with very few exceptions, agreed that dominant religion in the region has been conservative. See the voluminous work of Samuel S. Hill Jr., especially *Southern Churches in Crisis* (New York: Holt, Rinehart and Winston, 1966); Hill, ed., *Religion and the Solid South* (Nashville: Abingdon Press, 1972); and Ted Ownby, *Subduing Satan: Religion, Recreation, and Manhood in the Rural South, 1865–1920* (Chapel Hill: University of North Carolina Press, 1990). Wayne Flynt has been, perhaps, the most notable dissenter on this subject, but the essential validity of Hill's thesis is still accepted by scholars such as John B. Boles. See Boles's discussion of Hill, Flynt, and others in "The Discovery of Southern Religious History," in *Interpreting Southern History: Historiographical Essays in Honor of Sanford W. Higginbotham,* ed. John B. Boles and Evelyn Thomas Nolen (Baton Rouge: Louisiana State University Press, 1987), 512–15, 542–43, 512–13. See also Ted Ownby, "'Ethos without Ethic': Samuel S. Hill and Southern Religious History," in Feldman, *Reading Southern History,* 247–60. More recently, the dissenting view has been taken up by David L. Chappell in *A Stone of Hope: Prophetic Religion and the Death of Jim Crow* (Chapel Hill: University of North Carolina Press, 2004) and by Andrew M. Manis, "'City Mothers': Dorothy Tilly, Georgia Methodist Women, and Black Civil Rights," in Feldman, ed., *Before Brown.* For an account that is less sanguine about southern white religious/racial enlightenment, see Harvey, *Freedom's Coming.*

32. See Feldman, "Exporting 'The Southern Religion' and Shaping the Election of 2012."

33. On the tendency of Calvinism to devolve to the level of openly anti-democratic thought and behavior, see the career and writings of Armenian American Rousas John Rushdoony, an ultra-Calvinist of the Christian Reconstructionist persuasion who founded Dominionism, created homeschooling, and started the Chalcedon Foundation. In his book *Thy Kingdom Come,* Rushdoony writes that democracy and Christianity are incompatible: "Democracy is the great love of the failures and cowards of life," he wrote. "One faith, one law and one standard of justice did not mean democracy. The heresy of democracy has since then worked havoc in church and state. Christianity and democracy are inevitable enemies." Frank (Francis Jr.) Schaeffer, "Michelle Bachmann Was Inspired by My Dad and His Christian Reconstructionist Friends," http://www.alternet.org/ (accessed 9 August 2011) (first Rushdoony quotation in note). See also Schaeffer, *Sex, Mom*

and God: How the Bible's Strange Take on Sex Led to Crazy Politics—and How I Learned to Love Women (and Jesus) Anyway (New York: Da Capo Press, 2011) and Schaeffer, *Crazy for God*. See also Rushdoony, *Thy Kingdom Come: Studies in Daniel and Revelation* (Phillipsburg, NJ: Presbyterian and Reformed Publishing, 1970). Ironically Rushdoony's denunciation of *democracy* as a faulty religion for failures and the weak is the mirror image found in economic fundamentalist disdain for *Christianity* as the same, beginning with philosophical roots in the writings of Friedrich Nietzsche. Whether democracy or Christianity is the culprit—the safe haven for the "losers" of society—the ultimate culprit is still democracy, as anti-democratic fervor and vote suppression is the common end point to both religious fundamentalism and economic fundamentalism. Austrian economist and Chicago School neoliberals (and their progenitors) from Ludwig von Mises and Joseph Schumpeter to F. A. Hayek, Milton Friedman, and the atheist novelist Ayn Rand have all disparaged democracy often and harshly. Rejection of the concepts of social justice and social responsibility has not been far behind, as immortalized in their works and, especially, the words of libertarian enthusiast Margaret Thatcher. For specific works, quotes, and citations, see Feldman, "Putting Uncle Milton to Bed." "I don't want everyone to vote," Religious Right pioneer and Catholic Republican strategist Paul Weyrich bluntly informed fifteen thousand conservative preachers at a 1980 political training conference in Dallas. "Elections are not won by a majority of the people. They never have been since the beginning of our country and they are not now. As a matter of fact, our leverage in the elections quite candidly goes up as the voting populace goes down." Weyrich quoted in Feldman, *Painting Dixie Red*, 348n20.

Yet there were other routes that tied all of the elements of the two great meldings together: first economic rightism and white supremacy bound by the rope of anti-federal animus, and then economic rightism and religious fundamentalism glued by the mortar of anti-democratic angst. Rousas Rushdoony insisted that the United States was a Christian nation founded on biblical precepts and took his criticism of egalitarianism to the point of actually defending slavery. In this it is quite important that, for him and others swayed by his thought, an *economic* system (socialism) becomes the foil of slavery. "The law here is humane and unsentimental," he wrote. "It recognizes that some people are by nature slaves and will always be so.... Socialism, on the contrary, tries to give the slave all the advantages of his security together with the benefits of freedom, and in the process, destroys both the free and the enslaved." Such a defense paralleled that of the most unreconstructed exponents of classical economic thought, such as Bernard Mandeville, whose writing was so extreme that most of his eighteenth-century classical economic contemporaries, including Adam Smith, denounced him. Mandeville argued that unless the poor remained poor, they would not do an honest day's work without asking for inappropriately high wages. "To make the Society Happy," he wrote, "it is requisite that great numbers should be Ignorant as well as Poor," and the wants of the poor would be "but folly to cure." See Heilbroner, *The Worldly Philosophers*, 40, 60 (Mandeville quotations). See also Muller, *The Mind and the Market*, 42–43. George Grant, the former executive director of the Florida-based Coral Ridge Ministries (which has since changed its name to Truth in Action Ministries), is also on record praising slavery as benevolent and depicting the Civil War as a millennial clash between a devout Christian South and a godless North. Grant made these views known in a book he edited and provided a forward to, J. Steven Wilkins, *Call of Duty: The Sterling Nobility of Robert E. Lee* (Nashville: Cumberland House Publishing, 1997). A Dominionist, Grant was also quite open about his view of the goals of Dominionism: "It is dominion we are after. Not just a voice. . . . It is dominion we are after. Not just equal time. . . . World conquest." The Dominionist admiration of American slavery shares common ground with the beliefs of quack historian David Barton and serious literature professor and philosopher Melvin E. Bradford. Barton, a favorite of the modern Christian Right, and the United States-as-a-Christian-Nation School, explained that "God's laws concerning slavery provided parameters for treatment of slaves, which were for the benefit of all involved." Barton's praise for slavery and Christian Reconstruction coexist with his Orwellian tying of the modern Democratic Party to racism and the modern GOP to support for civil rights. See Rachel Tabachnick, "Meet the Christian Dominionist 'Prayer Warriors' Who Have Chosen Rick Perry as Their Vehicle to Power," http://www.alternet.org/, 15 August 2011 (accessed 19 August 2011). Here is where Christian Reconstruction meets racism meets hatred of the federal government meets extreme affection for libertarian economics and the neo-Confederacy. All were present in the extensive writings of George Wallace and Ronald Reagan favorite Melvin E. Bradford of Texas. Bradford was highly influenced by late nineteenth-century Southern Presbyterian and Christian Reconstructionist theologian Robert L. Dabney, whose views were carried forward by philosopher Richard M. Weaver and poet Donald Davidson of the Nashville Agrarians centered at Vanderbilt University in the 1930s. Not coincidentally, Bradford also disparaged egalitarianism, defended slavery, glorified the Confederacy, demonized Abraham Lincoln, and provided much of the philosophical underpinnings of the New Right. See Fred Arthur Bailey, "M. E. Bradford, the Reagan Right, and the Resurgence of Confederate Nationalism," in Feldman, *Painting Dixie Red*, 291–313, esp. p. 299. Also see Michelle Goldberg, "A Christian Plot for Domination?" *Daily Beast*, 14 August 2011 (second Rushdoony quotation, Grant quotations, and Barton quotation in note).

For the influence of Dominion theology beyond Christian Reconstructionism on figures such as Pat Robertson, see Garry Wills, *Under God: Religion and American Politics* (New York: Simon and Schuster, 2007). On the hatred of the U.S. government by leaders of the Christian Reconstructionist movement such as the Calvinist theologian Rousas Rushdoony, his son-in-law Gary North, and Calvinist pastor David Chilton, see Schaeffer, "Michelle Bachmann Was Inspired by My Dad." See the same article for their stress on the violent prohibitions and punishments of the Old Testament over the lessons of the New Testament, including the death penalty for homosexuality, cursing one's parents, taking the Lord's name in vain, and other offenses. Also on the subject of the death penalty for these things, see Goldberg, "A Christian Plot for Domination?" "Ten Commandments Judge" Roy Moore, for example, displayed obvious Dominionist beliefs and theocratic tendencies about "God's Law" superseding man-made law as well as recommending capital punishment for gays and lesbians before (and after) he was removed as chief justice of the Alabama Supreme Court. For more on Roy Moore, see Glenn Feldman, ed., *Politics and Religion in the White South* (Lexington: University Press of Kentucky, 2005). On the older ties during the 1930s and the late nineteenth century between laissez-faire economics and religious fundamentalism, see Jeff Sharlet, "Fundamentalism Springs Eternal for GOP," On Faith blog, *Washington Post*, 21 August 2011. On the current Religious Right view that rampant deregulation, unfettered profit making, and the privatization of everything from prisons to health care to public services and old-age insurance, the military, and pensions are "normal" because at least "corporations weren't the evil government" that was competing with Dominionists' desire to exert dominion over all the earth and subject it to God's Law, see Schaeffer in "Michelle Bachmann Was Inspired by My Dad." On the general subjects in this endnote, see also Michelle Goldberg, *Kingdom Coming: The Rise of Christian Nationalism* (New York: W. W. Norton, 2007); Kevin Phillips, *American Theocracy: The Peril and Politics of Radical Religion, Oil, and Borrowed Money in the 21st Century* (New York: Penguin, 2007); and Ryan Lizza, "Leap of Faith: The Making of a Republican Front Runner," *New Yorker*, 15 August 2011.

34. Clifton Fadiman, ed., *The Little Brown Book of Anecdotes* (Boston: Little, Brown, 1985), 560 (Vanderbilt quotation); Heilbroner, *The Worldly Philosophers*, 217 (Morgan quotation).

35. Heilbroner, *The Worldly Philosophers*, 215 (Vanderbilt and Morgan quotations). See also James A. Barnes, *Wealth of the American People* (New York: Prentice Hall, 1949), 630 and George A. Steiner and John F. Steiner, *Business, Government, and Society: A Managerial Perspective, Text and Cases*, 9th ed. (Boston: Irwin-McGraw-Hill, 2000), 11; and Philip S. Foner, *History of the Labor Movement in the United States*, vol. 2, *From the Founding of the A. F. of L. to American Imperialism* (New York: International Publishers, 1975), 50 (Gould quotation).

36. "American Labor History Notes" (APAAN, 489), 8, CLEAR (first quotation); Woodward, *Origins of the New South*, 128 (second quotation).

37. For Hayek on "social justice" and "the common good," see Muller, *The Mind and the Market*, 372 (quotations). See also Donald R. Stabile, *Work and Welfare: The Social Costs of Labor in the History of Economic Thought* (Westport, CT: Greenwood Press, 1996) and Roseanne Currarino, *The Labor Question in America: Economic Democracy in the Gilded Age* (Urbana: University of Illinois Press, 2010).

38. Heilbroner, *The Worldly Philosophers*, 68 (third quotation), also pp. 42–74 inclusive. See also Muller, *The Mind and the Market*, 52 (quoted), 58 (second and third quotations), 69 (fourth quotation), 141 (on Hegel); Frederic Bastiat, *Economic Sophisms*, translated from the French (Irving-on-Hudson, NY: Foundation for Economic Freedom, 1964).

39. But, of course, the choice for Mill was not as stark as communism or unfettered capitalism. Mill favored a capitalism reined in by the regulatory and reform hand of government oversight, what some call liberalism, others a kind of mild, English "socialism," and what is more commonly referred to as a "mixed capitalist economy." Heilbroner, *The Worldly Philosophers*, 82 (Ricardo quotation), 130–31 (Mill quotations).

40. Muller, *The Mind and the Market*, 79 (quotations).

41. Papers of the NAACP, part 7, series A, reels 3 and 21, AU and LC; NAACP, *Thirty Years of Lynching in the United States, 1889–1918* (New York: NAACP, 1969); see also W. Fitzhugh Brundage, *Lynching in the New South: Georgia and Virginia, 1880–1930* (Urbana: University of Illinois Press, 1993); Stewart E. Tolnay and E. M. Beck, *A Festival of Violence: An Analysis of Southern Lynchings, 1882–1930* (Urbana: University of Illinois Press, 1995); and Thomas J. Sugrue, *Sweet Land of Liberty: The Forgotten Struggle for Civil Rights in the North* (New York: Random House, 2009).

42. Papers of the NAACP, part 7, series A, reels 3 and 21, AU and LC; NAACP, *Thirty Years of Lynching in the United States*. See also James H. Madison, *A Lynching in the Heartland: Race and Memory in America* (New York: Palgrave Macmillan, 2001); Stephen J. Leonard, *Lynching in Colorado, 1859–1919* (Boulder: University Press of Colorado, 2002); and Christopher Waldrep, *The Many Faces of Judge Lynch: Extralegal Violence and Punishment in America* (New York: Palgrave Macmillan, 2002).

43. Massachusetts Republican senator Henry Cabot Lodge's "force bill" to provide for federal supervision of southern elections was defeated in the Senate in 1890 and posed no threat by 1894. In a series of "civil rights" decisions, the U.S. Supreme Court very narrowly interpreted the Fourteenth and Fifteenth amendments, making circumvention of the spirit of these laws quite possible. The famous "Civil Rights Cases" were actually five separate cases condensed into one issue. See *Civil Rights Cases*, 109 U.S. 3 (1883). See also the classic Malcolm Cook McMillan, *Constitutional Development in Alabama, 1798–1901: A Study in Politics, Sectionalism, and the Negro* (Chapel Hill: University of North Carolina Press, 1955), 230–32.

44. Hugh C. Bailey, *Liberalism in the New South: Southern Social Reformers and the Progressive Movement* (Coral Gables, FL: University of Miami Press, 1969), 51–52 (quotations). Other examples abound.

45. Northern sympathy and the absence of fear of intrusion from the federal government was a marked part of Alabama's 1901 deliberations on black suffrage. See the *Official Proceedings of the Constitutional Convention of the State of Alabama, May 21st, 1901 to Sept. 3, 1901* (Wetumpka, AL: Wetumpka Printing, 1940), 2:2247 (hereafter *Official Proceedings, 1901*). U.S. congressman and future senator Oscar W. Underwood asked for northern and federal latitude for Alabama to work out its own solutions to its race relations and, typically, tied the racial and the economic together in a chamber-of-commerce type of white supremacy. He asked for laissez-faire on race especially "if you are in favor of upholding the Negro race . . . of honest governments in the Southern states . . . yes, and the investments that you have brought there among us." See the *Congressional Record* 34, 56th Cong., 2nd Sess., 557 (January 1901), quoted in McMillan, *Constitutional Development in Alabama*, 291n41.

46. Many social workers, psychologists, and statisticians, some of them of Ivy League caliber, concurred. One journalist put it this way: "To reform his character is an almost hopeless task. . . . The Negro is a Negro. We must deal with him as he is." Quotations from Oshinsky, *"Worse than Slavery*," 94–96. See also Gilbert Osofsky, *The Burden of Race: A Documentary History of Negro-White Relations in America* (New York: HarperCollins, 1967), 184–87, 201–5, and I. A. Newby, *Jim Crow's Defense: Anti-Negro Thought in America* (Baton Rouge: Louisiana State University Press, 1965) 7. On the Alabama estimation of the North's "full sympathy" for their racial situation, see, e.g., *Official Proceedings, 1901*, 3:2885–86 (Thomas Goode Jones quoted).

47. See, e.g., the *(Birmingham) Alabama Independent*, 10 July 1969, p. 7. Of course, pockets of Republican strength existed in the South, most notably in the Mountain Republican strongholds that overlapped with pro-Union sentiment during the Civil War: east Tennessee, western North Carolina, northwest Georgia, north Alabama, northeast Mississippi, and various parts of Kentucky. See Alexander P. Lamis, *The Two-Party South* (New York: Oxford University Press, 1984). The famous line is, of course, from William Faulkner's *Requiem for a Nun*.

48. For discussions of this prevailing view of Reconstruction, see Gaston, *The New South Creed*, 130–31; Gaines M. Foster, *Ghosts of the Confederacy: Defeat, the Lost Cause, and the Emergence of the New South, 1865–1913* (New York: Oxford University Press, 1987); and numerous works by Fred Arthur Bailey, such as "Free Speech and the 'Lost Cause' in the Old Dominion," *Virginia Magazine of History and Biography* 103 (April 1995): 237–66. For the enduring importance of the Civil War in southern history, see, e.g., Susan-Mary Grant and Peter J. Parish, eds., *Legacy of Disunion: The Enduring Signifi-*

cance of the American Civil War (Baton Rouge: Louisiana State University Press, 2003); David R. Goldfield, *Still Fighting the Civil War: The American South and the Civil War* (Baton Rouge: Louisiana State University Press, 2002); and David W. Blight, *Race and Reunion: The Civil War in American Memory* (Cambridge, MA: Belknap Press, Harvard University Press, 2001).

Chapter 3

1. For a very good recitation of these reforms, see Flynt, *Alabama in the Twentieth Century*, and Flynt's section in William Warren Rogers, Robert David Ward, Leah Rawls Atkins, and Wayne Flynt, *Alabama: The History of a Deep South State* (Tuscaloosa: The University of Alabama Press, 1994).

2. This humanistic conception of history is perhaps most closely associated with R. G. Collingwood's classic, *The Idea of History* (Oxford: Clarendon Press, 1946).

3. As one recent student of Civil War general James Longstreet communicated to an audience of southern historians, "throughout my entire project I have had to be very careful of sources which prefer to generalize, rather than provide a detailed explanation of the dynamics and nuances of Southern culture." Christopher Martin, National University, Escondido, CA, to H-SOUTH@H-NET.MSU.EDU, 23 August 2011, 11:34 AM, and from Jim Crutchfield, 23 August 2011 at 13:22, both on Subject: Re: You Don't Know Dixie.

4. Charles S. Sydnor, "The Southern Experiment in Writing Social History," *Journal of Southern History* 11 (November 1945): 456.

5. "Having failed to establish a separate nation and having gone down to defeat on the field of battle, Southerners turned their attention to their own past with a concentration so great that the cult of history became a permanent and important ingredient of the Southern culture. . . . [T]he writing of history became an act of sectional allegiance and devotion. . . . If the South has often reacted churlishly and shortsightedly, the fault does not lie with history itself, but with a distorted historical tradition of which even the South's historians have been victims, but which only they can correct." John Hope Franklin, "As for Our History," reprinted in John Hope Franklin, *Race and History: Selected Essays, 1938–1988* (Baton Rouge: Louisiana State University Press, 1989), 63, 70.

6. The literature that takes this tack is extensive. See Cecelia Tichi, *Civic Passions: Seven Who Launched Progressive America* (Chapel Hill: University of North Carolina Press, 2011), as well as George E. Mowry, *The Era of Theodore Roosevelt and the Birth of Modern America, 1900–1912* (New York: Harper and Row, 1958). For a positive evaluation of southern Progressivism, see Dewey W. Grantham, *Southern Progressivism: The Reconciliation of Progress and Tradition* (Knoxville: University of Tennessee Press, 1983).

7. Gabriel Kolko, *The Triumph of Conservatism: A Reinterpretation of American History, 1900–1916* (New York: Free Press, 1963); James A. Weinstein, *The Corporate Ideal in the Liberal State, 1900–1918* (Boston: Beacon Press, 1968); Larry G. Gerber, *The Limits of Liberalism: Josephus Daniels, Henry Stimson, Bernard Baruch, David Richberg, Felix Frankfurter, and the Development of the Modern Political Economy* (New York: New York University Press, 1983).

8. Robert H. Wiebe, *The Search for Order, 1877–1920* (New York: Hill and Wang, 1967); George Brown Tindall, *The Persistent Tradition in New South Politics* (Baton Rouge: Louisiana State University Press, 1975), 52–56. Ellis W. Hawley carried this type of

analysis into the 1920s in *The Great War and the Search for a Modern Order: A History of the American People and Their Institutions, 1917–1933* (New York: St. Martin's Press, 1979).

9. Sheldon Hackney, *Populism to Progressivism in Alabama* (Princeton: Princeton University Press, 1969), 278, 312, 329–32.

10. Richard Hoftstadter, *The Age of Reform: From Bryan to FDR* (New York: Vintage Books, 1955).

11. Woodward, *Origins of the New South*.

12. William W. Rogers, *The One-Gallused Rebellion: Agrarianism in Alabama, 1865–1896* (Baton Rouge: Louisiana State University Press, 1970); Samuel L. Webb, *Two-Party Politics in the One-Party South: Alabama's Hill Country, 1874–1920* (Tuscaloosa: The University of Alabama Press, 1997).

13. William E. Leuchtenburg, *The Perils of Prosperity, 1914–1932* (Chicago: University of Chicago Press, 1958). On Progressivism during the 1920s, see Grantham, *Southern Progressivism*; George Brown Tindall, "Business Progressivism in the Twenties," *South Atlantic Quarterly* 62 (Winter 1963): 92–106; Tindall, *The Emergence of the New South*, 219, 224; Tindall, *The Ethnic Southerners* (Baton Rouge: Louisiana State University Press, 1976), 142–61. See also William A. Link, *The Paradox of Southern Progressivism, 1880–1930* (Chapel Hill: University of North Carolina Press, 1993) and Arthur S. Link, "What Happened to the Progressive Movement in the 1920s?" *American Historical Review* 64 (July 1959): 833–51.

14. Woodward, *Origins of the New South*, 369–95. Woodward was expanding on a theme set out five years earlier in Arthur S. Link, "The Progressive Movement in the South, 1870–1914," *North Carolina Historical Review* 23 (April 1946): 172–95. A recent example of this approach may be found in Gregory P. Downs, *Declarations of Dependence: The Long Reconstruction of Popular Politics in the South, 1861–1908* (Chapel Hill: University of North Carolina Press, 2011). Bruce Clayton is harder on these reformers than Woodward and Link, concluding that their commitment to racism "helped to increase the gap between blacks and whites," in *The Savage Ideal: Intolerance and Intellectual Leadership in the South, 1890–1914* (Baltimore: Johns Hopkins University Press, 1972), 181. John David Smith has asserted that southern historiography of the Progressive period paralleled the reformers' beliefs that white advancement was contingent on the settlement of the "Negro Question." Of course, this settlement would be on terms favorable to the white South. See Smith, "An Old Creed for the New South: Southern Historians and the Revival of the Proslavery Argument, 1890–1920," *Southern Studies* 18 (Spring 1979): 76, 87. J. Morgan Kousser also demurred by interpreting the period as reactionary. He focused on race control through disfranchisement and segregation as examples of such reaction in *The Shaping of Southern Politics: Suffrage Restriction and the Establishment of the One-Party South, 1880–1910* (New Haven: Yale University Press, 1974), 229. George M. Frederickson understood southern progressivism as inherently racist and in consonance with "conservative goals such as law and order, social harmony, and rule by a benevolent elite," in *White Supremacy: A Comparative Study in American and South African History* (New York: Oxford University Press, 1981), 296. Elsewhere, Kousser and others have narrowed their interpretation of southern progressivism even further, as "for middle-class whites only." See Kousser, "Progressivism—For Middle-Class Whites Only: North Carolina Education, 1880–1910," *Journal of Southern History* 46 (May 1980): 169–94, quotation on 192, and H. Leon Prather Jr., *Resurgent Politics and Educational Progressivism in*

the New South: North Carolina, 1890–1913 (Rutherford, NJ: Fairleigh Dickinson University Press, 1979), 277–83.

15. Even this generally accepted racial exclusion is related to debates over the basically liberal or conservative, positive or negative, nature of the Progressive Movement as a whole. Wayne Flynt has consistently argued that southern progressivism was a quite positive phenomenon. See, e.g., *Alabama in the 20th Century*, and Flynt's sections in Rogers et al., *Alabama*. In *Darkness at the Dawning: Race and Reform in the Progressive South*, (Philadelphia: J. J. Lippincott, 1972), 2–4, Jack Temple Kirby postulated that disfranchisement was the seminal "reform" of the era in the South, the prerequisite that allowed positive reforms to take place in a variety of areas. Kirby interpreted southern progressivism very positively; its reform ran "deeper and broader . . . than in other regions . . . simply because there was so much more to do in the impoverished South." Hugh C. Bailey admitted that Deep South reformers accepted racism and exploited it for their own advancement but warned against using race as the single measure of the era. "[F]or their time and place," Bailey claimed, "many of the Southern social reformers . . . were . . . liberal in racial matters." See *Liberalism in the New South: Southern Social Reformers and the Progressive Movement* (Coral Gables, FL: University of Miami Press, 1969), 12 and Bailey, *Edgar Gardner Murphy: Gentle Progressive* (Coral Gables, FL: University of Miami Press, 1968). On Alabama, see Martin T. Olliff, ed., *The Great War in the Heart of Dixie: Alabama during World War I* (Tuscaloosa: The University of Alabama Press, 2008).

16. "Zero-sum theory" is, of course, identified with economist Lester C. Thurrow. See *The Zero-Sum Society: Distribution and the Possibilities for Economic Change* (New York: Viking Press, 1981).

17. Confusion over the Progressive Movement is so extensive that historians have even considered abolishing the name "Progressive Era." See Richard L. Watson Jr., "From Populism through the New Deal," in *Interpreting Southern History: Historiographical Essays in Honor of Sanford W. Higginbotham*, ed. John B. Boles and Evelyn Thomas Nolen (Baton Rouge: Louisiana State University Press, 1987), 329.

18. On the length of the Alabama state constitution, see Kyle Whitmire, "Constitution Conundrum," *Birmingham Weekly* (7–14 November 2002): 6.

19. Rogers et al., *Alabama*, 335.

20. Hackney, *Populism to Progressivism in Alabama*, 177.

21. Malcolm Cook McMillan, *Constitutional Development in Alabama, 1798–1901: A Study in Politics, Sectionalism, and the Negro* (Chapel Hill: University of North Carolina Press, 1955), 259.

22. *Official Proceedings, 1901*, 3:2982 (Watts quoted), and Charles H. Greer of Perry County, 3:3079 (quotation). Patricians also expressed fear that north Alabama whites were learning how to manipulate ethnic votes through force and fraud. Some also expressed concern that the federal government might intervene in southern elections if they continued to be so blatantly controlled by force and fraud. Others simply objected that the practice of buying votes was becoming too expensive.

23. A number of works are relevant here. See Woodward, *Origins of the New South* and Ayers, *The Promise of the New South*. On Alabama alone, see Michael W. Fitzgerald, *The Union League Movement in the Deep South: Politics and Agricultural Change during Reconstruction* (Baton Rouge: Louisiana State University Press, 1989); Hackney, *Populism to Progressivism in Alabama*; Rogers, *The One-Gallused Rebellion*; Webb, *Two-Party Politics in the One-Party South*; Letwin, *The Challenge of Interracial Unionism*; and Kelly,

Race, Class, and Power in the Alabama Coalfields. South-wide, see Michael Hyman, *The Anti-Redeemers: Hill Country Political Dissenters in the Lower South from Redemption to Populism* (Baton Rouge: Louisiana State University Press, 1990) and Michael Perman, *Struggle for Mastery: Disfranchisement in the South, 1888–1908* (Chapel Hill: University of North Carolina Press, 2001). See also the excellent state studies: Jane Elizabeth Dailey, *Before Jim Crow: The Politics of Race in Postemancipation Virginia* (Chapel Hill: University of North Carolina Press, 2000) and Stephen Kantrowitz, *Ben Tillman and the Reconstruction of White Supremacy* (Chapel Hill: University of North Carolina Press, 2000). The literature on the Populist Movement is vast. At the very least, the following should be consulted: Lawrence Goodwyn, *The Populist Moment: A Short History of the Agrarian Revolt in America* (New York: Oxford University Press, 1978); Bruce M. Palmer, "*Man over Money": The Southern Populist Critique of American Capitalism* (Chapel Hill: University of North Carolina Press, 1980); and Barton C. Shaw, *The Wool-Hat Boys: Georgia's Populist Party* (Baton Rouge: Louisiana State University Press, 1984).

24. For a sample of Alabama concern about "black and tan" elements in what remained of the GOP, see W. C. Garrett and Charles A. Sears to Oscar W. Underwood, 11 February 1904, and *Birmingham News* clipping, ca. 10 February 1904, both in box 4, folder 3, Oscar W. Underwood Papers, ADAH (hereafter Underwood Papers).

25. *Official Proceedings, 1901,* 3:2841 (Heflin quotation); Denson in the *Minutes of the Democratic State Convention,* 29 March 1899, pp. 23, 25–27, ADAH. See also David Alan Harris, "Racists and Reformers: A Study of Progressivism in Alabama, 1896–1911" (Ph.D. diss., University of North Carolina at Chapel Hill, 1967), 133–34. Denson's ardor cooled as it became increasingly apparent that patrician promises to protect poor-white voting in a constitutional convention were empty. For samples of these pledges, see Hackney, *Populism to Progressivism in Alabama,* 159, 164–66, 168, 175 and Rogers et al., *Alabama,* 346. Hackney has written that "Progressives and Populists too for that matter, were no less racist or prejudiced than their fellow Alabamians" (326). I. L. Brock to O. D. Street, 13 September 1902, in Oliver Day Street Papers, W. Stanley Hoole Special Collections Library, UA (hereafter Street Papers, UA), quoted in Hackney, *Populism to Progressivism in Alabama,* 203. Wayne Flynt has concurred that "In some respects poor whites were harsher racists than yeomen or planters." *Dixie's Forgotten People: The South's Poor Whites* (Bloomington: Indiana University Press, 1979), 11.

26. John B. Knox, Anniston industrialist and former chair of the State Democratic Executive Committee, explained that "There is a difference . . . between the uneducated white man and the ignorant Negro. There is in the white man an inherited capacity for government, which is totally wanting in the Negro. . . . The Negro . . . is descended from a race lowest in intelligence and moral perceptions of all the races of men." *Official Proceedings, 1901,* 1:12. Future U.S. senator Captain Frank S. White agreed that "We have disfranchised the African in the past by doubtful methods, but in the future we will disfranchise [him] by law. The cancer that has been eating upon the body politic . . . must be taken away." *Minutes of the Democratic State Convention,* 25 April 1900, p. 5, ADAH.

27. The canonical traditional account of southern disfranchisement is Kousser, *The Shaping of Southern Politics.* Kousser's interpretation is essentially a longer, more quantitative version of C. Vann Woodward's original in *Origins of the New South.* Michael Perman basically echoed the Woodward and Kousser thesis in *Struggle for Mastery.* For a revisionist position on this question, see Glenn Feldman, *The Disfranchisement Myth: Poor Whites and Suffrage Restriction in Alabama* (Athens: University of Georgia Press, 2004). A

recent study by Donna A. Barnes has provided additional evidence for the revisionist position. See *The Louisiana Populist Movement, 1881–1900* (Baton Rouge: Louisiana State University Press, 2011), 233–34.

28. For scholarship that has generally cast the direct primary as a liberalizing, democratizing reform, see Allen W. Jones, "Political Reforms of the Progressive Era," *Alabama Review* 21 (July 1968): 175–76, 178–79, 206; Jones, "Political Reform and Party Factionalism in the Deep South: Alabama's 'Dead Shoes' Senatorial Primary of 1906," *Alabama Review* 26 (January 1973): 3–4, 32; McMillan, *Constitutional Development in Alabama*, 316–17; Rogers et al., *Alabama*, 355–56.

29. Charles M. Shelley quoted in Harris, "Racists and Reformers," 223–24. Congressman Shelley was joined by two plain-white representatives, former governor Joseph F. Johnston and Congressman Jesse F. Stallings.

30. Oates quoted in the *Birmingham Alabamian*, 21 February 1902, quoted in Jones, "A History of the Direct Primary in Alabama," 138. *Birmingham Age-Herald*, 20 January 1901, quoted in McMillan, *Constitutional Development in Alabama*, 245.

31. O'Neal was also a firm proponent of the New South Creed, replete with a desire to bury sectional feeling in the interest of attracting northern capital to build southern industrial growth. See, e.g., Emmett O'Neal, "Thanksgiving Proclamation by the Governor of Alabama," 18 November 1912 (Montgomery, 1912), Linn-Henley Research Center for Southern History, Birmingham Public Library, Birmingham, AL. On O'Neal, also see Jones, "Political Reforms of the Progressive Era," 194, and Rogers et al., *Alabama*, 381. Some very good work has been done on the topic of woman suffrage in the South. See Marjorie Spruill Wheeler, *New Women of the New South: Leaders of the Woman Suffrage Movement in the Southern States* (New York: Oxford University Press, 1993); Glenda Elizabeth Gilmore, *Gender and Jim Crow: Women and the Politics of White Supremacy in North Carolina, 1896–1920* (Chapel Hill: University of North Carolina Press, 1996); Elna C. Green, *Southern Strategies: Southern Women and the Woman Suffrage Question* (Chapel Hill: University of North Carolina Press, 1997); Anastasia Sims, *The Power of Femininity in the New South: Women's Organizations and Politics in North Carolina, 1880–1930* (Columbia: University of South Carolina Press, 1997); and Mary Martha Thomas, *The New Woman in Alabama: Social Reforms and Suffrage, 1890–1920* (Tuscaloosa: The University of Alabama Press, 1992).

32. Jones, "Political Reforms of the Progressive Era," 193–94.

33. Rogers et al., *Alabama*, 383–84. Of course, in addition to disfranchisement, the Progressive Era, broadly understood, was also notable for the strengthening of Jim Crow laws of segregation.

34. Hackney, *Populism to Progressivism in Alabama*, 159, 164–66, 168, 175; Rogers et al., *Alabama*, 346.

35. Harris, "Racists and Reformers," 358–59.

36. *Plessy v. Ferguson*, 163 U.S. 537 (1896). See also Harris, "Racists and Reformers," 357–61.

37. *Official Proceedings, 1901*, 3:3377.

38. James B. Sellers, *The Prohibition Movement in Alabama, 1702–1943* (Chapel Hill: University of North Carolina Press, 1943), 101.

39. Rogers et al., *Alabama*, 372–73.

40. See Mancini, *One Dies, Get Another*, 99–116; Lichtenstein, *Twice the Work of Free Labor*; and Oshinsky, "*Worse than Slavery*." For the percentages of blacks in the convict-

lease system, see Flynt, *Poor but Proud*, 137, and Harris, "Racists and Reformers," 284. Harris also details the various tortures employers used, such as the lash, solitary confinement, bread and water, freezing shower baths, crucifixion, yoke and buck, and water torture (71–72, 380). Dr. Russell S. Cunningham—company physician for TCI, longtime opponent of convict lease, and later lieutenant governor—calculated the death rate for black convicts at 400 percent higher than that of free black miners and 1,000 percent greater than that of free white miners. He filed the information in the 1897 "Cunningham Report." See Hackney, *Populism to Progressivism in Alabama*, 144–45. Dr. Shirley Bragg, a Lowndes County physician who served as president of the state Board of Convict Inspectors, declared in 1905 that county leasing should be "wiped out of existence and it cannot be done too soon. If the state wishes to kill its convicts it should do so directly." Quotation from Harris, "Racists and Reformers," 282, 287.

41. McMillan, *Constitutional Development in Alabama*, ix (1978 edition). Allen Johnston Going, in *Bourbon Democracy in Alabama, 1874–1890* (Tuscaloosa: The University of Alabama Press, 1951), wrote that "as long as the system supplied money to depleted state and county treasuries and as long as conditions were not notoriously bad, there was little chance of abolishing convict leasing" (190). But conditions *were* beyond bad; they were abominable. The lease brought $1.37 million in profits to the state between 1907 and 1910, according to Rogers et al., *Alabama*, 362.

42. Flynt, *Poor but Proud*, 267–69.

43. Rogers et al., *Alabama*, 393; Flynt, *Poor but Proud*, 137, 263. Governor Emmett O'Neal was instrumental in passing the new mine safety law. See Robert David Ward and William Warren Rogers, *Convicts, Coal, and the Banner Mine Tragedy* (Tuscaloosa: The University of Alabama Press, 1987). David Alan Harris described the state assumption of county convicts after 1900 as a reform that improved the fates of the convicts "just enough to quiet the demand" for abolition of the lease. See Harris, "Racists and Reformers," 291. Rogers and Ward also take vehement issue with the notion, put forth by Sheldon Hackney and other scholars, that Alabama governors Joseph F. Johnston, W. D. Jelks, and B. B. Comer did anything substantial to reform convict lease or guide it toward abolition. See Rogers et al., *Alabama*, 321, 356, 362. Harris agrees with Rogers and Ward about Comer; see "Racists and Reformers," 378. See also Hackney, *Populism to Progressivism in Alabama*, 144, 302.

44. Papers of the NAACP, part 7, series A, reels 3 and 21, Microforms and Documents Dept., Ralph Brown Draughon Library, Auburn University, Auburn, AL (hereafter MADD) and LC, Washington, DC. See also the statistics by state in NAACP, *Thirty Years of Lynching in the United States*. See also the Tuskegee Institute News Clipping Files: The Lynching File, reels 221 and 222, Tuskegee Institute (now Tuskegee University), Tuskegee, AL (hereafter TU).

45. *Montgomery Advertiser*, 3 April and 26 May 1911, 12 September 1912, 22 April 1914, and 5 January 1915; *Montgomery Evening Journal*, 13 August 1912; *Atlanta Constitution*, 31 December 1914; *Knoxville Sentinel*, 3 September 1914; *Pittsburgh Lead*, 4 January 1915. Governors Thomas Goode Jones, Joseph F. Johnston, W. D. Jelks, Emmett O'Neal, and Thomas E. Kilby all made efforts to stop lynching or prosecute its participants. See Hackney, *Populism to Progressivism in Alabama*, 145–46, 184, and McMillan, *Constitutional Development in Alabama*, 337–38.

46. *Congressional Record*, 63rd Cong., 2nd sess., LI, 2893, J. Thomas Heflin Scrap-

books, Dept. of Special Collections, Harwell Goodwin Davis Library, Samford University, Homewood, AL. See also *Montgomery Advertiser*, 14 April 1909 (quotation).

47. Glenn Feldman, "You Know What It Means to Have 9,000 Negroes Idle: Rethinking the Great 1908 Alabama Coal Strike," *Alabama Review* 74 (July 2011): 174–223.

48. Frank V. Evans, "Coal Miners' Strike in the Alabama Coal District in the Year 1908," folder: Strike of 1908, Records of the Alabama Coal Operators' Association/Alabama Mining Institute, Birmingham Public Library Archives, Birmingham, AL. See also *Birmingham Age-Herald*, 8–10, 25 August 1908.

49. *Birmingham News*, 25 and 31 August 1908; *Birmingham Age-Herald*, 4, 7, 24, and 30 August 1908; Flynt, *Poor but Proud*, 136–40, 141.

50. *Birmingham Age-Herald*, 8, 22, and 25 August 1908. A good deal of research is available on the Alabama coalfields. See Robert H. Woodrum, *Everybody Was Black Down There: Race and Industrial Change in the Alabama Coalfields* (Athens: University of Georgia Press, 2007); Brian Kelly, *Race, Class, and Power in the Alabama Coalfields, 1908–21* (Urbana: University of Illinois Press, 2001); Edwin L. Brown and Colin L. Davis, eds., *It Is Union and Liberty: Alabama Coal Miners and the UMW* (Tuscaloosa: The University of Alabama Press, 1999); Daniel Letwin, *The Challenge of Interracial Unionism: Alabama Coal Miners, 1878–1921* (Chapel Hill: University of North Carolina Press, 1998); and Brian Kelly, "Policing the 'Negro Eden': Racial Paternalism in the Alabama Coalfields, 1906–1921," *Alabama Review* 51 (July 1998): 163–83 and (October 1998): 243–65.

51. *Birmingham Labor Advocate*, 17 July, 7, 14, and 28 August, 25 September 1908; *UMW Journal*, 30 July 1908, p. 7; *Birmingham News*, 21 and 25 July, 24 August 1908; Richard A. Straw, "The Collapse of Biracial Unionism: The Alabama Coal Strike of 1908," *Alabama Historical Quarterly* 37 (Summer 1975): 98–99, 108, 112.

52. Straw, "The Collapse of Biracial Unionism," 112 (quotation). See also Daniel Letwin, "Interracial Unionism, Gender, and 'Social Equality' in the Alabama Coalfields, 1878–1908," *Journal of Southern History* 61 (August 1995): 551n98; Letwin, "The Early Years: Alabama Miners Organize, 1878–1908," in Brown and Davis, *It Is Union and Liberty*, 36. For other variations of the quote, see Philip H. Taft, *Organizing Dixie: Alabama Workers in the Industrial Era*, ed. Leon Fink (Westport, CT: Greenwood Press, 1981), 27; Kelly, *Race, Class, and Power in the Alabama Coalfields*, 23–24.

53. *Montgomery Advertiser*, 20 March 1921 (Kilby quotation).

54. Rogers et al., *Alabama*, 415, 418; Tindall, *Emergence of the New South*, 227.

55. Rogers et al., *Alabama*, 416, 418; Tindall, *Emergence of the New South*, 23, 224–25.

56. On Kilby and his alliance with the Alabama Power Company and the state's prohibitionists, see Frank P. Glass to Oscar W. Underwood, 14 January 1915, and Forney Johnston to Oscar W. Underwood, 12 January 1915, both in box 36, folder 8, Underwood Papers, ADAH. On race, see the *Montgomery Advertiser*, 20 March 1921. See also Jimmie Frank Gross, "Strikes in the Coal, Steel, and Railroad Industries in Birmingham from 1918–1922" (M.A. thesis, Auburn University, 1962), and Tindall, *Emergence of the New South*, 188–89.

57. Tindall, *Emergence of the New South*, 174–75.

58. Frederick Lewis Allen, *Only Yesterday: An Informal History of the 1920s* (New York: Harper & Brothers, 1931), Leuchtenburg, *The Perils of Prosperity, 1914–1932*, and John D. Hicks, *Republican Ascendancy* (New York: Harper & Brothers, 1960) all see a

break between the Progressive Era and World War I, arguing that the era's liberalism ended with American entry into war. Ellis W. Hawley argues continuity in the postwar period based on his understanding of an ongoing organizational revolution in *The Great War and the Search for a Modern Order: A History of the American People and Their Institutions, 1917–1933* (New York: St. Martin's Press, 1979). Continuity with progressivism before and after the war is argued by Arthur S. Link in "The Progressive Movement in the South."

59. See Glenda Elizabeth Gilmore, *Defying Dixie: The Radical Roots of Civil Rights, 1919–1950* (New York: W. W. Norton, 2008); Robert K. Murray, "The Red Scare," in *The Social Fabric: American Life from the Civil War to the Present*, ed. John H. Cary, Julius Weinberg, and Thomas L. Hartshorne (Boston: Little, Brown, 1987); Carole Marks, *Farewell, We're Good and Gone: The Great Black Migration* (Bloomington: Indiana University Press, 1989); Tindall, *Emergence of the New South*, 143–83; Wiebe, *The Search for Order*; Mary Beth Norton et al., *A People and a Nation: A History of the United States* (Boston: Houghton Mifflin, 1986), 2:666. Alan Wolfe has argued that the states' National Guard units engaged in rampant repression when they were activated to intervene in industrial conflicts. *The Seamy Side of Democracy: Repression in America* (New York: David McKay, 1973), 133–34.

60. Lloyd M. Hooper to Pate, 20 December 1918, "Negro Organizations," folder A, Program Administrative Files, 1917–1919, Alabama State Council of Defense Records, ADAH (quotations); Lloyd M. Hooper to Oscar W. Underwood, 6 February 1920, Underwood Papers. See also Thomas McAdory Owen, *History of Alabama and Dictionary of Alabama Biography* (Chicago: S. J. Clarke, 1921), 3:839–40 and Evans C. Johnson, *Oscar W. Underwood: A Political Biography* (Baton Rouge: Louisiana State University Press, 1980). For Wayne Flynt's assessment of Underwood's innate conservatism, see Rogers et al., *Alabama*, 435.

61. *Mobile Register*, 17 July 1919. See also Allan R. Millett and Peter Maslowski, *For the Common Defense: A Military History of the United States of America* (New York: Free Press, 1984), 365–67; Maurice Matloff, ed., *American Military History* (Washington, DC: Center of Military History, 1969, 1973), 407–9; and Russell F. Weigley, *The American Way of War: A History of United States Military Strategy and Planning* (Bloomington: Indiana University Press, 1977), 208, 217, 221.

62. Tindall, *Emergence of the New South*, 174.

63. On the lynching of Frank Foukal case, see *Andrews v. Alabama*, 1 Div. 363 (Alabama Court of Appeals, Baldwin Circuit, June 1, 1920), ADAH; "Foukal Murder Case" and "Foukal Lynching Case: Bay Minette," folder 469, box 1919–1920, Alabama Attorney General's Office, correspondence, 1919–20, ADAH; miscellaneous news clippings, reel 1, Horace C. Wilkinson Papers, Department of Special Collections, Harwell Goodwin Davis Library, Samford University, Homewood, AL. On the lynching of Alto Windham case, see *Durden v. Alabama*, 4 Div. 761 (Alabama Court of Appeals, Geneva Circuit, 1922), ADAH; *Whitehead v. Alabama*, 206 Ala. 290 (1921); and *Ex Parte Durden*, 208 Ala. 697 (1922). On the lynching of Willie Baird case, see *Robert Lancaster v. The State of Alabama*, Cause: 5277, Alabama Court of Appeals 1925, 6 Div. 490, Official Court Transcript, ADAH; *Report of the Cases Argued and Determined in the Supreme Court of Alabama during the October Term, 1920–1921*, Lawrence H. Lee, Reporter of Decisions (St. Paul: West Publishing Company, 1921), vol. 214, pp. 3–4, 28 May and 20

June 1925. See also p. 76, 10 December 1925. *Lancaster v. Alabama*, 6 Div. 490 (Alabama Court of Appeals, Marion Circuit, 1925); *Lancaster v. Alabama*, 214 Ala. 2 (1925); and *Lancaster v. Alabama*, 214 Ala. 76 (1925).

64. *Houston Post*, 3 and 8 July 1919 (second quotation); *Montgomery Advertiser*, 26 November 1919 (first quotation); *Mobile Register*, 10, 19, and 20 July 1919; *Birmingham News*, 19 July 1919; Tuskegee Institute News Clipping Files: The Lynching File, reels 221 and 222, TU. One fascinating example of a kind of exception to this rule occurred in the 1917 conviction of a thirty-three-year-old white transient for the killing of a Marion black man. The defendant pled guilty on advice of counsel and was given life imprisonment and recommended for parole after only three-and-a-half years. Interestingly, the judge in the case was later governor Benjamin Meek Miller. J. O. Benton to Charles Henderson, 15 September 1917, and "Statement of the Facts . . . Conviction of Harry Fox," ca. 15 September 1917, both in box SG 22539, folder 8: Convict Dept., Alabama Governors Papers, Papers of Charles Henderson, ADAH.

65. H. Key Milner to Thomas E. Kilby, 13 October 1919, 10 January 1921, and "Memorandum from Operative #57, Birmingham, Alabama, 5 January 1921," in the folder: Coal Strike, 1921, Thomas E. Kilby Papers, Alabama Governors Papers, ADAH. Henry Key Milner, "Scrapbook of Mardi Gras Balls," Birmingham Public Library Archives, Birmingham, AL. "Establishment violence" refers to the use of state troops, police, and other arms of government to safeguard forcibly the political and economic status quo. See Robert P. Ingalls, "Antiradical Violence in Birmingham during the 1930s," *Journal of Southern History* 47 (November 1981): 521–44 and H. Jon Rosenbaum and Peter C. Sederberg, "Vigilantism: An Analysis of Establishment Violence," in *Vigilante Politics*, ed. Rosenbaum and Sederberg (Philadelphia: University of Pennsylvania Press, 1976), 3–6.

66. *Acts of Alabama*, Act 108, 15 February 1919, pp. 95–96, Act 172, 18 February 1919, pp. x–xi, 166–67, Act 257, 29 August 1919, pp. 241–42, Acts 57 and 58, 11 February 1919, p. 30, Act 361, 19 September 1919, pp. 469–77, and Act 551, pp. 15, 808–9, Act 733, p. 1084, and Act 413, p. 30, all in 30 September 1919; see also Act 545.

67. Organized labor was especially disparaged in the South as a haven for criminals, anarchists, socialists, the irresponsible, the unpatriotic, and the un-southern. See, e.g., L. F. Thompson, Citizens Alliance, to Oscar W. Underwood, 15 and 26 March 1904, box 4, folder 6, Underwood Papers.

68. Glenn Feldman, *Politics, Society, and the Klan in Alabama, 1915–1949* (Tuscaloosa: The University of Alabama Press, 1999), 16–17, 20, 326. More generally on the Klan, see Rory McVeigh, *The Rise of the Ku Klux Klan: Right Wing Movements and National Politics* (Minneapolis: University of Minnesota Press, 2009).

69. The word "backward" here is used with some irony although in no way as a denial that the region, indeed, trailed the rest of the nation on a number of important points. The irony is that the South actually pioneered, or led, the nation in this regard—but in the same way that a lapped race car that is so far behind the pack "leads" a race.

70. Virginia Durr, interview by John Egerton, 6 February 1991, Southern Oral History Project: 34007, A-337, SHC. Hugo Black married Durr's sister, making them in-laws. For a view that dissents from received wisdom as to the extent that the KKK backed 1920s Alabama politicos such as Hugo Black, see Samuel L. Webb, "Hugo Black, Bibb Graves, and the Ku Klux Klan: A Revisionist View of the 1926 Alabama Democratic Primary," *Alabama Review* 57 (October 2004): 243–73.

Chapter 4

1. For statements on race's centrality from different perspectives, see U. B. Phillips, "The Central Theme of Southern History," *American Historical Review* 34 (October 1928): 30–43; V. O. Key Jr., *Southern Politics in State and Nation* (New York: Alfred A. Knopf, 1949; reprint: Knoxville: University of Tennessee Press, 1984); Carl N. Degler, "Racism in the United States: An Essay Review," *Journal of Southern History* 38 (February 1972): 102; and Joel Williamson, *The Crucible of Race: Black/White Relations in the American South since Emancipation* (New York: Oxford University Press, 1984).

2. *Alabama KKK Newsletter*, January 1929, p. 2, box 26, folder: Baptist and Catholic Intolerance, Religion, Oliver Day Street Papers, ADAH (hereafter Street Papers, ADAH). See Declaration in KKK-Prattville File, Boone Aiken Papers, Auburn, AL, BA; Proceedings of the Meeting Held at Municipal Auditorium, Birmingham, Alabama, 3 January 1929, pp. 27 and 48 (Heflin quotations), box 19, folder 3, State Democratic Executive Committee Records, ADAH (hereafter SDEC Records).

3. Race evoked the most primal emotions. See, e.g., the KKK pamphlet, KKK-Prattville File, BA. See also G. G. Guest to Oliver Day Street, 16 July 1928, and J. O. Hayes to Oliver Day Street, 25 June 1928, both in box 1277, folder 59, and R. J. Guest to O. D. Street, 12 November 1928, box 1277, folder 60, all three in Street Papers, UA.

4. William Robert Snell, "The Ku Klux Klan in Jefferson County, 1915–1930" (M.A. thesis, Samford University, 1967), 85–86; Newton and Newton, *Ku Klux Klan*, 525.

5. Eric Rauchway, "White Fright," *New Republic*, http://www.tnr.com/, 15 November 2007 (quotations) (accessed February 2012). See also Peter C. Murray, *Methodists and the Crucible of Race, 1930–1975* (Columbia: University of Missouri Press, 2004).

6. Snell, "Ku Klux Klan in Jefferson County," 85–86; Newton and Newton, *Ku Klux Klan*, 525.

7. *Alabama KKK Newsletter*, April 1928, p. 2, June 1928, p. 1, July 1928, p. 1, and January 1929, p. 4.

8. KKK Scrapbooks, #257, Birmingham Public Library Archives, Birmingham, AL; KKK File, reel 31, 1928, TU; *Montgomery Advertiser*, 22 January 1928; "The Klan Goes in for a 'Face-Lifting,'" *Literary Digest* 96 (10 March 1928): 16.

9. KKK File, reel 28, 1927, reel 31, 1928, TU; *Montgomery Advertiser*, 18 August 1927, 26 January 1928.

10. Neal R. Peirce, *The Deep South States of America: People, Power, and Politics in the Seven Deep South States* (New York: W. W. Norton, 1974), 303; *Montgomery Advertiser*, 18 August 1927 (quotations). For more on Heflin's ability to mesmerize rural audiences, see Paul Maxwell Smith, "Loyalists and States' Righters in the Democratic Party of Alabama, 1949–1954" (M.A. thesis, Auburn University, 1966). See also Mark Schultz, *The Rural Face of White Supremacy: Beyond Jim Crow* (Urbana: University of Illinois Press, 2005).

11. O'Connor to W. B. Bankhead, 13 September 1928, box 5, folder 13 and the pamphlet "Alabama Democracy, 1930: United Democracy and Party Harmony vs. Heflin Republicanism and Party Disruption," p. 21, box 3, folder 10, both in the John H. Bankhead II Papers, ADAH (hereafter Bankhead II Papers); Rogers et al., *Alabama*, 438; "Al Smith," *Kourier Magazine* 3 (June 1927): 12–13.

12. See the flyer "Call for Conference of Anti-Smith Democrats," J. F. Hines Papers, Samford University, Special Collections Library, Homewood, AL (hereafter Hines Pa-

pers); *Birmingham Age-Herald,* 22 July and 14 August 1928; *Birmingham News,* 14 August 1928; Rogers et al., *Alabama,* 438.

13. Ibid. Samuel Dawson aided Locke and Wilkinson, working closely with Alabama Republican boss Oliver Day Street. See Oliver D. Street to Walter H. Newton, 3 April and 8 May 1929, Oliver D. Street to Horace C. Wilkinson, 29 March 1929, Horace C. Wilkinson to Oliver D. Street, 10 April 1929, and Samuel Dawson to Oliver D. Street, 20 April 1929, all in box 300, folder: Alabama, "S," Republican National Committee Papers, Herbert Hoover Presidential Library, Iowa City, Iowa (hereafter HHPL).

14. *Birmingham Age-Herald* and the *Birmingham News,* both 14 August 1928.

15. Ibid. See also Gould Beech, interview by John Egerton, 9 August 1990, p. 6, Magnolia Springs, Alabama, Southern Oral History Project (UNC): 4007, A-342, SHC.

16. Hugh Gladney Grant Diary, p. 1, Hugh Gladney Grant Papers, Duke University; the flyer "Headquarters: Hoover-Curtis Campaign, Agricultural Group," Hines Papers; *Montgomery Advertiser,* 8 November 1928; Rogers et al., *Alabama,* 439; Newton and Newton, *Ku Klux Klan,* 52; J. Mills Thornton III, "Alabama Politics, J. Thomas Heflin, and the Expulsion Movement of 1929," *Alabama Review* 21 (April 1968): 100.

17. Marie Bankhead Owen to J. H. Bankhead II, 30 June 1927, box 1, folder 7, Bankhead II Papers; box 26, folder: Intolerance, Street Papers, ADAH; *Alabama KKK Newsletter,* July 1928, p. 3; *Birmingham News* and *Birmingham Age-Herald,* 4 November 1928; Ralph M. Tanner, "The Wonderful World of Tom Heflin," *Alabama Review* 36 (July 1983): 163–66; Arnold S. Rice, *The Ku Klux Klan in American Politics* (Washington, DC: Public Affairs Press, 1962), 89–90; Rogers et al., *Alabama,* 439; Chalmers, *Hooded Americanism,* 305.

18. Tindall, *Emergence of the New South,* 188–89; Paul M. Pruitt Jr., "The Killing of Father Coyle: Private Tragedy, Public Shame," *Alabama Heritage* 30 (Fall 1993): 24–37; Seymour Martin Lipset and Earl K. Raab, *The Politics of Unreason: Right-Wing Extremism in America, 1790–1970* (New York: Harper and Row, 1970); Richard M. Hofstadter, *The Paranoid Style in American Politics and Other Essays* (New York: Alfred A. Knopf, 1965); Wayne Flynt, *Cracker Messiah: Governor Sidney J. Catts of Florida* (Baton Rouge: Louisiana State University Press, 1977).

19. *Alabama KKK Newsletter,* July 1928, pp. 1, 4.

20. *Alabama KKK Newsletter,* October 1928, p. 3.

21. *Congressional Record* extracts, Senate, 18 February 1927, 20 January, 13 April 1928, J. Thomas Heflin Scrapbooks, MFS-652, Samford University, Special Collections Library, Homewood, AL (hereafter Heflin Scrapbooks).

22. *Congressional Record* extract, Senate, 18 January 1928, Heflin Scrapbooks, MFS-652; Hugh Gladney Grant Diary, pp. 1, 71.

23. *Alabama KKK Newsletter,* March 1927, pp. 2, 4, April 1928, p. 3, June 1928, p. 3, July 1928, and the leaflet "Read, Think, and Act," ca. 1928, by a "Christian Patriot," all in box 26, folder: Intolerance, Street Papers, ADAH; Cannack to J. Thomas Heflin, 23 February 1927, McKinney to J. Thomas Heflin, 7 February 1927, Johnson to J. Thomas Heflin, 30 January 1927, Weldon to J. Thomas Heflin, 28 February 1927, all in Heflin Scrapbooks; "Al Smith," *Kourier Magazine* 3 (June 1927): 12–14, and J.A.J., "Roman Treason against Our Homes," *Kourier Magazine* 3 (April 1927): 21.

24. *Birmingham Age-Herald,* 10 May and 5 September 1928.

25. Hugh Gladney Grant Diary, p. 1; *Alabama KKK Newsletter,* June 1928, p. 4.

26. Robert K. Murray, *Red Scare: A Study of National Hysteria, 1919–1920* (New

York: McGraw-Hill, 1964); John Higham, *Strangers in the Land: Patterns of American Nativism, 1860–1925* (New York: Atheneum, 1974); David M. Kennedy, *Over Here: The First World War and American Society* (New York: Oxford University Press, 1980), 31, 53, 146; Merle Curtie, *The Roots of American Loyalty* (New York: Atheneum, 1968), 224–25; Ellis W. Hawley, *The Great War and the Search for a Modern Order: A History of the American People and Their Institutions, 1917–1933* (New York: St. Martin's Press, 1979), 29, 50.

27. *Alabama KKK Newsletter*, April 1928, p. 3, July 1928, p. 3, September 1928; Frank Joseph Fede, *Italians of the Deep South: Their Impact on Birmingham and America's Heritage* (Montgomery: Black Belt Press, 1994); Glenn Feldman, *From Demagogue to Dixiecrat: Horace Wilkinson and the Politics of Race* (Lanham, MD: University Press of America, 1995), 35, 60, 81.

28. *Birmingham Age-Herald*, 11–12 September 1928; *Birmingham News*, 11–12 September, 4 November 1928.

29. *New York Times*, 11 July 1927.

30. "Let Us Keep the Issues Straight," *Alabama Christian Advocate*, box 5, folder 13, William Brockman Bankhead Personal Papers, ADAH; Alabama Women's League for White Supremacy clipping in box 210, folder: Birmingham City Commission, Alabama Governors Papers, Benjamin Meek Miller Papers, ADAH (hereafter Miller Papers); *Alabama KKK Newsletter*, September 1928, pp. 1, 4, November 1928; *Montgomery Advertiser*, 18 November 1927; *Birmingham News* and the *Birmingham Age-Herald*, 8 and 10 October 1928; Rogers et al., *Alabama*, 440; Rice, *Ku Klux Klan in American Politics*, 91; Albion Will Hixon, Uniontown, Alabama, to SDEC, 6 December 1927, box 19, folder 4, SDEC Records.

31. George H. Malone was the patriarch of a prominent Dothan banking family that would play a leading role in Alabama politics for decades. The Malones would bankroll conservative Democrats and the Dixiecrat revolt of 1948 and beyond before turning to the modern GOP. Wallace Malone Sr. and Jr. would be instrumental in these efforts. See G. H. Malone to Oliver D. Street, 11 April 1929, Oliver D. Street to Walter H. Newton, 20 April 1929, and *Montgomery Advertiser*, 21 April 1929 clipping attached to Oliver D. Street to Walter H. Newton, 23 April 1929. On Zue Musgrove Long, sister of Col. L. B. Musgrove, see Joe A. Thompson to Col. Horace A. Mann, 5 April 1929, all in box 300, folder: Alabama, "S," Republican National Committee Papers, HHPL. See also "A Resolution Adopted by Conference of Anti-Smith Democrats," 13 August 1928, Hines Papers; box 26, folder: Intolerance, Street Papers, ADAH; *Alabama KKK Newsletter*, January 1929, p. 3; *Birmingham News* and the *Birmingham Age-Herald*, 22 and 31 August, 14 September 1928; Rogers et al., *Alabama*, 438.

32. O. D. Street to Marshall, 10 October 1928, Ransom to O. D. Street, 20 September 1928, *Chicago Tribune* clipping 2 October 1928, and the circular "Governor Smith's Membership in the Roman Catholic Church and Its Proper Place as an Issue in This Campaign," all in box 26, folder: Intolerance, Street Papers, ADAH. See also Paschal G. (P. G.) Shook to Lewis L. Strauss, 25 September 1928, box: Campaign of 1928—Contributions & Finance, folder: Alabama, Lewis L. Strauss Papers, HHPL.

33. *New York Times*, 8 July 1928, p. 2; *Birmingham Age-Herald* and the *Birmingham News*, 8 July 1928; Snell, "Ku Klux Klan in Jefferson County," 76–77, 131; Rice, *Ku Klux Klan in American Politics*, 87.

34. *Birmingham News*, 14–15 August 1928.

35. *Birmingham Age-Herald* and the *Birmingham News*, both 14–15 August 1928.

36. KKK File, reel 31, 1928, TU; *Montgomery Advertiser,* 19 August 1927, 10 April 1928; Thornton, "Alabama Politics," 97; Rogers et al., *Alabama,* 439–41.

37. Roberts to J. Thomas Heflin, 21 January 1928, box 820, folder 57, Papers of J. Thomas Heflin, UA (hereafter Heflin Papers); Feldman, *From Demagogue to Dixiecrat,* 94; Hendon to editor, *Birmingham Age-Herald,* 20 January 1928, in *Birmingham Age-Herald,* 23 January 1928; *Birmingham News* and *Birmingham Age-Herald,* 9 May, 8 September 1928; Newton and Newton, *Ku Klux Klan,* 262–63, 376, 485; Rogers et al., *Alabama,* 439–41. For a view that dissents from received wisdom as to the extent that the KKK backed 1920s Alabama politicos, see Webb, "Hugo Black, Bibb Graves, and the Ku Klux Klan."

38. Parker to editor, *Birmingham News* in *Birmingham News* and the *Birmingham Age-Herald,* 2 September 1928.

39. The broadside, "Al Smith, the Negro Lover," box 19, folder 4 and box 106, folder: Anti-Smith Broadsides, both in SDEC Records; "A Resolution Adopted by Conference of Anti-Smith Democrats," 13 August 1928, Hines Papers; *Birmingham Age-Herald,* 4 September 1928; Hugh D. Reagen, "Race as a Factor in the Presidential Election of 1928 in Alabama," *Alabama Review* 19 (January 1966): 5–19.

40. *Congressional Record* extracts, 20 January, 7 February, 13 April, and 26 May 1928, Heflin Scrapbooks, MFS-652; "A Resolution Adopted by Conference of Anti-Smith Democrats," 13 August 1928, Hines Papers; *Birmingham Age-Herald* and *Birmingham News* clippings, 4 November 1928, in box 26, folder: Intolerance, Street Papers, ADAH; *Montgomery Advertiser,* 17 August 1928.

41. Adam to J. Thomas Heflin, 26 January 1928, box 820, folder 55, Heflin Papers; *Alabama KKK Newsletter,* April 1928, p. 3, October 1928, and Hassell to editor, *New York Observer,* 14 July 1928, all in box 26, folder: Intolerance, Street Papers, ADAH; "Al Smith," *Kourier Magazine* 3 (June 1927); 13–14; Thornton, "Alabama Politics," 101; Virginia Van der Veer Hamilton, *Hugo Black: The Alabama Years* (Baton Rouge: Louisiana State University Press, 1972), 245.

42. *Alabama KKK Newsletter,* September 1928.

43. KKK File, reel 31, 1928, TU; *Montgomery Advertiser,* 4 September 1928; Reagen, "Race as a Factor," 6.

44. George A. Akerson to O. D. Street, 15 April 1928, and O. D. Street to George A. Akerson, 21 April 1928, folder: C & T, Campaign and Transition, George A. Akerson Papers, HHPL; *Birmingham News,* 11 September 1928 (quotation).

45. *Birmingham Age-Herald,* 7 September and 8 October 1928; *Birmingham News,* 7 September, 8 October, and 5 November 1928; Reagen, "Race as a Factor," 6–7, 12–17.

46. *Birmingham Age-Herald,* 7 September and 8 October 1928; *Birmingham News,* 7 September, 8 October, and 5 November 1928; Reagen, "Race as a Factor," 6–7, 12–17.

47. "Senator J. Thomas Heflin on Present Political Issues," 1928 broadside of excerpts from the *Congressional Record* (first quotation) and Publicity Bureau, Alabama Democratic Campaign Committee, "The Republican Party & Herbert Hoover . . . 'The Negro,'" 1928 broadside (second quotation), both in oversized box 47, folder 10: Broadsides, Flyers, and Circulars, W. B. Bankhead Papers, ADAH.

48. *Birmingham Age-Herald* and *Birmingham News,* 2 September 1928; Reagen, "Race as a Factor," 6–7, 12–17. The infamous "force bill," calling for federal supervision of southern elections, was associated with Republican senator Henry Cabot Lodge of Massachusetts.

49. Pamphlet by R. B. Evins, "White Supremacy Endangered: The South Must Continue Democratic to Avoid Legislation to Enforce the Fifteenth Amendment" (Birmingham: Jefferson County Campaign Committee, 1928), Auburn University, Department of Special Collections, Auburn, AL; *Birmingham Age-Herald* and *Birmingham News*, 2–3 September 1928.

50. George Huddleston to Hamill, 4 October 1928, box 210, folder: Birmingham City Commission, Miller Papers; *Birmingham News* and *Birmingham Age-Herald*, 3 September 1928; Rogers et al., *Alabama*, 440.

51. *Birmingham News*, 4 and 6 November 1928 (first quotation); *Birmingham Age-Herald*, 16 November 1928; *Birmingham News* clipping transcript, 11 October 1928 (second quotation), attached to Mabel Jones West to Frank Dixon, 24 August 1942, box SG 12277, folder 29, Alabama Governors Papers, Frank M. Dixon Papers, ADAH (hereafter Dixon Papers).

52. Marie Bankhead Owen, "Hoover's Religion" broadside, 23 October 1928, and "Anonymous" to Cole Blease, ca. 1928 (quoted), both in box 5, folder 14, W. B. Bankhead Papers. On Brauer, see *Birmingham News* clipping transcript, 11 October 1928, attached to Mabel Jones West to Frank Dixon, 24 August 1942, box SG 12277, folder 29, Dixon Papers.

53. *Birmingham News*, 5–6 November 1928. Over the course of his long career, Bilbo served as both governor of and senator from Mississippi.

54. *Alabama Official and Statistical Register, 1931*, 511–12; KKK File, reel 36, 1930, TU; *Montgomery Advertiser*, 6 January 1930; *Birmingham News*, 14 September, 5, 7–8, and 10 November 1928; *Birmingham Age-Herald*, 14 September, 17 November 1928; *New York Times*, 12 August 1928, p. 12; Rogers et al., *Alabama*, 441; Rice, *Ku Klux Klan in American Politics*, 91; Thornton, "Alabama Politics," 101. The Black Belt had a long history of manipulating the black vote by force and fraud; see McMillan, *Constitutional Development in Alabama*.

55. *Birmingham News*, 7 November 1928. Paschal G. Shook, chairman of the Alabama Republican Finance Committee, was delighted in the signal "achievement to break the solid South, especially in view of the fact that the negro question, which has held it solid for many years, was pushed to the front." See P. G. Shook to Edwin C. Halter, 12 November 1928, box: Campaign of 1928—Contributions & Finance, folder: Alabama, Strauss Papers, HHPL.

56. Feldman, *Politics, Society, and the Klan in Alabama*, chapters 9 and 10, and Feldman, *From Demagogue to Dixiecrat*, 87–98. For example, the Reverend Bob Jones Sr., a Baptist minister, spoke throughout Alabama on behalf of Klan-backed political candidates and to Klan dens during the 1920s. Jones's speeches were often laced with nativism, jingoism, and anti-Catholicism. After the rise of the conservative Religious Right in the 1980s, the university he founded in Tennessee and then South Carolina—Bob Jones University—became a pilgrimage site for aspiring Republican presidential candidates. During the 2000 presidential campaign, the background of the university's founder, along with the more recent racial and sexual-orientation policies of the school, became a national issue. See Feldman, *Politics, Society, and the Klan in Alabama*, 38, 40, 65–66, 131, 170, 175, 182; *Mobile Register*, 25 February 2000; *Washington Post*, 18 February 2000; *Huntsville (AL) Times*, 16 February 2000; Rives Moore, The Interfaith Alliance, News Release, 18 February 2000; Libby Quaid, "Democrats Swipe at Ashcroft over Bob Jones Visit," Associated Press, 22 February 2000; Robert A. George, "Bush's Missed Opportu-

nity," Salon.com, 22 February 2000; John Leo, "The Company He Keeps," *U.S. News & World Report*, 6 March 2000; Janelle Carter, "Democrats in Congress Seek Condemnation of Bob Jones U.," Associated Press, 29 February 2000; Reg Henry, "Watch Out for a School Named Bob," *Pittsburgh Post-Gazette*, 14 March 2000; Jay Reeves, "Book Links Founder of Bob Jones U. with Alabama Klan," Associated Press, 18 March 2000; Libby Quaid, "Democrats Seizing on Bob Jones Issue," Associated Press, 14 April 2000; and Juliet Eilperin and Hanna Rosin, "Bob Jones: A Magnet School for Controversy," *Washington Post*, 25 February 2000.

57. Yet Hanson also recognized the long-term importance of the project. "The treatment must be a sparing administration gradually applied. . . . [W]e must not excite too many of their prejudices at once," he cautioned one of his more gifted Bourbon editors, "but must work at it very slowly and tactfully, violating as little as possible their sacred taboos." Victor Hanson to Grover C. Hall, 12 August 1927, box 67, folder 1, Grover C. Hall Papers, ADAH (first quotation) (hereafter Hall Papers). Charles Fell editorials in the *Birmingham Age-Herald*, 14–15 August 1928 (second quotation). Another considerable impediment to the South "going Republican" anytime soon was that in places like Alabama, the GOP was riven by considerable division, internal dissension, and petty political bickering. In Alabama most of this revolved around patronage issues and leadership disputes between national GOP committeeman and patronage referee Oliver Day Street and former national committeeman Joseph A. Thompson of Thompson Plantations in Roba, Alabama. See, e.g., the welter of correspondence in the Herbert Hoover Presidential Library pertaining to the Alabama GOP plagued by factionalism: Baughn to *Mobile Register*, press telegram, ca. 1929, Robert R. Pollack, Cullman, Alabama, to Herbert Hoover, 27 March 1929, C. P. Lunsford to Walter H. Newton, 6 April 1929, Walter H. Newton to C. P. Lunsford, 16 April 1929, Joseph O. Thompson to Herbert Hoover, 8 April 1929, Joe A. Thompson to Col. Horace Mann, 5 April 1929, S. L. Studdard to Walter H. Newton, 3 and 20 May 1929, Oliver Day Street to Walter H. Newton, 8 May 1929, all in the Republican National Committee Papers, box 300: Alabama, folder "S," HHPL.

Chapter 5

1. Forney Johnston, Alabama senator Oscar W. Underwood's chief lieutenant, placed the senator's name into nomination for president with a sensational attack on the hooded order and the proposition of an official party plank against the KKK. The Alabama delegation, dominated by a Big Mule/Black Belt alliance of wealthy industrialists, bankers, and planters, favored adoption of the plank because although they sympathized with the order's racist philosophy, they also saw the Klan as a populist political threat that had to be squelched. On this subject, see Feldman, *Politics, Society, and the Klan in Alabama*.

2. Tindall, *Emergence of the New South*, 544.

3. Ickes himself had served as president of the Chicago chapter of the NAACP. Quotations in ibid., 557 (first), 556 (second and fourth), 555 (third), 543 (fifth).

4. For more on this subject, see Anthony J. Badger's excellent work, *The New Deal: The Depression Years, 1933–1940* (New York: Farrar, Strauss, and Giroux, 1989).

5. George R. Leighton, "Birmingham, Alabama: The City of Perpetual Promise," *Harper's Magazine* 175 (August 1937): 239; Rogers et al., *Alabama*, 476, 481; Feldman, *From Demagogue to Dixiecrat*, 104; Feldman, *Politics, Society, and the Klan in Alabama*, 219.

6. Ottia Missie Sutton to B. M. Miller, 28 November 1934, Lucille Cherry to B. M. Miller, 9 September 1934 (first quotation), Pauline C. Houston to B. M. Miller, 8 December 1934 (second quotation), Luther Hicks to B. M. Miller, 7 June 1934 (third quotation), Earl Watson to B. M. Miller, 7 June 1934, W. J. Pruit to B. M. Miller, n.d., Ed Frisco to B. M. Miller, 10 June 1934, J. J. Henderson to B. M. Miller, 6 July 1934 (fourth quotation), and [No first name] Coopta to B. M. Miller, 16 June 1934, all correspondence in box SG 19954, folder 9: Alabama Relief Adm. Letters, Miller Papers.

7. Rogers et al., *Alabama*, 467 (first quotation); no name to B. M. Miller, 5 October 1934 (second quotation), box SG 19954, folder 9: Alabama Relief Adm. Letters, Miller Papers; Lorena Hickok to Harry L. Hopkins, 2 April 1934 (third quotation), Lorena Hickok Papers, FDR Presidential Library, Hyde Park, New York (hereafter FDR), quoted in Rogers et al., *Alabama*, 468.

8. George Brown Tindall, *The Disruption of the Solid South* (Athens: University of Georgia Press, 1972), 28; Tindall, *Emergence of the New South*, 607, 618 (quotation). Public opinion polls revealed strong support until the end of the 1930s. Tindall's estimation of the futility of opposing FDR applied to the first part of the decade.

9. The list of southern Senate majority leaders and House Speakers was extensive: Sam Rayburn of Texas, Joseph T. Robinson of Arkansas, James F. Byrnes of South Carolina, Alben W. Barkley of Kentucky, Pat Harrison of Mississippi, and William B. Bankhead of Alabama. Brother John Bankhead II, along with Hugo Black and Lister Hill, served as strong advocates of Roosevelt and the New Deal in the U.S. Senate. Alabamians George Huddleston, Luther Patrick, and Joseph Starnes toed the line with Will Bankhead in the House. Virginia Van der Veer Hamilton, *Lister Hill: Statesman from the South* (Chapel Hill: University of North Carolina Press, 1987), 72–73; Martha H. Swain, *Pat Harrison: The New Deal Years* (Jackson: University Press of Mississippi, 1978); Tindall, *Emergence of the New South*, 609–11.

10. Hamilton, *Lister Hill*, 72–73. The Alabama Power Company, citing the TVA as an unfair form of federal intrusion into the free market, kept the Wilson Dam (near Muscle Shoals) in court for five years before a settlement was reached. See Rogers et al., *Alabama*, 471, 486. See also Harvey H. Jackson III, *Rivers of History: Life on the Coosa, Tallapoosa, Cahaba, and Alabama* (Tuscaloosa: The University of Alabama Press, 1995) and Jackson, *Putting "Loafing Streams" to Work: The Building of Lay, Mitchell, Martin, and Jordan Dams* (Tuscaloosa: The University of Alabama Press, 1997). See also Leah Rawls Atkins, *Developed for the Service of Alabama: The Centennial History of the Alabama Power Company, 1906–2006* (Birmingham: Alabama Power Company, 2006).

11. Graves refused to use the state militia this way in a series of strikes during the 1930s in the coal and textile industries. See Brown and Davis, *It Is Union and Liberty*. Graves played, in the words of a leading Alabama historian, "as large a role in Montgomery as Roosevelt did in Washington" to help create a strong labor movement in the state. Wayne Flynt quoted in Rogers et al., *Alabama*, 500.

12. Sidney J. Smyer to James L. Hare, 23 and 26 October 1936, box 2981, folder 1A, James L. Hare Papers, UA. On Miller and industrialist calls to use the state militia, see Scott Roberts to B. M. Miller, 7, 10, and 12 September 1934, B. M. Miller to Scott Roberts, 7 and 11 September 1934, H. D. Agnew to B. M. Miller, George Lanier to B. M. Miller, and H. V. Carter and John Denson to B. M. Miller, all 6 September 1934, John Peach to H. D. Agnew, 25 August 1934, H. D. Agnew to Donald Comer, 5 September

1934, all in box SG 19956, folder 6: 1934 Strike Situation, Miller Papers; *Alabama: News Magazine of the Deep South*, 24 July 1939, p. 15 (hereafter *Alabama Magazine*); James L. Sledge III, "The Alabama Republican Party, 1865–1978" (Ph.D. diss., Auburn University, 1998), 122–23. Upon election, Frank Dixon promptly abolished the state Department of Labor and used the National Guard to break a strike. See Rogers et al., *Alabama*, 497, 498 (quotation), 499, and 501.

13. Feldman, *From Demagogue to Dixiecrat*, 99–120.

14. Wilkinson served as Bibb Graves's campaign manager in his successful 1934 bid for governor. Klan remnants could be found among the planter-industrialist clique, too, in the 1930s. James Marion "Jimmie" Jones had gained election to the city commission during the 1920s as a Horace Wilkinson product who belonged to, and was supported by, the KKK. Feldman, *From Demagogue to Dixiecrat*, 103, 106, 109 (first quotation). *(Birmingham) Alabama Herald*, 2 April and 17 December 1935 (second and third quotations) and 23 June 1934, 12 February, and 30 July 1935 (set of fourth quotations); Preston H. Haskell to James Simpson, 11 May 1935 and Garrison to Simpson and Mills to Simpson, both 10 May 1935, all in the James A. Simpson Papers, ADAH. The anti–civil service side ran ads such as one that appeared in the *Birmingham News* on 6 May 1935 urging voters against "Negroizing, Hansonizing, and Simpsonizing" Birmingham through the "despicable civil service bill." Victor Hanson, publisher of the *Birmingham News* and a charter member of the planter-industrialist clique, was also an opponent of Wilkinson's machine. See also Leah Rawls Atkins, "Senator James A. Simpson and Birmingham Politics of the 1930s: His Fight against the Spoilsmen and the Pie-Men," *Alabama Review* 41 (January 1988): 3–29. Hubert Baughn fought vigorously for the merit system from the pages of *Alabama Magazine*. See, e.g., 9 and 23 August 1937, both p. 16, 16 August 1937, p. 20, 17 January, 7 February, and 11 April 1938, all p. 15, 28 March 1938, p. 3, and 1 July 1940, p. 14. Barney Weeks, interview with Robert J. Norrell, 21 February 1989, pp. 33–35, CLEAR, outlines the close relationship between Bull Connor and U.S. Steel, with corporation attorney Jim Simpson serving as the liaison between the two in terms of keeping Alabama's working class divided along the lines of race.

15. Section 7(a) of the National Industrial Recovery Act (NIRA) of 1933 recognized the right to organize and engage in collective bargaining and established a minimum wage and maximum hours. Although the NIRA was struck down in May 1935 in *Schechter v. U.S.*, 295 U.S. 495 (1935), its first provisions were codified in the National Labor Relations Act (1935), also known for its sponsor as the Wagner Act, and its wage and hour provisions in the 1938 Fair Labor Standards Act, sponsored in part by Alabama senator Hugo Black. The Walsh-Healey Act of 1936 set a forty-hour work week and prevailing wages, and outlawed child labor. See Tindall, *Emergence of the New South*, 505–39. See also Wayne Flynt, "The New Deal and Southern Labor," in *The New Deal and the South*, ed. James C. Cobb and Michael V. Namorato (Jackson: University Press of Mississippi, 1984), 63–96.

16. For more, see, e.g., Eula Mae McGill, interview by the author, 12 March 1997, CLEAR.

17. Herbert R. Northrup, *Organized Labor and the Negro* (New York: Harper and Brothers, 1944), 3–5, 18–19; Tindall, *Emergence of the New South*, 571–72. On the AFL, see Nell Irvin Painter, *The Narrative of Hosea Hudson: His Life and Times as a Negro Communist in the South* (Cambridge, MA: Harvard University Press, 1979), 184.

18. In Alabama, for example, the percentage of African Americans who made up the new industrial unions was very high: steelworkers, 41 percent; ore miners, 56 percent; and coal miners, 63 percent. Rogers et al., *Alabama*, 503.

19. Walter Galenson, *The CIO Challenge to the AFL: A History of the American Labor Movement, 1935–1941* (Cambridge, MA: Harvard University Press, 1960), 341 (Franz Daniel quoted); Robert H. Zieger, *The CIO, 1935–1955* (Chapel Hill: University of North Carolina Press, 1995). On the resentment associated with the NRA codes, see Northrup, *Organized Labor and the Negro*, 175. New Deal–era black sociologist Ralph J. Bunche recognized the distracting role race played for the southern white voter: accounts by politicians of "black brutes raping white women presented to . . . breathless audiences" were "masterpieces of emotional appeal and sure vote-getters—especially when the price of cotton is down." Bunche, *The Political Status of the Negro in the Age of FDR*, ed. Dewey W. Grantham (Chicago: University of Chicago Press, 1973), 33. Bunche was, perhaps, a bit sanguine in imagining that emotional appeals were losing their resonance in the early 1970s. He did not realize the extent of the power of coded racial appeals or of a *new racism* that would tap other *politics of emotion* issues to augment race. Bunche estimated that race was losing its appeal to the "Southern mentality" in the early 1970s: "There are many in the South today, however, who have grown wary of the Negro diversion. The South is slowly awakening to the fact that it has many problems that are immediately more pressing than its black one" (32). See also Robert H. Woodrum, *Everybody Was Black Down There: Race and Industrial Change in the Alabama Coalfields* (Athens: University of Georgia Press, 2007).

20. See Brown and Davis, *It Is Union and Liberty*. See also Kelly, *Race, Class, and Power in the Alabama Coalfield* and Letwin, *The Challenge of Interracial Unionism*.

21. Painter, *Hosea Hudson*, 329. See also Robert J. Norrell, "Caste in Steel: Jim Crow Careers in Birmingham, Alabama," *Journal of American History* 73 (December 1986): 669–94, esp. 675–79. The Steelworkers Organizing Committee (SWOC) knew that job seniority preserved racial inequality at TCI but, according to SWOC organizer Albert C. Buttram, felt the union had to agree to it in order to retain the support of the mill's white workforce. Howard Strevel, a Tennessee transplant with racially egalitarian beliefs, admitted that the job seniority system was a "bad system" but remembered that "our people liked it because nobody could roll them" from a white job. It kept the white steelworker "as safe as he was in his mother's arms" (677). The CIO took over the ailing Amalgamated Association of Iron, Steel, and Tin Workers in June 1936 to create the SWOC, chaired by UMW vice president Philip Murray, former NRA director Noel R. Beddow as regional director, and the UMW's William Mitch in charge of the South. SWOC achieved successes at U.S. Steel in 1937 and at Woodward Iron, Sloss-Sheffield, TCI, Ingalls Iron, and other companies, amounting to 5,700 SWOC members in Alabama by 1940. See Marshall, *Labor in the South*, 185–88.

This topic is the recipient of much historiographical controversy. A contrary position to Norrell's has been enunciated in its most unrepressed form by Judith Stein in "Southern Workers in National Unions: Birmingham Steelworkers, 1936–1951," in *Organized Labor in the Twentieth-Century South*, ed. Robert H. Zieger (Knoxville: University of Tennessee Press, 1991), 183–222, and *Running Steel, Running America: Race, Economic Policy, and the Decline of Liberalism* (Chapel Hill: University of North Carolina Press, 1998), and other articles and reviews. See also the "New Southern Labor History" as enunciated by Robert Korstad and Nelson Lichtenstein in "Opportunities Found and Lost: Labor, Radicals, and the Early Civil Rights Movement," *Journal of American History* 75 (September 1988): 786–811; Eric Arnesen, "'Like Banquo's Ghost, It Will Not Down': The Race Question and the American Railroad Brotherhoods, 1880–1920," *American Historical Review* 99 (December 1994): 1601–33; and Arnesen, "Up from Exclusion: Black and White Workers, Race, and the State of Labor History," *Reviews in American History* 26 (March 1998): 146–74. While these studies do make a good point about the importance of class considerations in southern labor history, overall the Norrell position is more persuasive and has found substantial support in the work of McKiven, *Iron and Steel*; Alan Draper, *Conflict of Interests: Organized Labor and the Civil Rights Movement in the South, 1954–1968* (Ithaca, NY: ILR Press at Cornell University, 1994); Bruce Nelson, *Divided We Stand: American Workers and the Struggle for Black Equality* (Princeton: Princeton University Press, 2001); J. Mills Thornton III, *Divided Lines: Municipal Politics and the Struggle for Civil Rights in Montgomery, Birmingham, and Selma* (Tuscaloosa: The University of Alabama Press, 2002), 625n9; Paul D. Moreno, *Black Americans and Organized Labor: A New History* (Baton Rouge: Louisiana State University Press, 2006), and fiery support from Herbert Hill in "Myth-Making as Labor History: Herbert Gutman and the United Mine Workers of America," *International Journal of Politics, Culture, and Society* 2 (Winter 1988): 132–200 and in Hill's review of Judith Stein's work, "Race and the Steelworkers Union: White Privilege and Black Struggle; A Review Essay of Judith Stein's *Running Steel, Running America*," *New Politics* 8, n.s. (Winter 2002): 1–58.

22. Feldman, *From Demagogue to Dixiecrat*, 115.

23. Perry Thompson, interview by Hardy T. Frye, pp. 1, 16 (quoted), Interview #48 in the Hardy T. Frye Oral History Collection, AU.

24. Howard Strevel quoted in E. B. Rich and Howard Strevel, interview by Edwin L. Brown, Glenn Cole, and Ralph A. Johnson, 9 June 1988, p. 1(quotation), 3, 4, CLEAR.

25. Flynt, "The New Deal and Southern Labor," 63–96; Feldman, *From Demagogue to Dixiecrat*, 121; Rogers et al., *Alabama*, 481; George Packer, *Blood of the Liberals* (New York: Farrar, Strauss, and Giroux, 2000), 124; Pamela Elise Jones, "Alabama Coal Miners and the New Deal: A Fight for Recognition" (M.A. thesis, University of Alabama at Birmingham, 2004). Forney Johnston represented the Alabama coal operators in an April 1934 hearing in Washington at which the state mine owners successfully resisted raising their wages to meet the federally mandated NRA wage codes and preserved their average daily wage at $3.80, the lowest in America. See Marshall, *Labor in the South*, 145, 149. The monthly staff meetings at Alabama Fuel and Iron featured posters reading: "We are 100% Non-Union and Proud of It." Signs at the company gate read "We are Americans and believe in American principles. If you are here to interfere with our rights, this is the place to turn around" and "This is a happy and satisfied community. We need no paid advice. . . . We tolerate no agitators." See Stetson Kennedy, *Southern Exposure* (1946; reprint, Boca Raton: Florida Atlantic University Press, 1991), 291–92.

26. Harry H. Smith to B. M. Miller, 31 October 1933 (first quotation) and 3 November 1933 (second quotation), both in box SG 19950, folder: Strike Situation, Mobile, 1933, Miller Papers. For extensive denunciation by various business and industrial interests during the textile strikes, see Birmingham Chamber of Commerce to Bibb Graves, and I. W. Rouzer, Alabama Mining Institute, to Bibb Graves, both 4 September 1936, and the Anniston Chamber of Commerce to Bibb Graves, 5 September 1936. For expressions of support from various textile locals, other local unions, and central labor bodies, see the letters and resolutions to Graves, ca. 5 and 6 September 1936, all correspondence in

the same box and folder, Alabama Governors Papers, Bibb Graves Papers, ADAH (hereafter Graves Papers). See also Rogers et al., *Alabama*, 483 and Debbie Pendleton, "New Deal Labor Policy and Alabama Textile Unionism" (M.A. thesis, Auburn University, 1988), 23, 34.

27. Robert R. Moore to Bibb Graves, 22 September 1936, box SG 12183, folder: Talladega Mill Strike, Graves Papers.

28. Lucy Randolph Mason to Sidney Hillman, 11 September 1937 (first quotation) in Mason Papers, cited in Tindall, *Emergence of the New South*, 524. Other quotations in this paragraph are from this same page, although this passage owes much to pp. 524–33.

29. *Thornhill v. Alabama*, 310 U.S. 88 (1940) eventually struck down the Alabama statute against picketing. For examples of the repressive anti-union environment in Alabama, see Alan Draper, "The New Southern Labor History Revisited: The Success of the Mine, Mill and Smelter Workers Union in Birmingham, 1934–1938," *Journal of Southern History* 62 (February 1996): 87–108, especially 97–99 on Borden Burr's conduct representing Henry F. DeBardeleben and TCI at the November 1937 NLRB hearings. Burr was extremely proud of his designation as the University of Alabama's "All-American Alumnus." He held the record for consecutive attendance at Alabama's home football games and frequently manned the football chains. He had quarterbacked the 1899 Crimson Tide team and claimed to have invented the football huddle. Walter J. "Crack" Hannah, of Hannah Steel, was a leading strong-arm man for TCI and later inducted into the Alabama Business Hall of Fame. He was strongly suspected of taking active part in a heinous 1936 beating of Alabama communist Joseph Gelders that nearly resulted in death. See Beech interview.

30. Paul Moffett to Bibb Graves, 3 July 1937 (first quotation). "Business only wants a square deal [and] everybody [to] stop rocking the boat," the president of Ingalls Iron Works assured the governor, especially the "outside agitators." R. I. "Bob" Ingalls to Bibb Graves, 3 July 1937. For the other quotations about agitators and troublemakers and wanting to "handle problems in our own way," see W. P. Lay to Bibb Graves, 9 June 1937, and "See Our Signatures" (petition) to Bibb Graves, 9 June 1937, all correspondence in box SG 12180, folder 9: Gadsden Labor Problems, Graves Papers. See also Marshall, *Labor in the South*, 190 and Feldman, *Politics, Society, and the Klan in Alabama*, 277–78.

31. Story Grocery Company to Bibb Graves, 23 November 1936, box SG 12180, folder 9: Gadsden Labor Problems, Graves Papers.

32. E. W. Lankford, UMWA 5827, to Bibb Graves, 8 September 1937, and Lewis Bowen and Earle Parkhurst, "Report on Investigation Assault on Representatives of Labor in Gadsden on June 25, 1936," 26–27 June 1936, with attached affidavits and sworn statements, all in box SG 12180, folder 9: Gadsden Labor Problems, Graves Papers. John Temple Graves warned that collective bargaining could only be successful in places like Alabama if conducted with "a more Southern point of view." *Birmingham News*, 1 July 1936, in Marshall, *Labor in the South*, 189.

33. Badger, *The New Deal*, 251.

34. "K.K.K. vs. Labor: A Sampler," *Southern Exposure* 8, no. 2 (1980): 61 (Evans quotation); Robert P. Ingalls, "Anti-Labor Vigilantes in the South during the 1930s," *Southern Exposure* 12 (November/December 1978): 72–78, 77 (second quotation); Chalmers, *Hooded Americanism*, 320–23 (third and fourth quotations).

35. *Alabama Magazine*, 19 December 1938, p. 3. Baughn anticipated the "massive resistance" line by also stipulating that the "question of labor relations is Alabama's business

and not the concern of Washington or Massachusetts." Baughn enthusiastically printed denunciations of the CIO as the "Communist International Organization" by future Dixiecrats such as Oklahoma governor W. H. "Alfalfa Bill" Murray, in Birmingham to speak to the Constitutional Education League. See *Alabama Magazine,* 22 November 1937, p. 6. William Bradford Huie signed on as coeditor with Baughn of the newly created magazine in late 1936 but did not stay long. See *Alabama Magazine,* 30 November 1936, p. 3, and 23 August 1937, p. 2.

36. James Willoughby to Bibb Graves, 6 April 1937, box SG 12187, folder 9, Graves Papers. George W. Christians, commander in chief, Crusader White Shirts, to Thomas F. McMahon, president of the UTWA, 14 August 1934, box SG 19956, folder 6, Miller Papers.

37. "An American" to Bibb Graves, 18 June 1938, box SG 12187, folder 3: Communism, 1938, Graves Papers.

38. Galenson, *The CIO Challenge to the AFL,* 340.

39. Ibid., 340–41.

40. On AFL Red-baiting of the CIO, see Eula Mae McGill, interview by the author, 21 March 1997, p. 2, CLEAR. Marshall, *Labor in the South,* 151, 152 (Altman quotation). Although Mitch studiously discouraged both communists and Klan members from joining his organizations, he did embrace black civil rights and enlisted the aid of black organizers such as Walter Jones of the UMW. See Feldman, *Politics, Society, and the Klan in Alabama,* 274. See also Horace Huntley, "Iron Ore Miners and Mine Mill in Alabama, 1933–1952" (Ph.D. diss., University of Pittsburgh, 1977), and Horace Huntley and David Montgomery, eds., *Black Workers' Struggle for Equality in Birmingham* (Champaign: University of Illinois Press, 2004). *Birmingham Age-Herald,* 2 May 1934 and *Jasper Union News,* 21 May 1936, both quoted in Marshall, *Labor in the South,* 151, 152. Not all white workers were so enlightened. One white steelworker resisted membership entreaties by a SWOC organizer by flatly informing him, "I'm not going to join your damn nigger organization." See Norrell, "Caste in Steel," 673–74.

41. Charles B. Gomillion, interview by Hardy T. Frye, p. 8, Interview #19, Hardy T. Frye Oral History Collection, AU; John A. Salmond, "'Flag-bearers for Integration and Justice': Local Civil Rights Groups in the South, 1940–1954," in Feldman, *Before Brown,* 222–37; Tindall, *Emergence of the New South,* 633–34.

42. Painter, *Hosea Hudson,* 14.

43. Feldman, *Politics, Society, and the Klan in Alabama,* 239.

44. As with most myths, there was a kernel of truth at the center of the widespread belief. At a 1928 communist summit in Moscow, the Communist Party had indeed talked about the southern Black Belt of the United States as the weakest link in the Western world and called for an assault on capitalism through the liberation of the black race that predominated in the region (Painter, introduction to *Hosea Hudson,* 16). Still, it was a simple task for opponents of black advancement to extrapolate liberally and hang the whole enterprise, regardless of its myriad sources and indigenous roots, on an alien, communist, un-American conspiracy with political subversion at bottom.

45. *Birmingham Age-Herald,* 7 August 1931; *Birmingham News,* 7–10 August 1931.

46. J. W. Odum to Bibb Graves, 15 November 1938 (quotation), box SG 12200, folder: Scottsboro Cases, Hamp Draper to Bibb Graves, 15 September 1938, box SG 12187, folder 9: Convict Dept., 1937, and Thomas Maxwell, Tuscaloosa, to Bibb Graves, 26 January 1936, box SG 12187, folder 3: Communism, 1938, all three in Graves Papers. "We are the

policemen of the Negroes," a black preacher confided to nervous whites. "If we did not keep down their ambitions and *divert them into religion* there would be upheaval in the South" (italics added). Quoted in Gunnar Myrdal, *An American Dilemma: The Negro Problem and Modern Democracy*, 2 vols. (New York: Harper and Brothers, 1944), 876, cited in Tindall, *Emergence of the New South*, 566. See also Lynn Williams, "Stories and Images of Scottsboro: Creating Alabama's 'Terrible Public Image' through the Arts" (paper delivered at the Alabama Historical Association annual meeting, 18 April 1999, Montgomery). I am grateful to the author for making a copy available to me. Also see "Alabama Not Eager for Scottsboro Boys' Blood" and "The Scottsboro Case, 1932–1935," http://www.afroam.org/history/scott (accessed February 2012).

47. Birmingham, *Alabama Criminal Code*, Section 4092; Robin D. G. Kelley, *Hammer and Hoe: Alabama Communists during the Great Depression* (Chapel Hill: University of North Carolina Press, 1990), 72–74, 121–23. The Downs Sedition Ordinance was par for Birmingham's 1930s city commission. An ultraconservative body even though two of its three commissioners were closely allied with New Deal ally Horace Wilkinson and Governor Bibb Graves, the commission rejected federal relief, somehow managed to operate in the black, and outlawed bread lines because they were "unseemly." (*Birmingham*) *Southern Worker*, 29 November 1930. See also Painter, *Hosea Hudson*, 27 and Edwin Shannon LaMonte, *Politics and Welfare in Birmingham, 1900–1975* (Tuscaloosa: The University of Alabama Press, 1995), 92; Feldman, *Politics, Society, and the Klan in Alabama*, 238–58.

48. Blaine Owen Affidavit, 25 February 1937, part 15C, p. 6,324, United States Senate, Committee on Education and Labor, 75th Cong., 2nd sess., *Violation of Free Speech and Rights of Labor, Hearings before Subcommittee*, Microforms and Documents Department, AU; Joseph Gelders to Roger N. Baldwin, 14 August 1936, American Civil Liberties Union Records, Mudd Manuscript Library, Princeton University, Princeton, New Jersey (hereafter ACLU Records).

49. Papers of the NAACP, part 6, reel 2, part 7, series A, reel 7, and part 10, reel 23, LC and MADD; Kelley, *Hammer and Hoe*, 40–43; Bruce Crawford, "Bullets Fell on Alabama," *Nation* 141 (18 September 1935): 319–20; Feldman, *Politics, Society, and the Klan in Alabama*, 259–84. See also Theodore Rosengarten, *All God's Dangers: The Life of Nate Shaw* (New York: Vintage Books, 1974).

50. Bibb Graves to [Mr.] Lee, 21 October 1936, Joseph Gelders to Bibb Graves, 5 January 1937, and Bibb Graves to James Chappell, 22 January 1937, all in box SG 12179, folder: Re Joseph Gelders, Graves Papers. Hubert Baughn, writing as his editorialist persona Major Squirm, breezily referred to the near fatal Gelders assault as "a sound spanking." *Alabama Magazine*, 7 February 1938, p. 15. See also Durr interview, 2.

51. When a carload of communists associated with the National Committee for the Defense of Political Prisoners was overtaken, also in Chilton County, and had their car riddled with bullets, Graves refused to provide police protection and instead accused the communists of shooting up their own car as a publicity stunt. Garfield Hays to Bibb Graves, and Jack Conroy, Bruce Crawford, Emmett Gowen, Shirley Hopkins, and Alfred H. Hirsch to Bibb Graves, both on 31 July 1935, both in box SG 12165, folder 1: Communism, drawer 3, no. 1, all in Graves Papers; Delegation of NCDPP, "Report on Georgia-Alabama," 19 July 1934, pp. 8–9, ACLU Records; Crawford, "Bullets Fell on Alabama," 319–20.

52. Delegation of NCDPP, "Report on Georgia-Alabama," 8–9.

53. Packer, *Blood of the Liberals*, 112 (quotations), 113. George Brown Tindall has pointed to Florida governor David Scholz as one such undeserving recipient of the label in *Emergence of the New South*, 644. Anthony J. Badger explains that Theodore G. Bilbo and fellow Mississippian John Rankin, "[t]wo of the most violent Negrophobes in Congress," were also strong supporters of the New Deal because of its programs in cotton and rural electrification. See *The New Deal*, 270.

54. J. Mills Thornton III argues that the 1920s KKK was the actual seedbed of later Alabama liberalism in "Hugo Black and the Golden Age," *Alabama Law Review* 36 (1985): 899–913 (first quotation from article's title). John Egerton described Alabama as "progressive, forward-looking, essentially liberal" and asked a Depression-era journalist, "Mr. Beech, what in the world happened? . . . What happened there?" Beech interview, 16, 17. Wayne Flynt titled his chapter on politics and society in the 1940s and 1950s "The Flowering of Liberalism" in a popular textbook. He also put the point at which liberalism and race coalesced to the detriment of the New Deal coalition at the late 1950s, much later than the present study, and talked of only southern "conservatives" being alienated by this identification, not those who passed for southern liberals. See Rogers et al., *Alabama*, 524–44, quotation on p. 525. Washington journalist Stewart Alsop had claimed the "liberal oasis" moniker for Alabama in 1946. See John Egerton, *Speak Now against the Day: The Generation before the Civil Rights Movement* (New York: Alfred A. Knopf, 1994), 391. See also Margaret E. Armbrester, "John Temple Graves II: A Southern Liberal Views the New Deal," *Alabama Review* 32 (July 1979): 203–13. This piece does not mention race in musing over Graves's disillusionment with the New Deal.

55. Aubrey Williams, Clifford and Virginia Durr, and Gould Beech found themselves social pariahs for their liberal views. William Mitch was an Indiana socialist brought down South to inject liberalism into the ranks of organized labor. Herman Clarence Nixon, originally of Possum Trot in Calhoun County, taught political science at Vanderbilt and Tulane universities. Williams and Clifford Durr, of course, had careers as New Deal bureaucrats before returning home to Alabama. Hugo Black took a seat on the U.S. Supreme Court. On Mitch, see Painter, *Hosea Hudson*, 377n5. See also Tindall, *Emergence of the New South*, 506, 581, 593. The Durrs did suffer economically and socially in Montgomery for their liberalism.

56. Tindall, *Emergence of the New South*, 632, 633 (quoted).

57. Alabamians had pushed W. B. Bankhead for the vice-presidential spot on the 1940 ticket and considered FDR's choice of agriculture secretary Henry Wallace (after Justice William O. Douglas's initial declining) as a personal affront. See Rogers et al., *Alabama*, 472, 489.

58. Rogers et al., *Alabama*, 494 (quotation), 495, 496. For J. T. Graves's early New Deal liberalism, see *Birmingham Age-Herald*, 31 August 1935, p. 1, and 17 September 1935, p. 1.

59. "Big Jim" Folsom is perhaps the only major exception here. Folsom paid dearly for his racial liberalism; it helped end his political career in Alabama. Gould Beech noted this trend; Beech interview, 16–17, 19. See also *Anniston Star*, 29 April 1948, clipping in folder: 1948 Elections, Charles G. Dobbins Papers, AU, and Virginia Van der Veer Hamilton, "Lister Hill, Hugo Black, and the Albatross of Race," *Alabama Law Review* 36 (1985): 845–60.

60. Rogers et al., *Alabama*, 474 (first quotation), 489 (second quotation), 490–91 (third quotation), 491 (fourth quotation). "Once given what they viewed as their fair share of the fruits of capitalism, white workers turned against their black brothers and sisters," Wayne Flynt wrote. "Conservative unions denounced radical ones, and workers newly installed in the middle class quickly forgot the poor they left behind. Successful workers rationalized that they earned their way out of poverty whereas their less worthy companions slacked off or wasted their opportunities" (484).

61. Bailey quoted in *Raleigh News and Observer*, 8 July 1934, cited in Tindall, *Emergence of the New South*, 612.

62. Powell to B. M. Miller and Fleming to Franklin Roosevelt et al., both 31 October 1934, John LeFlore and Johnson to B. M. Miller, 27 October 1934, and other material all in box 250, folder: Lynching of Claude Neal, Miller Papers.

63. *Birmingham News* and *Birmingham Age-Herald*, both 31 January 1937, p. 3; Dan T. Carter, *Scottsboro: An American Tragedy* (Baton Rouge: Louisiana State University Press, 1969), 380–81.

64. Texas congressman Maury Maverick lived up to his last name as an exception here as did Tar Heel journalist Virginius Dabney. Costigan-Wagner Federal Anti-Lynching Bill, ca. 1934, part, series B, reels 7–11, NAACP Papers, MADD and LC; Harvard Sitkoff, *A New Deal for Blacks: The Emergence of Civil Rights as a National Issue* (New York: Oxford University Press, 1978), 272–90, 291 (Bailey quotation), 292–97; Tindall, *Emergence of the New South*, 551–52. See also the excellent work by Jacquelyn Dowd Hall, *Revolt against Chivalry: Jesse Daniel Ames and the Women's Campaign against Lynching* (New York: Columbia University Press, 1979).

65. Lamis, *The Two-Party South*, 8 (quotation).

66. Ibid.

67. "The Lynching Situation," *Kourier Magazine* 6 (October 1930): 11 (first quotation); Frank M. Dixon to Kenneth D. McKellar, 4 March 1940 (second quotation), box SG 12248, folder: Anti-Lynching Bill, Alabama Governors Papers, Frank M. Dixon, ADAH; Tindall, *Emergence of the New South*, 552; Henry M. Edmonds, J. G. Chappell, Jimmy Mills, and Forney Johnston to Bibb Graves, 10 December 1937 (third quotation), box SG 12194, folder 11, Graves Papers. While Presbyterian minister Edmonds was in sympathy with the letter as an appeal for a pardon, he specifically outlined his dissent from his co-signers on the anti-lynching question.

68. Forney Johnston to Grover C. Hall, 17 November 1938 (quotation) and James G. Chappell to Grover C. Hall, 18 November 1938, both in box 67, folder 1, Hall Papers. For Johnston's earlier activism against the 1928 bolters, the Klan, and politicos such as Horace Wilkinson, see Forney Johnston to R. B. Evins, 31 March 1930, box 31, folder 9, SDEC Records. See also Forney Johnston to Oscar W. Underwood, 12 January 1915, box 36, folder 8, Underwood Papers.

69. Quotations from Grover Hall to Bibb Graves, 14 November 1938, Grover Hall to James G. Chappell, 15 November 1938, both in box 67, folder 1, Hall Papers, and Hall editorial "O Scottsboro," ca. December 1937 in the *Montgomery Advertiser*, clipping in box SG 12194, folder 11, Graves Papers.

70. Gavagan Federal Anti-Lynching Bill, 1936–39, part 7, series B, reels 17–20, NAACP Papers, MADD and LC; Tindall, *Emergence of the New South*, 553.

71. James E. Shepard, president of the North Carolina College for Negroes, to Bibb

Graves, 29 November 1935, box SG 12187, folder 3: Communism, 1938, Graves Papers (quotation).

72. Francis Butler Simkins and Charles Pierce Roland, *A History of the South*, 4th ed. (New York: Alfred A. Knopf, 1972), 549; Tindall, *Emergence of the New South*, 544, 549.

73. Republicans, and later southern Democrats, attacked Social Security as "radical and even Communistic." See "Republicans Take Refuge under Mask of Platitudes, Declares Senator McAdoo," clipping, Speech of Hon. William Gibbs McAdoo by radio to Democratic dinner, San Francisco, 27 August 1936, box 17, folder 5, John H. Bankhead II Personal Papers, ADAH. See also Tindall, *Disruption of the Solid South*, 31 and *Emergence of the New South*, 544, 545, 547.

74. This phrase is ubiquitous in the parlance of southern whites, increasingly so as threats to traditional race relations increased throughout the twentieth century. See, e.g., Fred D. Oakley, Potts Camp, Mississippi, to Eleanor Roosevelt, 5 March 1944, folder: 190.1, Eleanor Roosevelt Papers, FDR (quotation) (hereafter ER Papers).

75. Charles G. Dobbins, "Alabama Governors and Editors, 1930–1955: A Memoir," *Alabama Review* 29 (April 1976): 154. An overly sanguine Dobbins Jr. also said in 1976 that "No longer is that true." Tindall, *Emergence of the New South*, 635.

76. *Birmingham Post*, 21 June 1934 (Vardaman quotation) and *Birmingham News*, 28 August 1938, both in the news clipping file: Political Parties—Republican—Birmingham and Jefferson County, Tutwiler Collection of Southern History, Birmingham Public Library, Birmingham, AL.

77. C. G. Snead to B. M. Miller, 31 March 1933, box SG 19947, folder 12, Miller Papers.

78. Beech interview, 25 (first quotation); *Alabama Magazine*, 28 November 1938, p. 18 (second quotation).

79. Cash, *The Mind of the South*, 420–21.

80. "Famous Quotations," White Citizens Council Pamphlet, Greenwood, Mississippi, Educational Fund of the White Citizens Council, box 1: Race Relations, folder: Association of Citizens Councils, Mississippi, Roland M. Harper Papers, UA. See also Badger, *The New Deal*, 270.

81. Radio Address of Gessner T. McCorvey, 14 September 1940, pp. 1, 2, and 5, box 81, folder 12 and Clinton L. McKinney to John D. McQueen, 6 June 1937, box 69, folder 14, both in SDEC Records.

82. Painter, *The Narrative of Hosea Hudson*, 101–2 (Dr. Thomson quotation), 114 (second quotation); Rogers et al., *Alabama*, 468.

83. Painter, *The Narrative of Hosea Hudson*, 137.

84. Beech interview, 7–8; *Alabama Magazine*, 28 November 1938, p. 18. Liberal thought such as this was exceedingly rare in Alabama yet it did emerge, occasionally, especially on economic issues. For examples, see Troy Whitaker, Gadsden, to the ed., *Alabama Magazine*, 14 December 1936, p. 15, and C. A. Thaxton to the ed., *Alabama Magazine*, 19 April 1937, p. 15.

85. Painter, *The Narrative of Hosea Hudson*, 141 (first quotation), 323 (second quotation).

86. Ibid., 131 (first quotation), 169 (second quotation). See also Lynne B. Feldman, *A Sense of Place: Birmingham's Black Middle-Class Community, 1880–1930* (Tuscaloosa: The University of Alabama Press, 1999).

87. Painter, *The Narrative of Hosea Hudson*, 356–57 (Jackson quotation), 331 (Hudson quotation); Thompson interview, 2, 20 (first quotation), 11. Jackson served as the editor of the *Birmingham World*.

88. Tindall, *Disruption of the Solid South*, 31–32.

89. On southern resentment over losing the two-thirds rule, see *Alabama Magazine*, 28 August 1939, p. 15 and 22 July 1940, p. 11. See also Tindall, *Emergence of the New South*, 556 (quotation), 619; Pamela Tyler, "'Blood on Your Hands': White Southerners' Criticism of Eleanor Roosevelt during World War II," in Feldman, *Before Brown*, 96–115.

90. The celebrated quote by "Cotton Ed" about his walkout at "Philadelphy" is found in Harry S. Ashmore, *An Epitaph for Dixie* (New York: W. W. Norton, 1958), 100–101. For the quote, see also Wayne Greenhaw, *Elephants in the Cottonfields: Ronald Reagan and the New Republican South* (New York: Macmillan, 1982), 49. Greenhaw, a journalist, correctly puts the starting point of southern disillusionment with the racial nature of the New Deal and Democratic liberalism at 1936, much earlier than many historians (49).

91. For commentary on this longstanding strategy, see Painter, *The Narrative of Hosea Hudson*, 47–48.

92. For more on the racial and class nature of the New Deal, see Badger, *The New Deal*, 271.

93. Dixon, author of two best-selling white supremacist novels that glorified the Reconstruction KKK—*The Clansman: An Historical Romance of the Ku-Klux Klan* (New York: Grosset & Dunlap, 1905) and *The Leopard's Spots: A Romance of the White Man's Burden* (New York: Doubleday, 1903)—was the uncle of later Alabama governor Frank M. Dixon. See also Tindall, *Emergence of the New South*, 616, 617 (quotation), 619; Tindall, *Disruption of the Solid South*, 32; and Kennedy, *Southern Exposure*, 128–29.

94. Tindall, *Emergence of the New South*, 617 (quotation).

95. *Alabama Magazine*, 22 November 1937, p. 1 (second quotation), 24 January 1938, p. 3 (first quotation), 17 April 1939, p. 15 (third quotation), 18 April 1938, p. 3, 14 March 1938, p. 3 (fourth quotation), 25 April 1938, p. 3 (fifth quotation). See also 24 January 1938, p. 3, 14 March 1938, p. 3, and 24 January 1938, p. 3. Fred R. Marun headed up the southern headquarters of the anti-FDR Constitutional Educational League in Birmingham (*Alabama Magazine*, 22 November 1937, p. 7).

96. Franklin D. Roosevelt, "Franklin Roosevelt's Address Announcing the Second New Deal," 31 October 1936, Madison Square Garden, New York City, FDR.

97. *Alabama Magazine*, 21 February 1938, p. 3 (first and third quotations), and 28 March 1938, p. 3 (second quotation). The magazine also frequently criticized what it termed FDR's "demagogic attacks on businessmen" as in the 14 March 1938 issue, p. 3. See also Feldman, *From Demagogue to Dixiecrat*, 108.

98. See, e.g., the Alabama Mills, Inc., advertisement in *Alabama Magazine*, 4 April 1938, p. 2 (quotations).

99. Black's bill became the Fair Labor Standards Act. *Alabama Magazine*, 16 August 1937, p. 3 (first quotation) and DeBardeleben's Alabama Fuel and Iron Company advertisement, *Alabama Magazine*, 22 November 1937, p. 2 (second quotation).

100. *Alabama Magazine*, 21 February 1938, p. 3 (first quotation) and 4 April 1938, p. 3 (other quotations).

101. *Alabama Magazine*, 4 April 1938, p. 3 (first quotation), 25 April 1938, p. 3 (second quotation), 17 April 1939, p. 3 (third quotation); B. H. Hartsfield to ed., *Alabama Magazine*, 14 November 1938, p. 11.

102. Bruce Shelton editorial in the *Tuscaloosa News* quoted with approval in *Alabama Magazine*, 10 April 1939, p. 15.

103. *Alabama Magazine*, 26 June 1939, p. 15 (first quotation), 21 October 1940, p. 19 (second quotation), and 9 December 1940, p. 15 (third quotation). The court case was *Smith v. Texas*, 311 U.S. 128 (1940). See also *Chambers v. Florida*, 309 U.S. 227 (1940).

104. Feldman, *Politics, Society, and the Klan in Alabama*, 219–84.

105. Rogers et al., *Alabama*, 497 (first quotation); Feldman, *From Demagogue to Dixiecrat*, 108 (second quotation).

106. Minutes of Meeting of the SDEC, Jefferson Davis Hotel, Montgomery, Alabama, 18 January 1936, box 75, folder 7, and also the "List of Persons Who Protested and List of Persons Who Supported," Borden Burr to John D. McQueen, 14 January 1936, and Mabel Jones West to John D. McQueen, 15 January 1936, documents in box 71, folder 12, all in the SDEC Records; Beech interview, 26 (quotation).

Chapter 6

1. Sledge, "The Alabama Republican Party," 126; Tindall, *Emergence of the New South*, 541, 542 (quotation), 557.

2. James Willoughby to Bibb Graves, 6 April 1937 (first quotation), box SG 12187, folder 3, Graves Papers; Badger, *The New Deal*, 271 (second quotation).

3. Tindall, *Emergence of the New South*, 611 (second quotation), 612 (first quotation), 613 (third quotation).

4. *Alabama Magazine*, 31 January 1938, p. 3 (quoted).

5. [Ala.] Citizens to W. B. Bankhead, ca. 1935 (quoted), LPR 66, box 41, folder 2, W. B. Bankhead Papers.

6. Ibid. (quoted). Actually, a number of the classical economists, such as Adam Smith, had attitudes toward organized labor and the environment that were far more progressive than their latter-day apostles. The Scottish father of free enterprise, for instance, believed strongly in state-sponsored public education, environmental protections, government assurance of the concept of a "living wage" as opposed to a minimum wage, and laws against price-fixing, collusion, rigged markets, and lopsided corporate investment in the political process. See, e.g., Stabile, *Work and Welfare*.

7. John C. Sheffield, Helena, Arkansas, "The Second Secession," February 1937, box 2, folder 5, LPR 33, Frank M. Dixon Personal Papers, also in box SG12491, folder 8, Sparks Papers, both in ADAH.

8. Ibid.

9. On the murder of Joseph Shoemaker, see Kennedy, *Southern Exposure*, 168–69.

10. "The Negro Goes Democratic," *Kourier Magazine* 12 (August 1936): 20 (first quotation); Wyn Craig Wade, *Fiery Cross: The Ku Klux Klan in America* (New York: Simon and Schuster, 1987), 259, 275 (other quotations). The song lyrics also appear in George Wolfskill and John A. Hudson, *All But the People: Franklin D. Roosevelt and His Critics, 1933–1939* (New York: Macmillan, 1969), 87. See also Elna C. Green, ed., *The New Deal and Beyond: Social Welfare in the South since 1930* (Athens: University of Georgia Press, 2003).

11. William Blanchard of Miami's White Front concurred that it "does not take half an eye to see that the negro is the most gross member of the human family. Only when . . . compelled by the alien race does he step forward. The rich dark continent will always re-

main the toy of conquerors until the master stoops so low as to share his blood with the slave." Kennedy, *Southern Exposure*, 80–81 (Evans quotation), 82 (Blanchard quotation).

12. Ibid., 84 (quotations).

13. Ibid., 81 (Ellender quotation), 82–83 (Blanchard quotations). See also Major Squirm column in *Alabama Magazine*, 24 April 1939, p. 15.

14. In fact, Street had displayed strong racist tendencies going back to at least 1901 when he favored retention of the poll tax and passage of a new constitution that would disfranchise black voters. Thomas Atkins Street had run as an unsuccessful Populist candidate for Alabama governor in 1896. The younger Street, also of Marshall County, was a Populist notable during the 1890s and then became a leading Republican patronage referee and officeholder. See Feldman, *Politics, Society, and the Klan in Alabama*, 160–92, esp. 178–79. Also see O. D. Street to Congressman Samuel Hobbs, 13 February 1943, box 10, folder: Political 1943 Correspondence, Street Papers, ADAH (quotation). See also the different collection of Oliver Day Street Papers at UA.

15. See, e.g., Major Squirm column in *Alabama Magazine*, 11 October 1937, p. 16.

16. Oliver Day Street to ed., *Birmingham News*, 15 January 1936 (first part of quotation), O. D. Street to ed., *Birmingham News*, ca. 1936 (last part of quotation). Street also warned the public that the New Deal was "part of a conspiracy engineered from socialist and communist sources," in O. D. Street to ed., *Birmingham Age-Herald*, 22 October 1934, all in box 31, folder: Political Scrap, Street Papers, ADAH.

17. J. G. Bass to Dear Sir, 1 October 1934, box 5, folder: Republican State Campaign Committee, and O. R. Hood, Gadsden, Alabama, to O. D. Street, ca. October 1941, box 10, folder: 1941 Republican Political Correspondence, both in Street Papers, ADAH.

18. J. G. Bass to Dear Sir, 1 October 1934 (first quotation) and J. G. Bass to Dear Sir, 9 October 1934 (second quotation), both in box 5, folder: Republican State Campaign Committee; Charles T. Lunsford, (Marion County), Alabama, to O. D. Street, 28 April 1936 (third quotation) and T. M. Nelson, Penala Plantation, to O. D. Street, 1 August 1935 (fourth quotation), both in box 5, folder: Political Support, 1936–1938, all in Street Papers, ADAH.

19. O. D. Street to ed., *Birmingham News*, ca. 18 May 1935, box 31, folder: Political Scrap, Street Papers, ADAH.

20. O. D. Street to Herbert Hoover, 29 June 1936 (first quotation), box 10, folder: Herbert Hoover letter, O. D. Street to ed., *Birmingham Age-Herald*, 31 May 1935 (second quotation), box 31, folder: Political Scrap, both in Street Papers, ADAH.

21. O. D. Street to ed., *Birmingham Age-Herald*, 29 July 1935, p. 4.

22. O. D. Street to ed., *Birmingham News*, ca. 1935 (first quotation), O. D. Street to ed., *Birmingham News*, 15 January 1936 (second and third quotations), both in box 31, folder: Political Scrap, Street Papers, ADAH

23. O. D. Street to the Honorable O. R. Hood, 17 October 1941, box 10, folder: 1941 Republican political correspondence (first quotation), and O. D. Street to Congressman Sam Hobbs, 13 February 1943, box 10, folder: 1943 correspondence (second quotation), both in Street Papers, ADAH.

24. O. D. Street to Thomas Lawson, attorney general of Alabama, 14 March 1941, box 10, folder: 1941 Republican Political Correspondence, Street Papers, ADAH. On Dilling, see O. D. Street to Mrs. Elizabeth Dilling, 3 January 1944, box 10, folder: Political 1943 Correspondence, Street Papers, ADAH, and Kennedy, *Southern Exposure*, 151, 207.

25. O. D. Street to B. L. Noonjin, 25 March 1944, box 10, folder: 1944 Political Correspondence (first quotation) and O. D. Street to ed., *Birmingham News,* ca. 10 January 1936 draft, box 31, folder: Political Scrap (second and third quotations), both in Street Papers, ADAH.

26. O. D. Street to Congressman Joseph Martin (R-Mass.), 6 March 1944, box 10, folder: 1944 Political Correspondence (quotation); O. D. Street to Tim Nelson, 8 August 1935, box 31, folder: Political Scrap; O. D. Street to Frank Knox, *Chicago Daily News,* 13 April 1937, box 10, folder: Correspondence 1937; O. D. Street to Joseph Martin, Republican National Committee, national chairman, 9 August 1940 (call for FDR's impeachment), box 10, folder: 1940 Republican Political Correspondence, all in Street Papers, ADAH.

27. Charles Fiedelson was the editor in question. See B. L. Noonjin to O. D. Street, 23 March 1944 (first quotation) and O. D. Street to Congressman Joseph Martin, 6 March 1944 (second quotation), both in box 10, folder: 1944 Political Correspondence, and O. D. Street to Frank Knox, *Chicago Daily News,* 13 April 1937, box 10, folder: Correspondence 1937 (third quotation), all in Street Papers, ADAH.

28. O. D. Street to ed., *Birmingham Age-Herald,* 3 August 1936, box 31, folder: Political Scrap, Street Papers, ADAH.

29. O. D. Street to Mrs. Elizabeth Dilling, Chicago, 3 January 1944, box 10, folder: Political 1943 Correspondence. Another reason Alabama Democrats were reticent about criticizing the New Deal too openly, according to the Republican chieftain, was that they were afraid of replaying the 1928 "bolt" in which they won an election for the Republicans only to see it stolen by Democratic-controlled machinery. See O. D. Street to B. L. Noonjin, 8 August 1940, box 10, folder: 1940 Republican Political Correspondence. By 1939, Street gloated that almost all Alabama Democrats were "now saying about Roosevelt" what he had long said, that "There are many Chinamen I would support over him." See O. D. Street to John Marshall, 8 August 1939, box 10, folder: Letter for John Marshall, all in Street Papers, ADAH. Street had enjoyed close relations with a number of key Alabama Democrats for years. See, e.g., Hugh Mallory, Selma, to O. D. Street, 17 January 1928, box 1276, folder 58, Street Papers, UA.

30. Frank M. Dixon to Senator Kenneth D. McKellar, 4 March 1940, box SG 12248, folder 8: Antilynching Bill, Washington, Dixon Papers.

31. Southern conservatives almost uniformly favored a concept of "representation" in democracy that squared with elected officials functioning as "agents" or a simple mirror to reflect the popular will, regardless of its wisdom or lack thereof. They did not warm to a competing concept of representation that understood elected representatives to function as the "trustees" of the electorate, bringing to bear their education and expert judgment in ways that might sometimes conflict with popular prejudices. For various categories of representation, see the classic Hanna Fenichel Pitkin, *The Concept of Representation* (Berkeley: University of California Press, 1967); Roland Pennock and John W. Chapman, eds., *Representation* (New York: Atherton Press, 1968); and Roger H. Davidson, *The Role of the Congressman* (New York: Pegasus, 1969).

32. Frank M. Dixon to Senator Kenneth D. McKellar, 4 March 1940, box SG 12248, folder 8: Antilynching Bill, Washington, Dixon Papers (quotations); Kenneth D. McKellar to Frank M. Dixon, 9 February 1940, same box and folder. See also the *Congressional Record,* 76th Cong., 3rd Sess., H.R. 801 (Wagner-Costigan Anti-Lynching Bill). Southern white race-based resentment about taxes was strong. If the poll tax were repealed, the

mayor of Chattanooga speculated around 1940, "the niggers in this town [would] bond us to death . . . have us in the poorhouse in two years. They don't pay taxes so they don't care how much you spend." Bunche, *The Political Status of the Negro in the Age of FDR*, xix. Rape was often supplied as a reason for southern lynching, but an extensive study concluded that between 1882 and 1938, 75 percent of lynchings had been carried out for reasons other than rape or attempted rape. See report by Monroe N. Work, Tuskegee Institute, "Lynching Compilation, 1882–1938," box SG 12248, folder 8: Antilynching Bill, Washington, Dixon Papers. In his letter to McKellar, Governor Dixon also made the regular complaint about regional freight rates that discriminated unfairly against the South and made it difficult to profit from lower regional wage rates. For this complaint, see also John C. Sheffield, "The Second Secession," February 1937, box 2, folder 5, Dixon Personal Papers, ADAH.

33. In January 1935, the U.S. Supreme Court struck down part of the NIRA in *Panama Refining Company v. Ryan*, 293 U.S. 388 (1935). On 27 May 1935 the Supremes struck down the NIRA completely in *Schechter v. U.S.*, 295 U.S. 495 (1935). A year after its *Panama Refining* decision, the high court invalidated the AAA in *U.S. v. Butler*, 297 U.S. 1 (1936).

34. Tindall, *Emergence of the New South*, 620.

35. *Congressional Record*, 75th Cong., 1st sess., Appendix, 661 (Glass quotations), cited also in Tindall, *Disruption of the Solid South* (Athens: University of Georgia Press, 1972), 33 and Tindall, *Emergence of the New South*, 621, 622, 624 (Manifesto quotation). Bailey also managed to get a couple of Republicans to sign the manifesto.

36. Kennedy, *Southern Exposure*, 2, 3 (quotation); Tindall, *Emergence of the New South*, 627 (quotation repeated).

37. Kennedy, *Southern Exposure*, 4–5. See also Cobb, *Industrialization and Southern Society*.

38. For the malformed nature of Alabama's tax structure, see McMillan, *Constitutional Development in Alabama*; Bailey Thompson, ed., *A Century of Controversy: Constitutional Reform in Alabama* (Tuscaloosa: The University of Alabama Press, 2002); and Kyle Whitmire, "Who Would Want the Job Anyway?" *Birmingham Weekly*, 14–21 November 2002, p. 8.

39. Per capita annual income in the Southeast was only $309 versus a $573 national average; southern farmers grossed only $186 per year as opposed to $528 by farmers in other regions. Kennedy, *Southern Exposure*, 2–12, 7 (first quotation), 11 (second quotation).

40. Ibid., 4; Tindall, *Emergence of the New South*, 637 (Foreman quotation), 641 (Pepper quotation), 626 (Roosevelt quotations). Charles Eckstat to Bibb Graves, 29 August 1935, box SG 12165, folder 2, Graves Papers. One of the "deviltries of medieval civilizations," like the U.S. South, was that "water will find its level and that negroes and whites living together in the South for centuries has not only failed to elevate the negro but has brought the white man down to the negro's own level . . . degenerated morality." Historian, Washington, D.C., to the Editor [no publication name], 1 May 1928, box 5, folder 13, W. B. Bankhead Papers.

41. Major Squirm column, *Alabama Magazine*, 1 May 1939, p. 15; Tindall, *Emergence of the New South*, 624, 627 (George quotation), 629 (Smith quotation).

42. Tindall, *Emergence of the New South*, 630 (first quotation), 633 (second quotation).

43. Durr interview, 9–10; Rogers et al., *Alabama*, 502 (Connor quotation); Feld-

man, *From Demagogue to Dixiecrat*, 109; Tindall, *Emergence of the New South*, 636–37; *Alabama Magazine*, 5 December 1938, p. 5. See also Thomas A. Krueger, *And Promises to Keep: The Southern Conference for Human Welfare, 1938–1948* (Nashville: Vanderbilt University Press, 1967) and Linda Reed, *Simple Decency & Common Sense: The Southern Conference Movement, 1938–1963* (Bloomington: Indiana University Press, 1991). On the background of conference attendees, see Patricia Sullivan's landmark study, *Days of Hope: Race and Democracy in the New Deal Era* (Chapel Hill: University of North Carolina Press, 1996), 98–101. See also Sullivan, ed., *Freedom Writer: Virginia Foster Durr, Letters from the Civil Rights Years* (New York: Routledge, 2003). Also see Egerton, *Speak Now against the Day*, 186, 292–93.

44. For a good recent study on the general topic of communism and race in the South, see Glenda Elizabeth Gilmore, *Defying Dixie: The Radical Roots of Civil Rights, 1919–1950* (New York: W. W. Norton, 2008).

45. On Gelders's background, see Sullivan, *Days of Hope*, 97. See also Tindall, *Emergence of the New South*, 637, 638 (quotation), 639.

46. *Alabama Magazine*, 28 November 1938, p. 18 (first quotation), p. 3 (second quotation).

47. *Alabama Magazine*, 5 December 1938, p. 14 (first quotation), 28 November 1938, p. 3 (second and third quotations).

48. *Alabama Magazine*, editorial, 5 December 1938, pp. 3–4 (quotations).

49. Ibid. (quotations).

50. *Alabama Magazine*, editorial, 28 November 1938, p. 3 (first quotation) and 5 December 1938, pp. 3–5 and 14 (other quotations).

51. *Alabama Magazine*, 5 December 1938, pp. 3–5, 14 (quotations).

52. Major Squirm column, *Alabama Magazine*, 12 December 1938, p. 15.

53. *Alabama Magazine*, 21 November 1938, p. 4. The Bourbon organ still insisted on emphasizing its low opinion of the KKK. See, e.g., Major Squirm column, *Alabama Magazine*, 5 December 1938, p. 14.

54. The women's group called for Charlton's resignation from their state executive committee because she obviously "no longer represents the people who placed her there." See George Londa to Mr. Bliven, 27 November 1938, Virginia Durr Papers, ADAH (hereafter V. Durr Papers); *Alabama Magazine*, 5 December 1938, p. 6 (quotations including in note).

55. *Selma Times-Journal* and *Montgomery Journal* editorials reprinted in and quoted from *Alabama Magazine*, 5 December 1938, pp. 10–12.

56. *Montgomery Advertiser* editorial reprinted in and quoted from *Alabama Magazine*, 5 December 1938, pp. 10–12.

57. *Huntsville Times, Decatur Daily,* and *Tuscaloosa News* editorials reprinted in and quoted from *Alabama Magazine*, 5 December 1938, pp. 11–14.

58. Leroy Gossett, Gadsden (Etowah County), to ed., *Alabama Magazine*, 12 and 26 December 1938, both p. 4 (first quotation); W. P. Gordon, Oneonta (Blount County), to ed., *Alabama Magazine*, 12 December 1938, p. 4 (second quotation), S. A. Riley, Birmingham, to ed., *Alabama Magazine*, 26 December 1938, p. 4 (third quotation).

59. In an index of just how popular the sobriquet "liberal" was during the period, the editor of the arch-conservative *Alabama Magazine* actually agreed with the sentiment of the disenchanted liberal educator: "Same here." *Alabama Magazine*, 5 December 1938, p. 11 (quoted).

60. Durr interview, 3, 11, 30 (quotation), 31.

61. Noonjin was born on an Etowah County farm and moved into Gadsden, where he had various business interests. *Alabama Magazine,* 26 December 1938, p. 6 (Noonjin quotations).

62. George Londa to Mr. Bliven, 27 November 1938, in V. Durr Papers.

63. Rogers et al., *Alabama,* 496–97; Tindall, *Emergence of the New South,* 636–39. I have made the same error in earlier works. See Feldman, *From Demagogue to Dixiecrat,* 109, 121, 139, and Feldman, *Politics, Society, and the Klan in Alabama,* 274. For more discussion on the SCHW and its successor, the Southern Conference Educational Fund, see Sullivan, *Days of Hope* and Reed, *Simple Decency & Common Sense.*

64. *Raleigh News and Observer,* 26 November 1938, in Tindall, *Emergence of the New South,* 637.

65. *Alabama Magazine,* 5 December 1938, p. 5 (Graves quotation and F. D. Patterson characterization), p. 7 (Bankhead response), p. 15 (Patrick quotation). A similar Graves quote about being "surprised and shocked" was reported on p. 12 of the same issue. Editorials reprinted from the *Selma Times-Journal* (p. 10) and the *Tuscaloosa News* (p. 13) also singled out F. D. Patterson for praise as exhibiting a proper African American response. On John Temple Graves and F. D. Patterson, see Durr interview, 18–19, 23. Gould Beech also remembered the mass exodus after the meeting; Beech interview, 20–21. See also Sullivan, *Days of Hope,* 100. University of North Carolina Press director W. T. Couch also backed off later from much of the racial sentiment expressed at the meeting. He felt compelled to write an apologetic publisher's introduction (arguing against the sudden abolition of segregation) for Rayford W. Logan's edited collection of essays from leading black minds titled *What the Negro Wants* (Chapel Hill: University of North Carolina Press, 1944). In other places Couch was even more aggressive in his defense of Jim Crow. See his correspondence with Stetson Kennedy in *Southern Exposure.* U.S. commissioner Louise Charlton was a notable exception. She stuck to her guns and even went so far as to issue a blistering public response to the "little Hitlers" who were the same "anti-labor, anti-education, anti-Roosevelt group of do-nothing critics" who used the "shopworn smokescreen" of attacks on black people. Charlton defended her service as chair of the meeting "to begin a regional program for lifting the level of human life" and predicted that one day "Birmingham and the South will count the conference as one of its golden achievements." For Cooper Green's and Louise Charlton's contrasting behaviors, see Egerton, *Speak Now against the Day,* 292, 293 (quotations in note).

66. Starnes was from Guntersville in Marshall County. See *Alabama Magazine,* 5 December 1938, p. 7. Congressman Starnes also agreed to speak to Mabel Jones West's Alabama Council of Women's Democratic Clubs organizational meeting of a new women's club that would devote itself to "promoting American principles in Alabama, damning and downing un-American activities" (10).

67. "Stalin baited his hook with a 'progressive' worm," Dies declared, and the New Deal "suckers swallowed bait, hook, line, and sinker." See Tindall, *Emergence of the New South,* 625.

68. Just a year before, Black had opposed the anti-lynch measure as a scheme that would somehow erode labor rights. *Alabama Magazine,* 5 December 1938, p. 7 (Bankhead quotations); Tindall, *Emergence of the New South,* 552.

69. See, e.g., the characterization of Huddleston in Rogers et al., *Alabama,* 494, 501.

70. Packer, *Blood of the Liberals,* 54–55 (first quotation), 56 (second quotation).

71. Ibid., 56 (first quotation), 57 (second and third quotations).

72. Ibid., 114 (first quotation), 116 (second quotation), 124 (third and fourth quotations).

73. *Congressional Record* quoted in ibid., 121.

74. Packer, *Blood of the Liberals*, 126, 178, 180. The quotation is from pp. 177 and 179, and it continues: "Class politics, played so surely by the charismatic Roosevelt, wooed the South from its old hostility to central authority and obscured the forces that were beginning to divide the Democratic Party. But once Roosevelt was dead and the war over . . . opponents of the New Deal saw their opportunity to turn the region against Washington by singing the old, sure song of race along with the new song of Communism." In an earlier, poignant passage on p. 120, Packer writes that "One can almost point to those weeks in Washington . . . [i]n the summer of 1935, . . . as the moment when liberalism, reaching the peak of its New Deal heyday, lost its connection to something vital from the past. . . . [T]o the harm of both, liberalism and populism, the braintruster with his briefcase and the one-galloused dirt farmer, parted ways." The SCHW itself held on for ten years, eventually devolving into the Southern Conference Education Fund under James Dombrowski, which continued work on voting and civil rights but at a more modest level. There was some activity on voting rights during the Depression decade, but almost all of it was disappointing. From 1932 to 1942, despite the best efforts of Black Belt African Americans led by Macon County's Charles Gomillion, only a hundred blacks joined the voter rolls. Between 1939 and 1942, black Birmingham attorney Arthur D. Shores filed suit three times for the NAACP against the Jefferson County Board of Voting Registrars. Malcolm and Pauline Dobbs, local SCHW leaders, led the African Americans to the steps of the Jefferson County Courthouse to register. But each time the board circumvented the suit simply by registering the individual plaintiff. In Mobile, state Democratic powerhouse Gessner T. McCorvey buried the hatchet with rival state chairman John D. McQueen long enough to cooperate in cracking down on black voting and the "disgraceful and nauseating scenes" of large numbers of African American voters being "bought up like so many sheep." Gomillion interview, 2; Norrell, "Caste in Steel," 669–94, esp. p. 680; Gessner T. McCorvey to John D. McQueen, 24 April 1935 (quotation in note) and 26 April 1935, both in box 64, folder 12, and Frank Boykin to John D. McQueen, 22 January 1935, box 64, folder 1, SDEC Records. On Pauline and Malcolm Dobbs, see Sullivan, *Days of Hope*, 205–6, 215, 216.

75. Henry H. Smith to B. M. Miller, 3 November 1933 (quotation attributed to McCorvey), box SG 19950, folder: Strike Situation, Mobile 1933, Miller Papers; *Alabama Magazine*, 28 March 1938, p. 3 (second quotation).

76. *Alabama Magazine*, 1 May 1939, p. 3, 28 August 1939, p. 15.

77. Painter, *The Narrative of Hosea Hudson*, 260, 266 (first quotation); *Alabama Magazine*, 14 November 1938, p. 3 (second quotation).

78. *Alabama Magazine*, 14 November 1938, p. 3.

79. O. D. Street to Wendell Willkie, 30 July 1940, box 10, folder: Republican Political Correspondence, Street Papers, ADAH. Willkie won only Winston County in Alabama, as FDR cruised to victory with a 200,000-plus vote margin. See Sledge, "The Alabama Republican Party, 1865–1978," 127–29.

80. Greenhaw, *Elephants in the Cottonfields*, 50; Tindall, *Disruption of the Solid South*, 34 (quotation).

81. Sample DeBardeleben-Alabama Fuel and Iron Company advertisements on be-

half of Willkie appeared in *Alabama Magazine*, 22 July 1940, p. 4 (first quotation) and 11 November 1940, p. 6 (second and third quotations).

82. *Alabama Magazine*, 15 July 1940, p. 3 (second quotation), 22 July 1940, pp. 3, 5 (first quotation).

83. Carr letter reprinted in its entirety in *Alabama Magazine*, 22 July 1940, pp. 5–7.

84. While Bankhead and his brother in the U.S. Senate had made no secret of their desire to see Will tapped for the vice-presidential spot, FDR bestowed that honor on Agriculture Secretary Henry A. Wallace after Supreme Court Justice William O. Douglas declined it. Wallace was far too liberal in every way to be acceptable to the South. *Alabama Magazine*, 29 July 1940, p. 5 (first quotation) and Major Squirm column, *Alabama Magazine*, 4 November 1940, p. 15 (second and third quotations).

85. *Alabama Magazine*, 29 July 1940, p. 5 (McMillan quotation), p. 6 (Thompson quotation), 7–10.

86. See *Alabama Magazine*, 5 August 1940, pp. 6, 7 (first quotation), 12 August 1940, p. 5, 19 August 1940, pp. 5–6. See L. W. Mabry, Mobile, to ed., *Alabama Magazine*, 4 November 1940, p. 14 (quoted).

87. Robert H. Malone, Dothan, to ed., *Alabama Magazine*, 4 November 1940, p. 14. Mrs. A. Y. Malone of Dothan served as a national Democratic committeewoman. See also *Alabama Magazine*, 14 November 1938, p. 15, and 19 August 1940, p. 4 (DeBardeleben quotation), pp. 5–7, 4 November 1940, p. 8, and 11 November 1940, p. 15. Reverend A. J. Dailey of Birmingham appeared as a featured speaker on the Willkie caravan.

88. Stops included Vernon and Prattville in central Alabama, the mining town of Jasper in northwest Alabama, and the north Alabama hamlets of Florence, Sheffield, Moulton, Russellville, and Haleyville. See *Alabama Magazine*, 11 November 1940, p. 6. For the attacks on the caravan, see *Alabama Magazine*, 4 November 1940, p. 8. Radio address delivered by Gessner T. McCorvey, SDEC chair, 14 September 1940, pp. 1, 2, 5 (quotations), LPR 99, box 81, folder 12, SDEC Records.

89. Key, *Southern Politics in State and Nation*, 5–6.

90. *Alabama Magazine*, 11 November 1940, pp. 3 (second quotation) and 5 (first quotation).

91. *Alabama Magazine* editorial, 4 November 1940, p. 3.

92. Gomillion interview, 6, 8.

93. On the instances mentioned, see Tyler, "'Blood on Your Hands'"; Tindall, *Emergence of the New South*, 625. The DAR incident involved, of course, the celebrated soprano Marian Anderson.

94. E. P. Crow, Atlanta, to Franklin D. Roosevelt, 18 February 1944 (first quotation), file: Colored Matters, January–March 1944, Official Files 93, Franklin Delano Roosevelt Papers, and "Disgusted" to Editor, clipping attached to Marion M. Crisp letter, 26 March 1944 (second quotation), folder: 190.1, ER Papers. Also see Loretta Carlisle, Houston, to Eleanor Roosevelt, 18 April 1944, and Fedora Marie Carpenter, Rayville, LA, to Eleanor Roosevelt, 29 February 1944; all correspondence in FDR. See also the informative essay by Pamela Tyler that was very useful in locating relevant sources on the First Lady: "'Blood on Your Hands.'"

95. Howard C. Smith to Senator Lister Hill, 4 January 1943 (first quotation) in Hamilton, *Lister Hill*, 115. "An Outraged Woman," Lakeland, to Eleanor Roosevelt, 28 February 1944 (second quotation) and Mrs. Paul T. Norris, Quinton, Alabama, to Eleanor Roosevelt, 4 April 1944 (third quotation), both in folder: 190.1, ER Papers.

96. On Jesse Daniel Ames, see the classic by Jacquelyn Dowd Hall, *Revolt against Chivalry*. On Julia Tutwiler and Hallie Farmer, see Flynt, *Alabama in the Twentieth Century*.

97. Alabamian to Mr. President, cc. Senators Bankhead and Hill, and Congressman Frank Boykin, 4 March 1943, box 376, folder 1, J. Lister Hill Papers, UA (first quotation) (hereafter Hill Papers). See also James Willoughby to Bibb Graves, 6 April 1937, box SG 12187, folder 3, Graves Papers (second quotation).

98. See Tyler, "'Blood on Your Hands,'" for more on these relationships. The quote is Rob Hall's from Sullivan, *Days of Hope*, 100.

99. *Congressional Record*, 78th Cong., 2nd Sess. (1944), vol. 90, part 6, 20 June 1944, p. 6,253 (first quotation), cited in Tyler, "'Blood on Your Hands,'" 111 (second quotation). See also Michael W. Fitzgerald, "'We Have Found a Moses': Theodore Bilbo, Black Nationalism, and the Greater Liberia Bill of 1939," *Journal of Southern History* 63 (May 1997): 293–320.

100. Tindall, *Emergence of the New South*, 617.

101. Miss Lillie M. Williams, Monroe, LA, to Eleanor Roosevelt, 15 March 1944, folder: 190.1, ER Papers, Mrs. J. T. Stephens, Selma, AL, to Franklin D. Roosevelt, 9 October 1944, Official Files 93, file: Colored Matters, October–December 1944, FDR Papers (first quotation), and Chester B. Collins, Ft. Worth, Texas, to Franklin D. Roosevelt, 26 May 1944, Official Files 93, file: Colored Matters, April–May 1944, FDR Papers (second quotation), all correspondence at FDR. On the low opinion of the worth of black life (and, for that matter, the lives of poor whites as well) during this period, consider the warden of Kilby Prison's estimation of the "number of dead heads here that are worthless to the state." Among his list, the warden included Abe Davis, prisoner #11472 of Dallas County. "This negro has heart trouble and is in very poor physical condition. He is worthless." Alex Duncan, prisoner #32823 of Russell County, also "has heart trouble and [is] in very poor physical condition. Worthless." Dock Wellborn, prisoner #36522 of Bullock County, had granuloma inguinale and is "bed ridden . . . with little prospect of recovery. This is one that it takes about two to wait on." The warden also included white males such as Daniel Clenny, prisoner #5582 of Madison County, who had Bright's disease and "the medicine he has to take cost the state approximately fifteen dollars per month. He is worthless." F. A. Boswell Jr., Warden, Kilby Prison, to Hamp Draper, 30 October 1937, box SG 12187, folder 8: Convict Department, #1, Graves Papers.

102. Speech of Horace C. Wilkinson to the Kiwanis Club of Ensley, Alabama, 31 December 1942, titled "The Mulatto Menace," reprinted in its entirety in the *Greensboro (AL) Southern Watchman*, 3 April 1943, p. 6; Chester B. Collins, Ft. Worth, to Franklin Roosevelt, 26 May 1944, Official Files 93, file: Colored Matters, April–May 1944, FDR Papers; and Mrs. Paul T. Norris, Quinton, AL, to Eleanor Roosevelt, 4 April 1944, folder: 190.1, ER Papers, both letters in FDR.

103. Mrs. J. T. Stephens, Selma, AL, to Franklin D. Roosevelt, 9 October 1944, box 6, file: Colored Matters, October–December 1944, Official Files 93, FDR Papers, and Mrs. Paul T. Norris, Quinton, AL, to Eleanor Roosevelt, 4 April 1944, folder: 190.1, ER Papers (quotation), both in FDR Library.

104. Tyler, "'Blood on Your Hands,'" 113 (quotation). See also Marion M. Crisp letter, 26 March 1944, folder: 190.1, ER Papers.

105. Eleanor Clubs mentioned in Mrs. Paul T. Norris, Quinton, AL, to Eleanor Roosevelt, 4 April 1944, and Willie King Jones, Austin, TX, to Eleanor Roosevelt, 8 April 1944, both in the ER Papers, and Mrs. J. T. Stephens, Selma, to Franklin D. Roosevelt,

9 October 1944, box 6, file: Colored Matters, October–December 1944, Official Files 93, FDR Papers, all in FDR Library, and also Alabamian to Mr. President, cc. Bankhead, Hill, Boykin, 4 March 1943, box 376, folder 1, Hill Papers. Also see Tindall, *Emergence of the New South*, 718 (Alexander quotation).

106. For more on the clubs, see Tyler, "'Blood on Your Hands'" and Bryant Simon, "Fearing Eleanor: Whiteness and Wartime Rumors in the South, 1940–1945" (paper presented at Cambridge University History Conference, April 1999).

107. Tyler, "'Blood on Your Hands,'" 111 (Bilbo quotation); "An Outraged Woman" to Eleanor Roosevelt, 28 February 1944 (third quotation), Bertie Mae Loner to Eleanor Roosevelt, 1 March 1944 (fourth quotation), and Miss Lillie M. Williams to Eleanor Roosevelt, 6 March 1944, all in folder: 190.1, ER Papers. See also *Daily Oklahoman* clipping, ca. 14 February 1944 (second quotation) along with Margery Triuz, Woodward, Oklahoma, to Franklin Roosevelt, 16 February 1944, and news clipping ca., 14 February 1944 (also second quotation) along with E. P. Crow to Franklin D. Roosevelt, 18 February 1944, file: Colored Matters, January–March 1944, OF 93, FDR Papers. All correspondence in the FDR Library.

108. Willie King Jones to Eleanor Roosevelt, 8 April 1944 (quotation), Alma Valda Lester to Eleanor Roosevelt, 29 February 1944, Fedora Marie Carpenter to Eleanor Roosevelt, 29 February 1944, and Loretta Carlisle to Eleanor Roosevelt, 5 April 1944. A twelve-year-old Louisiana girl said that she was so appalled at the thought of blacks and whites dancing that she was "not able to put into words" how shocking it was. "It may be the Yankees way," but it certainly was not acceptable in Southern culture. Alma Valda Lester to Eleanor Roosevelt, 29 February 1944; all letters in folder: 190.1, ER Papers.

109. Miss Lillie M. Williams to Eleanor Roosevelt, 6 March 1944 (first quotation) and Loretta Carlisle to Eleanor Roosevelt, 18 April 1944 (second quotation), both in folder: 190.1, ER Papers; also Chester B. Collins to Franklin D. Roosevelt, 26 May 1944, file: Colored Matters, April–May 1944, OF 93, FDR Papers. Montgomery's Virginia Durr confirms that the "love" white southerners held for blacks in their households and the feeling that they were the "best friends" of black people were deep and genuine. It wasn't until she spent her college years at Wellesley in the North that Mrs. Durr began to question the fundamental racial assumptions that had been instilled in her as a child in Alabama and the contradictory and destructive effects of segregating one's "best friends." See Durr interview.

110. Mr. and Mrs. George B. Rogers to Franklin D. Roosevelt, 23 December 1943 (first quotation) and *Orlando Morning Sentinel* editorial clipping, 19 March 1943 (second quotation), both in PPF 2, folder: Eleanor Roosevelt, 1943, FDR Papers. See also Tyler, "'Blood on Your Hands,'" 103 (Frank Daniels quotation), 107 (FBI quotation). Another Florida newspaper, the *Fort Myers News-Press*, intimated that a divorce suit or congressional pressure was a possibility. Kennedy, *Southern Exposure*, 86.

111. Tyler, "'Blood on Your Hands,'" 108 (first quotation). Also Mrs. A. W. Taylor to Franklin Roosevelt, 29 May 1944 (second and third quotations), file: Colored Matters, April–May 1944, OF 93, FDR Papers, FDR Library. After much urging from the NAACP, the Army Air Corps agreed to black aviation cadets and established an all-black flight unit at the Tuskegee Institute in Alabama. See Rogers et al., *Alabama*, 515, 516 and Robert J. Jakeman, *The Divided Skies: Establishing Segregated Flight Training at Tuskegee, Alabama, 1934–1942* (Tuscaloosa: The University of Alabama Press, 1992).

112. Mrs. Paul T. Norris, Quinton, AL, to Eleanor Roosevelt, 4 April 1944 (first quotation) and Alma Valda Lester to Eleanor Roosevelt, 29 February 1944, both in folder: 190.1, ER Papers; Tyler, "'Blood on Your Hands,'" 115 (second quotation).

113. Chappell, *A Stone of Hope* and Manis, "'City Mothers.'" For an account that is less sanguine about southern white religious/racial enlightenment, see Paul Harvey, *Freedom's Coming: Religious Culture and the Shaping of the South from the Civil War through the Civil Rights Era* (Chapel Hill: University of North Carolina Press, 2007).

114. Mrs. J. T. Stephens, Selma, AL, to Franklin D. Roosevelt, 9 October 1944, file: Colored Matters, October–December 1944 (first quotation) and Mrs. A. W. Taylor to Franklin Roosevelt, 29 May 1944, file: Colored Matters, April–May 1944 (third quotation), both in OF 93, FDR Papers. Also Philip C. McNeil, Mobile, to Eleanor Roosevelt, 10 April 1944, folder: 190.1, Criticism, ER Papers (second quotation). A Bowdon, Georgia, man said simply "The Lord" created segregation in H. R. Johnson to Eleanor Roosevelt, 17 April 1944, also in folder: 190.1 of the ER Papers; all correspondence at FDR. See also David M. Goldenberg, *The Curse of Ham: Race and Slavery in Early Judaism, Christianity, and Islam* (Princeton: Princeton University Press, 2006).

115. Fred D. Oakley, Potts Camp, Mississippi, to Eleanor Roosevelt, 5 March 1944, folder: 190.1, ER Papers (second quotation); Allida Black, *Casting Her Own Shadow: Eleanor Roosevelt and the Shaping of Postwar Liberalism* (New York: Columbia University Press, 1996), 87 (first quotation). See also Elna C. Green, ed., *Looking for the New Deal: Florida Women's Letters during the Great Depression* (Columbia: University of South Carolina Press, 2007).

116. Durr interview, 36; Tyler, "'Blood on Your Hands,'" 103 (first quotation), 10 (second quotation), 12 (third quotation), 18, manuscript version in possession of the author.

117. Miss Lillie M. Williams to Eleanor Roosevelt, 6 March 1944 (first quotation) and Fedora Marie Carpenter to Eleanor Roosevelt, 29 February 1944 (second quotation), both in folder: 190.1, ER Papers. Also *Greensboro Watchman* clipping, 23 March 1944, file: Colored Matters, January–March 1944 (third quotation) and Chester B. Collins to Franklin D. Roosevelt, 26 May 1944, file: Colored Matters, April–May 1944, both in OF 93, FDR Papers.

118. Congressman Charles McKenzie (D-LA) quoted in *Daily Oklahoman* clipping, ca. 14 February 1944; Margery Triuz, Woodward, OK, to Franklin Roosevelt, 16 February 1944, file: Colored Matters, January–March 1944, OF 93, FDR Papers.

119. Marion M. Crisp, Elaine, AR, to Eleanor Roosevelt, 26 March 1944 (quotation), and Fred D. Oakley, Potts Camp, MS, to Eleanor Roosevelt, 5 March 1944, both in folder: 190.1, ER Papers. The *Orlando Morning Sentinel* agreed that Eleanor was "too busy sticking her nose into too many people's business," 19 March 1943 clipping, file: Eleanor Roosevelt, 1943, PPF 2, FDR Papers. See also M. M. Moulthrop, mayor of Eufaula (Barbour County), to Eleanor Roosevelt, 20 July 1942, box 376, folder 1, Hill Papers.

120. Mrs. Paul T. Norris, Quinton, AL, to Eleanor Roosevelt, 4 April 1944, folder: 190.1, ER Papers (first quotation); M. M. Moulthrop, Mayor of Eufaula, AL, to Eleanor Roosevelt, 20 July 1942, box 376, folder 1, Hill Papers (second quotation).

121. J. H. Bradford, Uniontown, AL, letter, 21 February 1944, file: Colored Matters, January–March 1944, Official Files 93, FDR Papers, and Alabamian to Mr. President, cc. Bankhead, Hill, Boykin, 4 March 1943, box 376, folder 1, Hill Papers.

122. Tyler, "'Blood on Your Hands,'" 113 (J. T. Graves quotation). See also Bertie Mae Loner to Eleanor Roosevelt, 1 March 1944 (second quotation) and Fred D. Oakley to Eleanor Roosevelt, 5 March 1944, both in file: 190.1, ER Papers.

123. Mrs. J. T. Stephens to Franklin D. Roosevelt, 9 October 1944, box 6, file: Colored Matters, October–December 1944, Official Files 93, FDR Papers.

Chapter 7

1. Wayne Flynt section of Rogers et al., *Alabama*, 524–25. A very similar assessment is found in Webb, *Two-Party Politics in the One-Party South*, 1.

2. See Sullivan's excellent study: *Days of Hope*, 188–89, 191 (quotations).

3. John A. Salmond, *A Southern Rebel: The Life and Times of Aubrey Willis Williams, 1890–1965* (Chapel Hill: University of North Carolina Press, 1983), 181 (Williams quoted); Salmond, *The Conscience of a Lawyer: Clifford J. Durr and American Civil Liberties, 1899–1975* (Tuscaloosa: The University of Alabama Press, 1990), 92–94; Salmond, "'Flag-Bearers for Integration and Justice'"; Egerton, *Speak Now against the Day*, 259, 341–59.

4. Sullivan, *Days of Hope*, 187 (first quotation), 189 (CIO executive board quoted); Bunche, *The Political Status of the Negro in the Age of FDR*, 32. Bunche was, though, still a bit cynical, remarking in 1940 that "Like the Negro, the white South holds out its hands for alms and special privilege" (34).

5. Sullivan, *Days of Hope*, 188.

6. Ibid., 188–89 (quotation). See also the "lost opportunities" thesis most closely identified with Robert Korstad, Nelson Lichtenstein, and Michael Honey that laments the eclipse of a radical, labor-based early civil rights movement, betrayed by the alleged failure and indifference of liberal institutions such as unions. According to the thesis, a leftist, black, working-class-based civil rights movement, thwarted by liberal failure, resulted in a modern movement characterized by middle-class church leadership and destined for much more modest, bureaucratic, and legalistic accomplishments. See Korstad and Lichtenstein, "Opportunities Found and Lost" and Michael Honey, *Southern Labor and Black Civil Rights: Organizing Memphis Workers* (Urbana: University of Illinois Press, 1993).

7. William D. Barnard, "The Old Order Changes: Graves, Sparks, Folsom, and the Gubernatorial Election of 1942," *Alabama Review* 28 (July 1975): 163–84. See p. 174 (Graves election quote), and p. 182 (north Alabama and Black Belt quote). According to Barnard, and every other scholar who has looked at the South, the division in Alabama was quite stark: "The Democratic party in Alabama was split in the 1940s, as it had been in rough fashion since Reconstruction, into two factions. One, favoring an expansion of state services and identifying with Franklin Roosevelt's New Deal in the 1930s, drew its strength from the mining and farming regions of *north Alabama*, from organized labor, city and county officeholders, the elderly, and educators. The other, *favoring low taxes and economical government at all costs and vehemently anti–New Deal*, drew its support from the business and industrial community and from conservative agricultural interests, particularly in the *Black Belt*" (italics added) (163–64). Not only has the north Alabama–south Alabama dichotomy been overstated, as has been and will be discussed, there actually existed somewhat of an east Alabama-west Alabama cleavage apparent in things like politics and support for the Klan that has received little to no attention.

8. Barnard, "The Old Order Changes," 164n4 (quoted) cites Albert Burton Moore,

History of Alabama (1934; reprint, Tuscaloosa: Alabama Book Store, 1951), 774–77, as evidence for his exceedingly generous evaluation of Alabama's, and Bibb Graves's, relationship to the KKK. Actually, Alabama's societal and cultural support for the KKK had been very broad and deep. Violence occurred much earlier and in much greater frequency and intensity, and with far greater societal support, than has been traditionally portrayed. Bibb Graves actively worked to protect violent Klansmen from being punished by law enforcement. Opposition to the order emanating from the "better sorts" was, in large measure, conservative and an ongoing reaction to Reconstruction. It was mostly pragmatic and based on the most mercenary calculation of staving off federal interference on race relations and preserving the state's ability to attract outside investment. See Feldman, *Politics, Society, and the Klan in Alabama*.

9. Thornton, "Hugo Black and the Golden Age," 899–913.

10. Rogers at al., *Alabama*, 525, 526 (quotes about Sparks).

11. Sarah Newman Shouse, *Hillbilly Realist: Herman Clarence Nixon of Possum Trot* (Tuscaloosa: The University of Alabama Press, 1986), 168.

12. Egerton, *Speak Now against the Day*, 391 (quotation). See, e.g., Webb, *Two-Party Politics in the One-Party South*, 1.

13. Rogers et al., *Alabama*, 524 (Flynt title); Thornton, "Hugo Black and the Golden Age."

14. Beech interview, 16 and 17 (Egerton quoted).

15. Rogers et al., *Alabama*, 525–26. For more on Sparkman, see Susan Youngblood Ashmore, "Southern Accents: The Politics of Race and the Economic Opportunity Act of 1964," in *History and Hope in the Heart of Dixie: Scholarship, Activism, and Wayne Flynt in the Modern South*, ed. Gordon E. Harvey, Richard D. Starnes, and Glenn Feldman (Tuscaloosa: The University of Alabama Press, 2006), 33.

16. To his credit, Wayne Flynt recognized that "when Northern liberals and Southern conservatives increasingly linked liberalism to race relations, the New Deal coalition in Alabama began to unravel." Yet Flynt put this at a much later date than does the present study: "By the late 1950s liberalism had taken on a racial meaning in Alabama politics that made it unacceptable to most white voters." Rogers et al., *Alabama*, 525. In another spot in his narrative, Flynt put the date at which "race became central to state politics" as the "later 1940s. . . . The turning point . . . came in the Dixiecrat movement of 1948" (532).

17. Christopher MacGregor Scribner, "Federal Funding, Urban Renewal, and Race Relations: Birmingham in Transition, 1945–1955," *Alabama Review* 48 (October 1995): 269–95; Tindall, *Emergence of the New South*, 696–700; Rogers et al., *Alabama*, 512, 521–22.

18. Scribner, "Federal Funding, Urban Renewal, and Race Relations"; Tindall, *Emergence of the New South*, 696–700; Rogers et al., *Alabama*, 512, 521–22.

19. Rogers et al., *Alabama*, 511–13.

20. Brown and Davis, *It Is Union and Liberty*, 84–110; Allen W. Cronenberg, *Forth to the Mighty Conflict: Alabama and World War II* (Tuscaloosa: The University of Alabama Press, 1995); Rogers et al., *Alabama*, 512, 513, 514, 523; Tindall, *Emergence of the New South*, 701 (journalist quoted), 702. Dos Passos, a member of the "Lost Generation" of writers, is of course best known for his *U.S.A. Trilogy*.

21. Gomillion interview, 9. See Jakeman, *The Divided Skies*. See also Rogers et al., *Alabama*, 515–16 and Daniel Kryder, *Divided Arsenal: Race and the American State during World War II* (New York: Cambridge University Press, 2001).

22. A federal minimum-wage requirement was part of both the 1936 Walsh-Healey Act and the 1938 Fair Labor Standards Act, which had begun as the (Hugo) Black Wages and Hours Bill.

23. Wright, *Old South, New South*; Gilbert C. Fite, *Beyond the Fence Rows: A History of Farmland Industries, Inc., 1929–1978* (Columbia: University of Missouri Press, 1978); Pete Daniel, *Lost Revolutions: The South in the 1950s* (Chapel Hill: University of North Carolina Press, 2000); Cobb, *Industrialization and Southern Society*. In 1950 Alabama's farmers cultivated nearly twenty-one million acres of land (an all-time high). See also Rogers et al., *Alabama*, 519–20.

24. W.C.T. Carter to ed., *Collier's Weekly*, 14 July 1943 (quotation), box SG 12491, folder 7, Alabama Governors Papers, Chauncey Sparks Papers, ADAH (hereafter Sparks Papers).

25. See, e.g., Thurman Sensing, director of research for the Southern States Industrial Council, speech ca. 1944, "The South Has No Racial Problem," box SG 12491, folder 8, Sparks Papers (quotation).

26. Ibid. See also Kennedy, *Southern Exposure*, 199 (SSIC and Rankin quoted). See also John U. Barr to Frank M. Dixon, 30 December 1948, box 2, folder 5, Dixon Personal Papers.

27. During the war, Rankin responded to Carl Sandburg's call for conquest of the color line by denouncing the poet as "a communist-front propagandist" who was trying to "mongrelize America." Kennedy, *Southern Exposure*, 201 (Rankin quoted in note). *Congressional Record*, 78th Cong., 2nd Sess., 5054 (first Rankin quotation) cited in Tindall, *Emergence of the New South*, 715, also p. 444 (Edgerton quoted). See also Andrew Kersten, *Race, Jobs, and the War: The FEPC in the Midwest, 1941–46* (Champaign: University of Illinois Press, 2000); Bruce J. Schulman, *From Cottonbelt to Sunbelt: Federal Policy, Economic Development, and the Transformation of the South, 1938–1990* (New York: Oxford University Press, 1991), 24 (last quotation).

28. Frank M. Dixon to Ralph D. Williams, Defense Supplies Corporation, New York, printed in the *Montgomery Advertiser*, 24 July 1942, box 4, folder: Racial Question, 1942, range H, section 4, shelf e, Chauncey Sparks Personal Papers, ADAH (quoted).

29. *Alabama Magazine*, 9 October 1942, p. 3.

30. Among those who sent congratulations were Thomas McGough, a director of the SSIC and president of the Birmingham-based McGough Bakeries, Robert I. Ingalls of Ingalls Shipbuilding Corporation, I. W. "Ike" Rouzer, president of the Alabama Mining Institute, J. Bruce Henderson, Wilcox County state senator, Fred D. Renneker and H. G. Seibels, Birmingham insurance executives, Mrs. L. P. Munger and J. Frank Rushton Jr., also of Birmingham, Judge Walter B. Jones of Montgomery, Elbert S. Jemison of the Jemison Land Companies, Milton H. Fies of DeBardeleben Coal, W. Howell Morrow of Lanett, and Borden Burr, perhaps the state's leading anti-labor attorney. Congratulatory Letters Received by Governor Dixon on the Race Segregation Issue, list, ca. August 1942, box SG 12277, folder 30, Dixon Papers. Black support for Dixon's position was negligible. Only twelve notes of congratulation were cited in this list of hundreds of letters and telegrams, all coming from a group of black doctors, funeral directors, and Baptist and Methodist ministers in Gadsden. See also T. A. McGough to Frank M. Dixon, 25 July 1942, box SG 12276, folder 11 and Donald Comer to Frank M. Dixon, 6 August 1942, box SG 12276, folder 10, both in Dixon Papers. For more on McGough's background, see Kennedy, *Southern Exposure*, 200. For more on the new Wilkinson-Dixon alliance, see the

Atticus Mullin column in the *Montgomery Advertiser*, 31 July 1942, p. 7. The Alabama Mining Institute was staffed by some of Alabama's biggest mules. I. W. Rouzer served as president, Prince DeBardeleben and R. T. Daniel were vice presidents, and Charles F. DeBardeleben, Hugh Morrow, and Herbert Tutwiler served on the board of governors. See I. W. Rouzer to Frank M. Dixon, 13 August 1942, box SG 12276, folder 10, Dixon Papers. In 1943 Liberty National Life Insurance Company, under Frank P. Samford, merged with Brown-Service, the largest funeral insurance company in the world, to give Samford control of Alabama's largest (and the United States' tenth-largest), insurance firm. See *Alabama Magazine*, 28 July 1944, p. 7. See also Borden Burr to Gessner T. McCorvey, 4 November 1948, box 2, folder 5, Dixon Personal Papers.

31. Ben D. Turner, president, Mobile Chamber of Commerce, to Frank M. Dixon, 7 August 1942, Opelika Rotary Club Resolution to Frank M. Dixon, 11 August 1942, and S. Palmer Keith, president of the Bessemer Lions Club, to Frank M. Dixon, 4 August 1942, all in box SG 12276, folder 10, Dixon Papers. See also the Opelika Rotary Club, Bessemer Lions Club, Ensley Kiwanis Club, and Mobile Chamber of Commerce, all in the Congratulatory Letters Received by Governor Dixon on the Race Segregation Issue, list, ca. August 1942, box SG 12277, folder 30 and C. C. Williams, committeeman, Ensley Kiwanis Club, to Frank M. Dixon, 13 August 1942, box SG 12276, folder 11, all in Dixon Papers.

32. R. T. Brooke to Frank M. Dixon, 31 July 1942, box SG 12276, folder 11 (first quotation) and J. F. Duggar to Frank M. Dixon, 7 August 1942, box SG 12276, folder 10 (second quotation), both in Dixon Papers. See also Hugh F. McElderry, executive secretary, Talladega Chamber of Commerce, to Frank M. Dixon, 7 August 1942, same box, folder 10.

33. Virginia Durr to Clark and Mairi Jemison, September 1959, quoted and cited in Flynt, *Poor but Proud*, 335.

34. Virginia Durr to Judge Jones, n.d., box 1, folder 5, V. Durr Papers.

35. "Kluxers on the Prowl," *Newsweek* 34 (11 July 1949): 21–22 (first quotation); Tuskegee Institute News Clipping Files: Anti-Negro Groups File, reel 108, 1949, TU; *Montgomery Advertiser*, 13 June 1948 (second quotation).

36. Mrs. Henry W. Dunn, Gadsden, to Frank M. Dixon, 12 August 1942 (first quotation), Mrs. A. L. (Mary) White, Birmingham, to Frank M. Dixon, 30 July 1942 (second quotation), and Mrs. Minnie Callaway Claiborne, Bessemer, to Frank M. Dixon, 31 July 1942, all three in box SG 12276, folder 10, Dixon Papers. Also see Endorsement (West Blocton), ca. July 1942, and James A. Chappell to Frank M. Dixon, 30 July 1942 (third quotation), both in same box, folder 11, Dixon Papers.

37. S. Palmer Keith to Frank M. Dixon, 4 August 1942, box SG 12276, folder 10, Dixon Papers.

38. Frank M. Dixon to S. P. Galliard, 13 August 1942 (first Dixon quotation), Frank M. Dixon to Mrs. James A. Carney, Battle's Wharf, 5 August 1942 (second Dixon quotation), and Frank M. Dixon to Willis Pace Estis, 19 August 1942, all in box SG 12276, folder 10, Dixon Papers.

39. Beech interview, 20.

40. *Cullman Democrat*, 30 July 1942, clipping in box 4, folder: Racial Question, 1942, Sparks Personal Papers. See the miscellaneous newspaper clippings in box 8, range I, section 7, shelf b, Pete Jarman Papers, ADAH. Alabama's congressional delegation in 1942 included Frank Boykin, George Grant, H. B. Steagall, Sam Hobbs, Joseph Starnes, Pete

Jarman, Carter Manasco, John Sparkman, and John Newsome. See *Alabama Magazine*, 19 June 1942, p. 7. George Grant to Frank M. Dixon, 24 July 1942 (first quotation); also see the letters to Dixon from Joseph Starnes and Frank Boykin on the same date, John Sparkman on 25 July 1942, Sam Hobbs on 29 July 1942 (second quotation), H. B. Steagall on 4 August 1942, Pete Jarman on 14 September 1942, W. D. Malone to Frank M. Dixon, 31 July 1942, and John H. Bankhead to Wallace D. Malone, 29 July 1942. Mining magnate I. W. Rouzer was also against this "cramming [of] negro soldiers in southern camps." See Ike Rouzer to Joseph Starnes, 29 July 1942, all in box SG 12277, folder 30, and also the miscellaneous news clipping, ca. August 1942 (Bankhead quoted) in box SG 12276, folder 10, all in Dixon Papers. General Marshall declined the request.

41. "An American" (Atlantic City, NJ) to Frank M. Dixon, 24 July 1942 (first quotation), "An American Mother" (New York City) to Frank M. Dixon, 16 August 1942 (second quotation), and no name (Cleveland) to Frank M. Dixon, ca. 30 July 1942 (third quotation), all in box SG 12276, folder 11, Dixon Papers.

42. "An American" (Atlantic City, NJ) to Frank M. Dixon, 24 July 1942 (second quotation), W. C. Raines to Frank M. Dixon, 20 August 1942 (third quotation), and Rollins Leonard Winslow to Frank M. Dixon, 8 August 1942 (fourth quotation), all in box SG 12276, folder 11, and the *Philadelphia Inquirer*, 25 July 1942 (first quotation), clipping in box SG 12276, folder 10, all in Dixon Papers. See *Alabama Magazine*, 31 July 1942, p. 6.

43. G. F. Porter, secretary of the Dallas NAACP, to Frank M. Dixon, 28 July 1942 (first quotation) and unsigned letter (Raleigh, NC), ca. 30 July 1942 (second quotation). The North Carolina writer also damned Alabama as "a black state" and asked the state's whites to "try to be human wrather [sic] than a brute." The Alabama Farmer's Union, largely black and somewhat communist, also sent a resolution protesting Dixon's refusal of the War Production Board contract. See Gerald Harris, president, Alabama Farmer's Union, to Frank M. Dixon, 5 August 1942. Also see no name (Memphis) to Frank M. Dixon, ca. 30 July 1942. All four letters in box SG 12276, folder 11, Dixon Papers.

44. The *Selma Times-Journal* editorial "A Champion Arises," ca. 6 August 1942 (first quotation), urged Alabamians to turn quickly "to sources of strength or we shall be lost." For Ed Field as editor of the *Selma Times-Journal*, see *Alabama Magazine*, 16 March 1945, p. 15. See the *Pell City News*, 30 July 1942 (third quotation), clipping, and the *Mobile Post*, 7 August 1942, editorial "South Rallies behind Dixon," the *Decatur Daily* editorial, "Dixon Courage," and the *Dothan Eagle* editorial "Alabama Unintimidated," all ca. 30 July 1942, and all of the above in this note from box 4, folder: Racial Question, 1942, Sparks Personal Papers. Sam B. Sloane's *Sumter County Journal*, ca. 30 July 1942 (second quotation), clipping in box SG 12276, folder 11, Dixon Papers.

45. A. B. Hale to Frank M. Dixon, ca. 28 July 1942 (first quotation), box SG 12276, folder 11, Mrs. A. L. (Mary) White to Frank M. Dixon, 30 July 1942 (third quotation), box SG 12276, folder 10, and Mrs. James A. Carney, Battles Wharf, Alabama, to Frank M. Dixon, 3 August 1942, box SG 12276, folder 10, all in Dixon Papers. See also Levie Shelley to Judge Chauncey Sparks, 28 July 1942 (second quotation), box 4, folder: Racial Question, 1942, Sparks Personal Papers. A recent title that makes good use of this phrase is Jeffrey Frederick, *Stand Up for Alabama: Governor George C. Wallace* (Tuscaloosa: The University of Alabama Press, 2007).

46. "A Dangerous Order," Speech of Hon. John E. Rankin, House of Representatives, 1 December 1942, *Congressional Record* Extract (first quotation) and Horace C. Wil-

kinson to Frank M. Dixon, 29 August 1942, both in box SG 12277, folder 29, Dixon Papers. See also *Alabama Magazine*, 21 August 1942, p. 11, and 23 October 1942, p. 15 (second quotation from both). For Milton Webster of the FEPC repeatedly quoted, see the *Alabama Magazine*, 25 June 1942, pp. 6 and 15, and 31 March 1944, p. 5.

47. A. B. Hale to Frank M. Dixon, ca. 28 July 1942, box SG 12276, folder 10, Dixon Papers.

48. Benjamin B. Gossett, Charlotte, NC, to Frank M. Dixon, 13 August 1942 (first quotation) and J. F. Duggar to Frank M. Dixon, 7 August 1942 (third quotation), both in box SG 12276, folder 10, Dixon Papers. For the almost exact phrasing as the first quotation, see R. A. Bragg to Dixon et al., 24 July 1942, box 4, folder: Racial Question, 1942, Sparks Personal Papers and "A Champion Arises" (second quotation). Dixon agreed with the cultural assessments of his position: the federal position was "naturally repugnant to me" and represented "an extremely dangerous situation in this section . . . being forced on the Southern people." See Frank M. Dixon to Oliver Day Street, 19 August 1942, box 10, folder: 1942 Political Republican Correspondence, Street Papers, ADAH.

49. "Your Friend" to Frank M. Dixon, 5 August 1942 (first quotation) and *Dothan Eagle* editorial, ca. August 1942 (second quotation), reprinted in miscellaneous news clippings, both in box SG 12276, folder 10, Dixon Papers. Horace Hall pointedly criticized Col. Harry Ayers of the *Anniston Times*, Victor Hanson's *Birmingham News*, and his nephew Grover C. Hall Jr. of the *Montgomery Advertiser*. These "historical ignoramuses," Hall charged, apparently suffered under the delusion that journalistic laurels could best be won with "a dagger thrust deep into the backs of their own people" (part of second quotation).

50. I should make it clear that "Reconstruction Syndrome" is a term I coined in earlier works to describe the concept that has been used throughout this and other works. H. L. Hargrove to Frank M. Dixon, 10 August 1942, clipping enclosed of the *Mobile Post*, 7 August 1942 (Floridian quoted), J. F. Duggar to Frank M. Dixon, 7 August 1942 (second quotation), and for the fault lying with the "federal government [and] . . . the First Lady," see Miss Terrell Whitman to Frank M. Dixon, 8 August 1942, all three in box SG 12276, folder 10, Dixon Papers.

51. O. D. Street to Frank M. Dixon, 15 August 1942, box 10, folder: 1942, Political Republican Correspondence, Street Papers, ADAH. Nor was this a particularly new, or strictly southern, phenomenon. Nineteenth-century philosopher Georg Hegel wrote of the tension in German society between a landed aristocratic elite, the *junkers*, and the centralization of power in the "state," with alliances built into bureaucracies and universities with their intelligentsia. Hegel pled for people not to make the mistake of conceiving of "the state" as something alien, foreign, or external to them. See Muller, *The Mind and the Market*, 140–42, 161–63, and esp. 154–55.

52. Resolution of the Bessemer Lions Club, 28 July 1942, box SG 12276, folder 10, Dixon Papers.

53. "A Champion Arises" (Dixon quoted). Dixon's speech to the Southern Society of New York, 11 December 1942 (second quotation), copy of speech sent with R. H. Powell to Frank M. Dixon, 23 December 1942, box 1, folder 27, Dixon Personal Papers.

54. *Cullman Democrat*, 30 July 1942 (first quotation) and *Montgomery Advertiser*, 24 July 1942 (Dixon quotations), both clippings in box 4, folder: Racial Question, 1942, Sparks Personal Papers. Dixon's quotes also appear in the *Alabama Magazine*, 31 July 1942, p. 5.

376 / Notes to Pages 182-187

55. *Decatur Daily* editorial reprinted in the *Mobile Post*, 7 August 1942 (quoted), clipping in H. L. Hargrove to Frank M. Dixon, 10 August 1942, box SG 12276, folder 10, Dixon Papers. Other quotations all in *Alabama Magazine*, 31 July 1942, p. 6, see also p. 7. Final quotation is from a *Dothan Eagle* editorial.

56. *Decatur Daily* and *Dothan Eagle* quotations in *Alabama Magazine*, 7 August 1942, pp. 7, 11.

57. *Alabama Magazine*, 7 August 1942, p. 11. Grover C. Hall Jr.'s editorial has sometimes mistakenly been interpreted as a celebration of Alabama's predominant liberalism of the period instead of what it was, a warning to Dixon to right himself away from the provocative course set by Talmadge, Bilbo, and Blease and to take a quieter path toward preserving Jim Crow.

58. Col. Harry M. Ayers, a longtime anti-Klan critic of Wilkinson's, criticized the suggestion as "in effect . . . an invitation to a resurgence of the Ku Klux Klan." See the *Anniston Star* quoted in the *Alabama Magazine*, 31 July 1942, p. 6.

59. *Selma Times-Journal* editorial (first quotation) and *Alabama Magazine* (second quotation), both in the *Alabama Magazine*, 31 July 1942, p. 6.

60. Frank M. Dixon to Mrs. A. L. (Mary) White, 3 August 1942 (first quotation), in box SG 12276, folder 10, Dixon Papers; *Opp Weekly Journal*, 30 July 1942 (second quotation), clipping in box 4, folder: Racial Question, 1942, Sparks Personal Papers.

Chapter 8

1. Henry F. DeBardeleben to Congressman Joseph Starnes, 29 July 1942, box SG 12277, folder 30, Dixon Papers; *Alabama Magazine*, 3 July 1942, p. 3.

2. I. W. Rouzer to Joseph Starnes, 29 July 1942, box SG 12277, folder 30, Dixon Papers. Rouzer believed that blacks had "more rights, more freedom, and more downright security" in the South than "anyplace on the globe" and that all of that would be "reversed" if the present racial challenges continued. Rouzer also thought that it was the "Lady of the White House" who had "thoughtfully (or thoughtlessly) made a complete mess of her reign as the First Lady . . . [with] the blessing and help of all the half-baked reformers and 'wackies' of the nation . . . inspiring a false hope in the breast of the negro race by her stupid determination to break down the wall of social equality" and by doing "a pretty good job of stirring up" hard racial feelings.

3. Joseph Starnes to Frank M. Dixon, 24 July 1942, box SG 12277, folder 30, Dixon Papers.

4. *Alabama Magazine*, 12 and 19 June 1942, both p. 3. The press breakdown on the FEPC hearings was initially similar to that on the Frank Dixon issue, with the *Dothan Eagle*, the *Gadsden Times*, a number of the state weeklies, and John Temple Graves II's column in the *Birmingham Age-Herald* against it while Harry Ayers's *Anniston Times* and Victor Hanson's *Birmingham Age-Herald*, *Birmingham News*, and *Montgomery Advertiser* expressed support for it. See the *Alabama Magazine*, 25 June 1942, pp. 6–7, 15.

5. *Dothan Eagle* quoted in *Alabama Magazine*, 19 June 1942, p. 7 (second quotation), p. 3.

6. Major Squirm column in *Alabama Magazine*, 25 June 1942, p. 15 (first quotation), p. 3 (second quotation).

7. *Dothan Eagle* quoted in *Alabama Magazine*, 19 June 1942, p. 7 (first and second quotations) and standard editorial in 25 June 1942, p. 3 (third quotation). On John

Beecher's background, see the *Alabama Magazine*, 12 June 1942, p. 7. See also John Beecher and Steven Ford Brown, *One More River to Cross: The Selected Poems of John Beecher* (Montgomery, AL: NewSouth Books, 2003).

8. *Alabama Magazine*, 12 June 1942, p. 7 (first quotation). Major Squirm quotation from columns in issues on 12, 19, and 25 June 1942, all on p. 15. Baughn outed as Major Squirm by editor Barrett Shelton of the *Decatur Daily* in *Alabama Magazine*, 12 May 1944, p. 15.

9. *Alabama Magazine*, 25 June 1942, p. 7.

10. *Louisville Courier-Journal*, 21 June 1942 (Ethridge quoted). FDR created a second FEPC in May 1942 with twelve regional offices, including Dallas and Atlanta. But it died in 1946 for want of an additional congressional appropriation. See also Tindall, *Emergence of the New South*, 713–15.

11. *Alabama Magazine*, 4 and 11 September 1942, p. 6 in both. Cobbs, Hall, and Samford would soon leave the regular Democratic Party to lead the Alabama Dixiecrats and then, after that, the GOP.

12. Hubert Baughn admitted that race was "the fundamental issue" in the South. See Major Squirm column in the *Alabama Magazine*, 19 June 1942, p. 15.

13. Miss Lida Bestor Robinson to Frank M. Dixon, 29 July 1942, box SG 12276, folder 11 (first quotation), Mrs. Estelle Cassimus to Frank M. Dixon, 13 November 1942, box SG 12277, folder 29 (second quotation), both in Dixon Papers. Dave Smith, "The Dope on Dixie Cops," ca. August 1943, clipping in box SG 12491, folder 8, Sparks Papers (third quotation).

14. The writer also recommended disfranchisement for blacks "on the basis of demonstrable cranial sub-adultism" and pledged himself "prepared to work for the Lily White cause" whatever the cost. "A cure must be found for this cancer in our country." See Charles Eli Sexton to Chauncey Sparks, ca. 20 September 1943, box SG 12491, folder 7, Sparks Papers.

15. H. D. Kissinger, Kansas City, MO, to Chauncey Sparks, 28 August 1943, doggerel attached to letter, box SG 12491, folder 8, Sparks Papers.

16. In fact, the privileged in Alabama had welcomed the rejuvenation of the hooded order for about a decade until the political contest had become critical. See Feldman, *Politics, Society, and the Klan in Alabama*.

17. Mabel Jones West to Frank M. Dixon, 24 August 1942 (first quotation) and Frank M. Dixon to Mabel Jones West, 27 August 1942, both in box SG 12277, folder 29, Dixon Papers; Briget McCauley to Chauncey Sparks, 27 September 1943, box SG 12491, folder 7, Sparks Papers (second quotation); Elman Caldwell to Chauncey Sparks, 25 April 1943, box SG 12398, folder 19, Sparks Papers. Caldwell also admitted that he had taken part in "numerous horsewhipping[s] of those blacks and I hate the ground every Nigra walks upon," as he described himself as "a True Son of the South." He recommended that blacks be reduced to a "state of servility such as they were during the Ante Bellum days" because "[t]he Nigra is inferior and God did [not] intend that they should have" any more than the bare necessities. For the Wilkinson-Dixon alliance, see the Atticus Mullin column in the *Montgomery Advertiser*, 28 July 1942, in the *Opp Weekly Journal*, 30 July 1942, clipping in box 4, folder: Racial Question, 1942, Sparks Personal Papers. The comments of Archibald Rutledge, poet laureate of South Carolina, appear in Jason Morgan Ward, "'Negroes, the New Deal . . . and Karl Marx': Southern Antistatism in Depression and War," 9–10, manuscript in possession of the author. I thank Professor Ward for making

this paper available to me. Also Robert Erskine Kerr to Frank M. Dixon, 26 August 1942, box SG 12277, folder 29, Dixon Papers. One writer pleaded for the South to leave FDR's Democratic Party to vote for "a real true American, not one who is putting Africans in our place, and who will surely rule or ruin the white race." "One of the Insulted Whites from the South," working in D.C., to Chauncey Sparks, 13 August 1943, box SG 12409, folder 7, Sparks Papers.

18. *CIO News Digest* quoted in the *Alabama Magazine*, 14 August 1942, p. 3 (first quotation); the second quotation is from a news item in the same issue of the *Alabama Magazine*, p. 6. The rather tasteless criticism of Dixon's physical deformity was in reference to the fact that he had had a leg amputated while serving as a volunteer aviator in the French Air Force during World War I.

19. Harry H. Smith to Chauncey Sparks, 30 September 1943, box SG 12491, folder 7, Sparks Papers (first quotation); Monroe Stephens to Horace Wilkinson, 24 July 1942, box SG 12277, folder 30, Dixon Papers (second quotation). Stephens resided near the Alabama-Georgia line as had his family "on all sides" since 1838.

20. Gessner T. McCorvey to E. Ray Scott, 2 October 1942, box SG 12234, folder 21, Dixon Papers.

21. Ibid. Alabama's Bourbons applauded McCorvey because he "spoke the language of most Alabamians" and was willing to "stand up and fight for Southern principles of democracy" against the New Deal "conglomeration of radical rousers and social equality advocates." See *Alabama Magazine*, 13 November 1942, p. 6.

22. T. E. "Bull" Connor to Franklin D. Roosevelt, 6 August 1942, box 376, folder 3, Hill Papers. The Connor letter is also found in box SG 12491, folder 5, Sparks Papers.

23. Wilkinson-Dixon scatter sheet mentioned in the Atticus Mullin column in the *Montgomery Advertiser*, 28 July 1942, cited in the *Opp Weekly Journal*, 30 July 1942 (first quotation); Levie Shelley to Judge Chauncey Sparks, 28 July 1942 (second quotation), both in box 4, folder: Racial Question, 1942, Sparks Personal Papers; J. H. Tucker, Ensley, AL, to Frank M. Dixon, 1 August 1942, box SG 12276, folder 10, Dixon Papers. *Alabama Magazine*, 18 September 1942, p. 7 (PM quoted).

24. Horace C. Wilkinson, "Racial Relations! An Address Delivered before the Kiwanis Club of Bessemer, Alabama," 22 July 1942, box 376, folder 1, Hill Papers. A copy of the speech also appears in box 4, folder: Racial Question, 1942, Sparks Personal Papers.

25. Ibid. At one point during the speech Wilkinson displayed the sophistic art of denial: "These instances . . . are not mentioned for the purpose of arousing feeling against the negro race." By and large, white southerners rejected the "one-world liberalism" of Wendell Willkie. See Greenhaw, *Elephants in the Cottonfields*, 50.

26. See, e.g., Herbert R. Northrup, *The Negro in the Automobile Industry* (Philadelphia: Industrial Research Unit, Wharton School of Finance and Commerce, University of Pennsylvania, 1968), 17, 70–71; Lloyd H. Bailer, "Auto Unions and Negro Labor," 550–56, 562–66, cited in Northrup, *The Negro and the Automobile Industry*, 17; Norrell, "Caste in Steel, 669–94, e.g., pp. 681–82; Nelson, *Divided We Stand;* and Moreno, *Black Americans and Organized Labor.*

27. Resolution from W. H. Hollis, chair of the Negro Masonic Temple's Citizens Committee on Jobs and Training, to Chauncey Sparks, 4 December 1942, sent on 10 December 1942, box SG 12491, folder 8, Sparks Papers (quotation).

28. Mrs. J. B. Newman, Cheverly, Hyattsville, MD, to Chauncey Sparks, 30 August 1943 (first quotation). A black Missouri preacher wondered if the time would ever come

when members of his race would not be restricted to menial labor. See Rev. Outee A. Renfro Sr. to Chauncey Sparks, 31 August 1943, both in box SG 12491, folder 8, Sparks Papers. Neal Dugger, Ensley, to Frank M. Dixon, 31 July 1942, box SG 12276, folder 10, Dixon Papers (second quotation). See also Norrell on the "centrality of race to the experience of workers" in "Caste in Steel," 670.

29. A number of labor historians are in agreement on this issue. See Norrell, "Caste in Steel," 681; Irving Howe and B. J. Widdick, *The UAW and Walter Reuther* (New York: Random House, 1949), 228; Northrup, *The Negro and the Automobile Industry,* 57 (quoted); Bruce Nelson, "'CIO Meant One Thing for the Whites and Another Thing for Us': Steelworkers and Civil Rights, 1936–1974," in *Southern Labor in Transition,* ed. Robert H. Zieger (Knoxville: University of Tennessee Press, 1997), 113–45; and F. Ray Marshall, *The Negro and Organized Labor* (New York: John Wiley and Sons, 1965) on the UAW and race, 69, 83n53. On Philip Murray's view, see p. 114 and Norrell, "Caste in Steel," 681.

30. Willis Pace Estis, Pleasant Grove, to Frank M. Dixon, 17 August 1942, Virgil Powell to Frank M. Dixon, 4 August 1942 (first quotation) and 14 July 1942, and Neal Carroll to Frank M. Dixon, 3 August 1942, all in box SG 12276, folder 10, Dixon Papers; *Alabama Magazine,* 18 September 1942, p. 7 (Victor Bernstein cited on O'Connell quotation).

31. Norrell, "Caste in Steel," 670, 681 (first and second quotations), 682 (third quotation), 684.

32. Although the CIO pattern, even when flawed, was usually significantly more inclusive than the AFL model, the blacks who made up a full third of the workforce at Ingalls Company were so dissatisfied that they voted the USW (a CIO union) out and turned to the AFL—which was soon followed by another local union. Herman A. Taylor, oral interview by Terrence J. Weatherspoon, 8 October 1999, CLEAR (second quotation). Painter, *The Narrative of Hosea Hudson,* 325 (first quotation); Northrup, *Organized Labor and the Negro,* 181, 183; Marshall, *The Negro and Organized Labor,* 45–46. The Rowan section titled "Steel Industry" in Herbert R. Northrup et al., *Negro Employment in Basic Industry: A Study of Racial Policies in Six Industries* (Philadelphia: Industrial Research Unit, Wharton School of Finance and Commerce, University of Pennsylvania, 1970), 272, 275, reported that the black percentage of Alabama steelworkers plunged from nearly 38 percent in 1940 to 30.6 percent by the end of the 1950s. Local 1013 of the USW in Birmingham had over 6,000 members, one of the largest in the South (254–55). Norrell, Northrup, and Rowan are all in agreement about the racially restrictive steelworker practices of the time. See also Bruce Nelon, *Divided We Stand: American Workers and the Struggle for Black Equality* (Princeton: Princeton University Press, 2001) and Paul D. Moreno, *Black Americans and Organized Labor: A New History* (Baton Rouge: Louisiana State University Press, 2007).

33. Numan V. Bartley, *The Rise of Massive Resistance: Race and Politics in the South during the 1950s* (Baton Rouge: Louisiana State University Press, 1969), 345.

34. The percentage of African Americans who made up the Red Mountain ore miners fell from 70 percent in 1930 to less than 50 percent by the end of the 1940s. "The Economics of Employment Discrimination," in *Employment of Blacks in the South: A Perspective on the 1960s,* ed. F. Ray Marshall (Austin: University of Texas Press, 1978), 226; Norrell, "Caste in Steel," 684 (quotation), 685. See also Huntley, "Iron Ore Miners, and Mine Mill in Alabama" and Huntley and Montgomery, *Black Workers' Struggle for Equality in Birmingham.*

35. FDR issued Executive Order 9346 on 27 May 1943 that made the FEPC an independent agency answerable only to presidential authority, setting the stage for the complaint that led to the Supreme Court case. See *Executive Order 9346*, 8 Fed. Reg. 7183 (1943). See also *Steele v. Louisville and Nashville Railroad*, 245 Ala. 113 (1944), 323 U.S. 192 (1944), and 65 S.Ct. 226 (1944). *Hearings on H. Res. 102 Before the House Special Committee to Investigate Executive Agencies*, 78th Cong., 1st and 2nd Sess., pt. 2, pp. 2129–30 (1944). The Brotherhood of Locomotive Firemen continued to ignore rulings and enforce the illegitimate Southeastern Carriers Agreement until 1948. See Howard N. Risher, "The Negro in the Railroad Industry," in *Negro Employment in Land and Air Transport*, ed. Herbert R. Northrup and Howard W. Risher Jr. (Philadelphia: Industrial Research Unit, Wharton School, University of Pennsylvania Press, 1971), 35, 47, 62–66, 82, 106; Northrup, *Organized Labor and the Negro*, 45, 97; Herbert R. Northrup, Armand J. Thiebolt, and William N. Chernish, *The Negro in the Air Transport Industry* (Philadelphia: Industrial Research Unit, Wharton School, University of Pennsylvania Press, 1971), 23; Marshall, *The Negro and Organized Labor*, 90, 94–97, 128–29, 183; Norrell, "Caste in Steel," 680–81; and Galenson, *The United Brotherhood of Carpenters*.

36. Weeks interview by Robert J. Norrell; Barney Weeks, interview by Edwin L. Brown, I. N., and Ralph A. Johnson, ca. 1988, pp. 16–18, CLEAR. E. B. Rich and Howard Strevel, interview by Edwin L. Brown, Glenn Cole, and Ralph A. Johnson, 9 June 1988, CLEAR; Asa Trammell, interview by Edwin L. Brown, Glenn Cole, and Ralph A. Johnson, 23 June 1988, CLEAR. See also Herbert R. Northrup et al., *The Negro in the Rubber Tire Industry* (Philadelphia: Industrial Research Unit, Wharton School, University of Pennsylvania Press, 1969), 32–35; Northrup, *Organized Labor and the Negro*, 31, 32 (quotation), 215–16, 225–27; Herbert R. Northrup, "The Negro in the Paper Industry," in *Negro Employment in Southern Industry: A Study of Racial Policies in Five Industries*, ed. Herbert R. Northrup et al. (Philadelphia: Industrial Research Unit, Wharton School, University of Pennsylvania Press, 1970), 2–232, esp. p. 36.

37. Leon Alexander, interviews by Peggy Hamrick, 8 and 17 July 1984, Birmingham, AL, Archives of American Minority Cultures Collection, box 3008, "Working Lives Series," UA. See also Virgil Powell to Frank Dixon, 14 July 1942 (quotations), box SG 12276, folder 10, Dixon Papers. Also see Northrup, *The Negro in the Rubber Tire Industry*, 34–35 and Northrup, *Organized Labor and the Negro*, 159–60. For the impact of mechanization and resultant job loss, see Charles R. Perry, *Collective Bargaining and the Decline of the United Mine Workers* (Philadelphia: Industrial Research Unit, Wharton School, University of Pennsylvania Press, 1984), 54; Northrup et al., *Negro Employment in Southern Industry*, 64; and Brown and Davis, *It Is Union and Liberty*.

38. Tom Brokaw, *The Greatest Generation* (New York: Random House, 2004); Zieger, *The CIO*.

39. Major Squirm column in *Alabama Magazine*, 10 July 1942, p. 15.

40. Frank M. Dixon to Franklin D. Roosevelt, 21 October 1941, box SG 23766, Scrapbook: Sloss-Sheffield Strike, 1941, Dixon Papers (first quotation); Major Squirm column in *Alabama Magazine*, 25 September 1942, p. 15 (second quotation).

41. *Alabama Magazine*, 27 October 1941, p. 3 (first quotation) and 13 November 1942, p. 3 (second quotation).

42. *Dothan Eagle* editorial "The South Must 'Reconstruct' Again," ca. 22 October 1941, clipping in box SG 23766, Scrapbook: Sloss-Sheffield Strike, 1941, Dixon Papers.

43. C. B. King to Frank M. Dixon, 16 March 1942, box SG 12270, folder 2 (first quotation), and for a letter from an erstwhile union sympathizer now disillusioned, see John M. Gray, First National Bank of Scottsboro, to Frank M. Dixon, 25 October 1941, box SG 23766, Scrapbook: Sloss-Sheffield Strike, 1941, both in Dixon Papers; Norrell, "Caste in Steel," 680 (second quotation).

44. Jakeman, *The Divided Skies*.

45. "It just don't add up in the South" any southerner knew instinctively, as one circuit court bailiff complained. See Horace C. Wilkinson to Lister Hill, 24 August 1943, box 376, folder 2 (first quotation), G. J. Flowmoy to Lister Hill, 16 August 1942 (quotation in note) and J.W.A. Burton to Lister Hill, 25 October 1942, latter two in box 376, folder 1, all three in the Hill Papers. Miscellaneous news clipping, ca. August 1942, box SG 12276, folder 10, Dixon Papers (second quotation). See also Tindall, *Emergence of the New South*, 712.

46. The *Gadsden Times* took especial issue with northern blacks—the "'high-brow' . . . snooty element" that made up the New Deal's "'brown brain trust'" and was responsible for most of the social dislocation of the era. They may "drink oceans of Mrs. Roosevelt's tea" but would sooner die than rub elbows with blacks who had to work for a living. *Gadsden Times* quoted in *Alabama Magazine*, 24 July 1942, p. 9; Guy Hardwick to Frank M. Dixon, 24 July 1942, box SG 12276, folder 10, Dixon Papers.

47. Horace C. Wilkinson to Lister Hill, 24 August 1943, box 376, folder 2, Hill Papers (quoted). This was so especially in light of the fact that the South had been the "most loyal section of the nation [and] the backbone of the Democratic Party." The infringement upon the South's constitutional rights was a naked attempt to "take advantage of our patriotism." Horace C. Wilkinson to Joseph Starnes, 1 September 1943, box 376, folder 2, Hill Papers and the same letter also located in box SG 12491, folder 8, Sparks Papers. This truism held for the South's relations with its own central government as well. "In national politics," political scientist V. O. Key observed in 1949, the Democratic "party is the Solid South; it is, or at least it has been, the instrument for the conduct of the 'foreign relations' of the South with the rest of the nation." Key, *Southern Politics in State and Nation*, 315.

48. (Miss) Augusta P. Hope to Lister Hill, 15 August 1942 (first quotation) and J. Edgerton Brownie to Lister Hill, 10 October 1942. For additional white calls to draft blacks, see Lon F. Thompson, UMWA Local #5827, Piper, AL, to Lister Hill, 3 September 1942, Jim Howell to Lister Hill, 5 October 1942, and William E. Mickle to Lister Hill, 12 August 1942, all in box 376, folder 1, Hill Papers. Rev. R. T. Nelson to Chauncey Sparks, May 1944, box SG 12398, folder 19, Sparks Papers (second quotation); Charles B. Crow to [Captain] Powell, 4 November 1942, box 1, folder 9, Charles B. Crow Papers (third quotation) ADAH.

49. Willis Pace Estis to Frank M. Dixon, 17 August 1942, box SG 12276, folder 10 and Mrs. Estelle Cassimus to Frank M. Dixon, 13 November 1942 (second quotation), box SG 12277, folder 29, both in Dixon Papers. Mrs. Cassimus proposed that any black who asked a white woman out should be arrested. Lon F. Thompson, UMWA Local #5827, to Lister Hill, 3 September 1942, box 376, folder 1, Hill Papers (first quotation).

50. Dan T. Carter, *The Politics of Rage: George Wallace, the Origins of the New Conservatism, and the Transformation of American Politics* (New York: Simon and Schuster, 1995).

51. Charles Eli Sexton to Chauncey Sparks, 20 September 1943, box 12491, folder 7, Sparks Papers (quotations); John D. McQueen to Lister Hill, 15 September 1943, box 376, folder 2, Hill Papers. For Rankin, see *Alabama Magazine*, 24 July 1942, p. 9.

52. John D. McQueen to Lister Hill, 15 September 1943, box 376, folder 2, Hill Papers (first quotation). See also "One of the Insulted Whites from the South" to Chauncey Sparks, 13 August 1943 (second quotation), box SG 12409, folder 7, Sparks Papers; Frank B. King, Demopolis, to Frank M. Dixon, 2 August 1942, box SG 12276, folder 10, Dixon Papers; "A Longsuffering fellow-Southerner (Who will not vote for a 4th Term)" to Chauncey Sparks, 11 December 1943, box SG 12491, folder 8, Sparks Papers (third quotation).

53. *Alabama Magazine*, 19 June 1942, p. 14 (Huie quoted).

54. Charles Eli Sexton to Chauncey Sparks, 20 September 1943 (first quotation), box SG 12491, folder 7, Sparks Papers; Thomas M. Searles to Frank Dixon, 10 September 1942 (second quotation), box SG 12276, folder 10, Dixon Papers; Gessner T. McCorvey to E. Ray Scott, 2 October 1942, box SG 12234, folder 21, Dixon Papers (third [first McCorvey] quotation); miscellaneous news clipping, ca. August 1942, box SG 12276, folder 10, Dixon Papers (fourth [second McCorvey] quotation), and Harry H. Smith to Chauncey Sparks, 30 September 1943, box SG 12491, folder 7, Sparks Papers; John D. McQueen to Lister Hill, 15 September 1943, box 376, folder 2, Hill Papers (fifth quotation).

55. Wirt C. Davidson to Chauncey Sparks, ca. 25 August 1943, box SG 12491, folder 7, Sparks Papers.

56. Thomas E. Moore to Frank M. Dixon, 4 July 1943, box SG 12491, folder 7 (first quotation), and "Consider Its Friends," editorial in the *Greensboro Watchman*, 17 April 1943, box SG 12398, folder 19, Sparks Papers (second quotation). Also see Fred Arthur Bailey, "E. Merton Coulter and the Political Culture of Southern Historiography," 32–48, and Bailey, "Charles S. Sydnor's Quest for a Suitable Past," 88–111, in *Reading Southern History: Essays on Interpreters and Interpretations,* ed. Glenn Feldman (Tuscaloosa: The University of Alabama Press, 2001).

57. Maxilm'n B. Wellborn to Chauncey Sparks, 11 September 1944, box SG 12491, folder 6, Sparks Papers.

58. *Dothan Eagle*, 3 March 1944 (first quotation), clipping and *Montgomery Alabama Journal*, 22 March 1944 (second quotation), clipping, both in Scrapbook #24, p. 6, Sparks Personal Papers.

Chapter 9

1. The only hope for progressive government in the South, patrician-turned-textile union organizer Lucy Randolph Mason felt, "lies in the lower economic groups. . . . Yet this is the group so largely disfranchised by the poll tax." Tindall, *Emergence of the New South*, 557, 640 (quotation in note); *New York Times*, 22 August 1936; Tindall, *Disruption of the Solid South*, 34–35.

2. The eight were Alabama, Arkansas, Georgia, Mississippi, South Carolina, Tennessee, Texas, and Virginia. Tindall, *Emergence of the New South*, 640.

3. Stetson Kennedy, *Southern Exposure* (1946; reprint, Boca Raton: Florida Atlantic University Press, 1991), 92–95, 107.

4. Feldman, *The Disfranchisement Myth*.

5. Molton H. Gray, commander, George Ruffin Council of the National Council of Negro Veterans, to Lister Hill, 27 February 1944, and Esther V. Cooper, executive secretary of the Southern Negro Youth Congress, to Lister Hill, 15 March 1944, both in box 376, folder 2, Hill Papers.

6. *Alabama Magazine,* 4 September 1942, p. 3 (Dixon quotation and Baughn quotations); Frank M. Dixon to Carter Manasco, 27 August 1942, box SG 12278, folder 11, Dixon Papers.

7. *Alabama Magazine,* 4 September 1942, p. 3 (all quotations).

8. Luther Patrick to Frank M. Dixon, 29 August 1942, Pete Jarman to Frank M. Dixon, 15 October 1942, R. B. Vail to Frank M. Dixon, 29 August 1942 (first [Grant] quotation) and Frank M. Dixon to George O. Miller, 11 September 1942 (second quotation), all in box SG 12278, folder 11, Dixon Papers. *Alabama Magazine,* 4 February 1944, p. 10.

9. At last Hill had taken "a positive stand," one Bourbon organ wrote. It was the least he could do because it had been Hill's repeated "betrayal of the voters" that was partially responsible for the catalog of outrages piled upon the South by "New Deal radicals." Don Drennen to Lister Hill, 9 September 1942 (first quotation), Lister Hill to Don Drennen, 10 September 1942 (second quotation), and Lister Hill to Horace C. Wilkinson, 11 September 1942 (second quotation repeated), all in box 376, folder 1, Hill Papers; Major Squirm column in *Alabama Magazine,* 18 September 1942, p. 15; *Selma Times-Journal* editorial, ca. November 1942, clipping in box SG 12278, folder 10, Dixon Papers (quotation in note).

10. John Temple Graves to Frank M. Dixon, 2 September 1942 (first quotation) and Horace C. Wilkinson to John Temple Graves, 31 August 1942 (second quotation), both in box SG 12278, folder 11, Dixon Papers. In this letter, Wilkinson went on to explain that people were beginning to believe that they are "entitled to all the privileges of the Government without sharing any of its burdens; that they must be well housed and well clothed whether they toil or spin." See also *Alabama Magazine,* 4 September 1942, p. 3; Horace C. Wilkinson to Lister Hill, 31 August 1942, box 376, folder 1, Hill Papers; and Tyler, "'Blood on Your Hands.'"

11. Kennedy, *Southern Exposure,* 101 (quotation), 102, 108–11. See also Simkins and Roland, *A History of the South,* 549.

12. Gessner T. McCorvey to E. Ray Scott, 2 October 1942, box SG 12234, folder 21, Dixon Papers (first quotation). In another venue, McCorvey spoke of disallowing "a thriftless, shiftless, trifling element . . . an illiterate, ignorant group." See Gessner T. McCorvey Statement, 9 February 1945, box 83, folder 13, SDEC Records. Kennedy, *Southern Exposure,* 102 (first and second quotations); Tindall, *Emergence of the New South,* 640 (Hall quotation), 641.

13. Dixon quotation from Frank M. Dixon to Senator Tom Connally, 18 November 1942, and Frank M. Dixon to Homer Adkins, governor of Arkansas, 10 October 1942, both in box SG 12278, folder 10. See also Frank M. Dixon to Southern Governors, 30 September 1942, and Frank M. Dixon to Alabama Congressional Delegation, 3 October 1942, both in same box, folder 11, and all in Dixon Papers.

14. Harry Flood Byrd to Frank M. Dixon, 25 September 1942, Harry Flood Byrd to Thomas S. Lawson, 25 September 1942, and the Remarks of Hon. Harry Flood Byrd, *Congressional Record,* 22 September 1942, *Congressional Record Appendix,* p. A 3589, all in box SG 12278, folder 11, Dixon Papers. Address of Congressman Henry B. Steagall

before the Joint Session of the Legislature of Alabama, Montgomery, AL, 10 June 1943, p. 11, box 2346, folder: Alabama Here We Rest—The Future, Henry B. Steagall Congressional Papers, UA.

15. *Alabama Magazine,* 13 November 1942, p. 7, also see 9 October 1942, p. 5 (first and second quotations), 5 October 1945, p. 15 (third quotation). See also pp. 5 and 15 of the same issue for the *Dothan Eagle* and Major Squirm emphasizing the prescient threat to the Constitution.

16. "[A]nd I figger he'll be sorry erlong erbout nex' May," Major Squirm wrote about Patrick. Squirm was correct. See the column in *Alabama Magazine,* 5 October 1945, p. 15 and 14 April 1944, p. 3. All of the following letters to Frank M. Dixon: Sam Hobbs, 29 August 1942, John H. Bankhead, 1 September 1942, Frank Boykin, 3 October 1942, John H. Bankhead, Lister Hill, Sam Hobbs, Pete Jarman, and Joseph Starnes, all on 5 October 1942, George Grant and John Sparkman, both on 6 October 1942. All Dixon correspondence in box SG 12278, folder 11, Dixon Papers.

17. *Anniston Star* quoted in *Alabama Magazine,* 11 September 1942, p. 4 (first quotation); Gurley N. Vines to Frank M. Dixon, 18 November 1942, box SG 12278, folder 10 (second quotation) and Charles J. Searles to Frank M. Dixon, 8 October 1942, box SG 12278, folder 11 (third quotation), both in Dixon Papers.

18. Maxim'n B. Wellborn to Chauncey Sparks, 11 September 1944, box SG 12491, folder 6 (first quotation) and Oliver Day Street to Chauncey Sparks, 6 May 1943, box SG 12398, folder 19, both in Sparks Papers. See also Oliver Day Street to ed., *Birmingham News,* 10 February 1944, box 31, folder: Political Scrap, Street Papers, ADAH. Ruth B. Quigley (Mrs. George N. Quigley) to Lister Hill, 23 May 1944, box 376, folder 3, Hill Papers (second quotation).

19. Jed Harris, "Save Your Spleen for the Damyankee Poll Tax Appeasers," *PM Magazine,* 17 October 1942, clipping in box SG 12278, folder 11, Dixon Papers.

20. Kennedy, *Southern Exposure,* 121.

21. James Armstrong, interview by Cliff Kuhn, 16 July 1984, Birmingham, AL, Archives of American Minority Cultures Collection, "Working Lives Series," UA; Gomillion interview, 2–3 and Arthur D. Shores, interview by Hardy T. Frye, Interview #44, p. 1, both in the Hardy T. Frye Oral History Collection, AU; *Montgomery Advertiser,* 13 October 1945, clipping in Scrapbook #24, p. 44, range H, section 4, shelf e, Sparks Personal Papers. Rogers et al., *Alabama,* 514, 539–40. The John LeFlore Papers at the University of South Alabama Archives in Mobile contain a good deal of material on voter registration.

22. *Dothan Eagle,* 28 June 1944, editorial clipping in Scrapbook #24, p. 26, Sparks Personal Papers.

23. Bunche, *The Political Status of the Negro in the Age of FDR,* xix (first quotation), 401 (second quotation).

24. Rogers et al., *Alabama,* 526; Barnard, "The Old Order Changes," 163–84.

25. Barnard, "The Old Order Changes," 165 (first quotation), 169 (second quotation). Another Horace Wilkinson protégé, Smyer would become a leader for the Dixiecrats and, after that, the GOP.

26. Bailey, Glass, and O'Daniel were from North Carolina, Virginia, and Texas, respectively. Tindall, *Emergence of the New South,* 722. Staunch conservatives John L. McClellan of Arkansas and James O. Eastland of Mississippi were among this 1942 freshman class.

27. Miss Terrell Whitman to Frank M. Dixon, 8 August 1942, box SG 12276, folder 10, Dixon Papers (first quotation); Champ Pickens to Chauncey Sparks, 15 February 1943, box SG 12491, folder 8, Sparks Papers; M. M. Moulthrop, mayor of Eufaula, to Lister Hill, 21 July 1942, M. M. Moulthrop to Eleanor Roosevelt, 20 July 1942, William E. Mickle to Lister Hill, 12 August 1942 (second quotation), and G. J. Flowmoy to Lister Hill, 16 August 1942 (third quotation), all in box 376, folder 1, Hill Papers. Pete Daniel, "Going among Strangers: Southern Reactions to World War II," *Journal of American History* 77 (December 1990): 886–911.

28. Robin D. G. Kelley, "'We Are Not What We Seem': Rethinking Black Working-Class Opposition in the Jim Crow South," *Journal of American History* 80 (June 1993): 75–112, esp. 87, 104–5 (quotation).

29. Bunche, *The Political Status of the Negro in the Age of FDR*, 33. See also M. M. Moulthrop to Eleanor Roosevelt, 20 July 1942, box 376, folder 1, Hill Papers.

30. *Alabama Magazine*, 21 August 1942, p. 11 (first quotation); "One of the Insulted Whites from the South" to Chauncey Sparks, 13 August 1943 (second quotation), box SG 12409, folder 7, Sparks Papers.

31. A. Philip Randolph to Lister Hill, 16 October 1942, William E. Mickle to Lister Hill, 12 August 1942, G. J. Flowmoy to Lister Hill, 16 August 1942, all in box 376, folder 1, Hill Papers; *(Nashville) Southern Conference for Human Welfare Bulletin*, 20 August 1942, and Marie Ellis to Frank M. Dixon, 30 August 1942, both in box SG 12277, folder 29, Dixon Papers; Reese Adamson to Marshall Haynes, Louisville and Nashville Railroad, 13 December 1943, box SG 12491, folder 7 and Ray F. Bozeman to Chauncey Sparks, 5 September 1944, same box, folder 6, both in Sparks Papers; *Alabama Magazine*, 25 September 1942, p. 14; Norrell, "Caste in Steel," 681; Kennedy, *Southern Exposure*, 180.

32. Reese Adamson to Chauncey Sparks, 12 January 1944, box SG 12491, folder 7, Sparks Papers; *Alabama Magazine*, 3 July 1942, p. 5 (first *Gadsden Times* quotation) and 10 July 1942, p. 4 (second *Gadsden Times* quotation). Adamson eventually became a leading Republican in Alabama.

33. W. C. Beebe to Lister Hill, 1 June 1943, box 376, folder 2, Hill Papers; Sparks to Hon. Hayse Tucker and Hon. G. R. Swift, 25 May 1943, and Wesley E. Grubbs to H. W. Nixon, 2 June 1943, both in box SG 12491, folder 7, Sparks Papers; Rogers et al., *Alabama*, 514.

34. Block quote compiled from Chauncey Sparks to John P. Lewis, managing editor of *PM Magazine*, 24 June 1943, and Chauncey Sparks to Walter Davenport, associate editor of *Collier's*, ca. 24 June 1943, both in box SG 12491, folder 7, Sparks Papers. Only a year later a two-hour gun battle erupted at Mobile's Brookley Army Air Field between white military police and black soldiers. See Rogers et al., *Alabama*, 514.

35. J. Edgerton Brown to Lister Hill, 10 October 1942, box 376, folder 1, Hill Papers (second quotation); Wesley E. Grubbs to H. W. Nixon, 2 June 1943 (first quotation, quoting Bill Sergeant) and "Colonel Robert Joerg's Report to the Governor on . . . Mobile," 12 June 1943 (fourth quotation), both in box SG 12491, folder 7, Sparks Papers; *Mobile Labor Journal*, 2 July 1943, p. 2; *Alabama (CIO) News Digest*, 3 June 1943, p. 3 (third quotation); Statement of Dr. B. F. Ashe, regional director of the War Manpower Commission, 1 June 1943, series: WMC17, RG 211, NA-SE.

36. Rice Estes, SC, to Chauncey Sparks, 15 July 1943, box SG 12491, folder 7 (first quotation) and no name, Sweet Home, NY, to Sparks, 26 May 1943, same box, folder 8 (second quotation), both in Sparks Papers.

37. Sparks sponsored tax reform that placed a measure of the pitifully small Alabama tax burden on corporations and utilities. See Rogers et al., *Alabama*, 526; A. D. Quackenbush to Chauncey Sparks, 30 August 1943 (first and second quotations) and J. M. Radney to Chauncey Sparks, 25 June 1943 (third quotation). Sparks's attorney general congratulated him on his "courageous and manly stand." See John J. Haynes, attorney general to Chauncey Sparks, 25 June 1943. Other Alabamians denounced the "meddlesome criticism" and the "northern agitators [who] are responsible for 99% of our riots," and suggested that the governor's splendid reply be "placed in [the] Alabama Archives for public record." See, respectively, L. C. Irvine to Chauncey Sparks, 29 June 1943, Jones D. Gary, Texasville, to Chauncey Sparks, 28 June 1943, and R. W. Hawthorne, Pine Apple, to Chauncey Sparks, 25 June 1943, all of the correspondence in box SG 12491, folder 7, Sparks Papers.

38. Hamner Cobbs, "Appeasement Doesn't Pay," *Greensboro Watchman*, 17 April 1943, p. 4, clipping in box SG 12398, folder 19, Sparks Papers.

39. *Tuscaloosa News*, 25 June 1943, p. 4, clipping; *Montgomery Advertiser*, 27 May 1943, clipping; *Greensboro Watchman*, 17 July 1943, p. 5, all in Scrapbook #24, Sparks Personal Papers.

40. Chauncey Sparks, "Founder's Day—Tuskegee" speech, 4 April 1943, pp. 2, 6, 8, 9, 12, box SG 12398, folder 19, Sparks Papers.

41. Ibid.

42. *Birmingham News*, 18 April 1943, *Jacksonville News*, 4 February 1943, *(Montgomery) Alabama Journal*, ca. January 1943, *Talladega Daily Home*, 15 April 1943, *Anniston Star*, 12 April 1943, and the *Tallassee Tribune*, 6 May 1943, all editorial clippings in Scrapbook #24, Sparks Personal Papers. A Dothan lawyer praised Sparks's "tolerant approach and wise understanding." J. Hubert Farmer to Chauncey Sparks, 6 April 1943, box SG 12398, folder 19A, Sparks Papers.

43. Marvin H. Carter to Chauncey Sparks, 6 April 1943, box SG 12398, folder 19A (first quotation) and Ernest D. LeMay to Sparks, 3 September 1943, box SG 12491, folder 8 (second quotation), both in Sparks Papers.

44. Ed Field was thrilled with Patterson's remarks and wrote of them as a "Rebuke to Agitators," in the *Selma Times-Journal*, 27 April 1943, clipping in Scrapbook #24, Sparks Personal Papers (Patterson quoted). The Kilby inmate's words were almost certainly colored by the fact that he also asked for an early parole. David Daniel Dunbar, Kilby Prison, to Chauncey Sparks, ca. 10 April 1943, and for additional black praise see William B. Patterson to Chauncey Sparks, 7 April 1943, both in box SG 12398, folder 19A, and also Rev. E. M. Wilson to Chauncey Sparks, 1 May 1943, same box, folder 19. A black AFL organizer in Mobile assured the governor that labor was interested only in equal job opportunity and legal justice, not desegregation. See R. F. Finkley to Chauncey Sparks, 16 February 1943, box SG 12491, folder 8, all correspondence in note in Sparks Papers. The Rev. E. M. Wilson had backed Frank Dixon during the 1942 controversies, leading *Birmingham World* editor Emory O. Jackson and nine black preachers to request that the pulpit at the black Alabama State Baptist Convention be withheld from Wilson. See Emory Jackson to Prof. W. B. Campbell and Nine Black Preachers to W. B. Campbell, 28 July 1942, and the Rev. E. M. Wilson to Frank M. Dixon, 4 November 1942, box SG 12277, folder 29, Dixon Papers.

45. Oliver Day Street to Chauncey Sparks, 6 May 1943, box SG 12398, folder 19. In

the same box and folder 19A, see J. Thomas Heflin to Chauncey Sparks, 6 April 1943, Marvin H. Carter, Cotton Company, to Chauncey Sparks and Leon Schwarz, Mobile Mattress Company, to Chauncey Sparks, both on 6 April 1943, A. W. Vogtle, manager of DeBardeleben Coal Company, to Chauncey Sparks, Roy B. Williams, cotton buyer for Avondale Mills, to Chauncey Sparks, Harold McDermott, vice president and treasurer of Newcastle Coal Company, to Chauncey Sparks, C. G. Smith, secretary and treasurer, McQueen Smith Farms, to Chauncey Sparks, and Frank B. Clark, Clark and Company Mortgage Loans, to Chauncey Sparks, all five on 5 April 1943, all in the Sparks Papers.

46. M.S.M. Ashley to Chauncey Sparks, 5 April 1943 (quotation). The same critic exhorted white Alabamians to stop being "little Hitlers" at home. "It makes little sense" to send "American boys to die for the very same things which are being denied" here. Moses Saint Matthew Ashley to Chauncey Sparks, 6 April 1943; both Ashley letters in box SG 12398, folder 19A, Sparks Papers. Hamner Cobbs was certain that only the eastern black press had any critical words for Sparks. *Greensboro Watchman*, 17 April 1943, p. 3; see also *Birmingham Weekly Review*, 17 April 1943, p. 1, both editorial clippings in Scrapbook #24, Sparks Personal Papers.

47. *Baltimore Afro-American*, 10 April 1943, p. 1 and *Chicago Defender* columnist A. N. Fields, "Today's Talk," *Pittsburgh Courier*, 17 April 1943, p. 3 (quoted), both in Scrapbook #24, Sparks Personal Papers. Fields's column is also in box SG 12398, folder 19, Sparks Papers. He condemned Sparks's "attitude towards human life [a]s the natural counterpart of a slave tradition, and is economically and socially immoral."

48. *Pittsburgh Courier*, 17 April 1943, p. 1 and Hamner Cobbs, "Appeasement Doesn't Pay," *Greensboro Watchman*, 17 April 1943, pp. 3–4, both editorial clippings in Scrapbook #24, Sparks Personal Papers.

49. Gordon Bliss Jones to Hamner Cobbs, 20 July 1943, box SG 12491, folder 7, Sparks Papers; Cobbs, "Appeasement Doesn't Pay" (quoted).

50. Robert E. Lee Club of Reeltown, Alabama (Notasulga), to Chauncey Sparks, box SG 12398, folder 19A, Sparks Papers.

51. *Birmingham News*, 5 May 1944 (first quotation); *Birmingham Age-Herald*, 5 May 1944 (second quotation); and *Birmingham Post*, 3 April 1944, all three editorial clippings in Scrapbook #24, p. 22, Sparks Personal Papers; *Alabama Magazine*, 5 May 1944, p. 10, and 13 October 1944, p. 5 (for the *Birmingham Post* being a Republican newspaper along with all the other Scripps-Howard papers).

52. *Birmingham Age-Herald*, 4 May 1944, *Dothan Eagle*, 4 May 1944, and *Kansas City Plain Dealer*, 12 May 1944 (quotations), all three editorial clippings in Scrapbook #24, respectively on pp. 21, 22, and 25, Sparks Personal Papers. Northerners were not so supportive of the speech. See, e.g., Alonzo Dow Brewer to Chauncey Sparks, 7 September 1944, box SG 12491, folder 6, Sparks Papers.

53. Chauncey Sparks to FDR, 24 August 1944, box SG 12491, folder 5, Sparks Papers, a copy of the telegram in box 376, folder 3, Hill Papers. Also the *Birmingham Age-Herald*, 24 and 29 August 1944, *(Montgomery) Alabama Journal*, 25 August 1944, *Montgomery Advertiser*, 29 August 1944, *Anniston Star*, 24 August 1944, *Decatur Daily*, 28 August 1944, all clippings in Scrapbook #24, pp. 27–31, Sparks Personal Papers.

54. John H. Bankhead II to Chauncey Sparks, 31 August 1944, Chauncey Sparks to the Whole Alabama Delegation, 24 August 1944, George Andrews to Chauncey Sparks, 26 August 1944 (emphasized the political aspects of the order), Sam Hobbs to Chauncey

Sparks, 25 August 1944 (quotation), George Grant to Chauncey Sparks, 25 and 30 August 1944, John Newsome to Chauncey Sparks, 26 August 1944, John Sparkman to Chauncey Sparks, 30 August 1944, all in box SG 12491, folder 5, Sparks Papers.

55. Frank W. Boykin to Chauncey Sparks, 26 August 1944 (first quotation), Frank W. Boykin to Chauncey Sparks (telegram, 1:43 P.M.), 26 August 1944 (second quotation), both in box SG 12491, folder 5, Sparks Papers; *Alabama Magazine*, 8 September 1944, p. 3 (third quotation); Mary Wash Burks to Lister Hill, 26 August 1944, box 376, folder 3, Hill Papers.

56. *Sylacauga News*, 24 August 1944, clipping in Scrapbook #24, p. 27, Sparks Personal Papers (first quotation); George Andrews to Chauncey Sparks, 30 August 1944 (second quotation) and J. A. Tucker to Chauncey Sparks, 28 August 1944 (third quotation), both in box SG 12491, folder 5, Sparks Papers.

57. When the answer finally came it was sent from an underling, adding further insult to regional injury. Robert L. Patton to Chauncey Sparks, 1 September 1944, and Sparks Press Release Telegram, 28 August 1944, both in box SG 12491, folder 5, Sparks Papers. See also *Montgomery Advertiser, (Montgomery) Alabama Journal,* and *Dothan Eagle,* all 6 September 1944, clippings in Scrapbook #24, p. 36, Sparks Personal Papers.

58. Many others assented while some worried that the provocations would give impetus to a new Klan. See the *Birmingham News*, 26 August 1944, for Bull Connor's protests and the *Birmingham Age-Herald*, 29 August 1944 (first quotation), both in Scrapbook #24, pp. 29 and 31, respectively, Sparks Personal Papers. See also Bull Connor to Chauncey Sparks, 1 September 1944, and Carter Manasco to Franklin D. Roosevelt, 25 August 1944, both in box SG 12491, folder 5, Sparks Papers. Connor predicted "terror, bloodshed and calamity for both races," in Bull Connor to Lister Hill, 25 August 1944. See also Mary Wash Burks to Lister Hill, 26 August 1944, and Alwyn Vickers to Lister Hill, 31 August 1944 (second quotation), all three in box 376, folder 3, Hill Papers. Also Mrs. J. T. Stephens to Franklin D. Roosevelt, 9 October 1944, box 6, folder: Colored Matters, October–December 1944, Official Files 93, Franklin D. Roosevelt Papers, FDR Library.

59. For expressions of support, see W. I. "Bud" Gary to Chauncey Sparks, 26 August 1944, Edgar Sheffield, Sims Lumber Company, to Chauncey Sparks, 25 August 1944, Tom Pankey, The Pankey Companies, Brokers and Importers, to Chauncey Sparks, 25 August 1944, George Bliss Jones to George Grant, 28 August 1944 (first quotation), all in box SG 12491, folder 5, and J. Herbert Meighan, mayor of Gadsden, to Chauncey Sparks, 28 August 1944, same box, folder 6, Sparks Papers. See also the *Birmingham Post*, 3 April 1944 (third quotation) and *Ensley Industrial Press*, 12 October 1944 (second quotation), Scrapbook #24, pp. 20 and 40, respectively, in Sparks Personal Papers.

60. *Mobile Register*, 19 April 1944, clipping in Scrapbook #24, p. 18, Sparks Personal Papers (quotation).

61. *Birmingham News*, 26 August 1944, Scrapbook #24, p. 29 (first quotation, Bankhead). See also the similar argument in the *Birmingham Age-Herald*, 26 August 1944, same scrapbook, p. 24, Sparks Personal Papers; LB, Houston, to Chauncey Sparks, 28 August 1944 (second quotation) and Mrs. Gustave Frederick Martins, Montgomery, to Chauncey Sparks, 30 June 1944 (fourth quotation), both in box SG 12491, folder 8, Sparks Papers; C. H. Young, Anniston, to Lister Hill, 27 July 1944, box 376, folder 3, Hill Papers (third quotation).

62. *Birmingham Age-Herald*, 16 August 1944, clipping, and Bull Connor to Franklin D.

Roosevelt, 31 August 1944, both in box SG 12491, folder 5, Sparks Papers; *Birmingham Age-Herald,* 30 August 1944, and *Greensboro Southern Watchman,* 2 September 1944, both clippings in Scrapbook #24, pp. 32 and 36, respectively, Sparks Personal Papers.

63. (Miss) Maria DeVan Hurley to Chauncey Sparks, 27 April 1944, box SG 12491, folder 8, Sparks Papers (first quotation). One such pro-segregationist black was the Reverend D. V. Jemison, former pastor of the St. Louis Street Baptist Church in Mobile and president of the National Convention, which claimed to embody 13,000 blacks. See *Alabama Magazine,* 8 September 1944, p. 6 and 15 September 1944, p. 4 (second quotation).

64. For an example of the view that there was not much difference between the two major parties on race, see a moderate *Birmingham News* editor's disgust with Eleanor Roosevelt's racial activities and Republican Wendell Willkie speaking to the national NAACP convention in Los Angeles in James A. Chappell to Frank M. Dixon, 30 July 1942, box SG 12276, folder 11, Dixon Papers. *Talladega Daily Home,* 29 August 1944 (first quotation, Abernethy), *Gadsden Times,* 27 August 1944 (second quotation, Starnes), and *Greensboro Southern Watchman,* 26 August 1944 (third quotation) and 2 September 1944, all in Scrapbook #24, pp. 29, 30, 36 in Sparks Personal Papers; Joe Starnes to Chauncey Sparks, 2 September 1944 (Starnes quote repeated), box SG 12491, folder 5, Sparks Papers.

65. *Talladega Daily Home,* 28 August 1944, clipping in Scrapbook #24, p. 30, Sparks Personal Papers.

66. *Roanoke (AL) Leader,* ca. September 1944 (first quotation), L. Arnold, New York, to Chauncey Sparks, 25 August 1944 (second quotation), and N. Duke Kimbrough Jr., Birmingham, to Chauncey Sparks, 27 August 1944 (third quotation), all three in box SG 12491, folder 5, Sparks Papers. *Roanoke Leader* editorial reprinted in the *Covington News,* 28 September 1944, clipping in Scrapbook #24, p. 40, Sparks Personal Papers.

67. Forrest G. Jones, Montgomery, to Chauncey Sparks, 25 August 1944, box SG 12491, folder 5 (first quotation), and W. B. Houseal to Chauncey Sparks, 31 August 1944, same box, folder 6, both in Sparks Papers; *Birmingham Age-Herald,* 29 August 1944 (second quotation, Sparks) and *Clanton Union Banner,* 31 August 1944, both clippings in Scrapbook #24, pp. 31, 32, Sparks Personal Papers; *Alabama Magazine,* 1 September 1944, p. 5 (third quotation, Boykin); Peter Bryce Gilreath, Birmingham, to Lister Hill, 31 August 1944, box 376, folder 3, Hill Papers (fourth quotation).

68. The Black Belt's Pete Jarman demonstrated that he was on the same page as his colleague from the hill country: "Although neither a Negro hater or baiter . . . I hold no brief for . . . the uncalled for and unpardonable attitude of this Administration toward the intermingling of the races. In fact, I am a self-respecting Southern white man . . . who naturally recognizes the God given inferiority of the Negro to the white man. . . . No such Southerner who shares my appreciation of the purity of our Caucasian blood, on which I am more strongly impressed with the passage of the years . . . could possibly feel otherwise. . . . [Nor could] our Southern people, black and white, [who] deserve hearty congratulations [for resisting] . . . the apparent attempt to mongrelize the white citizenship of the South." Joe Starnes to Chauncey Sparks, 4 September 1944 (quotes in text) and Pete Jarman to Chauncey Sparks, 2 September 1944 (quote in note), both in box SG 12491, folder 5, Sparks Papers.

69. B. M. Miller, a large mule himself, had originally dubbed Hanson the "Number 1 Big Mule of Alabama." *Alabama Magazine,* 14 April 1944, p. 6 (quoted in note). See also Hamilton, *Lister Hill,* 119 (quote in text).

70. *Dothan Eagle* et al. criticism in the *Alabama Magazine*, 7 August 1942, pp. 7, 11; *Montgomery Advertiser*, 27 May 1943, clipping, and *Greensboro Watchman*, 17 July 1943, p. 5, all clippings in Scrapbook #24, Sparks Personal Papers.

71. For example, the *Birmingham News* called the order a "harmful mistake." See the *Alabama Magazine*, 1 September 1944, p. 11. The *Birmingham News* and the *Birmingham Age-Herald* had also argued that southern blacks were content with segregation. See both newspapers on 24 August 1944.

72. *Montgomery Advertiser*, 25 August 1944; also Scrapbook #24, p. 28, Sparks Personal Papers.

73. The *Montgomery Advertiser* editorial of 25 August 1944 was reprinted across the state in, among other papers, the *(Montgomery) Alabama Journal*, 25 August 1944, *Birmingham Age-Herald*, 29 August 1944, and *(Athens) Alabama Courier*, 31 August 1944. See the *Greensboro Southern Watchman*, 26 August 1944, also 2 September 1944 (first quotation, Grant); *Alabama Magazine*, 1 September 1944, p. 11 (second quotation). See also Scrapbook #24, pp. 31, 32, 35 Sparks Personal Papers.

74. J. T. Graves column reprinted in the *Pittsburgh Courier*, 16 September 1944, clipping in Scrapbook #24, p. 40, Sparks Personal Papers.

75. Lister Hill to Chauncey Sparks, 25 August 1944, box SG 12491, folder 5, Sparks Papers (first quotation). See also Lister Hill to E. G. Branch, 25 August 1944 (first quotation repeated), Lister Hill to A. B. Champion, 28 August 1944 (second quotation), C. C. Lee Jr. to Hill, 9 September 1944 (third quotation), Lister Hill to C. C. Lee Jr., 14 September 1944 (fourth quotation), Bull Connor to Lister Hill, 31 August 1944, and Lister Hill to Bull Connor, 4 September 1944 (fifth quotation), all in box 376, folder 3, Hill Papers.

76. Numerous racial and economic conservatives from around the South and the nation appealed to Dixon and Sparks in these years. See, e.g., Harry Flood Byrd to Frank M. Dixon, 25 September 1942, box SG 12278, folder 11, Dixon Papers, and D. Karrs, Carolina Beach, NC, to Chauncey Sparks, ca. 27 August 1944, box SG 12491, folder 5, and LB, Houston, TX, to Chauncey Sparks, 28 August 1944, same box, folder 8, both in Sparks Papers. See also Jay Taylor, "Who Will Do the Work?" manuscript sent to *Collier's Weekly* and Sparks, ca. December 1943, p. 4 (quotations), and Taylor, "An American Solution," manuscript sent to Sparks, 2 March 1944, p. 9 (last quotation), both in box SG 12491, folder 7, Sparks Papers.

77. Such veneration was plentiful during this era. Hubert Baughn's *Alabama Magazine*, e.g., was a diligent collector of such sentiment from around the country. See also Taylor, "Who Will Do the Work?" p. 4, and Taylor, "Rebuilding Our Democracy," manuscript sent to Sparks, ca. December 1943, p. 5 (quotation from both), box SG 12491, folder 7, Sparks Papers.

78. See Jerry Z. Muller, *Capitalism and the Jews* (Princeton: Princeton University Press, 2010); Taylor, "Who Will Do the Work?" p. 3 (quotations); and Abraham H. Foxman, *Jews and Money: The Story of a Stereotype* (New York: Palgrave Macmillan, 2010). For a much earlier, controversial exposition, see Werner Sombart, *The Jews and Modern Capitalism* (Leipzig: Duncker and Humblot, 1911). A German economist and sociologist, Sombart coined the term "creative destruction" used in Joseph Schumpeter's theories about innovation.

79. Taylor, "Who Will Do the Work?" pp. 3–5 (first quotation) and Taylor, "An American Solution," p. 10 (second quotation).

80. During the 2004 presidential election between John Kerry and George W. Bush, a Texas Republican-turned-Democrat confronted her older father, a Texas physician, about rampant charges of voter suppression efforts being waged by Republican operatives that targeted likely Democratic voters. "Those people shouldn't be voting anyway" was his response. Conversations with SYA, November 2004. Taylor, "Who Will Do the Work?" p. 3 (first quotation); Taylor, "Rebuilding Our Democracy," p. 6 (second quotation), p. 10 (quote about "darker skinned peoples"); Taylor, "An American Solution," p. 4 (remainder of third quotation).

81. Ayn Rand, *The Fountainhead* (Philadelphia: Blakiston Company, 1943) and Ayn Rand, *Atlas Shrugged* (New York: Random House, 1957). See also Taylor, "Rebuilding Our Democracy," pp. 2–3 (quotations), 7 and Taylor, "An American Solution," 11.

82. Eighteenth-century economic thinker Bernard Mandeville argued that unless the poor remained poor, they would not do an honest day's work without asking for inappropriately high wages. "To make the Society Happy," he wrote, "it is requisite that great numbers should be Ignorant as well as Poor," and the wants of the poor would be "but folly to cure." Heilbroner, *The Worldly Philosophers*, 40, 60. See also Muller, *The Mind and the Market*, 42–43. Taylor, "Who Will Do the Work?" pp. 1, 2, and 4 (first quotation); Taylor, "Rebuilding Our Democracy," pp. 4–6 (second quotation).

83. Robert Reich, "Republican Politics as Social Darwinism," *Huffington Post*, 26 September 2010.

84. See Jean H. Baker, *Margaret Sanger: A Life of Passion* (New York: Hill and Wang, 2011); Taylor, "An American Solution," 8, 9, 11 (quotations).

85. Charles Parsons to Chauncey Sparks, 1 September 1943 (first quotation), Twelve Members of Union, Columbia, SC, to Chauncey Sparks, 6 September 1943, J. Frank Norris to Chauncey Sparks, 1 September 1943 (second quotation), and Mrs. W. B. White, Grand View, TX, to Chauncey Sparks, 31 August 1943 (third quotation), all in box SG 12491, folder 8, Sparks Papers.

86. Leon W. Harris, Anderson, SC, to Chauncey Sparks, 31 August 1943, box SG 12491, folder 8, Sparks Papers.

87. (Miss) Shirley Whisenhunt, Ada, OK, to Chauncey Sparks, 31 August 1943, box SG 12491, folder 8, Sparks Papers.

88. M. D. Boland, Columbus, GA, to Sparks, 2 August 1943, box SG 12491, folder 8, Sparks Papers.

89. Atticus Mullin column in the *Montgomery Advertiser* quoted in the *Alabama Magazine*, 14 August 1942, p. 15 (first quotation); Major Squirm column in *Alabama Magazine*, 13 November 1942, p. 15 (second quotation).

90. Levie Shelley to Judge Chauncey Sparks, 28 July 1942, box 4, folder: Racial Question, 1942, Sparks Personal Papers; Charles Eli Sexton to Chauncey Sparks, 20 September 1943, box SG 12491, folder 7, and for representative complaint about African American influence in the national Democratic Party, see Hamner Cobbs's editorial, *Greensboro Watchman*, 17 April 1943, p. 6, clipping in box SG 12398, folder 19, both in the Sparks Papers. See also Lt. Paul Mur to Lister Hill, 13 July 1943, Lawrence E. McNeil to Lister Hill, 21 June 1943 (quotation), both in box 376, folder 2, and, for fear over Eleanor Clubs existing in Alabama, Augusta P. Hope to Eleanor Roosevelt, 15 August 1942, and Eleanor Roosevelt to Miss Hope, 22 August 1942, both in box 376, folder 1, all in Hill Papers.

91. Mrs. Minnie Callaway Claiborne to Frank M. Dixon, 31 July 1942 (first quotation) and S. Palmer Galliard to Frank M. Dixon, 12 August 1942 (second quotation),

both in box SG 12276, folder 10, Dixon Papers; W.C.T. Carter to ed., *Collier's Weekly,* 14 July 1943, box SG 12491, folder 7, Sparks Papers (third quotation).

92. Cobbs, "Appeasement Doesn't Pay," 4, 7 (first quotation); E. R. Barnes to Chauncey Sparks, 28 June 1943, box SG 12491, folder 7, Sparks Papers (second quotation).

93. Thomas E. Moore, Los Angeles, to Chauncey Sparks, 4 July 1943, box SG 12491, folder 7, Sparks Papers. A study that focuses on 1948 to the Nixon years with regard to the ties between southern segregationists and northern conservatives is Joseph E. Lowndes, *From the New Deal to the New Right: Race and the Southern Origins of Modern Conservatism* (New Haven: Yale University Press, 2008).

94. Robert Erskine Kerr to Frank M. Dixon, 26 August 1942, box SG 12277, folder 29, Dixon Papers (first quotation). See also "Your Friend," Marion, AL, to Frank M. Dixon, 5 August 1942 (second quotation), J. H. Tucker to Frank M. Dixon, 1 August 1942 (third quotation), and John M. Thomason to Frank M. Dixon, 25 July 1942, all three in box SG 12276, folder 10, Dixon Papers.

95. *Alabama Magazine,* 14 August 1942, p. 3.

96. Major Squirm column in *Alabama Magazine,* 18 September 1942, p. 15. For an example of Governor Dixon's aversion to the federal government, see Frank M. Dixon to Mrs. Estelle Cassimus, 24 November 1942, box SG 12277, folder 29, Dixon Papers.

97. F. E. Litchfield to Frank M. Dixon, 22 October 1941, box SG 23766, Scrapbook: Sloss-Sheffield Strike, 1941, Dixon Papers (first quotation); Mrs. J. B. Newman to Chauncey Sparks, 30 August 1943, box SG 12491, folder 8, Sparks Papers (second quotation).

98. Horace Hall, *Dothan Eagle,* ca. 22 October 1941 and Ed Field, *Selma Times-Journal,* 23 October 1941, p. 4, both editorial clippings in box SG 23766, Scrapbook: Sloss-Sheffield Strike, 1941, Dixon Papers. Another paper made clear the connections in the Alabama mind between Reconstruction, race, and now "socialism." It denounced the "machinations of meddlesome nit-wits," the interference of "outsiders," and "racial rabble-rousers." "We in the South are again face to face with an old problem. . . . Instead of the abolitionists and reconstructionists . . . the South is about to be blessed by the socialists under the protection of the New Deal." *Brewton Standard* editorial reprinted in *Alabama Magazine,* 14 August 1942, p. 7.

99. The South's legislative role, according to political scholar Paul Seabury, was "not only marginally decisive," it actually supplied the "bedrock of support" for the New Deal and wartime Democratic Party without which American policy "might well have been paralyzed." Tindall, *Emergence of the New South,* 687 (quotation in note), 691–92; Mrs. W. B. White to Chauncey Sparks, 31 August 1943, box SG 12491, folder 8, Sparks Papers (quotation in text).

100. Drew Pearson, "Merry-Go-Round," column in the *Boston Traveler,* 30 August 1943, box SG 12491, folder 8, Sparks Papers; Gessner T. McCorvey to E. Ray Scott, 2 October 1942, box SG 12234, folder 21, Dixon Papers. Criticism of Sparks was not common in the South, but it did exist. An Alabama woman who voted for Sparks was horrified by the idea of the governor impugning the First Lady "of all things" at the national Democratic convention: "[N]o gentleman, no Alabamian—would think of publicly making any such remarks about the wife of the President." Minnie Pearce Sargent (Mrs. Harvey Owen Sargent) to Chauncey Sparks, 30 August 1943; see also Rev. Outee A.

Renfro Sr., Kansas City, MO, to Chauncey Sparks, 31 August 1943, both in box SG 12491, folder 8, Sparks Papers.

101. C. L. Vance to Senator Alben Barkley, 20 November 1942 (first quotation), box SG 12277, folder 29, Dixon Papers; "One of the Insulted Whites from the South" to Chauncey Sparks, 13 August 1943 (second quotation), box SG 12409, folder 7, Sparks Papers.

102. Elmore D. Treaves Jr. to Chauncey Sparks, ca. 2 September 1943 (first quotation) and Leon W. Harris to Chauncey Sparks, 31 August 1943 (second quotation), both in box SG 12491, folder 8, Sparks Papers. The regional emphasis was clear in the posture of one of the loudest of the disgruntled Democrats soon to bolt to the States' Rights Party and then the GOP: Hamner Cobbs. He prided himself on the fact that the *Greensboro Watchman*, with its devout white supremacy and unfettered laissez-faire, was "A Southern Newspaper For People Who Believe in the South . . . weary of the ceaseless attacks on the South [and] . . . pro-Southern in everything which it publishes." *Greensboro Watchman*, 17 April 1943, p. 6, clipping in box SG 12398, folder 19, Sparks Papers.

103. "A Longsuffering fellow-Southerner" to Chauncey Sparks, 11 December 1943.

104. T. M. Murphree to Frank M. Dixon, 9 August 1942, box SG 12276, folder 10, Dixon Papers.

105. R. M. Harper to Frank M. Dixon, 1 August 1942, box SG 12276, folder 10, Dixon Papers.

106. Ibid.

Chapter 10

1. For the general labeling of Grover C. Hall Sr. as a "liberal" by the SCHW's *Southern Patriot*, the *Montgomery Advertiser*, and the planter-industrialist cabal, see *Alabama Magazine*, 4 August 1944, p. 11; David R. Davies, ed., *The Press and Race: Mississippi Journalists Confront the Movement* (Jackson: University Press of Mississippi, 2001), 9 (first quotation); C. Vann Woodward, *The Strange Career of Jim Crow* (1955; reprint, Baton Rouge: Louisiana State University Press, 1974), 166 (second quotation); Gunnar Myrdal, *An American Dilemma: The Negro Problem and American Democracy* 2 vols. (New York: Harper and Brothers, 1944) 440 (third quotation). Myrdal went on: "Part of the explanation is that Southern conservatism is 'reactionary' in the literal sense of the word. It has preserved an ideological allegiance not only to the *status quo*, but to *status quo ante*. The region is still carrying the heritage of slavery" (441). Black sociologist Ralph J. Bunche also made basically the same point, writing around 1940: "In no other section of the United States can such intense self-imposed political provincialism be found. The net result is a political naivete and backwardness. . . . The South pays a high price for its white supremacy in terms of a corrupt, undemocratic political system and extreme reaction in social legislation. In the final analysis, the nonvoting Negro remains the greatest single political influence in the Southern scene." Bunche, *The Political Status of the Negro in the Age of FDR*, 32.

2. For Dobbins, see Rogers et al., *Alabama*, 526; James G. Chappell to Chauncey Sparks, 8 April 1943, and Chauncey Sparks to J. C. Chappell, 10 April 1943, both in box SG 12501, folder 5, Sparks Papers.

3. Major Squirm column in *Alabama Magazine*, 19 June 1942, p. 15.

4. *Greensboro Watchman* editorial reprinted in *Alabama Magazine,* 21 August 1942, p. 12.

5. On this score the Selma editor singled out Hanson's *News, Age-Herald, Advertiser,* and the *Anniston Times.* "A Champion Arises" (quoted). This view of the *Birmingham News* et al. was shared by confidantes of Sparks. See Levie Shelley to Judge Chauncey Sparks, 28 July 1942, box 4, folder: Racial Question, 1942, range H, section 4, shelf e, Sparks Personal Papers.

6. Grover C. Hall Jr., "The Race Issue Must Not Be Alabama's Shame!" *Montgomery Advertiser,* 25 July 1942, editorial clipping in box 4, folder: Racial Question, 1942, Sparks Personal Papers.

7. Grover C. Hall Jr., "One More Word," *Montgomery Advertiser,* 31 July 1942, editorial clipping in box 4, folder: Racial Question, 1942, Sparks Personal Papers. In this editorial, a frustrated Hall also took a poke at the emotional nature of Alabama's politics by calling for "less fear and less hysteria" in dealing with race and for "reason rather than passion [to] dominate public discussion."

8. Major Squirm column in *Alabama Magazine,* 19 June 1942, p. 15 (quotation); "A Champion Arises." "[We have] followed a course of moderation in recording the frenzied gyrations of the irresponsibles [in Washington who have fomented]" challenges to southern white supremacy like the FEPC, Field maintained, and "[we have] ignored the hysterical yappings of the so-called 'liberals' within the South itself." *Selma Times-Journal,* ca. 6 August 1942, box 4, folder: Racial Question, 1942, Sparks Personal Papers.

9. "[A]ll self-respecting negroes of mature thinking" favored segregation, a female parole officer in Marion agreed. The color line was "fair to all" a Hope Hull man added. Resolution of the Bessemer Lions Club, 28 July 1942 (quotation), Miss Terrell Whitman, Marion, to Frank M. Dixon, 8 August 1942 (quoted in note), and J. F. Duggar, Hope Hull, to Frank Dixon, 7 August 1942 (quoted in note), all in box SG 12276, folder 10, Dixon Papers. On examples of the social penalty, see Jennifer E. Brooks, "Winning the Peace: Georgia Veterans and the Struggle to Define the Political Legacy of World War II," in Feldman, *Before Brown,* 238–67. John Bankhead and Chauncey Sparks made the argument that Jim Crow was in the best interest of all Alabamians (see the *Birmingham News,* 26 August 1944, and the *Baldwin Times,* 31 August 1944, respectively, in Scrapbook #24, pp. 29, 32, Sparks Personal Papers) as did Congressman Frank Boykin: Statement by Frank W. Boykin, representative, re: Maxwell Order, 26 August 1944, box SG 12491, folder 5, Sparks Papers. For one "self-respecting Negro" who opposed Jim Crow and was "humiliated" at being asked to move while on a Southern Railroad Company train, see James T. Mason, president of the Easonian Seminary, Birmingham, to Earnest Norris, president, SRRC, and Lister Hill, 3 October 1945, box 376, folder 4, Hill Papers.

10. I. W. Rouzer to Joseph Starnes, 29 July 1942, box SG 12277, folder 30 (first quotation) and the *Sumter County Journal,* ca. 30 July 1942, clipping in box SG 12276, folder 11 (third quotation), both in Dixon Papers; R. A. Bragg to Frank M. Dixon et al., 24 July 1942, box 4, folder: Racial Question, 1942, Sparks Personal Papers (second quotation).

11. Gurley N. Vines, deputy treasurer, Jefferson County Courthouse, to Frank M. Dixon, 18 November 1942, box SG 12278, folder 10 (first quotation) and Horace C. Wilkinson to John Temple Graves, 31 August 1942 (second quotation). Wilkinson used the phrase "our way of life" three times in this letter, same box, folder 11, both in Dixon Papers. Harry Worley to Chauncey Sparks, 7 April 1943, box SG 12398, folder 19A, Sparks Papers. The "seeds of hate" are being sown all over the South by the agitators, Ed Field's

Selma Times-Journal pontificated, and the harvest, when it came, would be terrible for both races "in our native land." See "A Champion Arises." Hamner Cobbs advertised his newspaper as strictly "Southern" in nature and posture. *Greensboro Watchman*, 17 April 1943, p. 6.

12. Myrdal, *An American Dilemma*, 471.

13. *Opp Weekly Journal*, 30 July 1942, and Levie Shelley to Judge Chauncey Sparks, 28 July 1942, both in box 4, folder: Racial Question, 1942, Sparks Personal Papers; southerner to Frank M. Dixon, 25 July 1942, box SG 12276, folder 11, Dixon Papers.

14. Arch-conservative Hubert Baughn referred to the race issue as "the fundamental issue" (see Major Squirm column in *Alabama Magazine*, 19 July 1942, p. 15) while the more moderate Grover C. Hall Jr. called it the "most vital issue." See "The Race Issue Must Not Be Alabama's Shame," *Montgomery Advertiser*, 25 July 1942, editorial clipping in box 4, folder: Racial Question, 1942, Sparks Personal Papers.

15. Marian D. Irish, "The Southern One-Party System and National Politics," *Journal of Politics* 4 (February 1942): 80.

16. Myrdal, *An American Dilemma*, 430. In his endnotes on the matter (1310n5), Myrdal also cited two liberal southern authors who recognized the broad and interrelated societal effect of the Reconstruction/racial trauma. Willis D. Weatherford asked: "Who among us has not seen how the presence of the Negro has molded our political history since emancipation? We have been slow to pass laws for compulsory school attendance, lest we tie ourselves to the task of classical education of the Negro . . . slow enough about extending the suffrage, lest the colored man should become too influential. No major political issue has faced the South in the last hundred years that has not been decided largely in light of the presence of the Negro." Willis D. Weatherford and Charles S. Johnson, *Race Relations: Adjustment of Whites and Negroes in the United States* (Boston: D.C. Heath and Company, 1934), 298. T. J. Woofter Jr. wrote: "It is . . . apparent that in excluding the Negro the South is, in a way, politically dominated by the Negro question. Before all others it looms as the bulwark of the one-party system. It was a determining factor in the prohibition vote. It affected the South's stand on woman suffrage and it ramifies into hundreds of questions of public policy, it influences the South's position on child labor, it is a stumbling block in the administration of compulsory school laws, standing as an ever-present shadow across the door of political councils." Thomas Jackson Woofter, *The Basis of Racial Adjustment* (1925; reprint, Freeport, NY: Books for Libraries Press, 1969), 166. Myrdal himself observed that "The conservative Southerner is not so likely to write books on the Negro problem as is his liberal compatriot. . . . [Yet even] they too usually complained about how the Negro problem has entered into all public questions of the region and hindered their consideration upon their own merits. But they consider this situation without remedy or, rather, hold that even a gradual enfranchisement . . . could only accentuate this 'plight'" (1310n5).

17. Thomas J. Searles to Frank M. Dixon, 10 September 1942 (first quotation), I. W. Rouzer to Joe Starnes, 12 August 1942 (second quotation), Oliver Day Street to Frank M. Dixon, 15 August 1942, and Rose McDavid Munger (Mrs. L. P. Munger) to Frank M. Dixon, 30 July 1942, all four in box SG 12276, folder 10, Dixon Papers. The Mungers became a leading GOP family. For additional references to "outsiders" meddling in southern racial affairs, see Oliver Day Street to Chauncey Sparks, 6 May 1943, box SG 12398, folder 19 and Harry Worley to Chauncey Sparks, 7 April 1943, same box, folder 19A, both in Sparks Papers.

18. Miss Lida Bestor Robinson to Dixon, 29 July 1942, box SG 12276, folder 11, Dixon Papers.

19. For example, Hamner Cobbs ran an editorial titled "75 Years Ago in the *Alabama Beacon*" from 18 April 1868 in the *Greensboro Southern Watchman*, 17 April 1943, p. 6, clipping in box SG 12398, folder 19, Sparks Papers (first quotation); "A Champion Arises" (second quotation).

20. On the freight rate issue, see the *Alabama Magazine*, 19 June 1942, p. 4; Thomas J. Searles to Frank M. Dixon, 10 September 1942, box SG 12276, folder 10, Dixon Papers (quoted). All of this refers to the "Reconstruction Syndrome" language and thought, a concept I have long used in my work and which has been discussed earlier. The closest thing I have ever found to a reference to such a mind-set is mention of a "Reconstruction complex" by World War II veteran R. W. Hayes testifying before the Georgia state legislative bill to restore the white primary in 1947, cited in Egerton, *Speak Now against the Day*, 389, cited in a draft of Brooks, "Winning the Peace," 20 (copyedited version in possession of the author).

21. R. A. Bragg to Frank M. Dixon et al., 24 July 1942, box 4, folder: Racial Question, 1942, Sparks Personal Papers (first quotation); C. L. Vance to Alvin M. Barkley, 20 November 1942, box SG 12277, folder 29, Dixon Papers (second quotation).

22. Speech of Hon. John E. Rankin, House of Representatives, 1 December 1942 (first quotation), *Congressional Record* extract and Frank M. Dixon to C. L. Vance, 25 November 1942 (second quotation), both in box SG 12277, folder 29, Dixon Papers. A north Alabama congressman agreed: the wartime actions and "damnable deceits" of the race "agitators . . . to push their dark agenda" and take advantage of the war were playing right "into the hands of America's enemies." *Alabama Magazine*, 4 September 1942, pp. 6–7 (Joe Starnes quotation).

23. *Gadsden Times* editorial reprinted in the *Alabama Magazine*, 11 September 1942, p. 4 (first quotation); C. L. Vance to Alvin M. Barkley, 20 November 1942, box SG 12277, folder 29, Dixon Papers (second quotation).

24. C. L. Vance to Alvin M. Barkley, 20 November 1942; *Alabama Magazine*, 14 August 1942, p. 3 (first quotation) and 25 June 1942, p. 3 (second quotation).

25. I. W. Rouzer to Joe Starnes, 12 August 1942 (first quotation) and I. W. Rouzer to Frank M. Dixon, 13 August 1942 (second quotation), both in box SG 12276, folder 10, Dixon Papers.

26. Judge W. M. Beck to Frank M. Dixon, 6 August 1942, Frank M. Dixon to Guy Hardwick, 3 August 1942, and Frank M. Dixon to Mrs. James A. Carney, 5 August 1942, all three in box SG 12276, folder 10, Dixon Papers.

27. Myrdal, *An American Dilemma*, 457.

28. Ibid.

29. "Politics of emotion" (such as the perennial "God, Guns, and Gays" issue in the South) is a concept used previously in my work that refers to the use of (not only race but other) emotional hot-button issues to distract plain whites from more rational, often material ("politics of reason") issues.

30. Alabama's U.S. congressman from Guntersville agreed that it was "no time for social reforming, racial agitation, racketeering, or [war] profiteering." See Joseph Starnes to I. W. Rouzer, 8 August 1942, box SG 12276, folder 10, Dixon Papers. Major Squirm column in *Alabama Magazine*, 18 September 1942, p. 15 (quotation in text).

31. *Alabama Magazine*, 3 July 1942, p. 3 (first quotation; italics added); *Gadsden Tribune*, 6 August 1942, editorial clipping in box 4, folder: Racial Question, 1942, Sparks Personal Papers (second quotation).

32. C. C. Williams, Ensley Kiwanis Club, to Frank M. Dixon, 13 August 1942, box SG 12276, folder 11, Dixon Papers (first quotation); John D. McQueen to Lister Hill, 15 September 1943, box 376, folder 2, Hill Papers (second quotation).

33. Mrs. Mamie Long, Montgomery, to Lister Hill, 4 September 1943, box 376, folder 2, Hill Papers (first quotation); Wirt C. Davidson, Jasper, to Chauncey Sparks, ca. 25 August 1943, box SG 12491, folder 7, Sparks Papers (second quotation). "[A]ll true Americans" hated the CIO's involvement in race discrimination matters, a rural Etowah County woman stipulated about race, economics, and patriotism. See Mrs. H. W. Dunn, Route 3, Gadsden, to Frank M. Dixon, 1 September 1942, box SG 12276, folder 10, Dixon Papers.

34. Bumper stickers declaring that one cannot be both a Christian and pro-choice were not uncommonly seen in places like Birmingham around 2004. George Norris column in *Memphis Commercial Appeal*, 8 July 1942, transcript typed by Roland M. Harper in box SG 12276, folder 10, Dixon Papers (first quotation); Levie Shelley to Judge Chauncey Sparks, 28 July 1942, box 4, folder: Racial Question, 1942, Sparks Personal Papers (second quotation).

35. *Philadelphia Inquirer*, 25 July 1942, clipping in box SG 12276, folder 10, Dixon Papers (first quotation); no name, Home Sweet Home, NY, to Chauncey Sparks, 26 May 1943, box SG 12491, folder 9, Sparks Papers (second quotation).

36. Horace C. Wilkinson, "Help Dixie's Cause! An Appeal to the People of Alabama to Help in the Fight to Preserve Our Way of Life," ca. 1948, box 7, folder 10, Alabama Pamphlets Collection, ADAH; Sarah Hart Brown, "Communism, Anti-Communism, and Massive Resistance: The Civil Rights Congress in Southern Perspective," 8 (copyedited manuscript in possession of the author [first quotation]). Brown's essay later appeared in Feldman, *Before Brown*, 170–97. John Dos Passos, *State of the Nation* (Boston: Houghton Mifflin, 1944), 82 (second quotation). See also Tindall, *Emergence of the New South*, 709 and Jay Taylor, "Rebuilding Our Democracy," ca. December 1943, p. 7 (third quotation), box SG 12491, folder 7, Sparks Papers.

37. John C. Sheffield, "The Second Secession," ca. February 1937, box 2, folder 5, Dixon Personal Papers. A later version of the Sheffield essay also appears, with date received of 15 December 1943, in box SG 12491, folder 8, Sparks Papers.

38. In 1940s Mississippi, for example, whites repeatedly got enraged, even engaging in mob violence, when instances of black and white sex, even consensual involving white women, became known. Yet "nothing was done" when white males had sex with black females, even in the case of a white man who raped a twelve-year-old babysitter, complained the Mississippi Regional Council of Negro Leadership, *Prospectus*, 13–14, cited in David R. Beito and Linda Royster Beito, "T.R.M. Howard: Pragmatism over Strict Integrationist Ideology in the Mississippi Delta, 1942–1954," 20 (copyedited page version). The Beitos' essay later appeared in Feldman, *Before Brown*, 68–95. See also E. M. Fitzroy to Lister Hill, 2 December 1944, box 376, folder 4, Hill Papers.

39. Kevin Alexander Gray, "'Segregation (and Hypocrisy) Forever': The Legacy of Strom Thurmond," *Counterpunch*, 8 March 2004, http://www.counterpunch.org/ (accessed February 2012); Beito and Beito, "T.R.M. Howard," 20. See also Fawn MacKay Brodie, *Thomas Jefferson: An Intimate History* (New York: W. W. Norton, 1974); Dumas

Malone and Steven Hochman, "A Note on Evidence: The Personal History of Madison Hemings," *Journal of Southern History* 41 (November 1975): 523–28.

40. Transcript of phone conversation, Sheriff W. L. Holcombe, Mobile, to State Senator Hayse Tucker, Montgomery, 31 May 1944, box SG 12491, folder 7, Sparks Papers (first quotation); *Dothan Eagle,* 30 March 1945, clipping in Scrapbook #24, p. 42, Sparks Personal Papers. Kennedy, *Southern Exposure,* 131–32 (second quotation). On the unrest in Mobile, see also Rogers et al., *Alabama,* 514 and Melton A. McLaurin, "Mobile Blacks and World War II: The Development of a Political Consciousness," in *Gulf Coast Politics in the Twentieth Century,* ed. Ted Carageorge (Pensacola: Historic Pensacola Preservation Board, 1974), 47–56.

41. Fred Fite, Hamilton attorney, to Lister Hill, 23 November 1945, box 376, folder 4, Hill Papers.

42. Memorandum, Re: Race, Governor's Office, 29 June 1944, and Charles E. Williams to Chauncey Sparks, 29 August 1944, both in box SG 12491, folder 8, Sparks Papers. See also no name, Hon. Roy L. Nolen to Lister Hill, 7 April 1944, box 376, folder 2 and David H. Ferguson to Lister Hill, 19 July 1944, same box, folder 3, both in Hill Papers. On hotel beds, see W. Hume Logan to Miss Dorothy Thompson, 24 April 1944, box SG 12491, folder 8, Sparks Papers.

43. Robert F. McKibbon to Lister Hill, 5 December 1945 (first quotation), box 376, folder 4, Hill Papers. See also Scrapbook #24, p. 44, Sparks Personal Papers. "This Morning" column, *Lafayette Sun,* 20 February 1946 (second quotation).

44. For northern white commiseration on this score, see Mr. and Mrs. James DeMille, Chicago, to Chauncey Sparks, 8 April 1944, box SG 12491, folder 8, Sparks Papers. "Would you like to spend your life's savings buying a home, and then have a negro move next door and immediately reduce your property value by 50% or over?" asked Everett R. Brown, M.D., to Claude Pepper, 25 February 1945, box 376, folder 4, Hill Papers.

45. Miss Lillie M. Williams to Eleanor Roosevelt, 6 March 1944, folder: 190.1, ER Papers (first quotation); Pete Jarman to Robert Patterson, Asst. Secretary of War, 19 September 1944, box SG 12491, folder 6, Sparks Papers (second quotation). See also George A. Denison, M.D., Jefferson County Health Officer, to Dr. Roy Kracke, director, medical school, 30 August 1944, series 17.1, box 1, folder 4, Dean-School of Medicine Papers, University of Alabama at Birmingham Archives (UAB).

46. Tom Heflin was long associated with the crack that he could detect federal officeholders upon crossing any county line "because they smelled so much like negroes." Radio speech by John H. Bankhead II on WBRC in Birmingham, transcript, 3 November 1930, p. 3, box 3, folder 10, Bankhead II Papers (quotation in note). Walton H. Craft to Chauncey Sparks, 6 September 1944, box SG 12491, folder 8, Sparks Papers (first quotation), copy of same letter in box 376, folder 3, Hill Papers; Kennedy, *Southern Exposure,* 132 (second quotation).

47. Reese Adamson to Hon. Marshall Haynes, 28 March 1944, box SG 12491, folder 8, Sparks Papers; Reese Adamson to Frank M. Dixon, 19 August 1948, box 2, folder 3, Dixon Personal Papers.

48. See chapter 2, note 31.

49. Miss Lida Bestor Robinson, Thomaston, to Frank M. Dixon, 29 July 1942, box SG 12276, folder 11, Dixon Papers; Mr. and Mrs. James DeMille to Chauncey Sparks, received 8 April 1944, box SG 12491, folder 8, Sparks Papers, both in ADAH.

50. "Your Friend," Marion, to Frank M. Dixon, 5 August 1942 (first quotation), John M. Thomason, Birmingham, to Frank M. Dixon, 25 July 1942 (second quotation), and Frank B. King to Frank M. Dixon, 2 August 1942, all three in box SG 12276, folder 10, Dixon Papers.

51. I. W. Rouzer to Joseph Starnes, 12 August 1942 (first quotation), Donald Comer to Frank M. Dixon, 6 August 1942 (second quotation), and S. Palmer Galliard to Frank M. Dixon, 12 August 1942 (third quotation), all three in box SG 12276, folder 10, Dixon Papers.

52. Mrs. H. W. Dunn, Route 3, Gadsden, to Frank M. Dixon, 1 September 1942 (quoted) and W. M. Beck, Judge, DeKalb County, to Frank M. Dixon, 6 August 1942, both in box SG 12276, folder 10, Dixon Papers.

53. Mrs. H. W. Dunn to Frank M. Dixon, 1 September 1942 (first quotation) and Owen Meredith, Tuscaloosa, to Frank M. Dixon, 11 August 1942 (second quotation), both in box SG 12276, folder 10, Dixon Papers.

54. Joseph L. Edgar to Eleanor Roosevelt, 6 September 1944 (second quotation) and Mrs. O. P. Garrett, Bessemer, to Chauncey Sparks, received 31 August 1944, both in box SG 12491, folder 6, Sparks Papers; Joseph L. Edgar to ed., *Alabama Sun,* 29 April 1944, box 376, folder 2, Hill Papers (first quotation).

55. A. R. Maxwell to Sparks, 21 September 1943, box SG 12491, folder 7, Sparks Papers.

56. L. B., Houston to Chauncey Sparks, 28 August 1944, box SG 12491, folder 8, Sparks Papers (first quotation); Joseph L. Edgar to ed., *Alabama Sun,* 29 April 1944 (second quotation).

57. Statement by Frank W. Boykin, representative, re: Maxwell Order, 26 August 1944, box SG 12491, folder 5, Sparks Papers (first quotation); *Alabama Magazine,* 2 February 1945, pp. 8 (second quotation), 9. See also Leah Rawls Atkins, *Developed for the Service of Alabama: The Centennial History of the Alabama Power Company, 1906–2006* (Birmingham: Alabama Power Company, 2006).

58. Manis, "'City Mothers,'" 42 (copyedited manuscript in possession of the author); James T. Mason, "An Appeal against the Rising Tide of Prejudice against the Negro in the South," ca. 2 September 1943, box SG 12491, folder 8, Sparks Papers (quoted).

59. White southerners implored liberal groups such as the Federal Council of Churches to "drop politics, preach the gospel, and follow the example of Paul, who said: 'preach nothing but Jesus Christ and Him crucified.'" W. Hume Logan to Miss Dorothy Thompson, 24 April 1944, box SG 12491, folder 8, Sparks Papers (quoted in note). Betty Carter, interview by John Egerton, 6 September 1990, p. 1, Greenville, MS, Interview # A-350, SHC (first quotation). Mays was the youngest of eight children on a South Carolina cotton farm; his father had been a slave. He earned a Ph.D. in 1935 from the University of Chicago, pastored an Atlanta church, and served as dean of Howard University for six years and as president of Morehouse College for twenty-seven. Benjamin E. Mays, *Born to Rebel: An Autobiography by Benjamin E. Mays* (New York: Charles Scribner's Sons, 1971), 241 (second quotation).

60. *Gadsden Times* editorial reprinted in the *Alabama Magazine,* 10 July 1942, p. 6.

61. *Greensboro Southern Watchman* quoted in *Alabama Magazine,* 3 July 1942, p. 5 (first quotation); *Gadsden Times* in *Alabama Magazine,* 10 July 1942, p. 6 (second quotation).

62. *Alabama Magazine,* 21 August 1942, p. 3.

63. *Alabama Magazine*, 13 July 1945, p. 3.

64. *Alabama Magazine*, 29 September 1944, p. 15 (first quotation) and 13 July 1945, p. 3 (second and third quotations).

65. *Alabama Magazine*, 15 June 1945, p. 3 (quotation) and 1 September 1944, p. 15. In the issue of 7 December 1945, p. 3, the Bourbon organ also damned the *News* and *Birmingham Age-Herald*, in a wild charge, for "pumping this district full of pro-union propaganda." For Hanson's retreat, see John Temple Graves to Chauncey Sparks, 21 August 1944, box SG 12501, folder 5, Sparks Papers. The main editorial targets in Hanson's papers were Charles Fiedelson, James Chappell, and Ted Van der Veer, while national columnists Drew Pearson and Walter Winchell also came in for criticism. See, e.g., *Alabama Magazine*, 2 February 1945, p. 15 and the Graves letter cited above in this note. See also the clippings in Scrapbook #24, p. 35, Sparks Personal Papers where Congressman George Grant, for example, also denounced the *Montgomery Advertiser* as liberal in the *Greensboro Southern Watchman*, 2 September 1944.

Chapter 11

1. Virginia and Clifford Durr were Montgomery liberals who lost all of that for their racial liberalism. See Barnard, *Outside the Magic Circle* and Sullivan, *Freedom Writer*.

2. Washington columnist Stewart Alsop made just such a contention. See Egerton, *Speak Now against the Day*, 391.

3. Two of the most closely connected studies to these categories are Joel R. Williamson, *The Crucible of Race: Black/White Relations in the American South since Emancipation* (New York: Oxford University Press, 1984) and Woodward, *The Strange Career of Jim Crow*. For example, Mississippi senator John Stennis was often praised as an opportunist and "a very decent man" while fellow senators James Eastland and Theodore Bilbo were denounced as Negrophobes who "felt it deep down in their bones." Yet as one Mississippi woman observed, Stennis basically "gave you a softened version of the same thing" Eastland did and they both ended up in the same place (Carter interview, 13). These distinctions continue today. For example, Jennifer E. Brooks discusses racial progressives and racial reactionaries as being distinct from a third category of racism, which she refers to as "Chamber of Commerce" (Brooks, "Winning the Peace," 46–47 [copyedited form in possession of the author]). The present study does not hew to these types of distinctions because the melding process during this period increasingly made racial conservatism and economic conservatism part of one and the same essential thing in the popular southern white mind.

4. Feldman, *Politics, Society, and the Klan in Alabama*.

5. Myrdal, *An American Dilemma*, 485.

6. Alwyn Viccard, Florida by way of forty years in Los Angeles, to Lister Hill, 31 August 1944, box SG 12491, folder 6, Sparks Papers; M. W. Smith Jr., M. W. Smith Lumber Company, Jackson, to Lister Hill, 29 March 1944, box 376, folder 2, C. H. Young, Anniston to Lister Hill, 27 July 1944 (first quotation), and F. W. Brown, Pell City, to Town Hall, New York City, 29 April 1944 (second quotation), both in box 376, folder 3, all three in Hill Papers.

7. William D. Barnard, *Dixiecrats and Democrats: Alabama Politics, 1942–1950* (Tuscaloosa: The University of Alabama Press, 1974), 58; Rogers et al., *Alabama*, 532.

8. *Montgomery Advertiser*, 25 and 31 July 1942.

9. *Wesleyan Christian Advocate,* 28 October 1948, p. 6 (first quotation) and 19 August 1948, pp. 6–7 (second quotation), both cited in Manis, "'City Mothers,'" 10–11 (copyedited form).

10. D. Alexander, Childersburg, Alabama, A Southern White Friend, "The Negro Disillusioned," pamphlet, ca. 6 May 1944, box SG 12491, folder 7, Sparks Papers.

11. Ibid.

12. Rogers et al., *Alabama,* 532 (quoted). The passage went on: "Ironically one of the nation's most articulate advocates of blacks, the poor, and the common person . . . lived and worked in Montgomery, Alabama."

13. Ibid., 528 (quotations). The newspaper had a national distribution of one million and issued eighty thousand copies to Alabama farmers per issue. Dies was, of course, chair of the notorious HUAC.

14. Wesley E. Grubbs, Mobile, to H. W. Nixon, 2 June 1943 (first quotation), box SG 12491, folder 7 and Hamner Cobbs, "Consider Its Friends," *Greensboro Southern Watchman,* 17 April 1943, p. 4, editorial clipping in box SG 12398, folder 19, both in Sparks Papers (second quotation). On p. 6 of the same issue, Cobbs advertised his journal as "a southern newspaper for people who believe in the South . . . weary of the ceaseless attacks upon the South . . . openly and proudly . . . pro-Southern in everything."

15. Frank Dixon accused "the President and Mrs. Roosevelt" of being "directly responsible" for disrupting the best-laid plans of the southern white friends of the Negro such as himself and Chauncey Sparks. See Frank M. Dixon to Chauncey Sparks, 31 August 1944. Hubert Baughn counted himself along with Sparks among the "Southern white friends" of the Negro. See Hubert Baughn to George Bliss Jones, secretary to the governor, 31 August 1944, both in box SG 12491, folder 5, Sparks Papers. See also *Alabama Magazine,* 8 September 1944, p. 3. For plenty of other white supremacist declarations of friendship for the Negro, see J. H. Bradford, Uniontown, AL, to Franklin D. Roosevelt, 21 February 1944, Official Files 93, file: Colored Matters, January–March 1944, Mrs. Alva W. Taylor Sr., Columbia, SC, to Franklin D. Roosevelt, ca. 29 May 1944, and Chester B. Collins to Franklin D. Roosevelt, 26 May 1944, both in Official Files 93, file: Colored Matters, April–May 1944, all three in FDR Papers, and Loretta Carlisle, Houston, to Eleanor Roosevelt, 18 April 1944 and Mrs. Paul T. Norris, Quinton (Walker County), AL, to Eleanor Roosevelt, 4 April 1944, both in file: 190.1, ER Papers.

16. Hall explained that white supremacy "carries with it the responsibility to be more democratic, more Christian, and more willing to accord justice and good will" to the inferior. *Montgomery Advertiser,* 25 July 1942 (first quotation and in note). See also W. H. Harrell, Billingsley, Autauga County, to Frank M. Dixon, 12 August 1942, box SG 12276, folder 10, Dixon Papers (second quotation).

17. F. W. Brown to Town Hall, NY, 29 April 1944 (first quotation) and Ruth B. Quigley (Mrs. George N. Quigley) to Lister Hill, 23 May 1944 (second quotation), both in box 376, folder 3, Hill Papers.

18. W. Hume Logan to Miss Dorothy Thompson, 24 April 1944, box SG 12491, folder 8, Sparks Papers.

19. Virginia Durr interview, Oral History Project, Columbia University, New York.

20. Southerner to Frank M. Dixon, 25 July 1942 (second quotation) and T. C. "Thug" Almon, probate judge, Morgan County, to Frank M. Dixon, 28 July 1942 (third quotation), both in box SG 12276, folder 11, Dixon Papers. Goodwill was based ultimately on segregation, argued a white Mobile attorney. See Harry H. Smith to Chauncey Sparks,

30 September 1943, and for a black desire for whites to act with "good will and cooperation" toward blacks, see S. J. Phillips, publisher of *Pulling Together* (Tuskegee) to Chauncey Sparks, 1 November 1943, both in box SG 12491, folder 7, Sparks Papers; *Alabama Magazine*, 21 April 1944, p. 14 (first quotation).

21. Champ Pickens to Chauncey Sparks, 15 February 1943, box SG 12491, folder 8, Sparks Papers.

22. R. A. Bragg to Frank M. Dixon et al., 24 July 1942, box 4, folder: Racial Question, 1942, Sparks Personal Papers (first quotation). See also George Norris column in the *Memphis Commercial Appeal*, 8 July 1942, transcript typed by Roland M. Harper, Tuscaloosa, box SG 12276, folder 10, Dixon Papers (second quotation).

23. So pervasive, in fact, that had the 1940s southern Right had access to the vast conservative echo chamber of talk-radio and Internet of the 1990s, it is possible they could have blocked *Brown v. Board of Education* and the Civil Rights and Voting Rights acts altogether. For "many good negroes" favoring segregation, see I. W. Rouzer to Joseph Starnes, 12 August 1942, box SG 12276, folder 10, Dixon Papers.

24. H. L. Hargrove to Frank M. Dixon, 10 August 1942 (first quotation) and Mrs. Minnie Callaway Claiborne to Frank M. Dixon, 31 July 1942 (second quotation), both in box SG 12276, folder 10, Dixon Papers. See also note 15 above.

25. "Race Segregation Strongly Defended," ca. 1942, clipping in box SG 12276, folder 11, Dixon Papers (quotation); Cobbs, "Appeasement Doesn't Pay," 4.

26. Frank M. Dixon to Virgil Powell, UMW miner in Bessemer, 17 July 1942 (quotation) and Frank M. Dixon to Neal Carroll, CIO miner in Bessemer, 4 August 1942, both in box SG 12276, folder 10, Dixon Papers.

27. Gessner T. McCorvey to E. Ray Scott, 2 October 1942, box SG 12234, folder 21, Dixon Papers.

28. *Brown v. Board of Education*, Board of Regents Topeka, Kansas, 347 U.S. 483 (1954).

29. Sullivan, *Days of Hope*, 166. Sullivan refers to these "traditional southern liberals" also as "moderates."

30. (Nashville) *SCHW Bulletin*, 20 August 1942, box SG 12277, folder 29, Dixon Papers.

31. "Things are very bad here" in north Alabama because the races were mixing in dining rooms and toilets at the nearby federal ordinance depot, but there was a "growing spirit of revolt and indignation among all classes of white people," an Anniston attorney reported. C. H. Young to Hill, 27 July 1944, box 376, folder 3, Hill Papers.

32. John Temple Graves, *The Fighting South* (New York: G. P. Putnam's Sons, 1943), 120. See also Tindall, *Emergence of the New South*, 718.

33. "[T]here is no power in the world—not even in all the mechanized armies of the earth, Allied and Axis," he assured nervous white southerners, "which could now force the . . . abandonment of the principle of segregation." *Louisville Courier-Journal*, 21 June 1942.

34. *Anniston Star* quoted in the *Alabama Magazine*, 11 September 1942, p. 4 (first quotation). Also *Anniston Star*, 12 April 1943 (second quotation) and 24 December 1944 (third quotation), both in Scrapbook #24, Sparks Personal Papers. Washington, D.C., columnist Drew Pearson described Ayers as one of the "Alabama liberal Democrats" for his opposition to Sparks's rump-party trial balloon in "Merry Go Round," column in the *Boston Traveler*, 30 August 1943, clipping in box SG 12491, folder 8, Sparks Papers. Even

Ayers's opposition to the 1930 rump Heflox/Klan movement in Alabama found its basis in praise for the Redeemers of 1874, "who drove the usurpers from power in Alabama and returned the government to its people" and the leading architects of Alabama's reactionary 1901 Constitution: Houston, Oates, Johnston, Morgan, Pettus, John B. Knox, Thomas W. Coleman et al. Ayers editorial, *Anniston Star,* ca. 23 October 1930, clipping in box 181, folder 462, Harry Mell Ayers Papers, W. Stanley Hoole Special Collections Library, UA.

35. James G. Chappell to Chauncey Sparks, 8 April 1943 (quotation) and Chauncey Sparks to J. C. Chappell, president of the *Birmingham News,* 10 April 1943, both in box SG 12501, folder 5, Sparks Papers.

36. Chauncey Sparks to John Temple Graves, 9 May 1944 (quoted), Memorandum to Chauncey Sparks from John W. Rish, Department of Revenue, Legal Division, 7 August 1944, and J. Clay Murphey to Chauncey Sparks, 4 August 1944, all three in box SG 12501, folder 5, Sparks Papers.

37. Sullivan, *Days of Hope,* 162 (Daniels quotation), 164 (Graves and McGill quotations). James Chappell of the *Birmingham News* also opposed the breakdown of segregation as something that would undermine the system "under which the White and Negro races have lived in peace together in the South since reconstruction days" and disparaged the FEPC and the activities of Eleanor Roosevelt and Wendell Willkie as serving to "arouse racial animosity." James A. Chappell to Frank M. Dixon, 30 July 1942, box SG 12276, folder 11, Dixon Papers. Also see Morton Sosna, *In Search of the Silent South: Southern Liberals and the Race Issue* (New York: Columbia University Press, 1977) and John T. Kneebone, *Southern Liberal Journalists and the Issue of Race, 1920–1944* (Chapel Hill: University of North Carolina Press, 1985). Couch, "Publisher's Introduction," in *What the Negro Wants,* xx.

38. Tindall, *Emergence of the New South,* 718–19, 720 (quotation), 721. On Lillian Smith's unorthodoxy, see also Carter interview, 19, 22.

39. Weeks interview by Robert J. Norrell, 10.

40. For example, even northern black commentators considered Graves a "long-time 'liberal' on racial matters." See the *Pittsburgh Courier,* 16 September 1944. See also Scrapbook #24, p. 40, Sparks Personal Papers. Graves lauded himself and Governor Sparks as "liberals" and "enlightened white Southern[ers]" for their racial view that insisted on Jim Crow yet which still "truly wished the Negro to get ahead, who hate the way he is cheated, denied, and discriminated against, but who are prejudiced against giving aid to his advancement" if it implies "a breakdown of segregation." John Temple Graves, "Advance Copy of 'This Morning' Column," re: Sparks's talk to group of Birmingham Negro ministers, ca. 7 May 1944. Sparks returned the praise, remarking that he believed both he and Graves were "thinkers and forward looking people." Chauncey Sparks to John Temple Graves, 9 May 1944, both in box SG 12501, folder 5: Race Problems, Sparks Papers.

41. *Alabama Magazine,* 25 June 1942, pp. 6–7, 15 and 15 June 1945, p. 3 (quotation). See also Armbrester, "John Temple Graves, II," 203–13.

42. Graves column reprinted in *Alabama Magazine,* 24 March 1944, p. 12.

43. Individual Negroes could qualify as a "grand old Negro and human being" and a patriot who is "winning a name for himself as an American and a Southerner rather than just as a Negro." But to do so they had to accede to the established rules of the racial game. Graves column reprinted in *Alabama Magazine,* 24 March 1944, p. 12 (first quotation); J. T. Graves to Chauncey Sparks, 28 June 1944 (second quotation and quota-

tion in note), box SG 12501, folder 5, Sparks Papers. See also Robert Durr to Sir, "Help Me Do This Job!" ca. November 1942, box 376, folder 1, Hill Papers.

44. *Alabama Magazine*, 7 August 1942, p. 11.

45. *Birmingham News*, 1 July 1936, quoted in Marshall, *Labor in the South*, 189 (Graves quoted). Graves column reprinted in *Alabama Magazine*, 24 March 1944, p. 12 (quoted).

46. On the SCHW, see the Durr interview, 18–19, 23. Also see *Alabama Magazine*, 19 December 1938, p. 3 (quotation).

47. Tyler, "'Blood on Your Hands,'" 22 (quotation) (copyedited version).

48. John Temple Graves to Frank M. Dixon, 2 September 1942, box SG 12278, folder 11, Dixon Papers. J. T. Graves column reprinted in the *Pittsburgh Courier*, 16 September 1944, clipping in Scrapbook #24, p. 40, Sparks Personal Papers.

49. P. P. Wilson to Lister Hill, 6 January 1945, box 376, folder 4, Hill Papers; Major Squirm column in *Alabama Magazine*, 2 March 1945, p. 15 (quotation).

50. Major Squirm column in *Alabama Magazine*, 25 June 1942, p. 15 (first quotation). "I don't propose to argue with any white man who does not think he is better than a negro." Horace C. Wilkinson to John Temple Graves, 31 August 1942, box SG 12278, folder 11, Dixon Papers (second quotation and quoted in note).

51. Those who admitted segregation was wrong were "so far removed from the great body of opinion in the white South that their moves fall short of the real service that could be done the Negro if the sum total of southern desire to help him could somehow be mustered." John Temple Graves, "This Morning" column in the *Asheville (NC) Citizen*, 26 July 1944, clipping, box SG 12501, folder 5, Sparks Papers (quoted in text and note).

52. Ibid. Graves also spoke often of his conviction that "there is an enormous reservoir of good will and help for Negroes among average Southern white people." See, e.g., J. T. Graves to Chauncey Sparks, 21 August 1944, box SG 12501, folder 5, Sparks Papers.

53. Graves, "This Morning."

54. Of course this is not to say that it did not exist at all. For example, the Reverend Charles K. Bell Jr., a white preacher from Anniston's Parker Memorial Baptist Church, worked very hard to save the life of a black soldier stationed in Britain who had been, Bell felt, falsely accused of rape. Reverend Charles K. Bell Jr. to Lister Hill, 12 June 1944, box 376, folder 3, Hill Papers. But the larger point is still intact.

55. Fitzgerald Hall to N. C. & St. L. Employees, 15 September 1942, box SG 12277, folder 29, Dixon Papers.

56. Ibid.

57. Ibid.

58. G. W. Glover, Dining Car Employees' Union, Local No. 478, to Fitzgerald Hall, 13 August 1942, and Fitzgerald Hall to G. W. Glover, 17 August 1942, both in box SG 12277, folder 29, Dixon Papers.

59. Fitzgerald Hall to N. C. & St. L. Employees, 15 September 1942. Hall felt UNC president Frank Porter Graham was a dangerous scalawag. The railroad baron asked Alabama governor Frank Dixon to use his influence with their mutual Alabama friend O. C. Carmichael, the chancellor of Vanderbilt University, to go up to Chapel Hill and "shut him up if possible." Fitzgerald Hall to Frank M. Dixon, ca. 26 September 1942, box SG 12277, folder 29, Dixon Papers.

60. Frank M. Dixon to Fitzgerald Hall, 18 September 1942 (second quotation) and

Fitzgerald Hall to Frank M. Dixon, ca. 26 September 1942 (first quotation), both in box SG 12277, folder 29, Dixon Papers.

61. Forney Johnston to Rev. William H. Marmion, rector, St. Mary's Church, 19 November 1942, box 4, folder: Racial Question, 1942, Sparks Personal Papers.

62. Ibid.

63. Forney Johnston to the Right Reverend Henry St. George Tucker, New York, 27 November 1942 (quoted), box 4, folder: Racial Question, 1942, Sparks Personal Papers.

64. Forney Johnston to Rev. William H. Marmion, rector, St. Mary's Church, 19 November 1942 (quoted) and, for complaints about Eleanor Roosevelt and Wendell Willkie, see Forney Johnston to the Right Reverend Henry St. George Tucker, 27 November 1942, both in box 4, folder: Racial Question, 1942, Sparks Personal Papers.

65. There was nothing quite so tragic as the plight of the northern mulatto who refused to reckon with this reality, "trying to become white by virtue of an act of Congress. He has abandoned his caste and knows in what is left of his negro soul that when he turns his vision to the white border he is a hybrid in God's effort to specialize the negro and the white. He knows that all the King's horses and all of the King's men can not restore to him the dignity and the uniqueness in our cosmic plan that he has unnecessarily abandoned, for a hopeless goal." Forney Johnston to Rev. William H. Marmion, 19 November 1942.

66. Forney Johnston to Rev. William H. Marmion, 19 November 1942. Johnston was in close touch with other leading paternalists throughout the South on the matter. See J. Melville Broughton, governor of North Carolina, to Forney Johnston, 31 December 1942, box 1, folder 13, Dixon Personal Papers.

Epilogue

1. Transcript of Richard Nixon, interview by Herbert Parmet, 16 November 1988, in possession of Dan T. Carter, quoted in Carter, *From George Wallace to Newt Gingrich: Race in the Conservative Counterrevolution, 1963–1994* (Baton Rouge: Louisiana State University Press, 1996), 27.

2. E. J. Dionne Jr., "The Shadow Class War: How 'Citizens United' Is Deforming Our Elections," *Commonweal*, 11 October 2010, http://commonwealmagazine.org/ (accessed February 2012). Coupled with this desire is a denial of the sordid yet critically important history of racism in places like Alabama. "Those who believe that Alabama experienced more racial animosity than other states," one Alabama conservative recently wrote, "are attentive students of media reports—but they ignore actual history. Chicago, Boston, and St. Louis are but a few examples of cities whose widespread and vicious racial injustice historically—and currently—exceeded any in Alabama." Comment by sanlot, 4 November 2010, on article by Thomas Spencer, "University of Alabama Plaza Dedicated to Students of George Wallace's 1963 Schoolhouse Stand," *Birmingham News*, 4 November 2010, http://www.al.com/ (accessed 7 November 2010).

3. Sean Hannity, *Let Freedom Ring: Winning the War of Liberty over Liberalism* (New York: William Morrow, 2002). Becky Perlow, "Catholic Bishops Launch Religious Liberty Campaign," CNN Blogs, http://religion.blogs.cnn.com/2012/06/25/catholic-bishops-launch-religious-liberty-campaign/ (accessed 26 July 2012).

4. Originating with GOP wunderkind Kevin P. Phillips in *The Emerging Republican*

Majority (New York: Arlington House, 1969), this analysis found itself echoed in several other best-selling political treatises of the time that forecast the demise of the Democratic Party from the left: principally Kirkpatrick Sale's *Power Shift* and Richard M. Scammon and Ben J. Wattenberg's *The Real Majority*. While still in galley form, the latter became must reading in the Nixon White House and apparently played a role in his administration's conceptualization of the "Silent Majority." First recommended to Nixon by a young speechwriter named Patrick J. Buchanan, *The Real Majority* echoed right-wing criticism of the Democratic Party but from the perspective of two Democratic journalists. They, as the party's conservative critics did, also reasoned that the Democrats had erred fatally in allowing themselves to be sucked into becoming not only the party of blacks due to its championship of civil rights but also the party of a whole host of un-American undesirables: women libbers pushing for abortion rights and the Equal Rights Amendment, homosexuals, Latino and other new and poverty-stricken immigrants, the urban poor, welfare dependents, war-protesting students in the streets, and Americans opposed to compulsory school prayer. They dubbed the subject "The Social Issue" and lamented that Democrats were on the losing end of it. See Kirkpatrick Sale, *Power Shift: The Rise of the Southern Rim and Its Challenge to the Eastern Establishment* (New York: Random House, 1975); Richard M. Scammon and Ben J. Wattenberg, *The Real Majority* (1970; New York: Primus, 1992); and Thomas Byrne Edsall and Mary D. Edsall, *Chain Reaction: The Impact of Race, Rights, and Taxes on American Politics* (1991; New York: W. W. Norton, 1992).

5. See Feldman, "Exporting 'The Southern Religion' and Shaping the Election of 2012.

6. See Feldman, *The Disfranchisement Myth*, 222n62.

7. For two very good biographies of Folsom, consult Carl Grafton and Anne Permaloff, *Big Mules and Branchheads: James E. Folsom and Political Power in Alabama* (Athens: University of Georgia Press, 1985) and George E. Sims, *The Little Man's Big Friend: James E. Folsom in Alabama Politics, 1946–1958* (Tuscaloosa: The University of Alabama Press, 1985). For more on Folsom, see also William D. Barnard, *Dixiecrats and Democrats: Alabama Politics, 1942–1950*, (Tuscaloosa: The University of Alabama Press, 1974).

8. *Birmingham News*, 12 July 1998, p. 1A.

9. *Birmingham News* and *Dothan Eagle*, 10 April 1949.

10. Alexander Heard, *A Two-Party South?* (Chapel Hill: University of North Carolina Press, 1952), 21–22.

11. Dwight David Eisenhower, Personal and confidential, to Edgar Newton Eisenhower, 8 November 1954, in *the Papers of Dwight David Eisenhower*, ed. Louis Galambos and D. van Ee, doc. 1147, http://www.eisenhowermemorial.org/presidential-papers/first-term/documents/1147.cfm (accessed 20 September 2011).

12. Lee Atwater gave a deathbed confession expressing remorse for using the race issue so blatantly to sink Dukakis's candidacy. Atwater confessed that his, GOP ad man Roger Ailes's (the later head of Fox News), and Jim Baker III's use of the Willie Horton ad was an effort to "strip the bark off the little bastard." According to Atwater, they wanted to make "Willie Horton . . . his [Dukakis's] running mate." John Brady, *Bad Boy: The Life and Politics of Lee Atwater* (Reading, MA: Addison-Wesley, 1997), 182 and 316 (Atwater quotations).

13. Transcript of Nixon interview, 27 (first quotation); Harry Dent to Richard Nixon, 13 October 1969, box 2, Harry Dent Files, Richard Nixon Presidential Materials, NA,

College Park, MD (second quotation); H. R. Haldeman Notes, 8 January 1970, box 41, H. R. Haldeman Papers, Nixon Presidential Materials, NA (third quotation). Dent, Haldeman, and other quotations in Carter, *From George Wallace to Newt Gingrich*, 28, 43, 44. For John Ehrlichman, see Dan T. Carter, "More than Race: Conservatism in the White South since V. O. Key," 6 (unpublished paper). Carter cites Ehrlichman's memoir, *Witness to Power: The Nixon Years* (New York: Simon and Schuster, 1982), 223. I am grateful to Professor Carter for making his paper available to me.

14. Phillips, *The Emerging Republican Majority*, 461–74. Phillips's quotation about the GOP not needing "Negro votes" (468), about GOP support for black voting rights (464). Phillips on his formula and Dan Carter's analysis in *From George Wallace to Newt Gingrich*, 43. George Brown Tindall dismissed Phillips's book as one of a recent spate of "wonders . . . major creations [that] have rolled off the psephological assembly lines . . . a nine-days' wonder . . . emerged from a shallow perspective . . . that perfectly illustrated the hazards of prophecy." Tindall, *Disruption of the Solid South*, 3, 5. Reg Murphy and Hal Gulliver prematurely wrote off the power of the plan in *The Southern Strategy* (New York: Charles Scribner's Sons, 1971), 269–73, and even mistakenly prophesied that "a future Southern Strategy would demand their [black voters] inclusion" (225).

15. Eminent historian Dan T. Carter is probably the leading figure in exposing the fact that race is so interwoven with ostensibly "nonracial" economic and other ideological positions in modern American politics that it serves as a subtle and powerful undercurrent for conservative ideology in the South and the non-South today. See, e.g., Carter, "Is There Still a South? And Does It Matter?" *Dissent* 53 (Summer 2007): 92–96. There is a longer version of the essay, "Is There Still a Dixie? The Southern Question and the Triumph of American Conservatism" (paper delivered at the University of Sussex, October 2006). I am grateful to Professor Carter for making a copy of this paper available to me. For a striking early combination of blending the racial, the moral, and the religious in what may be called the "New Racism," consider the comments of Alabama Dixiecrat congressman William Andrews, who said what many white southerners were thinking in reference to the 1962 *Engel v. Vitale* decision: "They put Negroes in the schools and now they've driven God out." Clive Webb, "A Continuity of Conservatism: The Limitations of Brown v. Board of Education," *Journal of Southern History* 70 (May 2004): 334.

16. Joanne Ricca, "The American Right" (paper delivered at the Annual Meeting of the United Association of College and Labor Educators, Los Angeles, California, April 2002), 11 (Dolan quotation) and 15 (Weyrich quotation); David B. Smith, "You're Talking about Them, Not Me, Right God," *Voice of Prophecy*, 27 July 2004, http://www.vop.com/ (accessed 29 July 2004) (second Dolan quotation); John Gallagher and Chris Bull, "Perfect Enemies: The Religious Right, the Gay Movement, and the Politics of the 1990s," *Washington Post*, ca. 1996 (second Dolan quotation repeated).

17. Dennis Crews, "Strange Bedfellows: Religion and Politics Are Becoming Too-Easy Partners in Today's—1984—America," *Yurica Report*, October 1984, http://www.yuricareport.com/ (accessed 14 October 2004) (Dolan quotation). One of the tragic ironies of Dolan's life and his right-wing, homophobic brand of Christianity was that he died in 1984 of AIDS as a closeted homosexual. See Smith, "You're Talking about Them."

18. Phillips, *The Emerging Republican Majority*, 462–63.

19. Harry Dent to Richard Nixon (memo), 13 October 1969, box 2, Harry Dent Files, Richard Nixon Presidential Materials, NA, in Carter, *From George Wallace to Newt Gingrich*, 28, 44. For Dent's coining and explanation of the term "compassionate con-

servatism" over two decades before it would go national, see Harry S. Dent, *The Prodigal South Returns to Power* (New York: John Wiley and Sons, 1978), 299.

20. Joe McGinnis, *The Selling of the President, 1968* (New York: Trident Press, 1969), 125.

21. Brady, *Bad Boy*, 70. On Atwater and Rove's relationship, see Robert Novak's syndicated column, *Birmingham News*, 26 December 2000, p. 15A. For Ailes's background and praise for his approach to "news," see Hannity, *Let Freedom Ring*, 258.

22. Brady, *Bad Boy*, 96, 70.

23. Ibid., 148.

24. Ibid., 70 (Atwater quoted), 147 (second quotation, Atwater), 147–48 (third quotation, Brady), and 148 (fourth quotation, Atwater). See also, e.g., pp. xvi, 153, and 158 for places to tap into voters' minds, pp. xvii and 38–39 for ties to Mary Matalin and Karl Rove, and p. 69 for affection for the Confederacy.

25. Carter, *From George Wallace to Newt Gingrich*, 118–19.

26. Greenhaw, *Elephants in the Cottonfields*, 97. For Wallace identifying himself as a Republican and his son, George Jr., serving as state treasurer in Alabama as a Republican, see *Birmingham News*, 6 November 2002, p. 1P. "Bull" Connor's nephew, James T. "Jabo" Waggoner, is a Democrat-turned-Republican state legislator who openly admits that the single most important factor in converting old southern Democrats to the modern Republican fold, at least in Alabama, has been race. Jabo Waggoner, interview by Melody P. Izard, Birmingham, AL, 14 January 2002, p. 1 (in possession of the author). Howard "Bo" Callaway, the Georgia political boss who left the Democratic Party to oversee the Republican "Southern Strategy" on the ground in the South during the Nixon years, agreed that George Wallace's ideas about race and the federal government were the same ideas that attracted southern whites to the modern GOP in droves. See Murphy and Gulliver, *The Southern Strategy*, 1.

27. Garry Wills, "Fringe Government," *New York Review of Books* 52 (October 6, 2005): 46–50. See the formal statement of Evangelicals and Catholics Together (ECT) with a list of original signatories, "Evangelicals & Catholics Together: The Christian Mission in the Third Millennium," *First Things* 43 (May 1994): 15–22. Tom Strode, "Land: Religious Right Has Won Fight with Secular Fundamentalists," *Baptist Press*, 26 January 2005 and Ralph Reed, *After the Revolution: How the Christian Coalition Is Impacting America* (Dallas: Word Publishing, 1996), 235–48. For the Orwellian use of abortion by the far right as the new civil rights, see, e.g., Greg Pierce, "Inside Politics: Civil Rights Award," *Washington Times*, 5 December 2006, http://www.washingtontimes.com/ (accessed 6 December 2006); John-Henry Westen, "Pastor Warren, Would You Permit a White Supremacist to Speak at Your Church?" *Christian Post*, 6 December 2006, http://www.christianpost.com/ (accessed 9 December 2006); Strode, "Land"; and Dimitri Cavalli, "A Liberal Mix of Religion and Politics," *Wall Street Journal*, 8 June 2007. Comments of Richard Land at the conference "Role of Religion in Public Life," James Madison Institute, Princeton University, Robert P. George, presiding, C-SPAN, 24 December 2005, http://www.c-span.org/ (accessed 25 December 2005). Ironically, Land would lose his daily radio show, sponsored by the Southern Baptist Convention (SBC), after he made racially insensitive remarks in the wake of the 2012 Trayvon Martin shooting controversy in Florida. Land is still the longtime president of the SBC's Ethics and Religious Liberty Commission. Jeremy Weber, "Richard Land Loses Radio Show over Trayvon Martin Comments," *Christianity Today*, 1 June 2012, http://blog.christianitytoday.com/ctliveblog

/archives/2012/06/richard_land_lo.html (accessed 26 July 2012). Of course, Lott's newfound and professed racial tolerance ignores a long personal history of intolerance, beginning with his apprenticeship to Mississippi Democrat (Dixiecrat) congressman William Colmer and continuing at the University of Mississippi and in the U.S. Congress. See Nicholas Lemann, "What Is the South?" *New Republic*, 29 January 2007, pp. 24–28.

28. *Engel v. Vitale*, 370 U.S. 421 (1962) dealt of course with public school prayer. *Roe v. Wade*, 410 U.S. 113 (1973). President John F. Kennedy, Executive Order 10980, 14 December 1961, established the Presidential Commission on the Status of Women. Title VII of the 1964 Civil Rights Act also addressed racial and gender discrimination in employment. Kennedy's Executive Order 10925, 6 March 1961, initiated the phrase "affirmative action" in dealing with racial discrimination matters and created the Commission on Equal Employment Opportunity.

29. Others, like conservative journalist Robert Novak, moved far to the right over time to become an apologist for more extreme views. His book, *The Agony of the GOP, 1964* (New York: Macmillan, 1965), reads almost as a primer in moderation and centrism next to his columns after 1992. The mutation of race prejudice was not complete, even in this transition viz the career of Rand acolyte Murray Rothbard, who supported Dixiecrat candidate Strom Thurmond for president in 1948. See David Leonhardt, "Free for All: A History of Libertarianism from the Austrians to Ayn Rand and Beyond," *New York Times Book Review*, 1 April 2007, p. 16. Bob Herbert, "The Howls of a Fading Species," *New York Times*, 1 June 2009 (Atwater quote).

30. On the focus-group-tested nature of the gay rights issue as a dynamite fund-raiser for the Religious Right, see conservative Andrew Sullivan's report of the Rev. Jim Wallis's discussions with Focus on the Family in "Wallis: Focus Admits Gays Not the Problem with American Families—Just a Fundraising Canard," http://www.rightwingwatch.org/, 5 June 2007 (accessed February 2012).

31. Of course George Wallace was too shrewd to be taken in by any of this. "I talked about the Supreme Court usurpation of power . . . about the big central government. Isn't that what everybody talks about now. Isn't that what Reagan got elected on? . . . Reagan got elected by one of the biggest votes . . . ever . . . by saying those very same things I said way back yonder." Jason Sokol, *There Goes My Everything: White Southerners in the Age of Civil Rights* (New York: Knopf, 2006), 252. On other occasions Wallace mused in similar language. Right-wing economics, religion, and militarism are deeply linked in fusionism or the Great Melding. Stephen Lendman argues that plain people observe Religious Right notables flaunting wealth as they identify with them and soak up a "prosperity gospel" that, they think, may make them rich, too. All the while "unrestrained free-market capitalism divinely sanctioned . . . create[s] a global marketplace of (non-Christian, non-believing) serfs . . . left to the mercy of . . . corporate predators." Thus military, economic, and religious allegiance is demanded for a neoliberal "Christian America where freedom means the freedom of the powerful to dominate the weak," as Chris Hedges writes. Lendman, "A Short History of the Christian Right." These arguments are reminiscent of liberal philosopher Isaiah Berlin's famous remark about unrestricted laissez-faire: "Freedom for wolves is death to the lambs." For a sample blogger who understands the chasm between the Religious Right and the New Testament, see Tom Degan, "Christ vs. Conservatism: A Serious Conflict," http://tomdegan.blogspot.com, 21 July 2006 (accessed 24 July 2006).

32. For an example of a young evangelical with progressive inclinations struggling to

understand how religion and libertarian economics ever became linked, see Stacia Brown, "Growing Up Evangelical: How Does Childhood Faith Influence Political Engagement?" *Sojourners*, 2 June 2005, pp. 20–25, http://www.sojo.net/ (accessed 3 June 2005).

33. David Brooks, "Dollars & Sense," *New York Times*, 26 January 2006, p. A23; Jason L. Riley, "President Bush Needs to Lead His Party on Race," *Wall Street Journal*, 16 January 2003, p. A12; Richard Benedatto, "GOP: 'We Were Wrong' to Play Racial Politics," *USA Today*, 14 July 2005, http://www.usatoday.com/ (accessed 15 July 2005) regarding RNC chair Ken Mehlman. In 2006 an Emory University study actually demonstrated a correlation between racial prejudice and Republican voter identification. See Shankar Vendatam, "Study Ties Political Leanings to Hidden Biases," *Washington Post*, 30 January 2006, p. A5. Former Christian Coalition director and Republican political strategist Ralph Reed recognized and publicly apologized for the "past complicity of the white church in the mistreatment of African-Americans and Jews . . . too large a blot on our history to deny. . . . George Wallace may have stood in the schoolhouse door, but evangelical clergy provided the framework for his actions." Of course, Reed's remarks must be tempered with the realization that he was simultaneously proposing a cross-color alliance between white and black religious conservatives that would also supersede class, a precursor to the Bush-Rove "faith-based initiative." Reed, *After the Revolution*, 236, 237 (quotations). See also Abdon W. Pallasch, "GOP Chairman: African Americans Not Given Good Reason to Vote for Party," *Chicago Sun-Times*, 20 April 2010.

34. Unfortunately there has been a recent spate of somewhat misguided scholarship that has argued against southern distinctiveness and the dominance of race in favor of allegedly "color-blind" and economic issues in the Republican partisan realignment of the South. See, in particular, Matthew D. Lassiter, *The Silent Majority: Suburban Politics in the Sunbelt South* (Princeton: Princeton University Press, 2006); Byron Shafer and Richard Johnston, *The End of Southern Exceptionalism: Class, Race and Partisan Change in the Postwar South* (Cambridge, MA: Harvard University Press, 2006); and Matthew D. Lassiter and Joseph Crespino, eds., *The Myth of Southern Exceptionalism* (New York: Oxford University Press, 2009). See my reviews of two of these works: Glenn Feldman, review of *The Myth of Southern Exceptionalism*, ed. Matthew D. Lassiter and Joseph Crespino, *Journal of Southern History* 77 (August 2011): 783–86 and Glenn Feldman, review of *The End of Southern Exceptionalism*, by Byron E. Shafer and Richard Johnston, *Journal of Southern History* 73 (August 2007): 146–48.

35. Andrew Rosenthal, "Do Most Mississippi Republicans Think Obama Is a Muslim?" *New York Times*, 13 March 2012 (quoted); Joe Garofoli, "52 Percent of Mississippi GOP Voters Think Obama Is a Muslim," *San Francisco Chronicle*, 12 March 2012; Chris Gentilviso, "Obama's Religion Still a Campaign Issue: Many Alabama, Mississippi Voters Believe President Is Muslim," *Huffington Post*, 12 March 2012. See also Beth Fouhy, "Voting in Alabama, Mississippi Could Clarify Race," Associated Press, 13 March 2012. Ultraconservative Catholic Rick Santorum, who appealed more to southern and midwestern evangelicals than Catholics, won the Republican primaries in Alabama, Mississippi, and Louisiana. See T. W. Farnum and Aaron Blake, "Santorum Wins Louisiana Primary," *Washington Post*, 24 March 2012 and Steve Weatherbe, "Why Does Santorum Appeal More to Evangelicals than Catholics?" *National Catholic Register*, 15 March 2012.

36. For the percentages in the text, see Alan Farm and Jennifer Agiesta, "Born-Again Voters Dominate Vote in AL, MS," Associated Press, 13 March 2012 (quoted). William

J. C. to Albert B., Jim W., Tom B., and the author, e-mail, 4 July 2012 (block quote), 9:50 P.M., in possession of the author.

37. Sean Wilentz, "The Worst President in U.S. History?" *Rolling Stone*, 21 April 2006; Jay Tolson, "Ten Worst Presidents: Introduction," *U.S. News & World Report*, 16 February 2007, http://www.usnews.com/ (accessed 17 February 2007); Catherine Dodge, "Bush Iraq Plan May Be Last Chance to Avoid History's 'Dustbin,'" Bloomberg News, http://www.Bloomberg.com/ (accessed 24 January 2007); "Politics," 22 January 2007; Eric Foner, "He's the Worst Ever," *Washington Post*, 3 December 2006, p. B1; Rick Shenkman, "George Bush's Misplaced Hope That Historians Will Rank Him Higher than His Contemporaries," History News Network, http://hnn.us/, 1 January 2007 (accessed 2 January 2007). For serious treatment given by the mainstream media of the absurdist charge that Obama is a socialist, see, e.g., David Crary, "Obama a Socialist? Many Scoff But Claim Persists," Associated Press, 4 June 2012. For disappointment in Obama from the Left, see Ezra Klein, "Barack Obama: Worst. Socialist. Ever," *Washington Post*, 7 May 2012, Work Blog, http://www.washingtonpost.com/blogs/ezra-klein/barack-obama-worst-socialist-ever/2012/05/07/gIQAbp9t7T_blog.html (accessed 8 May 2012); Steve Peoples, "Frustrated Liberals Want More from Obama," Associated Press, 7 June 2007; and Rex Nutting, "Obama's Four Biggest Failures," *Market Watch*, 25 June 2012, http://finance.yahoo.com/news/obama-four-biggest-failures-040048036.html (accessed 26 June 2012).

Select Bibliography of Primary Sources

Archives

Alabama Department of Archives and History (ADAH), Montgomery, Alabama

Alabama Attorney General's Office, Correspondence
Alabama Governors Papers
John H. Bankhead II Papers
John H. Bankhead II Personal Papers
William B. Bankhead Papers
William Brockman Bankhead Personal Papers
Matthew P. Blue Papers
Frank W. Boykin Papers
W. L. Bragg Papers
W. L. Bragg Speeches
Charles B. Crow Papers
Kate Cummings Diary
Curry Family Papers, Jabez L. M. Curry Papers
Dallas County Political Scrapbooks
Frank M. Dixon Papers
Frank M. Dixon Personal Papers
John Witherspoon DuBose Papers
Virginia Foster Durr Papers
James E. Folsom Papers
Ira Roe Foster Papers
Freedmen's Bureau Records
David Bibb Graves Papers
Reminiscences of Julius C. Greene
Charles Henderson Papers
Nannie Randolph Taylor Henley Papers
Hilary Abner Herbert Papers

George S. Houston Papers
Thomas E. Kilby Papers
Knights of the White Camellia Notebook
Labor Department Records (Alabama)
Robert D. Lindsay Papers
Robert McKee Papers
Benjamin Meek Miller Papers
Minutes of the Democratic State Convention
J. B. Moore Diary
Palmer Family Papers
Lewis E. Parsons Papers
Robert M. Patton Papers
Edmund Winston Pettus Papers
James A. Simpson Papers
William H. Smith Papers
Chauncey Sparks Papers
Chauncey Sparks Personal Papers
State Democratic Executive Committee Records (SDEC)
Oliver Day Street Papers
Wager Swayne Papers
Oscar W. Underwood Papers
Unprocessed Manuscripts Collection

Alabama Pamphlets Collection

Address of John A. Minnis
Constitution and Ritual of the Knights of the White Camellia
First Semi-Annual Report on Schools and Finances of Freedmen
Freedmen's Bureau Documents
Help Dixie's Cause! by Horace C. Wilkinson
Revised and Amended Precept of the Ku Klux Klan
Southern Relief Association of New York City Documents
States' Rights Information and Speakers Handbook

Alabama State Council of Defense Records, Program Administrative Files

*American Missionary Association Archives (AMA),
Fisk University, Nashville, Tennessee*

Miscellaneous correspondence

Auburn University Archives (AU), Auburn, Alabama

Ward Sykes Allen Papers
George William Andrews Collection
Charles E. Dobbins Papers
Charles G. Dobbins Papers

Hardy T. Frye Oral History Collection
Reminiscences of Julius C. Greene
Papers of the National Association for the Advancement of Colored People (NAACP)

Birmingham Public Library Archives (BPLA), Birmingham, Alabama

Alabama Coal Operators' Association/Alabama Mining Institute Records
Theophilus Eugene "Bull" Connor Papers
Cooper Green Mayoral Papers
KKK Scrapbooks
Henry Key Milner Scrapbooks
Philip H. Taft Research Notes

Blount County Historical Society (BCHS), Oneonta, Alabama

Ku Klux Klan materials

Boone Aiken Collection (BA), Auburn, Alabama

Declaration in KKK-Prattville File

Catholic University of America (CUA), Department of Archives and Manuscripts, Washington, D.C.

Philip Murray Papers

Center for Labor Education and Research Archives (CLEAR), School of Business, University of Alabama at Birmingham, Birmingham, Alabama

Oral History and Interviews Collection

Columbia University (CU), New York

Oral History Office

Duke University, Trinity College (DUKE), William R. Perkins Library, Durham, NC

James Locke Boardman Papers
Reminiscences of Sanders Dent
William R. Erwin Jr. Personal Files
Hugh Gladney Grant Papers
Trinity College Historical Society Papers
William Worth Belknap Papers

Duke University Department of Special Collections (DUKE-2), Durham, NC

Lucy Randolph Mason Papers

Franklin Delano Roosevelt Presidential Library (FDR), Hyde Park, New York

Lorena Hickok Papers
Eleanor Roosevelt Papers
Franklin Delano Roosevelt Papers

416 / Select Bibliography

Greene County Historical Society (GCHS), Eutaw, Alabama

Cemetery Markers
Miscellaneous clippings

Harry S. Truman Presidential Library (HST), Independence, Missouri

Papers of J. Howard McGrath
Papers of Philleo Nash
Papers of Harry S. Truman

Herbert Hoover Presidential Library (HHPL), Iowa City, Iowa

George A. Akerson Papers
Republican National Committee Papers
Lewis L. Strauss Papers

Historic Mobile Preservation Society (HMPS), Mobile, Alabama

Miscellaneous news clippings

Huntingdon College Archives and Special Collections (HUN), Montgomery, Alabama

Rev. Arad S. Lakin File

Library of Congress (LC), Washington, D.C.

Address of John A. Minnis
American Memory Project
Papers of the National Association for the Advancement of Colored People (NAACP)

Linn-Henley Research Center for Southern History (LH), Birmingham Public Library, Birmingham, Alabama

Thanksgiving Proclamation by the Governor of Alabama (Emmet O'Neal, 1912)

Louisiana State University Archives (LSU), T. Harry Williams Center for Oral History, Baton Rouge, Louisiana

Oral History Collection

Memphis Public Library Archives (MPL), Memphis, Tennessee

Kenneth D. McKellar Papers

Microforms and Documents Department (MADD), Ralph B. Draughon Library, Auburn University, Auburn, Alabama

La Follette Committee Hearings
Papers of the NAACP

Mississippi Department of Archives and History (MDAH), Jackson, Mississippi

James L. Alcorn and Family Collection

Missouri Historical Society (MHS), St. Louis, Missouri
Luther Ely Smith Family Papers

Mobile Municipal Archives (MMA), Mobile, Alabama
Miscellaneous newspaper clippings

Mobile Public Library Archives (MPLA), Mobile, Alabama
Folder: "KKK thru 1979"

Mudd Manuscript Library (PU), Princeton University, Princeton, New Jersey
American Civil Liberties Union (ACLU) Records

Museum of the City of Mobile (MCM), Mobile, Alabama
Ku Klux Klan folder; Rec.# 5714-4

National Archives (NA), Washington, D.C.
Records of the Assistant Commissioner for the State of Alabama, Bureau of Refugees, Freedmen, and Abandoned Lands, 1865–1870. Also cited as the Freedmen's Bureau Records

National Archives, Southeast Region (NASR), East Point, Georgia
Ku Klux Klan cases under the Enforcement Acts
Statement of Dr. B. F. Ashe, regional director of the War Manpower Commission

New York Public Library (NYPL), Special Collections, New York
Walter L. Fleming Collection

Samford University, Department of Special Collections (SU), Harwell Goodwin Davis Library, Homewood, Alabama
J. Thomas Heflin Scrapbooks
J. F. Hines Papers
Horace C. Wilkinson Papers

Southern Historical Collection (SHC), Louis Round Wilson Library, University of North Carolina at Chapel Hill
M. L. Patterson Papers
Southern Oral History Collection

Special Collections, Morris Library (SIU), Southern Illinois University at Carbondale, Carbondale, Illinois
Collection No. VFM-174 and VFM-175

Tuskegee University Archives (TU), Tuskegee, Alabama
Tuskegee Institute news clipping files: Anti-Negro Groups, Civil Rights File, KKK File, Lynching File

Tutwiler Collection of Southern History (TCSH), Birmingham Public Library, Birmingham, Alabama

Alabama Personalities File
News clippings files: Political Parties, Republican, Birmingham and Jefferson County
Notable Dixiecrat Personalities File

University of Alabama at Birmingham Archives (UAB), Birmingham, Alabama

Dean, School of Medicine, Papers
Luther Leonidas Hill Papers

University of Florida Archives (FLA), Samuel Proctor Oral History Program, Gainesville, Florida

Oral History Collection

University of South Alabama Archives (USA), Mobile, Alabama

John LeFlore Papers

University of West Alabama (UWA) (formerly Livingston University), Julia Tutwiler Library, Livingston, Alabama

Alabama Collection

W. Stanley Hoole Special Collections Library (UA), University of Alabama, Tuscaloosa, Alabama

Archives of American Minority Cultures Collection "Working Lives Series"
Col. Harry Mell Ayers Papers
Goodloe Family Papers
James L. Hare Papers
Roland M. Harper Papers
J. Lister Hill Papers
Samuel F. Hobbs Papers
Robert Jemison Jr. Papers
John Will Johnson Collection
Cabot Lull Collection
John J. Sparkman Papers
Henry B. Steagall Congressional Papers
Oliver Day Street Papers

Newspapers

Alabama Baptist, 1944
Alabama Beacon, 1868
Alabama Christian Advocate, 1928
(AL) CIO News Digest, 1942, 1943

Select Bibliography / 419

Alabama Daily State Journal, 1874
Alabama Sun, 1944
Alabama Temperance Association Bulletin, 1945
Alexander City Outlook
Andalusia Star, 1944
Anniston Star, 1942–44
Arkansas Gazette, 1948
Asheville (NC) Citizen, 1944
(Athens) Alabama Courier, 1944
Athens Weekly Post, 1868
Atlanta Constitution, 1914, 1946
Atlanta Daily World, 1946
(Atlanta Imperial) Knighthawk, 1924
Autauga Citizen, 1866, 1867
Baldwin Times, 1942, 1944
Baltimore Afro-American, 1943
Baltimore Manufacturers Record, 1914–23
Baton Rouge State-Times, 1944
Birmingham Afro-American, 1944
Birmingham Age-Herald, 1901, 1908, 1928–44
(Birmingham) Alabama Herald, 1935
Birmingham Alabamian, 1902
Birmingham Iron-Age, 1874
Birmingham Labor Advocate, 1908
Birmingham News, 1908, 1919, 1928–44, 1998, 2002
Birmingham Post, 1934, 1944
(Birmingham) Southern Worker, 1930
Birmingham Weekly, 2002
Birmingham Weekly Review, 1943, 1944
Birmingham World, 1942
Bladen Springs Herald, 1872
Boston Traveler, 1943
Brewton Standard, 1942
(Butler) Choctaw Herald, 1868, 1874
(Carrollton) West Alabamian, 1870, 1872
Centreville Press, 1944
Charleston News-Courier, 1944
Chattanooga News, 1944
Chicago Daily News, 1937
Chicago Defender, 1943
(Claiborne) Monroe Journal, 1867
Clanton Union Banner, 1944
Clarke County Democrat, 1868, 1874
Colbert County Reporter, 1944

Columbia (SC) Lighthouse and Informer, 1944
Columbus (GA) Recorder, 1944
Covington News, 1944
Cullman Democrat, 1942
Daily Oklahoman, 1944
Daily Selma Times, 1874
Dallas Morning News, 1944
(Dallas) Southern Weekly, 1944
Decatur Daily, 1938, 1942–44
DeKalb Times, 1944
(Demopolis) Southern Republican, 1869, 1870
Dothan Eagle, 1928, 1941–44
East Alabama Monitor, 1869
Ensley Industrial Press, 1944
Enterprise Chronicle, 1944
(Eufaula) Bluff City Times, 1869, 1872
Eufaula News, 1874
Eufaula Times, 1874
Eufaula Tri-Weekly Times, 1874
Eutaw Whig and Observer, 1874
Florence Journal, 1868
(Florence) Lauderdale Times, 1871, 1872
Florence Times-Journal, 1874
Fort Myers (FL) News-Press, 1943
Gadsden Times, 1942–48
Gadsden Tribune, 1942
(Greensboro) Alabama Beacon, 1867, 1870, 1874
Greensboro Southern Watchman, 1943–44
Greenville Advocate, 1868, 1874
(Grove Hill) Clarke County Democrat, 1874
Hale County News, 1944
Hale County Reporter, 1944
Henry County Register, 1870
Houston (TX) Informer, 1944
Houston (TX) Post, 1919
Huntsville Times, 1938, 2000
Huntsville Weekly Democrat, 1875
Jacksonville News, 1943
Jacksonville Republican, 1870, 1874
Jasper Union News, 1936
(Jefferson County) Southern Argus, 1874
Kansas City Plain Dealer, 1944
Kansas City Star, 1944

Knoxville (TN) Sentinel, 1914
LaFayette Sun, 1944
Lee County Bulletin, 1944
Livingston Journal, 1868
Los Angeles Tribune, 1944
Louisville (KY) Courier-Journal, 1942
Marengo News-Journal, 1874
Memphis Commercial Appeal, 1942
Memphis World, 1944
Mobile Daily Register, 1870
Mobile Daily Tribune, 1871
Mobile Labor Journal, 1943
Mobile Nationalist, 1869
Mobile Post, 1942
Mobile Press, 1943
Mobile Press-Register, 1942–44
Mobile Register, 1874, 1919, 1944, 2000
Mobile Republican, 1870, 1872
Monroeville Journal, 1870
Montgomery Advertiser, 1865–1910, 1911–15, 1919, 1921–44
(Montgomery) Alabama Journal, 1943–44
(Montgomery) Alabama State Journal, 1869, 1874
(Montgomery) Daily State Sentinel, 1868
Montgomery Evening Journal, 1912
Montgomery Examiner, 1944
Montgomery Journal, 1938
Montgomery Mail, 1870
Moulton Advertiser, 1868, 1874
(Moulton) The Union, 1867
(Nashville) Southern Conference for Human Welfare Bulletin, 1942
New Orleans Times-Picayune, 1944
New York Daily Worker, 1944
New York Herald-Tribune, 1944
(New York) People's Voice, 1944
New York Times, 1927, 1928, 1936
Norfolk (VA) Journal and Guide, 1944
(Notasulga) Universalist Herald, 1869
Opelika Times, 1874
(Opelika) Union Republican, 1869
Opelika Weekly Era and Whig, 1871
Opelika Weekly Locomotive, 1871
Opp Weekly Journal, 1942
Orlando Morning Sentinel, 1943

Pell City News, 1942
(Perry County) Marion Commonwealth, 1871, 1874
Philadelphia Inquirer, 1942
Pittsburgh Courier, 1943–44
Pittsburgh Lead, 1915
(Prattville) Autauga Citizen, 1874
Raleigh (NC) News and Observer, 1934, 1938
Richmond Times-Dispatch, 1944
Roanoke Leader, 1944
Rochester (NY) Union, 1874
Savannah Morning News, 1944
(Selma) Daily Messenger, 1868
Selma Echo, 1874
Selma Journal, 1907
(Selma) Southern Argus, 1869, 1874, 1875
Selma Times-Journal, 1938, 1941–44
Shelby County Democrat, 1944
Shelby County Guide, 1868
Shelby Guide, 1874
Southern Patriot, 1944
Sumter County Journal, 1942
Sylacauga Advance, 1944
Sylacauga News, 1944
(Talladega) Alabama Reporter, 1870
Talladega Daily Home, 1943–44
(Talladega) Democratic Watchtower, 1867
(Talladega) Our Mountain Home, 1874
Talladega Sun, 1869
Tallassee Tribune, 1943
Troy Messenger, 1870, 1874
(Troy) The Southern Advertiser, 1867
Tuscaloosa Independent Monitor, 1867, 1868
Tuscaloosa News, 1938, 1939, 1943–1944
Tuscaloosa Times, 1874
(Tuscumbia) North Alabamian and Times, 1872
Tuskaloosa Blade, 1872, 1874
Tuskegee News, 1866
(Tuskegee) Pulling Together, 1943
UMW Journal, 1908
Union Springs Herald, 1874
Union Springs Times, 1867
Washington Herald, 1944
Washington Post, 2000

Weekly Huntsville Advocate, 1870
Wesleyan Christian Advocate, 1944
(Wetumpka) Elmore Standard, 1867

Oral Histories and Interviews

Alexander, Leon. Interviews by Peggy Hamrick, 8 and 17 July 1984, Birmingham, Alabama. Archives of American Minority Cultures Collection, box 3008, "Working Lives Series," UA.

Armstrong, James. Interview by Cliff Kuhn, 16 July 1984, Birmingham, Alabama. Archives of American Minority Cultures Collection, "Working Lives Series," UA.

Baggett, James L. Interview by the author. 1 December 2003, Birmingham, Alabama. In possession of the author.

Beech, Gould. Interview by John Egerton, 9 August 1990, Magnolia Springs. Alabama Southern Oral History Project, SHC.

Carter, Betty. Interview by John Egerton, 6 September 1990, Greenville, Mississippi. Southern Oral History Project, SHC.

Davis, Harwell G. Interview by Arthur L. Walker, March 1974, Birmingham, Alabama. SU.

Durr, Virginia. Interview, Oral History Project, CU.

———. Interview by John Egerton, 6 February 1991. Southern Oral History Project, SHC.

Givhan, Robert Marcus. Interview by Melody Izard, 16 November 2007, Birmingham, Alabama. CLEAR.

Gomillion, Charles B. Interview by Hardy T. Frye. Interview #19, Hardy T. Frye Oral History Collection, AU.

McCorvey, Gessner T. Interview, 3 February 1948. Box 84, folder 13, SDEC Records, ADAH.

McGill, Eula Mae. Interview by the author, 12 March 1997, Birmingham, Alabama. CLEAR.

Rich, E. B., and Howard Strevel. Interview by Edwin L. Brown, Glenn Cole, and Ralph A. Johnson, Birmingham, Alabama, 9 June 1988. CLEAR.

Shores, Arthur D. Interview by Hardy T. Frye. Interview #44, Hardy T. Frye Oral History Collection, AU.

Sparks, Chauncey. Interview, 8 November 1946. Box SG 12521, folder 31, Sparks Papers, ADAH.

Taylor, Herman A. Interview by Terrence J. Weatherspoon, 8 October 1999, Birmingham, Alabama. In possession of the author.

Thompson, Perry. Interview by Hardy T. Frye. Interview #48, Hardy T. Frye Oral History Collection, AU.

Trammell, Asa. Interview by Edwin L. Brown, Glenn Cole, and Ralph A. Johnson, 23 June 1988, Birmingham, Alabama. CLEAR.

Weber, Palmer. Interview, Oral History Office, CU.

Weeks, Barney. Interview by Robert J. Norrell, 21 February 1989. Copy in CLEAR.
———. Interview by Edwin L. Brown, I. N., and Ralph A. Johnson, n.d., Birmingham, Alabama. Copy in CLEAR.
Williams, Aubrey W. Interview by Julian Pleasants, 11 September 1997, #4700: 0899, T. Harry Williams Center for Oral History, LSU and FLA.

Government Documents and Official Reports

Acts of Alabama, 1919.
Alabama Official and Statistical Register, 1947. Montgomery: Walker Printing Company, 1947.
Alabama Official and Statistical Register, 1951. Alexander City, AL: Outlook Publishing, 1951.
(Alabama) *State Senate Committee Report,* 14 December 1868. Reprinted in the *Moulton Advertiser,* 15 January 1869.
Birmingham, Alabama, *Criminal Code,* Section 4092.
Bragg, Dr. Shirley. "Report to the Governor, Alabama." January 1907. In Clarissa Olds Keeler, "The Crime of Crimes, or The Convict System Unmasked." Pamphlet in *From Slavery to Freedom: The African-American Pamphlet Collection, 1824–1909.* American Memory project, Library of Congress, Washington, DC, http://memory.loc.gov/ (accessed 5 January 2012).
Congressional Record and *Congressional Record Appendix.*
Executive Order 9346, 8 Fed. Reg. 7183 (1943).
Galambos, Louis, and D. van Ee. *The Papers of Dwight David Eisenhower.* Baltimore: Johns Hopkins University Press, 1996.
Minutes of the State Democratic Executive Committee (Alabama).
Official Proceedings of the Constitutional Convention of the State of Alabama, May 21st, 1901 to Sept. 3, 1901. Wetumpka, AL: Wetumpka Printing, 1940.
People for the American Way (PFAW) and the National Association for the Advancement of Colored People (NAACP). "The Long Shadow of Jim Crow: Voter Suppression in America, 2004." http://www.pfaw.org/ (accessed February 2012).
Proceedings of the Democratic State Convention (Alabama).
Report of the Assistant Commissioner of Alabama. Records of the Assistant Commissioner for the State of Alabama, Bureau of Refugees, Freedmen, and Abandoned Lands, 1865–1870.
United States Congress, *Affairs in Alabama.* H. Rept. 262, 43rd Cong., 2nd Sess., 1875.
———. *Civil Rights in Alabama.* Ex. Doc. 46, 43rd Cong., 2nd Sess., 1874.
———. *Hearings on H. Res. 102 Before the House Special Committee to Investigate Executive Agencies,* 78th Cong., 1st and 2nd Sess., pt. 2.
———. Joint Select Committee on the Condition of Affairs in the Late Insurrec-

tionary States. *Report of the Joint Select Committee to Inquire in to the Condition of Affairs in the Late Insurrectionary States So Far As Regards the Execution of the Laws, And Safety of the Lives and Property of the Citizens of the United States and Testimony Taken: Alabama, Volume III (or Volumes 8, 9, and 10).* 42nd Cong., 2nd Sess. Washington, DC: GPO, 1872.

———. *United States Troops in Alabama.* H. Ex. Doc. 110, 43rd Cong., 2nd sess., 1875.

United States. House of Representatives. 81st Cong., Committee of the Judiciary, Subcommittee No. 3, *Beatings and Cross-Burnings in Alabama Towns,* Investigation, 1949.

———. *Proceedings in the Ku Klux Trials at Columbia, S.C. in the United States Circuit Court, November Term, 1871.* New York: Negro Universities Press, 1969.

———. *Report on the Condition of the South by Carl Schurz, 1865.* 39th Cong., 1st Sess. New York: Arno Press, 1969.

———. *Report of the Joint Committee on Reconstruction at the 1st Session, 39th Congress.* Westport, CT: Negro Universities Press, 1969.

United States Senate. Committee on Education and Labor, 75th Cong., 2d sess. *Violation of Free Speech and Rights of Labor, Hearings Before Subcommittee.*

Court Cases and Legal Documents

George C. Adcock, E. Z. Yeager, and Gus Gulas v. Robert B. Albritton, et al., U.S. Supreme Court, October Term, 1948. Box SG 10034, folder: President Truman, Labor Department Records, State of Alabama, ADAH.

Andrews v. Alabama, 1 Div. 363 (Alabama Court of Appeals, Baldwin Circuit, June 1, 1920), ADAH.

Brown v. Board of Education, Board of Regents Topeka, Kansas, 347 U.S. 483 (1954).

Chambers v. Florida, 309 U.S. 227 (1940).

City of Birmingham v. Monk, 185 F.2d 859 (1950) and 341 U.S. 940 (1950).

Civil Rights Cases, 109 U.S. 3 (1883).

Davis v. Schell, 81 F. Supp. 872 (1949).

Durden v. Alabama, 4 Div. 761 (Alabama Court of Appeals, Geneva Circuit, 1922), ADAH.

Ex Parte Durden, 208 Ala. 697 (1922).

"Foukal Murder Case" and "Foukal Lynching Case: Bay Minette." Folder 469, box 1919–20, Alabama Attorney General's Office, correspondence, 1919–20, ADAH.

Horace C. Wilkinson v. Mobile Labor Journal, et al., 13 July 1948, Mobile County Circuit Court, transcript, box 2, folder 4, Dixon Personal Papers, ADAH.

Lancaster v. Alabama, 6 Div. 490 (Alabama Court of Appeals, Marion Circuit, 1925), ADAH.

Lancaster v. Alabama, 214 Ala. 2 (1925).

Lancaster v. Alabama, 214 Ala. 76 (1925).
Morgan v. Virginia, 328 U.S. 373 (1946).
Panama Refining Company v. Ryan, 293 U.S. 388 (1935).
Plessy v. Ferguson, 163 U.S. 537 (1896).
Ray v. Blair, 257 Ala. 151 (1952), 343 U.S. 154, 214, 901, 911 (1952), and 353 U.S. 231 (1952).
Red Lion Broadcasting v. FCC, 395 U.S. 367 (1969).
Report of the Cases Argued and Determined in the Supreme Court of Alabama During the October Term, 1920–1921. Lawrence H. Lee, Reporter of Decisions. St. Paul: West Publishing Company, 1921, 1925.
Robert Lancaster v. The State of Alabama, Cause: 5277, Alabama Court of Appeals 1925, 6 Div. 490, Official Court Transcript, ADAH.
Schechter v. U.S., 295 U.S. 495 (1935).
Smith v. Allwright, 321 U.S. 649 (1944).
Smith v. Texas, 311 U.S. 128 (1940).
Steele v. Louisville and Nashville Railroad, 245 Ala. 113 (1944), 323 U.S. 192 (1944), and 65 S.Ct. 226 (1944).
Thornhill v. Alabama, 310 U.S. 88 (1940).
U.S. v. Allen Alexander and Charles Smith, 6 April 1874, Case #127 A, B, NASR.
U.S. v. Butler, 297 U.S. 1 (1936).
U.S. v. California, 332 U.S. 19 (1947).
U.S. v. Elisha Eustis, John J. Jolly, and Edwin Reese, 26 April 1871, Case #75 A, B, C (NASR).
U.S. v. Frank Jackson, 15 January 1874, Case #157, NASR.
U.S. v. John Perkins, 20 April 1871, Case #78, NASR.
U.S. v. John Pettygrew, Hugh L. White, and William Harper, 6 January 1871, Case # 79 A, B, C, NASR.
Whitehead v. Alabama, 206 Ala. 290 (1921).
Wilkinson v. Ray, 258 Ala. 715 (1952).
Youngstown Sheet & Tube Company v. Sawyer, 343 U.S. 579 (1952).

Memoirs, Autobiographies, and Published Collections of Documents and Documentary Histories, Documentary Films

Dobbins, Charles G. "Alabama Governors and Editors, 1930–1955: A Memoir." *Alabama Review* 29 (April 1976): 135–54.
Drury, Allen. *A Senate Journal*. New York: McGraw-Hill, 1963.
Griffith, Lucille. *Alabama: A Documentary History to 1900*. Tuscaloosa: The University of Alabama Press, 1987.
Hoole, William Stanley, ed. *Reconstruction in West Alabama: The Memoirs of John L. Hunnicut*. Tuscaloosa: Confederate Publishing, 1959.
Mays, Benjamin E. *Born to Rebel: An Autobiography by Benjamin E. Mays*. New York: Charles Scribner's Sons, 1971.

Osofsky, Gilbert, *The Burden of Race: A Documentary History of Negro-White Relations in America*. New York: Harper and Row, 1967.

Painter, Nell Irvin. *The Narrative of Hosea Hudson: His Life and Times as a Negro Communist in the South*. Cambridge, MA: Harvard University Press, 1979.

Salmond, John A., ed. "Aubrey Williams Remembers: A Note on Franklin D. Roosevelt's Attitude toward Negro Rights." *Alabama Review* 25 (January 1972): 62–77.

Shut Up & Sing. Cabin Creek Films. 2006. Directed by Barbara Kopple and Cecilia Peck.

Struggles in Steel. Braddock Films, 1996. Directed by Tony Buba and Ray Henderson.

Sullivan, Patricia, ed. *Freedom Writer: Virginia Foster Durr, Letters from the Civil Rights Years*. New York: Routledge, 2003.

"White House Aide Clark M. Clifford Advises President Harry S Truman, 1947." Memorandum reprinted in Robert D. Griffith, ed., Major Problems in American History since 1945: Documents and Essays. Lexington: D. C. Heath and Company, 1992, pp. 147–52.

Index

Abernethy, Thomas, 181, 228–29; and Chauncey Sparks, 221; Dixiecrats, 182, 229; GOP, 182, 229; GOP campaign for governor, 299. *See also* Baughn, Hubert; Cobbs, Hamner; Dixiecrats; Field, Ed; Hall, Horace; Republicanism; Shelton, Barrett; Shelton, Bruce
accommodationism, 222. *See also* Washington, Booker T.
Adamson, Reese, 260, 385n32
affirmative action, 307; phrase initiated, 409n28. *See also* reverse discrimination
African Methodist Episcopal (AME), 224
Agrarians. *See* Nashville Agrarians; Vanderbilt University
Agricultural Adjustment Act (AAA), 89, 110, 119
agriculture. *See* Bankhead, John H., II; farmers; National Farmers Union; Populist Party; *Southern Farmer*; Tennessee Valley Authority
Ailes, Roger, 300, 304; creation of Fox News, 406n12; Willie Horton ad, 406n12. *See also* Southern Strategy
aliens. *See* foreigners; xenophobia
Alabama Constitution of 1901: 48–55, 209; malformed tax structure, 137. *See also* anti-democratic tendencies; disfranchisement; poll tax; voter suppression
Alabama Fuel and Iron Company. *See* DeBardeleben, Charles
Alabama Magazine, 119–20, 140, 186, 201–2, 211, 249; claims to want to be liberal, 363n59. *See also* Baughn, Hubert A.
Alabama Power Company, 92, 126, 263–64. *See also* Martin, Thomas W.
Alabama State Democratic Executive Committee (SDEC), 70, 121, 192, 256, 366n88 . *See also* 1928 bolt; Dixiecrats; Heflin, J. Thomas; Heflox ticket; Locke, Hugh; McCorvey, Gessner T.
Alabama Supreme Court, 322n43, 328n30. *See also* Moore, Roy
alcohol: as issue in 1928 bolt, 68–69, 75–76, 84. *See also* Baptists; Catholics; Gwaltney, L. L.; immigrants; Jones, Bob, Sr.; Methodists; Shuler, Rev. Robert; Tammany Hall; Women's Christian Temperance Union
Alexander, D., 266, 271–73
Alexander, Will W., 108, 158
Alger, Horatio, bootstrap theory, 33
Almon, "Thug," 275–76
Alsop, Stewart, 166, 355n54, 400n2; on Alabama as a liberal oasis, 166

Altman, John A., 101–2, 294. *See also* Folsom, James E.
American Civil Liberties Union (ACLU), 252
American Federation of Labor (AFL), 95, 101–2, 165, 353n40, 379n32; racial exclusion of versus CIO, 95, 197–99, 209, 379n32, 386n44
Americanism, xiii, xix, 2, 64, 70, 77, 101, 111, 112, 131, 144, 149, 258, 294; 100 percent Americanism, 85, 190. *See also* Ku Klux Klan
Ames, Jesse Daniel, 108, 155–56
Amnesty Act, 14–15
Anniston: race relations in, 402n31, 404n54
anti-democratic tendencies, 65, 70, 236, 289, 295, 391n80; in Calvinism, 328n33; of economic fundamentalists, 328n33; as part of the second Great Melding, xiv, xv, 35, 65, 86, 235–36, 295, 307–8; Progressivism in Alabama, 42, 51, 55, 64, 65; recent examples of, 35. *See also* Calvinism; economic fundamentalism; Great Melding (Second)
anti-intellectualism, 112, 231. *See also* republicanism; southern distinctiveness; voter suppression; Wallace, George C.
anti-Semitism, 129, 234–40. *See also* Jews
Arkansas, 69, 108, 139, 299, 348n9, 384n26; Brooks Hays, 139; desegregation of Central High School in Little Rock, 299; Joseph T. Robinson, 69, 108, 348n9; poll tax in, 382n2. *See also* Hays, Brooks; McClellan, John L.; Robinson, Joseph T., Sheffield, J. C.; Woodward, C. Vann
Armbrester, Margaret E., 355n54
Asheville. *See* South Carolina
Associated Industries of Alabama (AIA), 172, 188
Atlanta. *See* Georgia
Atlanta Constitution. *See* Grady, Henry W.; McGill, Ralph
Atwater, Lee, 300, 301, 304–5, 307; deathbed confession about Willie Horton ad, 309, 406n12; tutelage of protégés, 305, 408n21, 408n24. *See also* Bush, George H. W.; Dent, Harry; S. Dukakis, Michael; Eskew, Tucker; Horton, Willie; Matalin, Mary; Rove, Karl; Southern Strategy; Thurmond, J. Strom
Austrian School, xvii, 37–38, 235, 295, 328n33. *See also* economic fundamentalism
Ayers, Harry Mell, 182–83, 212, 221, 243, 279; against repeal of poll tax, 212; considered as liberal, 402n34; criticized by Horace Hall, 375n49; FEPC, 376n4; KKK, 376n58; praise for 1901 Alabama Constitution, 402n34; praise for Redeemers, 402n34

Bachmann, Michelle, xiii, 86
Badger, Anthony J., 347n4, 355n53, 358n92
Bailey, Hugh C., 335n15
Bailey, Josiah, 107, 108, 125, 136, 215, 384n26
Baker, James "Jim" III, 406n12
Baltimore. *See* Maryland
Baltimore Manufacturers Record. *See* Edmonds, Richard
Bankhead, John H., Sr., 72. *See also* Bankhead Family; Bankhead, John H., II; Bankhead, William B.; Owen, Marie Bankhead
Bankhead, John H., II, 61, 106, 139, 151, 193, 231, 232, 348n9, 366n84; desegregation of military, 176, 226, 282; lynching, 109; SCHW, 146; sees segregation as best for all, 227, 394n9; and Wallace Malone, 176. *See also* Bankhead Family; Bankhead, John H., Sr.; Bankhead, William B.; Owen, Marie Bankhead
Bankhead, William B., 106, 136, 151, 348n9, 355n57, 366n84. *See also* Bankhead Family; Bankhead, John H., Sr.; Bankhead, John H., II; Owen, Marie Bankhead
Bankhead Family, convict-lease and

Index / 431

dynasty estimated by C. Vann Woodward, 327n24. *See also* Bankhead Family; Bankhead, John H., Sr.; Bankhead, William B.; Owen, Marie Bankhead
Baptists, xiv, 11, 33, 71, 73, 75, 107, 191, 238, 261, 264, 346n56, 372n30; black, 228, 386n44, 389n63; liberal, 404n54; Southern Baptist Convention, 408n27. *See also* Barton, Rev. A. J.; Bell, Rev. Charles K.; Falwell, Jerry; Gingrich, Newt; Gwaltney, L. L.; Norris, J. Frank; Wilkinson, Horace C.
Barkley, Alben W., 348n9
Barnard, William D.: on Alabama as liberal, 165–66; on Bibb Graves's liberalism, 370n8; on North Alabama v. South Alabama, 370n7. *See also* North Alabama v. South Alabama dichotomy
Barr, John U., 172, 294. *See also* business; Dixiecrats
Bartley, Numan V., pocket-book ethics, 198
Barton, Rev. A. J., 71
Barton, David: distortions about civil rights and political parties, 328n33; praise for slavery, 328n33. *See also* Christian Reconstruction; Dominionism; religious fundamentalism; Religious Right
Bass, J. G., 131
Baughn, Hubert, 92, 94, 100, 120, 130, 228, 232, 256, 291; central importance of race, 377n12, 395n14; civil service, 349n14; desegregation of military, 210; Dixiecrats, 184; federal government, 352n35; friend to blacks, 250, 274, 401n15; goodwill toward blacks, 277; GOP, 150; Joseph Gelders flogging, 354n50; labor, 352n35; SCHW, 140; veneration of business, 390n77. *See also* Abernethy, Thomas; *Alabama Magazine*; Cobbs, Hamner; Dixiecrats; Field, Ed; Hall, Horace; Republicanism; Shelton, Barrett; Shelton, Bruce; business, veneration of
Beddow, Noel R., 107, 254, 350n21

Beech, Gould, 93, 112, 121, 123, 176, 274, 355nn54–55, 355n59, 364n65
Beecher, John 187
Bell, Rev. Charles K., Jr., 404n54
Berlin, Isaiah, 409n31
best sorts. *See* economics; labor; masses; race
best whites. *See* economics; labor; masses; race
Bethune, Mary McLeod, 89, 139
Big Mules. *See* Black Belt, alliance with Big Mules
Bilbo, Theodore, 83, 108, 113, 156–57, 158, 205, 207, 211, 249, 270, 291, 294, 346n53, 376n57; as New Dealer, 156–57, 158, 355n53; as true believer, 400n3
Billings, Dwight, 325n6
Birmingham, founding of, 25–26
Birmingham News and *Birmingham Age-Herald*: as allegedly pro-union, 400n65; on blacks as happy with segregation, 390n71
birth control, xv, 237
Black, Hugo, 42, 65, 72, 78, 93, 119, 121, 139, 146, 341n70, 349n15, 355nn54–55; labor, 65, 109, 349n15, 358n99, 372n22; New Deal, 93, 119, 348n9; KKK, 65, 121, 341n70, 345n37, 355n54; opposes federal anti-lynching bill, 109, 364n68; SCHW, 139; Supreme Court, 146, 355n55. *See also* Graves, Bibb; Roosevelt, Franklin D.
Black Belt, 7, 12, 15–18, 92, 142, 151–52, 157, 161, 188, 240; alliance with Big Mules, 48, 50–51, 77, 94, 347n1; anxiety about World War I in, 61; blacks "in their place," 275, 324n53; communism and the Thirties, 104, 107, 131, 162, 353n44; disfranchisement, 147; SCU in, 104; Dixiecrats, 296; Frank Dixon, 173, 178; KKK, 120–21, 130; 1928 bolt, 77–80; North Alabama versus South Alabama dichotomy, 6, 50–51, 165–66, 178, 370n7, 389n68; poll tax, 210–11; suppression of class consciousness,

117; voter fraud in, 48–49, 53, 55–56, 83, 346n54; voter registration, 147, 365n74. *See also* North Alabama v. South Alabama dichotomy
"blackification" (of bad behavior), 157
Blacks. *See* lynching; race; voter suppression
Blair, Algernon, 106
Blanchard, William, 129–30, 359n11
Blease, Cole, 82, 108, 249, 270, 376n57
Bob Jones University, 346n56
Boles, John B., 328n31
Bolt of 1928, 67–86. *See also* Heflin, J. Thomas; Ku Klux Klan; Locke, Hugh; Smith, Al; Street, Oliver Day; Wilkinson, Horace C.
Boswell, E. C. "Bud," 151, 152, 173–74
Boswell Amendment, referred to, 151
Bourbons. *See* Black Belt; Great Melding (First); Neo-Kluxism; New South movement; Reconstruction; Reconstruction Syndrome; Redemption
Boykin, Frank W., 176, 226, 230, 263
Bradford, M. E., xv, 308; anti-democratic beliefs of, 328n33; defense of slavery and, 328n33; ties to George Wallace, 328n33; ties to Ronald Reagan, 328n33
Bragg, Dr. Shirley, 337n40
Bragg, W. L., 15, 16, 323n49
Brando, Marlon, 44
Brandon, William, 80
Brock, I. L., 50
Brooks, David, 308–9
Brown v. Board of Education, 160, 190, 302, 402n23
Buchanan, Pat, 301, 405n4
Buckley, William F., 313n2. *See also* fusionism
Bulger, Thomas L., 56
Bunche, Ralph J., 164, 215–16, 350n19, 370n4, 393n1; on the South becoming liberal, 164
bureaucracy, 123, 128, 133, 173, 180–81, 187–88, 202, 225, 241, 282, 355n55, 370n6; Hegel on mistaking government as something alien, 375n51. *See also* New Deal
Burr, Borden, 121, 173; as a foe of labor, 352n29, 372n30
Bush, George H. W., 235, 300, 301, 304, 305
Bush, George W., xiv, 86, 235, 300, 301, 308, 309, 310, 391n80, 410n33
business: dividing labor on race, 241; purity of motives, 352n30; suspicion of "bigness" switched to federal government, xvii; veneration of, xix, 19, 23–26, 233–34, 326n10, 390n77; white supremacy of, 117, 120–22, 174–75, 187, 262. *See also* economic fundamentalism; economics; fascism, quasi-fascism; Hall, Horace; masses, divided on race; New South movement; social stratification; status quo society
business progressivism, 59. *See also* Tindall, George Brown
Byrd, Harry Flood, 125, 150, 172, 212, 294
Byrnes, James F. "Jimmy," 108–9, 294, 348n9; Dixiecrats, 109; GOP, 109; as a New Dealer, 108–9

Caldwell, Elman, 377n17
Calhoun, John C., 24, 116
California, 301
Callaway, Howard "Bo," on race and the GOP in the South, 408n26
Calvinism, xiv–xv, xvii, 21, 33–34, 38, 65, 67, 71, 132, 155, 156, 237, 261, 295; alcohol, 75; anti-democratic tendencies of, 328n33; extreme forms of, xv, 328n33; pro-business tilt of, 6; pro-slavery beliefs, 328n33; versus Catholicism, 75. *See also* Christian Reconstruction; Dominionism; Great Melding (Second); Puritans; religion; religious fundamentalism; Religious Right; Rushdoony, Rousas John
Carlton, David L., 325n6
Carmichael, A. A., 82, 294
Carmichael, O. C., 404n59

Index / 433

carpetbaggers, 40, 59, 80, 82, 161, 186, 206, 230, 242, 252, 256–57, 286, 288, 315n7, 320n35; labor, 148; Eleanor Roosevelt, 154; during Reconstruction, 3, 4, 6, 8, 13, 20. *See also* federal government; neo-carpetbaggers; neo-scalawags; outside agitators; Reconstruction; Reconstruction Syndrome; scalawags
Carr, Robert H., 150
Carter, Betty, 264, 400n3
Carter, Dan T., 204, 302, 406n13, 407n15. *See also* Gingrich, Newt; Southern Strategy; Wallace, George C.
Carter, Hodding, 247, 248, 264
Cash, W. J., 112, 324n55
Catholics, 6, 34, 59, 61, 100, 115; anti-Catholicism, 68–79, 84–85, 88, 130, 346n56; liberal, 261; modern, 294; 1928 bolt, 68–79, 84–85, 88, 130, 346n56; religious liberty campaign and bishops, 294; Religious Right, 303, 307, 328n33, 408n27, 410n35; versus Calvinism, 75. *See also* Dolan, Terry; Evangelicals & Catholics Together; Falwell, Jerry; George, Robert P.; Gingrich, Newt; Neuhaus, Richard John; Santorum, Rick; Street, Oliver Day; Weigel, George; Weyrich, Paul
Chapel, David L., 328n31
Chapel Hill. *See* North Carolina
Chappell, James A., 174, 176, 221, 248, 400n65; softness of liberalism of, 403n37
character clause. *See* anti-democratic tendencies; disfranchisement; voter suppression
Charleston. *See* South Carolina
Charlotte Observer. See Tompkins, Daniel Augustus
Charlton, Louise, 139, 142, 363n54, 364n65
Chicago School, 37–38, 235, 328n33. *See also* economic fundamentalism
Chilton, David, 326n13
Chotteau, Gerard, 12

Christian Americans, 118, 121, 129
Christian Reconstruction, xiv–xv, 6–7, 328n33. *See also* Calvinism; Dominionism; Rushdoony, Rousas John
civil rights. *See* federal government, retreat on civil rights; race; southern liberalism (softness of)
Civil War, 1; as not over, 203, 245–46; devastation of, 2–3, 22; enduring significance of, 8, 246. *See also* "our way of life"; Reconstruction; Reconstruction Syndrome; sovereignty of the South
Clanton, James H., 9–10, 319n28
class. *See* economic fundamentalism; economics; labor; masses, divided by race; middle class, blacks; race; race and class
class consciousness, 27. *See also* economic fundamentalism; economics; labor; masses, divided by race; politics of emotion; New Racism; race; race and class
class warfare, 153, 310
Clay, Henry, 24
Clayton, Bruce, 334n14
Clements, Marc Ray "Foots," 166
Clinton, Bill, 306
Cobb, James, C., 325n6
Cobbs, Hamner, 161, 173, 188, 208, 228–29, 249, 274, 391n90; close to Chauncey Sparks, 223, 387n46; desegregation as the ruin of civilization, 219; friend to blacks, 274, 277; goodwill toward blacks, 277; GOP, 182, 377n11; southern history, 206; newspaper as regional representative, 393n102, 394n11, 401n14; upset with Chauncey Sparks, 223. *See also* Abernethy, Thomas; Baughn, Hubert; Dixiecrats; Field, Ed; Hall, Horace; Republicanism; Shelton, Barrett; Shelton, Bruce
coded speech, 250–51, 295, 302, 303, 307. *See also* Nixon, Richard; Southern Strategy

Cole, Robert Rast, 172
Colmer, William, 408n27. *See also* Dixiecrats; Lott, Trent
"color-blind" issues, 234, 302–3, 410n34. *See also* sophistry of modern conservatism; southern distinctiveness; Suburban School
Comer, B. B., 42, 58, 65, convict-lease, 338n43
Comer, Donald, 105, 168; considered a liberal, 105; Dixiecrats, 106, 173, 262, 291, 294; participated in New Deal, 106. *See also* Republicanism
Commission on Interracial Cooperation, 108, 158
communism, 91, 104, 258, 331n39, 353n34; during Great Depression, 102–5; repression of, 101–5; rural, 104; SCHW, 139–40; as term for anything disliked, 247, 258. *See also* Connor, Theophilus Eugene "Bull"; Dos Passos, John; Downs Sedition Ordinance; Gelders, Joseph; Hall, Rob; Hudson, Hosea; Share Croppers Union; Simmons, Col. Roscoe
compassionate conservatism, 303, 407n19. *See also* Dent, Harry S.; Bush, George W.
Confederacy. *See* Civil War; neo-Confederate; Reconstruction Syndrome
conformity, 183, 250. *See also* Cultural IQ; culture; "our way of life"; patriotism
Congress of Industrial Organizations (CIO), 94–98, 114–15, 138–40, 182, 185, 191, 216, 218, 229–30, 350n21, 353n40, 378n18; CIO-PAC, 164–65; as communist and un-Christian, 154; as foreign and racially threatening, 100–2, 182, 241, 254, 350n18, 352n35, 379n32, 397n33; gap with local rank and file on race, 196–99; patriotism and suspect and wartime strikes of, 200–202, 397n33; rare labor dissatisfaction with, 379n32. *See also* Hillman, Sidney; labor; Lewis, John L.

Connally, Tom, 108, 125, 211
Connor, Theophilus Eugene "Bull," 66, 228, 291, 294; civil service, 94; Dixiecrats, 193; and Jim Simpson, 94, 349n14; letter to FDR, 192–93; pupil of Horace Wilkinson, 94; race and the GOP, 408n26; race-baited by Horace Wilkinson, 94; SCHW, 139, 142, 149, 156; U.S. Steel, 349n14; warnings of, 192–93, 226, 388n58. *See also* Simpson, James A.; Waggoner, James. T. "Jabo"; Wilkinson, Horace C.
conservatism, 202; extremism of modern, 121, 286; lust to revoke the New Deal, 292; reality and, 286; religion, 308, 399n59. *See also*: conformity; cultural conservatism; Cultural IQ; culture; extremism; Great Melding (First); Great Melding (Second); New Racism; politics of emotion; sophistry of modern conservatism; status quo society
conservative progressivism, 65
constitutionalism, xiii, xix, 100, 101, 112, 117, 126, 130, 131, 134, 136, 153, 210, 211, 230, 288, 294, 299, 381n47; Constitutional Democrats, 118; Constitutional Education League, 352n35, 358n95; Ron Paul and Social Security and Medicare as unconstitutional, 314n5; taxes, 245
continuity, xi; discontinuity, 44, 325n6; in Progressivism, 339n58. *See also* cultural conservatism; culture; Cultural IQ
contraception. *See* birth control
convict-lease system, 27–31, 56–57, 337n40; profits of, 338n41. *See also* Bankhead Family
Couch, W. T., 138, 281, 291, 364n65
craft unionism. *See* American Federation of Labor (AFL)
creative destruction, 390n78; Werner Sombart, 390n78
Crespino, Joseph, 410n34
crime. *See* "blackification" (of bad behavior); law and order; race, black or provocative bad behavior; rape

crop-lien system, 23
Crow, Charles B., 204. *See also* Owen, Marie Bankhead
cultural conservatism, xvi, 67, 128, 287, 289–90, 296; discussed, xvii, 178–83, 244–46. *See also* Calvinism; Nashville Agrarians; Social Darwinism
Cultural IQ, 111–12; discussed, 140, 178–80
culture, 110–20, 124–49, 238, 368n108; and Christianity, 127–28; cultural colonialism, 246; cultural continuity, 244–45, 246, 251–55; importance of, 161, 162, 178–83, 203, 206. *See also* conformity; Cultural IQ; "our way of life"; southern distinctiveness; sovereignty of the South
Cunningham, Russell S., 337n40
Curry, J. L. M., 324n55

Dabney, Robert L., 328n33
Dabney, Virginius, 139, 280, 356n64
Dalrymple, Dolly, 58
Dalrymple, William, 96
Daniel, Franz, 101
Daniel, R. T., 372n30
Daniels, Frank, 158, 159,
Daniels, Jonathan, 158, 280
Davis, Jefferson, 128, 206
DeBardeleben, Charles, 97, 106, 119–20, 211, 372n30; Dixiecrats, 199–20; GOP, 119–20, 365n81; New Deal, 150, 152; practices at Alabama Fuel and Iron Company, 351n25, 358n99, 365n81; Wendell Wilkie campaign, 150. *See also* Dixiecrats; Republicanism
DeBardeleben, Henry F., 97, 106, 211, 352n29; and Frank Dixon, 184. *See also* Fies, Milton H.
DeBardeleben, Henry Fairchild, 36
DeBardeleben, Prince, 372n30
DeBardeleben Coal and Coke, 211
Democratic and Conservative Party, xvi, 10–11, 14–15, 49, 69, 80, 256, 296, 315n7
Democratic Party: death of, 124; essential World War II role, 392n99; as party of the North, 229–30, 243–44; as party of undesirables, 295. *See also* Democratic and Conservative Party; Dixiecrats; New Deal; Kennedy, John; race; Reconstruction; Reconstruction Syndrome; Redemption; Republicanism; Roosevelt, Franklin D.; southern liberalism (softness of); Truman, Harry S.
Denniston, George H., 151
Denson, W. H., 48–50, 336n25
Dent, Harry S., 301, 303, 304, 305; coins term compassionate conservatism, 303, 407n19. *See also* Atwater, Lee; Nixon, Richard; Phillips, Kevin P.; Southern Strategy; Thurmond, Strom
Dewey, Thomas E., 149
Dies, Martin, Jr., 146, 230, 274, 364n67, 401n13. *See also* Starnes, Joseph
Dirksen, Everitt, 300
disfranchisement, 21, 30, 34, 38–41, 209; all-white or direct primary, 51; education, 53–55; 1901 Alabama Constitution, 48–55; poll tax, 208–14, 279; women's suffrage, 51–53. *See also* antidemocratic tendencies; Soldier Vote Bill; voter suppression
distinctiveness. *See* southern distinctiveness
Dixiecrats, xi–xii, xvi, 170, 172, 228, 239, 296, 352n35, 407n15; connection to modern Republican Party, 42, 80, 82, 106, 109, 120, 121, 133–34, 148, 152, 173, 175, 182, 206, 229, 235–36, 237, 242, 243, 260, 262, 281, 290, 293–94, 298–99, 300, 306, 344n31, 371n46, 377n11, 384n25, 408n27, 409n29; dream of national appeal, 293–94, 299; as perfect expression of the Great Melding, 191, 298, 308; pivotal Dothan dinner, 298–99; revolt as not a failure, 297–98; second revolt prevented, xiv, 66; states' rights philosophy, 277. *See also* Abernethy, Thomas; Baughn, Hubert; Cobbs, Hamner; Connor, Theophilus Eugene "Bull"; DeBardeleben, Charles; Dixon,

Frank M.; Field, Ed; Graves, John Temple, II; Hall, Grover C., Jr.; Hall, Horace; Malone, Wallace, Sr.; McCorvey, Gessner T.; Perez, Leander; Republicanism; Samford, Frank P.; states' rights; States' Rights Party; Thurmond, Strom; Wilkinson, Horace C.

Dixon, Frank M., 255, 261, 286, 291, 294–95, 361n32, 375n48, 376n4, 392n96; black allies, 386n44; Bourbons, 191–93, 214–15, 404n59; and Chauncey Sparks, 220–23; criticized, 374n43; defiance of FEPC, 170–85, 188, 217–21, 372n30; Dixiecrats, 152, 163, 170, 193; goodwill toward blacks, 274, 277; Grover Hall Jr.'s criticism misinterpreted by scholars, 182, 219–20, 231–32, 249–50, 270, 274–75, 376n57, 394n7; labor, 191, 197, 201–2, 214, 278, 348n12, 378n18; labor support, 214; lynching, 109; masculine politics, 214; Neo-Kluxism, 190–91, 372n30; during 1930s, 92–93, 286; 1928 bolt, 80; opposition to KKK, 80, 121, 190, 191; opposition to Soldier Vote Bill and, 209–12; poll tax, 209–12; as regional champion, 233, 244–45, 249–51, 254, 390n76; sees himself as friend to blacks, 401n15; sophistry of modern conservatism, 134–35. *See also* Dixiecrats; Dixon, Rev. Thomas W.; McCorvey, Gessner; Sparks, Chauncey; Wallace, George C.; Wilkinson, Horace C.

Dixon, Rev. Thomas W., 118, 191, 358n93; GOP, 191. *See also* Dixon, Frank M.; Ku Klux Klan

Dobbins, Charlie, 105, 111, 248, 357n75; considered as liberal, 166; considers Chauncey Sparks as liberal, 166, 248; liberal except on race, 266–67

Dobbins, Charles G., 111

Dobbs, Malcolm and Pauline, 365n74

Dobson, James, 86, 307, 308

Dolan, Terry, 303, 407n17

Dombrowski, James, 365n74; on the South as liberal, 164–65

Dominionism, xiv–xv, 86, 328n33; pro-slavery stance of, 328n33. *See also* Barton, David; Calvinism; Christian Reconstruction; Rushdoony, Rousas John

Dos Passos, John, 169, 258, 371n20

Double V Campaign, 203

Douglas, William O., 355n57, 366n84

Dowd, Mollie, 92, 139

Downs, William O., 106, 274; claims to be liberal, 105; protégé of Horace Wilkinson, 103; sees himself as friend to blacks, 274; sedition ordinance and, 103, 354n47

Downs Sedition Ordinance, 103, 354n47

Drennen, Don, 173, 210, 383n9

Drew, Daniel, 21, 33; Drew Theological Seminary, 33

Dukakis, Michael, 300, 406n12

Dunning School, 9, 84, 192

Dunning, William Archibald. *See* Dunning School; Reconstruction

Durr, Clifford, 93, 114, 123, 139, 140, 147, 156, 164, 355n55, 400n1; on the South becoming liberal, 164

Durr, Virginia, 65, 93, 114, 123, 139, 140, 144, 147, 156, 175, 209, 275, 341n70, 355n55, 368n109, 400n1

Dyer, L. C., 59–60, 62

Dyer Federal Anti-Lynching Bill, 59–60, 62

East Alabama v. West Alabama (observation), 370n7; mentioned, 17, 72, 191. *See also* North Alabama v. South Alabama dichotomy

Eastland, James O., 291, 384n26, 400n3

economic conservatism, xiii, xiv, 126, 174, 184, 188, 190–91, 202, 210, 218, 251, 255, 266, 278, 307, 400n3

economic fundamentalism, xiv, 33–34, 86, 185, 235, 295; anti-democratic tenets of, 328n33. *See also* Austrian School; Chicago School; creative destruction; economic conservatism; Friedman, Milton; Great Melding (First); Great Melding (Second);

Hayek, F. A.; libertarianism; Mises, Ludwig von; Rand, Ayn; trickle-down economics
economics: "better sorts," 216–17; class and race, 152, 233; class consciousness, 152, 233; "Report on Economic Conditions in the South," 136–37. *See also* business; economic fundamentalism; labor; New Deal; race and class (connected)
economic sophism, 37
Edgerton, John, 172
Edmonds, Henry M., 356n67
Edmonds, Richard, 23
education, 53–55. *See also* liberalism; public schools; race; taxes
Egerton, John, on Alabama as liberal, 166, 355n54
Ehrlichman, John D., 301
Eisenhower, Dwight D., 299–300; moderation of, 303–4
Eisenhower, Edgar, letter from Dwight Eisenhower, 299–300
Eisenhower, Milton, accused of being a communist with Dwight Eisenhower, 299
Ellender, Allen J., 130
Elliott, Carl, 166
Ellis, Handy: claims to be a liberal, 105; as a supporter of New Deal, 105. *See also* Dixiecrats
emotion, 167, 201, 204–5, 209, 302–3, 304–6, 308, 309, 342n3; in 1928 bolt, 70; of rural voters, 70. *See also* New Racism; politics of emotion
employment discrimination. *See* Fair Employment Practices Committee; Kennedy, John; War Manpower Board
Enforcement Acts. *See* Ku Klux Klan Acts
Engel v. Vitale, 307, 407n15, 409n28
Episcopalians, 75
Eskew, Tucker, 305
establishment violence, 63, 64, 341n65
Etheridge, Mark, 139, 187–88, 250, 282, 402n33
Evangelicals and Catholics Together (ECT), 408n27

Evans, Hiram, 70, 100, 129. *See also* Ku Klux Klan
exceptionalism. *See* southern distinctiveness
extremism, xiv, xv, xviii, xix, 42, 222, 236, 393n1; economic, 37–38, 65, 127, 153, 101, 295, 307–8, 328n33; Eisenhower on, 300; Goldwater on, 300; Kevin Phillips repelled by, 301; KKK as logical extreme of southern Progressivism, 41, 64; in opposition to New Deal, 122, 125, 129–31, 133, 135–36, 185, 233–34; morphed into mainstream conservatism, 121–22, 133, 309, 409n29; of modern GOP, xv, 86, 122, 233–34, 292–93, 295–96, 300–301, 309, 314n5, 409n29; in Progressivism in Alabama, 48; racial liberalism considered as, 141, 183, 280–81, 286, 375n48; southern roots of, xv, 309; in ultra-Calvinism, xiv–xv, 6–7, 295, 307–8, 328n33. *See also* economic fundamentalism; Great Melding (Second); Neo-Kluxism; New Racism; religious fundamentalism; Religious Right; Southern Religion; status quo society; Tea Party

Fair Deal, xvii
Fair Employment Practices Committee (FEPC), 170–85, 186–87, 194, 202, 211–12, 214, 217, 224, 265, 279, 282, 291, 297, 376n4, 380n35, 403n37; Ed Field's moderation, 394n8; Milton Webster, 374n46; FDR's second, 377n10; Frank Dixon's defiance of FEPC, 170–85, 188, 217–21, 372n30; as Reconstruction-like, 180. *See also* Dixon, Frank; Randolph, A. Philip; Roosevelt, Franklin D.
Fair Labor Standards Act (FLSA), 110–11, 372n22. *See also* Black, Hugo
Falwell, Jerry, xiv, 86, 294, 300, 307; Liberty University, 294
Farr, Reuben, 197
Farm Bureau, 137
Farmer, Hallie, 155

farmers, 3, 22, 46, 49, 65, 88, 90, 103–4, 119, 125, 137, 157, 163, 167–70, 222, 236, 258, 297, 300, 317n18, 362n39, 365n74; Andrew Mellon on, 237, 326n13; Bankhead-Jones Farm Act, 106; emotionalism and politics, 70; mechanization of farmland, 170; North Alabama, 372n23; poverty of, 103–4; SCU, 104. *See also* Bankhead, John H., II; National Farmers Union; Populist Party; *Southern Farmer*; Tennessee Valley Authority

fascism, 132, 177, 201, 257, 258; quasi-fascism, 236, 248, 294. *See also* Hitler, Adolf; Ku Klux Klan

Faulkner, William, 40

Federal Bureau of Investigation (FBI), 157–58

federal government: aid and monies from, xv, 20, 36, 59, 90–93, 105–7, 125, 142–43, 148–49, 165–67, 169, 230–31, 253, 266–67, 314n5, 324n56, 335n22, 345n48; conflated with the North, 276–77, 352n35; economic and labor regulations, 61, 95, 100, 137, 171–75, 178–79, 182–83, 185, 188, 191, 198, 201, 214, 217–18, 241, 245, 257, 261–62, 285–86, 307, 348n10, 351n25, 375n48; fear of and hostility to, xiii–xv, xviii, 2, 19–20, 40, 53, 64, 65, 68, 81, 85, 86, 110, 117, 120–22, 135, 148–49, 163, 167, 181, 189, 192–96, 202, 205, 207, 225, 226, 231, 235, 242, 249–57, 282, 294–99, 324n56, 328n33, 392n96, 398n46, 402n31; as a foreign entity, 20, 180, 203, 375n51; and George Wallace, 408n26; laws against lynching, 57–62, 107–9, 130, 134–35, 141–42, 145–46, 156, 259, 289; New Deal, 116–17, 125, 354n47, 372n22; poll tax, 211–13; prosecution of the KKK, 14; memory of Reconstruction and, 79–82, 125, 180–81, 242, 252, 256, 288, 293, 370n8; patronage of, 143, 163; during Reconstruction, 7–8, 11, 13–16, 19–20, 22, 324n56; retreat on civil rights, 17, 38, 221, 332n45; suspicion of "bigness" switched from business to, xvii; women's suffrage and, 51; voting laws, 295, 302, 332n43. *See also* economic fundamentalism; Great Melding (First); New Deal; Reconstruction; Reconstruction Syndrome; southern liberalism (softness of)

Field, Ed, 178, 181, 182, 242, 249, 374n44, 386n44; considered himself as moderate, 250, 27; Dixiecrats, 242; FEPC, 394n8, 394n11; GOP, 242. *See also* Abernethy, Thomas; Baughn, Hubert; Dixiecrats; Field, Ed; Hall, Horace; Republicanism; Shelton, Barrett; Shelton, Bruce

Field, Marshall, 274. *See also* Beech, Gould; Williams, Aubrey

Fies, Milton H., participated in the New Deal, 106, 372n30. *See also* DeBardeleben, Charles; DeBardeleben, Henry F.

Fisk, Jim, 33

Fleming, Walter, 9

Florida, 28, 83, 128, 129–30, 137, 138, 139, 155, 159, 164, 179, 209, 281, 297, 355n53, 368n110, 400n6; castration of Joseph Shoemaker, 128–29; Coral Ridge Ministries, 328n33; Florida Panhandle, 169; Jacksonville, 168; lynching of Claude Neal, 107–8; Miami, 129–30, 168, 359n111; Miami Republican National Convention, xvi, 129–30, 300; Panama City, 168; Tampa, 168; Trayvon Martin shooting, 408n27; Truth in Action Ministries, 328n33. *See also* Blanchard, William; Grant, George (pastor); Kennedy, Stetson; Pepper, Claude; Smith, Lillian

Florida White Front, 129–30

Flynt, Wayne, 48, 70, 337n40, 340n60, 356n60; on Alabama as liberal, 163–64, 166, 355n54, 370n1; on Aubrey Williams's liberalism, 401n12; on Bibb

Graves and labor, 348n11; Charlie Dobbins as liberal, 166; Chauncey Sparks as liberal, 166; flowering of liberalism, 166, 355n54; on liberalism in southern religion, 328n31; on North Alabama v. South Alabama, 163; on racism of plain whites, 335n15, 336n25; on southern Progressivism, 333n1, 335n15; race and liberalism, 371n16. *See also* Hall, Grover C., Jr.; North Alabama v. South Alabama dichotomy

folk theology, 85–86, 112–13, 160, 238–39, 261–64. *See also* gap between leadership and rank-and-file; religion

Folsom, James E., 214–15, 297; racial liberalism as an exception, 297, 355n59

"for blacks only." *See* Progressivism

foreigners, 2, 222; alcohol, 68, 71; blacks as, 244; labor unions, 63, 100–101; in social hierarchy, 31, 234, 247. *See also* outside agitators; xenophobia

Foreman, Clark, 137; on the South as liberal, 164–65

Forney, John H., 9–10, 319n28

Forrest, Nathan Bedford, 11, 82, 128, 319n28

"for whites only," thesis applied to southern Progressivism, 46–47, 63, 334n14. *See also* Link, Arthur S.; Woodward, C. Vann

Franklin, John Hope, 44, 333n5

freedmen. *See* race

Freedmen's Bureau, 3–4, 7, 20

freedom, xiv, xix, 2, 114, 148, 161, 188, 211, 235, 237, 294, 328n33, 409n31; for blacks, 215, 376n2; religious liberty campaign and bishops, 294; of speech, 100. *See also* economic fundamentalism; Reconstruction

Freeman, Douglas Southall, 125

Friedman, Milton, xv, 307; anti-democratic beliefs of, 328n33

friends of the Negro. *See* race, friends of the Negro

frontier mentality, 188–89

Fuller, Helen S., 139; on Alabama as liberal, 166

furnish system, 23

fusionism, xiii, 307, 409n31; southern roots of, xv, 313n2. *See also* Great Melding (First)

Galliard, S. Palmer, 211, 262

gangster rap (hip-hop culture), 215–16

gap between leadership and rank-and-file: in labor, 85–86, 96, 112–13, 160, 196–98, 202, 241; in religion, 85–86, 112–13, 160, 261–64. *See also* southern liberalism

Gary, Elbert H., 35

Gaston, Paul M., 32

gay rights, 35, 303, 308, 328n33, 396n29, 405n4, 407n17, 409n30; death penalty for homosexuality, 328n33

Gelders, Joseph, 104–5, 138–40, 156, 352n29, 354n50

gender, xvii, xix, 2, 41, 98, 101, 113, 121, 140, 154, 159, 171, 178, 194, 202, 213, 263, 267, 279, 284; connected to race, economics, and religion; 247; Eleanor Roosevelt, 155–56; interracial sex, 258–59; laws against discrimination, 307, 409n28; Neo-Kluxism, 85. *See also* Ames, Jesse Daniel; Farmer, Hallie; sex; Tutwiler, Julia

George, Robert P., 307, 408n27

George, Walter, 125, 138

Georgia, 23, 28, 91, 125, 137, 138, 139, 159, 239, 264, 271, 280, 305–6, 319n28, 378n19, 396n20, 408n26; Atlanta, 23, 25, 26, 38, 62, 70, 280, 377n10, 399n59; Atlanta race riot, 38, 399n59; Dixiecrats, 297; folk theology and racism in, 369n114; Goldwater, 300–301; labor, 101; Macon anti-New Deal meeting, 117–19, 129, 157; mountain Republicanism in northwest, 332n47; poll tax in, 382n2; Steve Nance, 101; voter suppression, 213. *See also* Callaway, Howard "Bo"; George, Walter; Gingrich, Newt; Gordon, John Brown; Grady, Henry W.; Macon anti-New Deal Meeting; Mays, Benjamin E.; Neal, Benjamin F.; Russell, Richard; Talmadge, Gene; Tilly, Dorothy; Wynne, Lewis R.

gerrymandering: See anti-democratic tendencies; disfranchisement; voter suppression

GI Bill, 169–70

Gingrich, Newt, 300, 305–6,

Glass, Carter, 108, 125, 136, 215, 384n26

Going, Allen Johnston, 338n41

Goldwater, Barry, 292, 298, 300, 301, 308

Gomillion, Charles, 213, 365n74

goodwill (on the part of whites). See race, goodwill on the part of whites

Goodwyn, Tyler, 80

Gordon, John Brown, 319n28

Gore, Thomas P., 125

Gospel of Wealth, 32

Gould, Jay, 33, 35

Grady, Henry W., 23

Graham, Frank Porter, 138, 404n59

grandfather clause. See anti-democratic tendencies; disfranchisement; voter suppression

Grant, George (congressman), 176, 210, 232, 400n65

Grant, George (pastor): Coral Ridge Ministries, 328n33; Truth-in-Action Ministries, 328n33

Grant, Ulysses S., 33

Graves, Bibb, 65, 72, 78, 106, 109, 165, 167, 193, 214–15, 354n47, 354n51; defiance of capital, 348n11; Joseph Gelders flogging, 104–5; KKK, 121, 166, 341n70, 345n37, 370n8; labor, 348n11, 351n26; New Deal, 92–94, 97–98, 348n11, 349n14, 351n26, 352n30, 354n21; other forms of vigilantism, 354n51, 370n8; SCHW, 139, 143, 145–47, 364n65; Scottsboro Boys, 103. See also Black, Hugo; Dowd, Mollie; Gelders, Joseph; Roosevelt, Franklin D.; Wilkinson, Horace C.

Graves, John Temple, II, 105, 232, 255, 279, 281–84, 355n54, 355n58; claims to be a liberal, 105, 403n40; considered a racial liberal, 403n40; desegregation of the military, 232; Dixiecrats, 106, 260, 281; on Eleanor Roosevelt, 162; FEPC, 376n4; goodwill, 404n52; labor, 99–100, 352n32; rules of southern society, 403n43, 404n51; SCHW, 146–47; softness of liberalism, 138, 232, 255, 279–84, 291–92; Soldier Vote Bill, 210, 283; talking out of both sides of mouth, 281–84, 404n50. See also Dixon, Frank; Sparks, Chauncey

Great Depression: devastation of, 90–91. See also Jews; New Deal; outside agitators; race; Roosevelt, Franklin D.

Great Melding (First), xii–xv, xvii, xix, 65–66, 86, 87, 116–17, 120, 123–24, 235–36, 266–67, 278, 293–94, 307, 308, 328n33; the Dixiecrat movement, 191, 298, 308; examples of, 118, 150, 217, 218, 245, 262; the FEPC, 170–73, 194; mentioned, 122, 128, 184, 188, 190, 193, 199–200, 202, 204, 210, 211, 234, 279, 283, 286, 299, 400n3, 409n31. See also economic fundamentalism; federal government; race

Great Melding (Second), xii–xv, xvii, xix, 34–35, 65, 86, 235–36, 293–94, 295, 307–8, 328n33, 409n31. See also anti-democratic tendencies; economic fundamentalism; religious fundamentalism

Green, Cooper, 121, 146, 364n65

Greenbackers, xiii, xv, 27, 95

Greenhaw, Wayne, 358n90

Greer, Charles H., 41

guns, 48–49, 104, 162, 283, 396n29; gun lobby, 311

Gwaltney, L. L.: considered liberal, 78; editor of the *Alabama Baptist*, 78

Hackney, Sheldon, 336n25, 338n43

Haggard, "Pastor Ted," 307, 308

Haldeman, H. R., 301
Hale, A. B., "stand up for Alabama" (slogan), 178
Hall, Fitzgerald, 285–88, 404n59; and Frank Dixon, 286; friend of the Negro, 285–88
Hall, Grover C., Sr., 74, 105, 106, 109–10, 211, 242, 248; considered liberal, 393n1; considers himself liberal, 105, 143; favors poll tax, 211; lynching, 109; participation in New Deal, 106; SCHW, 142–43;. *See also* Johnston, Forney; Gelders, Joseph; Ku Klux Klan; Scottsboro Boys
Hall, Grover C., Jr., 231, 291; criticism of Frank Dixon misinterpreted by scholars, 182, 219–20, 231–32, 249–50, 270, 274–75, 376n57, 394n7; criticized by Horace Hall, 182, 375n49; frustrated by emotion, 394n7; goodwill towards blacks rests on white supremacy, 401n20; race, 395n14; on white supremacy as compatible with Christianity, 401n16. *See also* Dixiecrats; Dixon, Frank; Hall, Horace; Republicanism
Hall, Horace, 173, 179, 182, 186, 188; criticized Grover Hall Jr., 182, 375n49; Dixiecrats, 173, 242; GOP, 242, 377n11; labor, 202, 242; ties between Christianity and business, 263; violence as justified, 242. *See also* Abernethy, Thomas; Baughn, Hubert; Dixiecrats; Field, Ed; Hall, Horace; Republicanism; Shelton, Barrett; Shelton, Bruce; Sparks, Chauncey
Hall, Jacquelyn Dowd, 356n64, 367n96
Hall, Rob, 139
Hampton, Wade, 138, 319n28
Hannah, Walter J., "Crack," 352n29
Hannity, Sean, 294
Hanson, Victor, 71, 81–82, 85, 224, 230–32, 248, 250, 264, 265, 347n57, 349n14, 375n49, 376n4, 389n69, 394n5, 400n65
Harding College, 294
Hardisty, Jean, 313n2. *See also* fusionism

Hare, James, 92
Harper, Roland M., 173, 245–46
Harris, David Alan, 338n43
Harrison, Pat, 348n9
Harvey, Paul, 3238n31, 369n113
Hawley, Ellis W., 339n58
Hayek, F. A., xv, 307, 331n7; antidemocratic beliefs of, 328n33
Hays, Brooks, 139
health. *See* public health
Hedges, Chris, 409n31
Heflin, J. Thomas, 222, 342n10, 398n46; anti-Catholicism of, 68, 70–74, 76–80; disfranchisement, 49; Heflox ticket and KKK, 402n34; hostility toward federal government, 398n46; KKK, 65, 402n34; lynching, 57; 1928 bolt, 68, 70–74, 76–80, 83; smell of blacks, 398n46;. *See also* Bankhead, John, II; Locke, Hugh; Wilkinson, Horace C.
Heflox ticket, 1930 senatorial election, 402n34. *See also* Heflin, J. Thomas; Ku Klux Klan; Locke, Hugh; Wilkinson, Horace C.
Hegel, Georg, 37; on mistaking government for something alien, 375n51
Henderson, Bruce, 372n30
Herbert, Hillary Abner, 15
Hickock, Lorena, 87
hierarchy. *See* Social Darwinism; social stratification; Sparks, Chauncey, rules and order in southern society; status quo society
Hill, Herbert, 350n21
Hill, Lister, 139, 155; economic liberalism of, 92, 138, 153, 166, 348n9, 383n9; feeds the monster of white supremacy, 232; race and, 106, 232; against repeal of poll tax, 212; against Soldier Vote Bill, 210; SCHW, 146; softness of his liberalism, xvi, 42, 66, 146, 147, 166–67, 247, 294, 296, 383n9; and Victor Hanson, 231. *See also* monster of white supremacy; New Deal; southern liberalism (softness of); Sparkman, John
Hill, Samuel S., Jr., 328n31

Hillman, Sidney, 164
hill country, 6, 9, 11–16, 26, 49–56, 66, 130–32, 138, 143–44, 151, 175–78, 181, 185, 207, 210, 223–24, 226–29, 259, 262, 264–65, 270, 275, 296, 389n68; anti-labor activities in, 98–100. See also North Alabama v. South Alabama dichotomy
Hillman, Sidney, 164
Hispanics, 405n4
historical and social scientific inquiry, nature of, 42–46
Hitler, Adolf, 158, 203, 223, 229, 254, 256, 271, 387n56; anti-labor forces compared to, 97–98, 364n65; Chauncey Sparks' actions compared to, 218; FDR compared to, 131; Frank Dixon compared to, 176–77; labor compared to, 132, 202, 262; liberals compared to, 144; racial liberals compared to, 175–76; references to Third Reich, 44, 177, 186
Hobbs, Samuel, 176
home rule, xiii, 17, 18, 65, 81, 161, 180
homosexuality. See gay rights
Honey, Michael, 370n6
Hooper, Lloyd M., 61–62
Hoover, Herbert, 71–74, 76, 79–81, 89, 124, 326n13; claiming the moniker of liberal, 105. See also Mellon, Andrew
Hoover, J. Edgar, 61, 158, 159
Hoovercrats. See Bolt of 1928; Heflin, J. Thomas; Locke, Hugh; Smith, Al; Street, Oliver Day; Republicanism; Wilkinson, Horace C.
Hopkins, Harry, 132
Horton, Willie (ad), 300, 305, 406n12. See also Ailes, Roger; Atwater, Lee; Baker, James, III; Bush, George H. W.
House Un-American Activities Committee (HUAC). See communism; Dies, Martin H., Jr.; Durr, Clifford; Gelders, Joseph; Starnes, Joseph; Virginia; Williams, Aubrey
Houston, TX, 168; Democratic National Convention at, 69–70, 75, 80

Houston, George S., 15, 16, 82, 152, 323n49, 402n34
Huddleston, George, softness of liberalism, 42, 66, 146–49, 294, 296, 348n9. See also New Deal; Packer, George; southern liberalism (softness of)
Hudson, Hosea, 95–96, 113–15, 139, 197–98; criticizes CIO on race, 95–96; expelled from CIO, 102; on racism of plain whites, 113–14; on timidity of black middle class, 114–15
Huie, William Bradford, 205, 352n35
Hunnicut, John, 13
Hunt, H. L., 300, 303. See also Eisenhower, Dwight D.

Ickes, Harold, xvii, 89, 129, 136, 347n3
Illinois, 38, 53, 71, 301
immigrants: as an issue in 1928 bolt, 68, 72–75; German Jews, 100–101; Irish, 72, 74, 301; Italians, 74, 301; Poles, 301; southern European, 75. See also alcohol; Baptists; Catholics; Gwaltney, L. L.; immigration; Jews; Jones, Bob, Sr.; Methodists; Shuler, Rev. Robert; Tammany Hall; Women's Christian Temperance Union
individualism. See rugged individualism
industrial unionism. See Congress of Industrial Organizations
Ingalls, Robert I., 169, 352n30, 372n30; on outside agitators, 352n30
"in their place." See Associated Industries of Alabama; National Association of Manufacturers; race, blacks kept "in their place"; Southern States Industrial Council; war production; women, kept in their place
interracial sex, gendered double-standard on, 258–59, 397n38. See also race; sex
ironies: of anti-democratic elements in political reforms of Progressive Era, 65, 341n69; of Ayn Rand and Ron Paul, xv, 314n5; of backward South as a trend-setter, 65, 341n69; Great Irony and, xi, xviii, 111; of no elemen-

tal change in South despite partisan realignment, xi–xii; of New Deal holding the seeds of its own destruction, xii, xvii, 87, 88, 148–49, 292; of politics being about culture not politics, xi, xviii, 111; of private southern warmth versus public social irresponsibility, 35–36; of robber barons misusing classical liberal economists, 36; of same elements causing Democratic solidarity and dissolution, xi, 292; of South getting more from New Deal than any section and turning against it, xvii. *See also* continuity; cultural conservatism; Cultural IQ; culture

iron laws: of biracial cooperation in labor, 195; of southern change and the federal role in, 196. *See also* federal government; labor; race; southern distinctiveness

Islam. *See* Muslims

Jackson, Andrew, 24
Jackson, Emory O., 115, 358n87, 386n44.
Jackson, Thomas H. "Stonewall," 128
Jarman, Pete, 176, 210, 260, 389n68
Javits, Jacob, 300
Jefferson, Thomas, 38, 287
Jeffersonian Democrats, 118
Jelks, W. D., 57; convict-lease, 338n43; opposition to lynching, 338n45
Jemison, Elbert S., 372n22
Jews, 6, 34, 44, 61, 84, 88, 234–35; German Jews, 100–101; New Deal, 100–101, 104, 115, 129, 132–33, 138, 146, 153, 156, 185, 193, 201, 261, 264, 301, 314n5, 410n33. *See also* anti-Semitism; New Deal; Roosevelt, Franklin D.
Jim Crow. *See* race; segregation
John Birch Society, 299
Johnson, Jack, 79; miscegenation, 79
Johnson, James Weldon, 62
Johnson, Lyndon Baines. *See* Kennedy, John

Johnston, Forney, 109–10, 287–91, 347n1, 351n25, 405nn65–66; friend of the Negro, 287–90; on lynching as act of friendship for the Negro, 289. *See also* Underwood, Oscar W.
Johnston, Joseph F., 337n29, 351n25; convict-lease, 338n43; opposition to lynching, 338n45
Johnston, Olin D., 138
Johnston, Richard, 410n34
Jones, Allen W., 337n28
Jones, Bob, Sr., 71, 74, 346n56. *See also* Bob Jones University; Ku Klux Klan
Jones, Bob (congressman), 166
Jones, James Marion, "Jimmie," 94, 142; as protégé of Horace Wilkinson, 94
Jones, Thomas Goode, 57, 63, 332n46; opposition to lynching, 338n45
Jones, Walter B. (judge), 188, 372n30
Jones, Walter, 148, 353n40

Kennedy, John: civil rights, 409n28; gender discrimination, 307, 409n28
Kennedy, Stetson, 364n65
Kentucky, 348n9; Harlan County, 28, 98; Louisville, 23, 25, 26; Mark Etheridge, 139, 187–88, 250, 282, 402n33; mountain Republicanism in, 332n47. *See also* Barkley, Alben W.; Clay, Henry; Etheridge, Mark
Kerry, John, 391n80
Key, V. O., Jr., 152, 342n1, 381n47
Kilby, Thomas E., 42, 57–63, 65, 222, 338n45, 339n56
Kilby Prison, 367n101, 386n44
King, Martin Luther, Jr., 134, 307
Kirby, John Temple, 117, 335n15
Knights of Labor, xiii, 27, 28, 294
Knox, John B., 336n26, 402n35
Korstad, Robert, 350n21, 370n6
Kousser, J. Morgan, 334n14, 336n27
Krugman, Paul, 313n2. *See also* fusionism
Ku Klux Klan, 1–20, 109, 142, 179, 197, 282, 294, 358n93, 388n58; Bourbons, 121, 128–30, 189–93, 222, 233, 242, 277, 283, 308, 358n93; communal

support for, 8–9, 12–13, 377n16; as logical extreme of southern Progressivism, 41, 64; 1928 bolt, 67–86; 100 percent Americanism, 85, 190; as populist, 41, 347n1; during Progressive Era, 41, 64; during Reconstruction, 8–20, 317n19, 358n93; during Twenties, 68–69, 77, 79, 81–84, 170, 287; labor and, 95, 100–101; opposition to, 64, 84–85, 269, 321n37, 376n58. *See also* Graves, Bibb; Heflin, J. Thomas; Locke, Hugh; Neo-Kluxism; Randolph, Ryland A.; Smith, Al; Street, Oliver Day; Wilkinson, Horace C.

Ku Klux Klan Acts, 14, 321n42

labor, 28, 195; anti-union beliefs, 26, 97–98, 288, 341n67; anti-unionism and race, 94–101, 202; anti-unionism and religion, 98; anti-unionism of Christian Americans, 118, 121, 129; child labor, 28, 35, 60; coal strikes, 57–59, 63; divided by race, 96, 113, 152, 195–98, 203; historiographical controversies in, 350n21; miners, 200; patriotism impugned, 200–202, 215, 234–35, 288; racial liberalism of, 96–97; racism within, 198–200, 204, 227, 240; during Reconstruction, 16; steelworkers, 197–98; strikes and, 57–59, 201–2; textile strikes, 83, 95, 97–98; trouble in Gadsden, 98–100; as undesirables, 341n67. *See also* American Federation of Labor; Beddow, Noel R.; Burr, Borden; class; class consciousness; Congress of Industrial Organizations; convict-lease system; DeBardeleben, Charles; DeBardeleben, Henry F.; employment discrimination; Fair Employment Practices Committee; gap between leadership and rank-and-file; iron laws; Knights of Labor; Lewis, John L.; National Labor Relations Act; patriotism; race; Strevel, Howard; United Mine Workers; War Manpower Board

La Follette, Bob, 300
LaHaye, Tim, 308
laissez-faire, xiv, xv, 17, 27, 32, 33, 36, 117, 120, 146, 161–62, 190, 220, 233, 255, 266, 294, 299; extreme forms of, 65, 100, 153, 164, 173, 393n102, 409n31; on race, 332n45; ties to religion and, 328n33
Land, Richard, 307, 408n27
Lassiter, Matthew D., 410n34
law and order, 17, 126, 302, 308, 334n14; low worth of convict life, 367n101
Lee, Robert E., 128, 138, 206, 224
LeFlore, John L. 213
Lendman, Stephen, 409n31
Lewis, John L., 95, 96, 100, 115, 148, 234, 236
liberalism: popularity of term in Depression, 105–10, 278, 363n59; once respectable if minority current, 278; religion, 308; schools as liberalizing agents, 206; SCHW, 245–49;. *See also* New Deal; southern liberalism (softness of)
libertarianism, xv, 32, 65, 86, 146, 233, 235, 294, 307, 313n2, 314n5, 326n10, 328n33, 409n32. *See also* economic fundamentalism
liberty. *See* freedom; libertarianism
Lichtenstein, Nelson, 350n21, 370n6
Lincoln, Abraham, xvii, 89, 153, 206, 300; assassination of, 266; castigated by M. E. Bradford, 328n33; party of, 115, 120, 124, 126–27, 130, 237, 243, 244
Lincoln, Mrs., 266
Lind, Michael, 313n2. *See also* fusionism
Lindsey, Brink, 313n2. *See also* fusionism; libertarianism
Link, Arthur S., 339n58; "for whites only" thesis, 46–47, 63, 334n14.
literacy tests. *See* anti-democratic tendencies; disfranchisement; voter suppression
Little Rock, AR, desegregation of Central High School, 299

Locke, Hugh, 93; 1928 bolt, 71, 76, 78; Heflox ticket and KKK, 402n34; and Horace Wilkinson, 93, 94, 106. *See also* Dixiecrats; Heflin, J. Thomas; Wilkinson, Horace C.
Lodge, Henry Cabot, 59–60, 332n43, 345n48
Lofgren, Mike, 314n5
Long, Zue Musgrove, 76
Lost Cause, 19, 83, 324n55
Lott, Trent, 306, 307, 408n27. *See also* Dixiecrats; Thurmond, Strom
Louisiana, 118, 130, 168, 294, 297, 368n108, 410n35; Eleanor Roosevelt, 158, 161; Dixiecrats, 297; Goldwater, 301; New Orleans, 25, 168, 172; Rev. Gerald L. K. Smith, 118, 291; Rick Santorum, 300, 410n35. *See also* Alexander, Will W.; Barr, John U.; Ellender, Allen J.; New Orleans; Perez, Leander; Smith, Rev. Gerald L. K.; Tulane University
Louisville and Nashville Railroad, 36, 279
Louisville Courier-Journal. *See* Etheridge, Mark
Lowndes, Joseph E., 392n90
Luke, William, 11–12, 323n48
lynching, 289; as act of friendship for the Negro, 289; campaign against, 57–64; as Christian act, 77; in effigy, 77; and rape, 130, 361n32; and sex, 259; Wagner-Costigan Bill, 108–10, 146. *See also* Ames, Jesse Daniel; Dyer, L. C.; Dyer Federal Anti-Lynching Bill; Kilby, Thomas E.; race; sophistry of modern conservatism; southern liberalism; Wagner-Costigan Federal Anti-Lynching Bill; Wilkinson, Horace C.

machismo. *See* masculinity
macho. *See* masculinity
Macon anti-New Deal Meeting, 117–19, 129, 157
Mallory, Hugh, S., 80
Malone, George H., 76, 344n31
Malone, Mrs. A. Y., 366n87

Malone, Robert, 151
Malone, Wallace D., Jr., 344n31
Malone, Wallace D., Sr., 173, 176, 263, 291, 344n31
Manasco, Carter, 176
Mandeville, Bernard, 237, 327n14, 328n33, 391n82
market values, xi, xvi, 128. *See also* economic fundamentalism
Marshall, George C., 176
Marshall, John, 24
Martin, James E., on foundation of the modern GOP, 298
Martin, Thomas W., connects business to Christianity, 263–64
Maryland, 23, 69, 223. *See also* Edmonds, Richard; Mencken, H. L.
masculinity: interracial sex and, 258–59; in southern politics, 177–78, 181–82, 214, 227, 240, 267. *See also* Dixon, Frank; sex; Sparks, Chauncey; Wallace, George C.
Mason, James T., 264
Mason, Lucy Randolph, 98, 138, 156, 383n1
Massachusetts, 7, 8, 10, 53, 332n43, 345n48; conflated with federal government, 352n35
masses: during disfranchisement, 49, 56; divided by race, 49, 56, 85–86, 135, 175, 184, 188–90, 195, 213, 219, 224, 227, 238–46, 262, 302–3; divided by religion, 238–39, 243; labor divided on race, 96, 113, 196–98; united by race, 15–16, 174–78, 322n46. *See also* labor, racism within; New Racism; politics of emotion
Matalin, Mary, 305, 408n24
Maverick, Maury, 138, 356n64
Mays, Benjamin, 264, 399n59
McArthur, F. D., 75, 79
McClellan, John L., 384n26
McCord, Leon, 74
McCorvey, Gessner T., 97, 184, 192–93, 243, 291, 294, 378n21; Dixiecrats, 152, 170–71; as friend to blacks, 274,

277; GOP, 152; labor, 149; poll tax, 211; violence, 206; voter suppression, 365n74, 383n12. *See also* Dixon, Frank; Wilkinson, Horace C.
McDuff, Milt, the Red Squad, 103
McDuffie, John, xvi, 66, 80, 106
McGill, Ralph, 139, 280
McGough, Thomas, 173, 372n30
McGough, William P., 151
McKee, Robert, 324n55
McKinney, Clinton, 113
McQueen, John D., 205, 365n74
Medicare, xv, 36; attacked by conservatives, 314n5; claimed by Ayn Rand and Ron Paul, 314n5
Mehlman, Ken, 309
Meighen, J. Herbert, referred to, 227
Mellon, Andrew, 126, 237, 326n13
Mencken, H. L., 69
Methodists, xiv, 11, 33, 69, 71–72, 76, 78, 271, 372n30; black, 224; liberal, 264
Meyer, Frank S., 313n2. *See also* fusionism
Miami, FL. *See* Florida
middle class: blacks, 115; pro-segregation, 389n63. *See also* class consciousness; communism; Hudson, Hosea; labor
Midwest, in possible coalition with Dixiecrats, 294
militarism. *See* Civil War; patriotism; politics of emotion; sovereignty of the South; terror; World War I; World War II
military, desegregation of, 203, 215, 225–29
military-industrial complex, 299–300. *See also* Eisenhower, Dwight D.
Mill, John Stuart, 37, 38, 331n39
Miller, Benjamin Meek, 80, 92–93, 97, 108, 112, 121, 341n64, 348n12; on Victor Hanson, 389n69
Milner, H. Key, 63
Mine, Mill, Smelters Union, 198, 379n34
Minnis, John A., 14, 321n42
miscegenation. *See* interracial sex
Mises, Ludwig von, 328n33
Mississippi, 28, 83, 108, 137, 150, 156, 158, 169, 172, 205, 207, 211, 212, 238, 248, 264, 294, 297, 301, 306, 307, 309, 310, 346n53, 348n9, 355n53, 408n27, 410n35; interracial sex and, 397n38; KKK in, 318n25, mountain Republicanism in northeast, 332n47; Pascagoula industry, 168; poll tax in, 382n2. *See also* Bilbo, Theodore; Carter, Betty; Carter, Hodding; Colmer, William; Eastland, James O.; Harrison, Pat; Lott, Trent; Rankin, John E.; Stennis, John
Mississippi Regional Council of Negro Leadership, 397n38
Missouri, 59–60, 62, 112; black labor in, 378n28; black religion in, 378n28. *See also* Dyer, L. C.; lynching
Mitch, William, 96–97, 102, 102, 138, 147, 148, 350n21, 353n40, 355n55
Mitchell, Arthur W., 116
Mitchell, John, 301, 302
Mobile, AL, 4, 9, 50, 59, 70, 97, 107, 149, 151, 199; race riot in, 217–18; violence in, 216, 385n34; war production and population growth in, 168–69
Monsanto Chemicals, 172, 211
monster of white supremacy: feeding of and ritual tribute, 145, 210, 232; god of white supremacy, 145. *See also* race
Montgomery Advertiser, 249. *See* Hall, Grover, Jr.; Hall, Grover, Sr.; Mullin, Atticus
Moore, R. R., 97
Moore, Roy, 328n33. *See also* Christian Reconstruction; Dominionism
moral authoritarianism, 237
moral chauvinism, 175, 266, 304, 305, 307–8
morality. *See* Calvinism; emotion; Ku Klux Klan; Mellon, Andrew; moral authoritarianism; moral chauvinism; New Racism; politics of emotion; religion; Religious Right; Social Darwinism; status quo society
Morgan, J. P., 24, 35

Morgan, Jimmy, 142
Morgan, John Tyler, 15, 402n34
Morrow, C. Howell, 372n22
Morrow, Hugh, 211, 372n30
movement conservatism, xiii, 60–61, 313n2. *See also* fusionism; Great Melding (First)
Mullin, Atticus, on rural politics and emotion, 70
Munger, Mrs. L. P. (Rose McDavid), 372n30, 395n17
Munger Family, 173, 395n17
Murray, Philip, 164, 196, 350n21; on South as liberal, 164
Murray, W. H., "Alfalfa Bill," 352n35
Muse, Vance, 118, 121, 129, 157
Muslims, 309, 310
Myrdal, Gunnar S., 139, 248, 252, 255, 393n1, 395n16

Nance, Steve, 101
Nashville Agrarians, 328n33
Nathan Bedford Forrest Klan, 77
National Association of Manufacturers (NAM), 172
National Association for the Advancement of Colored People (NAACP), 62, 84, 92, 97, 108, 124, 156, 177, 182, 193, 213, 229, 280, 283, 365n74, 368n111, 389n64; Harold Ickes, 347n3
National Farmers Union, 209; in Alabama, 374n43
National Labor Relations Act (NLRA), 100–11, 126; also known as the Wagner Act, 126, 185. *See also* Wagner, Robert A.
National Labor Relations Board (NLRB), 99, 151, 216, 352n29
National Industrial Recovery Act, 349n15: National Recovery Administration (NRA), 89, 95, 97, 110–11, 119–20, 125, 137, 185, 350n19, 350n21, 351n25
Neal, Benjamin F., 271
Neal, Claude: lynching of, 107–8

Negrophobes and paternalists, 268–77. *See also* southern liberalism (softness of)
Neo-Bourbonism. *See* Neo-Kluxism
neo-carpetbaggers, 154, 271. *See also* carpetbaggers; federal government; neo-scalawags; outside agitators; Reconstruction; Reconstruction Syndrome; scalawags
Neo-Confederates, 125, 148, 305, 328n33
Neo-Kluxism, 85, 128–29, 190; alliance with neo-Bourbons, 121, 128–29, 130, 154, 189–95, 233–34, 242, 308; mentioned, 140, 142, 222; related to modern GOP, 308. *See also* Ku Klux Klan; Republicanism
neo-scalawags, 252. *See also* carpetbaggers; federal government; neo-carpetbaggers; outside agitators; Reconstruction; Reconstruction Syndrome; scalawags
neoliberalism. *See* economic fundamentalism
Neuhaus, Richard John, 307
New Deal: conservative lust to revoke, 292; blacks included in, 89, 381n46; disgust with over economic liberalism, 125–29, 234; disgust with over racial inclusiveness, 123–49, 234; Macon anti-New Deal Meeting, 117–19, 129, 157; Republican opposition to, 130–33, 149–50, 357n73, 361n29, 362n35; taxes and, 131–32; as temporary, xii, xvii, 87, 88, 91, 105–6, 107, 116, 124–25, 146, 147–48, 167, 185, 210, 245, 255–56, 296. *See also* Bilbo, Theodore; Byrnes, James F.; Connor, Theophilus Eugene "Bull"; Downs, William O.; Graves, Bibb; Graves, John Temple, II; Great Melding (First); Great Melding (Second); Hill, Lister; Huddleston, George; McDuffie, John; Perez, Leander; race and class (connected); Roosevelt, Eleanor; Roosevelt, Franklin D.; southern liberalism (softness of); Starnes, Joseph; Thurmond, Strom

New Jersey, 176–77, 301
New Negroes, 302
New Negro movement, 124
New Orleans, 25, 168, 172
New Racism, 302–3, 306, 307–8, 350n19, 407n15
New South Creed, 19, 23, 26, 324n55, 337n31. *See also* Gaston, Paul M.; New South movement
New South movement, xi, 2, 6–7, 16, 19, 21–31, 33–36, 235–36, 292, 324n55, 325n6, 337n31. *See also* convict-lease system; Southern Religion
New York, 197; criticism of southern race relations from, 213, 218; 1924 Democratic National Convention, 88, 287
Nietzsche, Friedrich, 328n33
Nixon, E. D., 156
Nixon, Herman Clarence, 123, 138, 139, 355n55
Nixon, Richard, 292, 300, 301, 304, 307, 392n93, 405n4, 408n26; Southern Strategy, 301–2, 307, 309
Noonjin, B. Lonnie, 133, 144, 149, 364n61
Norquist, Grover, 86, 300; "starve the beast," 295
Norrell, Robert J., 350n21, 379n32
Norris, J. Frank, 238
North Alabama v. South Alabama dichotomy (as overstated), 6, 50–51, 143, 163, 165–67, 370n7; poll tax, 212; helped by South Alabama, 15–16; liberalism in, 143, 166; mentioned, 6, 15–17, 79, 97, 98, 144, 146, 169, 178, 181–82, 212, 216, 219, 227, 230, 250–51, 256, 261, 262, 275–76, 298, 335n22, 366n88, 396n22, 402n31; mountain Republicanism in, 332n47; during Reconstruction, 15–16. *See also* East Alabama v. West Alabama (observation)
North Carolina, 83, 98, 107, 108, 110, 125, 136, 138, 158, 159, 161, 280, 286, 325n6, 332n47, 364n65, 374n43, 404n59; Chapel Hill, 280, 404n59; Charlotte, 23, 25; Durham, 280; Gastonia textile strike, 98; mountain Republicanism in western, 332n47. *See also* Bailey, Josiah; Couch, W. T.; Daniels, Frank; Daniels, Jonathan; Glass, Carter; Graham, Frank Porter; Odum, Howard; Tompkins, Daniel Augustus
North, Gary, 328n33
Novak, Robert, 408n21, 409n29

Oates, W. C., 51, 402n34
Obama, Barack, 309–11, 411n37; alleged to be Muslim, 309–11; alleged to be socialist, 311, 411n37; and Jeremiah Wright, 310; War on Religion, 311
O'Daniel, Pappy, 215, 384n26
Odum, Howard, 280
Ogle, Belle, 91
O'Hehir, Andrew, 313n2. *See also* fusionism
Oklahoma, 125, 238, 352n35; Thomas P. Gore, 125. *See also* Murray, W. H. "Alfalfa Bill"
Oliver, W. B., 61, 81–82
O'Neal, Edward, 57
O'Neal, Emmett, 42, 51, 57, 63, 337n31, 338n43; opposition to lynching, 338n45
"our way of life," 110–13, 161, 178, 179, 181, 225, 251–55; South as a separate nation, 203, 251–54, 381n47. *See also* Civil War, as not over; conformity; cultural conservatism; culture; Cultural IQ; southern distinctiveness; sovereignty of the South
outside agitators (and outsiders), 2, 19, 58, 62, 64, 95, 98, 99, 101, 105, 172, 176–82, 186–88, 196, 210, 213, 217–18, 220, 222, 227, 239, 252, 262, 265–69, 271–73, 276–77, 280, 282–83, 286, 288, 351n25, 352n30, 386n37, 392n98, 395n17; in the form of the federal government, 134, 180, 252; linked in Reconstruction, New Deal, and civil rights, 19. *See also* carpetbaggers; federal govern-

ment; foreigners; neo-carpetbaggers; neo-scalawags; New Deal; race; Reconstruction; Reconstruction Syndrome; scalawags; xenophobia
Owen, Marie Bankhead, 82, 204. *See also* Bankhead Family; Bankhead, John H., Sr.; Bankhead, John H., II; Bankhead, William B.; Dixiecrats

Packer, George, 148, 149, 365n74
Palin, Sarah, xiii, 86, 300
Palmer, A. Mitchell, 61
patriarchy, 258–59. *See also* gender; interracial sex; status quo society; women
Patrick, Luther, 139, 148, 348n9; SCHW, 145–46, 212; for abolition of the poll tax, 212; for Soldier Vote Bill, 210; paid price for poll tax vote, 384n16
patriotism, xix, 181, 238, 241, 302, 381n47, 396n22; connected to religion, 254; defined as the interests of the privileged, 152–53; mentioned, 254; notion appropriated by the right, 253–58, 265; societies, 75. *See also* business; conformity; cultural conservatism; labor; "our way of life"; southern distinctiveness; New Racism; sovereignty of the South; status quo society
Patterson, F. D., 146, 222, 364n65, 386n44. *See also* Tuskegee Institute
Paul, Ron, 314n5
Pepper, Claude, 137, 138, 139, 209, 211
Perez, Leander, 294
Perman, Michael, 336n27
Perry, Rick, xiii, 86, 300
personal responsibility, xix, 32, 33, 36, 90, 302. *See also* Social Darwinism
Pettus, Edmund, 9, 10, 402n34
Philadelphia, 1936 Democratic National Convention, 115–16
Phillips, Kevin P., 301–5, 405n14, 407n14; Southern Strategy, 301–2
Phillips, U. B., 342n1
Pickens, Champ, 276
Piney Woods, 296
"Pittsburgh-Plus" base-point system, 24

plain folk. *See* economics; labor; masses, divided by race; race
Plains States, 311; in possible coalition with Dixiecrats, 294
plain whites. *See* economics; labor; masses; race
Plessy v. Ferguson, 56
pocket-book ethics, 198
Poillon, W. A., 4–5
politics of emotion, 255, 303–4, 350n19, 396n29. *See also* emotion; New Racism
poll tax, 208–14, 279, 382n2, 383n1. *See also* anti-democratic tendencies; disfranchisement; Soldier Vote Bill; voter suppression
poor whites: *See* economics; labor; masses; race
populism, xiv, 65, 67, 118, 163, 293, 295; KKK as populist, 41, 347n1
Populist Party, xiii, xv, 15, 19, 21, 27, 46, 49, 50, 68, 60, 76, 95, 124, 175, 294, 297, 324n55, 335n23, 335n25; Oliver Day Street, 130, 132, 133, 173, 180, 222, 360n14
Pratt, Daniel, 36
prayer. *See* public schools
Presbyterians, 33, 328n33; liberal, 356n67. *See also* Edmonds, Henry M.; Southern Presbyterians
propaganda, xvi, 62, 73, 75–76, 118, 201, 241; labor, 218, 400n65
property qualifications. *See* disfranchisement
Progressivism: in Alabama as "for blacks only," 41–66; in Alabama as perversion, 41–66. *See also* "for whites only"
public employees, xv
public health, 24, 110, 137
public schools, xv, 26, 36, 47, 84, 92, 104, 136, 179, 221, 234; as agents of racial liberalism, 206; cuts to, 118; for blacks, 30, 55–56, 104, 136, 207, 214, 220, 258, 307, 346n56, 395n16, 407n15, 410n33; home-schooling founded and, 328n33; prayer in, 303, 308, 405n4, 407n15, 409n28; during

450 / Index

Reconstruction, 10; taxes, 55, 275. *See also* Little Rock, AR; Reconstruction Syndrome; taxes
Puritans, 6, 237, 272

Quakers, 6, 34

race: blacks as happy in slavery, 227–28; blacks as happy under segregation, 222–23, 227–28, 276, 281, 286, 390n71, 402n23; black clerics as policemen of black masses, 353n46; blacks kept "in their place," 3, 8, 113, 132, 157, 159, 178–79, 256, 269, 275, 276–77; black middle class and, 115; black or provocative bad behavior, 215–16, 259–60; central importance of, 291–92, 342n1, 410n34; friends of the Negro, 17, 19, 115, 157, 159, 160, 162, 171, 176, 184–85, 194, 213–14, 219–22, 228, 231, 266–90, 368n109; goodwill on the part of whites, 220–21, 273–77, 282, 284–90, 401n16, 401n20; inherent smell of blacks, 260, 266, 273, 398n46; race-baiting in 1928 bolt, 77–86; racism denied, 405n2; racism of plain whites, 227; segregation as good for blacks and whites, 222, 223; slavery as good for blacks, 220, 245–46, 272–73, 275; voting, 30. *See also* coded speech; disfranchisement; interracial sex; masses, divided by race; military, desegregation of; monster of white supremacy; New Racism; Reconstruction Syndrome; religion, white supremacy; sophistry of modern conservatism; Southern Strategy; violence, as the underpinning of the southern status quo; voter suppression
race and class (connected), 15, 67–68, 95, 152, 171–72, 185–86, 202, 213, 217, 233, 247, 278, 279, 284, 358n92, 400n3, 407n15; economics, 247; gender, 171–72, 247; morality, 171–72; in labor, 94–101; in New Deal, 116–17, 123–24, 171–72; and other pillars of society, 171–72, 244, 247, 279, 287; separated, 284. *See also* Great Melding (First); status quo society
race riots, 61, 172, 222, 386n37. *See also* Georgia, Atlanta race riot; Mobile; Texas, Longview race riot
racism: *See* race
Rains, Albert, 167
Rand, Ayn, xv, 236, 295, 307, 409n29; anti-democratic beliefs of, 328n33; claiming Social Security and Medicare, 314n5
Randolph, A. Philip, 171
Randolph, Ryland A., 12–13, 15, 18–19, 321n38
Rankin, John E., 294; communism, 212, 372n27; FEPC, 172, 179; poll tax, 212; as New Dealer, 355n53; racial labels on blood vials, 205
rape, 10, 102–3, 110, 141, 155, 361n32, 397n38, 404n54; applied to Constitution, 212. *See also* gender; interracial sex; lynching, and rape; sex; violence; women
Rauschenbush, Walter, 34
Rayburn, Sam, 348n9
Reagan, Ronald, xiii, xiv, xv, 86, 235, 292, 295, 304, 308; and George Wallace, 409n31; and M. E. Bradford, 328n33; Reaganomics, 303. *See also* Bradford, M. E.; economic fundamentalism; Hayek, F. A.; Wallace, George C.
reality, 27, 217; distortion of, 73, 227–28, 257–58, 285–86, 304–5; historical inquiry, 42, 44; irrelevance of, 111, 285–86, 309; perception, 95, 139–40, 196, 201; self-deception, 274; sophistry of modern conservatism, 134. *See also* conservatism, extremism of modern
Reconstruction, xvii, xviii, 1–20, 180; amendments, 22; compared to socialism, 392n98; enduring import of,

245, 252, 254; labor 16; violence, 319nn31–32, 322n43. *See also* carpetbaggers; federal government; Ku Klux Klan; neo-carpetbaggers; neo-scalawags; outside agitators; race; Reconstruction; Reconstruction Syndrome; scalawags

Reconstruction Syndrome, 1, 2, 21–22, 81, 128, 179, 252, 375n50, 396n20. *See also* carpetbaggers; federal government; Ku Klux Klan; neo-carpetbaggers; neo-scalawags; outside agitators; race; Reconstruction; scalawags

Redemption, 14–20; Redeemer program, 294–95. *See also* carpetbaggers; federal government; Houston, George S.; neo-carpetbaggers; Lost Cause; neo-scalawags; New South Creed; New South movement; outside agitators; Reconstruction; Reconstruction Syndrome; scalawags

Reed, Ralph, 307, 309, 410n33

religion, 2, 308; conservatism of, 328n31; Church of God, 85; Holiness, 85; Pentecostal, 85; perverted during disfranchisement, 49; during Reconstruction, 19; war, 316n13; white supremacy, 112, 140–41, 160–61, 261–65, 272, 289, 377n17. *See also* Calvinism; Catholics; Christian Reconstruction; Dominionism; folk theology; gap between leadership and rank-and-file; religious fundamentalism; race; Religious Right; Rushdoony, Rousas John; status quo society

religious fundamentalism, xv, 34, 65, 84, 295, 328n33. *See also* Barton, David; Christian Reconstruction; Dabney, Robert L.; Dominionism; Great Melding (Second); economic fundamentalism; Religious Right; Rushdoony, Rousas John; Weaver, Richard M.

Religious Right, xiv, 34–35, 235, 292, 300, 301, 303, 306–9, 310, 328n33, 346n56, 409n30; anti-democratic tendencies of, 328n33; pro-slavery beliefs of, 328n33; Prosperity Gospel, 409n31. *See also* Barton, David; Calvinism; Christian Reconstruction; Dobson, James; Dominionism; Falwell, Jerry; Great Melding (Second); Moore, Roy; Neuhaus, Richard John; Reed, Ralph; Robertson, Pat; Rushdoony, Rousas John; Weyrich, Paul

Renneker, Fred D., 173, 372n30

"Report on Economic Conditions in the South," 136–37

representation: as reflexive of popular will, 183, 284, 361n31; various models of, 284

Republicanism, 118, 128, 213, 243, 326n13, 332n43, 345n48, 389n64; in Alabama, 49, 76–78, 93, 112, 130–33, 144–45, 149–50, 180, 224, 227, 360n14; anti-intellectualism and, 112, 231; black-and-tan, 49, 229; emotion, 86; Hoovercrats, 67–89; genius of, 84–86, 295; lily-white, 49; modern GOP as extreme, xv, 300, 309, 314n5; mountain, 332n47; move to modern GOP, xi, xii, xiii, xv, xvi, xvii, 1, 40, 65, 66, 86, 109, 120, 121, 128, 148, 150, 151, 171, 173, 175, 191, 194, 210, 228, 229, 232–37, 243, 244, 260, 281, 28–311, 328n33, 346n56, 385n32, 391n80, 405n4, 408n26, 410nn33–35; 1920s and, 89, 346n55, 347n57; opposition to the New Deal, 130–33, 149–50, 357n73, 361n29, 362n35; race, 132–33, 243, 410n33; Reconstruction and, xiii, xviii, 3–4, 8–13, 15, 16, 19–20, 40, 49, 68, 79–82, 84, 94, 125, 149, 152, 180, 212, 252, 316n13, 319n32, 322n45, 323nn47–48, 324n53; related to old Democratic and Conservative Party, xvi, 296. *See also* Bolt of 1928; Bush, George W.; "color-blind" issues; conformity; Cultural IQ; culture; DeBardeleben, Charles; extremism; Great Melding (First); Great Melding (Second); Hall, Grover C., Jr.; McCorvey,

Gessner; Neo-Kluxism; New Negroes; New Racism; Noonjin, Lonnie; politics of emotion; race; Reagan, Ronald; Reconstruction Syndrome; Religious Right; Samford, Frank P.; sophistry of modern conservatism; Southern Religion; Southern Strategy; status quo society; Street, Oliver Day; Suburban School; Vardaman, Claude O.

retrenchment, xiv, 17, 94, 303

reverse discrimination, 134. *See also* affirmative action

Ricardo, David, 37

robber barons, 32–35

Robert E. Lee Club, 224

Roberts, Kenneth, 166

Robertson, Pat, xiv, 300, 307, 308, 328n33

Robinson, Joseph T., 69, 108, 348n9

Robinson, Lewey V., 106

Robinson, Reid, 198

Rockefeller, Nelson, 300

Rockefeller Family, 241–42

Rocky Mountain West, 311; in possible coalition with Dixiecrats, 294

Roe v. Wade, 307, 409n28

Rogers, William Warren, 338n43

Romney, George, 300

Romney, Mitt, 310

Roosevelt, Eleanor, xvii, 89, 153, 181, 186–87; decorum and, 392n100; opposition to, 153–62, 181, 205–6, 237–38, 243, 252, 262–63, 271–72, 280, 368n108, 369n119, 381n46, 403n37; Southern Conference for Human Welfare, 138, 139, 143; southern women against, 155–56

Roosevelt, Franklin D., xi, xviii, 87–89, 91–93, 100, 106, 112, 365n74, 370n7; blacks and racial liberalism, xiii, 107, 110, 115, 124, 125, 129, 132, 142, 150, 153, 205–6, 209, 239, 281; business, 104, 119; court-packing scheme, 106, 136, 138; FEPC, 171, 186–87, 380n35; labor, 100, 115, 132, 348n11; New Deal as a threat to racial and economic status quo, 117, 123–24, 128, 171–72, 185–86; opposition to racial and economic liberalism of, 117–19, 121, 123–24, 130–33, 135–38, 141–43, 148–53, 189, 192–3, 205–6, 218, 225, 230, 237–39, 242–43, 250, 255, 281, 361n29, 364n65, 401n15; purge elections, 116, 137–38; and southern allies, 207, 348n9. *See also* Congress of Industrial Organizations; Fair Employment Practices Committee; Ickes, Harold; National Labor Relations Act; Roosevelt, Eleanor; Wallace, Henry A.; Williams, Aubrey W.

Roosevelt, Theodore, 293, 300

Rothbard, Murray, 308, 409n29

Rouzer, I. W. "Ike," 250–51, 262, 372n30; desegregation of military, 373n30; and Frank Dixon, 372n9; friend to blacks, 184–85, 376n2; opposes Eleanor Roosevelt, 376n2. *See also* DeBardeleben, Charles; DeBardeleben, Henry F.

Rove, Karl, 304, 305; and Lee Atwater, 408n21, 408n24

rugged individualism, 31, 90, 240; discussed, 2, 174, 225, 240. *See also* conservatism

rural. *See* farmers; Nashville Agrarians; Populists

Rushdoony, Rousas John, xiv, 328n33; anti-democratic beliefs of, 328n33; homeschooling, 328n33. *See also* Calvinism; Christian Reconstruction; Dominionism

Rushton, J. Frank, Jr., 372n22

Russell, Richard, 108

Sager, Ryan, 313n2. *See also* fusionism; libertarianism

Samford, Frank, P., 173, 188, 291, 294; GOP, 377n11; and insurance company, 372n30. *See also* Dixiecrats

Samford, Thomas P., 80

Sandburg, Carl, 372n27

Santorum, Rick, 300, 410n35
scalawags, 77, 82, 141, 187, 206, 257, 288, 315n7, 404n59; defined, 315n7; during Reconstruction, 3, 4, 6, 8, 15, 20, 40, 59. *See also* carpetbaggers; neo-carpetbaggers; neo-scalawags; Reconstruction; Reconstruction Syndrome
Scammon, Richard M., 405n4
Schaeffer, Francis, 326n13
Schecter v. U.S., 349n15
schools. *See* public schools
Schumpeter, Joseph, 326n10, 328n33, 390n78
Schurz, Carl, 4, 9
Schuyler, George S., 223
scientific management, 32
scientific racism, 31, 32, 38–40
Scottsboro Boys, 102–3, 105, 216; Forney Johnston, 109–10; and George Huddleston, 147; and Grover Hall Sr., 109–10
Scranton, William, 300
segregation. *See* race
Sensing, Thurman, 372n25
Serviceman's Readjustment Act of 1944. *See* GI Bill
sex, xv, 237; race, 189, 194, 204–6. *See also* birth control; gender; interracial marriage; lynching; miscegenation; race; rape; women
Shafer, Byron E., 410n34
Share Croppers Union (SCU), 104
Sharp, Laura, 151
Sheffield, J. C., 126–27
Shelley, Levie, 193
Shelton, Barrett, 182, 188, 377n8. *See also* Abernethy, Thomas; Baughn, Hubert; Field, Ed; Hall, Horace
Shelton, Bruce, 120. *See also* Abernethy, Thomas; Baughn, Hubert; Field, Ed; Hall, Horace
Sherman, William Tecumseh: burning of Atlanta, 25; march to the sea, 80
Shoemaker, Joseph, castration and death of, 128–29

Shores, Arthur D., 213, 365n74
Shuler, Rev. Robert, 76, 80
Silent Majority, 301, 405n4; as majority liberal South, 208–9
Simmons, Col. Roscoe, 258
Simpson, James A., 94, 193, 291, 349n14; and Bull Connor and U.S. Steel, 349n14. *See also* Connor, Theophilus Eugene "Bull"; Hanson, Victor
slavery, 2–3, 5–7, 10, 13, 19, 22, 43, 216, 220–21, 253, 275; 326n13, 328n33, 387n47, 393n1, 399n59; connected to socialism, 328n33; defenses of slavery, 160, 172, 220, 245–46, 271–72, 328n33; as good for blacks, 272; labor, 22–24; memory of, 80, 97; religious defenses of slavery, 34, 35, 271–72, 328n33; speech of Chauncey Sparks, 220–21, 275; voting, 30; white slavery, 128 *See also* Lincoln, Abraham; race; Rushdoony, Rousas John; Sparks, Chauncey; Stowe, Harriet Beecher
slippery-slope argument, 125, 207, 212, 219, 225, 257, 279
Smith, Adam: ideas misused, 32, 36–38; on labor, 359n6; on living wage, 359n6
Smith, Al, presidential candidacy of, 67–86, 130. *See also* Bolt of 1928; Heflin, J. Thomas; Ku Klux Klan; Locke, Hugh; Street, Oliver Day; Tammany Hall; Wilkinson, Horace C.
Smith, "Cotton Ed," 108, 116, 125, 358n90; on lynching, 259; versus Olin D. Johnston, 138
Smith, John David, 334n14
Smith, Lillian, 164, 281; on South becoming liberal, 164
Smith, Milton Hannibal, 36
Smith, Rev. Gerald L. K., 118, 291
Smyer, Sidney, 92, 215; Dixiecrats, 384n25; GOP, 384n25. *See also* Wilkinson, Horace C.
Social Darwinism, xv, 7, 31–33, 38, 80, 111, 132, 140, 233, 258. *See also* cultural conservatism; social stratification

socialism, 35–36; religion, 328n33; compared to Reconstruction, 392n98; Barack Obama, 311. See also communism; New Deal, opposition to

"Social Issue, The," 405n4

Social Security, xv, 36, 111, 148, 190, 202, 234; attacked by conservatives, 314n5, 357n73; claimed by Ayn Rand and Ron Paul, 314n5; Eisenhower on, 300. See also Paul, Ron; Rand, Ayn

social stratification, 156. See also conformity; cultural conservatism; race, blacks kept "in their place"; Social Darwinism; southern distinctiveness; status quo society; women, kept "in their place"

Soldier Vote Bill, 209–11, 283. See also Dixon, Frank; poll tax; Sparks, Chauncey

sophistry of modern conservatism, 134–35. See also federal government; lynching; race

South Alabama. See Black Belt; North Alabama v. South Alabama dichotomy

South Carolina, 14, 82, 98, 108, 109, 116, 125, 138, 150, 190, 207, 238, 259, 264, 294, 297, 301, 304, 305, 306, 319n28, 325n6, 348n9, 377n11, 399n59; Asheville, 62; Charleston, 62, 168; GOP pilgrimages to Bob Jones University, 346n56; KKK in during Reconstruction, 14; poll tax in, 382n2. See also Atwater, Lee; Blease, Cole; Byrnes, Jimmy; Calhoun, John C.; Carlton, David L.; Dent, Harry S.; Hampton, Wade; Johnston, Olin D.; Mays, Benjamin E.; Smith, "Cotton Ed"; Thurmond, Strom; Tillman, Ben

Southern Conference Education Fund, 365n74

Southern Conference on Human Welfare (SCHW), 124, 138–49; as cultural outliers, 278. See also Connor, Theophilus Eugene "Bull"; Gelders, Joseph; liberalism; Mason, Lucy Randolph; Roosevelt, Eleanor; southern liberalism (softness of)

southern distinctiveness, xvi; 44, 45, 203, 206, 220, 296, 309–10, 393n102, 410n34; irony of southern warmth and social responsibility, 35–36. See also anti-intellectualism; "color-blind" issues; Cultural IQ; culture; "our way of life"; sovereignty of the South; Suburban School; violence

Southern Farmer, 274, 401n13. See also Beech, Gould; Fields, Marshall; Warburg, J. P.; Williams, Aubrey W.

southern liberalism (softness of): xvi, 93–94, 104, 105–6, 145, 146–47, 247, 296; best friends of the Negro argument, 260–90; discussed, 65–66, 91, 93, 104–10, 117, 123–24, 136, 142, 145–49, 163–83, 185, 208–10, 212, 213, 220–32, 245, 247, 249–50, 266–90, 295–96, 355nn53–54, 357n84, 376n57; example of, 355n53, 357n84; goodwill on the part of whites, 220–21, 273–77, 282, 284–90, 401n16, 401n20; Grover Hall Jr.'s criticism of Frank Dixon misinterpreted by scholars, 182, 219–20, 231–32, 249–50, 270, 274–75, 376n57, 394n7; label claimed by many, 105; liberal except on race, 266–67; liberalism racialized, xvii, 123–24, 240–41, 247, 266–67, 278, 291, 293, 295–96; Montgomery Advertiser, 231; Neo-Kluxism, 222; poll tax and the South as inherently liberal, 208–9; popularity of term liberal in Depression, 105–10; Progressivism in Alabama, 42, 64. See also Altman, John; Ayers, Harry Mell; Beddow, Noel; Carmichael, A. A.; conservative progressivism; Couch, W. T.; Dobbins, Charlie; Downs, William O.; Ellis, Handy; federal government; Graves, Bibb; Graves, John Temple, II; Green, Cooper; Hall, Fitzgerald; Hall, Grover, Jr.; Hall, Grover, Sr.; Hanson, Victor; Hill, Lister; Huddleston, George; Johnston, Forney; liberalism; McDuffie, John; New Deal, as temporary; Patrick, Luther; Silent Majority;

Southern Conference on Human Welfare; Southern Religion; Sparkman, John; status quo society; Steagall, H. B.; Sumners, Hatton W.; Thurmond, Strom
Southern Presbyterians, 33, 328n33. *See also* Dabney, Robert L.
Southern Religion, The, xviii, 6–7, 34, 315n8, 317n16; in a general sense, 328n31
Southern States Industrial Council (SSIC), 172, 173, 372n25, 372n30. *See also* Barr, John U.; McGough, Thomas; Sensing, Thurman
Southern Strategy, 301–3, 309, 408n26; public denial of, 303; prematurely written off, 407n14. *See also* Ailes, Roger; Atwater, Lee; Baker, James III; Buchanan, Pat; Bush, George W.; Bush, George H. W.; Carter, Dan T.; coded speech; Dent, Harry S.; Dukakis, Michael; Ehrlichman, John; Horton, Willie; Nixon, Richard; Phillips, Kevin P.; Thurmond, Strom
southern way of Life. *See* culture; "our way of life"; sovereignty of the South
Southland. *See* culture; "our way of life"; sovereignty of the South
sovereignty of the South, 203, 251–54, 393n102, 394n11, 401n14. *See also* culture; "our way of life"; patriotism; southern distinctiveness
Sparkman, John: against repeal of poll tax, 212; softness of liberalism, xvi, 42, 66, 166–67, 294, 296; for Soldier Vote Bill, 210. *See also* Hill, Lister; New Deal; southern liberalism (softness of)
Sparks, Chauncey, 166, 178, 208, 214–27, 230–39, 243–51, 261, 275, 279–80, 281, 386n42, 388n57, 394n5, 402n34; blacks "in their place," 275; and Horace Wilkinson, 193; criticism of, 387n47, 387n52, 392n100; defense of slavery, 220–21, 275; liberalism of, 386n37; masculine politics, 386n37; rules and order in southern society, 220–21, 275; seen as liberal, 279–80; sees himself as friend to blacks, 401n15; sees himself as liberal, 279–80, 403n40; sees segregation as best for all, 394n9. *See also* Dixon, Frank; Wallace, George C.
Spencer, Herbert, 31, 32
Stallings, Jesse F., 337n29
"Stand Up for Alabama" (slogan), 227, 261, 374n45, 378n21; origins of term, 178. *See also* Dixon, Frank M.; Hale, A. B.; Sparks, Chauncey; Wallace, George C.
Starnes, Joseph, 176, 186, 229, 250–51, 396n22, 396n30; opposition to New Deal, 186, 229–30, 255; patriotism, 396n22; SCHW, 364nn65–66; support of the New Deal, 146, 348n9. *See also* Dies, Martin, Jr.
states' rights, xiii, xix, 2, 16–18, 34, 39, 64, 117, 134, 136, 185, 208, 240, 243, 254, 265, 282, 286, 299, 302; Chauncey Sparks, 221, 227; as euphemism for white supremacy, 294, 307, 309; Frank Dixon, 180, 184, 214; lynching, 109; New Deal, 256; poll tax, 279; Social Security, 148; women's suffrage, 51. *See also* constitutionalism; Dixiecrats; home rule; States' Rights Democratic Party
States' Rights Democratic Party, 124, 192, 277, 297, 393n102. *See also* Dixiecrats; states' rights
status quo society, 223, 247–65, 266, 268–69, 273, 283, 289; discussed, 95, 126, 135, 140, 155, 157, 167, 171–72, 181, 182, 202, 222, 224, 233, 237, 244, 247, 261, 266–69, 278, 279, 280, 286–89, 393n1; religion, 261–65; violence, 173; white supremacy, 111. *See also* southern liberalism (softness of); violence, as the underpinning of the southern status quo
Steagall, Henry, 82, 176, 212
Steele, Michael, 309
Stein, Judith., 350n21
Steiner, General Robert, 92, 173–74

Stennis, John, 400n3
Street, Oliver Day, 222; anti-Catholicism, 76–77; calls for FDR's impeachment, 361n26; GOP, 50, 149–50, 173, 180, 361n29; GOP patronage, 347n57; 1928 Bolt, 76–77, 343n13; New Deal as communism, 360n16; opposition to New Deal, 130–33, 360n16; as Populist, 50, 173, 180, 360n14; on Reconstruction, 180, 212–13; voter suppression, 180, 212–13, 360n14
Street, Thomas Atkins, 360n14
Strevel, Howard, 350n21
Stowe, Harriet Beecher, 187
Suburban School, 234, 302–3, 311, 410n34. *See also* "color-blind" issues; Crespino, Joseph; Lassiter, Matthew D.; race; sophistry of modern conservatism; southern distinctiveness
suburbs, 234, 311
Sullivan, Andrew, 409n30
Sullivan, Patricia, 164, 165, 278, 402n29; on SCHW, 362n43, 364n63; on South as liberal, 164, 165; on Southern Conference Educational Fund, 364n63. *See also* Durr, Virginia
Sumner, William Graham, 31
Sumners, Hatton W., 136
superiority, appeal of, 174–75
Supreme Court of the United States, 108, 109, 120, 133, 136, 277; "Civil Rights Cases," 332n43; dominated by liberals, 153, 194, 288; George Wallace, 409n31; Hugo Black, 139, 146, 355n55; labor, 199; New Deal, 362n33, 380n35. *See also* Black, Hugo; constitutionalism; Douglas, William O.
Swayne, Wager, 7
Sydnor, Charles S., 44

Talmadge, Eugene, 118, 129, 182, 277; on his own goodwill toward blacks, 277, 294
Tammany Hall, 68, 75, 79, 81. *See also* Smith, Al

taxes, 55–56, 57, 135, 241–42, 275; New Deal, 131–32; fanaticism about, 93; race, 361n32; tax fury, 302. *See also* "color-blind" issues; liberalism; public schools; Tea Party
Tea Party, xiii, xiv, xv, 7, 35, 65, 86, 235, 236, 253, 295, 300, 301, 308, 309. *See also* taxes
Ten Commandments, 308, 328n33. *See also* public schools, prayer in
Tennessee, 8, 28, 83, 137, 168, 172, 214, 257, 280, 286, 297, 328n33; Chattanooga, 25; Howard Strevel, 350n21; Knoxville, 25; mountain Republicanism in eastern, 332n47; Nashville, 25; original Bob Jones University, 346n56; poll tax in, 214, 382n2. *See also* Edgerton, John; Hall, Fitzgerald; Jackson, Andrew; Nashville Agrarians; Strevel, Howard; Vanderbilt University
Tennessee Coal and Iron Company (TCI), 24, 168
Tennessee Valley, 14–17, 51, 52, 54, 178, 181, 275. *See also* North Alabama v. South Alabama dichotomy
Tennessee Valley Authority (TVA), 92
Texas, 62, 83, 120, 136, 138, 150, 157, 168, 227–28, 238, 258, 263, 297, 328n33, 348n9, 356n64, 384n26, 391n80; Beaumont, 168; Brunswick, 168; Dallas, 376n10; Hatton Sumners, 136; H. L. Hunt, 300; Houston, 168; John H. Kirby, 117, 335n15; Longview race riot, 157; Orange, 168; poll tax in, 382n2; Tom Connally, 108, 125, 211. *See also* Baker, James III; Bradford, M. E.; Bush, George H. W.; Bush, George W.; Connally, Tom; Dies, Martin, Jr.; Houston, TX, Democratic National Convention at; Hunt, H. L.; Kirby, John H.; Maverick, Maury; Muse, Vance; Norris, J. Frank; Rayburn, Sam; Simmons, Roscoe; Sumners, Hatton
Thatcher, Margaret, xv, 328n33.
Thompson, Perry, 96

Thompson, R. DuPont, 151, 173
Thornhill v. Alabama, 352n29
Thornton, J. Mills: on Alabama as liberal, 166; golden age of liberalism, 166, 355n54; KKK as incubator of liberalism, 355n54
Thurmond, J. Strom, 109, 259, 294, 297, 301, 304, 305, 409n29
Thurrow, Lester C., 335n16
Tierney, John, 313n2. *See also* fusionism; libertarianism
Tillman, Ben, 249, 270
Tilly, Dorothy, 264
Tindall, George Brown, 59, 106, 138, 348n8, 355n53, 407n14
Tompkins, Daniel Augustus, 23
trickle-down economics, 327n14. *See also* economic fundamentalism
Truman, Harry S., xvii, 291–92, 297
Tulane University, 355n55
Tuskegee Airmen, 203, 368n111
Tuskegee Institute, 120, 146, 220–24, 248, 279; George Washington Carver, 276
Tutwiler, Herbert, 372n30
Tutwiler, Julia, 155
Tutwiler Hotel, 71
two-thirds rule, 115–16, 358n89

Underwood, Oscar W., 61, 147, 287, 347n1; conservatism of, 340n60; laissez-faire on race, 332n45. *See also* Johnston, Forney
Union. *See* federal government; Reconstruction; Reconstruction Syndrome
Union League, 3–4, 9
unions. *See* labor
Unitarians, 34
United Mine Workers, xiii, xv, 27, 57, 58, 95–97, 99, 101–2, 148, 204, 294, 350n21
United Steelworkers, 95–96, 350n21
University of North Carolina. *See* North Carolina, Chapel Hill
urban. *See* alcohol; immigrants; race; Tammany Hall
U.S. Post Office, attacks on, xv

U.S. Steel and Bull Connor; 349n14. *See also* Simpson, James E.

Vanderbilt, Cornelius, 35
Vanderbilt, William H., 33, 35
Vanderbilt University, 94, 328n33, 355n55, 404n59
Vardaman, Claude O., 112, 149
Veblen, Thorstein, 32
Vigilantism, 60–64; various groups, 8. *See also* Kilby, Thomas E.; Ku Klux Klan; Wilkinson, Horace C.
violence, 28, 38, 103–4, 162, 166, 175, 202, 215, 242, 269–70, 271, 273, 282–83, 317n18, 319n31, 320n35, 323nn47–48; on buses, streetcars, trains, 218–19; black clerics as policemen of black masses, 353n46; disappearance of, 324n53; economic, 33; forgotten about, 19; reaction to, 370n8; religious, 25; as underpinning of southern status quo, 5, 7–9, 28, 216–17, 242, 269–70, 273; black, 56, 205, 215, 353n46; women, 156. *See also* convict-lease system; disfranchisement; establishment violence; Hall, Horace; labor, strikes and; lynching; race; race riots; rape; Reconstruction; sophistry of modern conservatism; status quo society
Virginia, 83, 98, 118, 125, 136, 138, 150, 156, 189, 191, 212, 263, 280, 294, 384n26; Norfolk, 25; poll tax in, 382n2; Richmond, 25, 280; Virginia Dynasty, 24;. *See also* Byrd, Harry Flood; Dabney, Virginius; Dixon, Rev. Thomas W.; Glass, Carter; Jefferson, Thomas; Marshall, John; Mason, Lucy Randolph
Virginia Dynasty, 24
voter registration, 10. *See also* antidemocratic tendencies; disfranchisement; Durr, Virginia; LeFlore, John; McKinney, Clinton; poll tax; Shores, Arthur D.; Soldier Vote Bill; sophistry of modern conservatism

voter suppression, 10, 236, 323n47, 391n80. *See also* anti-democratic tendencies; disfranchisement; voter registration

Waggoner, James T. "Jabo," on race and GOP in the South, 408n26
Wagner, Robert A., 100–101, 108, 126
Wagner Act. *See* National Labor Relations Act; Wagner, Robert A.
Wagner-Costigan Federal Anti-Lynching Bill, 108–10, 146
Wallace, George C., xii, xvi, 66, 175, 204–5, 214, 233, 237, 290, 298, 305, 410n33; appeal to anti-intellectualism, 112; anticipated by Horace Wilkinson, 194; battles with Nixon for southern white vote, 292, 300–1, 307; connection to modern GOP, xvi, 243, 295, 301, 303, 306–7, 328n33, 408n26, 409n31; considers himself to be Republican, 307, 408n26; economic liberalism of, 42, 295; no difference between the major parties, 194; "stand up for Alabama" as slogan, 178; use of emotion, 204–5; use of masculinity and machismo politics, 177–78. *See also* Bradford, M. E.; Carter, Dan T.; Dixon, Frank; Reagan, Ronald; Republicanism; Nixon, Richard; Southern Strategy; Sparks, Chauncey; Wilkinson, Horace C.
Wallace, George C., Jr., 408n26
Wallace, Henry A., xvii, 164, 297, 355n57, 366n84; on South becoming liberal, 164
Wallis, Rev. Jim, 409n30
Walsh-Healey Act, 349n15, 372n22
Wall Street, 90, 303, 309
Wanniski, Jude, 300
Warburg, J. P., 274
Ward, George B., 142
Ward, Robert David, 338n43
War Manpower Board, 179, 184, 188, 196; state version of, 188
war production, 168–70
Washington, D.C. *See* federal government

Washington, Booker T., 32, 58, 220, 223
Wattenburg, Ben J., 405n4
Wayne, John, 303–4
Weaver, Richard M., 328n33
Webb, Samuel L.: on Alabama as liberal, 370n1; on North Alabama v. South Alabama, 370n1; on view of KKK backing for Bibb Graves and Hugo Black, 341n70, 345n47. *See also* North Alabama v. South Alabama dichotomy
Weigel, George, 307
Wesleyanism, 33, 261
West, Mabel Jones, 82, 121, 142, 146, 151, 156, 190, 364n66. *See also* Bolt of 1928; Ku Klux Klan
West Virginia, 28, 303
Weyrich, Paul, 300, 303, 306, 328n33
White, Frank S., 336n26
White, Walter, 89, 124, 156
White Citizens Councils, 172, 190,
White Legion, 103. *See also* Gelders, Joseph
white supremacy. *See* Great Melding (First); monster of white supremacy; New Racism; politics of emotion; race; status quo society
Wiener, Jonathan, 325n6
Wilkinson, Horace C., 42, 139, 291, 383n10; anticipating George Wallace, 194; anti-lynching cases, 57, 63; Dixiecrats, 106, 183, 190–95, 278, 283, 294, 372n30, 377n17; KKK, 65, 71, 283, 356n58; 1928 bolt, 71–72, 75–78, 343n13; neo-Bourbon-Dixiecrat alliance, 171–74, 177; exasperation with John Temple Graves, 404n50; New Deal, 93, 101, 103, 105–6, 170, 349n14, 354n47; "our way of life," 394n11; patriotism, 381n47; poll tax, 210–11; protégés of, 93, 101, 103, 105, 197, 384n25; race-baits Bull Connor, 94; Soldier Vote Bill, 210–11; speeches of, 193–95, 378n25. *See also* Connor, Theophilus Eugene "Bull"; Dixon, Frank; Downs, William O.; Folsom, James E.; Graves,

Bibb; Heflin, J. Thomas; Jones, Jimmie; Kilby, Thomas E.; Locke, Hugh; McCorvey, Gessner; Perez, Leander; Robinson, Lewey V.; Smyer, Sidney; Wallace, George C.
Williams, Aubrey, W., xvii, 89, 93, 112, 123, 139, 140, 143, 144, 147, 156, 164, 274, 355n55, 401n12; on South becoming liberal, 164
Willkie, Wendell, 148, 149–53, 378n25, 389n64, 403n37, 405n65; Alabama GOP, 151; caravan, 364n88; women involved in campaign, 151
Wilson, E. M., 222, 386n44
Wilson, Woodrow, 91
Wilson Dam, 348n10
Winchell, Walter, 400
Wiregrass, 50–54, 80, 112, 151, 162, 178, 183, 296, 298. See also North Alabama v. South Alabama dichotomy
Wolfe, Alan, 338n43
women: conservative, 155–56; Equal Rights Amendment, 405n4; feminism, 405n4; kept "in their place," 3, 41, 64; in 1928 bolt, 82–83; suffrage, 51, 53, 92. See also disfranchisement; Dowd, Mollie; Farmer, Hallie; gender; interracial sex; lynching; Owen, Marie Bankhead; Roosevelt, Eleanor; Tutwiler, Julia; West, Mabel Jones
Women's Christian Temperance Union, 71, 76
women's suffrage. See disfranchisement; gender; women, suffrage
Women's Trade Union League (WTUL), 139
Woodward, C. Vann, 27, 139, 248, 325n6, 327n24, 334n14, 336n27; "for whites only" thesis, 46–47, 63, 334n14. See also Link, Arthur S.
working class. See class; class consciousness; economics; labor
Works Progress Administration (WPA), 110–11
World War I, 46, 59, 60, 91–92, 131, 175, 199, 256
World War II, xvii, xviii, 64, 75, 151–52, 157, 163–64, 167–70, 175, 182, 187–90, 199, 203, 206–12, 229, 238–43, 253, 260, 267, 280–81, 287, 292, 296, 298
Wynne, Lewis R., 325n6

xenophobia, 60, 75, 84, 98, 101, 144, 244, 258, 262, 266, 280, 286. See also foreigners; outside agitators; Yankees

Yankees: See carpetbaggers; federal government; foreigners; neo-carpetbaggers; New Deal; outside agitators; race; Reconstruction; Reconstruction Syndrome; xenophobia

zero-sum theory, 335n16